# A Tour of the Interactive C...

| Interactive Demonstrations | Cases | Videos |
|---|---|---|
| **Chapter 1** An overview of the planning and control process | **Chapter 1** ValuComp Computers case requires use of fixed and variable cost information to prepare a budget | **Chapter 1** Peter Adkison, CEO of Wizards of the Coast, discusses how managerial accounting is used at his company |
| **Chapter 2** How direct material, direct labor, and manufacturing overhead are traced to a job-cost sheet, and the relation between the cost of jobs and balances in Work in Process, Finished Goods, and Cost of Goods Sold | **Chapter 2** The Spokane Ornamental Iron case tests students' knowledge of job-order costing | **Chapter 2** Automated manufacturing process at Toyota emphasizes how automation affects a firm's cost structure |
| **Chapter 3** The steps in process costing and the calculation of the cost of items completed and the cost of items in ending Work in Process | **Chapter 3** The Nature's Sweet case asks students to prepare a production cost report | |
| **Chapter 4** How variable costs, fixed costs and the selling price affect the break-even point | **Chapter 4** The Games Division of Mayfield Software case asks students to use the profit equation to calculate the break-even point | **Chapter 4** Larry Calkins, CFO of Holland America-Westours, discusses the fixed and variable costs of a cruise |
| **Chapter 5** (NEW) Affect on income of full versus variable costing | **Chapter 5** (NEW) Vector Manufacturing case requires preparation of an income statement using variable costing | |
| **Chapter 6** How allocation using a single overhead rate can distort the apparent profitability of products | **Chapter 6** The Andrews Consulting case uses ABM to analyze the process of acquiring technology at a consulting firm | **Chapter 6** Russ Albright, Finance Controller, discusses the use of ABM at Microsoft |
| **Chapter 7** How failure to use incremental analysis can lead to the "cost-allocation death spiral" | **Chapter 7** The West Coast Grocery Supply case uses incremental analysis to analyze whether or not West Coast should drop a product line | |
| **Chapter 8** (NEW) Demonstration of the Target Costing Process | **Chapter 8** (NEW) Nelson Plumbing Products case requires determination of the profit-maximizing price | |
| **Chapter 9** Using the trial-and-error approach to computing the internal rate of return when cash flows vary from period to period | **Chapter 9** The Medford Valley Resort case uses net present value to analyze the acquisition of a chair lift | |
| **Chapter 10** How changes in one budget can lead to automatic changes in other interdependent budgets using computer software | **Chapter 10** The Toscana Coffee case asks students to prepare a production budget for a coffee company | |
| **Chapter 11** How to calculate the controllable overhead variance and the overhead volume variance | **Chapter 11** The Crowley Industries case gives students practice in calculating standard cost variances | **Chapter 11** James Eschweiler, Director of Cost Accounting, discusses how Starbucks uses variance analysis to control the use of beans in its roasting process |
| **Chapter 12** Comparing two divisions of a company in terms of Economic Value Added | **Chapter 12** The Nelson Tool Company case asks students to classify performance measures into the four perspectives of a balanced scorecard | **Chapter 12** Stephen Lease, V.P. Corporate Planning, discusses how SAFECO uses a balanced scorecard to plan and evaluate performance |
| **Chapter 13** (NEW) Demonstration of the calculation of day's sales in accounts receivable | **Chapter 13** (NEW) The Ranger Company case requires vertical analysis of the company's income statement | |

# A NOTE TO STUDENTS ON HOW TO STUDY MANAGERIAL ACCOUNTING

Dear Students of Managerial Accounting:

In your business career, you'll be asked to plan operations, evaluate subordinates, and make a variety of decisions using accounting information. An understanding of managerial accounting will contribute to your success in these key activities, and this book, CD, and related Web site are designed to optimize learning the subject. To get the most out of these materials, I recommend that you take a three-step approach to the study of each chapter in *Managerial Accounting*:

- First, skim the chapter for a quick overview.
- Second, read the chapter carefully and pay particular attention to the illustrations. When you're finished, make sure you understand each of the learning objectives.
- Third, enhance and test your knowledge using the interactive CD and the Web site. These materials will also help you achieve one of your immediate goals—excellent performance on tests!

The CD will review the learning objectives, provide a matching exercise to test your understanding of key terms, and give a set of multiple-choice questions to test your knowledge of concepts and techniques. Demonstrations will illustrate the planning and control process, operation of a job-order costing system, overhead allocation, and other concepts and techniques in managerial accounting. Demonstrations, cases and critical thinking exercises will test your understanding of incremental analysis, activity-based management, the balanced scorecard, and other concepts and techniques in an interesting, interactive environment. Videos will highlight real companies and their use of managerial accounting. The Web site related to this book will provide additional material to test your understanding of managerial accounting.

A program on the Web site will *assess the learning style* that works best for you. Helpful tips will be provided on how to study managerial accounting given your particular learning style.

Best wishes for success,

Jim Jiambalvo

SECOND
EDITION

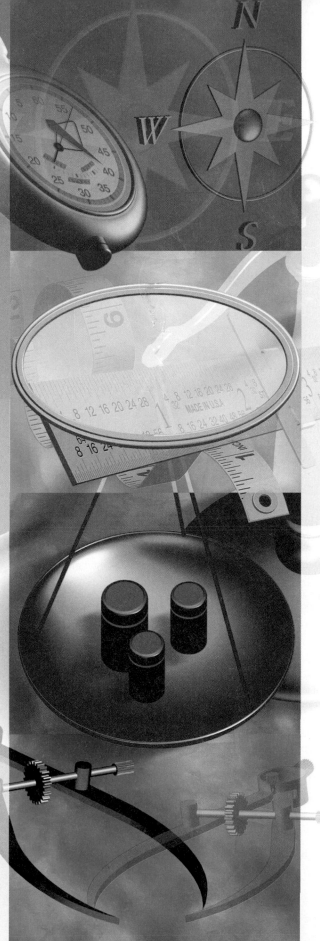

# MANAGERIAL ACCOUNTING

## James Jiambalvo
University of Washington

WILEY

JOHN WILEY & SONS, INC.

EXECUTIVE EDITOR   Jay O'Callaghan
SENIOR PRODUCTION EDITOR   Petrina Kulek
SENIOR DEVELOPMENT EDITOR   Marian Provenzano
SENIOR MARKETING MANAGER   Steven Herdegen
SENIOR DESIGNER   Karin Gerdes Kincheloe
TEXT DESIGNER   Lee Goldstein
ILLUSTRATION EDITOR   David Renwanz
PHOTO EDITOR   Jennifer MacMillan

This book was set in 10/12 New Aster by UG / GGS Information Services, Inc. and printed and bound by Von Hoffman. The cover was printed by Von Hoffman.

This book is printed on acid free paper.  ∞

To order books or for customer service please, call 1(800)-CALL-WILEY (225-5945).

ISBN 0-471-22876-1 (Domestic) 0-471-45183-5 (WIE)

Printed in the United States of America

10  9  8  7  6  5  4

To my wife, Cheryl

# ABOUT THE AUTHOR

 **PROFESSOR JAMES JIAMBALVO** joined the faculty at the University of Washington after receiving a Ph.D. in accounting from The Ohio State University. A CPA, he has audit experience with the firm that is now Deloitte & Touche and has served on D&T's national academic advisory board. Professor Jiambalvo's research has been published in top accounting journals, including *The Accounting Review, Contemporary Accounting Research*, the *Journal of Accounting and Economics*, and the *Journal of Accounting Research*. He is a past associate editor of *The Accounting Review* and has been a member of the editorial boards of *The Accounting Review, Contemporary Accounting Research; Auditing: A Journal of Practice and Theory*; and the *Journal of Management Accounting Research*.

Professor Jiambalvo has received the Burlington Northern Foundation Faculty Achievement Award, the Andrew V. Smith Faculty Development Award, and the Lex N. Gamble Award for Excellence in the Field of E-Commerce, and he was recognized for his teaching of managerial accounting with the MBA Professor of the Year Award. Professor Jiambalvo has taught numerous executive education courses, including courses for a number of software companies. At the University of Washington, he holds the PricewaterhouseCoopers and Alumni Endowed Professorship.

# PREFACE

This book is intended to drive home the fundamental ideas of managerial accounting and motivate students to actually *want* to study the subject. As you will see, the text has a number of unique features that help accomplish these goals. Based on my teaching experience and from what we have heard from professors using the first edition, we believe students and professors want a textbook that:

- Recognizes that most students will become managers, not accountants
- Focuses attention on decision making
- Motivates students to learn managerial accounting by connecting concepts and techniques to the real world
- Recognizes the growing importance of service businesses
- Is clear, concise, and can be covered in one semester

Here's how the second edition of managerial accounting reflects these desires.

**Recognizes that most students will become managers, not accountants.** Most students of introductory managerial accounting will pursue careers as managers, not accountants. Future managers most likely will not need to know the FIFO approach to process costing or how to calculate four overhead variances—so these and other less essential topics are not covered.

**Focuses more attention on decision making.** Instructors want their students to be able to solve the types of problems that face real managers. This requires that more emphasis be placed on decision making skills. Accordingly, three of the 13 chapters (Chapters 7, 8 and 10) focus specifically on decision making. Additionally, decision making, and the use of incremental analysis, are discussed in the first chapter and integrated throughout the book. By the time students get to Chapter 7 (The Use of Cost Information in Management Decision Making), they will already have a good understanding of costs that are relevant in making a decision. And after reading Chapter 7, working homework problems and discussing the material in class, they will have, we hope, a great understanding of decision making!

**Motivates students to learn managerial accounting by connecting concepts and techniques to the real world.** Business people often say that they wish they had known how important managerial accounting would be to their success on the job—they would have studied the subject harder in school! Here, every effort is made to convince students that managerial accounting is of critical importance in the real world. *Link to Practice* boxes relate the text material to real companies. Additionally, each chapter has several cases developed with feedback from managers who attested to their realism and relevance. An often-heard comment: "We had that exact situation at my company!" The interactive CD has videos with managers from Wizards of the Coast, Microsoft, Starbucks, and other companies showing the relevance of managerial accounting at their companies.

**Recognizes the growing importance of service businesses.** In the last twenty years, employment has shifted from manufacturing to the service sector. Now, more than 75% of all jobs are in the service economy. With this in mind, the second edition has added numerous examples of service companies in the chapter and end-of-chapter materials.

**Clear, concise, and can be covered in one semester.** According to students and faculty who used the first edition, a major and much appreciated strength of the text was the clear and concise writing style. This is continued here—discussions are to the point, ideas are illustrated, and examples are presented to make the ideas concrete. The 13 chapters can be comfortably covered in one semester.

# CHAPTER ORGANIZATION AND CONTENT

### Chapter 1: Managerial Accounting in the Information Age
This chapter describes how managerial accounting is used in planning, control, and decision making, and discusses two key ideas in managerial accounting: (1) decision making relies on incremental analysis and (2) you get what you measure! These two key ideas are integrated throughout the text and receive special attention in Chapter 7 (which covers decision making) and Chapter 12 (which covers performance evaluation). Because the book emphasizes the use of information in decision making, a number of cost terms are introduced in the first chapter (e.g., fixed, variable, sunk and opportunity cost). That way, students can begin discussing various decisions using the appropriate vocabulary right from the start. Later in Chapters 4 and 7, these cost terms are reinforced.

In addition, Chapter 1 discusses how information technology facilitates information flows up and down the value chain. And there is a discussion of business ethics and a framework for ethical decision making.

### Chapter 2: Job-Order Costing and Modern Manufacturing Practices
Using an example of a small custom boat builder, this chapter discusses cost classifications for manufacturing firms and how costs of manufactured products are reflected in a company's financial statements. Examples of job-order costing are presented for service companies as well as manufacturing firms. The chapter ends with a discussion of modern manufacturing practices and how they help companies succeed in a competitive global economy. Two of the Links to Practice are particularly interesting. One introduces the downside to the use of just-in-time manufacturing—supply chains may face critical disruptions due to terrorist attacks that shut down borders, air traffic, and ports. A second raises the intriguing question, "Considering that you get what you measure, can there be too much emphasis on quality?"

### Chapter 3: Process Costing
This chapter presents a relatively simple, straightforward treatment of process costing using the weighted-average approach. Students learn how to calculate the cost per equivalent unit and how to prepare a production cost report. They do not learn the more complex FIFO approach to process costing. The *Tech-Tonic Sports Drink* case at the end of the chapter confronts students with two ways to treat the cost of lost units: (1) include the entire cost of the lost units in cost of goods sold, or (2) assign part of the cost to cost of goods sold and part to ending inventory. The case can be used to discuss alternative accounting treatments, earnings management, and ethical issues in accounting.

### Chapter 4: Cost-Volume-Profit Analysis

This chapter presents the tools needed to analyze cost-volume-profit relationships and how they are used in planning, control, and decision making. Students learn how to use account analysis and the high-low method to estimate cost behavior. Regression analysis using Excel is presented in an appendix, and end-of-chapter material is available for instructors who wish to cover regression analysis. The chapter includes a discussion of operating leverage, shows how operating leverage affects the percentage change in profit for a given change in sales, and relates operating leverage to risk.

### Chapter 5: Variable Costing

This chapter explains the difference between variable and full costing and how, under full costing, excess production can be used to "bury" fixed production costs in ending inventory. There is also a discussion of the impact of just-in-time production on the difference between full and variable costing income.

### Chapter 6: Cost Allocation and Activity-Based Costing

The chapter explains *why* costs are allocated, then discusses the allocation process and problems related to allocation. This rather extensive background sets the stage for a thorough discussion of activity-based costing, since ABC addresses problems arising from using too few cost pools and only volume-related allocation bases. At this point in the book, students have a reasonable understanding of fixed and variable costs and the need for incremental analysis. This lets them grasp a major drawback with ABC in practice—namely, in practice, ABC is generally used to develop the *full cost* of products and services, and this information isn't consistent with the incremental analysis used in decision making. The chapter also notes a major benefit of ABC: namely, ABC may lead to improvements in cost control. This follows because with ABC, managers see costs broken out by a number of activities rather than buried in one or two overhead cost pools. The discussion of ABC's use in cost control naturally leads to a discussion of a related approach, activity-based management (ABM). ABM is discussed in more detail in an appendix to the chapter.

### Chapter 7: The Use of Cost Information in Management Decision Making.

By the time students get to Chapter 7, they already have a *fair* understanding of incremental analysis. After reading Chapter 7, they should have an *excellent* understanding. The chapter stresses the importance of qualitative considerations in management decisions. An appendix on the Theory of Constraints (TOC) applies TOC logic to analyze decisions related to inspections, batch sizes, and across-the-board cuts.

### Chapter 8: Pricing Decisions, Analyzing Customer Profitability, and Activity-Based Pricing

Pricing decisions are extremely important for most companies. This chapter covers the economic approach to determining the profit-maximizing price, incremental analysis related to pricing special orders, and the cost-plus approach to pricing. Target pricing is also discussed. Two topics related to activity-based costing (which is discussed in Chapter 6) are also covered: customer profitability analysis and activity-based pricing.

### Chapter 9: Capital Budgeting Decisions

This chapter shows how to take the time value of money into account when evaluating capital investment opportunities. Consistent with the idea that most users of the book will become managers rather than accountants, the treatment of taxes is simplified. Students learn that taxes play an important role in investment decisions, but are not required to learn complex tax rules (which may change before they have a chance to apply their knowledge). The chapter notes that managers may concentrate erroneously on the short-run profitability of investments rather than their net present values. This follows because you get what you measure! In other words, performance measures may drive managers to have a short-run focus. An appendix covers the use of Excel to calculate net present value and the internal rate of return.

### Chapter 10: Budgetary Planning and Control

The role of budgets in planning and control is presented in this chapter, and students learn how to prepare the various budget schedules that make up the master budget. Students also learn why flexible budgets are needed for performance evaluation. Importantly, there is a discussion on why budget-based compensation schemes can lead to budget padding and income shifting across periods. The Abruzzi Olive Oil Company case clearly conveys to students that budgets should be prepared using spreadsheets (exploring various budget assumptions is easy using a spreadsheet and very tedious using a hand-held calculator).

### Chapter 11: Standard Costs and Variance Analysis

In this chapter, students learn how to compute and interpret variances for direct material, direct labor, and manufacturing overhead. Consistent with our focus on future managers rather than future accountants, only two (rather than four) overhead variances are discussed: the controllable overhead variance and the overhead volume variance. To provide flexibility to instructors, recording of standard costs and variances in accounts is discussed in an appendix.

### Chapter 12: Decentralization and Performance Evaluation

This chapter discusses the pros and cons of decentralization and explains why companies evaluate the performance of subunits and subunit managers, really emphasizing the idea that *you get what you measure*. In particular, it focuses on why evaluation in terms of profit can lead to overinvestment (investing in projects with an expected return that is less than the cost of capital) while evaluation in terms of ROI can lead to underinvestment (failure to invest in projects with an expected return that is greater than the cost of capital). Residual income (and the related measure, economic value added or EVA) solves, to some extent, the problems of over- and underinvestment. The chapter ends with a discussion of the Balanced Scorecard.

### Chapter 13: Analyzing Financial Statements:
### A Managerial Perspective

This chapter reviews the three primary financial statements and explains that managers analyze them to control operations, to assess the financial stability of vendors, customers, and other business partners, and to assess how their companies appear to investors and creditors. In terms of analysis, the chapter covers horizontal, vertical, and ratio analysis. A discussion of earnings management indicates why it is important to compare cash flow from operations to net income. There is also a discussion of how the MD&A section of an annual report, credit reports, and news articles can be used to gain insight into a company's current and future financial performance.

# CHAPTER FEATURES

Here are the special features that are appreciated by instructors and students and contribute to a deep understanding of managerial accounting.

## VARIABLE COSTING

In 2006, the all-tube amplifier produced by ClausenTube received rave reviews and the company was able to sell all 5,000 units it produced, generating company profit of $3,500,000. Based on these results, the company increased production to 6,000 units in the subsequent year, but was only able to sell 4,800 units. This performance, however, was considered quite good given that the economy had slipped in the third and fourth quarters.

In early January of 2008, Robert Clausen, company president and founder, reviewed financial performance for 2007. Surprisingly, profit had increased slightly to $3,528,000. Robert was confused and wasted no time calling Leslie Anders, the company controller. "What's going on?" Robert asked in a voice that hinted at his irritation. "Sales are down, the production process and prices haven't changed and yet profit is up! How confident are you in the income numbers? There must be a significant error somewhere."

"I know this result looks bizarre," Leslie replied. "But it's not due to an error in the accounting department. It's due to the fact that our financial statements are prepared using what's called full, or absorption,

163

### Chapter Openers
Each chapter opens with an example from an hypothetical company posing an issue that a real manager might encounter, such as, "Is my costing system distorting product cost?" That issue is revisited later in the chapter after students have gained an understanding of the concepts and techniques needed to address it.

**LINK TO PRACTICE**

*Just-in-Time or Just-in-Case?*

Companies that have adopted just-in-time systems have found that they create shareholder value by reducing their investment in inventory and by eliminating costs associated with non-value-added activities. But now one of the leading advocates of JIT, Yossi Sheffi, director of Massachusetts Institute of Technology's Center for Transportation and Logistics, is suggesting that companies consider "just-in-case" options. The reason is that supply chains may face critical disruptions due to terrorist attacks and the reactions of governments to the attacks that can include shutting down borders, air traffic, and ports. Sheffi recommends that companies consider judiciously increasing their supplier base and dividing orders between domestic providers and foreign alternatives. Then, if borders get closed, domestic providers can still deliver goods. Strategic reserves of supplies also need to be considered "just in case" they're needed.

Terrorist attacks aren't the only reason companies need strategic reserves. Floods, strikes, bankruptcies, and road construction can also disrupt the supply chain. Smart companies will build these possibilities into their supply chain management strategies.

*Source:* "Just-in-Time Enters New Era," D.C. Denison, *The Boston Globe*, May 5, 2002, P. H2.

### Links to Practice
This feature relates the material to real-world companies and the issues they face.

---

**PROCESS COSTING AND INCREMENTAL ANALYSIS**

Recall from Chapter 1 that whenever we make a decision, we need to perform incremental analysis. That is, we need to determine the *change* in revenue and the *change* in cost, assuming a particular decision alternative is selected. If the net change is positive, the decision alternative is "good" since it will have a positive impact on firm profit. If the net change is negative, the decision alternative is "bad" in that it will have a negative impact on firm profit.

When using process costing information (or, for that matter, job-order costing information) to make a decision, we have to be careful to recognize that the

Decision Making/ Incremental Analysis

**REMEMBER—YOU GET WHAT YOU MEASURE!**

Before concluding our discussion of cost allocation, let's return to one of the key points raised in Chapter 1: You get what you measure! How does this point relate to cost allocation? Allocations affect the profit that managers have reported on their performance reports. Thus, managers pay attention to controlling the allocation base, since more use of the allocation base results in higher costs and lower profit.

### Two Key Ideas
The text stresses two key ideas: (1) decision making relies on incremental analysis and (2) performance measures affect the behavior of managers. This later idea is called *You Get What You Measure!* One or both of these ideas is referred to in every chapter. Icons are used to call attention to discussions related to them.

## Making Business Decisions and the Knowledge and Skills Checklist

At the end of each chapter a section called Making Business Decisions explicitly links the chapter material to decision making. Students are provided with a checklist of the knowledge and skills they've learned from the chapter that support their ability to make good business decisions.

### MAKING BUSINESS DECISIONS

Decision making relies on incremental analysis. A potential problem with cost allocation is that it may make a fixed cost appear to be a variable cost and, therefore, incremental. Suppose, for example, that fixed costs are allocated based on sales dollars. This makes it appear that if sales increase, the costs will increase. When making decisions using cost information that involves allocation—beware!

### KNOWLEDGE AND SKILLS CHECKLIST

*Knowledge and skills are needed to make good business decisions. Check off the knowledge and skills you've acquired from reading this chapter.*

❏ K/S 1. You have an expanded business vocabulary (see key terms).

❏ K/S 2. You can explain why costs are allocated.

❏ K/S 3. You can allocate service department costs to production departments.

❏ K/S 4. You recognize that cost allocation can lead to a number of significant problems.

❏ K/S 5. You understand activity-based costing (ABC) and can explain why it results in a cost that is different from that obtained using a traditional product costing approach.

❏ K/S 6. You can explain the difference between activity-based costing (ABC) and activity-based management (ABM).

## Chapter Summary by Learning Objective

There is a list of learning objectives at the start of each chapter and they are repeated next to the text where they are addressed. Importantly, at the end of each chapter there is a summary organized by learning objective so that students can efficiently review and assess whether or not they have mastered the material.

### SUMMARY OF LEARNING OBJECTIVES

**1** *Explain why indirect costs are allocated.* Indirect costs are allocated to provide information for decision making, to calculate the full cost of products, to reduce the frivolous use of common resources, and to encourage managers to evaluate the efficiency of internally provided services. From a decision making standpoint, the allocation should measure the opportunity cost of using a company resource. However, this is difficult to operationalize in practice, since opportunity costs often change quickly.

**2** *Describe the cost allocation process.* The cost allocation process has three steps: (1) identify the cost objectives, (2) form cost pools, and (3) select an allocation base to relate the costs to the cost objectives.

**3** *Discuss allocation of service department costs.* Service department costs are allocated to production departments, which in turn allocate these costs to products. The direct method allocates service department costs to production departments but not to other service departments.

**4** *Identify potential problems with cost allocation.* A number of problems are associated with

cost allocation in practice: (1) the allocated costs may not be controllable by the manager receiving the allocation; (2) allocations may be arbitrary; (3) allocations may make fixed costs appear to be variable; (4) allocations may be made using too few cost pools; and (5) allocation may be made using only volume-related allocation bases.

**5** *Discuss activity-based costing (ABC) and cost drivers.* Activity-based costing (ABC) is a costing method that recognizes that costs are caused by activities. Measures of the key activities that cause costs to be incurred are referred to as cost drivers. The cost drivers are used as the allocation bases to relate indirect costs to products. Unlike traditional systems, ABC does not focus solely on volume-related cost drivers.

**6** *Distinguish activity-based costing (ABC) from activity-based management (ABM).* Whereas ABC focuses on the costs of activities in order to develop the cost of goods and services produced by the activities, ABM focuses on the costs of activities in order to help manage the activities themselves (you can't manage what you can't measure).

## Solved Review Problems and Self-Testing Multiple Choice Questions.

End of chapter materials include a solved review problem and self-testing multiple-choice questions. The CD accompanying the text has additional self-testing materials.

### REVIEW PROBLEM

Little Gardener Company produces an environmentally safe general purpose plant food that can be used on flower beds and in vegetable gardens. The company operates two departments, Mixing and Packaging. Liquid plant food is prepared in the Mixing Department and packaged in 1-gallon containers in the Packaging Department. Material is added at the start of each process and labor and overhead are added evenly throughout the processes. All units are completed each month in Packaging. Therefore, there is no ending work in process in this department.

The following information is related to production in February:

| Unit Information (gallons) | Mixing | Packaging |
|---|---|---|
| Beginning work in process | | |
| (Mixing) | 2,000 | |
| (Packaging) | | –0– |
| Started during March | 60,000 | 61,000 |
| Ending work in process | | |
| (Mixing: 100% material, 60% conversion costs) | 1,000 | |
| (Packaging) | | –0– |

| Cost Information, Beginning Work in Process | | |
|---|---|---|
| Direct material | $4,000 | $ –0– |
| Direct labor | 800 | –0– |
| Manufacturing overhead | 1,120 | –0– |
| Transferred-in cost | –0– | –0– |

| Cost Added During February | | |
|---|---|---|
| Direct material | $120,000 | $18,300 |
| Direct labor | 30,000 | 3,050 |
| Manufacturing overhead | 42,000 | 6,100 |
| Transferred-in cost | –0– | ? |

**Required**
Prepare production cost reports for Mixing and Packaging for the month of February.

## PROBLEMS

**PROBLEM 1-1. Budgets in Managerial Accounting** Marie's Pie Company is in the process of preparing a production cost budget for May. Actual costs in April were:

**Marie's Pie Company
Production Costs
April 2006**

| Production | 15,000 Pies |
|---|---|
| Ingredient cost (variable) | $18,750 |
| Labor cost (variable) | 22,500 |
| Rent (fixed) | 5,000 |
| Depreciation (fixed) | 6,000 |
| Other (fixed) | 1,000 |
| Total | $53,250 |

*Required*

a. Using this information, prepare a budget for May. Assume that production will increase to 16,000 pies reflecting an anticipated sales increase related to a new marketing campaign.

b. Does the budget suggest that additional workers are needed? Suppose the wage rate is $20 per hour. How many additional labor hours are needed in May? What would happen if management did not anticipate the need for additional labor in May?

c. Calculate the actual cost per unit in April and the budgeted cost per unit in May. Explain why the cost per unit is expected to decrease.

## EXERCISES

**EXERCISE 9-1. Group Assignment** Explain why interest expense is not treated as a cash outflow in capital budgeting decisions made using net present value (NPV) analysis.

**EXERCISE 9-2. Writing Assignment** Pauline Hsu is the manager of the office products division of Lomar Enterprises. In this position, her annual bonus is based on an appraisal of return on investment (ROI) measured as Division Income ÷ End-of-Year Division Assets (net of accumulated depreciation).

Currently, Pauline is considering investing $25,000,000 in modernization of the division plant in Tennessee. She estimates that the project will generate cash savings of $5,500,000 per year for 8 years. The plant improvements will be depreciated over 8 years ($25,000,000 ÷ 8 years = $3,125,000). Thus, the annual effect on income will be $2,375,000 ($5,500,000 − $3,125,000).

*Required*

Using a discount rate of 12 percent, calculate the NPV of the modernization project. Then, calculate the ROI of the project each year over it's eight-year life. (Calculate ROI as affect on income divided by end of year book value. Note that the value of ROI is not defined at the end of year eight when book value is zero.) Finally, write a paragraph explaining why Pauline may not make the investment even though it has a positive NPV.

**EXERCISE 9-3. Internet Assignment** Go to Web site of Technology/Engineering Management, Inc. (http://www.temi.com/NewTechInvestments.htm) and read the note on justifying investments in new technology by Richard Mignogna, president of this consulting firm. What are the strategic benefits of investments in technology that, according to Mignogna, are seldom considered in investment decisions?

## CASES

### 1-1 LOCAL 635

Local 635 represents kitchen workers at hotels in several Midwestern cities. Part of their labor agreement states that workers "*shall receive one free meal per shift up to a cost of $8, with any cost over $8 being deducted from wages paid to said employee.*"

A labor dispute arose at the Riverside Hotel shortly after it was opened in June. Kitchen workers who ate dinner on the late shift found that their wages were reduced by $7 for each meal they consumed at the hotel during their dinner break. Josh Parker, a line cook, stated the widely held belief of the workers, "There's no way these dinners cost the Riverside Hotel $8 to make let alone $15. This is just another case of management trying to rip us off. Take last night. I had the prime rib dinner. The piece of meat cost about $5 and the salad less than $1. That's only $6 in total. Really, there aren't any other costs to speak of. The cook, well he's going to be working in the kitchen and getting paid for eight hours whether he makes my meal or not. This claim that my meal cost $15 is baloney!"

Management of the Riverside Hotel sees the situation differently. Take the case of Josh's dinner. In presenting the hotel's case to a labor arbitration board, Sandy Ross, manager of the hotel explained, "Look, that dinner goes for $25 on the menu so assigning a cost of $15 represents a very good value to the kitchen workers. The contention that the meal only costs $6 is nonsense. True, the meat costs $5 and the salad ingredients cost $1, but there's also the labor costs related to preparing the meal and numerous overhead costs like the cost of the oven that the prime rib is cooked in. That oven cost more than $18,000. And, there's heat, light, power, etc. Each meal we prepare should be assigned part of these overhead costs. And, don't

forget that when the worker finishes his or her meal, someone has to clean up. That costs money too. When you add up all of these items, a prime rib dinner easily adds up to $15!"

*Required*

a. List examples of costs, at the Riverside Hotel, that are variable, fixed, and sunk. Provide an example of an opportunity cost.

b. What is the source of conflict between labor and management? What changes would you recommend in the wording of the labor agreement?

### 1-2 HERBERT PLUMBING PRODUCTS

Herbert Products produces a variety of valves, connectors, and fixtures used in commercial and residential plumbing applications. Recently, a senior manager walked into the cost accounting department and asked Sara Fielding to tell him the cost of the D45 valve. Sara quickly replied "Why do you want to know?" Noticing that the manager appeared somewhat startled by this statement she explained that "The cost information you need depends on the decision you're going to make. You might be thinking of increasing a scheduled production run of 3,000 D45s by 100 units, or scheduling an *additional* production run, or you might even be thinking of dropping the product. For each of these decisions, the "cost" information is different."

*Required*

Using the concept of incremental analysis, expand on Sara's response of "Why do you want to know?" What cost information would be relevant to a decision to drop the product that would not be relevant to a decision to increase a production run by 100 units?

## Spreadsheet Exercises and Problems

Instructors can go to the instructor Web site for a list of exercises and problems that are well suited to spreadsheet analysis. For students who are not familiar with spreadsheets, each chapter identifies three to five exercises and problems with a spreadsheet icon; templates are available for these exercises and problems along with instructional material on how to approach their solution using a spreadsheet.

## Group Work, Writing Assignments, and Web Research

The first three exercises in each chapter address group work, writing, and Web research. Look for the following icons:

 group icon

 writing icon

 internet icon

## Cases

Each chapter has one to five cases and "solving" them develops critical thinking skills. The cases also provide additional opportunities for group work and/or written communication work. Several integrate other business disciplines such as management, finance, and marketing.

## Ethics

Chapter 1 presents a framework for considering ethical dilemmas. And the text has a number of problems and cases that address ethical issues.

### Interactive CD

This is *not* the typical CD that comes with most of today's textbooks! Students can use this interactive CD to deepen and test their understanding of Managerial Accounting in an environment that is stimulating, exciting, and fun! Students can work with the

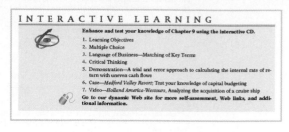

INTERACTIVE LEARNING

Enhance and test your knowledge of Chapter 9 using the interactive CD.
1. Learning Objectives
2. Multiple Choice
3. Language of Business—Matching of Key Terms
4. Critical Thinking
5. Demonstration—A trial and error approach to calculating the internal rate of return with uneven cash flows
6. Case—*Medford Valley Resort;* Test your knowledge of capital budgeting
7. Video—*Holland America-Westours,* Analyzing the acquisition of a cruise ship
Go to our dynamic Web site for more self-assessment, Web links, and additional information.

CD on their own, although instructors have the flexibility to demonstrate or assign material from the CD.

Here's what is included on the CD:

Multiple-choice self-testing

Key-term-matching exercises

Demonstrations of concepts and techniques (e.g., demonstration of the cost-allocation death spiral)

Critical thinking exercises—short-answer questions that require students to think deeply about managerial accounting concepts and techniques

Cases involving cost allocation, NPV, the balanced scorecard, and other topics

Videos, including use of managerial accounting at Wizards of the Coast, ABM at Microsoft, variance analysis at Starbucks, and more

# NEW IN THE SECOND EDITION

In the second edition, end-of-chapter exercises, problems, and cases have been increased by approximately 20 percent, with a significant number focusing on service companies. In terms of the text material, every chapter has been updated. The most significant changes, however, are as follows:

- A discussion of how information technology facilitates information flows up and down the value chain is presented in Chapter 1. The chapter also presents a framework for ethical decision making.

- Recognizing the importance of variable costing and pricing decisions, these topics are now addressed in separate chapters (Chapters 5 and 8). The chapter on pricing decisions also discusses customer profitability analysis and activity-based pricing.

- Several managerial accounting textbooks discuss the topic of financial statement analysis from the standpoint of an investor or creditor. In this edition, a new chapter (Chapter 13) discusses the analysis of financial statements from a *manager's* perspective. Managers analyze financial statements to control operations, to assess the financial viability of vendors, customers, and other business partners, and to assess how their companies appear to investors and creditors. The chapter provides students with the tools to address each of these uses of financial statement analysis.

- For instructors who wish to cover Activity-Based Management and the Theory of Constraints in more depth, appendices discussing these topics are provided in Chapters 6 and 7. Appendices also show how to use Excel to perform regression analysis to estimate fixed and variable costs (Chapter 4) and to calculate the net present value and the internal rate of return of an investment (Chapter 9).

# SUPPLEMENTS: The Teaching and Learning Package

A full range of supplements for both students and instructors is available.

## WEB SITE

**For instructors**, the Web site provides access to the Solutions Manual, Instructor's Manual, Computerized Test Bank, PowerPoint Presentations, text illustrations, and more. **For students**, the Web site provides a sample of the Study Guide, access to PowerPoint text illustrations, Excel templates, a Checklist of Key Figures, Web quizzing, and more. The Web site can be accessed at *http://www.wiley. com/college/jiambalvo*.

## INSTRUCTORS' RESOURCES

### Solutions Manual

Prepared by the author, the Solutions Manual provides detailed solutions for all end-of-chapter questions, exercises, problems, and cases. The solutions have been checked to ensure accuracy and print for exercises and problems is large for easy readability in lecture settings. (Also available at *http://www.wiley.com/college/ jiambalvo*.)

### Solutions Transparencies

The Solutions Transparencies feature detailed solutions to all exercises, problems, and cases. They use large, bold type for better projection and easy readability in large classroom settings.

### Instructor's Manual

The Instructor's Manual is a comprehensive resource guide designed to assist professors in preparing lectures and assignments. The manual includes chapter reviews, lecture outlines, assignment classification tables, teaching illustrations, vocabulary quizzes, multiple-choice quizzes, and additional exercises. (Also available at *http://www.wiley.com/college/jiambalvo*.)

### Test Bank

With a significant amount of *new* testing material, this new test bank consists of over 1,250 examination questions and exercises accompanied by answers and solutions. The types of questions include true-false, multiple choice, completion, short-answer essays and problems. (Also available at *http://www.wiley.com/college/ jiambalvo*.)

### Computerized Test Bank

Powered by Diploma© software, this *new* Computerized Test Bank allows instructors to create multiple versions of the same test by randomizing question order and the order of answers within multiple-choice questions. Instructors can also edit existing questions as well as add new content. The *new* computerized test bank is available on the Instructor Web site at at *http://www.wiley.com/ college/jiambalvo*.

### Checklist of Key Figures

The Checklist of Key Figures is a listing of key data figures within each solution to end-of-chapter problems. These check figures allow students to verify the accuracy of their answers as they work through assignments. The checklist is available on the Instructor Web site at *http://www.wiley.com/college/jiambalvo*.

## POWERPOINT PRESENTATIONS

The *new* Instructor PowerPoint Presentations are a designed to assist instructors in delivering effective classroom lectures. This lecture aid presents key concepts and images from the textbook in a concise and structured manner. Organized according to the text learning objectives this series of electronic transparencies can be used to enhance classroom discussion and visually reinforce managerial accounting concepts.

## VIDEOS

These videos, found on the CD-ROM accompanying the text, include frank discussions about real companies and the use of managerial accounting in their businesses.

### WebCT and Blackboard

WebCT or Blackboard offers an integrated set of course-management tools that enable instructors to easily design, develop, and manage Web-based and Web-enhanced courses. The Wiley Managerial Accounting, 2e WebCT, and Blackboard courses contain the basic course-management shell with all online resources for students. Your Wiley WebCT and Blackboard course can be customized to fit individual professor needs. Please contact your Wiley representative for more information.

# STUDENT RESOURCES

**Study Guide** The Study Guide will enhance student understanding of chapter material and improve student ability to solve homework assignments. In addition to a comprehensive review and reading tips, each chapter offers students the opportunity to practice their understanding of course concepts with true-false and multiple-choice questions, exercises, and cases. Solutions are provided for all practice materials.

**Excel Templates** These templates allow students to complete select end-of-chapter exercises and problems identified by a spreadsheet icon in the margin of the main text. Templates and instructional material on how to approach solutions using a spreadsheet are available free on the student Web site at *http://www.wiley. com/college/jiambalvo*.

**Working Papers** Working Papers are partially completed accounting forms for all end-of-chapter exercises, problems and cases. This is a convenient resource for organizing and completing homework assignments by demonstrating how to set up solution formats correctly.

**Web Quizzing** Self-assessment questions at the end of each chapter in the text can also be solved in an interactive environment on the student Web site at *http://www.wiley.com/college/jiambalvo*.

# ACKNOWLEDGMENTS

I am indebted to my colleagues at the University of Washington for enriching my understanding of managerial accounting. The team at Wiley provided expert help, guidance, and support throughout the publication process. In particular, Jay O'Callaghan, Executive Editor, and Marian Provenzano, Senior Development Editor, made a number of valuable suggestions for improving the second edition. Marian also made sure that the many parts came together in a cohesive and accurate whole. Other Wiley staff who contributed to the text and media are: Allie Keim, Media Editor; Ed Brislin, Associate Editor; Caroline Sieg and Petrina Kulek, Production Editors; Wendy Perez, Supplements Production Editor, David Renwanz, Illustration Editor; Jennifer MacMillan, Photo Editor, Karin Kincheloe, Designer; and Brian Kamins, Editorial Assistant. A note of thanks is also due to the staff at Multimedia Solutions (especially Scott Pehnke and Alan Ruthazer) for their creative and technical work in developing the interactive CD.

Other individuals whose input is greatly appreciated are indicated below.

## Executives Who Participated in Videos

Peter Adkison, COO, Wizards of the Coast

Larry Calkins, CFO, Holland America/Westours

Russ Albright, Finance Controller, Microsoft

Steve Lease, V.P. Corporate Planning, SAFECO

Jim Eshwiler, Director of Cost Accounting, Starbucks

## Ancillary Authors for the Second Edition

Jan Duffy, *Iowa State University*—Test Bank author

James Emig, *Villanova University*—Solutions Manual proofer

Jessica Johnson Frazier, *Eastern Kentucky University*—Study Guide author

Patricia Mounce, *Mississippi College*—Study Guide author

Scott Peterson, *Northern State University*—PowerPoint author

Rex Schildhouse, *University of Phoenix*—Excel Workbook author

Dick Wasson, *Southwestern College*—Instructor's Manual author

Jeff Wong, *University of Oregon*—PowerPoint Contributor

Carol Wysocki, *Washington State University*—Excel Working Papers author

## Reviewers

The development of this second edition of *Managerial Accounting*, benefited greatly from the comments and suggestions of colleagues who teach a managerial accounting course. I would like to acknowledge the contributions made by the following individuals:

Helen Adams
*University of Washington*

Sol. Ahiarah
*SUNY College at Buffalo*

Michael Alles
*Rutgers University*

Feliz Amenkhienan
*Radford University*

William Anderson
*Grove City College*

Vidya Awasthi
*Seattle University*

Kashi Balachandran
*New York University*

Phillip A. Blanchard
*The University of Arizona*

Myra Bruegger
*Southeastern Community College*

Karin Caruso
*Southern New Hampshire University*

Siew Chan
*University of Massachusetts-Boston*

Gloria Clark
*Winston-Salem State University*

Darlene Coarts
*University of Northern Iowa*

Brent Darwin
*Allan Hancock College*

Susan Davis
*Green River Community College*

Terry Elliott
*Morehead State University*

Laura Ellis
*University of Scranton*

Emanuel Emenyonu
*South Carolina State University*

James M. Emig
*Villanova University*

Michael Farina
*Cerritos College*

Reed Fisher
*Johnson State College*

Monica Frizzell
*Western Connecticut State University*

Susan Gardner
*Coker College*

Daniel Gibbons
*Waubonsee Community College*

Zhaoyang Gu
*Carnegie Mellon University*

Larry Hegstad
*Pacific Lutheran University*

Nancy Hill
*DePaul University*

Mark P. Holtzman
*Hofstra University*

Harry Hooper
*Santa Fe Community College*

Fredric Jacobs
*Michigan State University*

Sanford Kahn
*University of Cincinnati*

John Karayan
*Cal Poly Pomona*

Marsha Kertz
*San Jose State college of Business*

Sharon Koechling-Andrae
*Lincoln University*

Leon Korte
*The University of South Dakota*

Dennis Kovach
*Community College of Allegheny County*

Thomas Largay
*Thomas College*

Michel Lebas
*Hautes Estudes Com de Paris*

Roland Lipka
*Temple University*

Suzanne Lowensohn
*Colorado State University*

Suneel Maheshwari
*Marshall University*

Michael Matukonis
*SUNY Oneonta*

Janet McKnight
*University of Wisconsin-Stevens Point*

Betty McMechen
*Mesa State College*

John Metzcar
*Indiana Wesleyan University*

Tim Mills
*Eastern Illinois University*

Elizabeth Minibiole
*Northwood University*

Jamshed Mistry
*Worcester Polytechnic Institute*

Henry Moore
*Florida Community College*

Karen Nunez
*North Carolina State University*

George Otto
*Truman College*

Shirley Polejewski
*University of St. Thomas*

Craig Reeder
*Florida A&M University*

Barbara Reider
*University of Montana*

David Remmele
*University of Wisconsin-Whitewater*

Stefan Reichelstein
*Stanford University*

Lawrence Roman
*Cuyahoga Community College*

Nancy Ruhe
*West Virginia University*

Clayton Sager
*University of Wisconsin-Whitewater*

George Schmelzle
*Indiana University-Purdue University Fort Wayne*

Gowri Shankar
*University of Washington, Bothell*

Lewis Shaw
*Suffolk University*

Mehdi Sheikholeslami
*University of Wisconsin-Eau Claire*

Tommie Singleton
*University of North Alabama*

Richard Stec
*CCAC-North Campus*

Ephraim Sudit
*Rutgers University*

Diane Tanner
*University of North Florida*

Lakshmi U. Tatikonda
*University of Wisconsin-Oshkosh*

Mark Taylor
*Creighton University*

Steve Teeter
*Utah Valley State College*

Wendy Tietz
*Kent State University*

Alex Thevaranjan
*Syracuse University*

Ron Vogel
*College of Eastern Utah*

Jeffrey Wong
*Oregon State University*

Robert Wyatt
*Drury University*

**The first edition was reviewed by:**

Dennis Caplan
*Columbia University*

John S. Chandler
*University of Illinois at Urbana-Champaign*

Julie Chenier
*Louisiana State University*

Kenneth L. Coffey
*Johnson County Community College*

Charles Cullinan
*Bryant College*

R. Dan Edwards
*Seattle University*

Jackson F. Gillespie
*University of Delaware*

Robert Hilbelink
*Dordt College*

Timothy Hohmeier
*Keller Graduate School of Management*

Larry Killough
*Virginia Polytechnic Institute and State University*

Preisha Neidermeyer
*Union College*

Sandra S. Pelfrey
*Oakland University*

Franklin Plewa
*Idaho State University*

Anne Sergeant
*Iowa State University*

Teresa Speck
*Saint Mary's University of Minnesota*

Jack Topoil
*Community College of Philadelphia*

Dick Wasson
*Southwestern College*

Lorraine Wright
*North Carolina State University*

Gilroy J. Zuckerman
*North Carolina State University*

## Focus Group Participants

Kashi Balachandran
*New York University*

C.S. Agnes Cheng
*University of Houston*

Douglas Cloud
*Pepperdine University*

Charles Cullinan
*Bryant College*

Jill D'Aquila
*Iona College*

Hank Davis
*Eastern Illinois University*

Patricia Doherty
*Boston University*

Dean Edmiston
*Emporia State University*

John Harry Evans III
*University of Pittsburgh*

Ann Gabriel
*University of Notre Dame*

Joanna Ho
*University of California-Irvine*

Timothy Hohmeier
*Keller Graduate School of Management*

Robert Holtfreter
*Central Washington University*

Larry Killough
*Virginia Polytechnic Institute
and State University*

Eileen Peacock
*Oakland University*

Linda Ruchala
*University of Nebraska*

Kenneth Sinclair
*Lehigh University*

LaVerne Thompson
*St. Louis Community College-Meramac*

Wallace Wood
*University of Cincinnati*

## Other Contributors

Vidya Awasti, *Seattle University,*
Consultant—End-of-Chapter Material

Larry DuCharme, *University of
Washington*, Consultant—End-of-
Chapter Material

# CONTENTS

## Chapter 3
# PROCESS COSTING   79

## Chapter 4
# COST-VOLUME-PROFIT ANALYSIS                                           111

## Chapter 5
# VARIABLE COSTING                                                      163

## Chapter 6
## COST ALLOCATION AND ACTIVITY-BASED COSTING 187

## Chapter 7
## THE USE OF COST INFORMATION IN MANAGEMENT DECISION MAKING 235

## Chapter **8**
## PRICING DECISIONS, ANALYZING CUSTOMER PROFITABILITY, AND ACTIVITY-BASED PRICING   275

## Chapter **9**
## CAPITAL BUDGETING DECISIONS   297

## Chapter **10**
# BUDGETARY PLANNING AND CONTROL                    339

## Chapter **11**
# STANDARD COSTS AND VARIANCE ANALYSIS              381

## Chapter **12**
# DECENTRALIZATION AND PERFORMANCE EVALUATION    417

## Chapter **13**
## ANALYZING FINANCIAL STATEMENTS: A MANAGERIAL PERSPECTIVE  463

# LIST OF CASES

Each chapter of *Managerial Accounting* includes one or more cases that:

- Promote critical thinking and decision making skills.
- Provide an opportunity for group work and/or written communication work.
- Integrate information from other business disciplines.

**Chapter 1**

1–1: THE CASE OF LOCAL 635
A union is disputing "cost of meal" charges to hotel employees.

1–2: HERBERT PLUMBING PRODUCTS   A senior manager wants to know a product's cost. But the "cost" information needed depends on the decision the senior manager is facing.

**Chapter 2**

2–1: Ethics Case: BRIXTON SURGICAL DEVICES
To meet an aggressive earnings target, two senior executives are planning to increase production to "bury" fixed overhead costs in inventory.

2–2: CLK MARKETING RESEARCH
A marketing research firm is considering various costs when bidding on a job.

2–3: DYNAMIC HYDRAULIC SYSTEMS
A manufacturing firm is surprised that it is winning orders for complex products while the company is not price competitive on simple jobs that require less skilled (and lower-paid) workers.

2–4: DUPAGE POWDER COATING
A company's product costs are being distorted by its approach to overhead allocation.

**Chapter 3**

3–1: Tech-Tonic Sports Drink
A producer of a sports drink is considering alternative treatments for the cost of lost units.

3–2: JENSEN PVC, INC.
A company is considering lowering prices to increase sales and reduce unit costs by making better use of excess capacity.

**Chapter 4**

4–1: Ethics Case: WENDELL ROBERTS CONSULTING
A consultant's assumptions are biasing the calculation of damages related to a lawsuit.

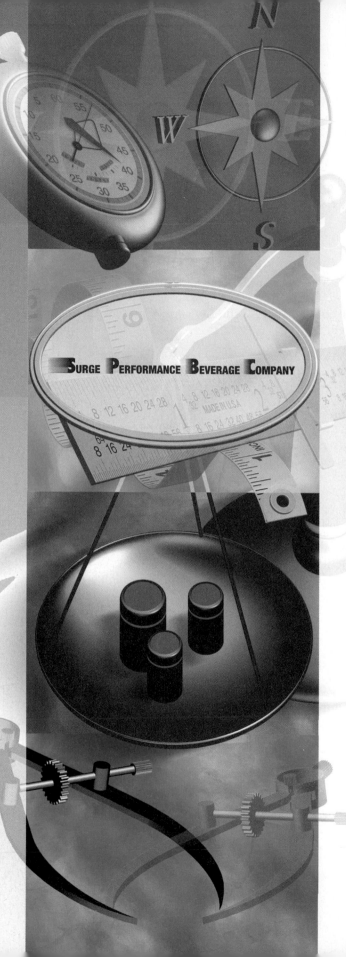

# chapter 1

## LEARNING OBJECTIVES

**1** State the primary goal of managerial accounting.

**2** Describe how budgets are used in planning.

**3** Describe how performance reports are used in the control process.

**4** Distinguish between financial and managerial accounting.

**5** Define cost terms used in planning, control, and decision making.

**6** Explain the two key ideas in managerial accounting.

**7** Discuss the impact of information technology on competition, business processes, and the interactions companies have with suppliers and customers.

**8** Describe a framework for ethical decision making.

**9** Discuss the duties of the controller, the treasurer, the chief information officer (CIO), and the chief financial officer (CFO).

# MANAGERIAL ACCOUNTING IN THE INFORMATION AGE

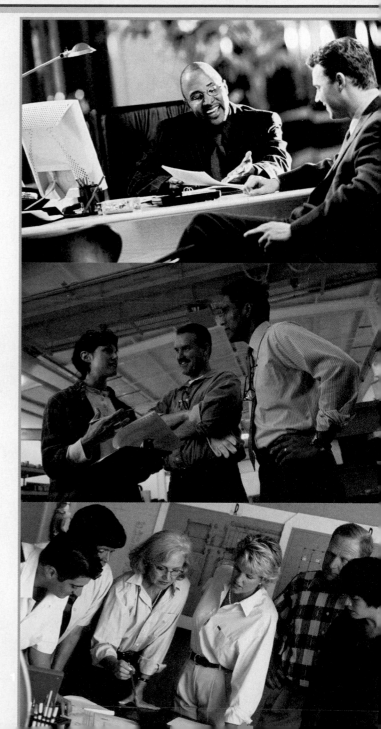

**W**hat type of job will you hold in the future? You may be a marketing manager for a consumer electronics firm, you may be the director of human resources for a biotech firm, or you may be the president of your own company. In these and other managerial positions you will have to plan operations, evaluate subordinates, and make a variety of decisions using accounting information. In some cases, you will find information from your firm's balance sheet, income statement, statement of retained earnings, and statement of cash flows to be useful. However, much of the information in these statements is more relevant to *external* users of accounting information, such as stockholders and creditors. In addition, you will need information prepared specifically for firm managers, the *internal* users of accounting information. This type of information is referred to as managerial accounting information.

If you are like most users of this book, you have already studied financial accounting. Financial accounting stresses accounting concepts and procedures that relate to preparing reports for external users of accounting information. In comparison, **managerial accounting** stresses accounting concepts and procedures that are relevant to preparing reports for internal users of accounting information. This book is devoted to the subject of managerial accounting, and this first

SURGE PERFORMANCE BEVERAGE COMPANY

1

See the video on the interactive CD that describes the use of managerial accounting at Wizards of the Coast.

State the primary goal of managerial accounting.

Describe how budgets are used in planning.

chapter provides an overview of the role of managerial accounting in planning, control, and decision making. The chapter also defines important cost concepts, and introduces key ideas that will be emphasized throughout the text. The chapter ends with a discussion of the information age and the impact of information technology on business, a framework for ethical decision making, and the role of the controller as the top management accountant. Lastly, you can enhance and test your knowledge of the chapter using the interactive CD that accompanies this book.

# GOAL OF MANAGERIAL ACCOUNTING

Virtually all managers need to plan and control their operations and make a variety of decisions. The goal of managerial accounting is to provide the information they need for *planning, control,* and *decision making.* If *your* goal is to be an effective manager, a thorough understanding of managerial accounting is essential.

## PLANNING

Planning is a key activity for all companies. A plan communicates a company's goals to employees aiding coordination of various functions such as sales and production. A plan also specifies the resources needed to achieve company goals.

**Budgets for Planning.** The financial plans prepared by managerial accountants are referred to as **budgets**. A wide variety of budgets may be prepared. For example, a *profit budget* indicates planned income, a *cash-flow budget* indicates planned cash inflows and outflows, and a *production budget* indicates the planned quantity of production and the expected costs.

Consider the production budget for Surge—Performance Beverage Company. In the coming year, the company plans to produce 5,000,000 12-ounce bottles. This amount is based on forecasted sales. To produce this volume, the company estimates it will spend $1,500,000 on bottles, $400,000 on ingredients, $150,000 on water, and pay workers at its bottling plant $300,000. It also expects to pay $60,000 for rent, incur $80,000 of depreciation of equipment, and pay $100,000 for other costs. The product cost budget presented in Illustration 1-1 summarizes

**Illustration 1-1**
Production cost budget

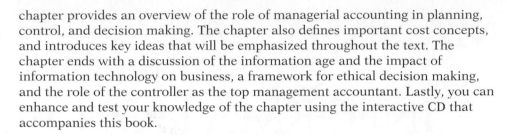

| **SURGE PERFORMANCE BEVERAGE COMPANY** | |
|---|---|
| **Budgeted Production Costs** | |
| **For the Year Ended December 31, 2006** | |
| **Budgeted Production** | **5,000,000 Bottles** |
| Cost of bottles | $1,500,000 |
| Ingredient cost | 400,000 |
| Water | 150,000 |
| Labor cost | 300,000 |
| Rent | 60,000 |
| Depreciation | 80,000 |
| Other | 100,000 |
| Total budgeted production cost | $2,590,000 |

this information. This budget informs the managers of Surge about how many bottles the company intends to produce and what the necessary resources will cost.

Describe how performance reports are used in the control process.

Managerial accounting information is used to plan and control operations and make decisions at Surge—Performance Beverage Company.

## CONTROL

Control of organizations is achieved by evaluating the performance of *managers* and the *operations* for which they are responsible. The distinction between evaluating managers and evaluating the operations they control is important. Managers are evaluated to determine how their performance should be rewarded or punished, which in turn motivates them to perform at a high level. Based on an evaluation indicating good performance, a manager might receive a substantial bonus. An evaluation indicating a manager performed poorly might lead to the manager being fired. In part because evaluations of managers are typically tied to compensation and promotion opportunities, managers work hard to ensure that they will receive favorable evaluations. (Of course, managers may also work hard because they love their jobs, receive respect from coworkers, or value the sense of accomplishment from a job well done!)

Operations are evaluated to provide information as to whether or not they should be changed (i.e., expanded, contracted, or modified in some way). An evaluation of an operation can be negative even when the evaluation of the manager responsible for the operation is basically positive. For example, the manager of one of the two bottling plants at Surge—Performance Beverage Company may do a good job of controlling costs and meeting deadlines given that the plant is old and out of date. Still, senior management may decide to close the plant because, given the outdated equipment in the plant, it is not an efficient operation. In this scenario, the manager receives a positive evaluation whereas the operation receives a negative evaluation.

Company plans often play an important role in the control process. Managers can compare actual results with planned results and decide if corrective action is necessary. If actual results differ from the plan, the plan may not have been followed properly; the plan may have not have been well thought out; or changing circumstances may have made the plan out of date.

Illustration 1-2 presents the major steps in the planning and control process. Once a plan has been made, actions are taken to implement it. These actions lead to results that are compared with the original plan. Based on this evaluation, managers are rewarded (e.g., given substantial bonuses or promoted if performance is judged to be good) or punished (e.g., given only a small bonus, given no bonus, or even fired if performance is judged to be poor). Also, based on the evaluation process, operations may be changed. Changes may consist of expanding (e.g., adding a second shift), contracting (e.g., closing a production plant), or improving operations (e.g., training employees to do a better job answering customer product inquiries). Changes may also consist of revising an unrealistic plan.

**Performance Reports for Control.** The reports used to evaluate the performance of managers and the operations they control are referred to as **performance reports**. Although there is no generally accepted method of preparing a performance report, such reports frequently involve a comparison of current period performance with performance in a prior period or with planned (budgeted) performance.

**Illustration 1-2**
Planning and control
process

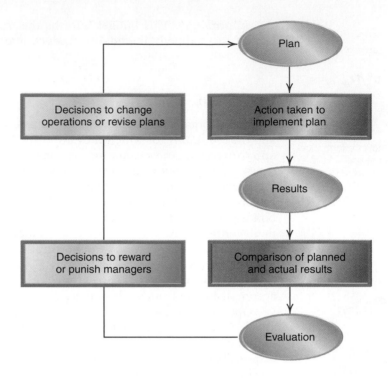

Suppose, for example, that during 2006, Surge—Performance Beverage Company actually produced 5,000,000 bottles and incurred the following costs:

| | |
|---|---|
| Cost of bottles | $1,650,000 |
| Ingredient cost | 450,000 |
| Water | 152,000 |
| Labor cost | 295,000 |
| Rent | 60,000 |
| Depreciation | 80,000 |
| Other | 101,000 |
| Total actual production cost | $2,788,000 |

A performance report comparing these actual costs to the budgeted costs is presented in Illustration 1-3.

Typically, performance reports only suggest areas that should be investigated; they do not provide definitive information on performance. For example, the performance report presented in Illustration 1-3 indicates that something may be amiss in the control of bottle and ingredient cost. Actual costs are $150,000 more than planned for bottles and $50,000 more than planned for ingredients. There are many possible reasons why these costs are greater than the amounts budgeted. Perhaps the price of bottles or key ingredients increased, or perhaps bottles were damaged in the production process. Management must investigate these possibilities before taking appropriate corrective action.

**Illustration 1-3**
Performance Report

**SURGE PERFORMANCE BEVERAGE COMPANY**

**Performance Report, Production Costs**
**For the Year Ended December 31, 2006**

|  | Actual | Budget | Difference (Actual Minus Budget) |
|---|---|---|---|
| Production (number of bottles) | 5,000,000 | 5,000,000 | -0- |
| Cost of bottles | $1,650,000 | $1,500,000 | $150,000 |
| Ingredient cost | 450,000 | 400,000 | 50,000 |
| Water | 152,000 | 150,000 | 2,000 |
| Labor Cost | 295,000 | 300,000 | (5,000) |
| Rent | 60,000 | 60,000 | -0- |
| Depreciation | 80,000 | 80,000 | -0- |
| Other | 101,000 | 100,000 | 1,000 |
| Total production cost | $2,788,000 | $2,590,000 | $198,000 |

Although performance reports may not provide definitive answers, they are still extremely useful. Managers can use them to "flag" areas that need closer attention and to avoid areas that are under control. It would not seem necessary, for example, to investigate labor, rent, depreciation, or other costs, because these costs are either equal to or relatively close to the planned level of cost. Typically, managers follow the principle of **management by exception** when using performance reports. This means that managers investigate departures from the plan that appear to be exceptional; they do not investigate minor departures from the plan.

## DECISION MAKING

As indicated in Illustration 1-2, decision making is an integral part of the planning and control process—decisions are made to reward or punish managers, and decisions are made to change operations or revise plans. Should a firm add a new product? Should it drop an existing product? Should it manufacture a component used in assembling its major product or contract with another company to produce the component? What price should a firm charge for a new product? These questions indicate just a few of the key decisions that confront companies. And how well they make these decisions will determine future profitability and, possibly, the survival of the company. Recognizing the importance of making good decisions, we'll devote all of Chapters 7 and 8 to the topic. And below you'll see that one of the two key ideas of managerial accounting relates to decision making and its focus on so-called incremental analysis. Finally, at the end of each chapter, there is a feature called MAKING BUSINESS DECISIONS. This feature will remind you of how the chapter material is linked to decision making, and it will summarize the knowledge and skills presented in the chapter that will help you make good decisions as a manager.

Distinguish between financial and managerial accounting.

# A COMPARISON OF MANAGERIAL AND FINANCIAL ACCOUNTING

As suggested in the opening of this chapter, there are important differences between managerial and financial accounting:

1. Managerial accounting is directed at internal rather than external users of accounting information.
2. Managerial accounting may deviate from generally accepted accounting principles (GAAP).
3. Managerial accounting may present more detailed information.
4. Managerial accounting may present more nonmonetary information.
5. Managerial accounting places more emphasis on the future.

**Internal versus External Users.** Financial accounting is aimed primarily at external users of accounting information, whereas managerial accounting is aimed primarily at internal users (i.e., company managers). External users include investors, creditors, and government agencies, who need information to make investment, lending, and regulation decisions. Their information needs differ from those of internal users, who need information for planning, control, and decision making.

**Need to Use GAAP.** Much of financial accounting information is required. The Securities and Exchange Commission (SEC) requires large, publicly traded companies to prepare reports in accordance with generally accepted accounting principles (GAAP). Even companies that are not under the jurisdiction of the SEC prepare financial accounting information in accordance with GAAP to satisfy creditors. Managerial accounting, on the other hand, is completely optional. It stresses information that is *useful* to internal managers for planning, control, and decision making. If a managerial accountant believes that deviating from GAAP will provide more useful information to managers, GAAP need not be followed.

**Detail of Information.** Financial accounting presents information in a highly summarized form. Net income, for example, is presented for the company as a whole. To run a company, however, managers need more detailed information, for example, information about the cost of operating individual departments in addition to the cost of operating the company as a whole.

**Emphasis on Nonmonetary Information.** Both managerial and financial accounting reports generally contain monetary information (information expressed in dollars such as revenue and expense). But, managerial accounting reports can also contain a substantial amount of nonmonetary information. The quantity of material consumed in production, the number of hours worked by the office staff, and the number of product defects are examples of important nonmonetary data that appear in managerial accounting reports.

**Emphasis on the Future.** Financial accounting is primarily concerned with presenting the results of past transactions. Managerial accounting, on the other hand, places considerable emphasis on the future. As indicated previously, one of the primary purposes of managerial accounting is planning. Thus, managerial accounting information often involves estimates of the costs and benefits of future transactions.

## SIMILARITIES BETWEEN FINANCIAL AND MANAGERIAL ACCOUNTING

We shouldn't overstate the differences between financial accounting and managerial accounting in terms of their respective user groups. Financial accounting reports are aimed *primarily* at external users, and managerial accounting reports are aimed *primarily* at internal users. However, managers also make significant use of financial accounting reports, and external users occasionally request financial information that is generally considered appropriate for internal users. For example, creditors may ask management to provide them with detailed cash-flow projections.

Define cost terms used in planning, control, and decision making.

# COST TERMS USED IN DISCUSSING PLANNING, CONTROL, AND DECISION MAKING

When managers discuss planning, control, and decision making, they frequently use the word *cost*. Unfortunately, what they mean by this word is often ambiguous. This section defines key cost terms so that you will have the accounting vocabulary necessary to discuss issues related to planning, control, and decision making. The discussion will be brief because we will return to these cost terms and examine them in detail in later chapters.

## VARIABLE AND FIXED COSTS

The classification of a cost as variable or fixed depends on whether the cost changes or remains the same in relation to the level of business activity.

**Variable Costs.** Costs that increase or decrease in proportion to increases or decreases in the level of business activity are **variable costs**. Material and direct labor are variable costs because they fluctuate with changes in production (business activity). Suppose that for Surge—Performance Beverage Company the cost of bottles, ingredients, water and labor are variable costs and in the prior month when production was 400,000 bottles, costs were $120,000 for bottles, $32,000 for ingredients, $12,000 for water and $24,000 for labor. How much variable cost should the company plan on for the current month if production is expected to increase by 20 percent to 480,000 bottles? Assuming the variable costs change in proportion to changes in activity, if production increases by 20 percent, these costs should also increase by 20 percent. Thus, the cost of bottles should increase to $144,000, the cost of ingredients should increase to $38,400, the cost of water to $14,400 and the cost of labor to $28,800.

|  | Prior Month | | Current Month | |
|---|---|---|---|---|
| Production | 400,000 Bottles | Per Unit | 480,000 Bottles | Per Unit |
| Variable costs: | | | | |
| Cost of bottles | $120,000 | $0.30 | $144,000 | $0.30 |
| Ingredient cost | 32,000 | 0.08 | 38,400 | 0.08 |
| Water | 12,000 | 0.03 | 14,400 | 0.03 |
| Labor cost | 24,000 | 0.06 | 28,800 | 0.06 |
| Total variable cost | $188,000 | $0.47 | $225,600 | $0.47 |

Note that although the *total variable cost* increases from $188,000 to $225,600 when production changes from 400,000 to 480,000 units, the *variable cost per unit* does not change. It remains $0.47 per bottle. With variable cost of $0.47 per bottle, variable cost increases by $37,600 (i.e., $0.47 × 80,000) when production increases by 80,000 bottles.

**Fixed Costs.**  Costs that do not change with changes in the level of business activity are **fixed costs**. Depreciation and rent are costs that typically do not change with changes in business activity. Suppose that in the prior month, Surge—Performance Beverage Company incurred $20,000 of fixed costs including $5,000 of rent, $6,667 of depreciation, and $8,333 of other miscellaneous fixed costs. If the company increases production to 480,000 bottles in the current month, the levels of rent, depreciation, and other fixed costs incurred should remain the same as when production was only 400,000 bottles. However, with fixed costs, the cost per unit does change when there are changes in production. When production increases, the constant amount of fixed cost is spread over a larger number of units. This drives down the fixed cost per unit. With an increase in production from 400,000 to 480,000 units, *total fixed costs* remains at $20,000. Note, however, that *fixed cost per unit* decreases from $0.0500 per unit to $0.0417 per unit.

| | Prior Month | | Current Month | |
|---|---|---|---|---|
| Production | 400,000 Bottles | Per Unit | 480,000 Bottles | Per Unit |
| Fixed costs: | | | | |
| Rent | $ 5,000 | $0.0125 | $ 5,000 | $0.0104 |
| Depreciation | 6,667 | 0.0167 | 6,667 | 0.0139 |
| Other | 8,333 | 0.0208 | 8,333 | 0.0174 |
| Total fixed cost | $20,000 | $0.0500 | $20,000 | $0.0417 |

## SUNK COSTS

Costs incurred in the past are referred to as **sunk costs**. These costs are not relevant to present decisions, because they do not change when these decisions are made. For example, suppose you buy a ticket to a play for $30. Before the play, you run into a friend who invites you to a party. If you go to the party you won't be able to attend the play. The cost of the ticket is irrelevant to the decision as to whether or not you should go to the party. What matters is how much you will enjoy the party versus the play and how much you can *sell* the ticket for (not how much you *paid* for it). Whether you go to the play or go to the party, you are out $30 (the price of the ticket to the play, which is sunk).

## OPPORTUNITY COSTS

The values of benefits foregone when one decision alternative is selected over another are **opportunity costs**. For example, suppose Surge—Performance Beverage Company refuses an order to produce 50,000 bottles for a grocery chain because taking on the order will require the company to miss delivery deadlines on orders already taken. Suppose the order would have generated $50,000 of additional revenue (the product sells for $1 per bottle) and $23,500 of additional costs. Then the opportunity cost (the net benefit foregone) associated with meeting current delivery deadlines is $26,500 ($50,000 − $23,500).

**Illustration 1-4**
Insurance as both a direct and indirect cost

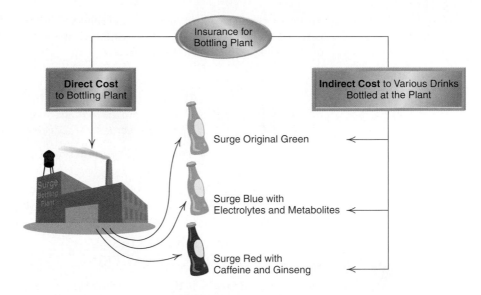

## DIRECT AND INDIRECT COSTS

Costs that are directly traceable to a product, activity, or department are **direct costs**. **Indirect costs** are those that either cannot be directly traced to a product, activity, or department, or are not worth tracing. The distinction between a direct and an indirect cost depends on the object of the cost tracing. For example, Surge—Performance Beverage Company has a production facility in Memphis for which it incurs insurance costs. The insurance cost related to the Memphis plant is obviously a direct cost of the Memphis plant. However, the insurance cost is an indirect cost of the individual types of sports drinks produced in the Memphis plant because *direct* tracing of the insurance cost to each type of drink is not possible. This situation is presented in Illustration 1-4.

## CONTROLLABLE AND NONCONTROLLABLE COSTS

A manager can influence a **controllable cost** but cannot influence a **noncontrollable cost**. The distinction between controllable and noncontrollable costs is especially important when evaluating manager performance. A manager should not be evaluated unfavorably if a noncontrollable cost sharply increases.

As an example of controllable and noncontrollable costs, consider a plant supervisor. This individual influences labor and material costs by scheduling workers and assuring an efficient production process. Thus, labor and material costs are the supervisor's controllable costs. However, the supervisor cannot determine insurance for a plant. A plant manager or an insurance specialist makes decisions regarding insurance. Therefore, insurance cost is a supervisor's noncontrollable cost but a plant manager's or an insurance specialist's controllable cost.

LEARNING OBJECTIVE **6**

Explain the two key ideas in managerial accounting.

# TWO KEY IDEAS IN MANAGERIAL ACCOUNTING

The subject of managerial accounting has many concepts. However, two ideas are fundamental to understanding the use of managerial accounting information in planning, control, and decision making. Keep these two ideas in mind as you progress through your business career—you'll find them to be invaluable! Because the ideas are so important, one or both will be emphasized in each chapter of the book and identified with an icon.

1. Decision making relies on incremental analysis—an analysis of the revenues that increase (decrease) and the costs that increase (decrease) if a decision is selected.

2. You get what you measure!

Decision Making/
Incremental Analysis

# DECISION MAKING RELIES ON INCREMENTAL ANALYSIS

Incremental analysis is the appropriate way to approach the solution to all business problems. Essentially, **incremental analysis** involves the calculation of the difference in revenue and the difference in cost between decision alternatives. The difference in revenue is the **incremental revenue** of one alternative over another, whereas the difference in cost is the **incremental cost** of one alternative over another. If an alternative yields an incremental profit (the difference between incremental revenue and incremental cost), it is the preferred alternative. In the simplified example that follows, decision alternative 1 should be selected because, compared with alternative 2, it yields an incremental profit of $3,000.

| | **Comparison of Decision Alternatives** | | | | |
|---|---|---|---|---|---|
| | **Alternative One** | | **Alternative Two** | | |
| Revenue | $15,000 | − | $10,000 | = $5,000 | Incremental Revenue |
| Cost | 8,000 | − | 6,000 | = 2,000 | Incremental Cost |
| Profit | $ 7,000 | − | $ 4,000 | = $3,000 | Incremental Profit |

Although the idea is simple, implementing it in practice can be difficult—that's why we devote all of Chapters 7 and 8 to decision making. For now, let's look at a decision facing Surge—Performance Beverage Company to gain a better understanding of incremental analysis.

Recall that at Surge—Performance Beverage Company, the budgeted annual production costs for 5,000,000 bottles was $2,590,000 as follows:

| Production | 5,000,000 bottles |
|---|---|
| Cost of bottles | $1,500,000 |
| Ingredient cost | 400,000 |
| Water | 150,000 |
| Labor cost | 300,000 |
| Rent | 60,000 |
| Depreciation | 80,000 |
| Other | 100,000 |
| Total production cost | $2,590,000 |
| Cost per unit | $0.518 |

Now, assume that Surge is approached by a dairy company that offers to buy 200,000 bottles in the coming year for $0.75 per bottle. The dairy plans on using the drink as an ingredient in a new line of frozen yogurt energy bars. In this case, there are two decision alternatives: (1) accept the offer, or (2) decline the offer. Currently, Surge sells its product only to grocery and health food stores at $1 per bottle.

If the offer is accepted, incremental revenue (the increase in revenue) will be $150,000 and incremental cost (the increase in cost) will be $94,000. Thus, the incremental profit of accepting the offer is $56,000. Assuming that the company has the capacity to produce the additional 200,000 bottles and that other orders will not have to be turned down if this large order is accepted, (i.e., assuming there are no opportunity costs), Surge—Performance Beverage Company should accept this order.

| | | |
|---|---:|---:|
| Incremental revenue ($.75 × 200,000 bottles) | | $150,000 |
| Less incremental costs: | | |
|    Increase in cost of bottles ($.30 × 200,000) | $60,000 | |
|    Increase in cost of ingredients ($.08 × 200,000) | 16,000 | |
|    Increase in cost of water ($.03 × 200,000) | 6,000 | |
|    Increase in cost of labor ($.06 × 200,000) | 12,000 | 94,000 |
| Incremental profit | | $ 56,000 |

Note that in the analysis, we use only four of the production cost items (cost of bottles, cost of ingredients, cost of water and cost of labor). These are the only costs that increase with the new order, because all other costs (rent, depreciation, and other) are fixed and will not increase with an increase in production. Therefore, they are not incremental costs and are not relevant to the decision at hand. Think about rent expense. If the special order is rejected, rent expense will be $60,000. If the special order is accepted, rent expense will still be $60,000. Since rent expense does not change, it is not incremental, and it is not relevant in analyzing the decision.

## YOU GET WHAT YOU MEASURE!

The second key idea in managerial accounting is "You get what you measure!" In other words, performance measures greatly influence the behavior of managers.

**You Get What You Measure**

**You get what you measure!**
*Performance Measures Drive Behavior*

Companies can select from a vast number of performance measures when deciding how they want to assess performance. Profit, market share, sales to new customers, product development time, number of defective units produced, and number of late deliveries are examples of measures in common use. Because rewards often depend on how well an employee performs on a particular measure, employees direct their attention to what is measured and may neglect what isn't measured.

For example, suppose that at Surge—Performance Beverage Company, sales to new customers is introduced as a primary measure of the performance of the sales manager. How would this influence the behavior of the sales manager? Most likely, this measure will lead the manager to spend more time developing business with new customers. Although that may be just what senior management wants from the performance measure, it could lead to problems. Suppose the sales manager greatly reduces the time spent attending to the needs of existing customers, and the company loses the business of several key accounts. To avoid this and other unintended consequences, companies need to develop a balanced set of performance measures and avoid placing too much emphasis on any single measure.

**LEARNING OBJECTIVE 7**

Discuss the impact of information technology on competition, business processes, and the interactions companies have with suppliers and customers.

# THE INFORMATION AGE AND MANAGERIAL ACCOUNTING

In recent years, advances in information technology have radically changed access to information and, in consequence, the business landscape—so much so, that the current business era is frequently referred to as the *information age*. Since managerial accounting is about *providing information* in order to plan and control operations and to make decisions, part and parcel of an understanding of managerial accounting is an understanding of the impact of information technology on competition, business processes, and the interactions companies have with suppliers and customers. These topics are discussed in this section.

## COMPETITION AND INFORMATION TECHNOLOGY

Business competition since the 1970s has been intense. Deregulation of airlines and banking, dropping of trade barriers in response to both the North American Free Trade Agreement (NAFTA) and the organization of the European Union, and economic development in Asia have all played a role. Now advances in information technology are redefining the meaning of intense competition. Consider the impact of exchanges: Web sites that are used to conduct auctions. ChemConnect, for example, operates a public on-line marketplace that brings together buyers and sellers of chemicals and plastics. Using their site, a company can place an order for a plastics stabilizer and receive a bid from a U.S. company in minutes, if not seconds. The problem for the potential U.S. supplier, however, is that it will be bidding against other U.S. companies as well as competitors from Asia and Europe whose prices will also be posted almost instantaneously. Local U.S. companies also face stiff competition from dot-coms operating in other states. In many cases, consumers will shop their local store to examine merchandise but then make their purchase over the Internet from an out-of-state dot-com with a lower price. But while advances in information technology have increased competition, they have also created opportunities and cost savings for firms that use information for strategic advantage in dealing with customers, suppliers, and improving internal processes.

## THE IMPACT OF INFORMATION TECHNOLOGY ON MANAGEMENT OF THE VALUE CHAIN

The **value chain** comprises a company's internal operations and its relationships and interactions with suppliers and customers that are aimed at creating maximum value for the least possible cost. Illustration 1-5 presents a picture of the

**Illustration 1-5**
The value chain for
Winston Clothiers

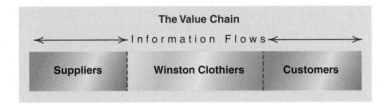

value chain for Winston Clothiers. Winston has 35 stores throughout the United States and annual sales of over $800 million. For Winston to be successful, its suppliers must provide high quality items, on time, to the right location, at a reasonable price. Also, Winston's own operations must be efficient. It must be able to market effectively and offer products that customers want. How can Winston ensure that this happens? The key is to take advantage of information flows up and down the value chain. This is where advances in information technology are having an impact. Note that in Illustration 1-5 the lines between suppliers and Winston and between customers and Winston are dashed lines. This represents the fact that the organizational boundaries are somewhat permeable because a lot of information is being transmitted both ways. Let's see some examples of how this works.

**Information Flows between Winston and Customers.** When customers make purchases, a Winston employee scans a bar code attached to the sale item thereby automatically transferring the sale information into a data base. This information can be used to update inventory records and ensure the company does not run out of "hot" items. The data base also provides information on slow moving merchandise that Winston can sell to a discount department store so that it doesn't take up valuable floor space. Further analysis of the sales data can reveal regional tastes in clothes helping Winston to buy the right styles for stores in different parts of the country. Winston may also track the buying patterns of customers who identify themselves by using Winston's credit card or a special customer discount card. This information can help Winston direct targeted selling messages to different customer types via email.

**Information Flows between Winston and Suppliers.** With several key suppliers, Winston has set up processes whereby the suppliers monitor Winston's sales of their merchandise using information from Winston's internal data base. Winston shares this information because the suppliers use it to improve their production scheduling, gain efficiencies, and pass along some of the related cost savings to Winston in the form of lower prices. Winston also tracks the status of its orders using its suppliers' Web sites. Thus, Winston knows the exact time merchandise will be arriving at each of its locations, and this information is available any time of the day. Winston uses this information, in part, to time its advertising campaigns.

**Using Information Technology to Gain Internal Efficiencies.** Internally, Winston uses information technology to automate purchasing and accounts payable, sales and customer billing, as well as other accounting and finance functions. While in the past the company could not close its books until one month after year end, it can now close in a week. This provide senior managers with timely information on the company's profitability and allows the company to provide timely financial reports to shareholders. The company has over 2,000 employees. Each employee has access to a company human resources (HR) Web site that provides comprehensive information on company policies and allows employees to select from a menu of alternative health and retirement plans. The launch of the Web site has eliminated the need for five full-time HR staff who previously responded to employee questions and processed paperwork.

## SOFTWARE SYSTEMS THAT IMPACT VALUE CHAIN MANAGEMENT

Companies use a variety of software systems to process information and improve the operation of the value chain. Here, we'll briefly discuss three systems: Enterprise Resource Planning (ERP) systems, Supply Chain Management (SCM) systems, and Customer Relationship Management systems (CRM).

**Enterprise Resource Planning Systems.** ERP systems grew out of material requirements planning (MRP) systems which have been used for more than 20 years. MRP systems computerized inventory control and production planning. Key features included an ability to prepare a master production schedule, a bill of materials, and generate purchase orders. **ERP** systems update MRP systems with better integration, relational databases, and graphical user interfaces. Features now encompass supporting accounting and finance, human resources, and various e-commerce applications including SCM and CRM which are discussed next.

**Supply Chain Management Systems.** Supply chain management (SCM) is the organization of activities between a company and its suppliers in an effort to provide for the profitable development, production, and delivery of goods to customers. By sharing information, production lead times and inventory holding costs have been reduced, while on-time deliveries to customers have been improved. **SCM** software systems support the planning of the best way to fill orders and help tracking of products and components among companies in the supply chain. Wal-Mart and Procter & Gamble (P&G) are two companies that have become well known for their cooperation in the use of SCM. When P&G products are scanned at a Wal-Mart store, P&G receives information on the sale via satellite and, thus, knows when to make more product and the specific Wal-Mart stores to which the product should be shipped. Related cost savings are passed on, at least in part, to Wal-Mart customers.

**Customer Relationship Management Systems. CRM** systems automate customer service and support. They also provide for customer data analysis and support e-commerce storefronts. While CRM is constantly evolving, it's already led to some remarkable changes in the way companies interact with customers. For example, Federal Express allows customers to track their packages on the Web. This service is becoming commonplace, but it didn't exist 10 years ago. Amazon.com uses CRM technology to make suggestions to customers based on their personal purchase histories. The ultimate development of CRM remains to be seen but undoubtedly mobile communication will play a significant role. Many companies are already experimenting with systems to send messages to cell phone users offering them special discounts and buying "opportunities."

## Savings from Taking Business Processes to the Web

Disney spends about $9 billion annually on goods and services. With that dollar level of spending, automation of key businesses processes can offer hefty savings. In 2000, Disney began a project called eSource, which allowed employees to buy everything from pencils to computers on-line via their desktop PCs. The system cost the company $20 million but saves approximately $40 million per year.

Dallas-based Texas Instrument spends $200 million annually on supplemental workers and consultants. The company implemented Cascadeworks software, which addresses staffing, consulting, and service agreements, and found that the system paid for itself in less than a year. Now when a supplemental worker's end term is entered into the system, computer access is automatically terminated. And with terms of employment captured by the system, final salary payments are made automatically.

*Sources: CFO, The Magazine for Senior Financial Executives*, November 2001, pp. 91–94. "Texas Instruments Goes Live with Powerful Services E-Procurement Solution From CascadeWorks," *CascadeWorks*, December 10, 2001. David Hannon, "Electronics Giant Centralizes Contract Labor Buy Online," *Reed Business Information*, February 21, 2002.

**LEARNING OBJECTIVE 8**

Describe a framework for ethical decision making.

# ETHICAL CONSIDERATIONS IN MANAGERIAL DECISION MAKING

Remember that when we discuss decision making throughout this book, we will focus on incremental analysis as the approach to making good decisions. However, in addition to performing incremental analysis, it is equally important that managers consider the ethical aspects of their decisions. Whey focus on ethics? First and foremost, ethical decision making is simply the "right thing to do." But additionally, when managers behave ethically, they gain the confidence of their customers, suppliers, subordinates, and company stockholders and that confidence is likely to translate into gains to the bottom line and the company stock price.

## ETHICAL AND UNETHICAL BEHAVIOR

Ethical behavior requires that managers recognize the difference between what's right and what's wrong and then make decisions consistent with what's right. In recent years, we've witnessed a plethora of disclosures, indictments, and convictions, indicating that key managers in major companies either can't tell right from wrong or don't care to make decisions consistent with what's right. Some examples:

> Enron managers mislead investors by hiding debt in so-called special purpose entities. Kenneth Lay, Enron's CEO, touted Enron's stock to employees just weeks before the energy company imploded leaving many with worthless 401(k) retirement accounts.

Arthur Anderson (formerly one of the world's largest audit firms and Enron's auditor) was found guilty of destroying literally thousands of audit records in an effort to keep them away from a Securities and Exchange Commission inquiry into Enron.

WorldCom, America's No. 2 long-distance company, disclosed the biggest case of fraudulent accounting in U.S. history with profits overstated by billions. The result—the company declared bankruptcy and began laying off 17,000 employees.

Dennis Kozlowski, who made more than $300 million as head of Tyco, was charged with conspiring with art dealers to avoid sales tax on art he bought for $13.2 million. Tyco's share price took a nosedive following the disclosure.

Sam Waksal, co-founder of ImClone Systems, was charged with insider trading for illegally tipping off family members prior to the public disclosure that the Food and Drug Administration had rejected ImClone's cancer drug.

In addition to these conspicuous and rather clear-cut examples of unethical behavior, some companies and individuals have been accused of paying unconscionably low wages to workers in Third World countries, using child labor, endangering the environment with toxic chemicals, and bribing officials to promote sales abroad. But are these accusations clearly indicative of ethical lapses? Low wages are better than no wages, and, while child labor is reprehensible, the additional income earned by a child may save a family from starvation. The point is that ethical dilemmas are often complex and the situations managers face are often gray rather than black and white. When this is the case, a framework for ethical decision making may help understanding of "what's right."

## A FRAMEWORK FOR ETHICAL DECISION MAKING

The following framework for ethical decision making consists of seven questions.[1] Hopefully answering these questions will serve as an aid in identifying "what's right." But certainly, answering them doesn't guarantee ethical decision making.

### A Seven-Question Framework for Ethical Decision Making
### When evaluating a decision ask:

1. What decision alternatives are available?
2. What individuals or organizations have a stake in the outcome of my decision?
3. Will an individual or an organization be harmed by any of the alternatives?
4. Which alternative will do the most good with the least harm?
5. Would someone I respect find any of the alternatives objectionable?

### After deciding on a course of action, but before taking action, ask:

6. At a "gut level," am I comfortable with the decision I am about to make?
7. Will I be comfortable telling my friends and family about this decision?

---

[1]Developing these questions was aided by three resources located on the Web. The first is *A Guide to Moral Decision Making* by Chris MacDonald in the Department of Bioethics at Dalhousie University (http://www.ethics.ubc.ca/chrismac/publications/guide.html.) The second is material developed by the *Center for Applied Ethics* at the University of British Columbia (*http://www.ethics.ubc.ca/resources/business/*), and the third is *Complete Guide to Ethics Management: An Ethics Toolkit for Managers*, by Carter MacNamera (http://www.mapnp.org/library/ethics/ethxgde.htm).

## Any Questions?

**Q)** Why focus on the Seven-Question Framework for ethical decision making? Many, if not most, companies have a written code of ethics, so when managers make decisions, they just need to consult their company's code to determine if their decision stacks up to what's right in their company's environment.

**A)** Managers should definitely be familiar with their company's code of ethics. However, codes of ethics aren't always a good guide to ethical behavior. Part of the problem is that codes often specify what can't be done rather than what should be done. And some codes focus more on ensuring that decisions are legal rather than right!

A number of exercises, problems, and cases in the end-of-chapter material present ethical dilemmas, and you should refer to this framework when preparing your answers to them. Alternatively, you may wish to consider other ethical perspectives. A large amount of material is available on the Web to help your understanding of ethical decision making.

Discuss the duties of the controller, the treasurer, the chief information officer (CIO), and the chief financial officer (CFO).

# THE CONTROLLER AS THE TOP MANAGEMENT ACCOUNTANT

Who is responsible for preparing the information needed for planning, control, and decision making? In most organizations, the top managerial accounting position is held by the controller. The **controller** prepares reports for planning and evaluating company activities (e.g., budgets and performance reports) and provides the information needed to make management decisions (e.g., decisions related to purchasing office equipment or decisions related to adding or dropping a product). The controller also has responsibility for all financial accounting reports and tax filings with the Internal Revenue Service and other taxing agencies, as well as coordinating the activities of the firm's external auditors.

A simplified example of the organization chart for the controller's office is shown in Illustration 1-6. Note that one of the areas reporting to the controller is

**Illustration 1-6**
Organization chart for the controller's office

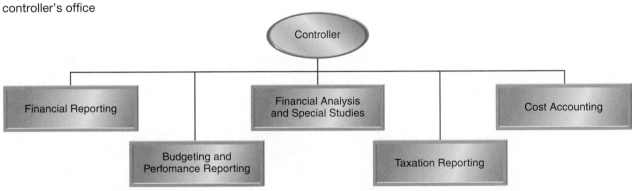

cost accounting. Most medium-sized and large manufacturing companies have such a department. Cost accountants estimate costs to facilitate management decisions and develop cost information for purposes of valuing inventory.

Many companies seeking to fill the position of controller send a clear message to applicants; "Bean counters need not apply!" This means that they want a managerial accountant who does more than concentrate on tracking costs ("counting beans"). They want an individual who will be an integral part of the top management team.

It is obvious that if you want a high-level career in managerial accounting you will need strong accounting skills. But this is not enough. To be an important player on the management team, you will need the skills required of all high-level executives: excellent written and oral communication skills, solid interpersonal skills, and a deep knowledge of the industry in which your firm competes.

In addition to the position of controller, many companies have positions called treasurer and chief information officer (CIO). The **treasurer** has custody of cash and funds invested in various marketable securities. In addition to money management duties, the treasurer is generally responsible for maintaining relationships with investors, banks, and other creditors. Thus, the treasurer plays a major role in managing cash and marketable securities, preparing cash forecasts, and obtaining financing from banks and other lenders. The **chief information officer (CIO)** is the person responsible for a company's information technology and computer systems. Both the controller and the treasurer report to the **chief financial officer (CFO)** who is the senior executive responsible for both accounting and financial operations. At some companies, the CIO also reports to the CFO. However, as we saw earlier, information technology is playing a critical role in managing the value chain and, therefore, it's not surprising that the CIO is frequently part of the senior management team reporting directly to the chief executive officer (CEO).

## *The Institute of Management Accounting*

The Institute of Management Accounting (IMA) is a professional organization that publishes *Strategic Finance* and *Management Accounting Quarterly*. Since 1973, the IMA has conducted a comprehensive examination to test what knowledge a management accountant must have in order to be successful in a complex and fast-changing business world. More than 3,000 individuals take the exam each year. Those who pass the exam are issued a Certificate in Management Accounting and are proud to indicate the designation CMA on resumes and business cards. For details on student and professional memberships in the IMA and information on the CMA examination, visit the IMA Web site (www.imanet.org).

One of the contributions of the IMA is the development of standards of ethical conduct and maintenance of an ethics hotline that members can call to discuss ethical conflicts.

### Japanese Companies Creating a New Executive Position—The CFO!

Unlike their U.S. counterparts, most Japanese companies don't have a chief financial officer (CFO), but the situation is changing. In 1999, Sony hired its first CFO and in 2002, Fujitsu, a large chip and computer company, did the same. Why the move to a CFO position? A lot has to do with Japan's economic woes. The number of Japanese companies that failed in 2002 is at the third highest level since the 1940s. Also, Japan's banks have their own financial problems, and no longer lend funds to companies just because they are part of the same *keiretsu* (a group of corporations that hold shares in each other's companies and provide mutual support). In this environment, the need for an executive who understands financial markets and who can communicate with investors is crucial, so more and more Japanese companies are hiring their first CFO.

*Source: CFO, The Magazine for Senior Financial Executives*, Carla Rapoport, July 2002, p. 54–58.

## MAKING BUSINESS DECISIONS

As we learned in the chapter, decisions are made to reward or punish managers and to change operations or revise plans. Should a company add a new product? Should it drop an existing product? Should a company outsource a business process or perform it internally? What price should a company charge for a new product? Appropriate answers to these types of questions are critical to firm profitability and much of this book will focus on how to address them. While "gut feel" will always play a role in decision making, so too will careful analysis. And the type of analysis we focus on is called incremental analysis which is an analysis of the costs and revenues that change when one decision alternative is selected over another.

### KNOWLEDGE AND SKILLS (K/S) CHECKLIST

*Knowledge and skills are needed to make good business decisions. Check off the knowledge and skills you've acquired from reading this chapter.*

☐ K/S 1. You have an expanded business vocabulary (see key terms).

☐ K/S 2. You understand that incremental analysis is used in decision making.

☐ K/S 3. You have a framework for ethical decision making.

☐ K/S 4. You know that performance measures impact manager behaviors.

☐ K/S 5. You understand that information technology is having a major impact on information flows up and down the value chain.

# S U M M A R Y OF L E A R N I N G O B J E C T I V E S

**1** *State the primary goal of managerial accounting.* The primary goal of managerial accounting is to provide information that helps managers plan and control company activities and make business decisions.

**2** *Describe how budgets are used in planning.* The financial plans prepared by managerial accountants are referred to as budgets. These plans help employees understand company goals and what resources are needed to achieve them.

**3** *Describe how performance reports are used in the control process.* Control of organizations is achieved by evaluating the performance of managers and the operations for which they are responsible. The reports used to evaluate the performance of managers and the operations they control are referred to as performance reports. Frequently, the reports compare current period performance with performance in a prior period or to planned (budgeted) performance. Since evaluations affect the rewards and punishments managers receive, the evaluation process causes them to work hard to receive good evaluations. Evaluations may also lead to modifications in operations, as needed.

**4** *Distinguish between financial and managerial accounting.* Managerial accounting differs from financial accounting in many ways. A key difference is that managerial accounting stresses information that is useful to firm managers, whereas financial accounting stresses information that is useful to external parties. In addition, financial accounting information must be prepared in accordance with GAAP, but managerial accounting information need not be.

**5** *Define cost terms used in planning, control, and decision making.* A number of cost terms are used in discussing planning, control, and decision making. The terms include; *variable cost* (a cost that changes in response to a change in business activity), *fixed cost* (a cost that does not change in response to a change in business activity), *sunk cost* (a cost incurred in the past), *opportunity cost* (a benefit foregone by selecting one decision alternative over another), *direct cost* (a cost that is directly traceable to a product, activity, or department), *indirect cost* (a cost that is not directly traceable to a product, activity, or department or is not worth tracing), *controllable cost* (a cost that a manager can influence), and

*noncontrollable cost* (a cost that a manager can not influence).

**6** *Explain the two key ideas in managerial accounting.* The first key idea is that "decision making relies on incremental analysis." This means that the solution to business problems involves the calculation of the difference in revenue (incremental revenue) and the difference in costs (incremental costs) between decision alternatives. The second key idea is that "you get what you measure!" In other words, how companies measure performance affects how managers behave. This can create problems if managers spend too much time focused on any single performance measure.

**7** *Discuss the impact of information technology on competition, business processes, and the interactions companies have with suppliers and customers.* Information technology (IT) allows buyers to reach suppliers with whom, in the past, it would have been too costly to contract. This has had a great impact on competition. Information technology is also having a profound effect on the entire value chain. Companies use IT to coordinate activities with suppliers and to gain information on customers. IT is also being used to improve the internal processes of companies.

**8** *Describe a framework for ethical decision making.* The framework for ethical decisions making consists of seven questions. See page 16.

**9** *Discuss the duties of the controller, the treasurer, the chief information officer, and the chief financial officer.* The controller is the top management accountant in most organizations. The controller is responsible for preparing reports for planning and evaluating company activities and for preparing information and reports needed to make management decisions. In contrast to the controller, the treasurer is responsible for maintaining relationships with investors, banks, and other creditors. The treasurer also has custody of cash and funds invested in various marketable securities. The chief information officer (CIO) is responsible for information technology. The controller and the treasurer report to the chief financial officer (CFO), who is the senior executive responsible for accounting and financial operations. The chief information officer (CIO) has historically reported to the CFO, but the trend is to have the CIO report to the chief executive officer (CEO).

# KEY TERMS

Budget (2)
Chief financial officer (CFO) (18)
Chief information officer (CIO) (18)
Controllable cost (9)
Controller (17)
Customer relationship
  management (CRM) systems (14)
Direct cost (9)
Enterprise resource planning
  (ERP) systems (14)

Fixed cost (8)
Incremental analysis (10)
Incremental costs (10)
Incremental revenue (10)
Indirect costs (9)
Management by exception (5)
Managerial accounting (1)
Noncontrollable costs (9)

Opportunity costs (8)
Performance report (3)
Supply chain management
  (SCM) systems (14)
Sunk costs (8)
Treasurer (18)
Value chain (12)
Variable cost (7)

# SELF ASSESSMENT   *(Answers Below)*

1. The primary goal of managerial accounting is to:
   a. Provide information to current and potential investors in the company.
   b. Provide information to creditors as well as current and prospective investors.
   c. Provide information to creditors, taxing authorities, and current and prospective investors.
   d. Provide information for planning, control, and decision making.

2. Match the following terms with the management activities described below:
   a. Planning.
   b. Control.
   c. Decision Making.
      (1) This management activity involves changing operations, revising plans, or rewarding/punishing managers.
      (2) This management activity compares actual results with planned outcomes as a basis for corrective action.
      (3) This management activity formulates goals, communicates them to employees, and specifies the resources needed to achieve them.

3. Which of the following statements about budgets is false?
   a. Budgets may be expressed in dollars, quantities, or both.
   b. Budgets may reflect projected revenues, projected expenses, projected cash flows, or projected quantities of inputs or outputs.
   c. Budgets must be prepared in accordance with GAAP.
   d. Budgets are useful both for planning and control.

4. Which of the following statements is false?
   a. Managerial accounting statements do not necessarily comply with GAAP.
   b. Financial accounting statements normally reflect more detail than would be found in managerial accounting reports.
   c. Managerial accounting reports emphasize future activities and future costs.
   d. Financial accounting data are directed primarily at external users rather than internal users.

5. Which of the following is most likely to be a variable cost?
   a. Depreciation.
   b. The cost of material used in production.
   c. Rent.
   d. Advertising.

6. Which of the following is most likely to be a fixed cost?
   a. The cost of material used in production.
   b. Rent.
   c. Assembly labor cost.
   d. Commissions.

7. Costs incurred in the past are:
   a. Opportunity costs.
   b. Direct costs.
   c. Sunk costs.
   d. Variable costs.

8. _____ costs are directly traceable to a product, activity, or department whereas _____ costs are not.

9. The salary a student forgoes while in college is an example of:

   a. Opportunity cost.
   b. Direct cost.
   c. Sunk cost.
   d. Variable cost.

10. List the two key managerial accounting ideas noted in the chapter.

11. The "information age" has impacted:

   a. Relationships and interactions with customers.
   b. Relationships and interactions with suppliers.
   c. Internal processes.
   d. All of the above.

12. Which of the following is not one of the seven questions in the framework for ethical decision making?:

   a. Will an individual or an organization be harmed by any of the decision alternatives?
   b. Would someone I respect find any of the alternatives objectionable?
   c. At a "gut" level, am I comfortable with the decision I am about to make?
   d. Are any of the alternatives illegal?

**Answers to Self Assessment**

**1.** d;   **2.** 1-c, 2-b, 3-a;   **3.** c;   **4.** b;   **5.** b;
**6.** b;   **7.** c;   **8.** Direct, indirect;   **9.** a;
**10.** Decision making relies on incremental analysis. You get what you measure!   **11.** d;   **12.** d.

# INTERACTIVE LEARNING

**Enhance and test your knowledge of Chapter 1 using the interactive CD.**

1. Learning Objectives
2. Multiple Choice
3. Language of Business—Matching of Key Terms
4. Critical Thinking
5. Demonstration—Planning and control process
6. Case—*ValuComp Computers*; Planning and control process
7. Video—Wizards of the Coast; Use of managerial accounting

**Go to our dynamic Web site for more self-assessment, Web links, and additional information.**

# QUESTIONS

1. What is the goal of managerial accounting?

2. Briefly describe the planning and control process.

3. In a performance report, current period performance is compared with some benchmark. What might be a useful benchmark?

4. List three differences between financial and managerial accounting.

5. List three examples of nonmonetary information that might appear in a managerial accounting report.

6. Explain the difference between fixed and variable costs.

7. Consider the manager of the home appliance department at a Sears store. For this manager, list a cost that is controllable and a cost that is non-controllable.

8. What is incremental analysis? How is the concept used in decision making?

9. What is meant by the statement "You get what you measure!"?

10. What is the title of the individual to whom the controller and the treasurer report?

11. How have changes in information technology impacted management of the value chain?

12. If an action is legal, is it necessarily ethical? Explain.

# EXERCISES

**EXERCISE 1-1. Group Assignment**  A key idea in this book is that *You get what you measure!* Essentially, this means that performance measures have a great influence on the behavior of managers.

*Required*

Select a company with which you are familiar. Identify three performance measures that the company might use. For each measure, identify a favorable outcome and an unfavorable outcome that might occur because the measure is used to evaluate manager performance.

**EXERCISE 1-2. Writing Assignment**  Nancy Peterson owns Lightning Printing, a copy business with several high-speed printers. One is a color printer that was purchased just last year at a cost of $25,000. Recently a sales person got Nancy to witness a demo of a new $23,000 color printing machine that promises higher speed and more accurate color representation. Nancy's interested but she can't get herself to trade in a perfectly good printer for which she paid $25,000 and replace it with one that will only cost $23,000.

*Required*

Write a paragraph explaining why the cost of the "old" printer is irrelevant to Nancy's decision.

**EXERCISE 1-3. Ethics/Internet Assignment**  Guthrie Wilson is an accountant at Bellwether Systems, a company that sells and installs customer relationship management (CRM) systems. The company sells third-party software at cost plus 20 percent and charges a fee of $200 per hour of installation/integration time spent on each engagement. Recently, Guthrie's boss asked him to charge 60 hours of time to the Bradley account when the time was actually worked servicing the IMG account. The rationale: "Look, IMG is a struggling start-up and they can barely afford our service. We ran over our time estimate due to some unforeseen problems, and they'll balk if we charge them for all of our time. Bradley, on the other hand, is a highly profitable company and we're providing services that are going to make them even more profitable. They'll have no problem with their bill."

*Required*

Go to the website for the Institute of Management Accounting (http://www.imanet.org). Click on *About IMA* and go to their Ethics Center. Click on the code of ethics and examine the IMA's ethical standards. What do the standards suggest that Guthrie should do to resolve the issue he's facing?

**EXERCISE 1-4. Budgets**  Megan Kelly is the chief financial officer of a chain of 25 drugstores. Explain how she can use budgets in both planning profit and controlling operations.

**EXERCISE 1-5. Performance Reports**  Which of the following statements related to performance reports is false?

_____ a. Performance reports may provide a comparison of actual performance with planned performance.

_____ b. Performance reports may provide a comparison of actual performance with performance in a prior period.

_____ c. If actual costs exceed planned costs in a performance report, this clearly indicates managerial incompetence.

_____ d. Performance reports are used to evaluate managers and the operations they control.

**EXERCISE 1-6. Performance Reports**    At ZX Fashions, the budgeted income statement for December, 2006 indicated sales of $100,000 and cost of sales of $60,000. Actual sales and cost of sales were $120,000 and $70,000, respectively. Should Margo Nelson, owner of the company, be concerned that cost of sales is $10,000 greater than planned? Explain the basis for your answer.

**EXERCISE 1-7. Financial vs. Managerial Accounting**    Consider a large manufacturing company like Boeing that rewards its sales force with bonuses based on sales. For this purpose, should the company record sales when orders are placed or, to be consistent with GAAP, wait until orders are delivered?

**EXERCISE 1-8. Cost Terms**    Identify each of the following statements with fixed costs or variable costs.

_____ a. A cost that varies in total with changes in the activity level.
_____ b. A cost that varies on a per-unit basis with changes in the activity level.
_____ c. A cost that remains fixed per unit with changes in the activity level.
_____ d. A cost that remains fixed in total with changes in the activity level.

**EXERCISE 1-9. Cost Terms**    Indicate whether each of the following costs is most likely a fixed cost or a variable cost.

_____ a. Assembly labor.
_____ b. The cost of material used in production.
_____ c. Rent.
_____ d. Depreciation.
_____ e. Fuel cost at an airline.

**EXERCISE 1-10. Cost Terms**    Explain how a cost can be controllable at one administrative level and noncontrollable at another administrative level.

**EXERCISE 1-11. Sunk Cost**    Anne, the manager of quality assurance at an electronics manufacturing firm, purchased a circuit-testing machine last year for $25,000. This year a new machine, which is faster and more reliable than Anne's current model, is available in the market. In deciding whether or not to purchase the new machine, should Anne consider how much she paid for the old machine? Should Anne consider the value of the old machine in the used equipment market?

**EXERCISE 1-12. Opportunity Costs**    Parrish Plumbing provides plumbing services to residential customers from Monday through Friday. Ken Parrish, the owner, believes that it is important for his employees to have Saturday and Sunday off to spend with their families. However, he also recognizes that this policy has implications for profitability, and he is considering staying open on Saturday.

Ken estimates that if his company stays open on Saturday, it can generate $2,000 of daily revenue each day for 52 days per year. The incremental daily costs will be $600 for labor, $400 for parts, $40 for transportation, and $100 for office staff. These costs do not include a share of monthly rent, or a share of depreciation related to office equipment.

Ken is determined not to have employees work on Sunday, but he would like to know the opportunity cost of not working on Saturday. Provide Ken with an estimate of the opportunity cost, and explain why you do not have to consider rent or depreciation of office equipment in your estimate.

**EXERCISE 1-13. Opportunity Cost**    Gordon made plans to visit a friend in Dallas during the Labor Day weekend. However, before the trip his employer asked him if he would work overtime for 16 hours at $25 per hour during the weekend. What will be the opportunity cost if Gordon decides to visit his friend in Dallas?

**EXERCISE 1-14. Incremental Analysis**    Akron Chemicals produces a chemical, PX44, which is used to retard fading in exterior house paint. In the past year, the company produced 200,000 gallons at a total cost of $1,000,000 ($5 per gallon). The company is currently considering an order for 10,000 gallons from a paint company in Japan (to date, Akron has not sold the product in markets outside the United States). Explain why the *incremental cost* associated with this order is likely to be less than $50,000.

**EXERCISE 1-15. Incremental Analysis**   In the past year, Western Components had sales of $8,000,000 and total production costs of $6,000,000. In the coming year, the company believes that sales and production can be increased by 30 percent, but this will require adding a second production shift to work from 4:00 P.M. to 1:00 A.M.

*Required*

a. Indicate three production costs that are likely to increase because of adding a second production shift.

b. What production cost most likely will not increase when the second shift is added?

**EXERCISE 1-16. You Get What You Measure!**   At the start of the current year, Ben Abbot, president of Abbot Products, told his managers that the company was going to begin tracking two new performance measures: customer satisfaction measured via a survey, and percent of orders delivered at the customer request date. Are these new measures likely to affect the behavior of managers? Suggest four possible responses.

**EXERCISE 1-17. Information Age**   In recent years, successful companies have begun to focus on managing *cross-company* processes with suppliers to reduce costs, increase speed, and improve quality. In its print advertisements, J.D. Edwards, a producer of ERP software systems notes that companies must "collaborate or die."

*Required*

Pick a company and discuss how it can collaborate with key suppliers to achieve mutually beneficial outcomes. Your discussion should indicate how information technology can play a role in collaboration.

# PROBLEMS

**PROBLEM 1-1. Budgets in Managerial Accounting**   Marie's Pie Company is in the process of preparing a production cost budget for May. Actual costs in April were:

**Marie's Pie Company**
**Production Costs**
**April 2006**

| Production | 15,000 Pies |
|---|---|
| Ingredient cost (variable) | $18,750 |
| Labor cost (variable) | 22,500 |
| Rent (fixed) | 5,000 |
| Depreciation (fixed) | 6,000 |
| Other (fixed) | 1,000 |
| Total | $53,250 |

*Required*

a. Using this information, prepare a budget for May. Assume that production will increase to 16,000 pies reflecting an anticipated sales increase related to a new marketing campaign.

b. Does the budget suggest that additional workers are needed? Suppose the wage rate is $20 per hour. How many additional labor hours are needed in May? What would happen if management did not anticipate the need for additional labor in May?

c. Calculate the actual cost per unit in April and the budgeted cost per unit in May. Explain why the cost per unit is expected to decrease.

**PROBLEM 1-2. Incremental Analysis**    Consider the production cost information for Marie's Pie Company in problem 1. The company is currently producing and selling 200,000 pies annually. The pies sell for $4.00 each. The company is considering lowering the price to $3.70. Suppose this action will increase sales to 250,000 pies.

***Required***

a. What is the incremental cost associated with producing an extra 50,000 pies?

b. What is the incremental revenue associated with the price reduction of $0.30 per pie?

c. Should Marie's lower the price of its pies?

**PROBLEM 1-3. Budgets in Managerial Accounting**    Kindra Walters, the sales manager of Office Furniture Solutions, prepared the following budget for 2006:

**Sales Department**
**Budgeted Costs, 2006**
**(Assuming Sales of $10,000,000)**

| | |
|---|---:|
| Salaries (fixed) | $400,000 |
| Commissions (variable) | 100,000 |
| Advertising (fixed) | 80,000 |
| Charge for office space (fixed) | 2,000 |
| Office supplies & forms ( variable) | 1,000 |
| Total | $583,000 |

After she submitted her budget, the president of Office Furniture Solutions reviewed it and recommended that advertising be increased to $100,000. Further, he wanted Kindra to assume a sales level of $11,000,000. This level of sales is to be achieved without adding to the sales force.

Kindra's sales group occupies approximately 250 square feet of office space out of total administrative office space of 20,000 square feet. The $2,000 space charge in Kindra's budget is her share (allocated based on relative square feet) of the company's total cost of rent, utilities, and janitorial costs for the administrative office building.

***Required***

Prepare a revised budget consistent with the president's recommendation.

**PROBLEM 1-4. Performance Reports**    Below is a performance report that compares budgeted and actual profit in the children's clothing department of Newport Beach Department Store for the month of December.

**Newport Beach Department Store**
**Children's Clothing**
**Performance Report**
**December 2006**

| | Budget | Actual | Difference |
|---|---:|---:|---:|
| Sales | $400,000 | $450,000 | $50,000 |
| Less: | | | |
|    Cost of merchandise | 200,000 | 270,000 | 70,000 |
|    Salaries of sales staff | 40,000 | 44,000 | 4,000 |
| Controllable profit | $160,000 | $136,000 | ($24,000) |

***Required***

a. Evaluate the department in terms of its increases in sales and expenses. Do you believe it would be useful to investigate either or both of the increases in expenses?

b. Consider storewide electricity cost. Would this cost be a controllable or a noncontrollable cost for the manager of children's clothing? Would it be useful to include a share of storewide electricity cost on the performance report for children's clothing?

**PROBLEM 1-5. Performance Reports**  At the end of 2006, Max Gunther, CFO for Abbot Products, received a report comparing budgeted and actual production costs for the company's plant in Northup, Oregon:

**Manufacturing Costs**
**Northup Plant**
**Budget versus Actual**
**2006**

|  | Budget | Actual | Difference |
|---|---|---|---|
| Materials | $2,000,000 | $2,200,000 | $200,000 |
| Direct labor | 1,500,000 | 1,600,000 | 100,000 |
| Supervisory salaries | 300,000 | 350,000 | 50,000 |
| Utilities | 40,000 | 41,000 | 1,000 |
| Machine maintenance | 160,000 | 163,000 | 3,000 |
| Depreciation of building | 40,000 | 40,000 | -0- |
| Depreciation of equipment | 135,000 | 137,000 | 2,000 |
| Janitorial | 90,000 | 105,000 | 15,000 |
| Total | $4,265,000 | $4,636,000 | $371,000 |

His first thought was that costs must be out of control since actual costs exceed the budget by more than $300,000. However, he quickly recalled that the budget was set assuming a production level of 50,000 units. The Northup plant actually produced 55,000 units in 2006.

*Required*

a. Given that production was greater than planned, should Max expect that all actual costs will be greater than budgeted? Which costs would you expect to increase and which costs would you expect to remain relatively constant?

b. Max is extremely busy—the company has six other plants. Therefore, he cannot spend time investigating every departure from the budget. With this in mind, which cost(s) should Max concentrate on in his investigation of budget differences?

**PROBLEM 1-6. Financial vs. Managerial Accounting**  SportShop.com sells sporting goods and athletic apparel over the Internet. In its first two years of business the company had relatively high sales but also suffered large losses. The company's income statement (filed with the Securities and Exchange Commission, mailed to stockholders, and available on the company's Web site) was as follows:

|  | 2006 | 2005 |
|---|---|---|
| Sales | $5,860,340 | $1,393,500 |
| Cost of sales | 4,568,421 | 1,165,247 |
| Gross profit | 1,291,919 | 228,253 |
| Selling, general and administrative expenses: |  |  |
| Payroll and payroll taxes | 945,672 | 654,783 |
| Option-based compensation | 485,622 | 125,367 |
| Occupancy & office expenses | 523,160 | 321,456 |
| Contract services and professional fees | 704,880 | 436,050 |
| Internet servicing expenses | 201,458 | 136,598 |
| General and administrative expenses | 687,482 | 359,657 |
| Advertising and promotion | 1,257,863 | 684,571 |
| Depreciation and amortization | 19,875 | 12,458 |
|  | 4,826,012 | 2,730,940 |
| (Loss) from operations | ($3,534,093) | ($2,502,687) |

*Required*

a. Assume you are a senior manager for SportShop.com. What forward looking information would you like to see in addition to the income statement which reports prior period profit and loss?

b. For internal reporting purposes, the company has capitalized certain costs related to employee training and advertising. Management's view is that these costs have increased the value of an important asset—the company's brand name. Would this be allowed for external reporting purposes under GAAP?

c. Is the information in the income statement sufficiently detailed for management's needs? Provide four examples of more detailed information that managers would likely request.

d. Suggest three nonmonetary measures that would be useful to managers of SportShop.com but not included in external financial reports.

e. SportShop.com currently reports its income statement on its Web site. Why might management of SportShop.com be reluctant to present nonmonetary information along with the income statement on the company's Web site?

**PROBLEM 1-7. You get what you measure!** Each year, the president of Quantum Electronics selects a single performance measure, and offers significant financial bonuses to all key employees if the company achieves a 10 percent improvement on the measure in comparison to the prior year. He recently expressed the opinion that "this focuses my managers on a single, specific target and gets them all working together to achieve a major objective that will increase shareholder value."

Phyllis Hamilton is a new member of the company's board of directors, and she has begun to question the president's approach to rewarding performance. In particular, she is concerned that placing too much emphasis on a single performance measure may lead managers to take actions that increase performance in terms of the measure but decrease the value of the firm.

*Required*

a. What negative consequence might occur if the performance measure is *sales to new customers ÷ total sales* in the current year versus the prior year? (Note: To receive a bonus, managers would need to *increase* this ratio compared with the prior year.)

b. What negative consequence might occur if the performance measure is *cost of goods sold ÷ sales* in the current year versus the prior year? (Note: To receive a bonus, managers would need to *decrease* this ratio compared with the prior year.)

c. What negative consequence might occur if the performance measure is *selling and administrative expenses ÷ sales* in the current year versus the prior year? (Note: To receive a bonus, managers would need to *decrease* this ratio compared with the prior year.)

**PROBLEM 1-8. Incremental Analysis** The Jefferson Plaza Hotel is a deluxe four star establishment. Late on Friday, it had 10 of its 200 rooms available when the desk clerk received a call from the Riley Hotel. The Riley Hotel made a booking error, and did not have room for three guests (each of whom had a "confirmed" room). The Riley wants to send their customers to the Jefferson, but pay the rate the guests would have been charged at the Riley ($120 per room) rather than paying the normal rate of $200 per room at the Jefferson.

*Required*

a. If the Jefferson Plaza accepts the guests, what will be the incremental revenue?

b. Provide examples of incremental costs that the Jefferson Plaza will incur if it accepts the guests.

c. In your opinion, will the incremental revenue be greater than the incremental cost?

# CASES

## 1-1 LOCAL 635

Local 635 represents kitchen workers at hotels in several Midwestern cities. Part of their labor agreement states that workers *"shall receive one free meal per shift up to a cost of $8, with any cost over $8 being deducted from wages paid to said employee."*

A labor dispute arose at the Riverside Hotel shortly after it was opened in June. Kitchen workers who ate dinner on the late shift found that their wages were reduced by $7 for each meal they consumed at the hotel during their dinner break. Josh Parker, a line cook, stated the widely held belief of the workers, "There's no way these dinners cost the Riverside Hotel $8 to make let alone $15. This is just another case of management trying to rip us off. Take last night. I had the prime rib dinner. The piece of meat cost about $5 and the salad less than $1. That's only $6 in total. Really, there aren't any other costs to speak of. The cook, well he's going to be working in the kitchen and getting paid for eight hours whether he makes my meal or not. This claim that my meal cost $15 is baloney!"

Management of the Riverside Hotel sees the situation differently. Take the case of Josh's dinner. In presenting the hotel's case to a labor arbitration board, Sandy Ross, manager of the hotel explained, "Look, that dinner goes for $25 on the menu so assigning a cost of $15 represents a very good value to the kitchen workers. The contention that the meal only costs $6 is nonsense. True, the meat costs $5 and the salad ingredients cost $1, but there's also the labor costs related to preparing the meal and numerous overhead costs like the cost of the oven that the prime rib is cooked in. That oven cost more than $18,000. And, there's heat, light, power, etc. Each meal we prepare should be assigned part of these overhead costs. And, don't forget that when the worker finishes his or her meal, someone has to clean up. That costs money too. When you add up all of these items, a prime rib dinner easily adds up to $15!"

### Required

a. List examples of costs, at the Riverside Hotel, that are variable, fixed, and sunk. Provide an example of an opportunity cost.

b. What is the source of conflict between labor and management? What changes would you recommend in the wording of the labor agreement?

## 1-2 HERBERT PLUMBING PRODUCTS

Herbert Products produces a variety of valves, connectors, and fixtures used in commercial and residential plumbing applications. Recently, a senior manager walked into the cost accounting department and asked Sara Fielding to tell him the cost of the D45 valve. Sara quickly replied "Why do you want to know?" Noticing that the manager appeared somewhat startled by this statement she explained that "The cost information you need depends on the decision you're going to make. You might be thinking of increasing a scheduled production run of 3,000 D45s by 100 units, or scheduling an *additional* production run, or you might even be thinking of dropping the product. For each of these decisions, the "cost" information that you need is different."

### Required

Using the concept of incremental analysis, expand on Sara's response of "Why do you want to know?" What cost information would be relevant to a decision to drop the product that would not be relevant to a decision to increase a production run by 100 units?

# chapter 2

## LEARNING OBJECTIVES

**1** Distinguish between manufacturing and nonmanufacturing costs and between product and period costs.

**2** Discuss the three inventory accounts of a manufacturing firm.

**3** Describe the flow of product costs in a manufacturing firm's accounts.

**4** Discuss the types of product costing systems.

**5** Explain the relation between the cost of jobs and the Work in Process Inventory, Finished Goods Inventory, and Cost of Goods Sold accounts.

**6** Describe how direct material, direct labor, and manufacturing overhead are assigned to jobs.

**7** Explain the role of a predetermined overhead rate in applying overhead to jobs.

**8** Explain why the difference between actual overhead and overhead allocated to jobs using a predetermined rate is closed to Cost of Goods Sold or is apportioned among Work in Process Inventory, Finished Goods Inventory, and Cost of Goods Sold.

**9** Discuss modern manufacturing practices and how they affect product costing.

# JOB-ORDER COSTING AND MODERN MANUFACTURING PRACTICES

While working in the software industry, Bob Williams spent his limited free time restoring an old wooden motorboat. After 15 years at Mayfield Software, Bob was able to retire and pursue his love affair with old boats on a full-time basis. He's now the new owner of Eastlake Motorboat Company, a small (and, heretofore, barely profitable) manufacturer of custom-built wooden motorboats patterned after the classic lake cruisers built in the 1930s through the 1950s.

During his first week on the job he had a lunch meeting with his accountant, Nancy Young, and expressed his interest in two key drivers of company success—cost estimation and pricing.

"Nancy, I know that before we take an order and set a price for a custom boat, we estimate material, labor, and overhead costs. What I want to do is look at what the boats are actually costing us and compare the actual costs to estimates. I think one of our problems may be that we are underestimating cost and pricing too low. How hard will it be to put together some cost data for a

number of recent orders so I can get a handle on this?"

"Not hard at all," Nancy replied. "We have what's called a job-order costing system that tracks the cost of each custom boat. I can get you the material later this afternoon."

"That's great, Nancy. And while you're at it, maybe you can bring me up to speed on how the costing system works. As you know, my background is in computer programming, and I'm afraid I don't know a lot about accounting. Do you think you can help me out with the basics?"

"You bet," Nancy assured him. "In fact, when we get back to the office, let's grab a cup of coffee and I'll begin your accounting education. Before long, you'll know the difference between product and period costs, fixed and variable costs, and how the job cost sheets relate to inventory on our balance sheet. Frankly, I'm really glad you're interested in the accounting side of things. The previous owner was great with boats but never paid much attention to financial information. That's probably one of the main reasons the company never really prospered."

To determine the cost of manufactured products like the boats made by Eastlake Motorboat, companies use a **product costing system**, an integrated set of documents, ledgers, accounts, and accounting procedures used to measure and record the cost of manufactured products. In this chapter, we consider cost classifications for manufacturing firms and how the costs of manufactured products are reflected in a company's financial statements. In particular, we consider a type of product costing system referred to as a job-order costing system. We will also see how service firms can use a job-order costing system to track the cost of services they provide to customers. Finally, we address modern manufacturing practices and how they are helping companies succeed in a competitive global economy. These practices are important to the study of managerial accounting because they affect the type and amount of costs and, to some extent, the design of the product costing system.

**Learning Objective 1**

Distinguish between manufacturing and nonmanufacturing costs and between product and period costs.

# COST CLASSIFICATIONS FOR MANUFACTURING FIRMS

Companies need to know the cost of their products so that they can set prices, calculate profit when products are sold, and assess the reasonableness of the costs incurred in purchasing or manufacturing products. Determining the cost of items a merchandising firm purchases from a supplier is relatively easy. The cost of the items is the purchase cost net of returns, allowances, and discounts plus related shipping costs. Determining the cost of items a manufacturing firm produces is more complex. Using both labor and machinery, a manufacturing firm converts raw materials into finished goods. Complexity arises because the costs of the resources used in production must be assigned to the units produced.

Merchandising and manufacturing firms are compared in Illustration 2-1. This section discusses the broad classifications of manufacturing and nonmanufacturing costs. It also discusses product and period costs, which are other ways in which costs can be classified.

## MANUFACTURING COSTS

**Manufacturing costs** (also known as product costs) are all the costs associated with the production of goods. They include three cost categories: direct material, direct labor, and manufacturing overhead.

**Direct Material.** **Direct material cost** is the cost of all materials and parts that are directly traced to items produced. For the Eastlake Motorboat Company, a manufacturer of motorboats, direct material includes the wood, the steering assembly, the motor, and a variety of other items.

Direct material cost often does not include the cost of minor materials, such as screws and glue. Although such minor material costs could be traced to a particular boat, tracing the costs may not be worth the time it would take to do so. Materials that are not directly traced to a product are referred to as **indirect materials**.

**Merchandising Firms (e.g., clothing store)**

Buy completed items from suppliers

Suppliers

Stock completed items

Warehouse or store

Sell items to customers

Customers

**Manufacturing Firms (e.g., boat producer)**

Buy raw materials from suppliers

Suppliers

Manufacture product in factory

Labor cost        Material cost

Production process

Other manufacturing cost

Stock completed items

Warehouse or store

Sell items to customers

Customers

**Illustration 2-1**
Comparison of merchandising and manufacturing firms

**Direct Labor.** **Direct labor cost** is the cost of labor that is directly traced to items produced. The Eastlake Motorboat Company's direct labor includes the labor cost of the workers directly involved in constructing each motorboat. It probably does not include the cost of production supervisors, such as the salary of Carl Jensen, the master builder. This manager supervises the production of 10 or more different boats at once. He spends five minutes to an hour on a job before directing his attention to another job or to other aspects of production, such as scheduling workers and ordering equipment. It would be very difficult, if not impossible, to directly trace the time Carl spends scheduling workers to individual jobs. And although it is possible to directly trace the time he spends supervising production of a particular job, it may not be worthwhile to do so. Labor costs that are not traced directly to products produced are referred to as **indirect labor costs**.

**Manufacturing Overhead.** **Manufacturing overhead** is the cost of all manufacturing activities other than direct material and direct labor. It includes indirect material and indirect labor, which were explained earlier, as well as a wide variety of other cost items. For the Eastlake Motorboat Company, manufacturing overhead includes the costs of screws, glue, varnish, supervisor salary, depreciation of tools, depreciation of the building where manufacturing takes place, utilities, and a number of other items. Illustration 2–2 lists some common manufacturing overhead costs.

**Illustration 2-2**
Common manufacturing
overhead costs

| | |
|---|---|
| Indirect factory labor | Power, heat, and light in the factory |
| Indirect material | Depreciation of factory equipment |
| Overtime premium | Depreciation of plant |
| Nightshift premium | Insurance on plant and factory |
| Vacation and holiday pay for factory workers | equipment |
| Social Security and Medicare taxes for factory workers | Repair of factory equipment |
| Health insurance for factory workers | Maintenance of factory building and grounds |
| | Property taxes related to the factory |

## NONMANUFACTURING COSTS

**Nonmanufacturing costs** (also known as period costs) can be defined simply as all costs that are not associated with the production of goods. These costs typically include selling and general and administrative costs.

**Selling Costs. Selling costs** include all the costs associated with securing and filling customer orders. Thus, selling costs include advertising costs, sales personnel salaries, depreciation of automobiles and office equipment used by the sales force, and costs of storing and shipping finished goods.

**General and Administrative Costs. General and administrative costs** are all the costs associated with the firm's general management. These costs include the salaries of the company president and accounting personnel, depreciation of the general office building, depreciation of office equipment used by general managers, and the cost of supplies used by clerical employees.

In many cases, a cost is classified by its use rather than by its specific nature. Consider janitorial costs. Janitorial costs associated with maintaining a production area are classified as a manufacturing cost (specifically, manufacturing overhead). In contrast, janitorial costs associated with maintaining the general office building are classified as a nonmanufacturing cost (specifically, general and administrative costs).

### Any Questions?

**Q** I see that in Illustration 2-2, overtime premium is listed as manufacturing overhead. Why is that? Can't we directly trace overtime to specific jobs worked on after 5 P.M., or on weekends or holidays when overtime is paid?

**A** The fact that a specific job is worked on after 5 P.M. or on a weekend or holiday doesn't necessarily mean that it's a job that *caused* overtime premium to be incurred. Plant supervisors try to schedule jobs in a way that's efficient. It could be that a particular job is worked on after 5 P.M. simply because it's efficient to make it the last job worked on during the day. Because of the difficulty of assigning overtime to specific jobs that *caused* it, most companies simply spread overtime premium among all jobs by including it in manufacturing overhead.

## PRODUCT AND PERIOD COSTS

As mentioned previously, costs that are classified as manufacturing and nonmanufacturing costs can also be classified as product and period costs. This latter distinction is made to emphasize differences in the timing of when costs are recognized as expenses. Product costs are identified with goods produced and expensed when goods are sold. Period costs are identified with accounting periods and expensed in the period incurred.

**Product Costs. Product costs** are those costs assigned to goods produced. Thus, the terms *product costs* and *manufacturing costs* are used interchangeably. Both include direct material, direct labor, and manufacturing overhead. Product costs are considered an asset (inventory) until the finished goods are sold. When the goods are sold, the product costs are expensed. Thus, direct labor cost incurred in 2005 to produce goods sold in 2006 does not reduce income until 2006, the year of the sale. This ensures a proper matching of revenue with the costs necessary to produce it.

**Period Costs. Period costs** are identified with accounting periods rather than with goods produced. Selling and general and administrative costs (nonmanufacturing costs) are period costs. We recognize period costs as expenses in the period incurred. For example, rent paid on an *office building* is a period cost and becomes an expense in the period incurred. In contrast, the rent paid on a *factory building* is a product cost and becomes an expense when goods are sold. Differences between product and period costs are summarized in Illustration 2-3.

**Ilustration 2-3**
Relationships among cost categories

|  | Type of Cost | When Expensed |
|---|---|---|
| **Manufacturing Costs** | **Product Cost** Direct material Direct labor Manufacturing overhead | Expensed when goods are sold |
| **Nonmanufacturing Costs** | **Period Cost** Selling cost General and administrative cost | Expensed in period in which they are incurred |

# PRODUCT COST INFORMATION IN FINANCIAL REPORTING AND DECISION MAKING

Manufacturing companies need product cost information in order to prepare financial statements in accordance with generally accepted accounting principles (GAAP). GAAP requires that inventory on the balance sheet and cost of goods sold on the income statement be presented using full cost information. **Full cost** means that product cost includes both variable and fixed manufacturing overhead as well as direct material and direct labor, which are generally variable costs.

## LINK TO PRACTICE

### Product and Period Costs at Dell

Dell is one of the three largest computer systems companies in the world, with manufacturing facilities in Austin, Texas; Nashville, Tennessee; Eldorado de Sol, Brazil; Xiamen, China; Limerick, Ireland; and Penang, Malaysia. The company's manufacturing process consists of assembly, functional testing, and quality control of its computer systems. Computer components, parts, and subassemblies are obtained from suppliers. Essentially, Dell has a build-to-order manufacturing process that allows it to quickly produce customized computer systems. Its flexi-

ble manufacturing process allows it to have low inventory levels and quickly incorporate new technologies into its product offerings.

Classify each of the following costs as a product or period cost for Dell.

1. Cost of components.
2. Cost of technical support provided to Dell customers.
3. Salary of CEO, Michael Dell.
4. Cost of shipping computers to customers.
5. Cost of assembling components.
6. Cost of testing components prior to assembly.
7. Depreciation related to assembly equipment.

**Answer** (1) Product, (2) Period, (3) Period, (4) Period, (5) Product, (6) Product, (7) Product.

**Decision Making/
Incremental Analysis**

Product cost information is also needed for a variety of managerial decisions. Often, the product cost information needed for management decision making is different from the product cost information produced for external financial reports. Recall from Chapter 1 that decision making relies on incremental analysis—an analysis of the revenues that increase (decrease) and the costs that increase (decrease) if a decision alternative is selected. In most cases, in order to perform incremental analysis, you need to separate fixed and variable cost components. For example, if Bob Williams, the owner of Eastlake Motorboat Company, wants to analyze the impact of increasing prices, he should take into account changes in both revenue and costs. When prices increase, the quantity demanded decreases and so production costs will decrease. However, unless production decreases substantially, most of the fixed costs, such as depreciation and rent on the factory, will not change. Thus, they are not incremental costs and do not affect the decision.

Later in the chapter, we'll return to the Eastlake Company example and the decision facing Bob Williams. For now, you should simply understand that product cost information produced for external reporting purposes may not be appropriate for management decisions unless it is modified or adjusted.

Discuss the three inventory accounts of a manufacturing firm.

# BALANCE SHEET PRESENTATION OF PRODUCT COSTS

As noted earlier, product costs are treated as an asset until the finished goods are sold. In this section, we learn how product costs appear on the balance sheet in three asset accounts related to inventory: Raw Materials, Work in Process, and Finished Goods. In the next section, we discuss how costs flow from one account to another. Then we turn our attention to how the costs are reflected on a company's income statement.

The **Raw Materials Inventory** account includes the cost of materials on hand that are used to produce a company's products. For the Eastlake Motorboat Company, steering assemblies, motors, wood, screws, varnish, and glue are included in Raw Materials Inventory.

**Work in Process Inventory** is the inventory account for the cost of goods that are only partially completed. For example, suppose that at the end of the year the Eastlake Motorboat Company has 10 partially completed boats. The cost of direct labor, direct material, and manufacturing overhead incurred to bring the boats to their current state of partial completion is included in Work in Process.

**Finished Goods Inventory** is the account for the cost of all items that are complete and ready to sell. Suppose that at the end of the year, the Eastlake Motorboat Company has two boats that are completed and ready to sell. Finished Goods includes the cost of direct material, direct labor, and manufacturing overhead incurred to bring those boats to their finished state. A simplified balance sheet showing the three inventory accounts is presented in Illustration 2-4.

**Illustration 2-4**
Balance sheet presentation of inventory accounts

## *Eastlake Motorboat Company*

### Balance Sheet
### As of December 31, 2006

| Assets | | | Liabilities and Stockholders' Equity | |
|---|---|---|---|---|
| Cash | | $ 20,000 | Accounts payable | $ 10,000 |
| Accounts receivable | | 40,000 | Notes payable | 60,000 |
| Inventory | | | Long-term debt | 100,000 |
| **Raw Materials** | $ 50,000 | | Common stock | 400,000 |
| **Work in Process** | 100,000 | | Retained earnings | 100,000 |
| **Finished Goods** | 60,000 | 210,000 | | |
| Equipment (net) | | 400,000 | Total liabilities and | |
| Total assets | | $670,000 | stockholders' equity | $670,000 |

Describe the flow of product costs in a manufacturing firm's accounts.

# FLOW OF PRODUCT COSTS IN ACCOUNTS

In an accounting system, product costs flow from one inventory account to another. Illustration 2-5 demonstrates the flow of product costs in the accounts.

The cost of *direct* material used reduces the Raw Material Inventory account and increases Work in Process Inventory. *Indirect* material used, however, is not added directly to Work in Process; instead, it is accumulated in Manufacturing Overhead. The amount of direct labor used increases Work in Process, but indirect labor is not added directly to Work in Process. Like indirect material, it is accumulated in Manufacturing Overhead. The cost accumulated in Manufacturing Overhead, which includes indirect material, indirect labor, and a variety of other overhead costs, is also added to Work in Process.

Once items are finished, the cost of the completed items is transferred from Work in Process into Finished Goods. The cost of items completed is referred to as **cost of goods manufactured**. When the completed items are sold, the cost of the items sold is transferred from Finished Goods into Cost of Goods Sold.

# INCOME STATEMENT PRESENTATION OF PRODUCT COSTS

When finished goods are sold, the cost of the inventory sold is considered an expense and must be removed from Finished Goods Inventory and charged to Cost of Goods Sold. This provides a matching of revenue (sales dollars) with the cost of producing the revenue (the cost of goods sold).

**Cost of Goods Manufactured.** Before cost of goods sold can be calculated, however, we must calculate cost of goods manufactured. Recall that cost of goods manufactured is the cost associated with all goods completed during a period. Cost of goods manufactured can be calculated using a simple formula. It is equal to the beginning balance in Work in Process plus current manufacturing costs (direct material, direct labor, and manufacturing overhead incurred in the current period) minus the ending balance in Work in Process.

**Cost of Goods Sold.** Once cost of goods manufactured is known, cost of goods sold can also be calculated using a simple formula. It is equal to the beginning balance in finished goods plus cost of goods manufactured minus the ending balance in finished goods.

**Illustration 2-5**
Flow of product costs in accounts

Illustration 2-6 presents a schedule of cost of goods manufactured and a simplified income statement showing cost of goods sold for the Eastlake Motorboat Company. Note that in the income statement the sum of the beginning balance in Finished Goods plus cost of goods manufactured is referred to as the **cost of goods available for sale**.

Discuss the types of product costing systems.

# TYPES OF COSTING SYSTEMS

As noted in the introduction to this chapter, companies use product costing systems (an integrated set of documents, ledgers, accounts, and accounting procedures) to measure and record the cost of manufactured products. There are two major product costing systems: job-order costing systems and process costing systems. The best system to use depends on the type of manufacturing.

**Illustration 2-6**
Schedule of cost of goods
manufactured and an
income statement showing
cost of goods sold

## *Eastlake* Motorboat Company

### Schedule of Cost of Goods Manufactured
### For the Year Ended December 31, 2006

| | | | |
|---|---:|---:|---:|
| Beginning balance in work in process | | | $    40,000 |
| Plus: current manufacturing costs: | | | |
| Direct material | | $1,400,000 | |
| Direct labor | | 600,000 | |
| Manufacturing overhead | | | |
| Heat, light, and power | $ 10,000 | | |
| Rent for production facility | 40,000 | | |
| Depreciation of equipment | 50,000 | | |
| Other | 100,000 | 200,000 | 2,200,000 |
| Total | | | 2,240,000 |
| Less ending balance in work in process | | | 100,000 |
| Cost of goods manufactured | | | **$2,140,000** |

### Income Statement
### For the Year Ended December 31, 2006

| | | |
|---|---:|---:|
| Sales | | $2,600,000 |
| Less cost of goods sold: | | |
| Beginning finished goods | $    80,000 | |
| Add cost of goods manufactured | 2,140,000 | |
| Cost of goods available for sale | 2,220,000 | |
| Less ending finished goods | 60,000 | **2,160,000** |
| Gross profit | | 440,000 |
| Less nonmanufacturing expenses: | | |
| Selling expenses | $ 150,000 | |
| General and administrative expenses | 210,000 | 360,000 |
| Net income | | $    80,000 |

Companies that produce individual products or batches of products that are unique use a **job-order costing system**. This is the case when a company manufactures goods to a customer's unique specifications. Companies using job-order systems include construction companies, producers of equipment and tools, shipbuilding companies, and printing companies. In the context of job-order costing, a **job** is an individual product or batch for which a company needs cost information. When the items that make up the job are completed and sold, the company can match the cost of the job with the revenue it produced and obtain an appropriate measure of gross profit.

Companies that use a **process costing system** generally produce large quantities of identical items. Such companies include metal producers, chemical producers, and producers of paints and plastics. Products like chemicals, paints, and plastics pass through uniform and continuous production operations. Costs are accumulated by each operation, and the unit cost of items is determined by divid-

### *Examples of Companies Using Job-Order and Process Costing Systems*

Which of the following companies use job-order systems and which ones use process costing systems to determine product cost?

**Companies**

| | |
|---|---|
| Pepsico Incorporated | Revlon Consumer Products Corporation |
| Cray Computer Corporation | Chris Craft Boat Company |
| Boeing Company | Goodyear Tire and Rubber Company |
| Starbucks Corporation | Anheuser-Busch Incorporated |

**Answer** Job-order companies—Cray Computer Corporation, Boeing Company, Chris Craft Boat Company. Process costing companies—Pepsico Incorporated, Starbucks Corporation, Revlon Consumer Products Corporation, Goodyear Tire and Rubber Company, Anheuser-Busch Incorporated.

ing the costs of the production operations by the large number of identical items produced.

$$\text{Unit cost of items produced} = \frac{\text{Total cost of production}}{\text{Total number of units produced}}$$

In a process costing system, there is no need to trace costs to specific items produced, since all items are identical. It is sufficient to assign each item its average unit cost of production. You will learn more about process costing systems in Chapter 3. The sections that follow focus on job-order costing.

**LEARNING OBJECTIVE 5**

Explain the relation between the cost of jobs and the Work in Process Inventory, Finished Goods Inventory, and Cost of Goods Sold accounts.

# OVERVIEW OF JOB COSTS AND FINANCIAL STATEMENT ACCOUNTS

As previously discussed, product costs include three cost items: direct material, direct labor, and manufacturing overhead. In a job-order costing system, the cost of a job is the sum of these three cost items. Thus, a job-order system must be able to relate these costs to specific jobs. (See Illustration 2-7.)

You should also recall that product costs are reflected in Work in Process Inventory and Finished Goods Inventory on the balance sheet and in Cost of Goods Sold on the income statement. In a job-order costing system, Work in Process will include the cost of all jobs that are currently being worked on (i.e., are in process). Finished Goods will include the cost of all jobs that are completed but not yet sold. Cost of Goods Sold will include the cost of all jobs that are sold during the accounting period. (See Illustration 2-8.)

**Illustration 2-7**
Relating product costs
to jobs

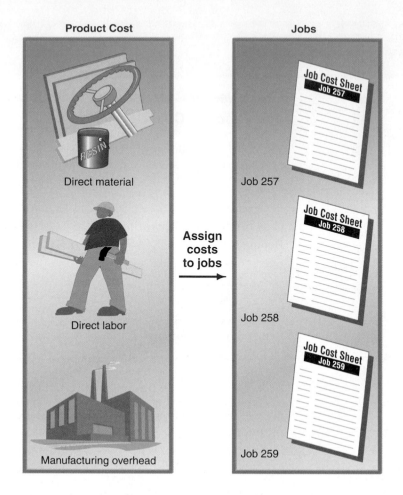

Cost flow through a job-order costing system is based on the status of jobs. First, direct material, direct labor, and manufacturing overhead costs related to jobs being worked on are added to the Work in Process Inventory account. When specific jobs are completed, the costs of those jobs (referred to as the costs of goods manufactured) are deducted from Work in Process Inventory and added to the Finished Goods Inventory account. When specific jobs are sold, the costs of those jobs are removed from Finished Goods Inventory and added to Cost of Goods Sold. These cost flows are indicated in Illustration 2-9.

As you read the following material, keep in mind the components of a job-costing system: (a) the items making up the costs of a job (direct material, direct labor, and manufacturing overhead) and (b) the way the status of jobs triggers the flow of costs through financial statement accounts (Work in Process, Finished Goods, and Cost of Goods Sold). These are basic structural elements that we build on in our discussion of the procedures of a job-order costing system.

**Illustration 2-8**
Job costs and financial
statement accounts

| Work in Process inventory | Finished Goods Inventory | Cost of Goods Sold |
|---|---|---|
| Cost of jobs being worked on | Cost of jobs completed but not yet sold | Cost of jobs sold |

**Illustration 2-9**
Flow of costs in job-order
system

| Work in Process Inventory | Finished Goods Inventory | Cost of Goods Sold |
|---|---|---|
| Direct material, direct labor, and manufacturing overhead related to jobs being worked on | Cost of jobs completed (cost of goods manufactured) | Cost of jobs sold |

Describe how direct material,
direct labor, and
manufacturing overhead are
assigned to jobs.

# JOB-ORDER COSTING SYSTEM

Job-order costing operations begin when a company decides to produce a specific product for stock (that is, with no specific buyer in mind for the item) or in response to an order for a custom product. For example, an electric motor manufacturer decides to build five model XL25 motors for stock, a print shop receives an order for 20,000 spring catalogs from a clothing manufacturer, or a residential construction company receives an order to build a summer home.

If the company decides to accept the order, a job cost sheet is prepared. A **job cost sheet** is a form, typically computer generated, used to accumulate the cost of producing the item or items ordered (i.e., the cost of the job). Illustration 2-10 shows a job cost sheet for a custom product to be built by Eastlake Motorboat Company. The job is identified by a job number: 20126. How specific amounts end up on the job cost sheet will be explained later. For now, simply note that the job cost sheet contains detailed information on the three categories of product costs: direct material, direct labor, and manufacturing overhead.

## DIRECT MATERIAL COST

A material requisition form is used to request the release of materials from a company's storage area. Illustration 2-11 shows a material requisition form for Eastlake Motorboat Company job 20126. The form lists the type, quantity, and cost of material, as well as the number of the job requiring the materials. Because the form includes the job number, it can be used to trace material cost to specific jobs. Requiring a supervisor's signature helps to prevent the unauthorized issuance of material.

Each material requisition form is listed in summary form on the job-cost sheet. For example, on material requisition form number 255, presented in Illustration 2-11, the total cost of items requested amounts to $1,542.68. When these items are released from storage, the total cost is posted to the job-cost sheet (see Illustration 2-10) and cross referenced by the material requisition number.

**Illustration 2-10**
Top of first page and
bottom of last page of job
cost sheets

## *Eastlake* Motorboat Company

**65 Shore Place**
**Kirkland, Washington 98006**

Job number: 20126    Requested delivery date: 5/30    Date Started: 4/15    Date Completed: 5/25

Customer: Mary and John Hughes, 647 Circle Drive, Redmond, Washington 98042

Description: 18 foot runabout, mahogany hull, 75 h.p. inboard, deluxe interior (cream/maroon)

| | Direct materials | | Direct labor | | | Manufacturing overhead |
|---|---|---|---|---|---|---|
| Date | Requisition number | Cost | Labor report number | Hours | Cost | $5.50 per direct labor hour |
| 4/15 | 255 | 1,542.68 | 105 | 16 | 296.00 | 88.00 |
| 4/16 | 261 | 5,450.00 | 106 | 24 | 432.00 | 132.00 |
| 4/17 | 266 | 225.42 | 107 | 32 | 576.00 | 176.00 |
| 4/18 | 272 | 1,820.65 | 108 | 15 | 262.50 | 82.50 |
| 4/19 | 282 | 436.80 | 109 | 17 | 297.50 | 93.50 |
| 4/22 | 289 | 854.64 | 110 | 8 | 140.00 | 44.00 |
| 4/23 | 295 | 1,620.22 | 111 | 10 | 175.00 | 55.00 |

(last page of job cost report)

| | | | | | | |
|---|---|---|---|---|---|---|
| 5/25 | 382 | 655.50 | 133 | 8 | 160.00 | 44.00 |
| | | Total 15,485.29 | | Total 385 | 6,750.00 | Total 2,117.50 |

Cost summary
Direct materials          $15,485.29
Direct labor                6,750.00
Manufacturing overhead      2,117.50
                          $24,352.79

llustration 2-11
Material requisition form

### *Eastlake*

Material requisition number    255

Job number 20126                           Date 4/15

| Item | Description | Cost |
|---|---|---|
| T5627 | Floor tarp | $   246.36 |
| L2005 | 432 feet mahogony planking | 1,296.32 |
| | | $1,542.68 |

Approved by: ___*Carl Jensen*___ Carl Jensen

Removal of materials from storage for use on a specific job decreases Raw Materials and increases Work in Process Inventory. Periodically (daily, weekly, or monthly), the total cost of materials issued to jobs is calculated and recorded in the company accounts. Suppose $60,000 of materials are issued to specific jobs. The entry to record this is:

| (date) | Work in Process Inventory | 60,000.00 | |
|---|---|---|---|
| | Raw Materials | | 60,000.00 |
| | To record raw materials used | | |

## DIRECT LABOR COST

Workers in a company that uses a job-order costing system fill out **time tickets** (also called job tickets or work tickets) to keep track of the amount of time spent on each job. Illustration 2-12 shows a time ticket for Eastlake Motorboat Company job 20126. If there are many workers on a particular job, individual time tickets may not be posted directly to job-cost sheets since that would produce too much detail. Illustration 2-13 presents a daily labor cost summary by job. As you can see, time ticket number 1587 is just one of two time tickets indicating work performed on job number 20126 on April 15. In total, on April 15, 16 hours were spent on job 20126 at a cost of $296.00. The total labor cost traced to job 20126 ($296.00) is the amount posted to the job cost sheet (see Illustration 2-10).

**Illustration 2-12**
Labor time ticket

### Eastlake

Time ticket number    1587
Employee number    21                    Grade    3
Job number    20126                      Date    4/15
Time start    8:00                       Time stop    5:00
Total hours    8

**Illustration 2-13**
Daily labor cost summary

## *Eastlake Motorboat Company*

**Daily labor report number: 105**        **Date: 4/15/2006**

| Job | Time ticket | Hours | Grade | Rate | Cost |
|---|---|---|---|---|---|
| 20118 | 1575 | 8 | 3 | 17.00 | 136.00 |
| 20118 | 1576 | 8 | 3 | 17.00 | 136.00 |
|  |  | 16 |  |  | 272.00 |
| 20119 | 1577 | 7 | 4 | 20.00 | 140.00 |
| 20120 | 1577 | 3 | 4 | 20.00 | 60.00 |
| 20120 | 1578 | 6 | 3 | 17.00 | 102.00 |
|  |  | 9 |  |  | 162.00 |
| 20121 | 1578 | 4 | 3 | 17.00 | 68.00 |
| 20121 | 1579 | 8 | 2 | 15.00 | 120.00 |
|  |  | 12 |  |  | 188.00 |
| 20123 | 1580 | 8 | 2 | 15.00 | 120.00 |
| 20123 | 1581 | 8 | 2 | 15.00 | 120.00 |
| 20123 | 1582 | 8 | 3 | 17.00 | 136.00 |
|  |  | 24 |  |  | 376.00 |
| 20124 | 1583 | 8 | 3 | 17.00 | 136.00 |
| 20124 | 1584 | 8 | 3 | 17.00 | 136.00 |
|  |  | 16 |  |  | 272.00 |
| 20125 | 1585 | 8 | 4 | 20.00 | 160.00 |
| 20125 | 1586 | 8 | 3 | 17.00 | 136.00 |
|  |  | 16 |  |  | 296.00 |
| 20126 | 1587 | 8 | 3 | 17.00 | 136.00 |
| 20126 | 1588 | 8 | 4 | 20.00 | 160.00 |
|  |  | 16 |  |  | 296.00 |

Total daily labor   $2,002.00

### *Journal Entry to Record Direct Labor*

Periodically, the amount of direct labor cost attributed to jobs being worked on must be debited to Work in Process. Suppose $10,000 of direct labor cost is incurred. The appropriate journal entry is:

| (date) | Work in Process Inventory | 10,000.00 | |
|---|---|---|---|
|  | Wages Payable | | 10,000.00 |
|  | To record direct labor cost | | |

# MANUFACTURING OVERHEAD

So far, we have traced raw material and direct labor costs to jobs. The final and more complex cost component to assign is manufacturing overhead, which we discuss in a general way here before going into more detail later in this chapter and in Chapter 6.

Recall that manufacturing overhead costs are not directly traced to goods produced. For that reason, an indirect method of assigning overhead costs to jobs is needed. The basic approach involves assigning overhead to jobs based on some characteristic that jobs share in common, such as direct labor hours or direct labor cost. The common characteristic is referred to as an **allocation base**. Essentially, the allocation base spreads the overhead among the various jobs.

An **overhead allocation rate** is calculated by dividing estimated overhead costs by the estimated quantity of the allocation base. For example, suppose Eastlake Motorboat Company anticipates $200,000 of manufacturing overhead and 36,364 direct labor hours during the year. With these estimates, Eastlake's accountant, Nancy Young, can calculate that $5.50 of overhead will be incurred for every direct labor hour worked ($200,000 ÷ 36,364). Based on this overhead rate, each job will receive $5.50 of overhead for every direct labor hour worked. The more labor hours spent on a job, the more overhead will be indirectly assigned to the job by means of the overhead rate. The amount of overhead assigned to jobs is referred to as **overhead applied**. Look back at Illustration 2-10 and note that Eastlake assigns overhead to jobs on the basis of labor hours. With an overhead rate of $5.50 and 385 labor hours, $2,117.50 of manufacturing overhead will be assigned to job number 20126.

### *Journal Entries to Record Manufacturing Overhead*

Recording manufacturing overhead is a two-step process. First, when actual overhead costs are incurred, they are debited to the Manufacturing Overhead account. Second, when overhead is applied to jobs, the Manufacturing Overhead account is credited, and Work in Process Inventory is debited.

**Step One.** Overhead costs include depreciation, utilities, and a variety of other costs. Therefore, the credit side of the entry to record manufacturing overhead can include a large number of accounts. Suppose $10,000 of depreciation, $1,000 of utility cost, and $55,000 of various other overhead costs are incurred. The journal entry to record these costs is:

| (date) | Manufacturing Overhead | 66,000.00 | |
|---|---|---|---|
| | Accumulated Depreciation | | 10,000.00 |
| | Utilities Payable | | 1,000.00 |
| | Various other accounts | | 55,000.00 |
| | To record overhead costs incurred. | | |

**Step Two.** The total amount of estimated overhead costs applied to jobs is calculated periodically, and an entry is made to take the cost out of Manufacturing Overhead and debit it to Work in Process. Suppose $60,000 of overhead is applied to jobs. The journal entry is:

| (date) | Work in Process Inventory | 60,000.00 | |
|---|---|---|---|
| | Manufacturing Overhead | | 60,000.00 |
| | To record overhead costs applied to jobs. | | |

## ASSIGNING COSTS TO JOBS: A SUMMARY

Direct material costs are traced to jobs using material requisition forms. Direct labor costs are traced to jobs using labor time tickets. Manufacturing overhead costs cannot be directly traced to jobs. Instead, they are assigned to jobs using an overhead rate that is multiplied by each job's measure of the allocation base. Illustration 2-14 summarizes the methods used to relate manufacturing costs to jobs.

**Illustration 2-14**
How manufacturing costs are related to jobs

**Illustration 2-15**
Analysis of estimated and actual costs for Eastlake Motorboat

## *Eastlake* Motorboat Company

| | Material | Labor | Overhead | | | |
|---|---|---|---|---|---|---|
| **Job 20126** | | | | Price | | 29,870 |
| Estimated | 14,380 | 6,549 | 2,055 | Est. margin | | 23% |
| Actual | 15,485 | 6,750 | 2,118 | Act. margin | | 18% |
| Difference | (1,105) | (201) | (63) | Difference | | −5% |
| **Job 20125** | | | | Price | | 41,550 |
| Estimated | 16,947 | 11,102 | 3,483 | Est. margin | | 24% |
| Actual | 19,655 | 10,325 | 3,340 | Act. margin | | 20% |
| Difference | (2,708) | 777 | 143 | Difference | | −4% |
| **Job 20124** | | | | Price | | 32,260 |
| Estimated | 15,265 | 6,628 | 2,081 | Est. margin | | 26% |
| Actual | 18,472 | 7,563 | 2,373 | Act. margin | | 12% |
| Difference | (3,207) | (935) | (292) | Difference | | −14% |
| **Job 20123** | | | | Price | | 37,021 |
| Estimated | 16,485 | 8,563 | 2,687 | Est. margin | | 25% |
| Actual | 21,547 | 10,258 | 3,219 | Act. margin | | 5% |
| Difference | (5,062) | (1,695) | (532) | Difference | | −20% |
| **Total Difference** | (12,082) | (2,054) | (744) | | | |
| % of estimate | 19% | 6% | 7% | | | |

*Note:* Actual overhead is applied using a predetermined rate times actual labor hours.

# EASTLAKE REVISITED: USING JOB COST INFORMATION

At this point we have reviewed a good deal of financial accounting information related to job-order costing systems. Of what use is all this information to management? Let's consider Eastlake Motorboat Company to illustrate.

Recall from the chapter opening vignette that Bob Williams, the new owner of Eastlake Motorboat, is concerned that his company is underestimating costs and setting prices too low for its custom boats. Using information from job-cost sheets, his accountant, Nancy Young, prepared an analysis of estimated and actual cost for four recent jobs (see Illustration 2-15). Using this information, Bob can see that his hunch is right: Actual costs are higher than estimated. The information indicates that, in particular, there has been a problem in estimating material costs; on average, these costs have been running 19 percent higher than estimated.

The problem is reflected in the difference between the estimated and actual profit margin percentages [(price − cost) ÷ price]. For example, consider job 20123. Based on estimated costs, the company would have earned a profit margin of 25 percent. However, owing primarily to the difference between estimated and actual material cost, the actual profit margin is only 5 percent.

Armed with the knowledge that costs have been underestimated, Bob can work to improve the estimation process, especially with respect to cost of materials. However, should he raise prices consistent with higher estimated cost? That's a complex question. The fact that his costs have been higher than planned doesn't necessarily mean prices have been too low.

**Decision Making/ Incremental Analysis**

As explained more fully in Chapter 8, in addition to considering production cost, managers need to consider what customers are willing to pay when setting prices. Let's look at job 20123. Suppose the customer for this boat was only willing to pay $37,021. Should Bob have turned down the sale? Probably not.

Remember that when making a decision we need to perform incremental analysis. Let's assume that overhead is composed primarily of fixed costs such as depreciation and rent. In this case, the incremental cost of the job is $21,547 for material and $10,258 for labor, which totals $31,805. Thus, the incremental profit on the job is $5,216 (selling price of $37,021, less the incremental cost of $31,805 for material and labor), and turning down the job would have hurt financial performance. In adjusting prices, Bob will have to be careful so that he doesn't end up turning down business that will actually improve profitability.

# RELATION BETWEEN THE COSTS OF JOBS AND THE FLOW OF COSTS IN WORK IN PROCESS, FINISHED GOODS, AND COST OF GOODS SOLD

Earlier in the chapter, we discussed in general terms how product costs flow in the accounts of a manufacturing firm (see Illustration 2-5). Now that we have a good understanding of the cost of a job, we can make a link between the cost of jobs and cost flows. When a company begins work on a job, production costs are applied to Work in Process using journal entries such as those illustrated earlier. When jobs are completed, Work in Process is reduced and Finished Goods is increased. When completed jobs are sold, Finished Goods is reduced by the cost of the completed jobs sold and the Cost of Goods Sold account is increased. Suppose the cost of jobs completed is $80,000 and the cost of jobs sold is $70,000. The journal entries are:

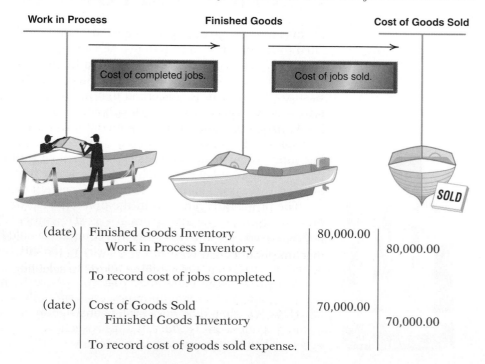

| (date) | Finished Goods Inventory | 80,000.00 | |
| | Work in Process Inventory | | 80,000.00 |
| | To record cost of jobs completed. | | |
| (date) | Cost of Goods Sold | 70,000.00 | |
| | Finished Goods Inventory | | 70,000.00 |
| | To record cost of goods sold expense. | | |

# ALLOCATING OVERHEAD TO JOBS: A CLOSER LOOK

We have seen how direct material, direct labor, and manufacturing overhead are accumulated in a job-order costing system. However, in discussing the process of assigning manufacturing overhead to specific jobs and recording overhead in various accounts, referred to as **overhead allocation**, we did not go into much detail. It's time for a more thorough discussion.

## OVERHEAD ALLOCATION RATES

Because cost items that make up overhead are related only indirectly to jobs being produced, some means of allocating or assigning overhead costs to jobs must be developed. As mentioned, overhead costs are allocated to jobs by means of an overhead allocation rate. The rate is calculated as the ratio of overhead costs to activity. Common measures of activity include direct labor hours, direct labor cost, machine hours, and direct material cost. Recall that the measure of these activities is referred to as the allocation base.

$$\text{Overhead allocation rate} = \frac{\text{Overhead cost}}{\text{Allocation base}}$$

Suppose a company had $50,000 of overhead cost and used 10,000 labor hours during the year. In this example, an average *actual* overhead cost per labor hour of $5 ($50,000 ÷ 10,000) can be calculated, and overhead can be assigned to jobs based on the amount of labor hours worked on each job. For example, if a particular job required 100 labor hours, it would receive an overhead allocation of $500 (100 × $5).

## THE OVERHEAD ALLOCATION BASE

In choosing among alternative allocation bases (such as direct labor hours, direct labor cost, machine hours, and direct material cost), keep in mind that jobs with greater quantities of an allocation base will receive larger allocations of overhead. For example, suppose machine hours are used as an allocation base and an overhead rate is calculated as $10 per machine hour. If one job uses 40 machine hours and another job uses 20 machine hours, the first job will receive an allocation of $400 and the second job will receive an allocation of only $200. This is appropriate if greater activity, as measured by machine time, generally requires the firm to incur more overhead cost.

The allocation base used should be strongly associated with overhead cost. That is, increases in overhead cost should coincide with increases in the allocation base. If increases in overhead are more closely associated with increases in machine hours than with increases in labor hours, it would be best to allocate overhead on the basis of machine hours. In selecting the allocation base, consider whether the production process is labor intensive or machine intensive. If an operation is labor intensive (i.e., large quantities of labor are used to produce most jobs), then direct labor hours or direct labor cost is likely to be a reasonable allocation base. If an operation is highly mechanized, then machine hours is likely to be a reasonable allocation base.

**You Get What You Measure**

In selecting an allocation base, you also need to remember that "You get what you measure!" Manufacturing managers try to reduce costs because it reflects well on their managerial skill. And if labor hours are used as the overhead allocation base, they may try to cut labor to reduce overhead charges to the jobs for which they are responsible. Similarly, if machine hours are used, they may try to reduce machine run time. But if labor or machine time are reduced, will overhead costs be reduced? That's not clear, because, at least in the short run, much of the overhead cost may be fixed. Thus, apparent cost savings may not be realized. In other words, the costing system will make it appear that costs are decreasing when in fact they are not.

## ACTIVITY-BASED COSTING (ABC) AND MULTIPLE OVERHEAD RATES

Many companies allocate overhead to jobs using a single overhead rate with an allocation base of direct labor. However, overhead costs are created by a variety of factors, and allocating costs just on the basis of labor, or any single allocation base, may seriously distort product costs.

**Activity-based costing (ABC)** is a method of assigning overhead costs to products using a number of different allocation bases. In the ABC approach, the major activities that create overhead costs are identified. The costs of the major activities are grouped into so-called **cost pools**. Multiple overhead rates are calculated by dividing the amount of each cost pool by a measure of its corresponding activity (referred to as a **cost driver**). Overhead is then assigned to a product based on how much of each activity (cost driver) it caused. The topic of ABC costing is examined in detail in Chapter 6.

**LEARNING OBJECTIVE 7**

Explain the role of a predetermined overhead rate in applying overhead to jobs.

## PREDETERMINED OVERHEAD RATES

Companies can develop overhead rates by dividing *actual* overhead by the *actual* level of the allocation base. Most companies do not follow this practice, however, because total actual overhead cost and the total actual level of the allocation base are not known until the end of the accounting period, making it impossible to determine the actual overhead rate until that time. In many cases, the price charged for a job depends on its cost. Thus, an immediate cost figure may be needed so that the company can determine the price to charge a customer. An immediate cost figure is also needed to determine the profitability of jobs.

Typically, then, overhead rates are based on *estimates* of overhead cost and *estimates* of the level of the allocation base rather than on *actual* costs and quantities. Overhead rates calculated in this way are referred to as **predetermined overhead rates** (also called budgeted overhead rates). Once the estimated overhead cost and estimated allocation base are established, the predetermined overhead rate is obtained by dividing the estimated overhead by the estimated level of the allocation base.

$$\text{Predetermined overhead rate} = \frac{\text{Estimated total overhead cost}}{\text{Estimated level of allocation base}}$$

Let's return to our example of Eastlake Motorboat Company. Suppose management estimates that $200,000 of total manufacturing overhead will be incurred in the coming year and that 36,364 labor hours will be required. In that case, the predetermined overhead rate is $5.50 per labor hour ($200,000 ÷

36,364) and a job requiring 100 direct labor hours to complete would be allocated $550 of overhead ($5.50 × 100 labor hours).

The estimated or budgeted overhead cost and the estimated level of the allocation base are generally estimated for a year so that the overhead allocation rate stays the same from month to month. If a shorter period, such as one month, were used, the overhead rate would fluctuate from month to month, causing identical jobs produced in different months to have different costs. This happens because some overhead charges only occur in certain months. For example, in summer months extra power costs may be incurred because the plant is air-conditioned. Another reason for fluctuation in a shorter period of time is that overhead includes both variable and fixed cost items. When *expected* levels of the allocation base decrease, the *expected* amount of variable overhead also decreases. However, the expected amount of fixed overhead does not decrease. Thus, the overhead rate is likely to be higher in slow months.

**Explain why the difference between actual overhead and overhead allocated to jobs using a predetermined rate is closed to Cost of Goods Sold or is apportioned among Work in Process Inventory, Finished Goods Inventory, and Cost of Goods Sold.**

## ELIMINATING OVERAPPLIED OR UNDERAPPLIED OVERHEAD

As indicated earlier, recording manufacturing overhead is a two-step process. First, the *actual* costs of various overhead items are accumulated in the Manufacturing Overhead account. Second, overhead is applied to individual jobs using the predetermined overhead rate. This increases Work in Process and decreases Manufacturing Overhead. Thus, two types of entries are made to the Manufacturing Overhead account: the debit entries record actual overhead costs incurred, and the credit entries record the amount of overhead applied to jobs in process.

| Manufacturing Overhead | |
| --- | --- |
| Actual overhead costs incurred | Overhead costs applied to jobs |

Unless *estimated* overhead equals *actual* overhead and the estimated level of the allocation base equals the actual level of the allocation base, the amount of overhead applied to jobs using a predetermined overhead rate will not equal actual overhead cost incurred. Because estimates are seldom perfectly accurate, there is likely to be a difference between the debits to manufacturing overhead (recording actual overhead costs) and the credits to manufacturing overhead (recording the amount of overhead applied to jobs using the predetermined overhead rate). The difference is referred to as **underapplied overhead** if actual overhead is greater than the amount of overhead applied and as **overapplied overhead** if actual overhead is less than the amount applied.

At the end of the accounting period, the amount of under- or overapplied overhead is equal to the balance in Manufacturing Overhead. This account must be closed, and accounts must be adjusted to reflect actual overhead costs. If a reasonable job of estimation has been done in developing the predetermined overhead rate, the amount of over- or underapplied overhead will not be large. In this case, most companies simply close the account and adjust Cost of Goods Sold.

For example, suppose a company had $50,000 of actual overhead and applied $48,000 to jobs using a predetermined overhead rate. In this case, overhead is underapplied by $2,000, the debit balance in the manufacturing overhead account. To close the account, the following journal entry is made.

| (date) | Cost of Goods Sold | 2,000.00 | |
| |     Manufacturing Overhead | | 2,000.00 |
| | To close manufacturing overhead and     eliminate underapplied overhead. | | |

Theoretically, the amount of under- or overapplied overhead should be apportioned among Work in Process, Finished Goods, and Cost of Goods Sold. This follows from the fact that use of a predetermined rate results in job costs that differ from the actual cost of jobs by the amount of over- or underapplied overhead. Because the cost of jobs is reflected in Work in Process, Finished Goods, and Cost of Goods Sold, all of these accounts should be adjusted to reflect actual overhead costs.

Apportioning costs among Work in Process, Finished Goods, and Cost of Goods Sold can be accomplished based on the relative cost recorded in these accounts. For example, suppose a company has Work in Process of $10,000, Finished Goods of $10,000, Cost of Goods Sold of $20,000, and underapplied overhead of $2,000. The apportionment rate would be $.05 for each dollar in the accounts (i.e., $2,000 ÷ $40,000). Thus, Work in Process would receive $500, Finished Goods would receive $500, and Cost of Goods sold $1,000. The following journal entry would be made.

| (date) | Work in Process Inventory | 500.00 | |
| | Finished Goods Inventory | 500.00 | |
| | Cost of Goods Sold | 1,000.00 | |
| |     Manufacturing Overhead | | 2,000.00 |
| | To apportion underapplied overhead. | | |

Whether the amount of over- or underapplied overhead is applied to Cost of Goods Sold or apportioned among Work in Process, Finished Goods, and Cost of Goods Sold depends on the dollar value of over- or underapplied overhead. If the amount is immaterial (i.e., relatively small), it is sufficient for practical purposes to simply debit (for underapplied overhead) or credit (for overapplied overhead) the amount to Cost of Goods Sold. If the amount is material (i.e., relatively large), it should be apportioned among Work in Process, Finished Goods, and Cost of Goods Sold.

# JOB-ORDER COSTING FOR SERVICE COMPANIES

All the examples used so far have involved manufacturing companies, but many service companies also use job-order costing. For example, a hospital might want to know the cost of treating a patient. In this case, the patient becomes a "job," and costs incurred in treating the patient (cost of physician and nursing care, cost of medicine, cost of X-rays, etc.) are accumulated on a report much like a job cost sheet used in a manufacturing setting. Repair shops also use job costing systems. When you bring your car in for service, the repair shop traces labor and parts to a job cost sheet that becomes your bill. Typically, these shops do not assign overhead to jobs. Rather, they mark up the charges for labor and parts to cover overhead and generate profit.

**Illustration 2-16**
Job cost sheet for a
service firm

**K/A** Kendall/Allan, Consulting

| Client | Design Works, Inc. |
| --- | --- |
| Engagement | Installation of billing system linked to existing G/L program. |

**Consultant time**

| Reference | Date | Name | Hours | Rate | Total |
| --- | --- | --- | --- | --- | --- |
| S325 | 15-Feb | S. Wilson | 8.0 | 45.50 | 364.00 |
| S325 | 15-Feb | H. Starr | 8.0 | 65.50 | 524.00 |
| S326 | 16-Feb | S. Wilson | 8.0 | 45.50 | 364.00 |
| S326 | 16-Jan | H. Starr | 8.0 | 65.50 | 524.00 |
| S326 | 16-Feb | J. Kendall | 3.5 | 125.00 | 437.50 |
| S327 | 19-Feb | S. Wilson | 8.0 | 45.50 | 364.00 |
| S328 | 20-Feb | S. Wilson | 4.5 | 45.50 | 204.75 |
| | | | | Total | 2,782.25 |

**Billable items**

| Reference | Description | | |
| --- | --- | --- | --- |
| E8102 | SQA software | | 5,868.25 |
| E8156 | SQA training manual | | 125.60 |
| | | Total | 5,993.85 |
| **Overhead** | (20% of consultant salary) | | 556.45 |
| | | Total cost | 9,332.55 |

Consider a job cost sheet for Kendall/Allan, a consulting firm that specializes in installing computer information systems. As indicated in Illustration 2-16, the company traces the time spent on each job by various consultants, as well as software and other miscellaneous items needed to complete each engagement (referred to by Kendall/Allan as "billable items"). Overhead is assigned on the basis of total consultant salary with an allocation rate of 20 percent. As you can see from examining this job cost sheet, if you understand job-order costing for manufacturing firms, you also understand job-order costing for service firms.

LEARNING OBJECTIVE 9

Discuss modern manufacturing practices and how they affect product costing.

# MODERN MANUFACTURING PRACTICES AND PRODUCT COSTING SYSTEMS

In the last two decades, U.S. companies have experienced stiff competition from foreign companies. To compete effectively in a global economy, many U.S. manufacturers have made fundamental changes in their operations and business philosophies. These changes in the manufacturing environment affect the types of costs that are incurred and, to some extent, the way the costs are recorded in the product costing system.

Here we briefly discuss three of the major changes: just-in-time production, computer-controlled manufacturing, and total quality management. The purpose of the discussion is to make sure you have a basic understanding of the setting in which companies are calculating product costs. In addition, you need to "speak the language" of top management and operating personnel if you want to have a significant impact on important decisions. Increasingly, the language includes references to just-in-time production, computer-controlled manufacturing, and total quality management.

## JUST-IN-TIME (JIT) PRODUCTION

Japanese companies, following the lead of Toyota Motor Company, were the first to use an innovative manufacturing system referred to as a **just-in-time (JIT)** system. One important goal of such manufacturing systems is to minimize inventories of Raw Materials and Work in Process. Companies with JIT systems make arrangements with suppliers to deliver materials just before they are needed in the production process. In addition, when products need to be manufactured on multiple production lines (first a production line that involves welding and then a production line that involves machining), production on one line is scheduled so that operations are completed just in time to meet the requirements of the next production line. With such a system, there is no buildup of raw material and work in process inventories to clog the factory floor. It is partly for this reason that JIT systems are also referred to as lean production systems. With JIT, there is no "fat" associated with wasted space and excess investment in inventory.

JIT is, however, much more than an effort to reduce companies' investments in inventory. The goals of a JIT system are to develop a balanced production system that is flexible and allows for smooth, rapid flow of materials. To achieve these goals, companies using JIT concentrate on improving quality (since quality problems disrupt the production system), eliminating production breakdowns, and preventing missed delivery deadlines by suppliers. To improve coordination with suppliers, many companies are using the Internet to link their production facilities to suppliers. (See the discussion in Chapter 1 on Supply Chain Management.) Dramatic improvements in manufacturing performance have been attributed to use of JIT production. Some companies report 90 percent reductions in production lead time, 90 percent reductions in work in process, and 80 percent reductions in space required for production.

JIT can also have an affect on product costing. What happens to over- or underapplied overhead when a company uses a JIT system? With a JIT system, Work in Process and Finished Goods Inventory balances are generally quite small compared to the balance in Cost of Goods Sold. Thus, the difference between assigning all of over- or underapplied overhead to Cost of Goods Sold or allocating it among Work in Process, Finished Goods, and Cost of Goods Sold is likely to be quite small. Thus, simply charging the amount to Cost of Goods Sold is expedient and appropriate.

## COMPUTER-CONTROLLED MANUFACTURING

In another major change, more and more companies are using highly automated **computer-controlled manufacturing systems**. Using computers to control equipment, including robots, generally increases the flexibility and accuracy of the production process. But while state-of-the-art equipment and computer-control systems may help firms meet the challenge of global competition, they also have a significant effect on the composition of product costs.

Survey data indicate that, on average, product costs in recent years have consisted of 53 percent material, 15 percent direct labor, and 32 percent overhead. Some highly automated companies, such as Hewlett-Packard, however, report that direct labor accounts for as little as 3 percent of total production costs.

### LINK TO PRACTICE

#### *Just-in-Time or Just-in-Case?*

Companies that have adopted just-in-time systems have found that they create shareholder value by reducing their investment in inventory and by eliminating costs associated with non-value-added activities. But now one of the leading advocates of JIT, Yossi Sheffi, director of Massachusetts Institute of Technology's Center for Transportation and Logistics, is suggesting that companies consider "just-in-case" options. The reason is that supply chains may face critical disruptions due to terrorist attacks and the reactions of governments to the attacks that can include shutting down borders, air traffic, and ports. Sheffi recommends that companies consider judiciously increasing their supplier base and dividing orders between domestic providers and foreign alternatives. Then, if borders get closed, domestic providers can still deliver goods. Strategic reserves of supplies also need to be considered "just in case" they're needed.

Terrorist attacks aren't the only reason companies need strategic reserves. Floods, strikes, bankruptcies, and road construction can also disrupt the supply chain. Smart companies will build these possibilities into their supply chain management strategies.

*Source:* "Just-in-Time Enters New Era," D.C. Denison, *The Boston Globe*, May 5, 2002, P. H2.

Decreasing labor costs are causing many companies to reconsider their overhead allocation bases. Currently, the most commonly used allocation bases for assigning overhead to jobs are direct labor hours and direct labor cost. However, in highly mechanized companies where direct labor is a small part of total manufacturing costs, using labor as an allocation base is generally not appropriate.

Computer-controlled manufacturing is used extensively at many companies.

### Computerized Manufacturing Heads for the Internet

Leisure boat building is a labor-intensive segment of the economy that has been slow to invest in new technology. But that situation is changing. Genmar Holdings, the second largest leisure boat manufacturer in the United States now has a compact, computer-controlled manufacturing system that pops out 18-foot hulls every 35 minutes. Previously, hull production took 8 hours. Pollution, waste, and labor are sharply reduced and quality is so high than Genmar is offering a lifetime guarantee instead of the industry standard five-year warranty.

An interesting aspect of the system is that it is controlled over the Internet by expert engineers located hundreds of miles from the Genmar plant. Genmar envisions this technology being used by manufacturing cells around the world. They can produce products close to where they will be used without having on-site expertise to run the systems.

*Source:* Barnaby Feder, "Computerized Manufacturing System Heads for the Internet; New Process Claims to have Potential to Make Factories Obsolete," *Milwaukee Journal Sentinel*, September 4, 2002, p. D3. "Genmar Wins Technology Awards for Manufacturing Process," *Genmar Holdings Inc.*, November 10, 2001. Kevin M. McCarthy, "Sailing Away." *U.S. Business Review Online*, January/February 2002.

**See the video on the interactive CD for an example of automated manufacturing at Toyota.**

Investing in state-of-the-art equipment also changes the mix of fixed and variable costs. When equipment is substituted for labor, fixed costs generally increase, and variable costs decrease.

## TOTAL QUALITY MANAGEMENT

To survive in an increasingly competitive environment, firms realize that they must produce high-quality products. An increasing number of companies have instituted **total quality management (TQM)** programs to ensure that their products are of the highest quality and that production processes are efficient. Currently, there is no generally agreed upon "right" way to institute a TQM program. However, most companies with TQM develop a company philosophy that stresses listening to the needs of customers, making products right the first time, reducing defective products that must be reworked, and encouraging workers to continuously improve their production processes.

Indeed, some TQM programs are referred to as continuous quality improvement programs. At Marlow Industries, a manufacturer of thermoelectric cooling devices, workers sign a Quality Pledge that reads: "I pledge to make a constant, conscious effort to do my job right today, better tomorrow, recognizing that my individual contribution is critical to the success of Marlow Industries."

The results of an effective TQM program can be impressive. At Sundstrand Data Control, a manufacturer of electronic instruments in Washington State, statistics show that the TQM program has reduced rework on some instrument production lines by 66 percent and scrap costs are down by 60 percent. The company

**You Get
What You Measure**

### Can There Be Too Much Emphasis on Quality?

In Chapter 1 we identified a key idea in managerial accounting: You get what you measure! Many companies have quality measures, but can there be too much emphasis on quality?

Consider the case of Wallace Company, a Texas-based industrial distributor of pipes, valves, and fittings that launched a "quality at all cost" campaign. Apparently, the campaign was successful, since the company won the prestigious Malcolm Baldrige National Quality Award. However, in the year the company won the award, it had a $691,000 loss on sales of $88 million. While racking up financial losses, the company was processing 100 requests a day for information about its quality programs! John Wallace, CEO, noted that "We spent too much time telling the story [*about quality*] and should have been out drumming up more business."

The point of this example is not to suggest that emphasis on high quality is a bad idea—far from it. For example, General Electric has a quality program aimed at reducing product defects, which is called the Six Sigma program. This program is cited as a major factor in GE's continuing earnings growth. However, companies must balance the emphasis on quality measures with an emphasis on measures of financial performance, measures of innovation, and measures of customer satisfaction. Otherwise, they may end up producing a high-quality product that customers don't want or for which customers are unwilling to pay a premium price.

also reduced cycle time (the time it takes to produce a product from beginning to end) by 90 percent.[1]

How does TQM affect product costing systems? Strong advocates would argue that without TQM, there is no need for product costing, since companies without TQM will not survive! Undoubtedly there is some truth to this position. In addition, TQM affects product costing by reducing the need to track the cost of scrap and rework related to each job. If TQM is able to reduce these costs to an insignificant level, the benefit of tracking the costs is unlikely to exceed the cost to the accounting system.[2]

---

[1]Steve Wilhelm, "Quality Program Keeps Spreading at Sundstrand," *Puget Sound Business Journal* 11, No. 52 (May 13, 1991), Sec. 1, p. 17.

[2]Many service firms such as banks, insurance companies, and hospital have adopted the TQM programs initially developed by manufacturers. TQM is especially popular in the health-care field.

# MAKING BUSINESS DECISIONS

When using job cost information to make a decision, care must be taken because some costs going into a job are fixed (e.g., depreciation on equipment that is included in manufacturing overhead) and some costs are variable (e.g., direct material costs). Thus, the *full cost* of a job is not the same as the *incremental* cost of a job.

## KNOWLEDGE AND SKILLS (K/S) CHECKLIST

*Knowledge and skills are needed to make good business decisions. Check off the knowledge and skills you've acquired from reading this chapter.*

☐ K/S 1. You have an expanded business vocabulary (see key terms).

☐ K/S 2. You know that the cost of a job for a manufacturing firm includes only direct material, direct labor, and manufacturing overhead. The cost of a job does not include selling and administrative costs, which are period costs.

☐ K/S 3. You know why companies use predetermined overhead rates.

☐ K/S 4. You know that the full cost of a job is not the incremental cost of a job.

☐ K/S 5. You are familiar with modern manufacturing practices such as just-in-time (JIT) production.

# SUMMARY OF LEARNING OBJECTIVES

**1** *Distinguish between manufacturing and non-manufacturing costs and between product and period costs.* Manufacturing costs include all the costs associated with the production of goods. They include direct material, direct labor, and manufacturing overhead. Nonmanufacturing costs are all the costs not associated with the production of goods. Selling and general and administrative costs are nonmanufacturing costs. Costs can also be classified as either product costs or period costs. Product costs are identical to manufacturing costs and include direct labor, direct material, and manufacturing overhead. Product costs are considered an asset (inventory) until finished goods are sold. When the goods are sold, the product costs are expensed. Period costs, on the other hand, are expensed in the period in which they are incurred. Period costs include both selling and general and administrative costs, which are also referred to as nonmanufacturing costs.

**2** *Discuss the three inventory accounts of a manufacturing firm.* The three inventory accounts

are Raw Materials Inventory, Work in Process Inventory, and Finished Goods Inventory. Raw Materials Inventory includes the cost of the materials on hand that are used to produce a company's products. Work in Process Inventory is the inventory account for the cost of goods that are only partially completed. Finished Goods Inventory is the account for the cost of all items that are complete and ready to sell.

**3** *Describe the flow of product costs in a manufacturing firm's accounts.* As they are incurred, product costs are assigned to Work in Process Inventory. When the items in work in process are completed, the cost of the completed items is removed from Work in Process and added to Finished Goods. When the Finished Goods are sold, the cost of the items sold is removed from Finished Goods and added to Cost of Goods Sold Expense. Thus, product costs become an expense when completed items are sold.

**4** *Discuss the types of product costing systems.* There are two types of product costing systems: job-order systems and process costing systems. Companies using job-order systems generally produce individual products or batches of products that are unique. Companies using process costing systems generally produce large quantities of identical items in a continuous production operation.

**⑤** *Explain the relation between the cost of jobs and the Work in Process Inventory, Finished Goods Inventory, and Cost of Goods Sold accounts.* Work in Process Inventory includes the cost of all jobs that are currently being worked on; Finished Goods Inventory includes the cost of all jobs that are completed but not yet sold; and Cost of Goods Sold includes the cost of all jobs that are sold during the accounting period.

**⑥** *Describe how direct material, direct labor, and manufacturing overhead are assigned to jobs.* Job cost sheets track the direct material, direct labor, and manufacturing overhead cost of each job. Direct material cost is traced to jobs by means of material requisition forms. Direct labor is traced to jobs by means of labor time tickets. Manufacturing overhead is applied to jobs using an overhead rate.

**⑦** *Explain the role of a predetermined overhead rate in applying overhead to jobs.* Most companies apply overhead to jobs using a predetermined overhead rate rather than an actual overhead rate. Actual overhead cannot be determined until the end of the accounting period, and companies cannot wait until the end of the period before applying overhead to jobs.

**⑧** *Explain why the difference between actual overhead and overhead allocated to jobs using a predetermined rate is closed to Cost of Goods Sold or is apportioned among Work in Process Inventory, Finished Goods Inventory, and Cost of Goods Sold.* If the amount of overhead applied to inventory does not equal actual overhead, the difference must be apportioned among Work in Process, Finished Goods, and Cost of Goods Sold. This adjusts the accounts to reflect actual overhead costs. If the amount of under- or overapplied overhead is small, the balance can be closed to Cost of Goods Sold.

**⑨** *Discuss modern manufacturing practices and how they affect product costing.* U.S. companies are facing stiff competition from companies abroad. In response, many have adopted manufacturing systems that minimize inventories of raw materials and work in process. In addition, many companies have become highly automated and have instituted total quality management programs. JIT production systems have reduced inventory levels, automation has increased levels of overhead and fixed costs, and total quality management programs have reduced product defects and waste.

# REVIEW PROBLEM

Herbert Plumbing Products produces a variety of valves, connectors, and fixtures used in commercial and residential plumbing applications. The company has a just-in-time inventory and production system, and has relatively small amounts of material, work in process, and finished goods inventory.

At the end of October, the company had $20,000 of raw material inventory. In addition, jobs 281 and 282 were in process and job 279 was complete and awaiting shipment. The job cost sheets for these jobs were as follows:

**End of October**

| | Direct Material | Direct Labor | Overhead | Total | Job Status |
|---|---|---|---|---|---|
| Job 279 | $50,000 | $15,000 | $30,000 | $ 95,000 | Finished but not shipped |
| Job 281 | 20,000 | 5,000 | 10,000 | 35,000 | In process |
| Job 282 | 60,000 | 20,000 | 40,000 | 120,000 | In process |

During November, the company began work on Jobs 283, 284, and 285. The status of the jobs at the end of November is as follows:

**End of November**

|  | Direct Material | Direct Labor | Overhead | Total | Job Status |
|---|---|---|---|---|---|
| Job 279 | $50,000 | $15,000 | $30,000 | $ 95,000 | Shipped |
| Job 281 | 25,000 | 8,000 | 16,000 | 49,000 | Shipped |
| Job 282 | 62,000 | 21,000 | 42,000 | 125,000 | Shipped |
| Job 283 | 30,000 | 20,000 | 40,000 | 90,000 | Shipped |
| Job 284 | 80,000 | 30,000 | 60,000 | 170,000 | Shipped |
| Job 285 | 15,000 | 10,000 | 20,000 | 45,000 | In process |

Also during November, Herbert Plumbing Products purchased $120,000 of materials and incurred $130,000 of actual overhead costs. The company charges over- or under-applied overhead to cost of goods sold.

**Required**
Assume that all material used in November is direct.
a. What is the balance in raw material inventory at the end of November?
b. What is the balance in work in process inventory at the end of November?
c. What is the balance in finished goods inventory at the end of November?
d. What is the cost of goods manufactured for the month of November?
e. What is cost of goods sold for the month of November?

**Answer**
a. The beginning balance in raw materials is $20,000.
   Purchases are $120,000.
   Inventory used in November:

| Job 281 | $ 5,000 |
|---|---|
| Job 282 | 2,000 |
| Job 283 | 30,000 |
| Job 284 | 80,000 |
| Job 285 | 15,000 |
| Total | $132,000 |

   Beginning balance + Purchases − Amount used = Ending Balance
          $20,000 + $120,000 − $132,000 = **$8,000**
b. The ending balance in Work in Process is the cost of jobs in process at the end of November. This is the cost of job 285, which is **$45,000**.
c. The ending balance in Finished Goods is the cost of jobs that are completed but not shipped. Since all completed jobs have been shipped, the balance is zero.
d. The beginning balance in Work in Process is:

| Job 281 | $ 35,000 |
|---|---|
| Job 282 | 120,000 |
| Total | **$155,000** |

   Additional costs added during November are:

| Material cost | | $132,000 per part a. |
|---|---|---|
| Direct labor cost | | |
| Job 281 | $ 3,000 | |
| Job 282 | 1,000 | |
| Job 283 | 20,000 | |
| Job 284 | 30,000 | |
| Job 285 | 10,000 | 64,000 |

Overhead

| | | |
|---|---|---|
| Job 281 | 6,000 | |
| Job 282 | 2,000 | |
| Job 283 | 40,000 | |
| Job 284 | 60,000 | |
| Job 285 | 20,000 | 128,000 |
| | Total | **$324,000** |

The ending balance in Work is Process is **$45,000** per part b.

Beginning balance in WIP + Current manufacturing costs − Ending balance in WIP = Cost of goods manufactured

$155,000 + $324,000 − $45,000 = **$434,000**.

e. Beginning balance in Finished Goods is the cost of job 279, which is $95,000.
Cost of goods manufactured is $434,000 per part d.
Ending balance in finished goods is zero per part c.

Beginning balance in finished goods + Cost of goods manufactured − Ending balance in finished goods = Cost of goods sold

$95,000 + $434,000 − 0 = $529,000

Alternatively, we could simply add up the cost of jobs shipped this period:

| | | |
|---|---|---|
| Job 279 | $95,000 | |
| Job 281 | 49,000 | |
| Job 282 | 125,000 | |
| Job 283 | 90,000 | |
| Job 284 | 170,000 | |
| | Total | $529,000 |

Note, however, that actual overhead is $130,000 while overhead applied to production at the standard rate of $2 per dollar of direct labor is $128,000 per part d. Thus, cost of goods sold must be increased by $2,000.

Cost of goods sold = $529,000 + $2,000 = **$531,000**

# KEY TERMS

Activity-based costing (ABC) (52)
Allocation base (47)
Computer-controlled
  manufacturing systems (57)
Cost driver (52)
Cost of goods available for sale (39)
Cost of goods manufactured (38)
Cost pools (52)
Direct labor cost (33)
Direct material cost (32)
Finished Goods Inventory (37)
Full cost (35)
General and administrative
  costs (34)

Indirect labor costs (33)
Indirect materials (32)
Job (40)
Job cost sheet (43)
Job-order costing system (40)
Just-in-time (JIT)
  manufacturing (56)
Manufacturing costs (32)
Manufacturing overhead (33)
Nonmanufacturing costs (34)
Overapplied overhead (53)
Overhead allocation (51)
Overhead allocation rate (47)

Overhead applied (47)
Period costs (35)
Predetermined overhead rate (52)
Process costing system (40)
Product costing systems (32)
Product costs (35)
Raw Materials Inventory (37)
Selling costs (34)
Time tickets (45)
Total quality management
  (TQM) (58)
Underapplied overhead (53)
Work in Process Inventory (37)

# S E L F   A S S E S S M E N T   *(Answers Below)*

1. Which of the following is a period cost?

   a. Raw materials costs.
   b. Manufacturing plant maintenance.
   c. Wages for production line workers.
   d. Salary for the vice president of finance.

2. Full costing includes which of the following in determining product cost?

   a. Only variable costs of production.
   b. Only fixed costs of production.
   c. Administrative overhead.
   d. All fixed and variable costs of production.

3. The inventory accounts of a manufacturing firm include:

   a. Raw materials.
   b. Finished goods.
   c. Work in process.
   d. All of the above.

4. Two common types of product costing systems are: _____ and _____.

5. Cost of Goods Sold is $200,000, the beginning balance in Finished Goods is $50,000, the ending balance in Finished Goods is $100,000, and the ending balance in Work in Process is $10,000. What is Cost of Goods Manufactured?

   a. $100,000.
   b. $250,000.
   c. $50,000.
   d. None of the above.

6. The beginning balance in Finished Goods is $50,000, the ending balance in Finished Goods is $100,000, and Cost of Goods Manufactured is $200,000. What is Cost of Goods Sold?

   a. $100,000.
   b. $250,000.
   c. $150,000.
   d. None of the above.

7. Which entity below would most likely use a job-order costing system?

   a. Textile manufacturer.
   b. Concrete block producer.
   c. Petroleum refiner.
   d. Antique automobile restorer.

8. The costs of all jobs not yet completed is in the _____ account.

9. The costs of all jobs completed but not yet sold is in the _____ account.

10. The components of a job-order costing system include which of the following?

    a. Documents and ledgers.
    b. Accounts receivable.
    c. Accounts and accounting procedures.
    d. a and b only.
    e. a and c only.

11. Three common allocation bases used to allocate manufacturing overhead are: (1) _____, (2) _____, and (3) _____.

12. Direct material is traced to jobs using:

    a. An overhead allocation base.
    b. Material requisition forms.
    c. Predetermined rates.
    d. All of the above.

13. The predetermined overhead rate is determined as:

    a. Estimated overhead costs divided by estimated allocation base.
    b. Actual overhead costs divided by estimated allocation base.
    c. Estimated overhead costs divided by actual allocation base.
    d. Actual overhead costs divided by actual allocation base.

14. Underapplied or overapplied overhead, if material in amount, is allocated to (1) _____, (2) _____, and (3) _____.

15. Overhead is overapplied if:

    a. The actual overhead rate is greater than the budgeted overhead rate.
    b. The Manufacturing Overhead account has a credit balance at the end of the period.
    c. The actual overhead rate is greater than the rate used in prior periods.
    d. The overhead rate is material.

16. Compared to traditional methods of allocating overhead, activity-based costing (ABC) uses:

    a. More allocation bases.
    b. Only allocation bases related to direct labor.
    c. Machine hours as an allocation base.
    d. None of the above.

17. Service companies:

    a. Do not use job-order costing.
    b. Often use job-order costing.
    c. Do not cost their services.
    d. Produce durable products.

18. Modern manufacturing practices include:

    a. Just-in-time production.
    b. Computer-controlled manufacturing.
    c. Total quality management.
    d. All of the above.

19. Total quality management (TQM) involves all of the following except:

    a. Satisfying customers' needs.
    b. Very close supervision of all employees.
    c. "A get it right the first time" philosophy.
    d. Encouraging continuous improvement.

20. All of the following are true about just-in-time (JIT) production except:

    a. JIT seeks to minimize inventories of raw materials and work in process.

    b. JIT is often referred to as "fat" production.
    c. JIT companies concentrate on improving quality.
    d. JIT companies need dependable suppliers.

**Answers to Self Assessment**

**1.** d; **2.** d; **3.** d; **4.** job-order and process costing; **5.** b; **6.** c; **7.** d; **8.** Work in Process; **9.** Finished Goods; **10.** e; **11.** direct labor hours, direct labor cost, and machine hours; **12.** b; **13.** a; **14.** Work in Process, Finished Goods, and Cost of Goods Sold; **15.** b; **16.** a; **17.** b; **18.** d; **19.** b; **20.** b.

# INTERACTIVE LEARNING

**Enhance and test your knowledge of Chapter 2 using the interactive CD.**

1. Learning Objectives
2. Multiple Choice
3. Language of Business—Matching of Key Terms
4. Critical Thinking
5. Demonstration—How direct material, direct labor, and manufacturing overhead are traced to a job cost sheet; relation between the cost of jobs and balances in Work in Process, Finished Goods, and Cost of Goods Sold
6. Case—*Spokane Ornamental Iron*; Test your knowledge of job-order costing
7. Video—Toyota; Automated manufacturing processes

**Go to our dynamic Web site for more self-assessment, Web links, and additional information.**

# QUESTIONS

1. Why is a product costing system necessary for a manufacturing company?

2. What is the difference between manufacturing and nonmanufacturing costs?

3. What is the difference between product and period costs?

4. What are the three categories of costs included in Work in Process Inventory?

5. Identify the two most common types of product costing systems and discuss the manufacturing environments associated with each system.

6. Differentiate among the following balance sheet inventory accounts: Raw Materials, Work in Process, and Finished Goods.

7. What jobs make up the cost of Work in Process Inventory?

8. What is a job cost sheet? What information does it contain?

9. What form is used to withdraw materials from the storeroom, and what information is normally on that form?

10. What information do you expect to find on a labor time ticket?

11. Why do companies apply overhead to jobs using a predetermined (budgeted) overhead rate instead of applying actual overhead to jobs?

12. Discuss an important characteristic of a good overhead allocation base.

13. Some modern, capital-intensive production facilities have significantly reduced the proportion of direct labor cost to total production cost. Discuss the effect this might have on the selection of an allocation base for the application of overhead.

14. When might it be necessary to assign underapplied overhead to Finished Goods, Work in Process, and Cost of Goods Sold?

15. Would an unexpected increase in sales and production result in underapplied or overapplied overhead? Explain.

16. As companies move to computer-controlled manufacturing systems, what happens to the mix of product costs (direct material, direct labor, and manufacturing overhead)?

# E X E R C I S E S

**EXERCISE 2-1. Group Assignment**   Consider three very similar companies. Company A allocates manufacturing overhead to jobs using labor hours as the allocation base; Company B allocates manufacturing overhead to jobs using machine hours as the allocation base; and Company C allocates manufacturing overhead to jobs using material cost as the allocation base.

*Required*
Explain why, in spite of the fact that the companies are very similar, supervisors at Company A are very focused on controlling labor whereas supervisors at Company B are very focused on controlling machine run time and supervisors at Company C are very focused on controlling material costs. Use the concept of "You get what you measure!" in your answer.

**EXERCISE 2-2. Writing Assignment**   At Binder Electronics, the balance in manufacturing overhead (which represents over- or underapplied overhead) is always closed to Cost of Goods Sold. This is done even when the balance is relatively large. Peter Lee, the controller, explains that this makes sense because Binder uses a just-in-time (JIT) manufacturing system and jobs are shipped to customers within hours of being completed.

*Required*
Write a paragraph elaborating on the justification provided by Peter Lee. Why is there no need to apportion the balance in manufacturing overhead among work in process, finished goods, and cost of goods sold?

**EXERCISE 2-3. Internet Assignment**   General Electric's quality program is called Six Sigma. Go to the company Web site (http://www.ge.com/commitment/quality/whatis.htm) and read about Six Sigma. Then locate the Six Sigma glossary (http://www.ge.com/commitment/quality/glossary.htm) and answer the following questions:

a. What does Six Sigma stand for?

b. What is the Pareto Principal?

c. What does it mean to "design for Six Sigma"?

**EXERCISE 2-4. Product Costing Systems**   For the list of product manufacturers below, indicate whether a job-cost system (J) or a process cost system (P) would be most appropriate.

- a. Beverage producer
- b. Pharmaceutical firm
- c. Print shop
- d. Producer of molds used by other manufacturing firms to shape their products
- e. Dog food producer
- f. Producer of computers assembled to customer order

**EXERCISE 2-5. Inventory-Related Accounts** Place Y (yes) beside the general ledger accounts related to inventory in a job-order cost system and N (no) by those that are not.

_____ a. Raw Materials
_____ b. General and Administrative Expense
_____ c. Work in Process
_____ d. Finished Goods
_____ e. Merchandise Inventory
_____ f. Cost of Goods Sold
_____ g. Manufacturing Overhead
_____ h. Advertising Expense

**EXERCISE 2-6. Recording Material Cost in Job-Order Costing** During the month of August, Binder Electronics had material requisitions for $250,000 of materials related to specific jobs and $20,000 of miscellaneous materials classified as overhead.

*Required*
Prepare journal entries to record the issuance of materials during August.

**EXERCISE 2-7. Recording Material Cost in Job-Order Costing** Five material requisitions (MR) forms were received by the materials storeroom of the Saint Louis Foundry during the first week of 2006. MR101 was for $750 of direct materials for job number 1501. MR102 was for $550 of direct materials for job number 1502. MR103 was for $110 of indirect materials issued to the factory floor. MR 104 was for $450 of direct materials issued to job number 1501. MR105 was for $600 of direct materials issued to job number 1503.

*Required*
Prepare summary journal entries to record the issuance of these materials. (*Hint:* There should be a separate journal entry for direct and indirect materials.):

**EXERCISE 2-8. Recording Labor Cost in Job-Order Costing** During the month of August, Binder Electronics had $65,000 of labor costs that were traced to specific jobs. The company also had $45,000 of indirect labor related to supervisory pay.

*Required*
Prepare journal entries to record labor cost during August.

**EXERCISE 2-9. Recording Labor Cost in Job-Order Costing** Wolk Products had the following labor time tickets for the month of February:

| Ticket # | Employee # | Pay Rate | Hours Worked | Job # |
|----------|-----------|----------|--------------|-------|
| 2101 | 011 | $ 8.00 | 120 | 201 |
| 2102 | 008 | 15.00 | 80 | 201 |
| 2103 | 011 | 8.00 | 40 | 201 |
| 2104 | 008 | 15.00 | 30 | 202 |
| 2105 | 008 | 15.00 | 50 | 203 |

*Required*

a. Calculate the amount of direct labor cost assigned to each job.

b. Summarize the labor time tickets and prepare a journal entry to record direct labor for the month.

**EXERCISE 2-10. Overhead Allocation Bases** Renton Manufacturing Company expects annual manufacturing overhead to be $600,000. The company also expects 60,000 direct labor hours costing $1,200,000 and machine run time of 30,000 hours.

*Required*

Calculate overhead allocation rates based on direct labor hours, direct labor cost, and machine time.

**EXERCISE 2-11. Service Company Allocation of Overhead**   Franklin Computer Repair treats each repair order as a job. Overhead is allocated based on the cost of technician time. At the start of the year, annual technician wages were estimated to be $800,000, and company overhead was estimated to be $400,000.

*Required*

a. Discuss why use of a predetermined overhead rate would be preferred to assigning actual overhead to repair jobs.

b. Suppose a job required parts costing $200 and technician time costing $100. What would be the total cost of the job?

**EXERCISE 2-12. Allocating Manufacturing Overhead to Jobs**   Jiffy Fabricators estimated the following annual values:

|  |  |  |
|---|---|---|
| 15 | Expected annual direct labor hours | 20,000 |
| 1.2 | Expected annual direct labor cost | $250,000 |
| 20 | Expected machine hours | 15,000 |
| .75 | Expected material cost for the year | $400,000 |
|  | Expected manufacturing overhead | $300,000 |

*Required*

a. Calculate overhead allocation rates using each of the four possible allocation bases provided.

b. Determine the cost of the following job (number 253) using each of the four overhead allocation rates.

**Job 253**

| | | |
|---|---|---|
| Direct materials | $2,500 | 125 |
| Direct labor (140 hrs @11/hr) | $1,540 | 62.6 |
| Machine hours used | 100 | |

**EXERCISE 2-13. Recording Actual Overhead and Overhead Applied to Jobs**
During the month of August, Binder Electronics applied overhead to jobs using an overhead rate of $2 per dollar of direct labor. Direct labor in August was $65,000. Actual overhead in August was $140,000. Assume that actual overhead was composed of the following items:

| | |
|---|---|
| Indirect materials | $ 20,000 |
| Indirect labor | 45,000 |
| Utilities | 5,000 |
| Depreciation | 50,000 |
| Repair expense | 20,000 |
| Total | $140,000 |

*Required*

a. Prepare a journal entry to record overhead applied to jobs.

b. Prepare a journal entry to record actual overhead.

**EXERCISE 2-14. Closing the Manufacturing Overhead Account**   Refer to the information in Exercise 13.

*Required*

a. Determine the balance in manufacturing overhead and prepare a journal entry to close the balance to cost of goods sold.

b. Why is it important to close the balance in manufacturing overhead?

c. What is the justification for assigning the balance in manufacturing overhead to Cost of Goods Sold rather than apportioning it to Work in Process, Finished Goods, and Cost of Goods Sold?

**EXERCISE 2-15. Cost of Jobs**   RonKen Company is a steel fabricator, and job 325 consists of producing 900 steel supports for Wendell Construction Company. Overhead is applied on the basis of direct labor hours, using a predetermined overhead rate of $15 per hour. Direct costs associated with Job 325 are: direct materials, $3,000; direct labor, 150 hours at $25 per hour.

*Required*
Calculate the cost of Job 325.

**EXERCISE 2-16. Service Company Use of Predetermined Overhead Rate**   Smith and Baker Legal Services employs five full-time attorneys and nine paraprofessionals. Budgeted salaries are $80,000 for each attorney and $30,000 for each paraprofessional. Budgeted indirect costs (e.g., rent, secretarial support, copying, etc.) are $150,000. The company traces the cost of attorney and paraprofessional time to each client and uses the total to assign indirect costs.

*Required*
What amount of indirect costs would be assigned if services to a client required $10,000 of attorney cost and $5,000 of paraprofessional cost?

**EXERCISE 2-17. Underapplied and Overapplied Manufacturing Overhead**   Injection Molding Services uses a job-order costing system. The account balances at the end of the period for the product cost-related accounts are as follows:

| | |
|---|---|
| Raw Materials Inventory | $200,000 |
| Work in Process Inventory | 400,000 |
| Finished Goods Inventory | 600,000 |
| Cost of Goods Sold | 800,000 |
| Manufacturing Overhead (credit) | 90,000 |

*Required*
Prepare journal entries to close the manufacturing overhead account assuming the amount ($90,000) is material.

# PROBLEMS

**PROBLEM 2-1. Cost of Goods Manufactured, Cost of Goods Sold, and Income**
The following information is available for Costa's Custom Glass for the fiscal year ending December 31, 2006.

| | |
|---|---|
| Beginning balance in Work in Process | $ 200,000 |
| Ending balance in Work in Process | 250,000 |
| Beginning balance in Finished Goods | 500,000 |
| Ending balance in Finished Goods | 400,000 |
| Direct material cost | 1,000,000 |
| Direct labor cost | 3,000,000 |
| Manufacturing overhead | 2,000,000 |
| Selling expenses | 300,000 |
| General and administrative expenses | 200,000 |
| Sales | 7,000,000 |

*Required*

a. Prepare a schedule of cost of goods manufactured.

b. Prepare an income statement for fiscal 2006. Ignore income taxes.

**PROBLEM 2-2. Cost of Goods Manufactured and Cost of Goods Sold**   Design Works International manufactures custom tiles. The following information relates to the fiscal year ending December 31, 2006.

| | |
|---|---:|
| Beginning balance in Raw Material Inventory | $ 200,000 |
| Purchases of raw material | 800,000 |
| Ending balance in Raw Material Inventory | 100,000 |
| Beginning balance in Work in Process | 400,000 |
| Ending balance in Work in Process | 200,000 |
| Direct labor cost | 1,000,000 |
| Manufacturing overhead applied | 500,000 |
| Beginning balance in Finished Goods | 600,000 |
| Ending balance in Finished Goods | 300,000 |
| Sales | 4,000,000 |
| Selling expenses | 250,000 |
| General and administrative expenses | 550,000 |

*Required*

a. Prepare a schedule of cost of goods manufactured. Assume there are no indirect material costs.

b. Prepare an income statement for fiscal 2006. Ignore income taxes.

 **PROBLEM 2-3. Job-Order Costing: Inventory Accounts and Cost of Goods Sold**   Smith Die Company manufactures cutting dies for the shoe industry. Each set of dies is custom designed to a customer's templates. During the first week of May, six orders were received from customers. They were assigned job numbers 1005–1010. The following transactions occurred during the first week of May.

Received shipment of steel from Eastern City Steel costing $4,800.

Received and paid for supplies (indirect materials) from Mallard Supply costing $2,200.

Material requisitions indicated that materials were issued to the factory floor as follows:

| Job No. | Direct Materials | Indirect Materials |
|---|---:|---:|
| 1005 | $   560 | |
| 1006 | 730 | |
| 1007 | 1,480 | |
| 1008 | 540 | |
| 1009 | 370 | |
| 1010 | 285 | |
| Totals | $3,965 | $799 |

The labor time ticket summary reflected the following costs for the week:

| Job No. | Direct Labor | Indirect Labor |
|---|---:|---:|
| 1005 | $1,420 | |
| 1006 | 1,840 | |
| 1007 | 3,220 | |
| 1008 | 1,200 | |
| 1009 | 720 | |
| 1010 | 560 | |
| Totals | $8,960 | $6,400 |

Overhead was applied to all jobs in process at 180 percent of direct labor cost.

Jobs 1005, 1006, 1007, and 1008 were completed and transferred to finished goods.

Jobs 1009 and 1010 were still in process at the end of the week.

Jobs 1005, 1006, 1007, and 1008 were shipped to customers and billed at 150 percent of total job cost.

### Required

a. Calculate the total cost of each job.

b. Prepare journal entries to record the above information.

**PROBLEM 2-4. Job Cost Sheets and Inventory Accounts** Renton Custom Windows produces custom windows for business and residential customers who supply Renton with architectural specifications.

**At the start of 2004, three jobs were in process:**

| Cost incurred as of 1/1/2004 | |
|---|---|
| Job 258 | $2,000 |
| Job 259 | 3,000 |
| Job 260 | 2,500 |

**Also at the start of 2004, 1 job was completed and awaiting shipment:**

| Cost incurred as of 1/1/2004 | |
|---|---|
| Job 257 | $6,000 |

**During 2004, the company incurred the following costs:**

| | |
|---|---|
| Direct material | $  500,000 |
| Direct labor | 1,000,000 |
| Manufacturing overhead | 2,000,000 |

**At the end of 2004, two jobs were in process:**

| Cost incurred as of 12/31/2004 | |
|---|---|
| Job 345 | $1,000 |
| Job 346 | 4,000 |

**In addition, four jobs were completed and awaiting shipment:**

| Cost incurred as of 12/31/2004 | |
|---|---|
| Job 341 | $1,000 |
| Job 342 | 4,000 |
| Job 343 | 1,000 |
| Job 344 | 4,000 |

### Required

a. What are the beginning and ending balances in Work in Process?

b. What are the beginning and ending balances in Finished Goods?

c. What is Cost of Goods Sold? What job numbers likely relate to the balance in Cost of Goods Sold?

**PROBLEM 2-5. Various Overhead Allocation Rates for Job-Order Costing** Allen Shoe Company has expected overhead costs of $10,000,000. The majority of the overhead costs are incurred providing production support to the direct labor force. Direct labor rates vary from $10 to $20 per hour, and more complex tasks are assigned to more skilled workers who have higher pay rates. Allen projects direct labor costs of $2,000,000 and 120,000 direct labor hours. More complex tasks require proportionally more support than do the less complex tasks.

Each model/size of shoe is produced in a single production run and constitutes a job. During the year, the company produced 10,000 pairs of the model K25, size 8 dress shoe. A total of 5,000 direct labor hours, costing $85,000, were assigned to the job.

*Required*

a. Determine the amount of overhead assigned to the model K25, size 8 dress shoe using both direct labor hours and direct labor cost as the allocation base.

b. Justify selection of either direct labor hours or direct labor cost as the allocation base.

**PROBLEM 2-6. Job Costs Using Different Overhead Rates**   Innovative Parts Company manufactures parts-to-order for antique cars. Innovative makes everything from fenders to engine blocks. Each customer order is treated as a job. They currently have two jobs, No. 9823 and No. 9824, which are complete, although overhead has not yet been applied. The company wants to know what each job's cost would be under alternative overhead allocation rates based on: (1) direct labor cost, (2) direct labor hours, and (3) machine hours. Estimates for this year are as follows:

|  |  |
|---|---|
| Direct labor cost | $120,000 |
| Direct labor hours | 8,000 |
| Machine hours | 5,000 |
| Overhead costs | $ 86,000 |

*(handwritten in margin: .716, 10.75, 17.2)*

Depreciation on machinery accounts for 75 percent of the overhead costs.

The job-cost sheets show the following:

|  | **Job 9823** | **Job 9824** |
|---|---|---|
| Direct material | $  855 | $1,650 |
| Direct labor cost | $1,020 | $1,020 |
| Direct labor hours | 85 | 68 |
| Machine hours | 100 | 200 |

*Required*

a. Determine the overhead allocation rate under the three suggested allocation bases.

b. Calculate the cost of Job 9823 and Job 9824 using each of the three bases.

c. Discuss which allocation base appears preferable.

**PROBLEM 2-7. Underapplied or Overapplied Overhead**   In the past year, Eagle Custom Cabinets had total revenue of $1,200,000, cost of goods sold of $700,000 (before adjustment for over- or underapplied overhead), administrative expenses of $300,000, and selling expenses of $100,000. During the year, overhead was applied using a predetermined rate of 50 percent of direct labor cost. Actual direct labor was $400,000. Actual overhead was $270,000. The ending balances in the inventory accounts (prior to adjustment for under applied overhead) are:

|  |  |
|---|---|
| Raw Materials Inventory | $24,000 |
| Work in Process Inventory | 60,000 |
| Finished Goods Inventory | 30,000 |

*Required*

a. Calculate net income treating the amount of underapplied overhead as immaterial and assigning it to Cost of Goods Sold.

b. Calculate net income treating the amount of underapplied overhead as material and apportioning it to the appropriate inventory accounts and Cost of Goods Sold.

c. Discuss the impact of the alternative treatments.

**PROBLEM 2-8. Underapplied or Overapplied Overhead**   Vista Window Company produces custom windows to specifications provided by architects. At the end of their accounting period, their account balances indicated the following:

|  |  |
|---|---|
| Raw Materials Inventory | $ 60,000 |
| Work in Process Inventory | 40,000 |
| Finished Goods Inventory | 20,000 |
| Cost of Goods Sold | 300,000 |
| Manufacturing Overhead (credit balance) | 24,000 |

*Required*

a. Determine the adjusted balances of the accounts if the balance in Manufacturing Overhead is considered immaterial in amount and assigned to Cost of Goods Sold.

b. Determine the adjusted balances of the accounts if the balance in Manufacturing Overhead is considered material in amount.

**PROBLEM 2-9. Job Costing (Service Example)**   White & Associates is an accounting firm that provides audit, tax, and accounting services to medium-sized retail companies. It employs 50 professionals (10 partners and 40 associates) who work directly with clients. The average expected total compensation per professional for the year is $106,000. The services of White are in high demand, and each professional works for clients to their maximum of 1,600 billable hours. All professional salaries are traced to individual client service summaries. All costs other than professional salaries are included in a single indirect cost pool (professional support). The indirect costs are assigned to service summaries using professional hours as the allocation base. The expected amount of indirect costs for the year is $4,200,000.

*Required*

a. Compute the budgeted indirect cost rate per hour of professional service.

b. White & Associates is bidding on tax and audit services for PC Station, Inc. that are expected to require 100 hours of professional service time. Calculate the estimated cost of the work using average professional wage rates and basing indirect costs on estimated service time.

**PROBLEM 2-10. Accounting for a Job-Order Cost System** Bob and Beth Ford retired from the food services industry and began catering wedding receptions on a limited basis. The major costs in setting up their business included: linens, $1,000; two complete silver services, $800; glass plates and cups, $1,200; and cake decorating tools and accessories, $400. It is expected that all of the above items will last 10 years with no salvage value. Bob and Beth do all of their food preparation in their apartment and have found that in an average month the utility bill is $100 higher than when they did not cater. All baking and cooking supplies are treated as "direct materials," and the only other cost incurred is liability insurance at $1,200 per year. All direct materials are purchased at a local grocery for cash, and Bob and Beth pay themselves an hourly wage of $25 per hour.
During the month of June, Bob and Beth catered five weddings.

|  | **Materials** | **Labor Hours** |
|---|---|---|
| Redfern wedding | $ 350 | 20 |
| Miller wedding | 700 | 35 |
| Walker wedding | 425 | 18 |
| DeSilva wedding | 1,500 | 80 |
| Estes wedding | 550 | 28 |

The overhead allocation base is labor hours with an estimated 1,000 hours per year, and billings are at 120 percent of job cost. Overhead allocations and markups are rounded to the nearest dollar.

*Required*

a. Prepare job cost sheets for each of the five catering jobs.

b. Calculate income for the month of June.

**PROBLEM 2-11. Recording Inventory Related Costs**    Fill in the missing information.

| Raw Materials | | | | | Work in Process | | |
|---|---|---|---|---|---|---|---|
| Beg. Bal. | 20,000 | | | Beg. Bal. | 70,000 | | |
| | | (a) | | Dir. Matl. | (a) | (b) | |
| Purchases | 30,000 | | | Dir. Labor | 50,000 | | |
| | | | | Overhead | 60,000 | | |
| End. Bal. | 10,000 | | | End. Bal. | 90,000 | | |

**Manufacturing Overhead**

| 65,000 | 60,000 |
|---|---|
| | (d) |

| Finished Goods | | | | Cost of Goods Sold | |
|---|---|---|---|---|---|
| Beg. Bal. | 100,000 | | | | |
| | | | | (c) | |
| | (b) | (c) | | | |
| | | | | (d) | |
| End. Bal. | 120,000 | | | | |

**PROBLEM 2-12. Recording Inventory Costs**    Vulcan Molding produces molded rubber components. At the start of the year, the company estimated that it would incur $2,000,000 of direct labor cost and $6,000,000 of manufacturing overhead. Overhead is allocated to production on the basis of direct labor cost.

Actual materials used during the year were $4,500,000, actual direct labor cost was $2,200,000, and actual overhead was $6,300,000.

*Required*

a. Calculate the overhead rate for the current year.

b. Prepare the journal entry to record use of direct material.

c. Prepare the journal entry to record direct labor.

d. Prepare the journal entry to record manufacturing overhead applied to production.

e. Prepare the journal entry to close the balance in manufacturing overhead to cost of goods sold.

**PROBLEM 2-13. Multiple Overhead Rates**    Vulcan Molding has three production departments: A, B, and C. At the start of the year, the company estimated that it would incur $2,000,000 of direct labor cost and $6,000,000 of manufacturing overhead as follows:

| | Dept. A | Dept. B | Dept. C | Total |
|---|---|---|---|---|
| Estimated overhead | $1,000,000 | $2,000,000 | $3,000,000 | $6,000,000 |
| Estimated direct labor | $500,000 | $500,000 | $1,000,000 | $2,000,000 |
| Overhead rate | $2.00 | $4.00 | $3.00 | $3.00 |

Along with many others, the following three jobs were worked on during the year:

| | Direct Labor Cost | | | |
|---|---|---|---|---|
| | Dept. A | Dept. B | Dept. C | Total |
| Job 201 | $8,000 | $2,000 | $4,000 | $14,000 |
| Job 202 | $4,000 | $6,000 | $8,000 | $18,000 |
| Job 203 | $1,000 | $4,000 | $1,000 | $6,000 |

*Required*

a. Calculate the overhead that would be assigned to each job assuming the company uses 1 plant-wide overhead allocation rate based on expected labor cost.

b. Calculate the overhead that would be assigned to each job assuming the company uses a separate overhead allocation rate for each production department based on direct labor cost.

c. Which is preferable—a single overhead rate or separate rates by production department? Explain.

**PROBLEM 2-14. Comprehensive Job-Order Costing Problem**   Lane Confectioners produce special orders of sugar candies and chocolates for airlines and hotels. During March, they purchased, on credit, 1,800 pounds of confectioners sugar @ $.90 per pound, 2,000 pounds of granulated sugar @ $.70 per pound, 800 pounds of chocolate @ $3.00 per pound, and 200 pounds of caramel @ $1.20 per pound from Seattle Confectionery Supply. In addition, they purchased for cash 60 dozen eggs @ $.70 per dozen, and 80 pounds of paraffin @ $.60 per pound from PMG Foods.

The *beginning* balances in the inventory accounts were:

| | |
|---|---|
| Raw Materials Inventory | $ 2,400 |
| Work in Process Inventory | 6,400 |
| Finished Goods Inventory | 8,600 |

The *ending* balances in the inventory accounts were:

| | |
|---|---|
| Raw Materials Inventory | $3,200 |
| Work in Process Inventory | 4,800 |
| Finished Goods Inventory | 5,400 |

Direct labor costs were $3,600 for 450 hours, indirect labor costs were $1,800, utilities were $340, rent was $600, and other overhead costs totaled $4,800. Manufacturing overhead is applied at $15 per direct labor hour. Sales during the month were $25,750, and selling and administration expenses were $8,000. (Assume that all of the above were noncash transactions.)

*Required*

a. Prepare journal entries to record the transactions for the month of March. Assume that over- or underapplied overhead is closed to Cost of Goods Sold.

b. Prepare an income statement for the month of March.

**PROBLEM 2-15. Selection of an Overhead Allocation Base**   Tilden Manufacturing expects the following overhead costs in 2004:

| | |
|---|---|
| Indirect material | $ 25,000 |
| Indirect labor | 40,000 |
| Depreciation of machinery | 100,000 |
| Repair and maintenance on machinery | 125,000 |
| Utilities and taxes | 35,000 |
| Total | $325,000 |

They expect to use 15,000 direct labor hours at a cost of $330,000 and 10,000 machine hours during the year.

*Required*

Justify the selection of an appropriate allocation base, and calculate the predetermined overhead allocation rate.

# CASES

## 2-1 ETHICS CASE: BRIXTON SURGICAL DEVICES

Brixton Surgical Devices, a public company with sales of over $800 million, is one of the worlds largest producers of surgical clamps, saws, screws, and stents. Its business involves production of both stock items and custom pieces for doctors at research hospitals.

At the end of the third quarter of 2006, it became clear to Ed Walters, chief operating officer, and Robin Smith, chief financial officer, that the company would not make the aggressive annual earnings target specified by the board of directors, and, in consequence, they would not receive bonuses that historically had averaged about 40 percent of their base compensation. That's when the two devised the following strategy.

"Here's what we'll do," suggested Ed. "We've never offered our customers a discount. Let's change that right now. We'll offer a 25 percent discount on all orders placed in October and November for delivery in December of 2006."

"That will certainly boost fourth quarter sales," said Robin. "But, you know, it won't really increase total sales. It'll just transfer some sales from the first quarter of 2007 to the fourth quarter of 2006. Of course, 2006 is where we need earnings to hit our bonus target. Hey, I've got another idea. We can also jack-up production of our stock items in the fourth quarter. With our high-priced production equipment, we've got a ton of overhead. But the more we produce, the more overhead we can bury in inventory. With lower unit costs, and higher sales, profit will go way up. Let's get going on execution. I've got to get the marketing people working on the promotion and you've got to update the production schedule. This could end up being our best year ever in terms of bonuses!"

### Required
Are the proposed actions of Ed and Robin ethical? What is the likely affect of the actions on shareholder value?

## 2-2 CLK MARKETING RESEARCH

CLK Marketing Research is a small firm located in Atlanta. On behalf of its clients, the firm conducts focus group meetings, telephone and mail opinion surveys, and evaluations of marketing strategies. The firm has three partners and six nonpartner professionals. At the start of the year, the company estimated total professional compensation (related to the three partners and six nonpartner professionals) to be $1,200,000.

To evaluate the profitability of its engagements, the firm traces actual professional compensation to each engagement along with so-called direct charges. Direct charges consist of travel costs and costs of conducting surveys (e.g., paper and postage). In addition, each engagement receives an allocation of overhead based on professional compensation charges. Overhead consists of all support costs including rent, utilities, and depreciation of office equipment. At the start of the year, these costs were estimated to be $360,000.

Recently, Celeste Norvell, a CLK partner, was asked to conduct a survey for BY2000, a new, high-tech company. Celeste is excited about this opportunity since she expects that this hot, small company will, in three to five years, become a hot, big company with premium billing opportunities. At this point, however, Celeste wants to quote a low fee since BY2000 has cash-flow problems and is clearly unwilling to pay CLK's normal rates.

On most jobs, CLK's fee is 1.5 times professional compensation. In addition, the company is reimbursed for all out-of-pocket costs related to travel and paper and postage costs for surveys. CLK is in high demand, and if the BY2000 job is undertaken, another potential client will be turned down for service.

Celeste estimates that the BY2000 engagement will require the following costs in addition to overhead support costs.

| | |
|---|---|
| Celeste Norvell (partner), 40 hours at a salary averaging $100 per hour | $4,000 |
| Bill Stern (professional staff) 100 hours at a salary of $30 per hour | 3,000 |
| Direct charges for actual travel, mailing, and postage | 2,200 |
| Total | $9,200 |

### Required
a. Calculate the expected *full cost* of the BY2000 engagement including an allocation of overhead.

b. What is the lowest amount that Celeste can bill on this engagement without hurting company profit?

c. In deciding on a price for the engagement, what should Celeste consider in addition to the amount calculated in (b)?

## 2-3 DYNAMIC HYDRAULIC SYSTEMS

Dynamic Hydraulic Systems (DHS) manufactures a variety of pumps, nozzles, hoses, and valves used in waste recovery systems. At the start of 2006, the company estimated that it would incur $10,000,000 of direct labor cost, $30,000,000 of direct material cost, and

$40,000,000 of manufacturing overhead ($5,000,000 of which would be variable and $35,000,000 fixed). Overhead is applied to jobs using a single allocation base, direct labor hours, and the rate is $100 per labor hour. At DHS, some manufacturing employees are highly skilled and are paid as much as $50 per hour. Less skilled workers earn as little as $15 per hour. In general, the jobs that require highly skilled workers are more complex and demand more support costs, such as cost related to setting up equipment for production.

During 2006, sales were unexpectedly low owing to increased competition from a Swedish firm that entered the U.S. market with aggressive pricing. In particular, DHS did not seem to be price competitive on jobs that called for less skilled (and lower paid) workers. This puzzled Dan Wilson, the plant manager. Talking to Bob Walters, vice president of finance, he expressed his confusion. "What's going on here? We're price competitive on the high-end jobs that are complex and require a lot of support in terms of engineering, material handling, and setting up equipment. But we're not competitive on the relatively simple jobs where, in my opinion, we are really efficient!"

To gain insight into the nature of the problem, the vice president asked Nancy Shell in accounting to analyze costs related to recent bids for "simple" and "complex" jobs. Nancy developed the following information:

### Job 358 (Relatively Simple)

| | |
|---|---|
| Direct material | $40,000 |
| Direct labor | |
| 210 hours × $20 | 4,200 |
| Overhead | |
| 210 hours × $100 | 21,000 |
| Total | $65,200 |

### Job 365 (Relatively Complex)

| | |
|---|---|
| Direct material | $60,000 |
| Direct labor | |
| 200 hours × $40 | 8,000 |
| Overhead | |
| 200 hours × $100 | 20,000 |
| Total | $88,000 |

As soon as he saw the analysis, Bob began to understand the nature of the problem. "Look what's happening, Nancy. The complex job has higher material cost and higher labor cost, but virtually the same amount of overhead as the simple job!"

*Required*

a. Expand on Bob's insight. In what way is overhead potentially distorted?

b. Should DHS lower prices to meet the competition from the Swedish firm? In answering this question, take into account the company's cost structure.

# 2-4 DUPAGE POWDER COATING

DuPage Powder Coating applies powder coating finishes to a variety of materials and parts used by small- and medium-sized manufacturing firms. Essentially, powder coating involves the application of powder (finely divided particles of organic polymer containing pigments, fillers, and additives) to a surface, after which the powder is fused into a continuous film by the application of heat or radiant energy. The process results in a durable finish that resists rust.

In prior years, finishes were applied by hand, and manufacturing overhead was allocated to jobs based on direct labor hours (the rate was $10 per hour based on overhead of $800,000 and 80,000 direct labor hours). At the start of the current year, the company purchased and installed a computer-controlled, electrostatic powder coating system at a cost of $1,500,000. With a five-year life, the equipment adds $300,000 a year to manufacturing overhead (thus, expected total overhead is now $1,100,000). However, labor has been reduced by 20,000 hours per year (because the equipment reduces the need for labor), and with an average wage rate of $20 per hour, $400,000 of wages are expected to be saved in the current year.

While the company purchased a computer-controlled system including a new spray chamber, it kept its old spray booth and manual equipment for use on small jobs.

DuPage Powder Coating has just received an order from Cedargreen Enterprises (a small manufacturer of outdoor furniture) to powder coat 4 tables and 16 chairs. On small orders such as this, DuPage uses its old spray booth and manual equipment rather than the new computer controlled system. Material cost for the job will be $400, and 6 labor hours are required.

*Required*

a. Based on the limited information, estimate the full cost of the job in the *current* year. Assume the company uses one, company-wide overhead rate.

b. What would have been the cost of the job in part (a) in the *prior* year?

c. Bill McCally, plant manager observed that "Last year, jobs like the one we did for Cedargreen Enterprises cost less. But, I know we're not less efficient at handling small jobs. We use the same equipment, the same labor, and the same products on small jobs this year as last year, and yet the accounting system is making small jobs look more expensive!"

Explain to Bill why the accounting system is making small jobs appear to be more costly in the current year.

d. Does the fact that small jobs have a higher cost in the current year suggest that prices for small jobs should be increased?

# chapter 3

## LEARNING OBJECTIVES

**1** Describe how products flow through departments and how costs flow through accounts.

**2** Discuss the concept of an equivalent unit.

**3** Calculate the cost per equivalent unit.

**4** Calculate the cost of goods completed and the ending Work in Process balance in a processing department.

**5** Describe a production cost report.

# PROCESS COSTING

Stacy Brannen was just completing a tour at Kent Chemical Company's Midwest plant. Only two weeks ago, she had graduated from State University with a degree in mechanical engineering, and now she was nearing the end of her first day on the job at Kent. The assistant plant manager, Bill Merton, conducted the tour and pointed out the steps involved in processing paints, stains, and wood preservatives.

Although the tour concentrated on the equipment used in the production processes, Stacy found herself wondering how the cost of products was determined. "Bill, can you give me a rough idea of how you calculate product costs?" she asked. "I noticed, for example, that to end up with a gallon of wood preservative ready to ship, we perform both mixing and packaging operations. With labor, material, and overhead added in these separate operations, is assigning costs to wood preservative a difficult job?"

"Well," Bill replied, "let's see if we can catch

Walter Hunt before he goes home for the day. He's the plant controller, and no one can do a better job than Walt of explaining how we do product costing at Kent Chemical."

The type of product costing system used at Kent Chemical Company is a process costing system. Such systems are in common use by companies that produce large numbers of homogeneous items in a continuous production process. Companies using process costing include producers of paints, plastics, cereals, cosmetics, and metals. Thus, well-known companies like DuPont, the Quaker Oats Company, and the Ralston Purina Company use process costing. This chapter introduces you to the essential elements of a process costing system.

# DIFFERENCE BETWEEN JOB-ORDER AND PROCESS COSTING SYSTEMS

As explained in Chapter 2, there are two primary systems for calculating the cost of inventory: a job-order system or a process costing system. In a job-order system, each unique product or batch is a "job" for which the company needs cost information. Therefore, it is necessary to trace manufacturing costs to specific jobs. When jobs are completed, the cost of the jobs is removed from Work in Process and included in Finished Goods. When completed jobs are sold, the cost of the jobs is removed from Finished Goods and included in Cost of Goods Sold.

Process costing, in contrast, is essentially a system of averaging. Dividing production costs by the total number of homogeneous items produced results in

**LINK TO PRACTICE**

### What Type of Costing System Is Used by Kimberly-Clark Corporation?

Kimberly-Clark produces a variety of well-known consumer products including Huggies® disposable diapers and Kleenex® brand facial tissues. What type of costing system do you think this company uses? Large quantities of identical units are produced in continuous production processes. So, to account for the cost of Huggies disposable diapers and the cost of Kleenex facial tissues, Kimberly-Clark uses process costing.

an average unit cost. When items are completed, multiplying the number of units completed by the average unit cost determines the cost to be removed from Work in Process Inventory and included in Finished Goods Inventory. When items are sold, multiplying the number of units sold by the average unit cost determines the cost to remove from Finished Goods Inventory and include in Cost of Goods Sold. Illustration 3-1 presents a comparison of job-order and process costing systems. The remainder of the chapter describes process costing systems in more detail.[1]

**Illustration 3-1**
Comparison of job-order and process costing systems

**Job-Order System—Use Costs of Specific Jobs**

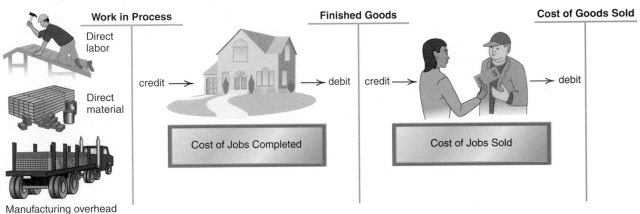

**Process Costing System—Use Average Unit Cost Information**

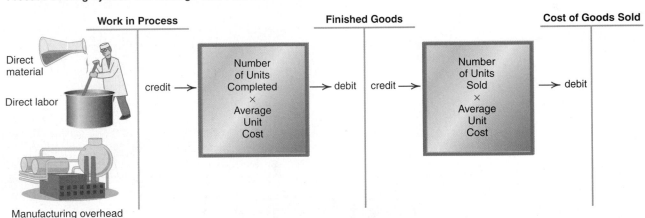

---

[1]In practice, firms frequently use a hybrid system that combines features of job-order costing and process costing. Thus, you should view job-order and process costing as two ends of a continuum of actual methods that are used in practice. A more detailed treatment of costing methods is provided in cost accounting textbooks.

Describe how products flow through departments and how costs flow through accounts.

# PRODUCT AND COST FLOWS

Just as a product passes through several departments before it is completed, costs flow through several accounts before the cost of the product is recorded in finished goods. Here, we discuss the flow of products through departments and the flow of costs through accounts in process costing companies.

## PRODUCT FLOWS THROUGH DEPARTMENTS

In the manufacturing operations of a company using process costing, a product typically must pass through two or more departments. The Kent Chemical Company manufactures wood preservative in two departments: mixing and packaging. After chemical materials are blended in the Mixing Department, the liquid preservative is transferred to the Packaging Department, where it is placed in plastic containers. Materials, labor, and overhead are added at different stages in each processing department.

Generally, identifying the stage when materials enter the production process is easy. In the Mixing Department, the chemical materials are added at the start of the process. Determining exactly when labor and overhead are added to the process is more difficult. Labor and overhead are often grouped together and referred to as **conversion costs**. These costs are often assumed to be added evenly throughout the process.

Illustration 3-2 shows how items flow through the two processing departments and how costs are incurred. As indicated, materials enter the Mixing Department at the start. However, conversion costs (labor and overhead) are assumed to enter mixing at a constant rate.

## COST FLOWS THROUGH ACCOUNTS

The product costs accumulated in a process costing system are essentially the same costs considered in job-order costing: direct material, direct labor, and manufacturing overhead. Additionally, a processing department may have a cost

**Illustration 3-2**
Flow of items through processing departments

### Virtual Plant Tours for Companies that Use Process Costing

Process costing is used by companies that produce large numbers of homogeneous items in a continuous production process. Have you ever been in a plant that has such a production process? If not, take a virtual plant tour of one or all of the following companies.

Canadian Springs is a producer and supplier of bottled water to homes and offices. Their tour is available at: http://www.canadiansprings.com/tour.cfm.

## ENDOT INDUSTRIES

Endot Industries is a manufacturer of polyethylene water pipe. Their tour is available at: http://www.endot.com/home/company_tour.asp.

Monitor Sugar Company is a manufacturer of sugar from beets. Their tour is available at: http://www.monitorsugar.com/tours.

For additional tours, including companies that would use job-order costing and some service operations, see the Web site *Plant Tours* on the Internet at: http://bradley.bradley.edu/~rf/plantour.htm.

Source: Logos are reprinted by permission of Canadian Springs, Endot Industries, and Monitor Sugar Company.

called **transferred-in cost**. This is the cost incurred in one processing department that is transferred to the next processing department. For example, at Kent Chemical the cost incurred in the Mixing Department is transferred to the Packaging Department.

Each processing department accumulates product cost in a separate departmental Work in Process account. The sum of the departmental Work in Process accounts is the amount in Work in Process for the entire company. The following entries illustrate the flow of costs between processing departments.

**Direct Material.** Suppose that $142,000 of direct materials are used during April in the Mixing Department of Kent Chemical Company. The following entry would be appropriate for this transaction:

| (date) | Work in Process, Mixing | 142,000 | |
| |     Raw Materials | | 142,000 |
| | | | |
| | To record use of raw material | | |

**Direct Labor.** Suppose that $62,200 of direct labor costs are incurred during April in the Mixing Department. The following entry would be appropriate for this transaction:

| (date) | Work in Process, Mixing | 62,200 | |
| |     Wages Payable | | 62,200 |
| | | | |
| | To record direct labor cost | | |

**Manufacturing Overhead.** To assign overhead to products in a process costing system, a company may use either actual overhead costs or a predetermined overhead rate. Unless the amount of overhead cost and the level of production are fairly constant from month to month, using actual overhead costs results in substantial fluctuations in the unit cost of goods produced. For this reason, most companies use a predetermined overhead rate.

Suppose that at the start of the year, the Mixing Department estimates it will incur $2,160,000 of overhead cost and $720,000 of direct labor cost. Using direct labor as an allocation base, the department calculates a predetermined overhead rate of $3 for each dollar of direct labor cost. Assuming $62,200 of direct labor cost was incurred in the month of April, $186,600 of overhead ($62,200 $\times$ $3 = $186,600) would be assigned to Work in Process that month.

| (date) | Work in Process, Mixing | 186,600 | |
| |     Manufacturing Overhead | | 186,600 |
| | | | |
| | To record manufacturing overhead | | |
| |     applied to Work in Process | | |

**Transferred-in Cost.** When one processing department completes its work, the items are transferred to the next department along with their related cost. As mentioned earlier, this cost is referred to as *transferred-in* cost. Suppose that during April, the Mixing Department completes units with a cost of $360,000. The completed units are transferred to the Packaging Department, and the related cost becomes a transferred-in cost to packaging. The entry to record the transfer is:

| (date) | Work in Process, Packaging | 360,000 | |
| |     Work in Process, Mixing | | 360,000 |
| | | | |
| | To record transfer of units from | | |
| |     Mixing to Packaging | | |

The flow of costs between departmental Work in Process accounts is presented in Illustration 3-3.

**Illustration 3-3**
Flow of cost between
processing departments

Discuss the concept of an
equivalent unit.

# CALCULATING UNIT COST

Process costing, as we have seen, is essentially a system of averaging. This section shows how to calculate an average unit cost in a process costing system.[2] First, however, we must explain an essential concept in process costing—the concept of an equivalent unit.

## EQUIVALENT UNITS

In calculating the average unit cost, it is necessary to convert the number of partially completed units in Work in Process to an equivalent number of whole units. Otherwise, the denominator in the average unit cost calculation will be misstated. When partially completed units are converted to a comparable number of completed units, they are referred to as **equivalent units**. For example, if 100 units in Work in Process are 50 percent completed, then they are equivalent to 50 completed units (100 × 50%), as shown in Illustration 3-4.

The number of equivalent units in Work in Process may be different for material and conversion costs. This is because material and conversion costs enter the production process at different times. For example, suppose that at the end of July, the Mixing Department at Kent Chemical has 100 gallons (units of production) of wood preservative in work in process that are 50 percent through the mixing process. Further, assume that materials enter into the process at the start, while conversion costs enter evenly throughout the process. Even though the units are

**Illustration 3-4**
How equivalent units
are calculated

---

[2]The approach we take is referred to as the weighted average method. Other approaches, such as the first-in, first-out method, are also used. These methods are discussed in cost accounting textbooks.

**Illustration 3-5**
Differences in equivalent units for material and conversion costs assuming material added at start of process

only halfway through the process, they have received 100 percent of material since material was added immediately at the start of the process (see Illustration 3-2). Therefore, with respect to material cost, there are 100 equivalent units in work in process. However, because the units are only halfway through the process, they have received only 50 percent of the labor and overhead needed for completion. Since the 100 gallons are only 50 percent complete with respect to conversion costs, there are 50 equivalent units for labor and overhead (see Illustration 3-5).

Calculate the cost per equivalent unit.

## COST PER EQUIVALENT UNIT

The average unit cost in a process costing system is referred to as a **cost per equivalent unit**. The formula for determining the cost per equivalent unit is:

$$\text{Cost per equivalent unit} = \frac{\text{Cost in beginning WIP} + \text{Cost incurred in current period}}{\text{Units completed} + \text{Equivalent units in ending WIP}}$$

The numerator contains the cost in beginning Work in Process (WIP) plus the cost incurred in the current period. This amount represents the total cost for which a processing department must account in each period. The total cost is divided by the units completed plus the equivalent units in ending Work in Process. The result is a cost per equivalent unit amount that can be used to spread the cost at the start of the period and the cost incurred during the period over the units completed and the units in process at the end of the period.

Calculate the cost of goods completed and the ending Work in Process balance in a processing department.

# CALCULATING AND APPLYING COST PER EQUIVALENT UNIT: MIXING DEPARTMENT EXAMPLE

Next, we consider cost per equivalent unit calculations for the Mixing Department of Kent Chemical Company. At the start of April, the Mixing Department has on hand beginning work in process inventory consisting of 10,000 gallons of wood

**Illustration 3-6**
Calculation of cost per equivalent unit, mixing department

| Cost | Material | Labor | Overhead | Total |
|---|---|---|---|---|
| Beginning WIP | $ 18,000 | $ 7,800 | $ 23,400 | $ 49,200 |
| Cost incurred during April | 142,000 | 62,200 | 186,600 | 390,800 |
| Total cost | $160,000 | $70,000 | $210,000 | $440,000 |
| **Units** | | | | |
| Units completed | 60,000 | 60,000 | 60,000 | |
| Equivalent units, ending WIP | 20,000 | 10,000 | 10,000 | |
| Total units | 80,000 | 70,000 | 70,000 | |
| **Cost per equivalent unit** | | | | |
| (Total cost ÷ total units) | $2   + | $1   + | $3   = | $6 |

preservative that are 80 percent complete. During the month, 70,000 gallons are started and 60,000 are completed. At the end of April, 20,000 gallons are on hand that are 50 percent complete. The cost in beginning Work in Process consists of $18,000 of material cost, $7,800 of labor cost, and $23,400 of overhead cost. During April, the Mixing Department incurs $142,000 of material cost and $62,200 of labor cost. Because the Mixing Department's predetermined overhead rate is $3 for each dollar of labor cost, $186,600 ($3 × $62,200) of overhead is applied to production during the month.

The cost per equivalent unit calculations for the Mixing Department are presented in Illustration 3-6. The cost of material includes the $18,000 in beginning Work in Process and the $142,000 of material cost incurred during April. The total of $160,000 is divided by 80,000 units, the sum of the number of units completed (60,000 gallons) and the equivalent units in ending Work in Process (20,000 gallons). Dividing total cost by the total number of units yields a cost per equivalent unit for materials of $2. A similar procedure is used to find the cost per equivalent unit for labor and overhead cost.

Let's look more closely at the equivalent units used in these calculations. Note that at the end of April there are 20,000 units on hand that are only 50 percent through the mixing process. However, since material cost enters at the start of the mixing process, the 20,000 units are 100 percent complete with respect to material cost. Thus, there are 20,000 equivalent units in ending Work in Process for materials. In contrast, for both labor and overhead, the 20,000 units on hand are only 50 percent complete, so they correspond to only 10,000 equivalent units.

As shown in the last line of Illustration 3-6, the total cost per equivalent unit is $6 consisting of $2 of material cost, $1 of labor cost, and $3 of overhead cost. These unit cost figures can be used to calculate the cost of goods completed and transferred out of the Mixing Department and the cost of ending Work in Process.

## COST TRANSFERRED OUT

Recall that 60,000 gallons were completed by the Mixing Department during April and transferred to the Packaging Department. We know that the unit cost is $6. Therefore, $360,000 of cost (60,000 gallons × $6) is related to the units completed and transferred out. The entry at the end of April to record the transfer was presented earlier and is repeated here:

| (date) | Work in Process, Packaging | 360,000 | |
| | Work in Process, Mixing | | 360,000 |
| | | | |
| | To record transfer of units from | | |
| | Mixing to Packaging | | |

## ENDING WORK IN PROCESS

The ending balance in Work in Process in the Mixing Department is $80,000. This balance is made up of 20,000 equivalent units for material at $2 per equivalent unit, 10,000 equivalent units for labor at $1, and 10,000 equivalent units for overhead at $3.

| Ending Balance in Work in Process, Mixing | |
| --- | --- |
| Material (20,000 equiv. units at $2) | $40,000 |
| Labor (10,000 equiv. units at $1) | 10,000 |
| Overhead (10,000 equiv. units at $3) | 30,000 |
| Total | $80,000 |

Here is a summary of the cost activity for the Mixing Department resulting in the $80,000 ending balance in Work in Process.

**Work in Process, Mixing**

| Beginning balance | 49,200 | |
| Material | 142,000 | 360,000 Cost transferred out |
| Cost added { Labor | 62,200 | |
| Overhead | 186,600 | |
| Ending balance | 80,000 | |

# PRODUCTION COST REPORT

LEARNING OBJECTIVE 5

Describe a production cost report.

A **production cost report** is an end-of-the-month report for a process costing system that provides a reconciliation of units and a reconciliation of costs as well as the details of the cost per equivalent unit calculations. The reconciliations help ensure that mistakes are not made in calculations. A production cost report for the Mixing Department of Kent Chemical Company is provided in Illustration 3-7. The unit cost calculations in the production report are identical to the ones just presented. We will concentrate now on the reconciliation of units and the reconciliation of costs.

## RECONCILIATION OF UNITS

Assuming no units are lost (e.g., due to evaporation, damage, or theft), the number of units in beginning work in process inventory plus the number of units started during the period should be equal to the number of units completed plus

**Illustration 3-7**
Production cost report,
mixing department

## Production Cost Report
## Mixing Department
## April 2006

### Unit Reconciliation

| | |
|---|---:|
| Units in Beg. WIP (100% material, 80% conversion costs) | 10,000 |
| Units started during April | 70,000 |
| Units to account for | 80,000 |
| Units completed and transferred to packaging | 60,000 |
| Units in ending WIP (100% material, 50% conversion costs) | 20,000 |
| Units accounted for | 80,000 |

### Cost Per Equivalent Unit Calculation

| | Material | Labor | Overhead | Total |
|---|---:|---:|---:|---:|
| **Cost** | | | | |
| Beginning WIP | $ 18,000 | $ 7,800 | $ 23,400 | $ 49,200 |
| Cost incurred during April | 142,000 | 62,200 | 186,600 | 390,800 |
| Total | $160,000 | $70,000 | $210,000 | $440,000 |
| **Units** | | | | |
| Units completed | 60,000 | 60,000 | 60,000 | |
| Equivalent units, ending WIP | 20,000 | 10,000 | 10,000 | |
| Total | 80,000 | 70,000 | 70,000 | |
| Cost per equivalent unit | $2 | $1 | $3 | $6 |

### Cost Reconciliation

| | | |
|---|---:|---:|
| Total cost to account for | | $440,000 |
| Cost of completed units transferred to Packaging (60,000 × $6) | | $360,000 |
| Cost of ending WIP | | |
| Material (20,000 equivalent units × $2) | $40,000 | |
| Labor (10,000 equivalent units × $1) | 10,000 | |
| Overhead (10,000 equivalent units × $3) | 30,000 | 80,000 |
| Total cost accounted for | | $440,000 |

the number of units in work in process at the end of the period. For the Mixing Department, 10,000 units were in beginning inventory and 70,000 units were started during the period, which means that 80,000 units must be accounted for. Since 60,000 units were completed and 20,000 units are in work in process at the end of the period, all of the units are accounted for.

## RECONCILIATION OF COSTS

For each period, the total cost that must be accounted for is the sum of the costs in beginning Work in Process and the costs incurred during the period. In the Mixing Department, this amounts to $440,000. The cost must be either transferred out with the completed units or remain in ending Work in Process inventory. The amount transferred out is $360,000 and the amount in ending Work in Process inventory is $80,000. Because their sum is $440,000, the total amount of cost is accounted for.

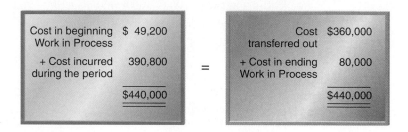

| Cost in beginning Work in Process | $ 49,200 | | Cost transferred out | $360,000 |
| + Cost incurred during the period | 390,800 | = | + Cost in ending Work in Process | 80,000 |
| | $440,000 | | | $440,000 |

# BASIC STEPS IN PROCESS COSTING: A SUMMARY

Unless process costing is approached in a systematic way, it is easy to get lost in the calculations. Here is a summary of the basic steps presented earlier. As you can see, each of the steps is performed when the production cost report is prepared.

**Step 1.**   Account for the number of physical units. The number of units at the start of the period plus the number of units started during the period should equal the number of units completed plus the number of units in ending Work in Process.

**Step 2.**   Calculate the cost per equivalent unit for material, labor, and overhead. Remember that cost (numerator in the calculation) includes both beginning cost and cost incurred during the period. The number of equivalent units (denominator in the calculation) includes both the number of units completed and the number of equivalent units in ending Work in Process.

**Step 3.**   Assign cost to items completed and items in ending Work in Process. The cost of items completed is simply the product of the *total* cost per equivalent unit and the number of units completed. The cost of items in Work in Process is the sum of the products of equivalent units in process and cost per equivalent unit for material, labor, and overhead.

**Step 4.**   Account for the amount of product cost. The cost of beginning inventory plus the cost incurred during the period should equal the amount of cost assigned to completed items plus the amount of cost assigned to items in ending Work in Process.

# KENT CHEMICAL REVISITED: ANSWERING STACY'S QUESTION

Recall that in the scenario at the beginning of the chapter, Stacy Brannen asked how the cost of products like wood preservative are calculated at Kent Chemical Company. At this point you should be able to answer that question. Essentially, material, labor, and overhead costs are accumulated in each processing department. In each department, the cost per equivalent unit is calculated for material, labor, and overhead (Step 2 in previous section). Then, the costs per equivalent unit are used to determine the cost of items completed and the cost of ending Work in Process (Step 3).

# DEALING WITH TRANSFERRED-IN COST: PACKAGING DEPARTMENT EXAMPLE

As previously noted, companies using process costing systems generally use several processes to make their products. When items are completed in one processing department, the cost of the completed units is transferred to the next processing department. This procedure is repeated until the units are completed in the last process. At that point, the cost of the items is transferred to finished goods.

Here, we consider an example to illustrate the method for dealing with cost transfers. The example involves the Packaging Department of Kent Chemical Company. To calculate product costs in the Packaging Department, we will use the same procedures already used to calculate product costs in the Mixing Department, thereby providing you with another opportunity to enhance your understanding of process costing.

**Step 1.** In working through the Packaging Department example, it will be helpful to examine the information provided in the Production Cost Report for the Packaging Department (see Illustration 3-8). At the start of April, the Packaging Department has 15,000 gallons that are 50 percent through the packaging operation. During the month of April, the department receives 60,000 gallons from the Mixing Department. There are now 75,000 gallons to account for. At the end of April, 5,000 gallons are 40 percent complete, and 70,000 gallons are completed and transferred to finished goods, which accounts for the total of 75,000 gallons. Reconciling the physical number of units is the first of the four steps in solving a process costing problem and is shown in the quantity reconciliation section of the Production Cost Report (Illustration 3-8).

**Step 2.** The second step is to calculate the cost per equivalent unit. The beginning balance in Work in Process includes $10,500 of material cost, $4,500 of labor, $9,000 of overhead, and $92,250 of cost transferred in from the Mixing Department. In addition, $49,500 of material cost, $27,900 of labor cost, $55,800 of overhead, and $360,000 of cost transferred in from the Mixing Department were incurred during the month of April. The sum of these costs is divided by the number of completed

**Illustration 3-8**
Production cost report,
packaging department

### Production Cost Report
### Packaging Department
### April 2006

**Unit Reconciliation**

| | |
|---|---|
| Units in Beg. WIP (100% material, 50% conversion costs) | 15,000 |
| Units received from Mixing during April | 60,000 |
| Units to account for | 75,000 |
| Units completed and transferred to packaging | 70,000 |
| Units in ending WIP (100% material, 40% conversion costs) | 5,000 |
| Units accounted for | 75,000 |

**Cost Per Equivalent Unit Calculation**

| | Material | Labor | Overhead | Trans. In | Total |
|---|---|---|---|---|---|
| **Cost** | | | | | |
| Beginning WIP | $10,500 | $ 4,500 | $ 9,000 | $ 92,250 | $116,250 |
| Cost incurred during April | 49,500 | 27,900 | 55,800 | 360,000 | 493,200 |
| Total | $60,000 | $32,400 | $64,800 | $452,250 | $609,450 |
| **Units** | | | | | |
| Units completed | 70,000 | 70,000 | 70,000 | 70,000 | |
| Equivalent units, ending WIP | 5,000 | 2,000 | 2,000 | 5,000 | |
| Total | 75,000 | 72,000 | 72,000 | 75,000 | |
| Cost per equivalent unit | $0.80 | $0.45 | $0.90 | $6.03 | $8.18 |

**Cost Reconciliation**

| | | |
|---|---|---|
| Total cost to account for | | $609,450 |
| Cost of completed units transferred to Finished Goods (70,000 × $8.18) | | $572,600 |
| Cost of ending WIP | | |
| Material (5,000 equivalent units × $0.80) | $ 4,000 | |
| Labor (2,000 equivalent units × $0.45) | 900 | |
| Overhead (2,000 equivalent units × $0.90) | 1,800 | |
| Transferred-in (5,000 equivalent units at $6.03) | 30,150 | 36,850 |
| Total cost accounted for | | $609,450 |

units plus the equivalent units in ending Work in Process for each cost category. As the Production Cost Report shows, this yields cost per equivalent unit values of $.80 for material, $.45 for labor, $.90 for overhead, and $6.03 for transferred-in cost. Note that the calculation for material assumes that material is added at the start of the packaging process—thus the 5,000 units in ending Work in Process are 100 percent complete with respect to materials.

Because it was not covered in the previous example, note especially the calculation of cost per equivalent unit for transferred-in cost. The sum of transferred-in cost in beginning Work in Process ($92,250) plus the cost transferred-in during April ($360,000) is the numerator of the calculation ($452,250). The denominator (75,000 units) is the sum of the units completed (70,000) plus the equivalent units in ending Work in Process (5,000). The result is a cost per equivalent unit for transferred-in cost of $6.03.

One aspect of the calculation may be confusing: the equivalent units in ending Work in Process. At the end of April, there are 5,000 units in process that are only 40 percent through the packaging process. However, these units are 100 percent complete with respect to transferred-in cost, because they were transferred in with all of the Mixing Department cost that they will receive. Therefore, there are 5,000 equivalent units in ending Work in Process for transferred-in cost.

**Step 3.** The third step in solving the process costing problem is to assign cost to items completed and items in ending Work in Process. The cost of the completed items is $572,600. As indicated in the production cost report (Illustration 3-8), this is computed as the cost per equivalent unit ($8.18) times the number of units completed (70,000). Once the units are completed in the Packaging Department, they include the cost of both the mixing operation and the packaging operation and they are ready to be transferred to Finished Goods. The entry to record the transfer is:

| (date) | Finished Goods | 572,600 | |
| |     Work in Process, Packaging | | 572,600 |
| | To record cost of units completed and transferred to Finished Goods | | |

The cost of ending Work in Process is composed of material, labor, overhead, and transferred-in cost. For each cost category, the equivalent units in ending Work in Process is multiplied by the cost per equivalent unit. As indicated in the production cost report, the sum of the cost categories is the ending balance of $36,850.

**Step 4.** The fourth and final step is to account for the amount of product cost. The cost of beginning inventory ($116,250) plus the amount of cost incurred during the period ($493,200) is the total cost that must be accounted for ($609,450). As indicated in the production cost report, this is accounted for by the cost of the completed items ($572,600) plus the cost of ending Work in Process ($36,850).

# PROCESS COSTING AND INCREMENTAL ANALYSIS

**Decision Making/ Incremental Analysis**

Recall from Chapter 1 that whenever we make a decision, we need to perform incremental analysis. That is, we need to the determine the *change* in revenue and the *change* in cost, assuming a particular decision alternative is selected. If the net change is positive, the decision alternative is "good" since it will have a positive impact on firm profit. If the net change is negative, the decision alternative is "bad" in that it will have a negative impact on firm profit.

When using process costing information (or, for that matter, job-order costing information) to make a decision, we have to be careful to recognize that the cost per unit is typically the average of fixed and variable costs. Thus, it does not measure the change in cost associated from producing an additional unit. Let's consider a simplified example to clarify this point. Later in Chapter 7, we'll go into more detail on decision making with product cost information.

Suppose that a company has no beginning work in process inventory and no ending work in process inventory for 2005. During 2005 the company incurs $100,000 of direct material cost, $200,000 of direct labor cost, and $300,000 of manufacturing overhead in producing 200,000 units that sell for $3.25 per unit. Further, let's assume that material and labor are variable costs and, for simplicity, that manufacturing overhead is completely fixed. In this case, the annual profit for 2005 is $50,000 as follows:

| | **200,000 Units** | **Per Equivalent Unit** |
|---|---|---|
| Direct material cost | $100,000 | $0.50 |
| Direct labor cost | 200,000 | 1.00 |
| Manufacturing overhead cost | 300,000 | 1.50 |
| Total | $600,000 | $3.00 |
| Current selling price | $3.25 | |

Profit = Sales − Cost
$\quad\quad$ = ($3.25 × 200,000) − $600,000
$\quad\quad$ = $50,000

Now, suppose the company is considering *decreasing* its price to $2.90 for 2006 and expects that demand for its product will increase 75,000 units to 275,000. Note that the price of $2.90 is less than the cost per equivalent unit in 2005 so it might appear that decreasing the price is a poor decision. However, to properly evaluate the decision, we must perform incremental analysis.

| | | |
|---|---|---|
| **New revenue** ($2.90 × 275,000) | | $797,500 |
| **Old revenue** ($3.25 × 200,000) | | 650,000 |
| **Change in revenue** | | $147,500 |
| **New Cost** | | |
| $\quad$ Material: variable ($0.50 × 275,000) | $137,500 | |
| $\quad$ Labor: variable ($1.00 × 275,000) | 275,000 | |
| $\quad$ Overhead: fixed | 300,000 | $712,500 |
| **Old Cost** | | 600,000 |
| **Change in cost** | | $112,500 |
| **Net change** | | $ 35,000 |

Note that with new price, revenue will increase by $147,500. However, costs will increase by only $112,500. Thus, there will be a net *benefit* of $35,000 associated with decreasing the price to $2.90 even though it is below the old cost per unit of $3.00. We can only see this by performing incremental analysis. And in performing incremental analysis, we must take into account that some of the costs are variable (material and labor) and some costs are fixed (manufacturing overhead). We would have made a serious error if we had assumed that the new cost would be $825,000 (i.e., $3.00 × 275,000). Costs won't increase by $3.00 per unit because $1.50 of the old unit cost is actually fixed.

# MAKING BUSINESS DECISIONS

Just as with job-order costing, process costing systems provide information on the *full* cost of units produced rather than their *incremental* cost. Since decision making relies on incremental analysis, care must be taken not to treat full cost as if it were incremental cost.

## KNOWLEDGE AND SKILLS (K/S) CHECKLIST

*Knowledge and skills are needed to make good business decisions. Check off the knowledge and skills you've acquired from reading this chapter.*

❏ K/S 1. You have an expanded business vocabulary (see key terms).

❏ K/S 2. You understand the concept of an equivalent unit.

❏ K/S 3. You can calculate the cost of units completed and the cost of ending Work in Process.

❏ K/S 4. You can reconcile units on a production cost report.

❏ K/S 5. You can reconcile costs on a production cost report.

# SUMMARY OF LEARNING OBJECTIVES

**1** *Describe how products flow through departments and how costs flow through accounts.* Process costing systems are used to accumulate the cost of inventory in companies that produce large numbers of identical items. Typically, several distinct processes are used to produce the items. When units are completed in one process, the cost of the units is transferred to the next process. This procedure is repeated until the units are completed in the last process. Along with transferred-in costs, each process may add its own material, labor, and overhead costs.

**2** *Discuss the concept of an equivalent unit.* Units in Work in Process are not equal to fully completed units. Therefore, in calculating the average cost per unit it is necessary to express these partially completed units in terms of equivalent whole units.

**3** *Calculate the cost per equivalent unit.* Process costing is essentially a system of averaging. The average unit cost is referred to as the cost per equivalent unit. It equals the sum of beginning Work in Process costs and current period costs

divided by the sum of units completed and equivalent units in ending Work in Process.

**4** *Calculate the cost of goods completed and the ending Work in Process balance in a processing department.* To calculate the cost of completed items, the total cost per equivalent unit is multiplied by the number of units completed. To calculate the cost of units in Work in Process, it is necessary to multiply the number of equivalent units in process by the cost per equivalent unit separately for each cost category (i.e., material, labor, overhead, and transferred-in cost). This is necessary because the units in Work in Process at the end of the period may be completed to different degrees with respect to each of these costs.

**5** *Describe a production cost report.* A production cost report provides a reconciliation of units in beginning inventory and units started to units in ending inventory and units completed. This report also provides a reconciliation of costs in beginning inventory and costs added during the period to costs in ending inventory and costs transferred out.

# R E V I E W    P R O B L E M

Little Gardener Company produces an environmentally safe general purpose plant food that can be used on flower beds and in vegetable gardens. The company operates two departments, Mixing and Packaging. Liquid plant food is prepared in the Mixing Department and packaged in 1-gallon containers in the Packaging Department. Material is added at the start of each process and labor and overhead are added evenly throughout the processes. All units are completed each month in Packaging. Therefore, there is no ending work in process in this department.

The following information is related to production in February:

| Unit Information (gallons) | Mixing | Packaging |
|---|---|---|
| Beginning work in process | | |
|   (Mixing) | 2,000 | |
|   (Packaging) | | –0– |
| Started during March | 60,000 | 61,000 |
| Ending work in process | | |
|   (Mixing: 100% material, 60% conversion costs) | 1,000 | |
|   (Packaging) | | –0– |

| Cost Information, Beginning Work in Process | | |
|---|---|---|
| Direct material | $4,000 | $ –0– |
| Direct labor | 800 | –0– |
| Manufacturing overhead | 1,120 | –0– |
| Transferred-in cost | –0– | –0– |

| Cost Added During February | | |
|---|---|---|
| Direct material | $120,000 | $18,300 |
| Direct labor | 30,000 | 3,050 |
| Manufacturing overhead | 42,000 | 6,100 |
| Transferred-in cost | –0– | ? |

**Required**

Prepare production cost reports for Mixing and Packaging for the month of February.

---

**Little Gardener Company**
**Production Cost Report**
**Mixing Department**
**February**

**Quantity Reconciliation**

| | |
|---|---|
| Units in beginning WIP | 2,000 |
| Units started during February | 60,000 |
|   Units to account for | 62,000 |
| Units completed | 61,000 |
| Units in ending WIP (100% material, 60% conversion costs) | 1,000 |
|   Units accounted for | 62,000 |

**Cost Per Equivalent Unit Calculation**

| Cost | Material | Labor | Overhead | Total |
|---|---|---|---|---|
| Beginning WIP | $ 4,000 | $ 800 | $ 1,120 | $ 5,920 |
| Cost incurred during February | 120,000 | 30,000 | 42,000 | 192,000 |
|   Total | $124,000 | $30,800 | $43,120 | $197,920 |

|  | Material | Labor | Overhead | Total |
|---|---|---|---|---|
| **Units** | | | | |
| Units completed | 61,000 | 61,000 | 61,000 | |
| Equivalent units, ending WIP | 1,000 | 600 | 600 | |
| Total | 62,000 | 61,600 | 61,600 | |
| Cost per equivalent unit | $2.00 | $0.50 | $0.70 | $3.20 |

**Cost Reconciliation**

| | |
|---|---|
| Total cost to account for | $197,920 |
| Cost of completed units transferred to Finished Goods (61,000 × $3.20) | $195,200 |
| Cost of ending WIP | |
| Material (1,000 equivalent units × $2) | $2,000 |
| Labor (600 equivalent units × $0.50) | 300 |
| Overhead (600 equivalent units × $0.70) | 420 |
| | 2,720 |
| Total cost accounted for | $197,920 |

---

**Little Gardener Company**
**Production Cost Report**
**Packaging Department**
**February**

**Quantity Reconciliation**

| | |
|---|---|
| Units in beginning WIP | –0– |
| Units started | 61,000 |
| Units to account for | 61,000 |
| Units completed | 61,000 |
| Units in ending WIP | –0– |
| Units accounted for | 61,000 |

**Cost Per Equivalent Unit Calculation**

|  | Material | Labor | Overhead | Trans. In | Total |
|---|---|---|---|---|---|
| **Cost** | | | | | |
| Beginning WIP | $ –0– | $ –0– | $ –0– | $ –0– | $ –0– |
| Cost incurred during February | 18,300 | 3,050 | 6,100 | 195,200 | 222,650 |
| Total | $18,300 | $3,050 | $6,100 | $195,200 | $222,650 |
| **Units** | | | | | |
| Units completed | 61,000 | 61,000 | 61,000 | 61,000 | |
| Equivalent units, ending WIP | –0– | –0– | –0– | –0– | |
| Total | 61,000 | 61,000 | 61,000 | 61,000 | |
| Cost per equivalent unit | $0.30 | $0.05 | $0.10 | $3.20 | $3.65 |

**Cost Reconciliation**

| | |
|---|---|
| Total cost to account for | $222,650 |
| Cost of completed units transferred to Finished Goods (61,000 × $3.65) | $222,650 |
| Cost of ending WIP | –0– |
| Total cost accounted for | $222,650 |

# KEY TERMS

Conversion costs (82)          Equivalent units (85)          Transferred-in costs (83)
Cost per equivalent unit (86)  Production cost report (88)

# SELF ASSESSMENT *(Answers Below)*

1. Which one(s) of the following characteristics are associated with a process costing system?

   a. Heterogeneous products.
   b. Homogeneous products.
   c. Continuous production.
   d. Discontinuous production.
   e. Costs are traced to jobs.
   f. Costs are traced to processing departments.

2. The best example of a business requiring a process costing system would be a(n):

   a. Custom cabinet shop.
   b. Antique furniture restorer.
   c. Soap manufacturer.
   d. Automobile repair shop.

3. The costs in a process cost system are traced to:

   a. Specific jobs.
   b. Specific customers.
   c. Specific company administrators.
   d. Specific production departments.

4. Match the following terms with the definitions shown below.

   a. Conversion costs.
   b. Equivalent units.
   c. Transferred-in costs.
   d. Cost per equivalent unit.
      (1) The costs associated with units received from a preceding department for further processing.
      (2) The unit cost in a process costing system.
      (3) The costs associated with changing units of direct materials into finished products; they include both direct labor and manufacturing overhead.
      (4) The quantity of partially completed units expressed in terms of whole units.

5. Determine the amount of conversion cost in the following list of costs.

   a. Direct material, $25,000.
   b. Direct labor, $35,000.
   c. Manufacturing overhead, $45,000.
   d. Selling expenses, $10,000.
   e. Administrative expenses, $50,000.

6. If raw materials are introduced into a production department at the beginning of the process, which statement is correct about the equivalent units in ending Work in Process for materials?

   a. All of the units in work in process are 100 percent complete with respect to materials.
   b. All of the units in work in process are 50 percent complete with respect to materials.
   c. Equivalent units of materials are not a function of when the materials are entered into the process.
   d. All of the preceding statements are correct.

7. A transfer of units from production department one to production department two would be recorded as a:

   a. Debit to Work in Process, Department 1; credit to Work in Process, Department 2.
   b. Debit to Work in Process, Department 2; credit to Work in Process, Department 1.
   c. Debit to Cost of Goods Sold; credit to Work in Process, Department 1.
   d. Debit to Cost of Goods Sold; credit to Work in Process, Department 2.

8. The Unit Reconciliation section of a production cost report includes all of the following except:

   a. Beginning units in process.
   b. Ending units in process.
   c. Units in finished goods.
   d. Units completed and transferred out.
   e. Units started during the period.

9. The units as shown in the unit reconciliation section of a production cost report are:

   a. Equivalent units of production.
   b. Units without regard to stage of completion.
   c. Units complete as to materials.
   d. Units complete as to prime costs.

10. Transferred-in costs occur in:

    a. All production departments.
    b. The first and last production departments.
    c. All production departments after the first.
    d. None of the above is correct.

**Answers to Self Assessment**
**1.** b, c, f;   **2.** c;   **3.** d;   **4.** (1)-c; (2)-d; (3)-a; (4)-b;
**5.** $80,000;   **6.** a;   **7.** b;   **8.** c;   **9.** b;   **10.** c.

# INTERACTIVE LEARNING

**Enhance and test your knowledge of Chapter 3 using the interactive CD.**

1. Learning Objectives
2. Multiple Choice
3. Language of Business—Matching of Key Terms
4. Critical Thinking
5. Demonstration—Steps in process costing
6. Case—*Nature's Sweet*; Preparing a production cost report

**Go to our dynamic Web site for more self-assessment, Web links, and additional information.**

# QUESTIONS

1. What are the two primary accounting systems used to record production costs?
2. Explain the concept of an "equivalent unit."
3. What is meant by the term *conversion costs*?
4. What is meant by the term *transferred-in cost*?
5. Why are units often in a different stage of completion with respect to raw materials and conversion costs?
6. What items are in the numerator and what items are in the denominator in the calculation of cost per equivalent unit?
7. What items of production cost make up the "costs to account for" in a production cost report?
8. What is accomplished by preparing a reconciliation of the physical units as a part of the production cost report?
9. Do transferred-in costs occur in all departments of a manufacturer using a process costing system? Explain.
10. What are the four steps involved in the preparation of a production cost report?

# EXERCISES

**EXERCISE 3-1. Group Assignment/Ethics** ArcTech is a manufacturer of semiconductors (referred to as chips). Their production process is complex and involves more than 100 steps starting with production of small, round silicon wafers, and ending with chips being put into individual packages that protect them and provide connections to the products for which the chips are developed. The company uses a process costing system and has always made the simplifying assumption that wafers in production, but not yet finished, are 50 percent complete with respect to conversion costs.

In the current year, the company has struggled due to a decline in computer sales and reduced demand for chips. To boost profit, the company has decided to start a very large number of wafers into production in the last few days of the year. Due to the use of ceramic carriers and other high-performance features, ArcTech's production process typically takes 30 days.

*Required*
Explain why starting a large number of wafers into production will boost profit even though the chips that ultimately result from the wafers are ones that have not been sold or even completed. Is the company's approach to boosting profit ethical?

**EXERCISE 3-2. Writing Assignment** Write a paragraph explaining the calculation of the cost per equivalent unit (i.e., explain what goes in the numerator and what goes in the denominator of the calculation). Be sure to explain why the denominator may be different for the cost per equivalent unit of material and the cost per equivalent unit of labor and overhead.

 **EXERCISE 3-3. Internet Assignment** Go to the Web site for Redhook Brewery (www.redhook.com), click on *breweries* and then *virtual tour* to view their production process.

*Required*

a. How many steps are there in the production process?

b. What characteristics of the production process suggest that Redhook uses process, as opposed to job-order, costing?

c. At what points are materials added to the production process?

d. Would you describe Redhook's production process as labor intensive or capital intensive?

 **EXERCISE 3-4. Unit Reconciliation** During July, Classic Car Wax Company completed 40,000 cans of wax. At the beginning of July, the company had 1,000 units that were 90 percent complete with respect to material and 45 percent complete with respect to conversion costs. During the month, the company started production of 43,000 units.

*Required*
How many units were in Work in Process at the end of July?

**EXERCISE 3-5. Unit Reconciliation** During August, Wilson Lubricant completed 40,000 gallons of product. At the start of August there were 10,000 gallons in Work in Process, and at the end of August, there were 12,000 gallons in Work in Process.

*Required*
How many gallons of product were started during the month of August?

**EXERCISE 3-6. Cost per Equivalent Unit** The balance in beginning Work in Process at Franz Silicon Compound Co. for direct labor was $120,000. During the month of May, an additional $500,000 of direct labor was incurred, and 10,000 pounds of compound were produced. At the end of May, 2,000 pounds of compound were in process and the units were 50 percent complete. At the start of May, the company had 5,000 pounds of compound that were 30 percent complete.

*Required*
Calculate the cost per equivalent unit for labor assuming that labor is added uniformly throughout the production process.

 **EXERCISE 3-7. Cost Reconciliation** During December, Western Solvent completed 30,000 units and at the end of December, there were 10,000 units in ending Work in Process that were 20 percent complete with respect to labor and overhead and 100 percent complete with respect to material.

During the month of December, the company incurred $140,000 of material cost, $60,000 of labor cost, and $87,000 of manufacturing overhead. Costs per equivalent unit for material, labor, and manufacturing overhead equal $5, $2, and $3 respectively.

*Required*
Calculate the amount of material cost, labor cost, and overhead cost in beginning Work in Process inventory.

**EXERCISE 3-8. Calculation of Equivalent Units** Sarsawa Tire Company produces tires used on small trailers. The month of April ended with 500 tires in-process, 80 percent complete as to direct materials and 50 percent complete as to conversion costs; 2,700 tires were transferred to finished goods during the month and 2,500 were started during the month. The beginning Work in Process Inventory was 60 percent complete as to direct materials and 40 percent complete as to conversion costs.

***Required***

Determine the denominators to be used in the calculations of cost per equivalent unit for materials and conversion costs.

**EXERCISE 3-9. Reconciliation of Units and Costs** At the start of July, Classic Car Wax Company had beginning Work in Process of 1,000 units that were 90 percent complete with respect to material and 45 percent complete with respect to conversion costs. The cost of the units was $7,200 ($5,400 of material and $1,800 of conversion costs). During the month, the company started production of 43,000 units and incurred $243,480 of material cost and $91,120 of labor and overhead. Cost per equivalent unit were $6.10 for material and $2.30 for labor and overhead (conversion costs). The cost of items completed was $336,000 ($244,000 for materials and $92,000 for labor and overhead). Units in ending Work in Process are 20 percent complete with respect to material and 10 percent complete with respect to conversion costs.

***Required***

a. Prepare a reconciliation of units.

b. What is the cost of ending Work in Process?

**EXERCISE 3-10. Costing Units Completed and Ending Work in Process** For the month of September, Wilber Pickle Company had cost per equivalent unit of $0.50 for materials (pickles, vinegar, spices, etc.) and $.90 for conversion costs (labor and overhead). At Wilber Pickle Company units are measured in quarts. The company began the month with 500 quarts of pickles. By the end of the month, the company had completed 4,000 quarts, and 800 quarts were in process. The in process units were 100 percent complete with respect to material and 80 percent complete with respect to labor and overhead.

***Required***

Determine the cost of the ending Work in Process Inventory and the cost of items completed and transferred to Finished Goods Inventory.

**EXERCISE 3-11. Costing Units Completed and Ending Work In Process** Howell Super Server produces a single model, the HM24, in a continuous production process. Eighty percent of materials are added at the beginning of production and the other 20 percent are added immediately before transfer to the finished goods warehouse. Conversion costs are assumed to be added evenly throughout the process. At the end of October 2006, there were four servers in process, 60 percent complete as to labor and overhead. Eighty-five servers were completed during the month. Assume that direct materials cost per equivalent unit during October was $2,500, labor cost per equivalent unit was $1,000, and overhead per equivalent unit was $2,000.

***Required***

Determine the cost of the ending Work in Process Inventory and the cost of items completed and transferred to Finished Goods Inventory.

**EXERCISE 3-12. Costing Units Completed and Ending Work in Process** At the start of October, Helbert Pure Extract had Work in Process Inventory consisting of 2,000 units that were 90 percent complete with respect to materials and 50 percent complete with respect to conversion costs. The cost of the units was $27,000 ($18,000 of material cost and $9,000 of labor and overhead). During October, the company started 40,000 units and incurred $404,180 of material cost and $371,880 of labor and overhead. The company completed 41,000 units during the month and 1,000 units were in process at the end of October. The units in ending Work in Process were 80 percent complete with respect to materials and 40 percent complete with respect to conversion costs.

### Required

a. Calculate the cost per equivalent unit for materials and conversion costs.

b. Calculate the cost of items completed during October.

c. Calculate the cost of ending Work in Process.

# PROBLEMS

**PROBLEM 3-1. Comprehensive Problem, One Department**   Regal Polish manufactures a single product in one department and uses a process costing system. At the start of May, there were 5,000 units in process that were 100 percent complete with respect to direct material and 50 percent complete with respect to conversion costs (labor and overhead). During the month, the company began production of 100,000 units and ending Work in Process Inventory consisted of 2,000 units that were 100 percent complete with respect to material and 80 percent complete with respect to conversion costs.

| Cost Information: | Beginning Work in Process | Costs Added in May |
|---|---|---|
| Direct material | $3,000 | $65,250 |
| Direct labor | 125 | 6,151 |
| Manufacturing overhead | 175 | 7,147 |
| | $3,300 | $78,548 |

### Required

a. Calculate the cost per equivalent unit for each of the three cost items and in total.

b. Calculate the cost of items completed in May and the cost of ending Work in Process.

c. Reconcile the sum of the two costs in part b to the sum of beginning Work in Process and costs added in May.

**PROBLEM 3-2. Comprehensive Problem, One Department**   Marquita Filters produces an air filter for use in jet aircraft. Parts are added at several points in their production process. In August, production began with 600 filters in Work in Process, 80 percent complete as to materials and 70 percent complete as to labor and overhead. During the month, an additional 3,200 units were started into production. Eight hundred filters were in Work in Process at the end of the month, and they were 60 percent complete as to materials and 50 percent complete as to labor and overhead.

   Cost information for August:

| | Beginning Work in Process Inventory | Cost Added in August |
|---|---|---|
| Direct material | $ 48,000 | $ 317,400 |
| Direct labor | 12,600 | 94,500 |
| Manufacturing overhead | 84,000 | 590,900 |
| Total | $144,600 | $1,002,800 |

### Required

a. Calculate the cost per equivalent unit for each of the three cost items and in total.

b. Calculate the cost of items completed in August and the cost of ending Work in Process Inventory.

c. Reconcile the sum of the two costs in part b to the sum of beginning Work in Process and the cost added in August.

**PROBLEM 3-3. Production Cost Report**   Olympic Laminators, Inc. is a specialized producer of laminated wood flooring. Their production process involves highly skilled workers and top quality hardwood veneers. Work in Process is relatively large because each 8′ × 10′ sheet of flooring is in process for up to three weeks because of drying time related to adhesives and multiple layers of material.

September began with 3,000 units (a unit is an 8′ × 10′ sheet) in process, on average 60 percent complete as to direct materials and 30 percent complete as to conversion costs; 4,000 units were started during the month and ending Work in Process Inventory consisted of 5,000 units that were on average 50 percent complete as to direct materials and 20 percent complete as to conversion costs.

| Cost Information: | Beginning Work in Process | Costs Added in September |
|---|---|---|
| Direct material | $144,000 | $216,000 |
| Direct labor | 120,000 | 531,000 |
| Manufacturing overhead | 20,000 | 52,000 |

*Required*

a. Prepare a production cost report for the month of September.

b. Prepare the journal entry to recognize the transfer of the units completed and transferred to finished goods during September.

**PROBLEM 3-4. Production Cost Report**   Aussie Yarn Co. is a U.S. producer of woolen yarn made from wool imported from Australia. Raw wool is processed, spun, and finished before being shipped out to knitting and weaving companies. Material is added in the beginning of processing and conversion costs are added evenly throughout processing.

Aussie began the month of August with 5,000 units in process that were 100 percent complete as to materials and 60 percent complete as to labor and overhead. They started 25,000 units into production during the month of which 4,000 remained in ending Work in Process Inventory and were 40 percent complete as to conversion costs. The cost data are as follows:

| | |
|---|---|
| Beginning Work in Process: | |
| Direct materials | $4,000 |
| Direct labor | 1,050 |
| Manufacturing overhead | 1,450 |
| Costs added during August: | |
| Direct materials | $22,280 |
| Direct labor | 9,990 |
| Manufacturing overhead | 11,522 |

*Required*
Prepare a production cost report for the month of August.

**PROBLEM 3-5. Journal Entries in Process Costing**   Lakeland Solvent produces a single product in two departments. The following costs relate to April:

| | Department 1 | Department 2 |
|---|---|---|
| WIP, March 31 | $ 26,000 | $ 46,000 |
| Costs added during April | | |
| Direct material | 80,000 | 20,000 |
| Direct labor | 45,000 | 55,000 |
| Manufacturing overhead | 230,000 | 110,000 |
| Transferred-in costs | N/A | ? |
| WIP, April 30 | –0– | 36,000 |

*Required*

Prepare journal entries to record:

a. The issuance of direct material.

b. The cost of direct labor (credit wages payable).

c. The application of manufacturing overhead.

d. The transfer of cost associated with units completed in both departments.

**PROBLEM 3-6. Journal Entries in Process Costing** Wilmont Box Company produces a single box used by AirSpeed, an express shipping company. Wilmont uses a just-in-time system and has almost no inventories of material, work in process, or finished goods. Indeed, the balances are so small that the company treats them as zero for purposes of its accounting reports.

During July, the company produced and shipped 100,000 boxes at a cost of $0.80 per box. The cost consisted of 50 percent material cost, 10 percent labor cost, and 40 percent manufacturing overhead.

*Required*

Prepare journal entries to record:

a. The issuance of direct material.

b. The cost of direct labor (credit wages payable).

c. The application of manufacturing overhead.

d. The completion of units in process and their transfer to finished goods.

e. Cost of goods sold.

**PROBLEM 3-7. Production Cost Report, Missing Data** Classic 50s Flooring produces linoleum flooring. Below is a partial production cost report for the Mixing Department. In the report, a unit is a gallon of linoleum cement (a mixture of linseed oil, pine resin, and wood flour).

**Production Cost Report**
**Mixing Department**
**June**

**Quantity Reconciliation**

| | |
|---|---:|
| Units in beginning WIP | 200 |
| Units started | 1,800 |
| Units to account for | 2,000 |
| Units completed | 1,700 |
| Units in ending WIP (100% material, 60% conversion costs) | (a) |
| Units accounted for | (b) |

**Cost Per Equivalent Unit Calculation**

| | Material | Labor | Overhead | Total |
|---|---:|---:|---:|---:|
| **Cost** | | | | |
| Beginning WIP | $ 450 | $ 1,152 | $ 2,304 | $ 3,906 |
| Cost incurred during February | 4,050 | 9,000 | 18,000 | 31,050 |
| Total | $4,500 | $10,152 | $20,304 | $34,956 |
| **Units** | | | | |
| Units completed | 1,700 | 1,700 | 1,700 | |
| Equivalent units, ending WIP | (c) | (d) | (e) | |
| Total | (f) | (g) | (h) | |
| Cost per equivalent unit | (i) | (j) | (k) | (l) |

*Required*
Fill in the missing data (items *a* through *l*).

**PROBLEM 3-8. Production Cost Report, Missing Information**   Marion Chemicals produces a chemical used as a base in paints. In the manufacturing process, all materials are added at the start of the process, whereas labor and overhead are added evenly throughout production.

*Required*
Fill in the missing information in Marion's Production Cost Report for the month of December.

**Marion Chemicals**
**Production Cost Report**
**December 2006**

**Unit Reconciliation**

| | |
|---|---|
| Units in beginning WIP (100% material, 20% conversion costs) | 20,000 |
| Units started during December | ? |
| Units to account for | ? |
| Units completed | ? |
| Units in ending WIP (100% material, 10% conversion costs) | 10,000 |
| Units accounted for | ? |

**Cost Per Equivalent Unit Calculation**

| | Material | Labor | Overhead | Total |
|---|---|---|---|---|
| **Cost** | | | | |
| Beginning WIP | $33,334.00 | $5,236.40 | $10,472.80 | $49,043.20 |
| Cost incurred in December | ? | ? | ? | ? |
| Total | ? | ? | ? | ? |
| **Units** | | | | |
| Units completed | ? | ? | ? | |
| Equivalent units, ending WIP | ? | ? | ? | |
| Total | ? | ? | ? | |
| Cost per equivalent unit | $1.6667 | $1.3091 | $2.6182 | ? |

**Cost Reconciliation**

| | | |
|---|---|---|
| Total cost to account for | | $2,817,594.30 |
| Cost of completed items | | $2,797,000.00 |
| Cost of ending WIP | | |
| Material | $? | |
| Labor | ? | |
| Overhead | ? | ? |
| Total cost accounted for | | $2,817,594.30 |

**PROBLEM 3-9. Comprehensive Problem, Two Departments**   Oral Care Toothpaste is manufactured in two departments: Mixing and Packing. Once the toothpaste mixture is completed in the Mixing Department it is sent to Packaging where a tube filling machine fills and seals individual tubes which are then passed to a machine that places tubes in individual boxes.

The following information is related to production in April:

| Unit Information | Mixing | Packing |
|---|---|---|
| Beginning Work in Process | | |
| (Mixing: 100% material, 80 % conversion costs) | 10,000 | |
| (Packing: 50% material, 40% conversion costs) | | 10,500 |
| Started during March | 600,000 | 590,000 |
| Ending Work in Process | | |
| (Mixing: 100% material, 70 % conversion costs) | 20,000 | |
| (Packing: 90% material, 80% conversion costs) | | 30,000 |
| **Cost Information, Beginning Work in Process** | | |
| Direct material | $4,000.00 | $630.00 |
| Direct labor | 800.00 | 42.00 |
| Manufacturing overhead | 1,680.00 | 84.00 |
| Transferred-in cost | – | 7,455.00 |
| **Cost Added During April** | | |
| Direct material | 246,100.00 | 77,045.00 |
| Direct labor | 65,640.00 | 5,903.00 |
| Manufacturing overhead | 119,120.00 | 11,890.00 |
| Transferred-in cost | – | 424,800.00 |

*Required*
Prepare production costs reports for Mixing and Packing for the month of April.

**PROBLEM 3-10. Comprehensive Problem, Two Departments** Carnival Caramel Company makes a high-quality caramel candy. The manufacturing process involves mixing ingredients (Mixing Department) and shaping the processed mixture into one-pound balls (Shaping Department), which are sold to retail outlets. No additional material is added in the shaping process. The following information is related to production in March:

| Unit Information | Mixing | Shaping |
|---|---|---|
| Beginning Work in Process | | |
| (Mixing: 100% material, 80% conversion costs) | 2,000 | |
| (Shaping: 70% conversion costs) | | 3,000 |
| Started during March | 40,000 | ? |
| Ending Work in Process | | |
| (Mixing: 100% material, 60% conversion costs) | 1,000 | |
| (Shaping: 50% conversion costs) | | 500 |
| **Cost Information, Beginning Work in Process** | | |
| Direct material | $ 2,000.00 | – |
| Direct labor | 800.00 | $ 450.00 |
| Manufacturing overhead | 960.00 | 290.00 |
| Transferred-in cost | – | 6,360.00 |
| **Cost Added During March** | | |
| Direct material | $40,840.00 | – |
| Direct labor | 20,832.00 | $11,800.00 |
| Manufacturing overhead | 23,168.00 | 8,022.50 |
| Transferred-in cost | – | ? |

*Required*
Prepare production cost reports for Mixing and Shaping for the month of March. In your calculations, round to four decimal places.

# CASES

## Case 3-1  TECH-TONIC SPORTS DRINK

The Western Beverage Company is marketing a new product, Tech-Tonic Sports Drink Syrup. The product sells for $15 per gallon, and in recent months the company has had sales of more than 500,000 gallons per month. Consumers mix 1 part syrup with 5 parts water to make a drink that *"replenishes vital bodily fluids following exertion."*

At the start of April, there were 150,000 gallons in beginning Work in Process. The product was 100 percent complete with respect to material and 50 percent complete with respect to conversion costs. During April, 600,000 gallons were started. Of the 750,000 units to account for, 150,000 gallons remained in process at the end of April. These units were 100 percent complete with respect to material and 20 percent complete with respect to conversion costs; 300,000 gallons were completed during April and, unfortunately, 300,000 gallons were lost owing to worker error. The production process calls for sodium to be added at the start of the process. On two separate occasions, a new worker added too much sodium

and batches were ruined. The errors were not identified until the end of the production process when batches were tested for quality assurance. Needless to say, the worker was fired.

The controller of Western Beverage, Gunther Bergman, is considering two ways to treat the cost of the "lost" units. One approach, is to "bury" the cost in the units completed and the units in process. This would result in cost of units completed of $1,528,182 and cost of ending Work in Process of $292,818 calculated as follows.

### Approach No. 1

**Tech-Tonic Sports Drink Syrup**
**Production Cost Report**
**April 2006**

**Quantity Reconciliation**

| | |
|---|---:|
| Units in beginning WIP (100% material, 50% conversion costs) | 150,000 |
| Units started | 600,000 |
| Units to account for | 750,000 |
| Units completed | 300,000 |
| Units in ending WIP (100% material, 20% conversion costs) | 150,000 |
| Lost units | 300,000 |
| Units accounted for | 750,000 |

**Cost Per Equivalent Unit Calculation**

| | Material | Labor | Overhead | Total |
|---|---:|---:|---:|---:|
| **Cost** | | | | |
| Beginning WIP | $105,000 | $ 45,000 | $ 90,000 | $ 240,000 |
| Cost incurred during April | 420,000 | 387,000 | 774,000 | 1,581,000 |
| Total | $525,000 | $432,000 | $864,000 | $1,821,000 |
| **Units** | | | | |
| Units completed | 300,000 | 300,000 | 300,000 | |
| Equivalent units, ending WIP | 150,000 | 30,000 | 30,000 | |
| Total | 450,000 | 330,000 | 330,000 | |
| Cost per equivalent unit | $1.17 | $1.31 | $2.62 | $5.10 |

**Cost Reconciliation**

| | | | |
|---|---|---:|---:|
| Total cost to account for | | | $1,821,000 |
| Cost of completed units transferred to Finished Goods (300,000 × $5.10) | | | $1,530,000 |
| Cost of ending WIP | | | |
| Material (150,000 equivalent units × $1.17) | | $175,500 | |
| Labor (30,000 equivalent units × $1.31) | | 39,300 | |
| Overhead (30,000 equivalent units × $2.62) | | 78,600 | 293,400 |
| | | | $1,823,400 |
| Difference due to rounding | | | (2,400) |
| Total cost accounted for | | | $1,821,000 |

A second approach involves identifying the lost units in the cost per equivalent unit calculation and assigning part of production cost to them. This cost would then be charged to Cost of Goods sold expense for April. The result is a cost of units completed equal to $827,143, cost of Work in Process equal to $166,714, and cost of lost units equal to $827,143 (which will be charged to Cost of Goods Sold).

*Approach No. 2*

**Tech-Tonic Sports Drink Syrup**
**Production Cost Report**
**April 2006**

**Quantity Reconciliation**

| | |
|---|---:|
| Units in beginning WIP (100% material, 50% conversion costs) | 150,000 |
| Units started | 600,000 |
| Units to account for | 750,000 |
| Units completed | 300,000 |
| Units in ending WIP (100% material, 20% conversion costs) | 150,000 |
| Lost units | 300,000 |
| Units accounted for | 750,000 |

**Cost Per Equivalent Unit Calculation**

| | Material | Labor | Overhead | Total |
|---|---:|---:|---:|---:|
| **Cost** | | | | |
| Beginning WIP | $105,000 | $ 45,000 | $ 90,000 | $ 240,000 |
| Cost incurred during April | 420,000 | 387,000 | 774,000 | 1,581,000 |
| Total | $525,000 | $432,000 | $864,000 | $1,821,000 |

**Cost Per Equivalent Unit Calculation**

| | Material | Labor | Overhead | Total |
|---|---:|---:|---:|---:|
| **Units** | | | | |
| Units completed | 300,000 | 300,000 | 300,000 | |
| Equivalent units, ending WIP | 150,000 | 30,000 | 30,000 | |
| Lost units | 300,000 | 300,000 | 300,000 | |
| Total | 750,000 | 630,000 | 630,000 | |
| Cost per equivalent unit | $0.70 | $0.69 | $1.37 | $2.76 |

**Cost Reconciliation**

| | | |
|---|---:|---:|
| Total cost to account for | | $1,821,000 |
| Cost of completed units transferred to Finished Goods (300,000 × $2.76) | | $828,000 |
| Cost of lost units (300,000 × $2.76) | | 828,000 |
| Cost of ending WIP | | |
| Material (150,000 equivalent units × $0.70) | $105,000 | |
| Labor (30,000 equivalent units × $0.69) | 20,700 | |
| Overhead (30,000 equivalent units × $1.37) | 41,100 | 166,800 |
| | | $1,822,800 |
| Difference due to rounding | | ⟨1,800⟩ |
| Total cost accounted for | | $1,821,000 |

## Required:

a. Assume that 80 percent of the units completed in April are sold in that month. What will be the difference in reported profit between the two approaches?

b. Which approach is most appropriate from a conceptual standpoint?

c. Senior managers at Western Beverage receive monthly bonuses determined as a percent of profit in excess of a targeted level of profit. Which method will they favor?

# Case 3-2  JENSEN PVC, INC.

Jensen PVC, Inc., produces poly vinyl chloride (PVC) irrigation pipes. In 2005, the cost of producing a foot of pipe was $0.25 and the selling price was $0.32 per foot. In 2006, production costs increased to $0.33 per foot although the selling price remained at $0.32.

|  | 2005 | 2006 |
|---|---|---|
| Selling price | $0.32 | $0.32 |
| Production cost | 0.25 | 0.33 |

The increase in cost was obvious. Material and labor had remained fairly constant per foot of pipe, but overhead costs, which were $0.12 per foot in 2005, had increased to $0.20 in 2006. The problem was that most overhead costs were fixed but output had decreased due to weak crop prices and a corresponding decrease in spending on irrigation projects.

Bob Elger, CFO of Jensen, reviewed the data generated by the company's process costing system. In 2005, overhead costs in all of the company's departments (mixing, extrusion, cutting, and packing) were $1,200,000 and pipe production was 10,000,000 feet. In 2006, overhead costs were still approximately $1,200,000, but pipe production decreased to 6,000,000 feet. At a recent meeting of the senior management team, Bob noted that "The problem is that we're not making use of capacity. We could easily produce 15,000,000 feet of pipe given our state of the art equipment, but we're operating at less than 50% of capacity."

## Required

Bob estimates that to sell 15,000,000 feet of pipe in the current market, the company would have to lower its price to $0.28 per foot, which is even lower than its current cost per foot of $0.33. Would decreasing the price be a good decision?

# chapter 4

## LEARNING OBJECTIVES

1. Identify common cost behavior patterns.

2. Estimate the relation between cost and activity using account analysis and the high-low method.

3. Perform cost-volume-profit analysis for single products.

4. Perform cost-volume-profit analysis for multiple products.

5. Discuss the effect of operating leverage.

6. Use the contribution margin per unit of the constraint to analyze situations involving a resource constraint.

# COST-VOLUME-PROFIT ANALYSIS

M ary Stuart is the vice president of operations for CodeConnect, a company that manufactures and sells bar code readers. As a senior manager, she must answer a variety of questions dealing with planning, control, and decision making. Consider the following questions that Mary has faced:

**Planning:** Last year, CodeConnect sold 20,000 bar code readers at $200 per unit. The cost of manufacturing these items was $2,940,000, and selling and administrative costs were $800,000. Total profit was $260,000. In the coming year, the company expects to sell 25,000 units. What level of profit should be in the budget for the coming year?

**Control:** In April, production costs were $250,000. In May, costs increased to $265,000, but production also increased from 1,750 units in April to 2,000 units in May. Did the manager responsible for production costs do a good job of controlling costs in May?

**Decision making:** The current price for a bar code reader is $200 per unit. If the price is increased to $225 per unit, sales will drop from 20,000 to 17,000. Should the price be increased?

The answer to each of these questions depends on how costs and, therefore, profit change when volume changes. The analysis of how costs and profit change when volume changes is referred to as **cost-volume-profit (C-V-P) analysis**. In this chapter, we develop the tools to analyze cost-volume-profit relations. These tools will enable you to answer questions like the ones listed above—questions managers face on a daily basis.

Identify common cost behavior patterns.

# COMMON COST BEHAVIOR PATTERNS

To perform cost-volume-profit (C-V-P) analysis, you need to know how costs behave when business activity (e.g., production volume and sales volume) changes. This section describes some common patterns of cost behavior. These patterns may not provide exact descriptions of how costs behave in response to changes in volume or activity, but they are generally reasonable approximations involving variable costs, fixed costs, mixed costs, and step costs.

## VARIABLE COSTS

As mentioned in Chapter 1, **variable costs** are costs that change in response to changes in volume or activity. Some common variable costs are direct and indirect materials, direct labor, energy, and sales commissions. Managers typically assume that variable costs change *in proportion* to changes in activity. Thus, if activity increases by 10 percent, variable costs are assumed to increase by 10 percent. Exactly how activity should be measured in analyzing a variable cost depends on the situation. At McDonald's restaurants, food costs vary with the number of customers served. At United Airlines, fuel costs vary with the number of miles flown. In these situations, number of customers and number of miles are good measures of activity.

Let's consider an example using CodeConnect, the company introduced in the beginning of the chapter. Suppose that CodeConnect has variable production costs equal to $91 per bar code reader. In this case, total variable cost at a production level of 1,000 units (the measure of activity) is equal to $91,000 ($91 × 1,000), while total variable cost at 2,000 units is equal to $182,000 ($91 × 2,000). A graph of the relation between total variable cost and production is provided in Illustration 4-1. The slope of the straight line in the figure measures the change in cost per unit change in activity. Note that while total variable cost increases with production, variable cost per unit remains at $91.

## FIXED COSTS

**See the video on the interactive CD for a discussion of the fixed and variable costs of a cruise at Holland America, Westours.**

Recall from Chapter 1 that **fixed costs** are costs that do not change in response to changes in activity levels. Some typical fixed costs are depreciation, supervisory salaries, and building maintenance. Suppose that CodeConnect has $94,000 of fixed costs per month. A graph of the relation between the company's fixed cost and production is provided in Illustration 4-2. As you can see, whatever the number of units produced, the amount of total fixed cost remains at $94,000. However, the amount of fixed cost per unit does change with changes in the level of activity. When activity increases, the amount of fixed cost per unit decreases because the fixed cost is spread over more units. For example, at 1,000 units, the fixed cost per unit is $94 ($94,000 ÷ 1,000), whereas at 2,000 units, the fixed cost per unit is only $47 ($94,000 ÷ 2,000).

**Illustration 4-1**
Variable cost behavior
at CodeConnect

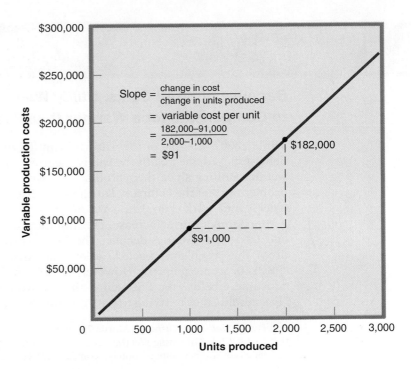

**Discretionary versus Committed Fixed Costs.** In the short run, some fixed costs can be changed while others cannot. **Discretionary fixed costs** are those fixed costs that management can easily change in the short run. Examples include advertising, research and development, and repair and maintenance costs. Some companies cut back on these expenditures when sales drop so that profit trends stay roughly constant. That, however, may be shortsighted since a cut in research and

**Illustration 4-2**
Fixed cost behavior
at CodeConnect

development can have a negative effect on long-run profitability, and a cut in repair and maintenance can have a negative effect on the life of valuable equipment. **Committed fixed costs**, on the other hand, are those fixed costs that cannot be easily changed in a relatively brief period of time. Such costs include rent, depreciation of buildings and equipment, and insurance related to buildings and equipment.

## MIXED COSTS

**Mixed costs** are costs that contain both a variable cost element and a fixed cost element. These costs are sometimes referred to as **semivariable costs**. For example, a salesperson may be paid $80,000 per year (fixed amount) plus commissions equal to 1 percent of sales (variable amount). In this case, the salesperson's total compensation is a mixed cost. Total production cost is also a mixed cost since it is composed of material, labor, and both fixed and variable overhead cost items.

Suppose the total production cost of CodeConnect is composed of $94,000 of fixed cost per month and $91 of variable cost per unit. In this case, total production cost is a mixed cost. A graph of the cost is presented in Illustration 4-3. Note that the total cost line intersects the vertical axis at $94,000 (just below the $100,000 point). This is the amount of fixed cost per month. From this point, total cost increases by $91 for every unit produced. Thus, at 3,000 units, the total cost is $367,000, composed of $94,000 of fixed cost and $273,000 of variable cost ($91 × 3,000).

## STEP COSTS

**Step costs** are those costs that are fixed for a range of volume but increase to a higher level when the upper bound of the range is exceeded. At that point the costs again remain fixed until another upper bound is exceeded. As an example, suppose

**Illustration 4-3**
Mixed cost behavior

**Illustration 4-4**
Step cost behavior

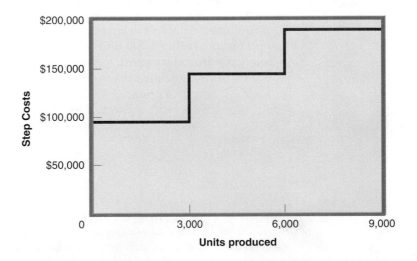

that CodeConnect can produce up to 3,000 bar code readers with fixed costs of $94,000. However, to produce 3,001 to 6,000 bar code readers the company must add a second shift. Fixed costs related to supervisory salaries, heat, light, and other fixed costs are expected to increase to $144,000. To produce more than 6,000 bar code readers the company must add a third shift and fixed costs are expected to increase to $194,000. A graph of these step costs are presented in Illustration 4-4.

## Any Questions?

**Q** Is labor always a variable cost?

**A** While we typically think of labor as a variable cost, it could also be a fixed cost or a step cost. In some countries like Japan and Korea, companies are very reluctant to lay off workers when business decreases and they are hesitant to increase labor when demand increases. Thus, for many companies in Japan and Korea labor is a fixed cost. In the United States, companies are more willing to hire and fire with fluctuations in demand, making labor more reasonably approximated as a variable cost. But some U.S. companies are so highly automated that they can accommodate wide fluctuations in volume with the same work force, and for them, labor is more reasonably approximated as a fixed cost. To determine whether labor is variable or fixed for a particular company, you must analyze the unique situation facing the company. Also, keep in mind the notion of a relevant range. Within a particular range of activity, labor may be fixed but it may jump to a higher level if the company exceeds the upper limit of the range.

**LEARNING OBJECTIVE 2**

Estimate the relation between cost and activity using account analysis and the high-low method.

# COST ESTIMATION METHODS

In order to predict how much cost will be incurred at various activity levels (a critical part of C-V-P analysis), you must know how much of the total cost is fixed and how much is variable. In many cases, cost information is not broken out in terms of fixed and variable cost components; therefore, you must know how to estimate fixed and variable costs from available information. In this section, we cover three techniques for estimating the amount of fixed and variable cost: account analysis, the high-low method, and regression analysis.

## ACCOUNT ANALYSIS

**Account analysis** is the most common approach to estimating fixed and variable costs. This method requires that the manager use professional judgment to classify costs as either fixed or variable. The total of the costs classified as variable can then be divided by a measure of activity to calculate the variable cost per unit of activity. The total of the costs classified as fixed provides the estimate of fixed cost.

To illustrate, let's return to the CodeConnect example. For the month of May, the cost of producing 2,000 units of the DX375 bar code reader was $265,000. Account analysis would require a detailed analysis of the accounts that comprise the $265,000 of production costs. Suppose the costs were as follows:

| May | |
|---|---:|
| Production in units | 2,000 |
| Production cost | |
|   Component cost | $130,600 |
|   Assembly labor | 32,400 |
|   Utilities | 7,100 |
|   Rent | 22,000 |
|   Depreciation of assembly equipment | 72,900 |
|     Total production cost | $265,000 |

**Illustration 4-5**
Estimate of variable
and fixed costs

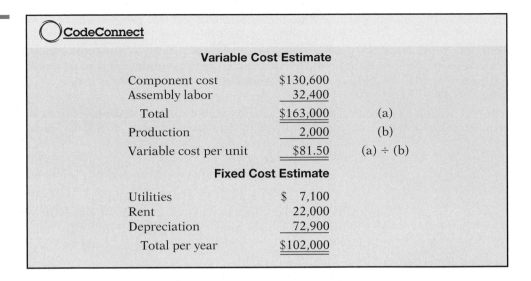

CodeConnect

**Variable Cost Estimate**

| | | |
|---|---:|---|
| Component cost | $130,600 | |
| Assembly labor | 32,400 | |
| Total | $163,000 | (a) |
| Production | 2,000 | (b) |
| Variable cost per unit | $81.50 | (a) ÷ (b) |

**Fixed Cost Estimate**

| | | |
|---|---:|---|
| Utilities | $ 7,100 | |
| Rent | 22,000 | |
| Depreciation | 72,900 | |
| Total per year | $102,000 | |

Using professional judgment, you may decide that component cost and assembly labor are variable costs and all other items are fixed costs. In this case, variable and fixed costs are estimated as in Illustration 4-5. Total production costs would be estimated as $102,000 of fixed cost per month plus $81.50 of variable cost for each unit produced.

Although Illustration 4-5 classifies each individual cost item as either 100 percent fixed or 100 percent variable, the account analysis method does not require that this be so. For example, there may be reason to believe that at least part of utilities are also variable. In this case, the manager can use his or her judgment to refine estimates using account analysis. Suppose the manager believes that approximately 50 percent of utilities are variable. As indicated in Illustration 4-6, the revised estimate of total variable cost would then amount to $166,550, or $83.28 per unit, whereas the revised estimate of fixed costs per month would amount to $98,450.

**Illustration 4-6**
Revisited estimate
of variable and
fixed costs

CodeConnect

**Variable Cost Estimate**

| | | |
|---|---:|---|
| Component cost | $130,600 | |
| Assembly labor | 32,400 | |
| Utilities (50% of $7,100) | 3,550 | |
| Total | $166,550 | (a) |
| Production | 2,000 | (b) |
| Variable cost per unit | $83.28 | (a) ÷ (b) |

**Fixed Cost Estimate**

| | | |
|---|---:|---|
| Utilities (50% of $7,100) | $ 3,550 | |
| Rent | 22,000 | |
| Depreciation | 72,900 | |
| Total per month | $98,450 | |

With these estimates we can project what costs will be at various levels of production. For example, how much cost can CodeConnect expect to incur if 2,500 units are produced? With 2,500 units, variable costs are estimated as $208,200 and fixed costs per month are estimated as $98,450. Therefore, total cost of $306,650 would be expected, as shown:

| Expected Monthly Cost of 2,500 Units; DX375 Bar Code Reader | |
|---|---|
| Variable cost (2,500 × $83.28) | $208,200 |
| Fixed cost per month | 98,450 |
| Total | $306,650 |

The account analysis method is subjective in that different managers viewing the same set of facts may reach different conclusions regarding which costs are fixed and which costs are variable. Despite this limitation, most managers consider it an important tool for estimating fixed and variable costs.

## SCATTERGRAPHS

In some cases, you may have cost information from several reporting periods available in order to estimate how costs change in response to changes in activity. Weekly, monthly, or quarterly reports are particularly useful sources of cost information. In contrast, annual reports are not as useful because the relation between costs and activity is generally not consistent or stable over several years.

Suppose the monthly production and cost information provided in Illustration 4-7 is available for CodeConnect. We can gain insight into the relation between production cost and activity by plotting these costs and activity levels. The plot of the data is referred to as a **scattergraph**. The scattergraph for the data in Illustration 4-7 is presented in Illustration 4-8.

Typically, as in Illustration 4-8, scattergraphs are prepared with costs measured on the vertical axis and activity level measured on the horizontal axis. Each point on the scattergraph represents one pair of cost and activity values. The

**Illustration 4-7**
Monthly production
cost information

⊘CodeConnect

| Month | Production | Cost |
|---|---|---|
| January | 750 | $  170,000 |
| February | 1,000 | 175,000 |
| March | 1,250 | 205,000 |
| April | 1,750 | 250,000 |
| May | 2,000 | 265,000 |
| June | 2,250 | 275,000 |
| July | 3,000 | 400,000 |
| August | 2,750 | 350,000 |
| September | 2,500 | 300,000 |
| October | 1,250 | 210,000 |
| November | 1,000 | 190,000 |
| December | 500 | 150,000 |
| Total | 20,000 | $2,940,000 |

**Illustration 4-8**
Scattergraph of cost and
production information

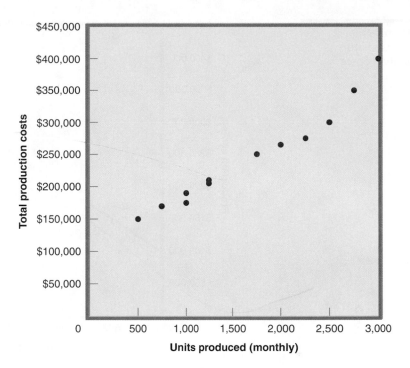

graphical features in spreadsheet programs such as Excel® make the preparation of a scattergraph very easy. Essentially, all you need to do is input the data, and then you can rely on the spreadsheet to accurately plot it.

The methods we use to estimate cost behavior assume that costs are linear. In other words, they assume that costs are well represented by straight lines. A scattergraph is useful in assessing whether this assumption is reasonable. The plot in Illustration 4-8 suggests that a linear approximation is quite reasonable since the data points line up in an approximately linear fashion. The scattergraph is also useful in assessing whether there are any outliers. Outliers are data points that are markedly at odds with the trend of other data points. Here, there are no obvious outliers.

## HIGH-LOW METHOD

With the same type of data as that described previously, we can estimate the fixed and variable components of cost at various activity levels using the **high-low method**. This method fits a straight line to the data points representing the highest and lowest levels of activity. The slope of the line is the estimate of variable cost (because the slope measures the change in cost per unit change in activity), and the intercept (where the line meets the cost axis) is the estimate of fixed cost.

We'll use the data in Illustration 4-7 to describe the high-low method. Note in Illustration 4-7 that the highest level of activity is a production level of 3,000 units in July with a corresponding cost of $400,000. The lowest level of activity is a production level of 500 units in December with a corresponding cost of $150,000. Thus, a line connecting these points looks like the one in Illustration 4-9.

We can calculate the slope of the line in Illustration 4-9 fairly easily. The slope is equal to the change in cost divided by the change in activity. In moving from the lowest level of activity to the highest level of activity, the cost changes by

**Illustration 4-9**
High-low estimate
of production costs

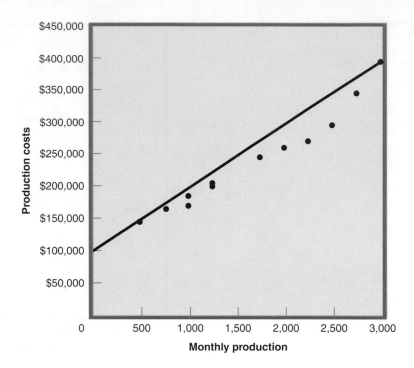

$250,000 and activity changes by 2,500 units. Thus, the estimate of variable cost (the slope) is $100 per unit.

$$\text{Estimate of Variable cost} = \frac{\text{Change in cost}}{\text{Change in activity}}$$

$$\text{Estimate of variable cost} = \frac{\text{Cost at highest level of activity} - \text{Cost at lowest level of activity}}{\text{Highest level of activity} - \text{Lowest level of activity}}$$

$$\text{Estimate of Variable cost} = \frac{\$400,000 - \$150,000}{3,000 - 500}$$

$$\text{Estimate of Variable cost} = \frac{\$250,000}{2,500} = \$100 \text{ per unit}$$

Once we obtain an estimate of variable cost, we can use it to calculate an estimate of fixed cost (the intercept of the line). The fixed cost equals the difference between total cost and estimated variable cost. For example, at the lowest level of activity (500 units), total cost is $150,000. Since variable cost is $100 per unit, variable cost is $50,000 of the total cost. Thus, the remaining cost of $100,000 must be the amount of fixed cost. As indicated in the following calculation, we arrive at the same fixed cost amount ($100,000) whether we work with the lowest or the highest level of activity.

| **Estimate Using Lowest Activity** | | **Estimate Using Highest Activity** | |
|---|---|---|---|
| Total cost | $150,000 | Total cost | $400,000 |
| Less: Estimated variable cost (500 × $100) | 50,000 | Less: Estimated variable cost (3,000 × $100) | 300,000 |
| Estimated fixed cost per month | $100,000 | Estimated fixed cost per month | $100,000 |

Be sure to note that because monthly data—the data from Illustration 4-7—are used in this example, the fixed costs calculated are the fixed costs *per month*. If annual data were used, the fixed costs calculated would be the fixed costs *per year*.

Refer back to Illustration 4-9 which shows the high-low line for the cost and activity data from Illustration 4-7. We can describe the total cost at any point along this line by using the following equation:

Total cost = Fixed cost + (Variable cost per unit × Activity level in units)

Thus, we can use the equation to derive an estimate of total cost for a given activity level. For example, at an activity level of 1,500 units, we would estimate that $250,000 of cost would be incurred:

$$\text{Total cost} = \$100,000 + (\$100 \times 1,500)$$
$$= \$100,000 + \$150,000$$
$$= \$250,000$$

Looking at Illustration 4-9 should suggest a weakness of the high-low method. Notice that the cost line passes through the high and low data points but the other data points lie below the cost line. In other words, the estimate represented by the line does not adequately fit the available data.

A significant weakness of the high-low method, then, is that it uses only two data points. These two points may not be truly representative of the general relation between cost and activity. The two points may represent unusually high and unusually low levels of activity, and costs at these levels may also be unusual. For example, at the highest level of activity, part-time workers may be used to supplement the normal workforce. They may not work as efficiently as other workers, and costs may be unusually high. Thus, when additional data are available, using more than two data points for estimates is advisable.

## REGRESSION ANALYSIS

**Regression analysis** is a statistical technique that uses all the available data points to estimate the intercept and slope of a cost equation. The line fitted to the data by regression is the best straight-line fit to the data. Software programs to perform regression analysis are widely available and are included in spreadsheet programs like Excel®. How to use Excel® to conduct regression analysis is explained in the appendix to this chapter. The topic of regression analysis is covered in introductory statistics classes. For our purposes, we simply note that application of regression analysis to the data in Illustration 4-7 yields the following equation.

Total cost = Fixed cost + (Variable cost per unit × Activity level in units)

Total cost = $93,619 + ($90.83 × Activity level in units)

Thus, at a production level of 1,500 units, the amount of total cost estimated is $229,864.

$$\text{Total cost} = \$93,619 \text{ of fixed cost} + (\$90.83 \times 1,500)$$
$$= \$229,864$$

This is less than the $250,000 estimated using the high-low cost equation.

A graph of the regression analysis estimate of cost is presented in Illustration 4-10. Notice that the regression line fits the available data better than the line

**Illustration 4-10**
Regression analysis
estimate of
production cost

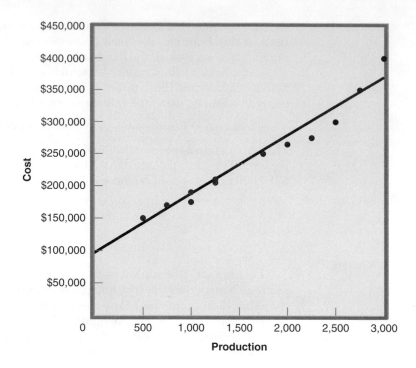

estimated with the high-low method. Because the regression line is more consistent with the past data of the company, it will probably provide more accurate predictions of future costs.

## THE RELEVANT RANGE

When working with estimates of fixed and variable costs, remember that they are only valid for a limited range of activity. The **relevant range** is the range of activity for which estimates and predictions are likely to be accurate. Outside the relevant range, the estimates of fixed and variable costs may not be very useful. Generally, managers are not confident using estimates of fixed and variable costs when called upon to make predictions for activity levels that have not been encountered in the past. That's because the activity levels are outside the range where they believe the estimates are accurate. For example, a manager at Code-Connect would not feel confident using the regression estimates of $93,619 fixed cost and $90.83 variable cost per unit to estimate total cost for a production level of 4,000 units. As indicated in Illustration 4-7, the highest prior level of production was 3,000 units and, thus, 4,000 units is outside the relevant range.

In some cases, actual costs behave in a manner that is different from the common cost behavior patterns that we have discussed. All of those patterns imply linear (straight-line) relations between cost and activity. In the real world, some costs are nonlinear. When companies produce unusually large quantities, for example, production may not be efficient, resulting in costs increasing more rapidly than the rate implied by a straight line. This may not be a serious limitation for a straight-line approach as long as the predictions and estimates are restricted to the relevant range. Consider Illustration 4-11. Note that although the relation between cost and activity is nonlinear, within the relevant range a straight line would closely approximate the relation between cost and activity.

**Illustration 4-11**
Relevant range

Relevant range

Cost

Activity

Perform cost-volume-profit
analysis for single products.

# COST-VOLUME-PROFIT ANALYSIS

Once fixed and variable costs have been estimated, cost-volume-profit analysis (C-V-P) can be conducted. Basically, C-V-P analysis is any analysis that explores the relation among costs, volume or activity levels, and profit.

## THE PROFIT EQUATION

Fundamental to C-V-P analysis is the profit equation. The **profit equation** states that profit is equal to revenue (selling price times quantity), minus variable cost (variable cost per unit times quantity), minus total fixed cost.

$$\text{Profit} = \text{SP}\,(x) - \text{VC}\,(x) - \text{TFC}$$

where    $x$ = Quantity of units produced and sold

SP = Selling price per unit

VC = Variable cost per unit

TFC = Total fixed cost

## BREAK-EVEN POINT

One of the primary uses of C-V-P analysis is to calculate the break-even point. The **break-even point** is the number of units that must be sold for a company to break even—to neither earn a profit nor incur a loss. The break-even point is shown in the profit graph presented in Illustration 4-12. At the point where sales revenue equals total cost (composed of fixed and variable costs), the company breaks even.

**Illustration 4-12**
Profit graph
and break-even point

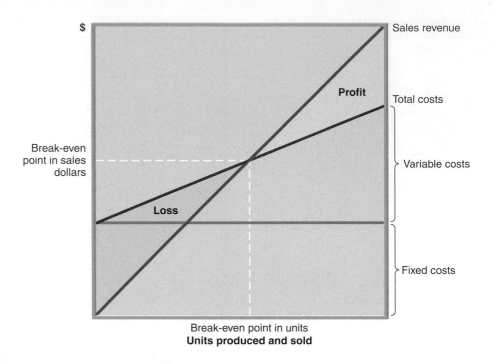

To calculate the break-even point, we simply set the profit equation equal to zero, because by definition the break-even point is the point at which profit is zero. Then we insert the appropriate selling price, variable cost, and fixed cost information and solve for the quantity ($x$).

Let's consider an example. Mary Stuart, the VP of operations at CodeConnect, wants to know the break-even point for the company's model DX375 bar code reader. This will help her assess the possibility of incurring a loss for this product. Suppose CodeConnect sells this model for $200 per unit. Variable costs are estimated to be $90.83 per unit, and total fixed costs are estimated to be $160,285 per month, composed of $93,619 of fixed production costs (estimated above) and $66,666 fixed selling and administrative costs.

| | |
|---|---:|
| Selling price per unit | $200.00 |
| Variable cost per unit | 90.83 |
| Fixed production cost per month | $ 93,619 |
| Fixed selling and administrative costs | 66,666 |
| Total fixed costs | $160,285 |

How many units must be sold to break even in a given month? To answer this question, we solve the profit equation for a particular value of $x$.

$$0 = \$200\,(x) - \$90.83\,(x) - \$160,285$$

$$0 = \$109.17\,(x) - \$160,285$$

$$\$109.17\,(x) = \$160,285$$

$$x = 1,468 \text{ units}$$

Solving for $x$ yields a break-even quantity of 1,468 units. If management prefers to have the break-even quantity expressed in dollars of sales rather than in units, the quantity is simply multiplied by the selling price of $200 to yield $293,600.

### How Do You Get to the Break-Even Point When You Have a $26.7 Billion Loss?

If your company was operating below the break-even point, what initiatives would you pursue to achieve break even? Insight into possible courses of action can be obtained from the case of Nortel Networks Corporation. In 2001, Nortel, a world leader in products and services that support the Internet and other public and private data, voice, and multimedia communications networks, had a $26.7 billion loss (including a special charge of $15.8 billion). By April 2002, the company had implemented plans that it hoped would get the company to the break-even point by the end of the year. Plans called for (1) cutting the payroll by 3,000 employees, (2) consolidating operations in fewer buildings, (3) shutting down Web sites that were not longer needed, and (4) cutting the number of executives at the vice-president level or above from 750 to less than 300. Note that most of the savings are coming from cuts in what were most likely considered to be fixed costs.

*Source:* "Nortel on Track to Break-Even by December without More Cuts," *Ottawa Citizen*, April 24, 2002, Business, p. D3. Andrew Zipern, "Nortel to Cut 3,500 More Jobs," *The New York Times*, May 30, 2002. Jim Duffy, "Nortel Narrows Loss on Lower Revenues," *Network World Fusion*, July 18, 2002.

**Margin of Safety.**  Obviously, managers are very concerned that they have a level of sales greater than break-even sales. To express how close they expect to be to the break-even level, managers may calculate the margin of safety. The **margin of safety** is the difference between the expected level of sales and break-even sales. For example, the monthly break-even level of sales for Model DX375 is $293,600. If management expects to have sales of $350,000, the margin of safety is $56,400 (i.e., $350,000 − $293,600). Given that the margin of safety is relatively high, Mary Stuart can be reasonably confident that the Model DX375 will break even.

## CONTRIBUTION MARGIN

The profit equation can be rewritten by combining the terms containing $x$ in them to yield the **contribution margin**—the difference between the selling price (SP) and variable cost per unit (VC).

$$\text{Profit} = \text{SP}(x) - \text{VC}(x) - \text{TFC}$$

$$\text{Profit} = (\text{SP} - \text{VC})(x) - \text{TFC}$$

$$\text{Profit} = \text{Contribution margin}(x) - \text{TFC}$$

The contribution margin measures the amount each unit sold contributes to covering fixed costs and increasing profit. This may not be obvious at first glance, but consider what happens when sales and production increase by one unit. The firm benefits from revenue equal to the selling price, but it also incurs increased costs equal to the variable cost per unit. Fixed costs are unaffected by changes in volume, so they do not affect the *incremental* profit associated with selling an additional unit.

If we solve the profit equation for the sales quantity in units ($x$), we get the following expression.

$$X = \frac{\text{Profit} + \text{TFC}}{\text{SP} - \text{VC}}$$

or

$$X = \frac{\text{Profit} + \text{TFC}}{\text{Contribution margin}}$$

This is a handy formula for calculating the break-even point and solving for the quantity needed to earn various profit levels. For CodeConnect, the amount of fixed cost is $160,285 per month. With a selling price of $200 and variable costs of $90.83, the contribution margin is $109.17. Using the formula implies that 1,468 units must be sold to break even each month.

$$1,468 = \frac{0 + \$160,285}{\$109.17} = \frac{\text{Profit} + \text{TFC}}{\text{Contribution margin}}$$

Now suppose that the management of CodeConnect wants to know how many units must be sold to achieve a profit of $40,000 in a given month. Using the formula implies that 1,835 units must be sold to achieve a profit of $40,000.

$$1,835 = \frac{\$40,000 + \$160,285}{\$109.17}$$

## CONTRIBUTION MARGIN RATIO

The **contribution margin ratio** provides a measure of the contribution of every sales dollar to covering fixed cost and generating a profit. It is equal to the contribution margin per unit divided by the selling price.

$$\text{Contribution margin ratio} = \frac{\text{SP} - \text{VC}}{\text{SP}}$$

Consider a company whose product has a selling price of $20 and requires variable costs of $15. In this case, the contribution margin ratio is 25 percent. Because the contribution margin per dollar of sales is 25 percent, for every additional dollar of sales, the company will earn $.25.

$$\text{Contribution margin ratio} = \frac{\$20 - \$15}{\$20} = 25\%$$

We can express the profit equation in terms of the contribution margin ratio as:

$$\text{Sales (in dollars)} = \frac{\text{Profit} + \text{TFC}}{\text{Contribution margin ratio}}$$

This formula can be used to calculate the amount of sales dollars needed to earn a profit of $40,000 in a given month for CodeConnect. Its contribution margin ratio is .5459 (contribution margin of $109.17 ÷ selling price of $200). Thus, sales of $366,890 are needed.

$$\$366,890 = \frac{\$40,000 + \$160,285}{.5459}$$

### "WHAT IF" ANALYSIS

The profit equation also can show how profit will be affected by various options under consideration by management. Such analysis is sometimes referred to as **"what if" analysis** because it examines *what* will happen *if* a particular action is taken.

**Change in Fixed and Variable Costs.** Suppose CodeConnect is currently selling 3,000 units per month at a price of $200. Variable costs per unit are $90.83 and total fixed costs are $160,285 per month. Management is considering a change in the production process that will increase fixed costs per month by $50,000 to $210,285, but decrease variable costs to only $80 per unit. How would this change affect monthly profit? Using the profit equation, and assuming that there will be no change in the selling price or the quantity sold, profit under the alternative will be equal to $149,715:

$$\text{Profit} = \$200 \, (3{,}000) - \$80 \, (3{,}000) - \$210{,}285 = \$149{,}715$$

Without the change, profit will equal $167,225:

$$\text{Profit} = \$200 \, (3{,}000) - \$90.83 \, (3{,}000) - \$160{,}285 = \$167{,}225.$$

The change in the production process would actually lower profit, so it appears not to be advisable.

**Change in Selling Price.** Any one of the variables in the profit equation can be considered in light of changes in the other variables. For example, suppose CodeConnect's management wants to know what the selling price would have to be to earn a profit of $200,000 if 3,000 units are sold in a given month. To answer this question, all of the relevant information is organized in terms of the profit equation, and then the equation is solved for the selling price.

$$\$200{,}000 = \text{SP} \, (3{,}000) - \$90.83 \, (3{,}000) - \$160{,}285$$

$$\text{SP} \, (3{,}000) = \$632{,}775$$

$$\text{SP} = \$210.93$$

# MULTIPRODUCT ANALYSIS

The previous examples illustrated C-V-P analysis for a single product. But C-V-P analysis can be extended easily to cover multiple products. In the following sections, we examine the use of the contribution margin and the contribution margin ratio in performing C-V-P analysis for a company with multiple products.

## CONTRIBUTION MARGIN APPROACH

If the products a company sells are similar (e.g., various flavors of ice cream, various types of calculators, various models of similar boats), the weighted average contribution margin per unit can be used in C-V-P analysis. Let's consider a simple example. Suppose the Hightech Calculator Company produces two types of calculators. Model A sells for $30 and requires $15 of variable cost per unit. Model B sells for $50 and requires $20 of variable cost per unit. Further, Hightech

**Illustration 4-13**
Calculation of weighted
average contribution

|  | Contribution Margin Model A | Contribution Margin Model B |
|---|---|---|
| Selling Price | $30 | $50 |
| Variable cost | 15 | 20 |
| Contribution margin | $15 | $30 |

typically sells two Model A's for one Model B sold. To calculate the weighted average contribution margin, the fact that twice as many A's as B's are sold must be taken into account. Since two Model A's are sold for each Model B, the contribution margin of A is multiplied by 2, and the contribution margin of B is multiplied by 1. The sum is then divided by 3 units to yield the weighted average contribution margin per unit of $20. (See Illustration 4-13.)

$$\text{Weighted average contribution margin} = \frac{2(\$15) + 1(\$30)}{3} = \$20 \text{ per unit}$$

Now, suppose the Hightech Company has fixed costs equal to $100,000. How many calculators must be sold for the company to break even? Working with the weighted average contribution margin, the break-even point is 5,000 calculators.

$$\text{Break-even sales in units} = \frac{\text{Profit} + \text{Total Fixed Costs}}{\text{Weighted average contribution margin}}$$

$$5,000 = \frac{0 + 100,000}{\$20}$$

These 5,000 units would be made up of the typical two-to-one mix. Thus, Hightech must sell 3,333 Model A's (two-thirds of 5,000) and 1,667 (one-third of 5,000) Model B's to break even.

## CONTRIBUTION MARGIN RATIO APPROACH

If the products that a company sells are substantially different, C-V-P analysis should be performed using the contribution margin ratio. Consider a large store like Wal-Mart, which sells literally thousands of different products. In this setting, it does not make sense to ask how many *units* must be sold to break even or how many *units* must be sold to generate a profit of $100,000. Because the costs and selling prices of the various items sold are considerably different, analyzing these types of questions in terms of number of units is not useful. Instead, these questions are addressed in terms of sales dollars. It is perfectly reasonable to ask how much *sales* must be to break even or how much *sales* must be to generate a profit of $100,000. To answer these questions, the contribution margin ratio rather than the contribution margin per unit is used.

Suppose the Packaged Software Products Division of Mayfield Software is interested in using C-V-P analysis to analyze its product lines. The division has three major product lines—games, learning software, and personal finance software products. All have different costs and selling prices. After performing a detailed study of fixed and variable costs in the prior year, the company prepared the analysis of product-line profitability shown in Illustration 4-14.

**Illustration 4-14**
Profitability analysis
of product lines

**Mayfield Software**

### Packaged Software Products Division
### Profitability Analysis
### For the Year Ended December 31, 2006

| Packaged Software Products | Games | Learning | Personal Finance | Total |
|---|---|---|---|---|
| Sales | $20,000,000 | $15,000,000 | $12,000,000 | $47,000,000 |
| Less variable costs: | | | | |
|   Material/packaging costs | 2,000,000 | 1,200,000 | 1,440,000 | 4,640,000 |
|   Order processing labor | 1,000,000 | 900,000 | 720,000 | 2,620,000 |
|   Billing labor and materials | 800,000 | 450,000 | 600,000 | 1,850,000 |
|   Shipping costs | 1,200,000 | 750,000 | 720,000 | 2,670,000 |
|   Sales commissions | 400,000 | 300,000 | 240,000 | 940,000 |
|   Total variable costs | 5,400,000 | 3,600,000 | 3,720,000 | 12,720,000 |
| Contribution margin | 14,600,000 | 11,400,000 | 8,280,000 | 34,280,000 |
| Contribution margin ratio | 0.73 | 0.76 | 0.69 | 0.73 |
| Direct fixed costs | | | | |
|   Research and development | 2,500,000 | 1,800,000 | 1,900,000 | 6,200,000 |
|   Marketing | 6,000,000 | 4,500,000 | 3,000,000 | 13,500,000 |
|   Facilities charges | 1,200,000 | 900,000 | 720,000 | 2,820,000 |
|   Total direct fixed costs | 9,700,000 | 7,200,000 | 5,620,000 | 22,520,000 |
| Product line profit | $ 4,900,000 | $ 4,200,000 | $ 2,660,000 | 11,760,000 |
| Common fixed costs | | | | |
| Management salaries | | | | 700,000 |
| Other common costs | | | | 1,500,000 |
|   Total common fixed costs | | | | 2,200,000 |
| Packaged Software Products profit | | | | $ 9,560,000 |

*[Handwritten annotation: "Total Fixed Costs" with a bracket pointing to Total direct fixed costs and Total common fixed costs]*

Let's review the report. From sales of each product line, the division subtracts variable costs to identify the contribution margin. The contribution margin is then divided by sales to identify the contribution margin ratio. The same procedure can be followed to identify the contribution margin ratio for the entire division. Given the information in the report, what is the break-even level of sales for the Packaged Software Products Division?

To answer this question, the total amount of fixed costs is divided by the contribution margin ratio for the division. Total fixed costs are composed of the direct fixed costs associated with the three product lines plus the common fixed costs. Common fixed costs are related to resources that are shared but not directly identifiable with the product lines. An example is the salary of the division manager. Because the contribution margin ratio for the division is .73 and total fixed

## LINK TO PRACTICE

### *Deciding to Use the Contribution Margin per Unit or the Contribution Margin Ratio*

**Baskin-Robbins**

At an ice cream company like Baskin-Robbins, it is very reasonable for managers to use either the weighted average contribution margin per unit or the weighted average contribution margin ratio in C-V-P analysis. For example, a manager might want to know the effect on profit of a 1,000,000 gallon increase in sales. Assuming the weighted average contribution margin is $5 per gallon, profit is expected to increase by $5,000,000. A manager might also want to know the effect on profit of a $1,000,000 increase in sales. Assuming a weighted average contribution margin ratio of $0.30, profit is expected to increase by $300,000.

**Sears**

A manager of a Sears store would focus on the weighted average contribution margin ratio, not the weighted average contribution margin per unit. Unlike the units at an ice cream store, the various units at a Sears store are quite different. It doesn't make sense to use a weighted average contribution margin *per unit* when the units are as diverse as refrigerators and shirts. Instead, a manager of a Sears store will focus on the weighted average contribution margin ratio. It would be reasonable for a manager at Sears to ask "What is the weighted average contribution margin ratio for our store?" and use that number to estimate the increase in profit if the store can increase sales by $20,000,000. Assuming the contribution margin ratio is .20, the expected increase would be $4,000,000.

costs are $24,720,000 ($22,520,000 direct fixed cost + $2,200,000 common fixed cost), the break-even point is sales of $33,863,014.

$$\text{Break-even point} = \frac{\text{Total fixed costs}}{\text{Contribution margin ratio}}$$

$$\text{Break-even point} = \frac{\$24,720,000}{.73} = \$33,863,014$$

The contribution margin ratio can also be used to analyze the effect on net income of a change in total company sales. Suppose in the coming year, management believes that total company sales will increase by 20 percent and is interested in assessing the effect of this increase on overall company profitability. A 20 percent increase in sales is $9,400,000 (20 percent of $47,000,000). The weighted average contribution margin ratio of .73 indicates that the company generates $0.73 of incremental profit on each dollar of sales. Thus, income will increase by .73 × $9,400,000 = $6,862,000.

Note that this approach makes one very important assumption: that when overall sales increase, sales of games, learning software, and personal finance software products will increase in the same proportion as current sales. If this assumption is not warranted, then the contribution margin ratios of the three product lines must be weighted by their share of the increase. For example, suppose the company believes sales will increase by $9,400,000 but expects the increase will be made up of a $4,000,000 increase in game sales, a $4,000,000 increase in sales of learning products, and a $1,400,000 increase in sales of personal finance products. To calculate the effect on net income, the contribution margin ratios of the specific departments must be used. The expected increase in profit is $6,926,000.

| Department | Increase in Sales | Contribution Margin Ratio | Increase in Profit |
|---|---|---|---|
| Games | $4,000,000 | .73 | $2,920,000 |
| Learning | 4,000,000 | .76 | 3,040,000 |
| Personal Finance | 1,400,000 | .69 | 966,000 |
| Total increase in profit | | | $6,926,000 |

Why did this analysis yield a larger increase in net income than the preceding analysis? The preceding analysis assumed the increase in sales would be proportionate to the current mix of Games, Learning, and Personal Finance products; the current analysis assumes that of the $9,400,000 increase in sales only $1,400,000 is due to Personal Finance software. Since Personal Finance software is the product line with the lowest contribution margin ratio, profit will be more if proportionately less of this product line is sold.

## Which Firm Has the Higher Contribution Margin Ratio?

Listed below are six pairs of firms with different contribution margin ratios (contribution margin per dollar of sales). For each pair, identify the firm with the higher contribution margin ratio. (Answer at bottom.)

**Companies**

McDonald's versus UAL (United Airlines)

Ford Motor Company versus Kroger (a large grocery chain)

Oracle (a large software company) versus Sears

Nordstrom (a chain of clothing stores) versus E*Trade (an online brokerage firm)

Coca-Cola versus Wal-Mart Stores

**Answer** United Airlines; Ford Motor Company; Oracle; E*Trade; Coca-Cola.

# ASSUMPTIONS IN C-V-P ANALYSIS

Whenever C-V-P analysis is performed, a number of assumptions are made that affect the validity of the analysis. Perhaps the primary assumption is that costs can be accurately separated into their fixed and variable components. In some companies, this a very difficult and costly task. A further assumption is that the fixed costs remain fixed and the variable costs per unit do not change over the activity levels of interest. With large changes in activity, this assumption may not be valid. When performing multiproduct C-V-P analysis, an important assumption is that the mix remains constant. In spite of these assumptions, most managers find C-V-P analysis to be a useful tool for exploring various profit targets and for performing "what if" analysis.

# CodeConnect EXAMPLE REVISITED: ANSWERING MARY'S QUESTIONS

Recall that at the beginning of the chapter, Mary Stuart of CodeConnect was faced with several questions related to planning, control, and decision making. Let's go back to these questions and make sure we can answer them.

**Planning:** Last year, CodeConnect sold 20,000 bar code readers at $200 per unit. The cost of manufacturing these items was $2,940,000, and selling and administrative costs were $800,000. Total profit was $260,000. In the coming year, the company expects to sell 25,000 units. What level of profit should be in the budget for the coming year?

Assume that the $2,940,000 of production costs consist of variable production costs of $90.83 per unit and fixed production costs of $1,123,428 per year. Further, assume that all selling and administrative costs are fixed and equal to $800,000 per year. In this case, expected profit is

$$\text{Selling price } (x) - \text{Variable cost } (x) - \text{Fixed costs} = \text{Profit}$$

$$\$200\,(25,000) - \$90.83\,(25,000) - \$1,123,428 - \$800,000 = \$805,822$$

**Control:** In April, production costs were $250,000. In May, costs increased to $265,000, but production also increased from 1,750 units in April to 2,000 units in May. Did the manager responsible for product costs do a good job of controlling costs in May?

Assume that production costs are estimated to be $90.83 per unit of variable cost and $93,619 of fixed costs per month. Then, the expected cost for producing 2,000 bar code readers is

$$\text{Variable cost } (x) + \text{Fixed cost} = \text{Total cost}$$

$$\$90.83\,(2,000) + \$93,619 = \$275,279$$

Because actual costs are somewhat less than expected costs, it appears (based on this limited analysis) that the manager responsible for product costs has done a good job of controlling them.

**Decision making:** The current price for a bar code reader is $200 per unit. If the price is increased to $225 per unit, sales will drop from 20,000 to 17,000. Should the price be increased?

**Decision Making/ Incremental Analysis**

Before answering this question, recall an idea we discussed in Chapter 1: All decisions rely on incremental analysis. For the pricing decision, we can perform an incremental analysis using the contribution margin. Currently, the contribution margin per unit is $109.17 (i.e., $200 − $90.83). Thus, the *total* contribution margin is 20,000 units times $109.17, which equals $2,183,400. If the selling price increases to $225, the contribution margin per unit will increase to $134.17 (i.e., $225 − $90.83). Thus, the *total* contribution margin will increase to $134.17 times 17,000 units, which is $2,280,890. The increase suggests that increasing the selling price is warranted although the effect on profit will be relatively minor. Why aren't fixed costs considered in this analysis? The fixed costs in this decision don't enter into the analysis because they are not incremental costs. Irrespective of the price, the company will have the same level of fixed costs.

### Incremental Analysis

| Total contribution margin | = (Selling price − Variable cost) × Number of units | | |
|---|---|---|---|
| $2,183,400 | = ($200 − $90.83) | × | 20,000 Original price of $200 |
| $2,280,890 | = ($225 − $90.83) | × | 17,000 New price of $225 |
| $ 97,490 | = Incremental profit with new price | | |

**5**

Discuss the effect of operating leverage.

# OPERATING LEVERAGE

We will cover two additional topics before concluding our discussion of C-V-P analysis. First, we'll discuss the concept of operating leverage, and then we'll address constraints on output. **Operating leverage** relates to the level of fixed versus variable costs in a firm's cost structure. Firms that have relatively high levels of fixed cost are said to have high operating leverage. To some extent, firms can control their level of operating leverage. For example, a firm can invest in an automated production system using robotics, thus increasing its fixed costs while reducing labor, which is a variable cost. The level of operating leverage is important because it affects the change in profit when sales change. Consider two firms with the same level of profit but different mixes of fixed and variable cost.

| | Firm 1 | Firm 2 | |
|---|---|---|---|
| Sales | $10,000,000 | $10,000,000 | 12,000,000 |
| Variable cost | 5,000,000 | 7,000,000 | |
| Contribution margin | 5,000,000 | 3,000,000 | |
| Fixed costs | 3,000,000 | 1,000,000 | |
| Profit | $ 2,000,000 | $ 2,000,000 | |

Suppose there is a 20 percent increase in sales. Which firm will have the greatest increase in profit? If Firm 1 has a 20 percent increase in sales, its profit will increase by $1,000,000 (i.e., 20% × the contribution margin) which represents a 50 percent increase in profit. Firm 2, on the other hand will have a profit increase of only $600,000 or 30 percent. Now, suppose there is a 20 percent decrease in sales. Which firm will have the greatest decrease in profit? Again, the answer is Firm 1. This is because it has relatively more fixed costs (higher operating leverage).

Firms that have high operating leverage are generally thought to be more risky because they tend to have large fluctuations in profit when sales fluctuate. However, suppose you are very confident that your firm's sales are going to increase. In that case you would want high operating leverage because the large positive fluctuation in sales will lead to a large positive fluctuation in profit. Unfortunately, many, if not most, managers are not highly confident that their firm's sales will only increase.

A final point on operating leverage: because of fixed costs in the cost structure, when sales increase by 10 percent, profit will increase by more than 10 percent. The only time that you expect profit to increase by the same percent as sales is when all costs are variable. If all costs vary in proportion to sales (i.e., all costs are variable), then profit will vary in proportion to sales.

## LINK TO PRACTICE

### Webvan Folds in the United States while in the UK, Tesco Prospers: Was Failure to Balance Fixed and Variable Costs the Cause of Webvan's Demise?

In July 2001, Webvan, the largest on-line grocery delivery service in the United States announced it would file for Chapter 11. It's failure, unlike the failure of many dot-coms, wasn't due to having a service nobody wanted. Indeed, its service appealed to many U.S. consumers and the company received positive reviews from most customers. In the UK, Tesco has a profitable business as an on-line grocer suggesting that money could also be made in the United States. Webvan's problem, according to Tim Jackson, a reporter for the *Financial Times* (London), was the company's failure to balance fixed and variable costs.

Webvan had margins [(sales minus cost of sales) ÷ sales] of 12 percent compared with the 4 percent standard in the grocery business. But to achieve its high margins, it had to revolutionize the way grocery shopping worked. The company built enormous warehouses, 18 times the size of an average supermarket, where workers could "pick and pack" as in an industrial distribution center. So, variable cost savings were achieved from a major investment in buildings and equipment that generated huge fixed costs. To cover the fixed costs the company needed tremendous sales volume and investors proved to be unwilling to pump more money into the company as it tried to build its customer base.

In comparison, Tesco, a large UK food retailer, has a profitable on-line grocery business. It's "secret"—a less radical business model with higher variable costs but less need for massive investment in plant and equipment and, thus, lower fixed costs. Tesco's success seems to indicate that excessive operating leverage may have doomed Webvan.

*Source:* Tim Jackson, "Bold But Doomed Venture: Unsupportable Fixed Costs were Behind Webvan's Failure to Deliver the Goods," *Financial Times* (London), Tuesday, July 10, 2001, Inside Track Section, p. 17. Joanna Glasner, "Why Webvan Drove off a Cliff," *Wired News*, July 10, 2001. Suzanne Kapner, "Early Winner in Online Food; Local and Simple Ways Work for British Grocer," *The New York Times*, July 20, 2001.

**Use the contribution margin per unit of the constraint to analyze situations involving a resource constraint.**

# CONSTRAINTS

In many cases (e.g., owing to shortages of space, equipment, or labor) there are constraints on how many items can be produced or how much service can be provided. Under such constraints, the focus shifts from the *contribution margin per unit* to the *contribution margin per unit of the constraint*. For example, suppose a company can produce either Product A or Product B using the same equipment. The contribution margin of A is $200, whereas the contribution margin of B is only $100. However, there are only 1,000 machine hours available, and Product A requires 10 hours of machine time to produce one unit while Product B requires only 2 hours per unit. In this simplified case, the company would only produce Product B. Although its contribution margin is smaller ($100 versus $200), it contributes $50 per machine hour, whereas Product A contributes only $20 per machine hour. In total, with 1,000 available machine hours, Product A can generate $20,000 of contribution margin while B can generate $50,000 of contribution margin.

|  | Product A | Product B |
| --- | --- | --- |
| Selling price | $500 | $300 |
| Variable cost | 300 | 200 |
| Contribution margin | $200 | $100 |
| Time to produce 1 unit | 10 hours | 2 hours |
| Contribution margin per hour | $20 | $50 |
| Contribution margin given 1,000 available hours | $20,000 | $50,000 |

# MAKING BUSINESS DECISIONS

In the chapter, we learned how to estimate fixed and variable costs using account analysis, the high-low method, and regression analysis (this latter method is covered in the appendix). All of these methods make the assumption that prior costs are good predictors of future costs. However, decisions that involve significant increases in sales or production may cause prior "fixed" costs to jump to a higher level. This might be due, for example, to the need to hire an additional supervisor.

## KNOWLEDGE AND SKILLS CHECKLIST

*Knowledge and skills are needed to make good business decisions. Check off the knowledge and skills you've acquired from reading this chapter.*

❏ K/S 1. You have an expanded business vocabulary (see key terms).

❏ K/S 2. You can perform account analysis.

❏ K/S 3. You can use the high-low method—and you recognize its limitations.

❏ K/S 4. You can use the profit equation to calculate expected profit for various levels of sales.

❏ K/S 5. You can perform multiproduct cost-volume-profit analysis.

❏ K/S 6. You can use the contribution margin per unit to analyze the effect of selling additional units.

❏ K/S 7. You can use the contribution margin ratio to analyze the effect of increasing sales dollars.

❏ K/S 8. You know how operating leverage affects the relation between percentage changes in sales and percentage changes in profit.

# S U M M A R Y OF LEARNING OBJECTIVES

**1** *Identify common cost behavior patterns.* Common cost behavior patterns include those involving variable, fixed, mixed, and step costs. Variable costs are costs that change in proportion to changes in volume or activity. Fixed costs are constant across activity levels. Mixed costs contain both a variable cost component and a fixed cost component. Step costs are fixed for a range of volume but increase to a higher level when the upper bound of the range is exceeded.

**2** *Estimate the relation between cost and activity using account analysis and the high-low method.* Managers use account analysis, the high-low method, and regression analysis to estimate the relation between cost and activity. Account analysis requires that the manager use his or her judgment to classify costs as either fixed or variable. The high-low method fits a straight line to the costs at the highest and the lowest activity levels. Regression analysis provides the best straight-line fit to prior cost/activity data.

**3** *Perform cost-volume-profit analysis for single products.* Once fixed and variable costs have been estimated, cost-volume-profit analysis can be performed. C-V-P analysis makes use of the profit equation

$$\text{Profit} = \text{SP}(x) - \text{VC}(x) - \text{TFC}$$

to perform "what if" analysis. The effect of changing various components of the equation can be explored by solving the equation for the variable affected by the change. Specific examples include solving for the break-even point or solving the equation to determine the level of volume re-

quired to achieve a certain level of profit. The number of units that must be sold or the sales dollars needed to achieve a specified profit level can be determined using the following formulas:

$$\text{Number of units} = \frac{\text{Fixed cost} + \text{Profit}}{\text{Contribution margin}}$$

$$\text{Sales dollars} = \frac{\text{Fixed cost} + \text{Profit}}{\text{Contribution margin ratio}}$$

**4** *Perform cost-volume-profit analysis for multiple products.* The case of multiple products is easily addressed by using the weighted average contribution margin per unit or the weighted average contribution margin ratio.

**5** *Discuss the effect of operating leverage.* Operating leverage relates to the level of fixed versus variable costs in a company's cost structure. The higher the level of fixed costs, the greater the operating leverage. Also, the higher the operating leverage, the greater the percentage change in profit for a given percentage change in sales. Firms with high operating leverage are generally considered to be more risky than firms with low operating leverage.

**6** *Use the contribution margin per unit of the constraint to analyze situations involving a resource constraint.* When there is a constraint, the focus shifts from the contribution margin per unit to the contribution margin per unit of the constraint. The product that has the highest contribution margin per unit of the constraint should be produced because it will generate the greatest contribution to covering fixed costs and generating a profit.

# A P P E N D I X

## USING REGRESSION IN EXCEL® TO ESTIMATE FIXED AND VARIABLE COSTS

In this appendix, we will see how to use the Regression function in Excel® to estimate fixed and variable costs using the data for CodeConnect presented in Illustration 4-7. As you will see, the spreadsheet program makes *performing* regression analysis very easy. However, it doesn't make *understanding* regression analysis easy! While we will discuss the interpretation of the output of the regression program, it would be wise to consult the treatment of regression analysis in an introductory statistics book before doing any real-world analysis.

## SETTING UP THE SPREADSHEET

In a normal installation of Excel®, data analysis programs such as Regression are not installed. So, before trying to perform regression, make sure you have installed the data analysis programs.

Once you have installed the data analysis programs, open a spreadsheet and enter the cost and production data from Illustration 4-7 in columns A and B. Now go under *Tools* and scroll down to *Data Analysis* (see Illustration A4-1). When the *Data Analysis* box opens up, scroll down to *Regression* and click *OK* (see Illustration A4-2).

Once the Regression program opens, under *Input Y*, scroll down from A1 to A13. Note that this includes the heading "Cost." Under *Input X*, scroll down from B1 to B13. Note that this includes the heading "Production." Click on Labels, which indicates that you have labels for Production and Cost data columns.

Under *Output options*, click on *New workbook*. Under *residuals*, click on *Line fit plot*. This indicates that you want a plot of the data and the regression line. At this point, your spreadsheet should look like the one in Illustration A4-3. Now click on *OK* and the Regression program will yield the output presented in Illustration A4-4.

**Illustration A4-1**
Under *Tools*,
Select *Data Analysis*

**Illustration A4-2**
Under *Data Analysis*,
Select *Regression*

**Illustration A4-3**
Regression Program

**Illustration A4-4**
Regression Output

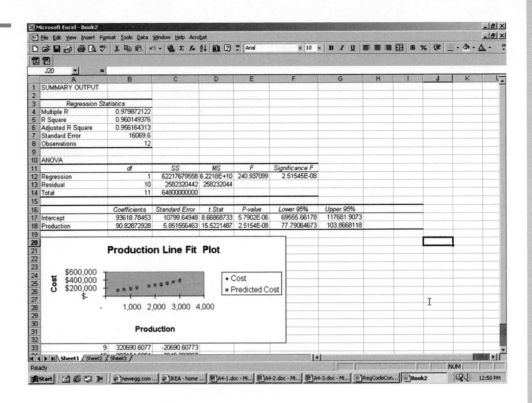

## INTERPRETING THE OUTPUT OF THE *REGRESSION* PROGRAM

Let's interpret the most critical elements of the regression output.

**The Plot.**  The plot of the data and the plot of the regression line indicate that the data line up quite close to the regression line. This suggests that a straight-line fit to the data will be quite successful.

**R Square.**  R Square is a statistical measure of how well the regression line fits the data. Specifically, it measures the percent of variance in the dependent variable (cost in the current case) explained by the independent variable (production). R Square ranges from a low of 0, indicating that there is no linear relation between cost and production, to a high of 1, indicating that there is a perfect linear relation between cost and production. In the current case, R Square is .96 which is quite high. This reinforces our conclusion from looking at the plot of the data that there is a strong linear relation between cost and production.

**Intercept and Slope of the Regression Line.**  The intercept of the regression line is interpreted as the estimate of fixed cost while the slope of the regression line is interpreted as the variable cost per unit. The output from the regression indicates that the intercept is $93,618.78 while the coefficient on production (the slope of the regression line) is $90.83. Thus, the regression line indicates that:

$$Cost = \$93{,}618.78 + \$90.83 \text{ (Production)}$$

**P-Value.** The p-values corresponding to the intercept and the slope measure the probability of observing values as large as the estimated coefficients when the true values are zero. In other words, there is some probability that even when the true fixed cost is zero we will observe an estimate as large as $93,618.78. We would, of course, like this probability to be quite low (at least less than .05). In the current case the probability is very low (.00000579022). Likewise, the probability that we will observe an estimate as large as $90.83 when the true variable cost per unit is zero is also very low (.0000000251545). Thus, it seems highly unlikely that either the true fixed cost is zero or that the true variable cost per unit is zero.

# R E V I E W   P R O B L E M

The Antibody Research Institute (ARI) is a biotechnology company that develops humanized antibodies to treat various diseases. Antibodies are proteins that bind with a foreign substance such as a virus and render it inactive. The company operates a research lab in Boston and currently employs 23 scientists. Most of the company's work involves development of humanized antibodies for specific pharmaceutical companies. Revenue comes from this contract work and from royalties on products that ultimately make use of ARI developed antibodies.

In the coming year, the company expects to incur the following costs:

**Expense Summary**

| | |
|---|---:|
| Salaries of 23 research scientists | $2,760,000 |
| Administrative salaries | 785,000 |
| Depreciation of building and equipment | 3,200,000 |
| Laboratory supplies | 765,000 |
| Utilities and other miscellaneous (fixed) expenses | 285,000 |
| Total | $7,795,000 |

Annual contract revenue is projected to be $4,000,000. The company also anticipates royalties related to the sale of Oxacine, which is a product that will come to market next year. Oxacine is marketed by Reach Pharmaceuticals and makes use of an antibody developed under contract with ARI. The product is scheduled to sell for $120 per unit and ARI will receive a royalty of 20 percent of sales. ARI, in turn, has a contractual commitment to pay 10 percent of royalties it receives (i.e. 10% of the 20%) to the scientists who were on the team that developed the antibody.

**Required**

a. How many units of Oxacine must be sold for ARI to achieve its break-even point?
b. Reach Pharmaceuticals has projected annual sales of 180,000 units of Oxacine. Assuming this level of sales, what will be the before-tax profit of ARI?
c. What if Reach Pharmaceuticals sells only 160,000 units of Oxacine? Assuming that the average salary of scientists is $120,000, how many scientists must be "downsized" to achieve the break-even point?
d. Do you consider ARI to be high or low with respect to operating leverage? Explain.

**Answer**

a. $4,000,000 + .20 ($120)(Q) − .10(.20)($120)(Q) − $7,795,000 = $–0–
   $21.6(Q) = $3,795,000
   Q = 175,694.44
b. $4,000,000 + .20 ($120)(180,000) − .10(.20)($120)(180,000) − $7,795,000 = $93,000
c. $4,000,000 + .20 ($120)(160,000) − .05($120)(160,000) − $7,795,000 = ($339,000)
   Average salary = $2,760,000 ÷ 23 = $120,000
   ($339,000) ÷ $120,000 = (2.825)
   This implies that approximately 3 scientists must be "downsized."

d. ARI is extremely high with respect to operating leverage since costs other than royalty payments to scientists are generally fixed. The fact that the costs are fixed does not mean, however, that they cannot be cut. Some costs such as the salaries of the scientists are discretionary fixed costs. Other costs such as depreciation are committed fixed costs.

# KEY TERMS

Account analysis (116)
Break-even point (123)
Committed fixed costs (114)
Contribution margin (125)
Contribution margin ratio (126)
Cost-volume-profit (C-V-P)
  analysis (112)

Discretionary fixed costs (113)
Fixed costs (112)
High-low method (119)
Margin of safety (125)
Mixed costs (114)
Operating leverage (133)
Profit equation (123)

Regression analysis (121)
Relevant range (122)
Scattergraph (118)
Semivariable costs (114)
Step costs (114)
Variable costs (112)
"What-if" analysis (127)

# SELF ASSESSMENT *(Answers Below)*

1. At Wendell Corporation, the selling price per unit is $800 and variable cost per unit is $500. Fixed costs are $1,000,000 per year. In this case, the contribution margin per unit is:

   a. $300
   b. $0.375
   c. 2,500 units.
   d. None of the above.

2. At Wendell Corporation, the selling price per unit is $800 and variable cost per unit is $500. Fixed costs are $1,000,000 per year. Assuming sales of $3,000,000, profit will be:

   a. $125,000
   b. $680,000
   c. $750,000
   d. None of the above.

3. The contribution margin ratio measures:

   a. Profit per unit.
   b. Contribution margin per dollar of sales.
   c. Profit per dollar of sales.
   d. The ratio of variable to fixed costs.

4. In March, Olympus Company had the following costs related to producing 10,000 units:

   | | |
   |---|---|
   | Direct materials | $60,000 |
   | Direct labor | 20,000 |
   | Rent | 5,000 |
   | Depreciation | 4,000 |

   Estimate variable cost per unit using account analysis.

   a. $8.90        c. $2.90
   b. $2.00        d. $8.00

5. Using the following production/cost data, estimate variable cost per unit using the high-low method

   | Month | Production | Cost |
   |---|---|---|
   | January | 2,000 | $20,000 |
   | February | 2,500 | $21,000 |
   | March | 3,000 | $23,000 |
   | April | 1,900 | $18,500 |

   a. $4.00
   b. $3.70
   c. $4.20
   d. $4.09

6. At Wendell Corporation, the selling price per unit is $800 and variable cost per unit is $500. Fixed costs are $1,000,000 per year. In this case, the break-even point is approximately:

   a. 3,333 units.
   b. 6,667 units.
   c. 5,500 units.
   d. None of the above.

7. Consider the sales and variable cost information for the three departments at Olson Drug in May:

   | | Drugs | Cosmetics | Housewares |
   |---|---|---|---|
   | Sales | $80,000 | $40,000 | $30,000 |
   | Variable cost | 40,000 | 15,000 | 25,000 |
   | Contribution margin | $40,000 | $25,000 | $ 5,000 |

   Based on this information, estimate the increase in profit for a $10,000 increase in sales (assuming the sales mix stays the same).

   a. $4,667        c. $3,334
   b. $5,667        d. None of the above.

8. Consider the sales and variable cost information in Question 7. Assuming that total fixed costs at Olson Drug are $30,000 per month, what is the break-even level of sales in dollars?

    a. $86,326
    b. $45,876
    c. $72,284
    d. $64,286

9. If a firm has relatively high operating leverage, it has:

    a. Relatively high variable costs.
    b. Relatively high fixed costs.
    c. Relatively low operating expenses.
    d. Relatively high operating expenses.

10. Product A has a contribution margin per unit of $500 and requires 2 hours of machine time. Product B has a contribution margin per unit of $1,000 and requires 5 hours of machine time. How much of each product should be produced given there are 100 hours of available machine time?

    a. 50 units of A.
    b. 25 units of B.
    c. 50 units of A and 25 units of B.
    d. None of the above is correct.

**Answers to Self Assessment**

**1.** a;     **2.** a;     **3.** b;     **4.** d;     **5.** d;     **6.** a;
**7.** a;     **8.** d;     **9.** b;     **10.** a.

# INTERACTIVE LEARNING

**Enhance and test your knowledge of Chapter 4 using the interactive CD.**

1. Learning Objectives
2. Multiple Choice
3. Language of Business—Matching of Key Terms
4. Critical Thinking
5. Demonstration—How variable costs, fixed costs, and the selling price affect the break-even point
6. Case—*The Games Division of Mayfield Software*; Calculating the break-even point
7. Video—Holland America West Tours; Fixed and variable costs of a cruise

**Go to our dynamic Web site for more self-assessment, Web links, and additional information.**

# QUESTIONS

1. Distinguish between variable and fixed costs.
2. Define the term *mixed cost* and provide an example of such a cost.
3. Distinguish between discretionary and committed fixed costs.
4. Provide two examples of costs that are likely to be variable costs.
5. Provide two examples of costs that are likely to be fixed costs.
6. Explain why total compensation paid to the sales force is likely to be a mixed cost.
7. Explain why telecom cost is likely to be a mixed cost.
8. In a scattergraph of production and costs, what would be the horizontal axis; cost or production?

9. Explain how one uses account analysis to estimate fixed and variable costs.
10. In fitting a straight line using the high-low method, should you use the highest and lowest costs or the highest and lowest activity levels?
11. Explain the concept of a relevant range.
12. What is the difference between the contribution margin and the contribution margin ratio?
13. What is the profit equation?
14. In a multiproduct setting, when would it *not* be appropriate to focus on a weighted average contribution *per unit*?
15. What are the assumptions in C-V-P analysis?

**16.** Which company would have higher operating leverage: a software company that makes large investments in research and development, or a manufacturing company that uses expensive materials and relies on highly skilled manual labor rather than automation?

**17.** In a situation where there is a production constraint, which product should be produced: the one with the highest contribution margin, or the one with the highest contribution margin per unit of constraint?

# E X E R C I S E S

**EXERCISE 4-1. Group Assignment**    Paul Drayton is planning on opening a 3,000 square foot restaurant in the Westlake Mall. As a small business owner, Paul is concerned about controlling his mix of fixed and variable costs. As Paul noted, "If I have too much fixed cost and sales don't take off right away, I'll have tremendous losses and may even go bust?"

*Required*
Expand on Paul's comment. Why is it crucial that small businesses limit their exposure to fixed costs? Identify a way that Paul can turn potential fixed costs into variable costs?

**EXERCISE 4-2. Writing Assignment**    During the 1990s, profits at Microsoft grew by an average of 47.5 percent per year, far faster than the 38.1 percent average annual growth in sales. Since profit growth drives stock prices, its not surprising that the huge increases in the bottom line translated into huge increases in Microsoft's stock price.

*Required*
Write a paragraph explaining how Microsoft managed to grow profits at a rate substantially higher than rate of growth for sales. Be sure to comment on the cost structure at Microsoft.

**EXERCISE 4-3. Internet Assignment**    Go to the Web site for Men's Wearhouse (http://www.menswearhouse.com). From there, go to Investor Relations and locate the company's annual report. Examine the line item "Gross Margin" on the company income statement. Explain why the *Gross margin* divided by *Net sales* is likely to *underestimate* the company's weighted average contribution margin ratio.

Now go to the Web site for Best Buy (http://www.bestbuy.com/) and locate their annual report. Consider their gross profit, which is equivalent to a gross margin. Explain why dividing their *Gross profit* by *Revenues* may provide a reasonable estimate of the firm's weighted average contribution margin ratio.

**EXERCISE 4-4. Cost Behavior**    Information for three costs incurred at Newton Manufacturing in the first quarter follows:

|  | Month | Amount | Units Produced |
|---|---|---|---|
| Depreciation | January | $500,000 | 3,000 |
|  | February | $500,000 | 4,500 |
|  | March | $500,000 | 6,000 |
| Direct labor | January | $120,000 | 3,000 |
|  | February | $180,000 | 4,500 |
|  | March | $240,000 | 6,000 |
| Telecommunications | January | $25,000 | 3,000 |
|  | February | $32,500 | 4,500 |
|  | March | $40,000 | 6,000 |

*Required*

Plot each cost making the vertical axis *cost* and the horizontal axis *units produced*. Classify each cost as either fixed, variable, or mixed.

**EXERCISE 4-5.  High-Low Method**   The Newton Manufacturing Company wants to predict machine repair expense at different levels of activity. The following data have been gathered:

| Month | Machine Repair Expense | Machine Hours |
|---|---|---|
| May | $ 8,000 | 2,000 |
| June | $12,000 | 4,000 |
| July | $20,000 | 8,000 |
| August | $16,000 | 6,000 |
| September | $10,000 | 3,000 |

*Required*

Determine the fixed and variable components of repair expense using the high-low method. Use machine hours as the measure of activity.

**EXERCISE 4-6.  High-Low method**   Brandon Janitorial Services is interested in estimating fixed and variable costs. The following data are available:

| | Cost | Sales |
|---|---|---|
| January | $18,000 | $20,000 |
| February | 21,200 | 22,000 |
| March | 21,500 | 24,000 |
| April | 23,400 | 21,000 |
| May | 21,500 | 26,000 |
| June | 23,400 | 27,000 |
| July | 21,500 | 24,000 |
| August | 18,400 | 19,000 |
| September | 19,200 | 22,000 |
| October | 20,400 | 24,000 |
| November | 23,600 | 27,000 |
| December | 23,800 | 28,000 |

*Required*

a. Use the high-low method to estimate fixed cost per month and variable costs per dollar of sales [i.e., estimate a and b in the equation Cost = a + (b × Sales) using the high-low method].

b. Explain why 1-b is equal to the contribution margin ratio.

c. Brandon Janitorial is considering an advertising campaign that is expected to increase annual sales by $50,000. Ignoring the cost of the advertising campaign, what is the expected increase in profit associated with the advertising campaign?

d. (optional) Repeat part a using regression analysis. In light of the result, how would you answer Part c?

**EXERCISE 4-7.  Scattergraph**   Icom.com is interested in estimating the relationship between customer service costs and sales. The following data are available:

| Month | Customer Service Cost | Sales |
|---|---|---|
| May | $ 6,000 | $100,000 |
| June | $ 6,500 | $140,000 |
| July | $ 7,300 | $170,000 |
| August | $10,200 | $200,000 |
| September | $10,800 | $225,000 |

*Required*

a. Prepare a scattergraph of customer service cost (vertical axis) and sales (horizontal axis).

b. Comment on whether there appears to be a linear relation between cost and sales and whether any of the observations appear to be outliers.

**EXERCISE 4-8. Account Analysis**   Icom.com is interested in estimating the cost involved in hiring new employees. The following information is available regarding the costs of operating the Human Resource department at Icom.com in May when there were 50 new hires.

**Human Resource Department**
**May 2006**

| | |
|---|---:|
| Staff salaries | $25,000 |
| Manager salary | 7,000 |
| Office supplies | 200 |
| Depreciation of office equipment | 300 |
| Share of building cost (based on square feet occupied by Human Resources) | 1,500 |
| Total | $34,000 |

*Required*

a. Use account analysis to determine fixed cost per month and variable cost per new hire.

b. The company is planning to hire 60 employees in June. Estimate the total cost of Human Resources for June.

c. What is the expected incremental cost associated with hiring 10 more employees than were hired in May?

**EXERCISE 4-9. Account analysis**   Brandon Janitorial Services is interested in estimating fixed and variable costs. The following data are available for the month of December.

| | Sales | Cost |
|---|---:|---:|
| **December** | $28,000 | $23,800 |
| **Detail of Cost** | | |
| Cleaning supplies | | $    800 |
| Employee wages | | 15,800 |
| Rent | | 800 |
| Utilities | | 600 |
| Depreciation | | 200 |
| Owner's salary | | 5,600 |
| Total | | $23,800 |

*Required*

a. Use account analysis to estimate fixed cost per month and variable costs per dollar of sales [i.e., estimate a and b in the equation Cost = a + (b × Sales)]

b. Based on your answer to part a, what is your estimate of the contribution margin ratio at Brandon?

**EXERCISE 4-10. Account analysis**   Wilson Manufacturing is interested in estimating fixed and variable manufacturing costs using data from October. Based on judgment, the plant manager classified each manufacturing cost as fixed, variable, or part fixed and part variable.

|  | **Units Produced** | **Cost** |
|---|---|---|
| **October** | 1,000 | $85,000 |

| **Detail of Cost** |  | **Cost Behavior** |
|---|---|---|
| Material | $30,000 | Variable |
| Direct labor | 20,000 | Variable |
| Depreciation | 10,000 | Fixed |
| Phone | 200 | Fixed |
| Other utilities | 2,800 | 20% Fixed |
| Supervisory salaries | 11,000 | 80% Fixed |
| Equipment repair | 5,000 | 10% Fixed |
| Indirect materials | 400 | Variable |
| Factory maintenance | 5,600 | 90% Fixed |
| Total | $85,000 | |

### Required

a. Use account analysis to estimate fixed cost per month and variable costs per unit produced.

b. Based on your answer to Part a, what is your estimate of the incremental cost of producing 100 units?

**EXERCISE 4-11. C-V-P Analysis, Profit Equation**    Xenoc, Inc. produces stereo speakers. The selling price per pair of speakers is $800. The variable cost of production is $300 and the fixed cost per month is $50,000.

### Required

a. Calculate the break-even point for a month.

b. How many pairs of speakers must be sold to earn a monthly profit of $20,000?

**EXERCISE 4-12. C-V-P Analysis, Profit Equation**    Kramer Groceries has estimated that fixed costs per month are $200,000 and variable cost per dollar of sales is $0.80.

### Required

a. What is the break-even point per month in sales?

b. What level of sales is needed for a monthly profit of $60,000?

c. For the month of April, the company anticipates sales of $1,400,000. What is the expected level of profit?

**EXERCISE 4-13. Contribution Margin**    Xenoc, Inc. produces stereo speakers. The selling price per pair of speakers is $800. The variable cost of production is $300 and the fixed cost per month is $50,000.

### Required

a. Calculate the contribution margin associated with a pair of speakers.

b. In August, the company sold five more pairs of speakers than planned. What is expected affect on profit related to selling the additional speakers?

**EXERCISE 4-14. Contribution Margin Ratio**    Xenoc, Inc. produces stereo speakers. The selling price per pair of speakers is $800. The variable cost of production is $300 and the fixed cost per month is $50,000.

### Required

a. Calculate the contribution margin ratio for Xenoc associated with a pair of speakers.

b. In October, the company had sales that were $5,000 higher than planned. What is the expected effect on profit related to the additional sales?

**EXERCISE 4-15. Margin of Safety**    Xenoc, Inc. produces stereo speakers. The selling price per pair of speakers is $800. The variable cost of production is $300 and the fixed cost per month are $50,000. For November, the company expects to sell 120 pairs of speakers.

*Required*

a. Calculate expected profit.

b. Calculate the margin of safety in dollars.

**EXERCISE 4-16. "What If" Analysis**    Xenoc, Inc. produces stereo speakers. The selling price per pair of speakers is $800. The variable cost of production is $300 and the fixed cost per month is $50,000.

*Required*

Calculate the expected profit for November assuming the company sells 120 pairs of speakers as planned (see Exercise 15), but the selling price changes to $1,000.

**EXERCISE 4-17. Multiproduct, Contribution Margin**    National Tennis Racquet Co. produces and sells three models:

|  | Smasher | Basher | Dinker | Total |
|---|---|---|---|---|
| **Units sold** | **1,000** | **2,000** | **2,000** | **5,000** |
| Sales | $100,000 | $120,000 | $80,000 | $300,000 |
| Less variable costs | 50,000 | 48,000 | 24,000 | 122,000 |
| Contribution margin | 50,000 | 72,000 | 56,000 | 178,000 |
| Less common fixed costs |  |  |  | 103,000 |
| Profit |  |  |  | $ 75,000 |

*Required*

a. What is the weighted average contribution margin per unit?

b. Calculate the break-even point in units assuming the current mix.

c. What would be the number of Smashers, Bashers, and Dinkers in the break-even level of sales?

**EXERCISE 4-18. Multiproduct, Contribution Margin Ratio**    National Tennis Racquet Co. produces and sells three models:

|  | Smasher | Basher | Dinker | Total |
|---|---|---|---|---|
| **Units sold** | **1,000** | **2,000** | **2,000** | **5,000** |
| Sales | $100,000 | $120,000 | $80,000 | $300,000 |
| Less variable costs | 50,000 | 48,000 | 24,000 | 122,000 |
| Contribution margin | 50,000 | 72,000 | 56,000 | 178,000 |
| Less common fixed costs |  |  |  | 103,000 |
| Profit |  |  |  | $ 75,000 |

*Required*

a. What is the weighted average contribution margin ratio?

b. What level of sales (in dollars) would be needed to earn a profit of $100,000 assuming the current mix?

c. What would be the sales (in dollars) of Smashers, Bashers, and Dinkers for total sales calculated in Part b?

**EXERCISE 4-19. Multiproduct, Contribution Margin Ratio**    Saldina Hardware is organized into three departments. The following sales and cost data are available for the prior year:

|  | Department A | Department B | Department C | Total |
|---|---|---|---|---|
| Sales | $265,000 | $850,000 | $900,000 | $2,015,000 |
| Less variable costs | 106,000 | 510,000 | 720,000 | 1,336,000 |
| Contribution margin | 159,000 | 340,000 | 180,000 | 679,000 |
| Less fixed costs | 60,000 | 85,000 | 92,000 | 237,000 |
| Profit | $ 99,000 | $255,000 | $ 88,000 | $ 442,000 |

*Required*

a. What is the weighted average contribution margin ratio?

b. What level of sales is needed to earn a profit of $500,000 assuming the current mix?

c. Saldina Hardware places an advertisement in the local paper each week. All else equal, which department would you emphasize in the advertisement?

**EXERCISE 4-20. Operating Leverage**   Refer to the data in Exercise 19.

*Required*

a. Calculate profit as a percent of sales in the prior year.

b. Suppose sales in the current year increase by 20 percent. Calculate profit as a percent of sales for the new level of sales and explain why the percent is greater than the one calculated in Part a.

**EXERCISE 4-21. Constraints**   Howard Products produces two products:

|  | Product A | Product B |
|---|---|---|
| Selling price | $80 | $70 |
| Less variable costs | 20 | 40 |
| Contribution margin | $60 | $30 |

Product A requires 5 labor hours and product B requires 2 labor hours. The company has only 320 available labor hours per week. Further, the company can sell all it can produce of either product.

*Required*

a. Which product(s) should the company produce?

b. What would be the incremental benefit of obtaining 10 additional labor hours?

# P R O B L E M S

**PROBLEM 4-1. Cost Behavior**   Royal Desert Hotel is interested in estimating fixed and variable costs so that the company can make more accurate projections of costs and profit. The hotel is in a resort area that is particularly busy from November through February. In July and August, however, the hotel has only a 50 percent occupancy rate.

*Required*
Classify each of the following costs as fixed (F), variable (V), or mixed (M) with respect to the number of hotel guests per month:

_____ a. Depreciation of the building
_____ b. Salaries of restaurant staff
_____ c. Salaries of administrative staff (hotel manager, desk clerks, accountants, etc.)
_____ d. Soap, shampoo, and other toiletries in rooms
_____ e. Laundry costs (cost of linens, cleaning products, depreciation of laundry equipment, etc.)
_____ f. Food and beverage costs
_____ g. Grounds maintenance

**PROBLEM 4-2. Account Analysis**   Rykor Electronics produces a high-end compact disc player that sells for $1,200. Total operating expenses for July were as follows:

| Units produced and sold | 140 |
|---|---|
| Component cost | $ 68,000 |
| Supplies | 1,540 |
| Assembly labor | 22,800 |
| Rent | 2,000 |
| Supervisor salary | 5,000 |
| Electricity | 200 |
| Telephone | 220 |
| Gas | 100 |
| Shipping | 1,400 |
| Advertising | 2,000 |
| Administrative costs | 12,500 |
| Total | $115,760 |

*Required*

a. Use account analysis to determine fixed cost per month and variable cost per CD player.

b. Project total cost for August assuming production and sales of 150 units.

c. What is the contribution margin per CD player?

d. Estimate total profit assuming production and sales of 150 units.

e. Rykor is considering an order for 100 CD players, to be produced in the next 10 months, from a customer in Australia. The selling price will be $800 per unit (well under the normal selling price). However, the Rykor brand name will not be attached to the product. What will be the impact on company profit associated with this order?

**PROBLEM 4-3. High-Low, Break-Even**   Rykor Electronics produces a high-end compact disc player that sells for $1,200. Total operating expenses for the past 12 months are as follows:

| | Units Produced and Sold | Cost |
|---|---|---|
| August | 125 | $107,670 |
| September | 145 | 116,990 |
| October | 150 | 124,500 |
| November | 160 | 126,500 |
| December | 165 | 134,700 |
| January | 140 | 112,400 |
| February | 145 | 120,600 |
| March | 135 | 110,400 |
| April | 130 | 111,140 |
| May | 135 | 114,200 |
| June | 145 | 116,700 |
| July | 140 | 115,760 |

*Required*

a. Use the high-low method to estimate fixed and variable costs.

b. Based on these estimates, calculate the break-even level of sales in units.

c. Calculate the margin of safety for the coming August assuming estimated sales of 150 units.

d. Estimate total profit assuming production and sales of 150 units.

e. Comment on the limitations of the high-low method in estimating costs for Rykor Electronics.

**PROBLEM 4-4. Regression Analysis (see Appendix)**  Rykor Electronics produces a high-end compact disc player that sells for $1,200. Total operating expenses for the past 12 months are as follows:

|  | Units Produced and Sold | Cost |
|---|---|---|
| August | 125 | $107,670 |
| September | 145 | 116,990 |
| October | 150 | 124,500 |
| November | 160 | 126,500 |
| December | 165 | 134,700 |
| January | 140 | 112,400 |
| February | 145 | 120,600 |
| March | 135 | 110,400 |
| April | 130 | 111,140 |
| May | 135 | 114,200 |
| June | 145 | 116,700 |
| July | 140 | 115,760 |

*Required*

a. Use regression analysis to estimate fixed and variable costs.

b. Compare your estimates to those obtained using account analysis (Problem 2) or the high-low method (Problem 3). Which method provides the best estimates of fixed and variable costs?

**PROBLEM 4-5. Break-Even, "What If"**  David Peterson is the owner/pilot of Peterson Island Air. The company flies a round trip daily from Seattle's Lake Union to a resort in the Gulf Islands in Canada. In 2005, the company reported an annual income before taxes of $1,760 although that included a deduction of $34,000 reflecting David's "salary."

| | | |
|---|---|---|
| **Revenue** | | |
| ($250 × 1,248 passengers) | | $312,000.00 |
| Less costs: | | |
| Pilot (owner's salary) | $ 34,000.00 | |
| Fuel (41,600 gallons × $2.40) | 99,840.00 | |
| Maintenance (variable) | 124,800.00 | |
| Depreciation of plane | 20,000.00 | |
| Depreciation of office equipment | 600.00 | |
| Rent expense | 24,000.00 | |
| Insurance | 5,000.00 | |
| Miscellaneous (fixed) | 2,000.00 | 310,240.00 |
| Income before taxes | | $  1,760.00 |

Revenue of $312,000 reflects six round trips per week for 52 weeks with an average of four passengers paying $250 each per round-trip (6 × 52 × 4 × $250 = $312,000). The flight to the resort is 400 miles one way. With 312 round-trips (6 per week × 52 weeks), that amounts to 249,600 miles. The plane averages 7 miles per gallon.

*Required*

a. How many round trips is David currently flying and how many round-trips are needed in total to break even?

b. How many round-trips are needed so that David can draw a salary of $80,000 and still not show a loss?

c. What is the average before tax profit of a round-trip flight in 2005?

d. What is the incremental profit associated with adding a round-trip flight?

**PROBLEM 4-6. Account Analysis, High-Low, Contribution Margin**    Information on occupancy and costs at the Regal Hotel for April, May, and June are indicated below:

|  | April | May | June |
|---|---|---|---|
| Occupancy | 1,500 | 1,650 | 1,800 |
| Day manager salary | $ 4,000 | $ 4,000 | $ 4,000 |
| Night manager salary | 3,500 | 3,500 | 3,500 |
| Cleaning staff | 15,000 | 15,300 | 15,600 |
| Depreciation | 10,000 | 10,000 | 10,000 |
| Complimentary continental breakfast: | | | |
| food and beverages | 4,500 | 5,000 | 5,500 |
|  | $37,000 | $37,800 | $38,600 |

*Required*

a. Calculate the fixed costs per month and the variable cost per occupied room using account analysis for April.

b. Calculate the fixed costs per month and the variable cost per occupied room using the high-low method.

c. Average room rates are $85 per night. What is the contribution margin per occupied room? In answering this question, use your variable cost estimate from Part b.

**PROBLEM 4-7. Fixed and Variable Costs, The Profit Equation**    Last year, Cindy Mathers had a booth at the three-day Bellevue Craft Fair where she sold a variety of silver jewelry handcrafted in India. Her before-tax profit was as follows:

| | |
|---|---|
| Sales | $15,520 |
| Cost of jewelry sold | 9,312 |
| Gross margin | 6,208 |
| Registration fee | 1,000 |
| Booth rental (5% sales) | 776 |
| Salary of Jane Kramer | 300 |
| Before tax profit | $ 4,132 |

Jane Kramer is a friend who takes care of the booth for approximately 5 hours from 9 A.M. until 2 P.M. Cindy takes over from 2 P.M. until closing at 9 P.M.

Cindy has added several new designs to her collection and anticipates that in the coming year, her sales will increase by 20 percent to $18,624. In light of this, she has forecasted before-tax profit as follows:

| | |
|---|---|
| Before tax profit in prior year | $ 4,132 |
| Sales in prior year | 15,520 |
| Before tax profit per dollar of sales | .26624 |
| Forecasted sales | $18,624 |
| Profit per dollar of sales | .26624 |
| Forecasted before-tax profit | $ 4,958 |

*Required*

a. What is the fundamental assumption that Cindy is making and why is it obviously *wrong*.

b. Prepare a more appropriate forecast of before-tax profit related to the Bellevue Craft Fair.

**PROBLEM 4-8. The Profit Equation**    Premier Custom Computers is a small company that assembles PCs to customer specifications. The company buys all of its component parts from TechWarehouse.Com. In the past year, the company had the following before tax profit:

| | | |
|---|---:|---:|
| Sales | | $1,250,000 |
| Less: | | |
| Cost of components | $875,000 | |
| Staff salaries | 180,000 | |
| Rent | 24,000 | |
| Utilities | 3,600 | |
| Advertising | 2,000 | 1,084,600 |
| Operating profit before bonuses | | 165,400 |
| Staff bonuses | | 66,160 |
| Profit before taxes and owner "draw" | | $ 99,240 |

The company, owned by Patricia Wells, has six full-time employees. These employees are each paid a base salary of $30,000 per year. In addition, they receive a bonus equal to 40 percent of operating profits before bonuses. Owner "draw" is the amount Patricia pays herself out of company profits.

The company is in the process of planning profit for the coming year. TechWarehouse.Com has agreed that their prices to Premier will be reduced by 20 percent on all purchases over $900,000.

***Required***

Estimate profit before taxes and owner "draw" for five levels of sales: $1,000,000; $1,100,000; $1,200,000; $1,300,000; $1,400,000.

 **PROBLEM 4-9. High-Low, Profit Equation**   Xenoc, Inc. produces stereo speakers. Each unit (a pair of speakers) sells for $800. Below is information on production/sales and costs for 2004.

| | Production and Sales in Units | Production Costs | Selling and Admin. Costs |
|---|---:|---:|---:|
| January | 95 | $ 78,500 | $ 13,800 |
| February | 100 | 80,000 | 14,000 |
| March | 105 | 81,500 | 14,200 |
| April | 108 | 82,400 | 14,320 |
| May | 107 | 82,100 | 14,280 |
| June | 110 | 83,000 | 14,400 |
| July | 107 | 82,100 | 14,280 |
| August | 115 | 84,500 | 14,600 |
| September | 105 | 81,500 | 14,200 |
| October | 110 | 83,000 | 14,400 |
| November | 120 | 86,000 | 14,800 |
| December | 150 | 95,000 | 16,000 |
| Total | 1,332 | $ 999,600 | $ 173,280 |
| | | | |
| Average cost per unit | | $750.45045 | $130.09009 |

***Required***

a. Use the high-low method to identify the fixed and variable cost components for both production costs and selling and administrative costs.

b. The company estimates that production and sales in 2005 will be 1,400 units. Based on this estimate, forecast income before taxes for 2005.

**PROBLEM 4-10. Multiproduct C-V-P**   Ballard HiFi sells audio and video equipment and car stereo products. After performing a study of fixed and variable costs in the prior year, the company prepared a product-line profit statement as follows:

**Ballard HiFi**
**Profitability Analysis**
**For the Year Ended 12/31/06**

|  | Audio | Video | Car | Total |
|---|---|---|---|---|
| Sales | $3,000,000 | $1,800,000 | $1,200,000 | $6,000,000 |
| Less variable costs: | | | | |
| Cost of merchandise | 1,800,000 | 1,260,000 | 600,000 | 3,660,000 |
| Salary part-time staff | 120,000 | 80,000 | 30,000 | 230,000 |
| Total variable costs | 1,920,000 | 1,340,000 | 630,000 | 3,890,000 |
| Contribution margin | 1,080,000 | 460,000 | 570,000 | 2,110,000 |
| Less direct fixed costs: | | | | |
| Salary, full-time staff | 300,000 | 250,000 | 210,000 | 760,000 |
| Less common fixed costs: | | | | |
| Advertising | | | | 110,000 |
| Utilities | | | | 20,000 |
| Other administrative costs | | | | 560,000 |
| Total common fixed costs | | | | 690,000 |
| Profit | | | | $ 660,000 |

*Required*

a. Calculate the contribution margin ratios for the audio, video, and car product lines.

b. What would be the effect on profit of a $100,000 increase in sales of audio equipment compared with a $100,000 increase in sales of video equipment, or a $100,000 increase in sales of car equipment? Based on this limited information, which product line would you recommend expanding?

c. Calculate the break-even level of sales for the company as a whole.

d. Calculate sales needed to achieve a profit of $1,500,000 assuming the current mix.

e. Determine the sales of audio, video, and car products in the total sales amount calculated for Part d.

**PROBLEM 4-11. Multiproduct, Contribution Margin Ratio** RealTimeService offers computer consulting, training, and repair services. For the most recent fiscal year, profit was $230,000 as follows:

|  | Consulting | Training | Repair | Total |
|---|---|---|---|---|
| Sales | $500,000 | $400,000 | $300,000 | $1,200,000 |
| Less variable costs: | | | | |
| Salaries | 250,000 | 160,000 | 180,000 | 590,000 |
| Supplies/parts | 20,000 | 30,000 | 60,000 | 110,000 |
| Other | 1,000 | 2,000 | 4,000 | 7,000 |
| Contribution margin | 229,000 | 208,000 | 56,000 | 493,000 |
| Less common fixed costs: | | | | |
| Rent | | | | 40,000 |
| Owner's salary | | | | 200,000 |
| Utilities | | | | 15,000 |
| Other | | | | 8,000 |
| Profit | | | | $ 230,000 |

*Required*

a. Jon Cisco, the owner of RealTimeService, believes that in the coming year he can increase sales by 20 percent. Assuming the current mix of services, what will be the percentage increase in profit associated with a 20 percent increase in sales? Why will profit increase at a greater percent than sales?

b. If Jon were to focus on the contribution margin per unit (rather than the contribution margin ratio), what would be a likely unit of service?

**PROBLEM 4-12. Operating Leverage** Sercon, Inc. and Zercon, Inc. are two companies in the pharmaceutical industry. Sercon has relatively high fixed costs related to research and development. Zercon, on the other hand, does little research and development. Instead, the company pays for the right to produce and market drugs that have been developed by other companies. The amount paid is a percent of sales. Thus, Zercon has relatively high variable costs and relatively low fixed costs.

|  | **Sercon, Inc.** | **Zercon, Inc.** |
|---|---|---|
| Sales | $80,000,000 | $80,000,000 |
| Less variable costs | 20,000,000 | 50,000,000 |
| Less fixed costs | 50,000,000 | 20,000,000 |
| Profit | $10,000,000 | $10,000,000 |

*Required*

a. Which company has the highest operating leverage?

b. Calculate the expected percentage change in profit for a 10 percent increase (and for a 10 percent decrease) in sales for each company.

c. Which company is more risky?

**PROBLEM 4-13. Value of Loosening a Constraint** For the past three years, Xenoc, Inc. has produced the model X100 stereo speaker. The model is in high demand, and the company can sell as many pairs as it can produce. The selling price per pair is $800. Variable costs of production are $300 and fixed costs per year are $600,000.

Each pair of speakers requires four hours of assembly time. Currently, the company has four assembly workers who are highly skilled and can work a total of 8,000 hours per year. With a tight labor market, the company finds it difficult to hire additional assembly workers with the skill needed to assemble the X100.

Jens Kritchner, the owner of Xenoc, is considering offering assembly workers an overtime premium (wages in excess of regular hourly wages) to get them to work more than 8,000 hours per year. In thinking about how much to offer, Jens performed the following calculation:

| | |
|---|---|
| Sales (2,000 units × $800) | $1,600,000 |
| Less variable costs (2,000 × $300) | 600,000 |
| Less fixed costs | 600,000 |
| Profit | $ 400,000 |
| Profit ÷ assembly hours | |
| ($400,000 ÷ 8,000) | $50 per assembly hour |

After seeing this calculation, Jens decided to offer overtime premium of $25 per hour to his assembly workers. Jens reasoned that "This is a great deal. Both the workers and I make an extra $25 when they work an hour of overtime!"

*Required*

a. How much would profit increase if four more assembly hours were available at the regular hourly wage for assembly workers?

b. Compare your answer in Part a to the answer that Jens would provide to the question in Part a (i.e., $50 × 4 = $200). What is the flaw in Jen's calculation of the value of additional assembly time?

c. Suppose Jens pays assembly workers $25 per hour of overtime premium. On average, what will be the incremental benefit to Jens of an hour of extra assembly time?

**PROBLEM 4-14. Constraints**   Pacer Running Shoes produces two models: the Master (a shoe aimed at competitive runners) and the Finisher (a shoe aimed at fitness buffs). Sales and costs for the most recent year are indicated:

|  | **Master** | **Finisher** |
|---|---|---|
| Sales (pairs) | 10,000 | 60,000 |
| Sales | $1,400,000 | $5,700,000 |
| Variable costs | 300,000 | 600,000 |
| Contribution margin | 1,100,000 | 5,100,000 |
| Fixed costs | 100,000 | 1,200,000 |
| Profit | $1,000,000 | $3,900,000 |
| Assembly time per pair | 2 hours | 1.5 hours |
| Profit per assembly hour | $50.00 | $43.33 |
| CM per assembly hour | $55.00 | $56.67 |

*Required*

a. Suppose the company has 110,000 assembly hours available. Further, management believes that at least 2,000 pairs of each model must be produced so that the company has a presence in both market segments. How many pairs of each model should be produced in the coming year?

b. Suppose management decides that at least 4,000 pairs of each model must be produced. What is the opportunity cost of this decision versus requiring only 2,000 pairs?

**PROBLEM 4-15. Regression Analysis (see Appendix), Profit Equation**   Bob Walker is a vice president of finance for Casper's Seafood, a chain of 12 restaurants on the East coast including five restaurants in Florida. The company is considering a plan whereby customers will be mailed coupons, in the month of their birthday, entitling them to 20 percent off of their total bill. The cost of the mailing (printing, paper, postage, etc.) is estimated to be $400,000. Bob estimates that the campaign will result in an annual increase in sales of $2,500,000 at normal prices ($2,000,000 after the 20 percent discount).

As part of his analysis of the financial impact of the plan Bob ran a regression of total monthly operating costs on sales using data from the past year. The results of this analysis are indicated in the Summary Output table:

|  | **Operating costs** | **Sales** |
|---|---|---|
| January | $ 3,366,650 | $ 3,641,000 |
| February | 3,352,250 | 3,565,000 |
| March | 3,541,500 | 3,910,000 |
| April | 3,566,625 | 4,002,500 |
| May | 3,502,500 | 4,250,000 |
| June | 3,793,800 | 4,352,000 |
| July | 3,912,000 | 4,380,000 |
| August | 3,760,550 | 4,247,000 |
| September | 3,633,250 | 4,125,000 |
| October | 3,589,600 | 3,984,000 |
| November | 3,375,250 | 3,765,000 |
| December | 3,682,250 | 4,165,000 |
|  | $43,076,225 | $48,386,500 |

**Summary Output**

| Regression Statistics | | df | SS | MS | F |
|---|---|---|---|---|---|
| Multiple R | 0.89547667 | | | | |
| R Square | 0.80187846 | | | | |
| Adjusted R Squ | 0.78206631 | | | | |
| Standard Error | 83006.2325 | | | | |
| Observations | 12 | | | | |
| | | | | | |
| ANOVA | | | | | |
| | | df | SS | MS | F |
| Regression | | 1 | 2.78868E+11 | 2.7887E+11 | 40.4740682 |
| Residual | | 10 | 68900346361 | 6890034636 | |
| Total | | 11 | 3.47768E+11 | | |
| | | | | | |
| | Coefficients | Standard Error | t State | P-value | |
| Intercept | 1214820.06 | 374061.8848 | 3.24764459 | 0.00875534 | |
| Sales | 0.58897387 | 0.092577959 | 6.36192331 | 8.2247E-05 | |

*Required*

Based on the limited information provided, provide Bob with an estimate of the net effect of the coupon campaign on annual profit (ignore taxes).

# CASES

## 4-1 ETHICS CASE: WENDELL ROBERTS CONSULTING

Quality Grocers (QG) operates a grocery store in the Westwood Mall and had income from operations in 2004 of $2,267,305. In 2005, Westwood Mall allowed another grocery store to open in the mall in violation of its lease agreement with QG. The result was that sales of QG declined by 30 percent and profit dropped to only $355,000.

**Income From Operations, 2004**

| | |
|---|---|
| Sales | $42,128,687 |
| Less cost of goods sold | 33,702,950 |
| Gross margin | 8,425,737 |
| Selling and administrative costs | 6,158,432 |
| Income from operations | $ 2,267,305 |

**Income From Operations, 2005**

| | |
|---|---|
| Sales | $29,490,081 |
| Less cost of goods sold | 23,592,065 |
| Gross margin | 5,898,016 |
| Selling and administrative costs | 5,542,589 |
| Income from operations | $ 355,427 |

QG has decided to sue Westwood Mall for damages and has hired Wendell Roberts Consulting to help with the calculation. Herold Williams is the consultant assigned to the engagement and he calculated damages as follows.

First, based on analysis of sales trends, he estimated that sales would have increased by 20 percent to $50,554,424. From this estimate, he subtracted cost of goods sold equal to 80 percent, which is the same percent as in 2004. He then assumed that selling and administrative costs are essentially fixed and subtracted 2004 costs with a minor increase of $100,000. That led to forecasted income from operations of $3,852,453.

**Forecasted Income From Operations, 2004**

| | |
|---|---|
| Sales | $50,554,424 |
| Less cost of goods sold | 40,443,539 |
| Gross margin | 10,110,885 |
| Selling and administrative costs | 6,258,432 |
| Income from operations | $ 3,852,453 |

Williams then calculated damages to be forecasted income minus actual income resulting in a claim of $3,497,026 (i.e., $3,852,453 − $355,427).

QG management reviewed the calculation and had only one question, "Why did you assume that selling and administrative costs are fixed? About 40 percent of them are variable." Williams responded that he assumed they were fixed because that made the claim larger. "Look," he said. "If you want some real money from this claim, you need to make assumptions that generate real money. And the more costs you assume are fixed, the higher the claim."

*Required*

a. Explain why Williams' assumption leads to a higher claim. Is his behavior ethical?

b. Recalculate the claim assuming 40 percent of selling and administrative costs are variable.

# 4-2 ROTHMUELLER MUSEUM

In 1928, Francis P. Rothmueller, a Northwest railroad magnate, established an endowment to fund the Rothmueller Museum in Minneapolis. Whereas the museum currently has a 30 million dollar endowment, it also has substantial operating costs and continues to add to its eclectic collection that encompasses paintings, photographs, drawings, and design objects post-1900. Annual earnings from the endowment (approximately $2,100,000 in 2004) are not sufficient to cover operations and acquisitions, and the museum's trustees and president are conscious of the need to generate income from admissions, special exhibits, and museum store sales.

Alice Morgan, photographic curator, is in the process of planning an exhibition of Ansel Adams photographs, which will run from September through November of 2005. Below is a preliminary budget, prepared by Alice, of revenue and costs associated with the exhibition:

| | | | |
|---|---|---|---|
| Revenue (9,000 × $12) | | $108,000 | 1 |
| Less: | | | |
| Lease of photographs from other museums and collectors | $80,000 | | 2 |
| Packing and transportation of photographs from other museums and collectors | 4,000 | | 3 |
| Event insurance | 2,000 | | 4 |
| Alice Morgan salary (25%) | 12,000 | | 5 |
| William Jacob salary (25%) | 8,000 | | 6 |
| Guard service | 9,000 | | 7 |
| Installation costs | 1,000 | | 8 |
| Advertising | 5,000 | | 9 |
| Exhibition printed programs | 2,000 | 123,000 | 10 |
| Profit (loss) | | $(15,000) | |

1. Estimated attendance is 9,000 and admission to the exhibit is $12.
2. Some photographs will come from the Rothmueller collection while others will be leased from other museums and collectors.
3. Cost of packing and transportation to and from Rothmueller.
4. Insurance to cover photographs during the run of the exhibition.
5. Twenty-five percent of annual salary for Alice Morgan, head photography curator.
6. Twenty-five percent of annual salary for William Jacob, assistant photography curator.
7. Cost of guard service for exhibition.
8. Painting of exhibition room to off-white background.
9. Advertising in newspapers and public radio.
10. Cost of programs describing the work of Ansel Adams and pictures at exhibition.

*Additional Information*

In preparing the budget, Alice assigned 25 percent of her and her assistant's annual salaries to the exhibition since they will each spend approximately three months on the project.

An admission fee of $5 is charged to enter the museum, and attendance at the exhibition is an additional $12 per person. Approximately one-fifth of the individuals who are estimated to attend the exhibition would have come to the museum whether or not the exhibition was being held. (Alternatively, four-fifth's of the individuals are coming specifically to attend the exhibition.)

Analysis of prior data indicate that 20 percent of individuals make a purchase at the museum store, and the average purchase price is $7. The store has a 30 percent gross margin (sales minus cost of sales) and profit (sales minus cost of sales minus staff salaries and other operating costs) per dollar of sales of 5 percent.

*Required*

a. Prepare an analysis of the financial impact of the exhibition on the Rothmueller Museum assuming attendance is 9,000. Does offering the exhibition appear to be a good decision from a financial standpoint?

b. How many people must attend the exhibition for its financial impact to be profit neutral (i.e., the museum will be no better off nor no worse off financially)?

# 4-3 MAYFIELD SOFTWARE, CUSTOMER TRAINING

Marie Stefano is the group director of customer training for Mayfield Software. In this capacity, she runs a center in Kirkland, Washington that provides training to employees of companies that use Mayfield's inventory control, customer management, and accounting software products. Her group employs a receptionist, an office manager/bookkeeper, and she has arrangements with several part-time trainers who are hired on an as needed basis (they are all retired employees of Mayfield Software). Trainers are paid $3,000 per day-long class. Mayfield is a decentralized company and Marie is given considerable authority to advertise and conduct classes as she sees fit.

During 2004, the group conducted 810 day-long classes with an average enrollment of 16 students paying $300. The group's Report of Operating Results for 2004 is detailed next.

**Report of Operating Results, 2004**

| | |
|---|---:|
| Revenue | $3,888,000 |
| Less operating costs: | |
| Trainer costs | 2,430,000 |
| Director salary | 150,000 |
| Receptionist | 45,000 |
| Office manager | 65,000 |
| Utilities, phone, etc. | 18,000 |
| Lease expense related to computers, servers, etc. | 240,000 |
| Rent | 72,000 |
| Operating manuals for participants | 324,000 |
| Postage, envelopes, paper, etc. | 8,424 |
| Advertising | 56,248 |
| Total operating costs | 3,408,672 |
| Profit before central charges | 479,328 |
| Central charges | 583,200 |
| Group profit | $ (103,872) |

*Additional facts*

1. All equipment is leased on a yearly basis. Costs include 80 workstations for students (one workstation for every seat in each of the four 20-student classrooms), plus servers and other miscellaneous equipment. While average class enrollment is 16 students, some classes are full (20 students) and classes are cancelled if enrollment is less than 12 students. Classes are typically held Monday through Friday although some classes are held on Saturdays and Sundays.

### Krog's Metalfab
### Income from Operations, 2003 and 2004

| 2003 | January | February | March | April | May | June |
|---|---:|---:|---:|---:|---:|---:|
| Sales | $500,260 | $348,260 | $360,250 | $302,685 | $434,650 | $510,650 |
| Less: | | | | | | |
| Cost of goods sold | 391,254 | 440,304 | 333,107 | 320,074 | 370,285 | 405,271 |
| Selling expense | 21,200 | 15,670 | 15,500 | 13,260 | 18,386 | 21,430 |
| Administrative expense | 20,250 | 20,250 | 20,250 | 20,250 | 20,250 | 20,250 |
| Total expense | 432,704 | 476,224 | 368,857 | 353,584 | 408,921 | 446,951 |
| Income from operations | $ 67,556 | ($127,964) | ($ 8,607) | ($ 50,899) | $ 25,729 | $ 63,699 |
| **2004** | **January** | **February** | **March** | **April** | **May** | **June** |
| Sales | $446,252 | $235,362 | $290,370 | $215,265 | $277,165 | $315,441 |
| Less: | | | | | | |
| Cost of goods sold | 394,560 | 310,478 | 329,585 | 299,840 | 326,598 | 342,512 |
| Selling expense | 19,300 | 10,864 | 13,065 | 10,061 | 12,537 | 14,068 |
| Administrative expense | 22,250 | 23,465 | 23,860 | 24,600 | 23,695 | 24,740 |
| Total expense | 436,110 | 344,807 | 366,510 | 334,501 | 362,830 | 381,320 |
| Income from operations | $ 10,142 | ($109,445) | ($ 76,140) | ($119,236) | ($ 85,665) | ($ 65,879) |

2. Rent relates to the training center in Kirkland, which is not part of Mayfield's main campus that is located in Bellevue, Washington.

3. Advertising costs relate to the cost of monthly advertisements in trade journals such as *TechWorker* and *Inventory Management*. These ads provide information on upcoming training sessions.

4. Operating manuals are provided to each participant.

5. Postage, envelopes, and paper costs relate, primarily, to billing companies for employees who participate in classes. This cost varies with the number of participants.

6. Central charges are assigned to each group at Mayfield Software based on actual sales. The allocation relates to costs incurred for the benefit of the company as a whole including salaries of the CEO and company president, legal costs, cost related to the company's central office building, brand advertising, etc. The charge is 15 percent of revenue.

### Required

a. As indicated, the training group suffered a loss in 2004. Thus, unbeknownst to Marie, management of Mayfield is considering shutting the training center down. Given the results of 2004, what would be the effect on Mayfield Software's total company profit in 2005 if the training center is closed at the start of the year?

b. Given the current room configuration and approach to allocation of central charges (15 percent of revenue), calculate the number of classes that must be offered (with an average enrollment of 16 students) for Marie's group to break even on the Report of Operating Results.

c. Recalculate your answer to Part b assuming Marie can lower the amount paid to instructors to $2,000 per class? Should Marie seriously pursue this option?

d. Mayfield Software is releasing version 4.0 of "CustomerTrack" in 2005. Marie believes that this will create a demand for 30 additional day-long classes with an average enrollment of 16 students per class.

What effect will this have on "group profit" on Marie's Report of Operating Results? Assume instructors will be paid $3,000 per class.

## 4-4 KROG'S METALFAB, INC.

John Krog is President, Chairman of the Board, Production Supervisor, and majority shareholder of Krog's Metalfab, Inc. He formed the company in 1991 to manufacture custom-built aluminum storm windows for sale to contractors in the greater Chicago area. Since that time the company has experienced tremendous growth and currently operates two plants: one in Chicago, the main production facility, and a smaller plant in Moline, Illinois. The company now produces a wide variety of metal windows, framing materials, ladders, and other products related to the construction industry. Recently, the company developed a new line of

| July | August | September | October | November | December | Total |
|---|---|---|---|---|---|---|
| $560,625 | $602,210 | $420,210 | $330,025 | $329,009 | $380,260 | $5,079,094 |
| | | | | | | |
| 421,256 | 439,890 | 369,555 | 331,252 | 332,125 | 353,125 | 4,507,498 |
| 23,550 | 24,980 | 17,753 | 14,340 | 14,258 | 16,341 | 216,668 |
| 20,250 | 20,250 | 20,250 | 20,250 | 20,250 | 20,250 | 243,000 |
| 465,056 | 485,120 | 407,558 | 365,842 | 366,633 | 389,716 | 4,967,166 |
| $ 95,569 | $117,090 | $ 12,652 | ($ 35,817) | ($ 37,624) | ($ 9,456) | $ 111,928 |

| July | August | September | October | November | December | Total |
|---|---|---|---|---|---|---|
| $356,662 | $452,245 | $362,772 | $314,427 | $263,273 | $316,265 | $3,845,499 |
| | | | | | | |
| 356,880 | 394,570 | 361,258 | 339,652 | 319,586 | 342,500 | 4,118,019 |
| 15,716 | 19,540 | 15,961 | 14,027 | 11,981 | 14,101 | 171,221 |
| 23,695 | 23,472 | 23,620 | 22,741 | 22,659 | 22,940 | 281,737 |
| 396,291 | 437,582 | 400,839 | 376,420 | 354,226 | 379,541 | 4,570,977 |
| ($ 39,629) | $ 14,663 | ($ 38,067) | ($ 61,993) | ($ 90,953) | ($ 63,276) | ($ 725,478) |

bronze-finished storm windows and initial buyer reaction has been quite favorable. The company's future seemed bright but on January 3, 2004, a light fixture overheated causing a fire that virtually destroyed the entire Chicago plant. Three days later, Krog had moved 50 percent of his Chicago workforce to the Moline plant. Workers were housed in hotels, paid overtime wages, and provided with bus transportation home on weekends. Still, the company could not meet delivery schedules because of reduced operating capacity, and total business began to decline. At the end of 2004, Krog felt that the worst was over. A new plant had been leased in Chicago and the company was almost back to normal.

Finally, Krog could turn his attention to a matter of considerable importance: settlement with the insurance company. The company's policy stipulated that the building and equipment loss be calculated at replacement cost. This settlement had been fairly straightforward and the proceeds had aided the rapid rebuilding of the company. A valued feature of the insurance policy was "lost profit" coverage. This coverage was to "compensate the company for profits lost due to reduced operating capacity related to fire or flood damage." The period of "lost profit" was limited to 12 months. Interpreting the exact nature of this coverage proved to be difficult. The insurance company agreed to reimburse Krog for the overtime premium, transportation, and housing costs related to operating out of the Moline plant. These expenses obviously minimized the damages related to the 12 months of lost or reduced profits. But, was the company entitled to any additional compensation?

Krog got out the latest edition of *Construction Today*. According to this respected trade journal, sales of products similar to products produced by Krog's Metalfab had increased by 7 percent during 2004. Krog felt that were it not for the fire, his company could also have increased sales by this percentage.

Income statement information is available for 2003 (the year prior to the fire) and 2004 (the year during which the company sustained "lost profit"). The expenses in 2004 include excess operating costs of $240,000. Krog has documentation supporting these items, which include overtime costs, hotel costs, meals, and such related to operating out of Moline. The insurance company is quite willing to pay for these costs since they reduced potential lost profit.

The chief accountant at Krog, Peter Newell, has estimated lost profit to be only $34,961. Thus, he does not feel that it's worthwhile spending a lot of company resources trying to collect more than the $240,000. Peter arrived at his calculation as follows.

| | |
|---|---|
| Sales in 2003 | $5,079,094 |
| Predicted sales in 2004 assuming a 7% increase | $5,434,630 |
| Actual sales in 2004 | 3,845,499 |
| (A) Lost sales | 1,589,131 |
| (B) Profit in 2003 as a percent of 2003 sales ($111,928 ÷ 5,079,094) | .0220 |
| Lost profit (A × B) | $   34,961 |

**Table 1   Revenue and cost data, Seattle Espresso**

| | January | February | March | April | May | June |
|---|---|---|---|---|---|---|
| Number of transactions | 10,800 | 10,044 | 10,080 | 8,700 | 7,200 | 5,568 |
| Hours of business | 360 | 324 | 360 | 348 | 360 | 348 |
| Avg. trans. per hour | 30 | 31 | 28 | 25 | 20 | 16 |
| Revenue | 43,200 | 40,176 | 40,320 | 34,800 | 28,800 | 22,272 |
| Costs | | | | | | |
| Cost of goods sold | 17,280 | 16,070 | 16,128 | 13,920 | 11,520 | 8,909 |
| Labor | 2,520 | 2,268 | 2,520 | 2,436 | 2,520 | 2,436 |
| Utilities | 400 | 450 | 325 | 300 | 280 | 275 |
| Depreciation | 2,000 | 2,000 | 2,000 | 2,000 | 2,000 | 2,000 |
| Rent | 700 | 700 | 700 | 700 | 700 | 700 |
| Other | 250 | 265 | 280 | 225 | 240 | 220 |
| Total cost | 23,150 | 21,753 | 21,953 | 19,581 | 17,260 | 14,540 |
| Avg. cost per transactions | 2.14 | 2.17 | 2.18 | 2.25 | 2.40 | 2.61 |

**Required**

a. Mr. Krog is not convinced by Peter's analysis and has turned to you, an outside consultant, to provide a preliminary estimate of lost profit. Using the limited information contained in the financial statements for 2003 and 2004, estimate lost profit. (Hint: You can proceed as follows.)

**Step 1.** Determine the level of fixed and variable costs in 2003 as a function of sales. You can use account analysis, the high-low method, or regression if you are familiar with that technique.

**Step 2.** Predict what sales would have been in 2004 if there was no fire. Using this level of sales and the fixed and variable cost information from step 1, estimate what profit would have been in 2004.

**Step 3.** The difference between actual profit in 2004 and the amount estimated in step 2 is lost profit.

b. Based on your preliminary analysis, do you recommend that Mr. Krog aggressively pursue a substantial claim for lost profit?

c. What is the fundamental flaw in Peter Newell's analysis?

# 4-5 SEATTLE ESPRESSO, INC.

Seattle Espresso Inc. operates 25 espresso bars in West Coast hotels. The bars are typically staffed by one person and, historically, have been quite profitable. In recent months, however, sales have fallen sharply because of increased competition. For example, at the start of the year, the location in the Carlton Hotel had an average of 30 transactions per hour. In the most recent month, there were only 15 transactions per hour. The decline appears to be due to customer reluctance to wait in line at Seattle Espresso since the opening, in late February, of two nearby competing espresso bars.

At a recent staff meeting, Angelo Steffano, founder and CEO of Seattle Espresso, made the following suggestion. "How about adding another staff person to the Carlton bar? Then our customers won't be waiting in line and we can recover our lost business. I'd be surprised if sales didn't get back to 30 transactions per hour if we had two staffers working the bar." As the meeting ended, the company controller, Sandra Costello, volunteered to analyze the financial impact of increasing staffing at the Carlton Hotel location.

**Required**

Do you recommend staffing the Carlton Hotel location with two people? Using the revenue and cost data in Table 1, calculate the effect on profit of implementing Steffano's suggestion.

| July | August | September | October | November | December |
|---|---|---|---|---|---|
| 5,400 | 5,040 | 5,568 | 5,760 | 5,220 | 5,400 |
| 360 | 360 | 348 | 360 | 348 | 360 |
| 15 | 14 | 16 | 16 | 15 | 15 |
| 21,600 | 20,160 | 22,272 | 23,040 | 20,880 | 21,600 |
| 8,640 | 8,064 | 8,909 | 9,216 | 8,352 | 8,640 |
| 2,520 | 2,520 | 2,436 | 2,520 | 2,436 | 2,520 |
| 290 | 340 | 325 | 330 | 370 | 390 |
| 2,000 | 2,000 | 2,000 | 2,000 | 2,000 | 2,000 |
| 700 | 700 | 700 | 700 | 700 | 700 |
| 230 | 245 | 260 | 210 | 270 | 240 |
| 14,380 | 13,869 | 14,630 | 14,976 | 14,128 | 14,490 |
| 2.66 | 2.75 | 2.63 | 2.60 | 2.71 | 2.68 |

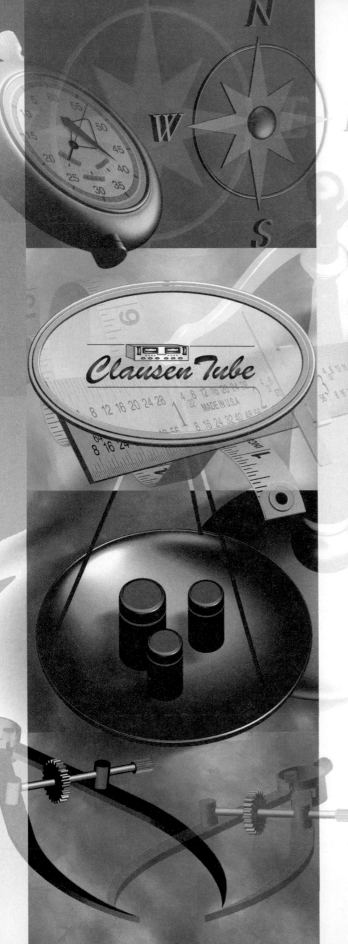

# chapter 5

## LEARNING OBJECTIVES

**1** Explain the difference between full (absorption) and variable costing.

**2** Prepare an income statement using variable costing.

**3** Discuss the effect of production on full and variable costing income.

**4** Explain the impact of JIT (just-in-time) on the difference between full and variable costing income.

**5** Discuss the benefits of variable costing for internal reporting purposes.

# VARIABLE COSTING

In 2006, the all-tube amplifier produced by ClausenTube received rave reviews and the company was able to sell all 5,000 units it produced, generating company profit of $3,500,000. Based on these results, the company increased production to 6,000 units in the subsequent year, but was only able to sell 4,800 units. This performance, however, was considered quite good given that the economy had slipped in the third and fourth quarters.

In early January of 2008, Robert Clausen, company president and founder, reviewed financial performance for 2007. Surprisingly, profit had actually increased slightly to $3,528,000. Robert was confused and wasted no time calling Leslie Anders, the company controller. "What's

going on?" Robert asked in a voice that hinted at his irritation. "Sales are down, the production process and prices haven't changed and yet profit is up! How confident are you in the income numbers? There must be a significant error somewhere."

"I know this result looks bizarre," Leslie replied. "But it's not due to an error in the accounting department. It's due to the fact that our financial statements are prepared using what's called full, or absorption, costing. That's the method most companies use for external reporting to shareholders and creditors. If your schedule permits, let's meet this afternoon and I'll show you an analysis that explains what happened. There's a method called variable costing that we could use for internal reporting purposes which wouldn't produce such puzzling results. Maybe we should consider adopting it. I really think it can help us do a better job managing the business."

In this chapter, we will discuss the differences between full costing and variable costing and gain an understanding of why profit is up at ClausenTube even though sales are down. We will also see how a variable costing income statement can support accurate planning and good decision making; two activities that are jeopardized if managers rely on full cost information.

Explain the difference between full (absorption) and variable costing.

# FULL (ABSORPTION) AND VARIABLE COSTING

Income statements of manufacturing firms prepared for *external* purposes use full costing (also called **absorption costing**). In **full costing**, inventory costs include direct material, direct labor, and all manufacturing overhead. Direct material and direct labor are generally variable costs, but manufacturing overhead includes both variable and fixed cost elements. Thus, fixed and variable costs are commingled, or combined, and it is very difficult to untangle the costs to perform "what if" analysis that requires separating fixed and variable costs. An alternative to full costing for internal reporting purposes is variable costing. In **variable costing**, only variable production costs are included in inventory costs. All fixed production costs are treated as period costs and expensed in the period incurred.

As shown in Illustration 5-1, the only difference between the two methods is their treatment of fixed manufacturing overhead. Under the full costing method, these costs are included in inventory. They enter into the determination of expense only when the inventory is sold. Under the variable costing method, fixed manufacturing costs enter into the determination of expense in the same way as other, nonmanufacturing period costs. Consider depreciation, which usually is a fixed cost component of manufacturing overhead. Under full costing, some portion of depreciation for the period remains in ending inventory when not all of the items produced are sold. Under the variable costing method, however, the total amount of depreciation is treated as an expense of the period.

Prepare an income statement using variable costing.

## VARIABLE COSTING INCOME STATEMENT

If variable costing is used, an income statement can be prepared that classifies all expenses in terms of their cost behavior—either fixed or variable. With the variable expenses separated from the fixed expenses, a contribution margin can be presented. The contribution margin information will allow readers of the income statement to make reasonable estimates of how much profit will change with a change in sales.

**Illustration 5-1**
Comparison of full
and variable costing

**Full Costing**

Product Costs

| Direct Labor | Direct Material | Variable Manufacturing Overhead | Fixed Manufacturing Overhead |

Period Costs

| Selling Costs | Administrative Costs |

Inventory —— Cost of Goods Sold ——→ Expense

**Variable Costing**

Product Costs

| Direct Labor | Direct Material | Variable Manufacturing Overhead |

Period Costs

| Fixed Manufacturing Overhead | Selling Costs | Administrative Costs |

Inventory —— Variable Cost of Goods Sold ——→ Expense

A comparison of a variable costing income statement and an income statement typical for a manufacturing firm using full costing is presented in Illustration 5-2. Suppose sales of Ciello Dress Manufacturing Company are expected to increase by $10,000,000. What is the expected increase in profit? Using the variable costing income statement, we can easily calculate the contribution margin ratio as the contribution margin divided by sales, which equals 65 percent. If sales increase by $10,000,000, profit is estimated to increase by $6,500,000.

**Illustration 5-2**
Comparison of income statements prepared using variable and full costing

---

### Income Statement Prepared Using Variable Costing

**Ciello Dress Manufacturing Company**
**Income Statement**
**For the Period Ending December 31, 2006**

**In Thousands**

| | | |
|---|---:|---:|
| Sales | | $100,000 |
| Less: Variable costs | | |
| Variable cost of goods sold | $20,000 | |
| Variable selling expense | 10,000 | |
| Variable administrative expense | 5,000 | 35,000 |
| Contribution margin | | 65,000 |
| Less: Fixed costs | | |
| Fixed manufacturing expense | 10,000 | |
| Fixed selling expense | 8,000 | |
| Fixed administrative expense | 7,000 | 25,000 |
| Net income | | $ 40,000 |

### Income Statement Prepared Using Full Costing

**Ciello Dress Manufacturing Company**
**Income Statement**
**For the Period Ended December 31, 2006**

**In Thousands**

| | | |
|---|---:|---:|
| Sales | | $100,000 |
| Less: Cost of goods sold | | 30,000 |
| Gross margin | | 70,000 |
| Less: Selling and administrative expense | | |
| Selling expense | $18,000 | |
| Administrative expense | 12,000 | 30,000 |
| Net income | | $ 40,000 |

---

**LEARNING OBJECTIVE 3**

Discuss the effect of production on full and variable costing income.

# EFFECTS OF PRODUCTION ON INCOME FOR FULL VERSUS VARIABLE COSTING: The ClausenTube Example

To examine in detail the differences between full and variable costing, let's consider the case of ClausenTube presented at the start of the chapter. The amplifiers produced by the company sell for $2,000 per unit. The variable production costs of each unit includes the following: direct material (various tubes and other components), $600; direct labor, $225; and variable manufacturing overhead, $75. In addition, $1,200,000 of fixed manufacturing overhead is incurred each year. Selling expense is composed of $40 per unit of variable expense and $100,000 of fixed expense. Administrative expenses are all fixed and equal to $500,000.

| | | |
|---|---:|---:|
| Selling price per unit | | $2,000 |
| Variable production costs per unit: | | |
|    Direct material | $600 | |
|    Direct labor | 225 | |
|    Variable overhead | 75 | 900 |
| Variable selling expense per unit | | 40 |
| Contribution margin per unit | | $1,060 |
| Fixed manufacturing overhead per year | | $1,200,000 |
| Fixed selling expense | | $100,000 |
| Fixed administrative expense | | $500,000 |

## QUANTITY PRODUCED EQUALS QUANTITY SOLD

In 2006, there is no beginning inventory of finished goods, 5,000 units are produced, and 5,000 units are sold. Illustration 5-3 provides a comparison of full costing and variable costing income statements for this situation. The full cost of production is $5,700,000. This includes $4,500,000 of variable production cost ($900 × 5,000 units) and $1,200,000 of fixed manufacturing overhead. With 5,000 units produced, this results in a unit cost of $1,140.

**Illustration 5-3**
Full versus variable costing
when units produced
equal units sold

**ClausenTube**
**Income Statements**
**For the Year Ended December 31, 2006**

**Full Costing**

| | | |
|---|---:|---:|
| Sales ($2,000 × 5,000 units) | | $10,000,000 |
| Cost of goods sold ($1,140 × 5,000 units) | | 5,700,000 |
| Gross margin | | 4,300,000 |
| Less selling and administrative expense: | | |
|   Selling expense | $ 300,000 | |
|   Administrative expense | 500,000 | 800,000 |
| Net income | | $ 3,500,000 |

Notes: Units produced and sold both equal 5,000
Selling expense = $100,000 + ($40 × 5,000 units).

**Variable Costing**

| | | |
|---|---:|---:|
| Sales ($2,000 × 5,000 units) | | $10,000,000 |
| Less variable costs: | | |
|   Variable cost of goods sold ($900 × 5,000 units) | $4,500,000 | |
|   Variable selling costs ($40 × 5,000) | 200,000 | 4,700,000 |
| Contribution margin | | 5,300,000 |
| Less fixed costs: | | |
|   Fixed production costs | 1,200,000 | |
|   Fixed selling costs | 100,000 | |
|   Fixed administrative costs | 500,000 | 1,800,000 |
| Net income | | $ 3,500,000 |

Note: Units produced and sold both equal 5,000.

Unit cost under full costing = Total production cost ÷ Number of units produced

= $5,700,000 ÷ 5,000

= $1,140 per unit

Because 5,000 units are sold, cost of goods sold is $5,700,000.

Selling expense is equal to $100,000 of fixed selling expense plus $40 per unit of variable selling expense for a total of $300,000.

| | |
|---|---|
| Variable selling expense ($40 × 5,000 units) | $200,000 |
| Fixed selling expense | 100,000 |
| Total selling expense | $300,000 |

Taking into account fixed administrative expense of $500,000, net income is $3,500,000.

Now let's consider the variable costing income statement in Illustration 5-3. The variable cost of production is only $900 per unit and variable selling expense is $40 per unit. With 5,000 units sold, variable expenses are $4,700,000. Thus, as indicated in the illustration, the contribution margin is $5,300,000. With fixed production cost of $1,200,000, fixed selling expense of $100,000 and fixed administrative expense of $500,000, net income is equal to $3,500,000, which is the same as net income calculated using full costing.

As we've just seen, when the quantity produced equals the quantity sold, there is no difference between net income calculated using full, versus variable, costing. Since all units produced are sold, no fixed cost ends up in ending inventory. Thus, the only difference between the two methods in this situation is that variable costing breaks out total costs into both fixed and variable costs and provides a contribution margin. That, however, is not a trivial difference since the contribution margin can be very helpful in planning and decision making. Suppose, for example, that ClausenTube is considering an advertising campaign that will cost $100,000 and is expected to increase sales by $200,000. What will be the impact on income (a planning question) and should the company undertake the marketing plan (a decision question)?

**Decision Making/ Incremental Analysis**

Using the variable costing income statement, we can easily calculate the contribution margin ratio to be 0.53:

$$\frac{\text{Contribution margin}}{\text{Sales}} = \frac{\$5,300,000}{\$10,000,000} = 0.53$$

With this information, we can estimate that if sales increase by $200,000, profit will increase by $6,000.

| | |
|---|---|
| Increase in sales | $200,000 |
| Contribution margin ratio | × 0.53 |
| Increase in contribution margin | 106,000 |
| Less increased marketing costs | 100,000 |
| Increase in profit | $ 6,000 |

Given that the impact on profit is positive, deciding to undertake the marketing plan is appropriate and ClausenTube can update its financial plans accordingly.

Now, suppose that the variable costing income statement is not available and ClausenTube managers rely on the information in the full costing income statement. How will they calculate the impact of the marketing plan? There are two assumptions they might make—both of which are wrong! First, they might assume that the cost of goods sold is entirely variable and, further, is the only variable cost. In this case, they will estimate that profit will increase by $0.43 for every dollar of sales which, as we know, is too low.

$$\frac{\text{Gross margin}}{\text{Sales}} = \frac{\$4,300,000}{\$10,000,000} = 0.43$$

Second, they might assume that *all* costs are variable in which case net income is equivalent to the contribution margin. In this case, they will estimate that profit will increase by only $0.35 for every dollar of sales which is also too low.

$$\frac{\text{Net income}}{\text{Sales}} = \frac{\$3,500,000}{\$10,000,000} = 0.35$$

The point is that having a variable costing income statement can be very useful for planning and decision making. Not having one may lead managers to make assumptions that are incorrect, leading to poor plans and poor decisions.

## QUANTITY PRODUCED IS GREATER THAN QUANTITY SOLD

In the previous section, we saw that when the quantity produced is equal to the quantity sold, there is no difference between income computed using full costing or using variable costing. Such is not the case if the quantity produced is *greater* than the quantity sold. In this case, income will be greater using full costing as opposed to variable costing. Let's see why this is the case.

Recall that in 2007, ClausenTube increased production to 6,000 units but only sold 4,800 due to a weakening economy. Illustration 5-4 provides a comparison of full costing and variable costing income statements for this situation. The full cost of production is $6,600,000. This includes $5,400,000 of variable production cost ($900 × 6,000 units) and $1,200,000 of fixed manufacturing overhead. With 6,000 units produced, this results in a unit cost of $1,100.

### Any Questions?

**Q** If variable costing is so great for internal reporting purposes, why isn't it used for external reporting purposes? Don't external users want useful information?

**A** Generally accepted accounting principles (GAAP) imply that variable costing is not acceptable for external reporting purposes. Since it's not allowed, it isn't used! But that leads one to wonder why this is the case. Shouldn't GAAP be formulated to provide useful information? Perhaps a better answer is that company managers may be concerned that variable cost information will prove helpful to competitors who, with the variable cost information, will have better insight into their company's cost structure.

**Illustration 5-4**
Full versus variable costing when units produced are greater than units sold

**ClausenTube**
**Income Statements**
**For the Year Ended December 31, 2007**

**Full Costing**

| | | |
|---|---:|---:|
| Sales ($2,000 × 4,800 units) | | $9,600,000 |
| Cost of goods sold ($1,100 × 4,800 units) | | 5,280,000 |
| Gross margin | | 4,320,000 |
| Less selling and administrative expense: | | |
|   Selling expense | $ 292,000 | |
|   Administrative expense | 500,000 | 792,000 |
| Net income | | $3,528,000 |

Notes: 6,000 units produced and 4,800 units sold
Selling expense = $100,000 + ($40 × 4,800 units).

**Variable Costing**

| | | |
|---|---:|---:|
| Sales ($2,000 × 4,800 units) | | $9,600,000 |
| Less variable costs: | | |
|   Variable cost of goods sold ($900 × 4,800 units) | $4,320,000 | |
|   Variable selling costs ($40 × 4,800) | 192,000 | 4,512,000 |
| Contribution margin | | 5,088,000 |
| Less fixed costs: | | |
|   Fixed production costs | 1,200,000 | |
|   Fixed selling costs | 100,000 | |
|   Fixed administrative costs | 500,000 | 1,800,000 |
| Net income | | $3,288,000 |

Note: 6,000 units produced and 4,800 units sold.

Unit cost under full costing = Total production cost ÷ Number of units produced

$$= \$6,600,000 \div 6,000$$

$$= \$1,100 \text{ per unit}$$

In the previous year, the unit cost was $1,140. Unit costs have decreased because production has increased, spreading fixed costs out over more units. Because 4,800 units are sold, cost of goods sold is $5,280,000. Net income amounts to $3,528,000.

Now let's consider the variable costing income statement in Illustration 5-4. The variable cost of production is only $900 per unit and variable selling costs are $40 per unit. With 4,800 units sold, variable expenses are $4,512,000. Thus, as indicated in the illustration, the contribution margin is $5,088,000. With fixed production costs of $1,200,000, fixed selling costs of $100,000 and fixed administrative costs of $500,000, net income is equal to $3,288,000, which is $240,000 less than the income computed using full costing.

Let's see why income is higher using full costing. Recall that the difference between full and variable costing is that under full costing, inventory cost includes fixed manufacturing overhead whereas under variable costing, fixed manufacturing overhead is expensed as a period cost. Illustration 5-5 presents a

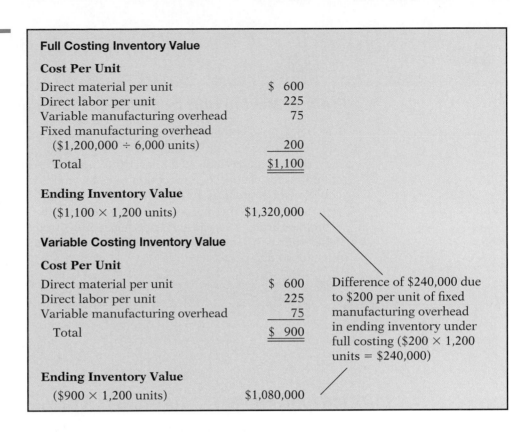

**Full Costing Inventory Value**

**Cost Per Unit**

| | |
|---|---|
| Direct material per unit | $ 600 |
| Direct labor per unit | 225 |
| Variable manufacturing overhead | 75 |
| Fixed manufacturing overhead ($1,200,000 ÷ 6,000 units) | 200 |
| Total | $1,100 |

**Ending Inventory Value**

($1,100 × 1,200 units)    $1,320,000

**Variable Costing Inventory Value**

**Cost Per Unit**

| | |
|---|---|
| Direct material per unit | $ 600 |
| Direct labor per unit | 225 |
| Variable manufacturing overhead | 75 |
| Total | $ 900 |

**Ending Inventory Value**

($900 × 1,200 units)    $1,080,000

Difference of $240,000 due to $200 per unit of fixed manufacturing overhead in ending inventory under full costing ($200 × 1,200 units = $240,000)

comparison. Note that the $240,000 difference in ending inventory values completely accounts for the difference in income under the two methods.

## QUANTITY PRODUCED IS LESS THAN QUANTITY SOLD

We have just seen that if the quantity produced equals the quantity sold, then full and variable costing yield the same reported income. If the quantity produced is greater than the quantity sold, full costing yields a higher income, because some fixed manufacturing overhead is in ending inventory under full costing while the entire amount is treated as a period expense under variable costing. Now, what is the case if the quantity produced is less than the quantity sold? To sell more than produced, a company must have some beginning inventory. The recorded value of that beginning inventory will be greater with full costing since full costing includes fixed manufacturing overhead and variable costing does not. Thus, when the beginning inventory is charged to cost of goods sold, the charge will be higher under full costing. The result—income is lower under full costing when the quantity produced is less than the quantity sold.

To summarize, here are the comparative effects of production on income for the two methods:

| Condition | Result |
|---|---|
| Units produced equal units sold | No difference in income |
| Units produced exceed units sold | Full costing yields higher income |
| Units produced are less than units sold | Variable costing yields higher income |

### *Profit at Maytag Hurt by Reduced Production*

In 2002, Maytag announced that production was being reduced since the company had excess inventory and, therefore, didn't need to produce as much. Further, the company indicated that third quarter profit would be hurt by the reduction. It's clear why a reduction in *sales* would hurt profit, but why would a reduction in *production* hurt profit? The reason is that Maytag uses full costing for financial reporting purposes. With a reduction in production, fixed manufacturing overhead is spread out over fewer units and unit cost increases. With a higher unit cost, cost of goods sold will be high and profit low when the costly units are sold.

*Sources:* The *New York Times*, August 13, 2002, Section C, p. 4. www.maytagcorp.com .

## EXPLAINING WHAT HAPPENED AT ClausenTube

Recall the scenario at the start of the chapter. Robert Clausen had just called his controller and asked her to explain why profit increased even though the company sold fewer units in 2007 compared to 2006 and had not changed its price or its production processes. Hopefully, the answer is now apparent. In 2007, the company produced a lot more units than it sold. The high level of production reduced cost per unit because fixed manufacturing overhead was spread out over more units. The low unit cost led to a low cost of goods sold value but the company ended up with a substantial ending inventory balance.

If the company had been using variable costing, Robert would have seen profit decline just as he expected. Note that per Illustration 5-3, income under variable costing in 2006 when sales were 5,000 units was $3,500,000. Per Illustration 5-4, income under variable costing in 2007 when sales were only 4,800 units was only $3,288,000. That's because variable costing does not allow fixed manufacturing overhead to be "buried" in ending inventory. Rather, with variable costing, the entire amount is treated as a period expense.

Explain the impact of JIT on the difference between full and variable costing income.

## IMPACT OF JIT ON THE INCOME EFFECTS OF FULL VERSUS VARIABLE COSTING

As discussed in Chapter 2, many companies have adopted just-in-time (JIT) inventory management systems. And companies that use JIT may have very low inventory levels since they don't produce until they are ready to sell their products. The result is that the units they produce are approximately equal to the units they sell and, thus, the difference between variable costing income and full costing income is likely to be very small for companies that use JIT.

# BENEFITS OF VARIABLE COSTING FOR INTERNAL REPORTING

Discuss the benefits of variable costing for internal reporting purposes.

There are two primary benefits associated with using variable costing for internal reporting purposes. Both are discussed in this section.

### VARIABLE COSTING FACILITATES C-V-P ANALYSIS

Variable costing separates fixed and variable costs, a necessary step in performing cost-volume-profit (C-V-P) analysis and, relatedly, planning and decision making. We discussed this point earlier, but it's worth repeating. Managers simply can't estimate accurately the impact of changes in volume on cost and profit unless they know which costs are fixed and which costs are variable. Consider the full costing income statement in Illustration 5-4 and ask yourself "What would be the impact on profit of a $100,000 increase in sales?" Unfortunately, the question cannot be answered with any assurance using the full cost information. We don't know which costs are fixed and which are variable so we don't know which ones will increase with the increase in sales.

Now, consider the variable costing income statement. We can easily see that the contribution margin ratio is .53 (i.e., $5,088,000 ÷ $9,600,000). Thus, we can easily estimate a $53,000 increase in profit with a $100,000 increase in sales.

### VARIABLE COSTING LIMITS MANAGEMENT OF EARNINGS WITH PRODUCTION VOLUME

Another reason why variable costing may be preferred for internal purposes is that it does not allow managers to artificially inflate profit by producing more units than they can sell. Suppose a manager expects sales to be 1,000 units. The selling price is $100 per unit, variable production costs are $50 per unit, and fixed production costs are $45,000. If the manager produced 1,000 units, profit would be equal to $5,000 (i.e., 1,000 × ($100 − $50) − $45,000) under both the full costing method and the variable costing method. The manager may realize, however, that if the full costing method is used, part of the fixed costs can be assigned to ending inventory, thereby transferring the expense to a future period. Thus, if the manager produces 2,000 units, profit will be $22,500 higher because half of the fixed costs will be included in the 1,000 units remaining in ending inventory. Of course, this is a short run strategy, because eventually the inventory buildup will be noticed. However, the manager may hope to be working for a different company by that time with a great "track record" as a manager at the former company. Note that the strategy of producing more than you can sell will not increase income under the variable costing method, because under that method, none of the fixed costs can be included in ending inventory.

## MAKING BUSINESS DECISIONS

A variable costing income statement facilitates decision making by breaking out the total contribution margin. If we divide the contribution margin by sales, we have the contribution margin ratio, and we can use it to analyze the impact of changes in sales on profit.

Since many decisions affect sales, being able to estimate the impact of changes in sales on profit greatly facilitates decision making.

## KNOWLEDGE AND SKILLS (K/S) CHECKLIST

*Knowledge and skills are needed to make good business decisions. Check off the knowledge and skills you've acquired from reading this chapter.*

❑ K/S 1. You have an expanded business vocabulary (see key terms).

❑ K/S 2. You can prepare a variable costing income statement.

❑ K/S 3. You can explain why the difference between income calculated using full costing versus variable costing depends on the quantity produced versus the quantity sold.

❑ K/S 4. You can use information in a variable costing income statement to calculate a contribution margin ratio and perform cost-volume-profit analysis.

# SUMMARY OF LEARNING OBJECTIVES

**1** *Explain the difference between full (absorption) and variable costing.* In full costing, product cost includes direct material, direct labor, and variable and fixed manufacturing overhead. In variable costing, fixed manufacturing overhead is not included in product cost. Rather, it is treated as a period expense.

**2** *Prepare an income statement using variable costing.* In a variable costing income statement, variable and fixed costs are segregated. All variable expenses are deducted from sales to yield a contribution margin. Then fixed expenses are deducted from the contribution margin to yield net income.

**3** *Discuss the effect of production on full and variable costing income.* If the quantity produced equals the quantity sold, there is no differ-

ence in income. If the quantity produced exceeds the quantity sold, full costing income is higher than variable costing income. If the quantity produced is less than the quantity sold, full costing income is less than variable costing income.

**4** *Explain the impact of JIT on the difference between full and variable costing income.* With a JIT system, there is often little difference between the quantity produced and the quantity sold. Thus, there is only a small difference between full and variable costing income.

**5** *Discuss the benefits of variable costing for internal reporting purposes.* Variable costing results in a contribution margin, which is useful in planning and decision making. Also, variable costing income cannot be managed up by producing more units than needed.

# REVIEW PROBLEM

Butler Manufacturing produces fireproof data storage containers that sell for $6,000 each. The company has the following cost structure:

| | |
|---|---|
| **Manufacturing costs:** | |
| Direct material per unit | $ 1,000 |
| Direct labor per unit | 2,000 |
| Variable manufacturing overhead per unit | 500 |
| Total variable manufacturing costs per unit | $ 3,500 |
| Fixed manufacturing overhead per year | $2,000,000 |
| **Selling costs:** | |
| Variable selling costs per dollar of sales | $ 0.10 |
| Fixed selling costs per year | $ 600,000 |
| **Administrative costs:** | |
| Fixed Administrative costs per year | $ 800,000 |

At the start of 2006, there were no beginning inventories. During 2006, the company produced and sold 2,000 units. During 2007, the company produced 2,500 units but still sold only 2,000 units.

**Required**
a. Calculate the full manufacturing cost per unit for 2006 and 2007.
b. Prepare full costing income statements for 2006 and 2007.
c. Calculate the variable manufacturing cost per unit for 2006 and 2007.
d. Prepare variable costing income statements for 2006 and 2007.
e. Reconcile the difference in net income for 2007 between the full costing and the variable costing approaches.

**Answer**

a. **Full manufacturing cost per unit in 2006**

| | |
|---|---:|
| Direct material per unit | $1,000 |
| Direct labor per unit | 2,000 |
| Variable manufacturing overhead per unit | 500 |
| Fixed manufacturing overhead per unit ($2,000,000 ÷ 2,000 units) | 1,000 |
| Total | $4,500 |

**Full manufacturing cost per unit in 2007**

| | |
|---|---:|
| Direct material per unit | $1,000 |
| Direct labor per unit | 2,000 |
| Variable manufacturing overhead per unit | 500 |
| Fixed manufacturing overhead per unit ($2,000,000 ÷ 2,500 units) | 800 |
| Total | $4,300 |

b. **Income for 2006 Using Full Costing**

| | | |
|---|---:|---:|
| Sales ($6,000 × 2,000 units) | | $12,000,000 |
| Cost of goods sold ($4,500 × 2,000 units) | | 9,000,000 |
| Gross margin | | 3,000,000 |
| Less selling and administrative expense: | | |
| Selling expense ($600,000 + .10 × $12,000,000) | $1,800,000 | |
| Administrative expense | 800,000 | 2,600,000 |
| Net income | | $    400,000 |

Note: Units produced and sold both equal 2,000.

**Income for 2007 Using Full Costing**

| | | |
|---|---:|---:|
| Sales ($6,000 × 2,000 units) | | $12,000,000 |
| Cost of goods sold ($4,300 × 2,000 units) | | 8,600,000 |
| Gross margin | | 3,400,000 |
| Less selling and administrative expense: | | |
| Selling expense ($600,000 + .10 × $12,000,000) | $1,800,000 | |
| Administrative expense | 800,000 | 2,600,000 |
| Net income | | $    800,000 |

Note: 2,500 units produced and 2,000 units sold

c. **Variable manufacturing cost per unit in 2006 and 2007**

| | | |
|---|---:|---:|
| Direct material per unit | $ | 1,000 |
| Direct labor per unit | | 2,000 |
| Variable manufacturing overhead per unit | | 500 |
| Total | $ | 3,500 |

d. **Income for 2006 and 2007 Using Variable Costing**

| | | |
|---|---:|---:|
| Sales ($6,000 × 2,000 units) | | $12,000,000 |
| Less variable costs: | | |
|   Variable cost of goods sold ($3,500 × 2,000 units) | $7,000,000 | |
|   Variable selling costs (.10 × $12,000,000) | 1,200,000 | 8,200,000 |
| Contribution margin | | 3,800,000 |
| Less fixed costs: | | |
|   Fixed production costs | 2,000,000 | |
|   Fixed selling costs | 600,000 | |
|   Fixed administrative costs | 800,000 | 3,400,000 |
| Net income | | $ 400,000 |

e. $800 of fixed manufacturing overhead per unit × 500 units in ending inventory = $400,000.

# KEY TERMS

Absorption costing (164)
Full costing (164)
Variable costing (164)

# SELF ASSESSMENT *(Answers Below)*

1. Full costing differs from variable costing in that:
   a. Full costing excludes selling costs from consideration.
   b. Full costing excludes administrative costs from consideration.
   c. Full costing includes variable manufacturing overhead in inventory.
   d. Full costing includes fixed manufacturing overhead in inventory.

2. If units produced exceed units sold:
   a. Full costing yields a higher income than variable costing.
   b. Full costing yields a lower income than variable costing.
   c. Full costing and variable costing yield the same income.

3. Use of a just-in-time inventory management system is likely to:
   a. Increase the difference between variable and full costing income.
   b. Decrease the difference between variable and full costing income.
   c. Have no effect on the difference between variable and full costing income.

4. A benefit of variable costing for internal reporting purposes is that it:
   a. Facilitates C-V-P analysis.
   b. Limits the ability to inflate income by producing more units than needed for current sales.
   c. Both a and b are correct.
   d. Neither a nor b is correct.

5. If units produced is less than units sold:
   a. Full costing yields a higher income than variable costing.
   b. Full costing yields a lower income than variable costing.
   c. Full costing and variable costing yield the same income.

*The following information applies to Questions 6–10.*

Ajax Manufacturing has the following cost structure:

| | |
|---|---:|
| Direct material | $10 |
| Direct labor | 20 |
| Variable manufacturing overhead | 5 |
|   Total variable manufacturing costs per unit | $35 |
| Fixed manufacturing overhead per year | $100,000 |
| Fixed selling and administrative expense per year | $200,000 |

**6.** Assume that Ajax produces 10,000 items and sells 8,000 items. In this case, the full costing value of ending inventory is:

a. $70,000.
b. $90,000.
c. $130,000.
d. $140,000.

**7.** Assume that Ajax produces 10,000 items and sells 8,000 items. In this case, the variable costing value of ending inventory is:

a. $70,000.
b. $90,000.
c. $130,000.
d. $140,000.

**8.** Assume that Ajax produces 10,000 items and sells 8,000 items. In this case, the full costing value of cost of goods sold is:

a. $360,000.
b. $350,000.
c. $300,000.
d. $280,000.

**9.** Assume that Ajax produces 10,000 items and sells 8,000 items. In this case, the variable cost of goods sold is:

a. $360,000.
b. $350,000.
c. $300,000.
d. $280,000.

**10.** Assume that Ajax produces 10,000 items and sells 8,000 items. The selling price of Ajax's product is $90 per unit. In this case, the contribution margin on the income statement prepared using variable costing is:

a. $350,000.
b. $440,000.
c. $550,000.
d. $700,000.

**Answers to Self Assessment**
**1.** d.   **2.** a.   **3.** b.   **4.** c   **5.** b   **6.** b   **7.** a.
**8.** a.   **9.** d.   **10.** b.

# INTERACTIVE LEARNING

Enhance and test your knowledge of Chapter 5 using the interactive CD.

**1.** Learning Objectives
**2.** Multiple Choice
**3.** Language of Business—Matching of Key Terms
**4.** Critical Thinking
**5.** Demonstration—Full versus variable costing
**6.** Case—*Vector Manufacturing*; Preparing a variable costing income statement

**Go to our dynamic Web site for more self-assessment, Web links, and additional information.**

# QUESTIONS

**1.** Explain the difference between variable costing and full costing.

**2.** Explain why income computed under full costing will exceed income computed under variable costing if production exceeds sales.

**3.** What are the benefits of variable costing for internal reporting purposes?

**4.** Why would the difference between income computed under full costing and income computed under variable costing be relatively small if a company used a JIT inventory management system?

**5.** Explain why the ending inventory balance (assuming it is not zero) computed under full costing will always be greater than the ending inventory balance computed under variable costing.

# EXERCISES

**EXERCISE 5-1. Group Assignment** A key idea in this book is that *Decision making relies on incremental analysis.*

**Required**
Explain how the use of variable costing can support appropriate decisions using incremental analysis.

**EXERCISE 5-2. Writing Assignment** In a normal year, Wilson Industries has $20,000,000 of fixed manufacturing costs and produces 50,000 units. In the current year, demand for its product has decreased and it appears that the company will only be able to sell 40,000 units. Senior managers are concerned, in part, because their bonuses are tied to reported profit. In light of this, they are considering keeping production at 50,000 units.

**Required**
Write a paragraph explaining why increasing production beyond the quantity needed for current sales will increase profit, and calculate the impact of producing 10,000 "extra" units. Is the managers' proposed action in the best interest of shareholders?

**EXERCISE 5-3. Internet Assignment** Search the Web using the term *variable costing*. You will find numerous sites where accounting professors discuss variable and full costing (also called absorption costing). Find a site that discusses the pros and cons of variable costing and compare the discussion to the treatment in the chapter.

**The Following Information Relates to Exercises 5-4–5-10.**
Xenoc, Inc. produces stereo speakers. The selling price per pair of speakers is $1,500. Costs involved in production are:

| | |
|---|---|
| Direct material | $100 |
| Direct labor | 150 |
| Variable manufacturing overhead | 50 |
| Total variable manufacturing costs per unit | $300 |
| Fixed manufacturing overhead per year | $600,000 |

In addition, the company has fixed selling and administrative costs:

| | |
|---|---|
| Fixed selling costs per year | $200,000 |
| Fixed administrative costs per year | $100,000 |

**EXERCISE 5-4.** During the year, Xenoc produces 1,000 pairs of speakers and sells 900 pairs. What is the value of ending inventory using full costing?

**EXERCISE 5-5.** During the year, Xenoc produces 1,000 pairs of speakers and sells 900 pairs. What is the value of ending inventory using variable costing?

**EXERCISE 5-6.** During the year, Xenoc produces 1,000 pairs of speakers and sells 900 pairs. What is cost of goods sold using full costing?

**EXERCISE 5-7.** During the year, Xenoc produces 1,000 pairs of speakers and sells 900 pairs. What is variable cost of goods sold?

**EXERCISE 5-8.** During the year, Xenoc produces 1,000 pairs of speakers and sells 900 pairs. What is net income using full costing?

**EXERCISE 5-9.** During the year, Xenoc produces 1,000 pairs of speakers and sells 900 pairs. What is net income using variable costing?

**EXERCISE 5-10.** During the year, Xenoc produces 1,000 pairs of speakers and sells 900 pairs. How much fixed manufacturing overhead is in ending inventory under full costing? Compare this amount to the difference in the net incomes calculated in Exercises 8 and 9.

# PROBLEMS

**PROBLEM 5-1. Variable and Full Costing: Sales Constant but Production Fluctuates**   Spencer Electronics produces a wireless home lighting device that allows consumers to turn on home lights from their cars and light a safe path into and through their homes. Information on the first three years of business is as follows:

|  | 2006 | 2007 | 2008 | Total |
|---|---|---|---|---|
| Units sold | 10,000 | 10,000 | 10,000 | 30,000 |
| Units produced | 10,000 | 12,000 | 8,000 | 30,000 |
| Fixed production costs | $600,000 | $600,000 | $600,000 | |
| Variable production costs per unit | $    100 | $    100 | $    100 | |
| Selling price per unit | $    200 | $    200 | $    200 | |
| Fixed selling and administrative expense | $200,000 | $200,000 | $200,000 | |

*Required*

a. Calculate profit and the value of ending inventory for each year using full costing.

b. Explain why profit fluctuates from year to year even though the number of units sold, the selling price, and the cost structure remain constant.

c. Calculate profit and the value of ending inventory for each year using variable costing.

d. Explain why, using variable costing, profit does not fluctuate from year to year.

**PROBLEM 5-2. Variable and Full Costing: Earnings Management with Full Costing; Changes in Production and Sales**   Firemaster BBQ produces stainless steel propane gas grills. The company has been in operation for three years and sales have declined each year due to increased competition. The following information is available:

|  | 2006 | 2007 | 2008 | Total |
|---|---|---|---|---|
| Units sold | 20,000 | 18,000 | 16,000 | 54,000 |
| Units produced | 20,000 | 20,000 | 14,000 | 54,000 |
| Fixed production costs | $20,000,000 | $20,000,000 | $20,000,000 | |
| Variable production costs per unit | $    800 | $    800 | $    800 | |
| Selling price per unit | $    2,000 | $    2,000 | $    2,000 | |
| Fixed selling and administrative expense | $    300,000 | $    300,000 | $    300,000 | |

*Required*

a. Calculate profit and the value of ending inventory (using LIFO) for each year under full costing.

b. Calculate profit and the value of ending inventory for each year under variable costing.

c. Explain how management of Firemaster could manipulate earnings in 2007 by producing more units than are actually needed to meet demand. Could this approach to earnings management be repeated year after year?

**PROBLEM 5-3. Variable and Full Costing: Income Effect of Clearing Excess Inventory**   The following information is available for Skipper Pools, a manufacturer of above-ground swimming pool kits:

|                                                | 2006 | 2007 | Total |
|------------------------------------------------|------|------|-------|
| Units produced                                 | 10,000 | 6,000 | 16,000 |
| Units sold                                     | 8,000 | 8,000 | 16,000 |
| Selling price per unit                         | $   3,000 | $   3,000 | |
| Direct material per unit                       | $      700 | $      700 | |
| Direct labor per unit                          | $   1,300 | $   1,300 | |
| Variable manufacturing overhead per unit       | $      200 | $      200 | |
| Fixed manufacturing overhead per year          | $2,000,000 | $2,000,000 | |
| Fixed selling and administrative expense per year | $1,000,000 | $1,000,000 | |

In its first year of operation, the company produced 10,000 kits, but was only able to sell 8,000 units. In its second year, the company needed to get rid of excess inventory (the extra 2,000 units produced but not sold in 2006) so it cut back production to 6,000 units.

*Required*

a. Calculate profit for both years using full costing.

b. Note that profit has declined in 2007. Is company performance actually worse in 2007 compared to 2006?

c. Calculate profit for both years using variable costing.

d. Does variable costing profit present a more realistic view of firm performance in the two years? Explain.

**PROBLEM 5-4. Reconciling Variable and Full Costing Income**   Miller Heating Company is a small manufacturer of auxiliary heaters. The units sell for $100 each. In 2006, the company produced 1,200 units and sold 1,000 units. Below are variable and full costing income statements for 2006.

**Income Statement Prepared Using Variable Costing**
**Miller Heating Company**
**Income Statement**
**For the Year Ending December 31, 2006**

| | | |
|---|---|---|
| Sales | | $100,000 |
| Less variable costs: | | |
|    Variable cost of goods sold | $20,000 | |
|    Variable selling expense | 10,000 | 30,000 |
| Contribution margin | | 70,000 |
| Less fixed costs: | | |
|    Fixed manufacturing expense | 24,000 | |
|    Fixed selling expense | 8,000 | |
|    Fixed administrative expense | 12,000 | 44,000 |
| Net income | | $ 26,000 |

**Income Statement Prepared Using Full Costing**
**Miller Heating Company**
**Income Statement**
**For the Year Ending December 31, 2006**

| | | |
|---|---|---|
| Sales | | $100,000 |
| Less cost of goods sold | | 40,000 |
| Gross margin | | 60,000 |
| Less selling and administrative expenses: | | |
|    Selling expense | $18,000 | |
|    Administrative expense | 12,000 | 30,000 |
| Net income | | $ 30,000 |

*Required*

Reconcile the difference in profit between the two income statements.

**PROBLEM 5-5. Using Information from a Variable Costing Income Statement to Make a Decision**  Below is a variable costing income statement for Wilner Glass Company, a maker of bottles for the beverage industry. For the coming year, the company is considering hiring two additional sales representatives at $60,000 each for base salary plus 3 percent of their sales for commissions. The company anticipates that each sales representative will generate $800,000 of incremental sales.

**Wilner Glass Company**
**Income Statement**
**For the Year Ending 12/31/2006**

| | | |
|---|---:|---:|
| Sales | | $18,000,000 |
| Less: | | |
|    Variable cost of goods sold | $6,300,000 | |
|    Variable selling expense | 3,600,000 | 9,900,000 |
| Contribution margin | | 8,100,000 |
| Less: | | |
|    Fixed production expense | 2,400,000 | |
|    Fixed selling expense | 1,600,000 | |
|    Fixed administrative expense | 2,800,000 | 6,800,000 |
| Net income | | $ 1,300,000 |

*Required*

a. Calculate the impact on profit of the proposed hiring decision. Should the company hire the two additional sales representatives?

b. Consider the analysis of the decision performed by the company's chief accountant and compare it to your analysis in part a. What is the fundamental flaw in the chief accountant's work?

**Analysis by Chief Accountant**

| | |
|---|---:|
| Incremental sales | $1,600,000 |
| Income per dollar of sales in 2006 ($1,300,000 ÷ $18,000,000) | 0.072 |
| | 115,200 |
| Less increase in base salary | 120,000 |
| Affect on profit | $    (4,800) |

**PROBLEM 5-6. Variable versus Full Costing Income and Earnings Management**  Renton Tractor Company was formed at the start of 2004, and produces a small garden tractor. The selling price is $5,000, variable production costs are $2,000 per unit, fixed production costs are $6,000,000 per year, and fixed selling and administrative costs are $2,000,000 per year. Data below indicate net income for 2004–2006 under full costing.

In 2004 and 2005, Edward Vendon was the president of Renton Tractor. The board of directors was generally pleased with the company's performance under his leadership—the company hit the break-even point in its first year of operation and had a modest profit in 2005. Edward quit at the end of 2005 and went on to start an e-commerce company selling used cars on the Internet. His replacement, Zac Dalton was, apparently, not as successful as Ed. Zac argued that he was improving the company by getting rid of excess inventory, but the board noted that the company showed a $2,000,000 loss in the first year of his leadership.

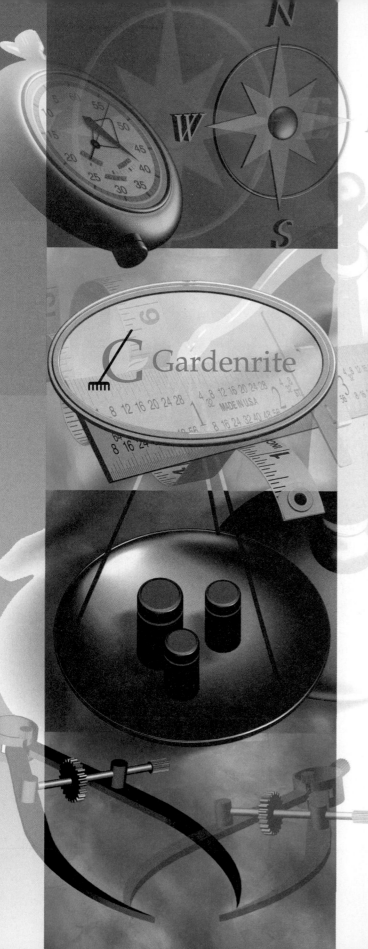

# chapter 6

# COST ALLOCATION AND ACTIVITY-BASED COSTING

**G**ardenrite Manufacturing Company produces garden tools and lawn maintenance products that are sold through a national chain of hardware stores. The company manufactures more than 60 products. Approximately 80 percent of its revenue comes from selling small home garden tools such as rakes, pruners, and spades. The company also manufactures high-quality lawn mowers, edgers, and blowers that are popular with professional lawn service companies, but sales of these products have not been a major source of revenue.

In recent months, Ben Jakes, the CFO at Gardenrite, has become concerned about the apparent profitability of several products. In particular, some high-volume products like the Model 250 spade are barely breaking even, whereas some low-volume products like the new Model 900 mower are selling for much more than the cost of production. The high profit earned by the Model 900 mower is particularly surprising. The company only recently began manufacturing mowers, and Ben expected production inefficiencies, associated with any new

product line, to keep profit margins low. Ben knows that manufacturing overhead is allocated to products based on labor cost. The approach is simple, but he suspects it may be causing allocations of cost that are too high for spades and too low for mowers.

Firms that produce more than one product or provide more than one type of service invariably have indirect costs because resources are shared by the products or services (e.g., two different products may be manufactured using the same piece of equipment). Various departments may also have common or shared resources (e.g., the marketing and human resources departments may share a high-speed copy machine). Because indirect costs associated with shared resources cannot be directly traced to products or services, some means of assigning them must be developed. The process of assigning indirect costs is referred to as **cost allocation**, which we first discussed in Chapter 2. Unfortunately, cost allocation frequently results in problems like the one faced by Ben Jakes. To prepare yourself to deal with them, you need a good understanding of why and how costs are allocated. Providing you with that understanding is the purpose of this chapter. One of the key points of the chapter is that costs are allocated for a variety of purposes; allocations that are adequate for one purpose may not be adequate for another purpose.

Many managers have expressed concern that the way overhead is typically allocated may seriously distort product cost for manufacturing firms. The problem arises because most product costing systems allocate overhead using measures related to production volume. This is the case at Gardenrite, where manufacturing overhead is allocated based on labor cost. However, many overhead costs are not proportional to volume. Activity-based costing (ABC) is an approach to allocating overhead costs that addresses this problem. We briefly discussed ABC in Chapter 2. Here you will gain a better understanding of the general process of cost allocation, which allows for a more detailed treatment of ABC.

In our discussion of ABC, we will build on the Gardenrite Manufacturing Company example. However, it is important to note that ABC is not restricted to manufacturing firms. Banks, hospitals, insurance companies and other service firms find that ABC provides insight into the costs of providing services to customers. Several of the problems and cases at the end of this chapter are in a service firm context and will provide you with an opportunity to generalize the ideas of ABC to this important business setting.

Explain why indirect costs are allocated.

# PURPOSES OF COST ALLOCATION

Companies allocate costs to products, services, and departments for four major reasons: (1) to provide information needed to make appropriate decisions, (2) to reduce the frivolous use of common resources, (3) to encourage managers to evaluate the efficiency of internally provided services, and (4) to calculate the "full cost" of products for financial reporting purposes and for determining cost-based prices (see Illustration 6-1). We will now discuss each of these purposes.

**Illustration 6-1**
Reasons why firms allocate costs

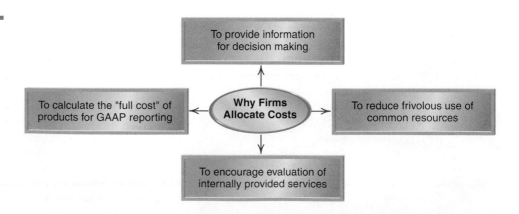

## TO PROVIDE INFORMATION FOR DECISION MAKING

When managers use a company resource and receive an allocation of its cost, they are, in essence, receiving a charge for use. For example, when Malinda Smith, a product manager at Connection Software, asks the art department to design a prototype box for a product under development, she will likely receive an allocation, on her product-line profit and loss statement, of costs incurred in the art department. The more art work she orders, the more cost she will receive, reducing the profit for which she is responsible. But what is the appropriate allocation?

*From a decision making standpoint, the allocated cost should measure the opportunity cost of using a company resource.* Let's see why this is the case. Suppose the art department has excess capacity and the design work does not create additional costs other than very minor material cost. In this case, the opportunity cost is approximately zero, and the appropriate allocation is also zero. Malinda's company, after all, does not want to discourage her from using the art department's services since this use does not lead to additional costs.

Suppose, however, the art department is extremely busy. If it takes on Malinda's job, other work will be delayed. In fact, a different product-line manager will be forced to go outside the company to get art work done on time, incurring a cost of $5,000. In this case, Malinda's use of a company resource has led to a $5,000 opportunity cost. Thus, $5,000 would be an appropriate allocation, or charge, to Malinda's operation. If she does not believe that the art department's services represent a $5,000 benefit to her operation, then she will not demand these services, and the other product manager can make use of them and avoid incurring $5,000 of costs outside the company.

Although allocated costs should measure the opportunity cost of using a company resource, in practice this is difficult to operationalize. One reason is that the opportunity cost may quickly change. For example, on Wednesday, the art department may be dealing with a rush job and working overtime. But by Friday, the rush job may be completed, and there may be excess capacity. Thus, the opportunity cost would be much higher on Wednesday than on Friday.

Still, the opportunity cost idea is a useful benchmark. Whenever you are discussing allocations of cost, you should ask yourself, "How close is this allocation to the opportunity cost of use?" The closer it is, the better the allocation.

## TO REDUCE FRIVOLOUS USE OF COMMON RESOURCES

As already noted, allocated costs serve as charges, or fees, for use of internal resources or services. Consider a company that purchases a computer to be used by all three of its divisions. Almost all of the costs associated with running the computer are fixed, and they amount to $100,000 per year. Some accountants would argue that because these costs are fixed, the divisions should not be charged for using the computer, since use creates no incremental cost. However, if the three divisions do not incur any charge for using the computer, they may tend to use the computer for frivolous or nonessential purposes (e.g., playing computer games, sending unnecessary e-mail, or preparing computer-generated reports that are not really needed).

This situation may not seem to be that detrimental to the company's welfare. After all, the costs associated with the computer are primarily fixed. If frivolous use does not create additional costs, why discourage it? The reason is that frivolous use may have hidden costs. The primary hidden cost in the example is slower service to departments that need to use the computer when it is being used unnecessarily by another department. In other words, an opportunity cost is associated with the use of the computer. Reports that take minutes to prepare when the computer is being used efficiently may take hours to produce when the computer is being used to prepare reports that are not important.

One way to eliminate frivolous use is to charge for the use of centrally provided services. And one of the most common ways to charge for use is to allocate the cost of the service. For example, suppose Division 1 plans to use the computer for 1,000 hours per year, Division 2 plans to use it for 1,000 hours, and Division 3 for 2,000 hours. A charge of $25 per hour ($100,000 ÷ 4,000 hours) could be assessed. Note that this rate would allocate the entire cost of the computer ($100,000) among the three users, assuming that their plans worked out as expected. Divisions 1 and 2 would each be charged $25,000, and Division 3 would be charged $50,000. If division managers knew that this method of cost allocation would be used, they would have an incentive to reduce their division's frivolous use of the computer, because use of the computer reduces the reported profit of their division.

## TO ENCOURAGE EVALUATION OF SERVICES

Cost allocation is also useful because it encourages managers to evaluate the services for which they are being charged. If no costs are allocated to users of centrally administered services, such as computer services or janitorial services, then the users of the services do not have an incentive to evaluate these services carefully. After all, the services are free. However, if the users are charged for the services (i.e., if they receive an allocation of the cost of the services), then the users have a strong incentive to look critically at the services and consider the possibility of lower-cost alternatives. If lower-cost alternatives exist, the users will certainly bring them to the company's attention. The company can then evaluate whether the services are being provided in an efficient manner.

Consider the example of the three divisions using a central computer system. Because the three divisions are being charged for using the system (through an allocation of its costs), the managers of the divisions have an incentive to evaluate the cost and quality of the service being provided. Suppose the manager of Division 3 determines that similar computing services can be purchased outside the company for less than the $50,000 currently being allocated to Division 3 for its use of the central computer system. The manager of Division 3 will bring this matter to high-level company officials, who will encourage the manager of the computer system to lower that operation's costs, perhaps by reducing staffing. If the costs of the computer system cannot be lowered, the company may consider replacing the computer system with separate computers for the divisions or buying computer services outside the company.

## TO PROVIDE "FULL COST" INFORMATION

As we have mentioned, GAAP requires full costing for external reporting purposes. Indirect production costs must be allocated to goods produced to meet this requirement. In addition, full cost information is required when a company has an agreement whereby the amount of revenue received depends on the amount of

### Cost-Plus Contract for Ad Agency

When we think of companies that have cost-plus contracts with the federal government, defense contractors like Boeing, Lockheed Martin, or Allied Signal come to mind. So it's somewhat surprising to see the Madison Avenue firm of Ogilvy & Mather in the news with a $152 million cost-plus-fixed-fee contract. The firm was hired in July, 2002 to handle an anti-drug ad campaign by the Office of National Drug Control Policy.

The direct costs of the ad campaign, including the cost of TV and radio spots, will be relatively easy to identify. However, a considerable amount of cost allocation will be required to determine "full cost." The salary of Ogilvy & Mather's CEO, the cost of office space, and the cost of word processing and design equipment are examples of costs that cannot be *directly* traced to the government work—thus, allocation is required.

This is the second time that Ogilvy has been hired to work for the federal drug czar's office. Earlier, Ogilvy agreed to a $1.8 million deal to settle claims that it overcharged the drug office on it's first contract. Ogilvy executives argued that the overcharges were clerical errors related to their lack of experience with federal rules. Indeed the rules are complex as you can see if you go to the Web site for the Code of Federal Regulations and read through the voluminous and complex regulations under Title 48, Chapter 99.

*Sources: USA Today*, "Anti-Drug Ad Contract Award Surprises Some," July 9, 2002, pg. 3B. "Mismanagement alleged in National Anti-Drug Campaign," www.cnn.com/2000/ALLPOLITICS/Stories, October 5, 2000. AdAge.com, "Ogilvy & Mather. Honesty Mistake or Fraud?," August 20, 2001.

cost incurred. For example, defense contractors with the federal government often have contracts that specify they will be paid the cost of production as well as some fixed amount or percentage of cost. Such contracts are commonly called "cost-plus" contracts. An interesting feature of these contracts is that the cost of production specified often includes not only manufacturing costs but also a share of general and administrative costs. Thus, a substantial amount of cost allocation is required to assign indirect manufacturing costs and indirect general and administrative costs to the contract work.

A major problem with cost-plus contracts is that they create an incentive to allocate as much cost as possible to the goods produced on a cost-plus basis and little cost to goods that are not produced on a cost-plus basis. The more cost allocated to cost-plus contracts, the higher the amount paid to the company.

In spite of this limitation, cost-plus contracts serve a useful purpose. Without the assurance that they will be reimbursed for their costs and that they will earn some profit, many manufacturers would not be willing to bear the financial risks associated with producing state-of-the-art products for the government, using untried technologies. For example, not many companies would be willing to develop a new fighter aircraft without assurance that they would be reimbursed for all costs incurred in its development.

Describe the cost allocation process.

# PROCESS OF COST ALLOCATION

We have seen that cost allocation is often necessary. But how is it achieved? The cost allocation process has three steps: (1) identify the cost objectives, (2) form cost pools, and (3) select an allocation base to relate the cost pools to the cost objectives. The three steps are shown in Illustration 6-2.

**Illustration 6-2**
The cost allocation process

## DETERMINING THE COST OBJECTIVE

The first step in the cost allocation process is to determine the product, service, or department that is to receive the allocation. The object of the allocation is referred to as the **cost objective**. For example, if a company allocates depreciation of a drilling press to products such as flanges and brackets, the products are the cost objectives. If computer-processing costs are allocated to the contracts worked on by a computer-aided design group, the contracts are the cost objectives. If a bank allocates general and administrative costs to product lines (e.g., loan services and estate-planning services), the product lines are the cost objectives (see Illustration 6-3).

## FORMING COST POOLS

The second step in the cost allocation process is to form **cost pools**. A cost pool is a grouping of individual costs whose total is allocated using one allocation base. For example, all of the costs in the maintenance department could be treated as a

**Illustration 6-3**
Cost objectives

cost pool. In this case, the cost pool would include the wages of workers in the maintenance department, supplies, small tools, and a variety of additional cost items. Cost pools are often formed along departmental lines (for example, maintenance department costs in one cost pool and personnel department costs in another cost pool). They may also be formed according to major activities. For example, costs related to equipment setups, a major activity in most manufacturing firms, are in one cost pool, and costs related to inspecting products for defects, another major activity, are in another cost pool.

The overriding concern in forming a cost pool is to ensure that the costs in the pool are homogeneous, or similar. One way to determine whether these costs are homogeneous is to compare the allocations with the allocations that result from breaking the pool up into smaller pools and using a variety of allocation bases. If there is not a substantial difference in the allocations, then, for practical purposes, the costs in the pool are considered to be homogeneous.

Some manufacturing companies include all manufacturing overhead (power costs, computing costs, material handling costs, etc.) in a single cost pool. However, allocations from a large pool containing costs related to very different activities are not likely to provide useful information. (We discuss this problem later in the chapter.) Although use of a single cost pool for overhead seems too broad, exactly how many cost pools are appropriate is not clear. Managers must make a cost-benefit decision. More pools involve more analysis and recordkeeping, which is costly. However, more pools also result in the benefit of more accurate information.

## SELECTING AN ALLOCATION BASE

The third step in the allocation process is to select an allocation base that relates the cost pool to the cost objectives. The allocation base must be some characteristic that is common to all of the cost objectives. If the cost objectives are manufactured products, then direct labor hours, direct labor cost, and machine hours are examples of characteristics that could be used as allocation bases. If the cost objectives are the divisions of a multidivisional firm, then sales dollars, total assets, and divisional profit are examples of characteristics that could be used as allocation bases.

Deciding which of the possible allocation bases to use is not an easy matter. Ideally, the allocation base selected should relate costs to cost objectives that *caused* the costs to be incurred. In this case, the allocation is based on a **cause-and-effect relationship**. For example, if additional activity in a production department causes an increase in the costs incurred by the maintenance department, then the allocation base selected should result in the additional costs being allocated to the production department when there is additional activity. Direct labor hours, direct labor cost, or machine hours in the production department would be likely choices for the allocation base because they represent the increase in activity that leads to the increase in cost in the Maintenance Department. However, it would be difficult to argue that one of these allocation bases is better than another on cause-and-effect grounds. As we will see next, this is one of the problems of cost allocation. A number of allocation bases may appear to be equally valid, but they may result in substantially different costs being assigned to the cost objectives.

Let's consider an example. Pratt Equipment Company has two producing departments, Assembly and Finishing, that receive allocations of indirect costs from the Maintenance department. In the coming year, the Maintenance Department expects to incur variable costs of $200,000. These costs are related to both the labor hours and the machine hours incurred in the producing departments. The quantities of labor and machine hours are indicated here. With labor hours as the allocation base, the allocation rate is $4 per labor hour, and the Assembly Department receives an $80,000 allocation of cost from the Maintenance Department. However, with machine hours as the allocation base, the allocation rate is $10 per machine hour, and the Assembly Department receives a $110,000 allocation of cost from the Maintenance Department. The $30,000 difference in the allocations occurs even though both labor hours and machine hours are reasonable allocation bases to use.

|  | Labor Hours | Allocations | Machine Hours | Allocations |
|---|---|---|---|---|
| Assembly | 20,000 | $ 80,000 | 11,000 | $110,000 |
| Finishing | 30,000 | 120,000 | 9,000 | 90,000 |
| Total | 50,000 | $200,000 | 20,000 | $200,000 |
| Allocation Rate | $4 per labor hour | | $10 per machine hour | |

When indirect costs are fixed, establishing cause-and-effect relationships between costs and cost objectives is not feasible. In these cases, accountants turn to other criteria, such as relative benefits, ability to bear costs, and equity. Unfortunately, these terms are rather vague and difficult to implement in an unambiguous manner.

The **relative benefits approach to allocation** suggests that the base should result in more costs being allocated to the cost objectives that benefit most from incurring the cost. This might suggest, for example, that computer costs should be allocated to departments based on time spent using the computer, since greater use implies greater benefit. However, this could result in fixed computer cost being allocated to departments that did not exist when the computer was acquired (and so could not have caused the cost of the computer to be incurred).

The **ability to bear costs** notion suggests that the allocation base should result in more costs being allocated to products, services, or departments that are more profitable. Because they are more profitable, they can *bear* the increased costs from the higher allocations.

The **equity approach to allocation** suggests that the base should result in allocations that are perceived to be fair or equitable. Obviously, this is a difficult criterion to apply, because different individuals have different perceptions of what is equitable.

Discuss allocation of service department costs.

# ALLOCATING SERVICE DEPARTMENT COSTS

The organizational units in most manufacturing firms can be classified as either production departments or service departments. Production departments engage in direct manufacturing activity, whereas service departments provide indirect support. For example, in a furniture manufacturing company, the assembly and finishing departments are production departments, whereas maintenance, janitorial, personnel, cafeteria, cost accounting, and power are service departments.

Cost pools are often formed by service departments, and these costs are allocated to production departments—the cost objectives. Ultimately, production departments allocate their costs to specific products.

## DIRECT METHOD OF ALLOCATING SERVICE DEPARTMENT COSTS

The method of allocating service department costs that we cover is called the direct method. In the **direct method of allocating cost**, service department costs are allocated to production departments but not to other service departments.[1] Thus, even though the Janitorial Department provides a service to the Personnel Department, under the direct method no janitorial costs are allocated to the Personnel Department. The process is diagrammed in Illustration 6-4. The illustration includes no arrow between janitorial costs and personnel costs because there is no allocation of costs between the Janitorial Service Department and the Personnel Department.

We'll consider an example involving the Bradley Furniture Company. Suppose the company's janitorial costs are $100,000. The company decides to allocate these costs to Assembly and Finishing based on the number of square feet in each production department. Since Assembly has 20,000 square feet and Finishing has 30,000 square feet, the allocation rate is $2 per square foot ($100,000 ÷ 50,000 square feet). Assembly receives an allocation of $40,000 (20,000 square feet × $2), and Finishing receives an allocation of $60,000 (30,000 square feet × $2) .

Now suppose the personnel costs at Bradley are $200,000. These costs are allocated based on the number of employees in each production department. The Assembly Department has 60 employees, and the Finishing Department has 40 employees. Thus, the allocation rate for personnel costs is $2,000 per employee ($200,000 ÷ 100 employees). The Assembly Department receives an allocation of

**Illustration 6-4**
Allocating service department costs with the direct method

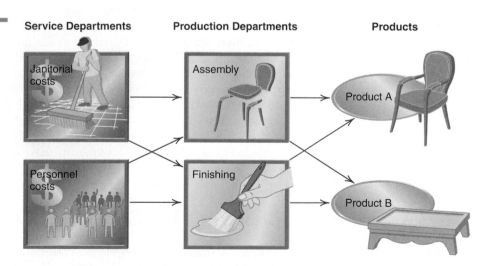

| Service Departments | Production Departments | Products |
|---|---|---|

---

[1]Alternatives to the direct method that recognize that service departments make use of each other's resources (including the sequential and the reciprocal methods) are covered in cost accounting texts.

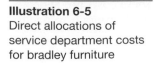

**Illustration 6-5**
Direct allocations of
service department costs
for bradley furniture

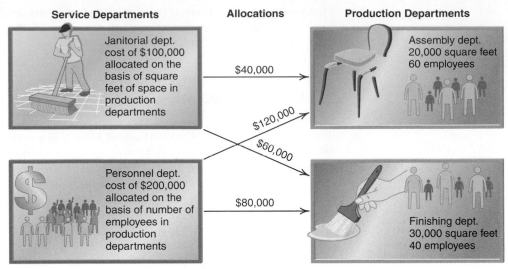

$120,000 (60 × $2,000), and the Finishing Department receives an allocation of
$80,000 (40 × $2,000). The allocations are presented in Illustration 6-5.

## ALLOCATING BUDGETED AND ACTUAL SERVICE DEPARTMENT COSTS

It is generally a good idea to allocate budgeted rather than actual service department costs. If budgeted costs are allocated, service departments cannot pass on the cost of inefficiencies and waste. For example, suppose at the start of the year, budgeted costs in the Janitorial Department are $100,000, and the accounting department informs Assembly and Finishing that they will receive allocations of $2 per square foot ($100,000 ÷ 50,000 square feet).

But suppose that the Janitorial Department actually incurs $130,000 of cost ($30,000 more than planned) owing to a lack of good cost control. If actual costs are allocated, the Janitorial Department can pass the extra costs on to the production departments by allocating $2.60 per square foot ($130,000 ÷ 50,000 square feet). The managers of Assembly and Finishing would strongly resist the higher charge. Obviously, they would not want their costs to be increased simply because some other department was not performing its job efficiently. This problem is avoided if only budgeted costs are allocated; in that case, the Janitorial Department must stick to the allocation of $2 per square foot.

Identify potential problems
with cost allocation.

# PROBLEMS WITH COST ALLOCATION

Our discussion so far has focused on ideas about how costs should be allocated. In practice, when costs are allocated, a number of problems may arise. Here we discuss problems brought about by (1) allocations of costs that are not controllable, (2) arbitrary allocations, (3) allocations of fixed costs that make the fixed costs appear to be variable costs, (4) allocations of manufacturing overhead to products using too few overhead cost pools, and (5) use of only volume-related allocation bases.

## RESPONSIBILITY ACCOUNTING AND CONTROLLABLE COSTS

In Chapter 1 we learned that one of the primary uses of managerial accounting is to evaluate the performance of managers and the operations under their control. Performance evaluation is facilitated by a system of accounting that traces revenues and costs to organizational units (e.g., departments and divisions) and individuals (e.g., plant manager, supervisor of assembly workers, vice president of operation), with related responsibility for generating revenue and controlling costs. Such a system is referred to as a **responsibility accounting system**.

Consider a company that produces tennis rackets and tennis clothes in two separate plants. The company could prepare monthly production cost reports that list the total amount of material, labor, and overhead cost for the two plants combined. However, this would *not* be consistent with responsibility accounting because the reports would not trace the production costs to the plants responsible for controlling them. A responsibility accounting system would require not only that the costs of producing the tennis rackets and tennis clothes be traced to their respective plants but also that the costs in each plant be traced to the departments or other units responsible for those costs. For example, within the plant producing the tennis rackets, labor costs should be traced to each foreman responsible for an identifiable group or team of workers (e.g., assembly workers and finishing workers).

Cost allocation is generally required in a responsibility accounting system because one organizational unit is often responsible for the costs incurred by another organizational unit. For example, activity in a Production Department increases the costs incurred in the Machine Repair Department. Because the Production Department is responsible for the incurrence of costs in the Machine Repair Department, the Production Department's performance reports should reflect some share of the Machine Repair Department cost. This can be achieved by allocating Machine Repair Department costs to the Production Department.

Some allocations of costs, however, are not consistent with a responsibility accounting system. Most accountants believe that managers should be held responsible only for costs they can control. These costs, called **controllable costs**, are affected by the manager's decisions. Allocating the cost of a building to the performance report of a supervisor responsible for controlling labor costs is not appropriate because the supervisor cannot control building costs.

If allocated costs beyond the manager's control appear on the manager's performance reports, they may cause considerable frustration. Managers want their performance evaluations to reflect their own strengths and weaknesses. In some cases, managers are allocated costs beyond their control simply to make them aware that the costs exist and must be covered by the firm's revenue. In such situations, the costs should be clearly labeled noncontrollable, indicating to the manager that company officials are aware that the items are not affected by his or her decisions. This should minimize possible resentment.

## ARBITRARY ALLOCATIONS

In practice, cost allocations are the topic of numerous and often heated discussions. Managers may feel that their departments receive unnecessarily large allocations of indirect costs, causing the departments to appear less profitable. Governmental agencies that have cost-plus contracts may feel that products produced by contractors on a cost-plus basis receive allocations of indirect costs that are unfairly high. Unfortunately, such discussions are likely to continue in the future. The reason is that allocations of costs are to a great extent inherently arbitrary.

In almost all cost allocation situations, determining the one "true," "correct," or "valid" allocation is not possible. As noted earlier in the chapter, various allocation bases (e.g., labor hours, labor cost, and machine hours) may be equally justifiable but may result in substantially different allocations. These situations naturally lead managers to support the allocation that makes their performance look best and reject allocations that cast an unfavorable light on their performance.

## UNITIZED FIXED COSTS AND LUMP-SUM ALLOCATIONS

One of the most significant problems associated with cost allocation is due to the fact that the allocation process may make fixed costs appear to be variable costs. This happens when fixed costs are **unitized**—that is, stated on a per unit basis. To illustrate the problem, consider the Jones Tool Company, which has two divisions. At the start of each year, the company estimates the amount of general and administrative costs that are incurred centrally on behalf of the operations of both divisions. Such costs include administrative salaries, clerical costs, central accounting costs, and a variety of others, all of which are essentially fixed in the short run. In the current year, these costs are expected to amount to $2,000,000. Jones has decided that it would be useful for the divisions to know that these costs are being incurred on their behalf. Therefore, it allocates the costs among the divisions based on their relative sales. In the current year, divisional sales are expected to be $50,000,000. Thus, Jones has decided to allocate general and administrative costs to the divisions at a rate of $0.04 per dollar of sales (i.e., $2,000,000 ÷ $50,000,000).

We have said that the general and administrative costs are essentially fixed, but how will they appear to the division managers? Let's look, for instance, at Bob Gallegos, the manager of the Carpenter Division, which produces a variety of carpenter tools (e.g., hammers, saws, and drills). Bob observes that as divisional revenue increases, the allocated costs increase. Thus, to him, the costs appear to be variable. This may lead Bob to make decisions that are not in the best interest of the company as a whole but that appear to maximize divisional profitability. For example, suppose the Carpenter Division is considering producing a new hammer that will sell for $20. At this price, the division expects to sell 100,000 units. Production of the hammer will require $12 of direct material cost, $6 of direct labor cost, and an increase in manufacturing overhead costs of $130,000. An analysis of the effect on the profit of the Carpenter Division is presented in Illustration 6-6.

As indicated in the illustration, sale of the hammer is expected to result in an increase of $2,000,000 in sales. There will also be a $1,800,000 increase in variable costs (direct material and direct labor) and a $130,000 increase in manufac-

**Illustration 6-6**
Problem of unitized fixed costs

| | | |
|---|---:|---:|
| Sales of hammers | | |
| (100,000 × $20) | | $2,000,000 |
| Less: additional costs | | |
| Direct material (100,000 × $12) | $1,200,000 | |
| Direct labor (100,000 × $6) | 600,000 | |
| Additional manufacturing overhead cost | 130,000 | 1,930,000 |
| Real increase in profit | | $70,000 |
| Less: allocated fixed costs | | |
| ($2,000,000 increase in sales × $.04) | | 80,000 |
| Perceived loss on sale of hammers | | ($10,000) |

turing overhead cost. Thus, production and sale of the hammer will result in a $70,000 increase in profit. From this information, the hammer appears to be a profitable addition to the product line of the division. However, will the manager of the division be motivated to produce the hammer? Probably not.

The reason is that, with the increase in sales, the division will receive a larger allocation of central general and administrative costs. With an allocation rate of $.04 per dollar of sales and an expected increase in sales of $2,000,000, the division would expect its allocated costs to increase by $80,000. To the manager of the division, the additional allocated costs appear to be variable even though, in fact, they are fixed (that is, central administration salaries, clerical costs, and accounting costs will not increase if the hammer is produced). The result is that the manager of the division would expect production of the hammer to result in a loss of $10,000 ($70,000 − $80,000) for the division.

To remedy this problem, allocations of *fixed costs* must be made in such a way that they *appear fixed* to the managers whose departments receive the allocations. This is achieved by **lump-sum allocations** of fixed costs. A lump-sum allocation is an allocation of a predetermined amount that is not affected by changes in the activity level of the organizational unit receiving the allocation. Resources are acquired taking into account the long-run needs of users. Thus, allocations of fixed costs should be based on the projected long-run needs that lead managers to incur the costs. For example, suppose Jones Tool Company purchases a computer to serve each of its two divisions. Purchase of the computer results in annual fixed costs of $40,000. In deciding what type of computer to purchase, management estimated that the Carpenter Division would use the computer for 2,000 hours per year and the Specialty Tools Division would use the computer for 3,000 hours per year. Thus, allocating $16,000 to the Carpenter Division ($40,000 × 2/5) and $24,000 to the Specialty Tools Division ($40,000 × 3/5) is appropriate.

Lump-sum allocations should generally remain the same year after year, even though, over time, the activity of the organizational units involved may deviate from expectations. Suppose, for example, that the Carpenter Division expanded and required 3,000 hours of computer time per year, whereas the Specialty Tools Division lost business and required only 2,000 hours. Should the lump-sum allocations of the two divisions be reversed? Probably not. Reversing the allocations would make it appear to the managers of the two divisions that their allocations do indeed depend on their activity levels. In other words, the fixed costs would again appear to be variable. If lump-sum allocations of *fixed* costs are to *appear fixed*, the amount of the allocation must not depend on changes in activity.

It follows that, with lump-sum allocations, the allocations of a division do not depend on the activity level of other divisions. Suppose the activity of the Carpenter Division stayed at 2,000 hours, but the activity level of the Specialty Tools Division decreased from 3,000 hours to 2,000 hours. If the cost of the computer were allocated based on current activity levels, the amount allocated to the Carpenter Division would increase from $16,000 to $20,000, in spite of the fact that its use of the computer had not changed. Obviously, this could cause considerable dissatisfaction on the part of the manager of the Carpenter Division. It could also make planning more difficult, because the costs of the division would depend on the activity of other divisions. This is not the case with a lump-sum allocation. Once the amount of the lump-sum is determined, it does not vary in response to changes in activity.

How can lump-sum allocations improve a manager's decisions? Refer back to the decision Bob Gallegos at the Carpenter Division of Jones Tool Company faced regarding sale of a new hammer. If the general and administrative costs at Jones

Tool Company are allocated on a lump-sum basis and the amount allocated to the Carpenter Division is $700,000 regardless of its activity, then Bob will perceive that general and administrative costs are indeed fixed. Thus, he will correctly determine that, in the interest of maximizing divisional profit, the hammer should be produced because it contributes $70,000 toward covering the allocated costs that will be incurred whether or not the hammer is produced.

## THE PROBLEM OF TOO FEW COST POOLS

Some companies assign overhead to products using only one or two overhead cost pools. Although the approach has the benefit of being simple and easy to use, product costs may be seriously distorted when only a small number of cost pools are used.

Consider the problem in the context of the Electra Manufacturing Company, which manufactures products in two departments: Assembly and Finishing. Electra has total manufacturing overhead of $1,000,000, and each year the company incurs 50,000 labor hours. If the company includes all overhead in one cost pool and allocates overhead using labor hours, the overhead rate will be $20 per labor hour ($1,000,000 ÷ 50,000 labor hours). But suppose that of the $1,000,000 of overhead, $600,000 is incurred in Assembly and $400,000 is incurred in Finishing. Furthermore, Assembly requires 40,000 labor hours, and Finishing requires only 10,000 labor hours. You can see that overhead per labor hour is much more expensive in the Finishing Department: $15 per labor hour in Assembly and $40 per labor hour in Finishing. (See Illustration 6-7.)

Now, assume that Electra has two products (A and B) that require 10 labor hours each. Product A requires two hours of assembly time and eight hours of finishing, whereas Product B requires eight hours of assembly time and two hours of finishing. How much overhead will be allocated to each product if all overhead is included in a single cost pool and allocated on the basis of labor hours? The answer is that both products will receive the same allocation. They both require 10 hours of total labor, and use of a single cost pool allocates the average cost per labor hour. Both will be allocated $200 of overhead ($20 × 10 labor hours).

Which product is being undercosted and which product is being overcosted? Product A is undercosted because it requires relatively more production time in finishing, which is a high-cost department in terms of overhead cost. Product B is overcosted because it requires relatively more production time in assembly, which is a cheap department in terms of overhead. Still, Product B receives the same charge per labor hour as Product A when only a single cost pool is used. Electra's problem is easily solved by setting up separate cost pools for overhead in each department.

---

**Illustration 6-7**
Overhead rates using one versus two cost pools

**One cost pool**

$$\frac{\text{Total overhead}}{\text{Total labor hours}} = \frac{\$1,000,000}{50,000} = \$20 \text{ per labor hour}$$

**Two cost pools (one for Assembly and one for Finishing)**

$$\frac{\text{Assembly overhead}}{\text{Assembly labor hours}} = \frac{\$600,000}{40,000} = \begin{array}{c}\$15 \text{ per assembly} \\ \text{labor hour}\end{array}$$

$$\frac{\text{Finishing overhead}}{\text{Finishing labor hours}} = \frac{\$400,000}{10,000} = \begin{array}{c}\$40 \text{ per finishing} \\ \text{labor hour}\end{array}$$

In general, product costs will be more accurate when more overhead cost pools are used. And decisions that rely on product cost information, such as product pricing decisions, will be improved. However, the more pools that are formed, the more costly will be the cost of record keeping. Companies must make a cost-benefit tradeoff. Is the cost of forming more cost pools worth the benefit of improved information? Similar questions must always be addressed when considering improvements in accounting information.

## USING ONLY VOLUME-RELATED ALLOCATION BASES

We now turn to a final problem involved in cost allocations. Some manufacturing companies allocate manufacturing overhead to products using only measures of production volume (e.g., direct labor or machine hours) as allocation bases. However, not all overhead costs vary with volume. We discuss this issue in the next section along with activity-based costing (ABC), because ABC solves the problem.

Discuss activity-based costing (ABC) and cost drivers.

# ACTIVITY-BASED COSTING

**Activity-based costing (ABC)** is a relatively recent development in managerial accounting, and it has received a tremendous amount of attention from both academics and practitioners interested in improving managerial accounting information.[2] We introduced ABC in Chapter 2, dealing with job-order costing. Now we discuss it in more detail.

### THE PROBLEM OF USING ONLY MEASURES OF PRODUCTION VOLUME TO ALLOCATE OVERHEAD

Manufacturing companies commonly use direct labor hours, direct labor cost, and machine hours as allocation bases when assigning overhead to products. Each of these items is a measure of production volume. Because most companies continue to allocate overhead using only measures of production volume as allocation bases, we refer to this approach as the "traditional approach." The problem with the traditional approach is that it assumes that all overhead costs are proportional to production volume. By "proportional," we mean that, for example, when volume increases by 20 percent, overhead increases by 20 percent; when volume increases by 50 percent, overhead increases by 50 percent, and so forth. However, many overhead costs (such as the cost of setting up equipment for a production run, the cost of inspecting raw materials, and the cost of handling materials) are not proportional to volume. In fact, many overhead costs are affected by product complexity rather than volume. The result is that simple high-volume products are often overcosted, whereas complex low-volume products are undercosted.

Consider the overhead costs created by starting up a production line. Both a high-volume product (which is associated with a large amount of labor and machine time) and a low-volume product (which is associated with a small amount of labor and machine time) may require the same amount of setup time and setup cost. However, since setup costs (along with all other overhead) are allocated only

[2]Credit for developing activity-based costing is usually given to Robin Cooper and Robert Kaplan. See R. Cooper, "The Rise of Activity-Based Costing—Part One: What Is an Activity-Based Cost System?" *Journal of Cost Management*, Summer 1988, pp. 45–54, and R. Cooper and R. Kaplan, "How Cost Accounting Distorts Product Costs," *Management Accounting*, April 1988, pp. 20–27.

### The Activity-Based Costing Portal

http://www.offtech.com.au/abc/Home.asp

This site offers a free ABC magazine, links to articles, and a forum for discussion of ABC related topics. A special feature allows students to submit questions on ABC.
   Articles recently featured on the site include:

- *A Procedure for Smooth Implementation of Activity Based Costing in Small Companies*
- *The Association Between Activity-Based Costing and Improvement in Financial Performance*
- *Using Activity-Based Costing to Manage More Effectively*
- *Activity-Based Costing Approach to Equipment Selection Problem for Flexible Manufacturing Systems*
- *Quality, Cost, and Value-Added in Comprehensive Institutions of Higher Education*

on the basis of production volume, the high-volume product will receive a larger *allocation* of setup cost. Thus, the high-volume product is overcosted. Let's see how the ABC approach avoids this problem.

## THE ABC APPROACH

In the ABC approach, companies identify the major activities that cause overhead costs to be incurred. Some of these activities are related to production volume, but others are not. The costs of the resources consumed performing these activities are grouped into cost pools. Finally, the costs are assigned to products using a measure of activity referred to as a **cost driver** (an allocation base in an ABC system). The steps involved in the ABC approach, then, are:

Step 1 — Identify major activities

Step 2 — Group costs of activities into cost pools

Step 3 — Identify measures of activities—the cost drivers

Step 4 — Relate costs to products using the cost drivers

**Illustration 6-8**
Common activities and
associated cost drivers

| Major Activities | Associated Costs | Cost Driver |
|---|---|---|
| Processing purchase orders for materials and parts | Labor cost for workers determining order quantities, contacting vendors, and preparing purchase orders | Number of purchase orders processed |
| Handling material and parts | Labor cost for workers handling material and parts, depreciation of equipment used to move material and parts (e.g., depreciation of fork lift trucks), etc. | Number of material requisitions |
| Inspecting incoming material and parts | Labor cost for workers performing inspections, depreciation of equipment used to test strength of materials, tolerances, etc. | Number of receipts |
| Setting up equipment | Labor cost for workers involved in setups, depreciation of equipment used to adjust equipment | Number of setups |
| Producing goods using manufacturing equipment | Depreciation on manufacturing equipment | Number of machine hours |
| Supervising assembly workers | Salary of assembly supervisors | Number of assembly labor hours |
| Inspecting finished goods | Labor cost for finished goods inspectors, depreciation of equipment used to test whether finished goods meet customer specifications, etc. | Number of inspections |
| Packing customer orders | Labor cost for packing workers, cost of packing materials, etc. | Number of boxes shipped |

Some common activities and associated cost drivers are listed in Illustration 6-8. Note that some of the cost drivers are volume related; machine hours and assembly labor hours are examples. Other cost drivers are not related to production volume; one example is the number of inspections. Some low-volume products that involve complex or fragile parts may need a large number of inspections, whereas some high-volume products that involve simple or rugged parts may need relatively few inspections. Number of setups, as suggested earlier, is another cost driver that may not be related to volume. Both low-volume and high-volume products may require the same number of setups.

Each firm must decide how many separate activities (and related cost pools and cost drivers) to identify. If too many activities are identified, the system will be unnecessarily costly and confusing. For example, consider a company that produces 200 products and identifies 100 key activities. This company must account for 20,000 (200 × 100) product-activity relations. On the other hand, if too few activities are used, the ABC system is not likely to produce accurate data. Most companies that design ABC systems use 25 to 100 distinct activities.[3]

---

[3]See R. Cooper, R. Kaplan, L. Maisel, E. Morrissey, and R. Oehm, "Implementing Activity-Based Cost Management: Moving from Analysis to Action," *Institute of Management Accountants*, 1992, p. 13.

## RELATING COST POOLS TO PRODUCTS USING COST DRIVERS

Let's take a moment to look at the last step in the ABC approach; relating cost pools to products using cost drivers as the allocation bases. Understanding how this step is accomplished will allow us to move on to a comprehensive example.

Lacet Electronics produces a variety of electronic products ranging from simple hand-held calculators to hard disk drives. Inspection to ensure that products are of high quality is a major activity at Lacet. In the coming year, the company expects to incur inspection costs of $2,500,000. Forty workers are employed in the inspection process, and they are expected to perform 1,000,000 product inspections in the coming year. Using inspection cost as a cost pool and the number of inspections as a cost driver, the company arrives at a rate of $2.50 per inspection for purposes of allocating inspection costs to products.

Lacet produces 20,000 Model ZX disk drives. Each drive is inspected three times during the production process, and various functions are tested for conformance with rigorous standards set by the company. How much of the total $2,500,000 inspection cost will be allocated to the Model ZX? With 20,000 disk drives and three inspections per drive, a total of 60,000 inspections will be performed. A rate of $2.50 per inspection implies that $7.50 of inspection cost will be allocated to each disk drive ($2.50 rate × 3 inspections) for a total of $150,000 ($7.50 × 20,000). A similar approach will be taken to determine the amount of inspection cost to be allocated to the other products produced by Lacet.

| | |
|---|---|
| Budgeted inspection cost | $2,500,000 |
| Divided by budgeted number of inspections | 1,000,000 |
| Cost per inspection | $2.50 |
| Times number of inspections per unit for the Model ZX disk drive | 3 |
| Inspection cost per unit for Model ZX | $7.50 |

## THE ABC APPROACH AT GARDENRITE MANUFACTURING: A COMPREHENSIVE EXAMPLE

Our comprehensive example of the ABC approach uses the situation faced by the Gardenrite Manufacturing Company presented at the start of the chapter. As you read through the example, make sure you can explain why using the ABC approach reduces the cost of the high-volume product (the Model 250 spade) and increases the cost of the low-volume product (the Model 900 mower).

**Gardenrite's Costs under the Traditional Approach.** For product costing purposes, Gardenrite traces labor and material costs directly to products produced. Manufacturing overhead is allocated to products based on labor cost. At the start of 2006, estimated manufacturing overhead was $40,000,000, and estimated labor cost was $8,000,000. Thus, the overhead allocation rate was $5 per dollar of labor.

For 2006, the following costs and revenues are expected from sale of the Model 250 spade and the Model 900 mower.

|  | Model 250 Spade | Model 900 Mower |
|---|---|---|
| Number of units | 85,000 | 800 |
| Sales revenue | $765,000 | $240,000 |
| Direct labor | 91,800 | 12,000 |
| Direct material | 153,000 | 48,000 |
| Overhead | 459,000 | 60,000 |
| Total cost | 703,800 | 120,000 |
| Gross profit | $ 61,200 | $120,000 |
| Cost per unit | $8.28 | $150.00 |
| Gross profit per unit | $.72 | $150.00 |
| Gross profit as a % of sales | 8.00% | 50.00% |

Note that the overhead allocated to the Model 250 spade, $459,000, is equal to the overhead rate of $5 per dollar of labor times the $91,800 of direct labor incurred in production of the spade.

The production process for spades is fairly simple. The company uses one supplier for the metal handle and blade. The company produces shafts on an automatic lathe, and the handles, blades, and shafts are assembled by hand at a single workstation.

Two years ago, the company began manufacturing lawn mowers. The production process for lawn mowers is much more complicated than that used for spades. Twenty suppliers are used to provide the 50 components involved in producing the Model 900 mower. Furthermore, assembly of mowers makes use of 15 separate assembly workstations.

Recall that Ben Jakes, the CFO at Gardenrite, suspects that the low gross profit (less than 10 percent of sales) for spades may be due to problems with the costing system in use. Furthermore, he is somewhat surprised that the company is able to earn such a high gross profit on mowers (50 percent of sales). Since the company only recently began manufacturing mowers, he expected production inefficiencies to keep gross profit low for at least three years.

**Gardenrite's Costs under the ABC Approach.** The CFO is right to be concerned about the product costing system at Gardenrite. The company's approach to allocating overhead assumes that all overhead is proportional to a single measure of production volume—labor cost. However, overhead is likely caused by several key activities.

Suppose the CFO authorizes a study of how the costs of the Model 250 spade and the Model 900 mower will change if an ABC approach is taken. The study determines that the $40,000,000 of overhead cost is related to the four cost drivers identified in Illustration 6-9. As indicated in the illustration, setup costs are related to the number of setups, material handling costs are related to the number of material requisitions, and depreciation of equipment is related to the number of machine hours required to produce products. All other overhead is categorized in a cost pool simply referred to as "Other." Gardenrite has decided that "manufacturing complexity" is a major factor contributing to the incurrence of other overhead costs. The cost driver for complexity is the number of workstations required to produce a product. Products that require many workstations to produce are more complex and cause more overhead.

**Illustration 6-9**
Overhead cost items
and cost drivers

| Overhead Cost Items | Annual Cost | Cost Driver | Estimated Annual Value | Cost per Driver Unit |
|---|---|---|---|---|
| Setup costs | $4,000,000 | Number of setups | 1,000 | $4,000 per setup |
| Material handling costs | $2,000,000 | Number of material requisitions | 2,000 | $1,000 per requisition |
| Depreciation of equipment | $10,000,000 | Number of machine hours | 20,000 | $500 per machine hour |
| Other | $24,000,000 | Number of workstations used in production of a product | 3,000 workstations used across all products | $8,000 per workstation |

Manufacturing spades requires two setups and three material requisitions. Forty machine hours are used to produce the 85,000 Model 250 spades. Assembly of spades requires one workstation. Production of the 800 Model 900 mowers requires five setups and 50 material requisitions. One hundred machine hours are used to produce the 800 mowers. Assembly of mowers requires 15 workstations. This information is summarized in Illustration 6-10.

Using this information, we can calculate the cost per unit of Model 250 spades and the cost per unit of Model 900 mowers assuming the company changes to an ABC system. The calculations are presented in Illustration 6-11. With the ABC approach, the cost of the Model 250 spade drops from $8.28 to $3.34 per unit, whereas the cost of the Model 900 mower increases from $150 to $375 per unit.

| | Model 250 Spade | Model 900 Mower |
|---|---|---|
| Cost per unit using traditional approach to allocating overhead | $8.28 | $150.00 |
| Cost per unit using ABC approach to allocating overhead | $3.34 | $375.00 |

Recall that the Model 250 spades sell for $9 per unit. Thus, the ABC approach reveals that this high-volume product is very profitable. However, the Model 900 mower sells for only $300 per unit. The ABC approach reveals that the selling

**Illustration 6-10**
Production information
for 85,000 spades
and 800 mowers

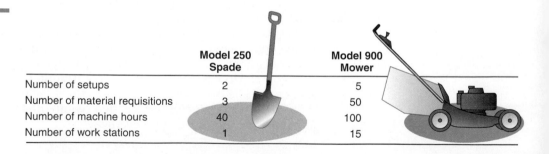

| | Model 250 Spade | Model 900 Mower |
|---|---|---|
| Number of setups | 2 | 5 |
| Number of material requisitions | 3 | 50 |
| Number of machine hours | 40 | 100 |
| Number of work stations | 1 | 15 |

**Illustration 6-11**
Costs of model 250 spade
and model 900 mower
using an ABC approach

| | Model 250 Spade | | Model 900 Mower |
|---|---|---|---|
| Number of units | 85,000 | Number of units | 800 |
| Direct labor | $ 91,800 | Direct labor | $ 12,000 |
| Direct material | 153,000 | Direct material | 48,000 |
| Overhead: | | Overhead: | |
|   Setup cost ($4,000 × 2) | 8,000 |   Setup cost ($4,000 × 5) | 20,000 |
|   Material handling cost ($1,000 × 3) | 3,000 |   Material handling cost ($1,000 × 50) | 50,000 |
|   Depreciation of equipment | 20,000 |   Depreciation of equipment | 50,000 |
|     ($500 × 40) | |     ($500 × 100) | |
|   Other ($8,000 × 1) | 8,000 |   Other ($8,000 × 15) | 120,000 |
| Total overhead | 39,000 | Total overhead | 240,000 |
| Total cost | $283,800 | Total cost | $300,000 |
| Cost per unit | $3.34 | Cost per unit | $375.00 |
| Selling price per unit | $9.00 | Selling price per unit | $300.00 |
| Gross profit per unit | $5.66 | Gross profit (loss) per unit | ($75.00) |
| Gross profit as a % of sales | 63% | Gross profit (loss) as a % of sales | (25%) |

price does not even cover the full cost of this low-volume product.[4] The CFO's intuition that the traditional product costing system at Gardenrite might be providing misleading information was correct. Because the traditional system only allocated costs using a volume-related allocation base, the high-volume product (spades) was overcosted and did not appear to be particularly profitable. The low-volume product (mowers) was undercosted and appeared to be highly profitable, when in fact it was not covering its full costs.

## PROS AND CONS OF ABC

Although, as you can see, ABC offers some real advantages, it is not without problems. This section describes two major benefits of ABC and two major limitations.

**Benefits.** ABC is less likely than traditional costing systems to undercost complex, low-volume products and overcost simple, high-volume products. This follows because ABC uses more cost drivers to assign costs and the drivers are not necessarily volume related.

A second benefit is that ABC may lead to improvements in cost control. With ABC, managers see costs broken out by a number of activities rather than buried in one or two overhead cost pools. Unless managers know the costs of setups, inspections, order taking, stocking, moving inventory, and other key activities, they are not likely to see a need to improve efficiency and reduce these costs.

---

[4]The fact that costs exceed revenue for the Model 900 mower does not *necessarily* imply that the product should be immediately dropped. Some of the costs included in the cost of the mower (like depreciation) will exist whether or not the mower is produced. See the discussion in Chapter 7 dealing with cost information and management decisions.

Recall that under its traditional overhead allocation system, managers at Gardenrite knew that overhead was $5 per labor dollar. What they didn't know was the cost of the key activities that determine total overhead. With the ABC system, however, they now know that (1) setup costs are $4,000,000 in total or $4,000 per setup; (2) material handling costs are $2,000,000 in total or $1,000 per requisition; (3) depreciation of equipment is $10,000,000 in total or $500 per machine hour and (4) other overhead costs are $24,000,000. With this information, managers are likely to be spurred to action leading to process improvements and increased efficiency. One can easily imagine a manager saying "Wow, I had no idea we were spending $2 million on material handling. We've got to be able to get this cost down below $1,000 per requisition. Let's take a look at the steps involved in material handling and cost them out. Now that I think of it, we have 15 people working the receiving dock and they don't seem that busy. Maybe that's a place to start."

**Limitations.** A major disadvantage of ABC is its expense; an ABC system is more costly to develop and maintain than a traditional costing system. Consider an ABC system with 20 cost pools applied to 100 different products. Assigning costs to each of the 20 pools will be costly, and then 2,000 allocations will have to be made (20 pools × 100 products) to assign costs to products.

Perhaps the major limitation of ABC is that, in practice, it is used to develop the *full cost* of products. Because full costs include allocations of costs that are fixed (e.g., depreciation of plant and equipment and supervisory salaries), the cost per unit generated by the ABC system does not measure the incremental costs needed to produce an item. And incremental information is what is needed to make decisions. (Remember that Chapter 1 made this point: Decision making relies on incremental analysis.)

**Decision Making/
Incremental Analysis**

Consider the example of the mower produced by Gardenrite analyzed in the previous section. The ABC system indicated that the cost per unit was $375 and that the selling price was only $300. However, will Gardenrite's costs really increase by $375 if another mower is produced? The answer is no. Much of the cost of producing the mower relates to depreciation on equipment that has already been incurred. This cost is not just fixed, it's also sunk, and sunk costs are not relevant for decisions since they're not incremental. Thus, in many cases, ABC does not provide clear-cut information applicable to decision making. Do the disadvantages of ABC outweigh the advantages? After assessing the pros and cons, we can reasonably conclude that, for companies that don't use the information in an overly simplistic way (i.e., treat the full cost information as if it were incremental cost information), an ABC system is likely to be quite beneficial.

## Any Questions?

**Q** According to the book, a major limitation of ABC is that it doesn't distinguish between fixed and variable costs. Isn't there a simple fix to this problem? Just separate fixed costs and variable costs in each cost pool and allocate the variable costs per unit of each cost driver to products, but don't allocate the fixed costs on a per unit basis.

**A** Your idea is a good one. Most likely, managers would find the variable cost per setup, the variable cost per material requisition, the variable cost per inspection, etc. to be very useful information. Unfortunately, the "simple fix" you suggest isn't common in practice. Perhaps this is due to the fact that, in practice, the fix isn't all that simple—a great deal of analysis would be needed to separate fixed and variable costs in each overhead cost pool.

See the video on the interactive CD to learn how Microsoft uses ABM to improve efficiency and effectiveness.

# ACTIVITY-BASED MANAGEMENT (ABM)

**Activity-based management (ABM)** is a management tool that involves analyzing and costing activities with the goal of improving efficiency and effectiveness. As you would expect, ABM is closely related to ABC, but the two schemes differ in their primary goals. Whereas ABC focuses on activities with the goal of measuring the costs of products and services produced by them, ABM focuses on activities with the goal of managing the activities themselves. This difference is shown graphically in Illustration 6-12.

To clarify the difference, consider activities involved in setting up equipment for a production run. ABC seeks to measure the cost of setups and then assign a cost to products based on how many setups each product requires. The goal of ABM, however, is to improve the efficiency and effectiveness of the activities. Thus, for example, ABM would focus on ways to improve the setup process and ways to eliminate the demand for setup activity (thus reducing setup cost).

Managers using ABM want to know the costs of activities because this information may provide insight into how well the activities are being performed. For example, by knowing the cost of setups, managers can benchmark performance by comparing setup costs at one plant to setup costs at another plant. If the costs per setup are much higher at Plant A than at Plant B (and the plants are producing similar items), there is a good chance that costs are out of control in Plant A. In essence, ABM supports the management dictum, "You can't manage what you can't measure." In other words, you need to know the costs of activities before you can do a good job managing them. ABM is discussed in more detail in the appendix to this chapter.

**Illustration 6-12**
Comparison of ABC and ABM

**ABC focus is better costing of products and services.**
**Resources are traced to activities to facilitate costing of products and services.**

| Resources | → | Activities | → | Costing of products and services |

**ABM focus is improvement of efficiency and effectiveness of activities.**
**Resources are traced to activities to facilitate evaluation of activities.**

| Resources | → | Activities | → | Evaluation of activities |

# REMEMBER—YOU GET WHAT YOU MEASURE!

Before concluding our discussion of cost allocation, let's return to one of the key points raised in Chapter 1: You get what you measure! How does this point relate to cost allocation? Allocations affect the profit that managers have reported on their performance reports. Thus, managers pay attention to controlling the allocation base, since more use of the allocation base results in higher costs and lower profit.

Consider two companies that are initially identical. Company A allocates production overhead based on labor hours, whereas Company B allocates production overhead based on machine hours. Managers at both companies must make decisions about how much labor and equipment to use in their production processes. All else being equal, the managers at Company A will view labor as more expensive, because when they use more labor to make products, the products receive higher allocations of overhead. Managers at Company B will view equipment as more expensive because when they use more machine time to produce products, the products receive higher allocations of overhead. Thus, over time, we might expect the managers of Company A to increase use of equipment and the managers of Company B to increase use of labor to produce their products.

Similarly, if you calculate overhead using the number of setups as the allocation base, managers are likely to want to reduce the number of setups. If you calculate overhead using the number of inspections as the allocation base, managers are likely to want to reduce the number of inspections. And if you calculate overhead using labor costs as the allocation base, managers are likely to want to reduce labor costs. These actions, which are driven by the way companies measure profit, are not necessarily good or bad. For example, it may be useful to *reduce* the number of inspections in order to reduce cost, but it might also be useful to *increase* the number of inspections in order to increase product quality. The point is not that the number of setups, the number of inspections, or labor costs are or are not good allocation bases. The point is that the choice of an allocation base affects other management decisions in ways that may not be obvious.

# MAKING BUSINESS DECISIONS

Decision making relies on incremental analysis. A potential problem with cost allocation is that it may make a fixed cost appear to be a variable cost and, therefore, incremental. Suppose, for example, that fixed costs are allocated based on sales dollars. This makes it appear that if sales increase, the costs will increase. When making decisions using cost information that involves allocation—beware!

## KNOWLEDGE AND SKILLS (K/S) CHECKLIST

*Knowledge and skills are needed to make good business decisions. Check off the knowledge and skills you've acquired from reading this chapter.*

❏ K/S 1. You have an expanded business vocabulary (see key terms).

❏ K/S 2. You can explain why costs are allocated.

❏ K/S 3. You can allocate service department costs to production departments.

❏ K/S 4. You recognize that cost allocation can lead to a number of significant problems.

❏ K/S 5. You understand activity-based costing (ABC) and can explain why it results in a cost that is different from that obtained using a traditional product costing approach.

❏ K/S 6. You can explain the difference between activity-based costing (ABC) and activity-based management (ABM).

# SUMMARY OF LEARNING OBJECTIVES

**1** *Explain why indirect costs are allocated.* Indirect costs are allocated to provide information for decision making, to calculate the full cost of products, to reduce the frivolous use of common resources, and to encourage managers to evaluate the efficiency of internally provided services. From a decision making standpoint, the allocation should measure the opportunity cost of using a company resource. However, this is difficult to operationalize in practice, since opportunity costs often change quickly.

**2** *Describe the cost allocation process.* The cost allocation process has three steps: (1) identify the cost objectives, (2) form cost pools, and (3) select an allocation base to relate the costs to the cost objectives.

**3** *Discuss allocation of service department costs.* Service department costs are allocated to production departments, which in turn allocate these costs to products. The direct method allocates service department costs to production departments but not to other service departments.

**4** *Identify potential problems with cost allocation.* A number of problems are associated with

cost allocation in practice: (1) the allocated costs may not be controllable by the manager receiving the allocation; (2) allocations may be arbitrary; (3) allocations may make fixed costs appear to be variable; (4) allocations may be made using too few cost pools; and (5) allocation may be made using only volume-related allocation bases.

**5** *Discuss activity-based costing (ABC) and cost drivers.* Activity-based costing (ABC) is a costing method that recognizes that costs are caused by activities. Measures of the key activities that cause costs to be incurred are referred to as cost drivers. The cost drivers are used as the allocation bases to relate indirect costs to products. Unlike traditional systems, ABC does not focus solely on volume-related cost drivers.

**6** *Distinguish activity-based costing (ABC) from activity-based management (ABM).* Whereas ABC focuses on the costs of activities in order to develop the cost of goods and services produced by the activities, ABM focuses on the costs of activities in order to help manage the activities themselves (you can't manage what you can't measure).

# APPENDIX

**Understand the four-steps involved in an ABM study.**

## ACTIVITY-BASED MANAGEMENT

Activity-based management is a method of activity analysis aimed at improving the efficiency and effectiveness of business processes. Let's look at two process improvement examples that will help make the goal of ABM more concrete. Then we'll discuss a four-step approach to conducting an ABM study.

Consider the activity *shipping goods to stores* conducted by a large retailer with multiple stores. This activity involves having suppliers unload deliveries at the company's warehouse. Subsequently, goods are moved from the warehouse to the company's trucks and sent to stores. How could this process be improved? Wal-Mart uses *cross-docking* whereby deliveries from suppliers are loaded directly from suppliers' trucks onto Wal-Mart trucks and then sent to stores. With this approach, there is no need to move products into and around a warehouse.

As another example, consider the activity *checking into a hotel*. A number of hotels have improved this process using computer technology. Based on information obtained from initial visits, a computerized database knows customer preferences for room location and for a smoking versus nonsmoking room. Credit card information, addresses, and phone numbers are also in the database. With this information readily available, hotel workers at the registration desk can check customers in more rapidly and in a way that recognizes their individual preferences, leading to gains in customer loyalty.

Hopefully, these two examples have provided some insight into the goal of an ABM study—process improvement. Now, let's discuss a four step process for conducting one. In our discussion, we'll consider the case of Mattress Warehouse, a discount store that sells beds and mattresses. The company has a single warehouse and 15 stores in the Dallas/Fort Worth area. Stores do not hold inventory except for display. Thus, all shipments originate from the warehouse. The company offers free delivery within 100 miles of any store and for the first time in its 25 year history has decided to study the delivery process to determine its cost and identify potential improvements. Solutions Analysis, a consulting firm, has been hired to undertake the study.

## STEP 1: DETERMINE MAJOR ACTIVITIES

The first step in the ABM study is to determine major activities. This is usually accomplished through interviews and observation. Solutions Analysis has determined that the key activities are:

   a. Determine customer locations, determine availability of stock, and prepare delivery schedules.
   b. Pick orders from warehouse.
   c. Load trucks.
   d. Deliver merchandise.
   e. Return merchandise to stock if not acceptable to customer or customer not home to receive delivery.
   f. Wash delivery trucks (performed each night).
   g. Schedule trucks for routine service (e.g., oil change) and nonroutine repairs.

## STEP 2: IDENTIFY RESOURCES USED BY EACH ACTIVITY

The second step is to identify the resources used by each activity. Let's consider the resources used by activities (e) and (f).

**Return Merchandise to Stock If Not Acceptable to Customer or Customer Not Home to Receive Delivery.** Solutions Analysis has determined that in a typical month, 25 orders are returned because customers receive a slightly different mattress or box spring than expected. For example, a customer may have picked out a mattress in the store with blue stitching but the one delivered has red stitching. Or, the model name on the mattress delivered is different (due to a change by the manufacturer) from the model name on the mattress in the store although items are identical in all other respects. Additionally, 40 orders are returned each month due to customers not being home to receive delivery. The monthly cost of this activity is $2,050.

**Wash Delivery Trucks.** Solutions Analysis has determined that each of the 15 delivery trucks is washed each night. Costs include the salaries of three employees, supplies, depreciation, water and other miscellaneous costs. The total cost is $8,450 each month.

| **Monthly Cost of Returning Merchandise to Stock when Not Acceptable to the Customer or the Customer is Not Home to Receive Delivery.** | |
|---|---:|
| Salaries related to returning merchandise to stock 15 hours × $20 | $ 300 |
| Costs to process paperwork for corrected shipment | 250 |
| Salaries to re-pick shipment 10 hours × $20 | 200 |
| Transportation cost to re-ship order (includes, fuel, repair cost, and driver salary) | 1,300 |
| Total | $2,050 |
| **Monthly Cost to Wash 15 Delivery Trucks.** | |
| Monthly salaries (three full-time employees) | $7,500 |
| Supplies | 450 |
| Depreciation of equipment | 300 |
| Water and other miscellaneous costs | 200 |
| Total | $8,450 |

## STEP 3: EVALUATE THE PERFORMANCE OF THE ACTIVITIES

Once Solutions Analysis has determined the cost of key activities, they can turn their attention to an evaluation of them. This is the third step in an ABM study. One way they can do this is by benchmarking the activities against similar activities performed by other clients they have dealt with. For example, Solutions Analysis now knows that it costs the company $101,400 a year ($8,450 × 12 months) to wash its 15 trucks. That's $6,760 per truck. From their work with other retail companies that perform delivery services, they have calculated an average cost of under $3,000 per truck. Thus, the cost of this activity to Mattress Warehouse appears to be too high.

## STEP 4: IDENTIFY WAYS TO IMPROVE THE EFFICIENCY AND/OR EFFECTIVENESS OF THE ACTIVITIES

The most satisfying part of the ABM process is identifying ways to improve the efficiency and/or effectiveness of activities, the fourth and last step of the ABM process. Pause for a minute and consider the two activities analyzed. Can you suggest any process improvements?

To identify process improvements, the consultants at Solutions Analysis would think about best practices they've identified at other clients, they would brainstorm with each other, and they would solicit input from managers at Mattress Warehouse. Possible improvements are listed in Illustration A6-1.

**Illustration A6-1**
Possible process improvements for mattress warehouse

- Ask the sales force to discuss the possibility of minor variations in stitching color with customers. If customers have a strong preference, confirm current colors with the warehouse before shipping. This should reduce returns.
- Have a clerk call customers the day before a delivery to confirm that the customers will be home. This should reduce the problem of customers not being home to accept deliveries.
- Reduce staffing in the wash operation from three full-time employees to two full-time employees. This will save approximately $2,500 per month. Alternatively, consider outsourcing the wash operation.

# CONCLUSION

Hopefully, this brief treatment of ABM has provided you with insight into the nature of an ABM study.[1] Unlike ABC, which is focused on better costing of goods and services, ABM is focused on process improvements. Still, ABM like ABC requires costing activities. Once activities are costed, a manager conducting an ABM study can identify the so-called "low hanging fruit." That is, the manager can identify activities whose costs are large and apparently out of line. These are the activities that deserve immediate management attention.

One reason ABM studies have become so popular is that they often generate very substantial financial returns. Consider the case of Mattress Warehouse. If it turns out that eliminating one employee from the wash operation is appropriate, the company will save $2,500 per month or $30,000 per year. Over five years, that's $150,000. To analyze the wash operation, a consultant from Solutions Analysis likely spent less than 8 hours and billed Mattress Warehouse less than $4,000.

# REVIEW PROBLEM

Bender Electric Motors produces electric motors used by home appliance and other manufacturing companies. Each motor is built to customer specifications although the number of units requested may vary from 1 to as many as 2,000.

Bender has recently adopted an activity-based costing system with the following overhead costs and drivers.

| Cost Pool | Annual Amount | Annual Driver |
|---|---|---|
| Direct labor related | $   400,000 | $1,000,000 direct labor cost |
| Material ordering | 100,000 | 5,000 purchase orders |
| Material inspection | 600,000 | 4,000 receiving reports |
| Equipment setup | 200,000 | 1,000 setups |
| Quality control | 400,000 | 2,000 inspections of motors |
| Machine related | 800,000 | 40,000 machine hours |
| Miscellaneous | 400,000 | $4,000,000 of product costs other than miscellaneous overhead |
| Total overhead | $2,900,000 | |

Recently, the company received an order from Kromer's Department Stores for 10 identical motors for use in a holiday display. Bender estimates the following costs and activities related to the order:

| | |
|---|---|
| Material cost | $500 |
| Labor cost | $200 |
| Purchase orders | 2 |

[1]The following books will provide you with additional information on activity-based management: Judith J. Baker, *Activity-Based Costing and Activity-Based Management for Health Care*, Aspen Publishers, (1998); James A. Brimson and John Antos, *Activity-Based Management*, John Wiley and Sons, (1994); and Robin Cooper, Robert Kaplan, Lawrence Maisel, Eileen Morrissey, and Ronald Oehm, *Implementing Activity-Based Cost Management: Moving From Analysis to Action*, Institute of Management Accountants, (1992).

| | |
|---|---|
| Receiving reports | 2 |
| Setups | 1 |
| Inspections | 1 |
| Machine hours | 10 |

Note that the costs indicated are *for all 10 motors*—they are *not* per motor.

**Required**
a. Calculate the cost of the Kromer job using the new ABC system.
b. Calculate the cost of the Kromer job assuming the company used a traditional costing system with labor cost as the only allocation base.
c. Briefly explain why costs are higher or lower using the ABC system in part a compared to the traditional system in part b.

**Answer**

a.

| Cost Pool | Overhead Rate |
|---|---|
| Direct labor related | $ 0.40 per direct labor dollar |
| Material ordering | $ 20.00 per purchase order |
| Material inspection | $150.00 per receiving report |
| Equipment setup | $200.00 per setup |
| Quality control | $200.00 per inspection |
| Machine related | $ 20.00 per machine hour |
| Miscellaneous | $ 0.10 per dollar of product costs other than misc. |

**ABC Cost of Kromer Job**

| | |
|---|---|
| Material | $ 500 |
| Labor | 200 |
| Overhead: | |
| Labor related ($0.40 × $200) | 80 |
| Material ordering ($20 × 2) | 40 |
| Material inspection ($150 × 2) | 300 |
| Setup ($200 × 1) | 200 |
| Quality control ($200 × 1) | 200 |
| Machine related ($20 × 10) | 200 |
| Miscellaneous (= .10 × cost other than misc.) | 172 |
| Total overhead | 1,192 |
| Total cost | $1,892 |

Cost other than misc. = $1,720

b.

**Traditional Overhead Rate**

| | |
|---|---|
| Total overhead | $2,900,000 |
| Total labor cost | $1,000,000 |
| Rate | $2.90 per labor dollar |

**Traditional Cost of Kromer Job**

| | |
|---|---|
| Material | $ 500 |
| Labor | 200 |
| Overhead ($2.90 × $200) | 580 |
| Total cost | $1,280 |

c. Costs are higher with ABC because the Kromer job is relatively small and makes use of a number of activities whose costs are not proportionate to volume.

# K E Y   T E R M S

Ability to bear costs (194)
Activity-based costing (ABC) (203)
Activity-based management (ABM) (209)
Cause-and-effect relationship (193)
Controllable cost (197)
Cost allocation (188)

Cost driver (202)
Cost objective (192)
Cost pools (192)
Direct method of allocating cost (195)
Equity approach to allocation (194)

Lump-sum allocations (199)
Relative benefits approach to allocation (194)
Responsibility accounting system (197)
Unitized (198)

# S E L F   A S S E S S M E N T   *(Answers Below)*

1. Costs are allocated:

   a. To provide information useful for decision making.
   b. To reduce frivolous use of resources.
   c. To encourage evaluation of internally provided services.
   d. To calculate the "full cost" of products/services for GAAP reporting.
   e. All of the above are reasons to allocate costs.

2. There are, in order, three steps in the cost allocation process. List them:
   (1) _____, (2) _____,
   (3) _____.

3. In the cost allocation process, the cost objective is:

   a. The allocation base used to allocate the costs.
   b. A grouping of individual costs whose total is allocated using one allocation base.
   c. The product, service, or department that is to receive the allocation.
   d. None of the above.

4. An important concern in forming a cost pool is to:

   a. Avoid placing similar costs in the same pool.
   b. Limit the number of costs that make up the pool.
   c. Ensure that the costs in the pool are homogeneous, or similar.
   d. None of the above.

5. In the cost allocation process, an allocation base:

   a. Must be some characteristic that is common to all of the cost objectives.
   b. Ideally should result in cost being allocated based on a cause-and-effect relationship.
   c. Both a and b.
   d. None of the above.

6. The direct method of allocating costs:

   a. Allocates service department costs to other service departments.
   b. Allocates only direct costs.

   c. Allocates service department costs to producing departments only.
   d. Both b and c.

7. To prevent service departments from passing on the excess cost related to inefficiencies:

   a. Budgeted costs should be allocated.
   b. Actual costs should be allocated.
   c. No costs should be allocated.
   d. None of the above.

8. When fixed costs are stated on a per unit basis:

   a. Fixed costs are said to be "unitized."
   b. Fixed costs may appear to be variable to managers receiving allocations.
   c. Decision making is greatly improved.
   d. Both a and b.

9. One way to avoid the problems associated with unitized fixed costs is to:

   a. Not allocate fixed costs.
   b. Use a lump-sum method of allocating fixed costs.
   c. Combine fixed and variable costs in a single cost pool.
   d. None of the above.

10. Allocation of indirect costs:

    a. Can be done with great accuracy and precision, if the proper techniques are used.
    b. Is an inherently arbitrary process, a characteristic that can lead to problems.
    c. Can often be justified in a variety of ways that lead to substantially different costs being allocated.
    d. Both b and c.

11. Controllable costs for the manager of Production Department A include:

    a. Costs of the finance department
    b. Costs of material and labor used in Department A.
    c. All costs related to Department A's final product.
    d. All the above.

**12.** In allocating costs to products, more accurate costing is generally obtained by:

    a. Allocating costs using labor hours as the allocation base.

    b. Having more than one cost pool.

    c. Always using allocation bases that are based on production volume.

    d. None of the above.

**13.** Cost drivers in activity-based costing:

    a. Are always related to production volume.

    b. Are workers who influence cost control.

    c. Often assign more costs to low-volume products than traditional allocation methods.

    d. None of the above.

**14.** Most companies that use an activity-based costing system use:

    a. No cost pools.

    b. One or two cost pools.

    c. Two to five cost pools.

    d. More than five cost pools.

**15.** Activity-based cost systems:

    a. Always lead to improvements in cost control.

    b. Are less expensive to develop and maintain than traditional costing systems.

    c. Allow managers to see the costs of key activities.

    d. Are used to develop the full cost of products, which provides clear information for decision making.

**16.** Activity-based management:

    a. Is the same as activity-based costing.

    b. Has the goal of managing activities that cause costs.

    c. Focuses only on the costs of activities.

    d. Supports the management dictum, "You can always manage what you can't measure."

**Answers to Self Assessment**

**1.** e;　**2.** (1) Identify the cost objectives, (2) form cost pools, and (3) select an allocation base to relate the cost pools to the cost objectives;　**3.** c;　**4.** c; **5.** c;　**6.** c;　**7.** a;　**8.** d;　**9.** b;　**10.** d; **11.** b;　**12.** b;　**13.** c;　**14.** d;　**15.** c;　**16.** b

# INTERACTIVE LEARNING

**Enhance and test your knowledge of Chapter 6 using the interactive CD.**

**1.** Learning Objectives

**2.** Multiple Choice

**3.** Language of Business—Matching of Key Terms

**4.** Critical Thinking

**5.** Demonstration—How allocation using a single overhead rate can distort the apparent profitability of products

**6.** Case—*Andrews Consulting;* Use ABM to analyze the process of acquiring technology at a consulting firm

**7.** Video—Activity-based management (ABM) at Microsoft

**Go to our dynamic Web site for more self-assessment, Web links, and additional information.**

# QUESTIONS

**1.** List four reasons why indirect costs are allocated.

**2.** Is the following statement true? "Cost allocation refers to the process of assigning *direct* costs." Discuss.

**3.** Allocated costs are, in effect, a charge for the use of internal resources or services. What are some possible advantages obtained from charging for internal resources and services?

4. What is a "cost-plus" contract? Describe how a cost-plus contract may influence selection of an allocation base.

5. Explain what a cost objective is and give two examples.

6. What is a "cost pool?"

7. Explain one possible advantage to having two cost pools for each service department; one for variable costs and one for fixed costs.

8. If a company is allocating cafeteria costs to all departments within the company, what allocation base might result in a cause-and-effect relationship?

9. If cause-and-effect relationships cannot be established when choosing an allocation base, accountants use other criteria to select an allocation base. What are three such criteria?

10. Why is it generally a good idea to allocate budgeted, rather than actual, service department costs?

11. What is a responsibility accounting system?

12. Why might noncontrollable costs be allocated to a department?

13. What major problem can be created by unitizing fixed costs for allocation? How might you avoid such a problem?

14. Briefly explain how traditional methods of allocating overhead to products might underallocate costs to low production-volume products.

15. How does activity-based costing differ from the traditional costing approach?

16. When would activity-based costing give more accurate costs than traditional costing systems?

17. What are the limitations of activity-based costing?

18. How does activity-based management differ from activity-based costing?

# EXERCISES

**EXERCISE 6-1. Group Assignment**   Explain how the allocation process can make a fixed cost appear variable, leading to a poor decision.

**EXERCISE 6-2. Writing Assignment**   Mansard Hotels has 5 luxury hotels located in Boston, New York, Chicago, San Francisco, and Los Angeles. For internal reporting purposes, each hotel has an income statement showing its revenue and direct expenses. Additionally, the company allocates to each hotel a share of general administrative and advertising costs (e.g., salary of the company president, salary of the company CFO, hotel chain advertising, etc.) based on relative revenue.

*Required*
Write a paragraph explaining why the allocation of general administrative and advertising costs to the specific hotels is potentially useful or potentially harmful.

**EXERCISE 6-3. Internet Assignment**   At research hospitals, indirect costs must be allocated among research, clinical, and educational activities. Examples of indirect costs include the cost of buildings, administrative overhead, utilities, computing, and telecommunications. A discussion of the process used by the Harvard Medical Center and affiliated hospitals is provided at:

http://research.bidmc.harvard.edu/research/costofresearch.asp

*Required*
Go to the Web site and identify the recommended allocation base for building depreciation, telecommunications, and administrative and general costs. Are these allocations consistent with "cause and effect" or "relative benefits?"

**EXERCISE 6-4. Reasons for Allocating Indirect Costs** Star Production Company has a security department that provides security services to other departments within the company. Department managers are responsible for working with the head of security to ensure that their departments are protected. Explain why Star might want to allocate security department costs to other departments.

**EXERCISE 6-5. Choice of Allocation Base (Cost Driver) For Service Departments** Keller Insurance Company has six service departments:

Human Resources (hires employees and manages benefits)
Duplicating (performs copy services)
Janitorial (provides routine cleaning services)
Accounting (provides accounting services)
Graphic Design (designs forms)
Food Services (provides free breakfast and lunch to employees)

The services are used by the company's three subsidiaries (Keller Home Insurance, Keller Auto Insurance, and Keller Business Insurance).

*Required*

a. Suggest allocation bases to be used in allocating the service department costs to the three subsidiaries.

b. Food Services are used by employees in the Human Resources Department. Would a share of Food Service costs be allocated to Human Resources under the direct method of allocation?

**EXERCISE 6-6. Cost Allocation Process** Apex Company's Copy Department, which does almost all of the photocopying for the Sales Department and the Administrative Department, budgets the following costs for the year, based on the expected activity of 5,000,000 copies:

| | |
|---|---|
| Salaries (fixed) | $60,000 |
| Employee benefits (fixed) | 15,000 |
| Depreciation of copy machines (fixed) | 15,000 |
| Utilities (fixed) | 2,000 |
| Paper (variable, 1 cent per copy) | 50,000 |
| Toner (variable, 1 cent per copy) | 50,000 |

The costs are assigned to two cost pools, one for fixed and one for variable costs. The costs are then assigned to the Sales Department and the Administrative Department. Fixed costs are assigned on a lump-sum basis, 30 percent to sales and 70 percent to administration. The variable costs are assigned at a rate of 2 cents per copy.

*Required*

Assuming 4,000,000 copies were made during the year, 1,500,000 for Sales and 2,500,000 for Administration, calculate the Copy Department costs allocated to Sales and Administration.

**EXERCISE 6-7. Allocation of Service Department Costs** The building maintenance department for Wells Manufacturing Company budgets annual costs of $3,000,000 based on the expected operating level for the coming year. The costs are allocated to two production departments. Wells is considering two allocation bases for assignment of costs to departments: (1) square footage and (2) direct labor hours. The following data relate to the potential allocation bases:

|                   | Production Dept. 1 | Production Dept. 2 |
|-------------------|:------------------:|:------------------:|
| Square footage    | 20,000             | 30,000             |
| Direct labor hours| 30,000             | 20,000             |

***Required***

Calculate the costs allocated to the production departments using each allocation base. Comment on which allocation base is preferable.

**EXERCISE 6-8. Allocation of Service Department Costs**   Marvin Company has three service departments (S1, S2, S3) and two production departments (P1, P2). The following data relate to Marvin's allocation of service department costs:

|     | Budgeted Costs | Number of Employees |
|-----|:--------------:|:-------------------:|
| S1  | $3,000,000     | 75                  |
| S2  | 2,000,000      | 50                  |
| S3  | 1,000,000      | 25                  |
| P1  |                | 150                 |
| P2  |                | 225                 |

Service department costs are allocated by the direct method. The number of employees is used as the allocation base for all service department costs.

***Required***

a.  Allocate service department costs to production departments.

b. Calculate the total service department cost allocated to each production department.

**EXERCISE 6-9. Problems Associated with Cost Allocation**   High Country Outerwear received an offer from a motorcycle company to purchase 1,000 waterproof riding suits for $175 each. High Country's accountants determine that the following costs apply to the production of a riding suit:

|                        |          |
|------------------------|---------:|
| Direct material        | $ 80     |
| Direct labor           | 40       |
| Manufacturing overhead | 62       |
| Total                  | $182     |

Of the $62 of overhead, $10 is variable and $52 relates to fixed costs. The $52 of fixed overhead is allocated as $1.30 per direct labor dollar.

***Required***

a.  What will be the effect on profit if the order is accepted?

b.  Explain why managers who focus on reported cost per unit may be inclined to turn down the order.

**EXERCISE 6-10. Responsibility Accounting, Controllable Costs**   Rex Kerr, the manager of the service department at the Dirt Bike Sales and Service Company, is evaluated based on the profit performance of his department. The profit of the department is down this year because the service department's share of allocated general and administrative costs (allocated based on relative sales dollars) is much higher than last year. In the current year, service revenue has increased slightly while sales of dirt bikes have decreased substantially.

***Required***

a. Explain why the allocation of general and administrative costs to the service department is higher in the current year.

b. Discuss how this situation relates to a responsibility accounting system and controllable costs.

**EXERCISE 6-11. Problems with Cost Allocation**  Keller Insurance Company has six service departments (Human Resources, Duplicating, Janitorial, Accounting, Graphic Design and Food Services) whose costs are allocated to the company's three subsidiaries (Keller Home Insurance, Keller Auto Insurance, and Keller Business Insurance) on the basis of their relative sales.

*Required*

a. Suppose you are the president of Keller Auto Insurance. Will you perceive the allocated service department costs to be fixed costs, variable costs, or mixed costs?

b. In performing incremental analysis, will the president of Keller Auto Insurance tend to overestimate or underestimate incremental costs? Explain.

**EXERCISE 6-12. Problems Associated with Too Few Cost Pools**  Mott Manufacturing allocates factory overhead using one cost pool with direct labor hours as the allocation base. Mott has two production departments (P1 & P2). The new accountant at Mott estimates that next year the total factory overhead costs will be $3,000,000 and approximately 400,000 direct labor hours will be worked. The accountant also estimates that P1 will use 100,000 direct labor hours and there will be about $2,000,000 in overhead costs in P1. P2 will use 300,000 direct labor hours and there will be $1,000,000 in overhead costs in P2. Mott has two products: A1 and B1. It takes two direct labor hours in P1 and three direct labor hours in P2 to complete one unit of A1. It takes one direct labor hour in P1 and four direct labor hours in P2 to complete one unit of B1.

*Required*
Which product will be undercosted and which will be overcosted with the one cost pool system? Support your answer with appropriate calculations.

**EXERCISE 6-13. Cost Allocation and Opportunity Cost**  Keller Insurance Company has a graphic design department that designs insurance forms and other documents used by the company's three subsidiaries (Keller Home Insurance, Keller Auto Insurance, and Keller Business Insurance). For practical purposes, the costs of the graphic design department are primarily fixed and relate to the salaries of the department's two employees.

*Required*
Analyze the following three independent cases:

a. Assume there is no allocation of graphic design costs to the subsidiaries. Jobs requested by the subsidiaries are completed promptly (generally by the next business day). How does the allocation (which is zero) compare to the opportunity cost of using design services?

b. Assume there is no allocation of graphic design costs to the subsidiaries. Jobs requested by the subsidiaries generally take weeks to complete; the subsidiaries often go outside the company for design services. How does the allocation (which is zero) compare to the opportunity cost of using design services?

c.  Assume subsidiaries receive an allocation of $50 per design hour. Jobs requested by the subsidiaries generally take weeks to complete; the subsidiaries often go outside the company for design services rather than wait for jobs to be completed. They generally pay $70 per hour outside the company. How does the allocation ($50 per design hour) compare to the opportunity cost of using design services?

d. Assume subsidiaries receive an allocation of $50 per design hour. Although the graphic design department is busy, jobs requested by the subsidiaries are completed promptly (generally by the next business day). How does the allocation ($50 per design hour) compare to the opportunity cost of using design services?

**EXERCISE 6-14. Activity-Based Costing** The following are six cost pools estab-lished for a company using activity-based costing. The pools are related to the com-pany's products using cost drivers.

**Cost Pools:**

(1) Inspection of raw materials

(2) Production equipment repairs and maintenance

(3) Raw materials storage

(4) Plant heat, light, water, and power

(5) Finished product quality control

(6) Production line setups

*Required*

For each of the preceding cost pools, identify a possible cost driver.

**EXERCISE 6-15. Relating Cost Pools to Products Using Cost Drivers** Power Electronics manufactures portable power supply units. Power has recently decided to use an activity-based approach to cost its products. Production line setups is a major activity at Power. Next year Power expects to perform 1,000 setups at a total cost of $1,500,000. Power plans to produce 750 units of product EP150, which will require 2 setups. How much setup cost will be allocated to each *unit* of EP150 produced?

**EXERCISE 6-16. Activity-Based Management** Eldon Company has two produc-tion plants. Recently, the company conducted a study to determine the cost of pro-cessing orders for parts at each of the plants. How might an operations manager use this information to manage the cost of processing orders?

**EXERCISE 6-17. Activity-Based Management** PorcheParts.com supplies parts for older Porches. Customer orders are placed over the Internet and are generally filled in one or two days using express mail services.

Mary Ortega, a consultant with ABM Services has been asked to conduct an ABM study of inventory management at PorcheParts.com. In this regard she has deter-mined that the cost of filling customer orders in the past year consisted primarily of $250,000 of salary expense related to five workers who "pick" parts from the ware-house and $300,000 of salary expense related to six workers who pack the orders for shipment. In the past year, the company filled 100,000 orders.

Based on work performed for a chain of auto supply stores, Mary has determined a benchmark cost of $4 per order.

*Required*

a. Comment on the advisability of comparing the costs at PorcheParts.com to those at an auto supply chain store.

b. Mary has observed the following: Workers go to a box that contains individual cus-tomer order sheets. They take the bottom order (the "oldest") and go into the ware-house with a handcart and a box. They then fill the order and carry the parts to a packing station. Can you suggest ways of improving this process?

# P R O B L E M S

**PROBLEM 6-1. Number of Cost Pools** Icon.com sells software and provides con-sulting services to companies that conduct business over the Internet. The company is organized into two lines of business (software and consulting), and profit statements are prepared as follows:

|  | Software | Consulting |
|---|---|---|
| Sales | $10,000,000 | $5,000,000 |
| Less direct costs | 5,000,000 | 3,000,000 |
| Less allocated costs | 3,000,000 | 1,000,000 |
| Income before taxes | $ 2,000,000 | $1,000,000 |

Direct costs include costs that are easily associated with each line of business. For software, this includes the salary of programmers, the cost of computers used by programmers, and the cost of CDs sold to customers. For consulting, direct costs include consultant salaries, computer costs, and travel costs. Allocated costs include costs that are not directly traced to the business units. These costs include employee benefits, rent, telecommunications costs, and general and administrative costs such as the salary of the CEO of Icon.com.

At the start of 2006, allocated costs were estimated as follows:

| Employee benefits | $1,000,000 |
|---|---|
| Rent | 600,000 |
| Telecommunications | 400,000 |
| General and administrative costs | 2,000,000 |
| Total | $4,000,000 |

In the past, allocations have been based on headcount (the number of employees in each business unit). Software had 300 employees and consulting had 100 employees. The new controller of Icon.com believes that the key driver of employee benefits and telecommunications costs is headcount. However, rent is driven by space occupied, and general and administrative costs are driven by relative sales. Icon.com rents 30,000 square feet; approximately 15,000 is occupied by software employees, and 15,000 by consulting personnel.

### Required

a. Prepare profit reports for software and consulting assuming the company allocates costs using headcount, space occupied, and sales as allocation bases. Compare the new levels of profit to the levels that result using a single allocation base (headcount).

b. Which provides the best information on profitability—a single overhead cost pool with headcount as the allocation base, or multiple cost pools using headcount, sales, and space occupied?

**PROBLEM 6-2. Allocated Cost and Opportunity Cost** Binder Manufacturing produces small electric motors used by appliance manufacturers. In the past year, the company has experienced severe excess capacity due to competition from a foreign company that has entered Binder's market.

The company is currently bidding on a potential order from Dacon Appliances for 5,000 Model 350 motors. The estimated cost of each motor is $50, as follows:

| Direct material | $20 |
|---|---|
| Direct labor | 10 |
| Overhead | 20 |
| Total | $50 |

The predetermined overhead rate is $2 per direct labor dollar. This was estimated by dividing estimated annual overhead ($10,000,000) by estimated annual direct labor ($5,000,000). The $10,000,000 of overhead is composed of $4,000,000 of variable costs and $6,000,000 of fixed costs. The largest fixed cost relates to depreciation of plant and equipment.

### Required

a. With respect to overhead, what is the opportunity cost of producing a Model 350 motor?

b. Suppose Binder can win the Dacon business by bidding a price of $48 per motor (but no higher price will result in a winning bid). Should Binder bid $48?

c. Discuss how an allocation of overhead based on opportunity cost would facilitate an appropriate bidding decision.

**PROBLEM 6-3. Cost-Plus Contracts, Allocations and Ethics**    Pelton Instrumentation manufactures a variety of electronic instruments that are used in military and civilian applications. Sales to the military are generally on a cost-plus profit basis with profit equal to 10 percent of cost.

Instruments used in military applications require more direct labor time because "fail-safe" devices must be installed. (These devices are generally omitted in civilian applications.)

At the start of the year, Pelton estimates that the company will incur $50,000,000 of overhead, $5,000,000 of direct labor, and 500,000 machine hours.

Consider the Model KV10 gauge that is produced for both civilian and military uses:

|  | Civilian | Military |
|---|---|---|
| Direct material | $2,000 | $2,500 |
| Direct labor | $600 | $900 |
| Machine hours | 80 | 80 |

*Required*

a. Calculate the cost of civilian and military versions of Model KV10 using both direct labor dollars and machine hours as alternative allocation bases.

b. Explain why Pelton Instruments may decide to use direct labor as an overhead allocation base.

c. Is it ethical for Pelton to select an allocation base that tends to allocate more of overhead costs to government contracts? Explain.

**PROBLEM 6-4. Allocating Service Department Costs**    World Airlines has three service departments: (1) ticketing, (2) baggage handling, and (3) engine maintenance. The service department costs are estimated for separate cost pools formed by department and are allocated to two revenue-producing departments: (1) domestic flights and (2) international flights. World does not differentiate between fixed and variable costs in making allocations. The following data relate to the allocations:

|  | Budgeted Data | |
|---|---|---|
|  | Costs | Air Miles |
| Ticketing | $4,000,000 | |
| Baggage handling | $2,000,000 | |
| Engine maintenance | $6,000,000 | |
| Domestic flights | | 5,000,000 |
| International flights | | 20,000,000 |

*Required*

a. Allocate the service department costs to the revenue-producing departments using air miles as the allocation base.

b. Evaluate the cause-and-effect relationship resulting from the use of air miles as the allocation base. In which of the cost pools do you think the cause-and-effect relationship is the strongest? Suggest alternative allocation bases for the two remaining cost pools with the weakest cause-and-effect relationship.

**PROBLEM 6-5. Allocating Service Department Costs**    Armstrong Industries produces electronic equipment for the marine industry. Armstrong has two service departments (maintenance and computing) and two production departments (assembly and testing). Maintenance costs are allocated on the basis of square footage occupied, and computing costs are allocated on the basis of the number of computer terminals. The following data relate to allocations of service department costs:

|  | Maintenance | Computing | Assembly | Testing |
|---|---|---|---|---|
| Service department costs | $400,000 | $600,000 |  |  |
| Square footage |  |  | 70,000 | 30,000 |
| Terminals |  |  | 5 | 10 |

*Required*

Allocate the service department costs to production departments using the direct method.

**PROBLEM 6-6. Choice of Allocation Base, Problems with Cost Allocation** Tilden Financial Services has two divisions: Financial Planning and Business Consulting. The firm's accountants are in the process of selecting an allocation base to allocate centrally provided personnel costs to the divisions. Two allocation bases have been proposed—salary and headcount (number of employees). Personnel costs are expected to be $1,000,000. The following data relate to the allocation:

|  | Financial Planning | Business Consulting |
|---|---|---|
| Salaries | $10,000,000 | $5,000,000 |
| Headcount | 150 | 50 |

*Required*

a. Prepare a schedule showing the allocations to the two divisions using each allocation base.

b. Referring to your answer to a, explain why allocations are sometimes considered arbitrary.

**PROBLEM 6-7. Cost Allocation and Apparent Profitability** Jarvis Paint Company applies paint finishes to auto parts. In the past, most finishes were applied by hand, and the overhead allocation rate in the prior year was $10 per labor hour ($2,000,000 overhead ÷ 200,000 labor hours). In the current year, overhead increased by $400,000 due to acquisition of new painting equipment. Labor, however, decreased by 50,000 hours because the equipment allows for rapid application of paint.

One of the company's many customers is Shelly Auto Supply. This company is relatively small and the time to paint an order of parts is typically less than 8 labor hours. On such jobs (less than 8 labor hours), the new equipment is not used, and thus the jobs are relatively labor intensive.

*Required*

a. Assume that in the current year, the company continues to allocate overhead based on labor hours. What would be the overhead cost of an 8-labor-hour job requested by Shelly Auto Supply? How does this compare to the overhead cost charged to such a job in the prior year?

b. Assume that the price charged for small jobs does not change in the current year. Are small jobs less profitable than they were in the past?

**PROBLEM 6-8. Activity-Based Costing** The Summit Manufacturing Company produces two products. One is a recreational whitewater kayak molded from plastic and designed to perform as a durable whitewater play boat. The other product is a high-performance competition kayak molded with high-tech fiberglass materials that are very light. The recreation boat is uniform in its dimensions and style. However, the competition boat is custom designed to fit the individual (e.g., rocker and cockpit size are adjusted).

Most of the sales come from the recreation boat, but recently sales of the competition boat have been increasing. The following information is related to the products for the most recent year.

| | Recreation Kayak | Competition Kayak |
|---|---|---|
| Sales and production (number of boats) | 900 | 100 |
| Sales price per boat | $600 | $660 |
| Unit costs: | | |
|    Direct materials | 150 | 200 |
|    Direct labor | 100 | 100 |
|    Overhead* | 135 | 135 |
| Total unit cost | 385 | 435 |
| Gross profit | $215 | $225 |

*Overhead costs:

| | |
|---|---|
| Building depreciation | $ 25,000 |
| Equipment depreciation | 25,000 |
| Materials ordering | 15,000 |
| Quality control | 10,000 |
| Maintenance and security | 10,000 |
| Setup and drafting | 20,000 |
| Supervision | 30,000 |
|   Total | $135,000 |

Overhead rate based on direct labor dollars:

| | |
|---|---|
| Total overhead | $135,000 |
| Total labor ($100 × 900) + ($100 × 100) | $100,000 |
| Rate (overhead labor) | $1.35 per direct labor dollar |

Victoria Mason, the president of Summit Manufacturing, is concerned that the traditional cost system used by Summit may not be providing accurate cost information and that the sales price of the competition boat might not be enough to cover its true costs.

### Required

a. The traditional system that Summit is using assigns 90 percent of the $135,000 total overhead to the recreational boats because 90 percent of the direct labor dollars are spent on the recreational boats. Discuss why this might not be an accurate way to assign overhead to boats.

b. Discuss how Summit might be able to improve cost allocation by using an ABC system.

c. Assume that Summit retains a consultant to create an activity-based costing system, and the consultant develops the following data:

| | | | Driver Activity | |
|---|---|---|---|---|
| | | | Rec. | Comp. |
| Cost Pool | Amount | Driver | Boats | Boats |
| Building | $25,000 | Square footage | 6,000 | 1,000 |
| Equipment | 25,000 | Machine hours | 3,400 | 600 |
| Materials ordering | 15,000 | Number of orders | 200 | 100 |
| Quality control | 10,000 | Number of inspections | 300 | 150 |
| Maintenance & security | 10,000 | Square footage | 6,000 | 1,000 |
| Setup and drafting | 20,000 | Number of setups | 20 | 40 |
| Supervision | 30,000 | Direct labor cost | $90,000 | $10,000 |
| | $135,000 | | | |

Determine the overhead allocation to each line of boats using an activity-based costing approach and compute the total unit costs for each model boat.

d. Discuss why activity-based allocations are different from those generated by the traditional allocation method used by Summit.

**PROBLEM 6-9. Activity-Based Costing**  Computech Company manufactures mouse devices for computers. They make 12 different models as well as several other types of computer components. They have recently adopted an activity-based costing system to assign manufacturing overhead to products. The following data relate to one of their products, the wireless Remote Mouse, and the ABC cost pools:

**Remote Mouse:**

| | |
|---|---|
| Annual production | 20,000 units |
| Direct materials per unit | $31 |
| Direct labor per unit | $6 |

**Manufacturing overhead cost pools:**

| Cost Pool | Cost | Cost Driver |
|---|---|---|
| Materials ordering | $    800,000 | Number of purchase orders |
| Materials inspection | 400,000 | Number of receiving reports |
| Equipment setup | 2,000,000 | Number of setups |
| Quality control | 900,000 | Number of inspections |
| Other | 15,000,000 | Direct labor cost |
| Total mfg. overhead | $19,100,000 | |

Activity information related to cost drivers:

| | Annual Activity | |
|---|---|---|
| Cost Pool | All Products | Remote Mouse |
| Materials ordering | 100,000 orders | 1,000 |
| Materials inspection | 2,000 receiving reports | 300 |
| Equipment setup | 100 setups | 1 |
| Quality control | 4,000 inspections | 400 |
| Other | $10,000,000 direct labor | $120,000 |

*Required*

a. Calculate the overhead rate per unit of activity for each of the five cost pools.

b. Calculate the *total* overhead assigned to the production of the Remote Mouse.

c. Calculate the *overhead cost per unit* for the Remote Mouse.

d. Calculate the *total unit cost* for the Remote Mouse.

e. Suppose that Computech allocates overhead by a traditional production volume-based method using direct labor dollars as the allocation base and one cost pool. Determine the overhead rate per direct labor dollar and the per unit overhead assigned to the Remote Mouse. Discuss the difference in cost allocations between the traditional method and the activity-based costing approach.

**PROBLEM 6-10. Activity-Based Management**  Baxter Consulting is a consulting firm with 10 offices. Within the company is a travel group that arranges flights and hotel accommodations for the over 1,000 consultants. The cost of operating the travel group (excluding the costs associated with actual travel such as hotel cost and air fare) amounts to approximately $800,000.

Recently, Baxter has conducted an ABM study that has determined the following:

a. Each consultant takes approximately 20 business trips per year.

b. On average, 30 percent of trips are rescheduled due to conflicts and poor planning.

c. The travel group employs 14 individuals at $45,000 each to book travel. In addition, there is a travel manager and an assistant travel manager.

d. Benchmarking with a Baxter client indicates that the client incurs $30 cost per completed trip to book travel.

***Required***

a. Evaluate the cost incurred by Baxter compared to the benchmark cost.

b. Baxter is planning a process improvement initiative aimed at reducing scheduling conflicts. What would be the savings if rescheduling could be reduced by 50 percent? Assume that the only variable cost in travel services is the wages paid to employees who book travel.

**PROBLEM 6-11. (Appendix) Activity-Based Management**    First National Bank of Denver is conducting an ABM study of its teller operations. In this regard, the company has identified the following major activities performed by bank tellers:

a. Process deposits

b. Process withdrawals

c. Process requests for certificates of deposits

d. Answer customer questions related to balances, overdrafts, interest rates, etc.

e. Print out customer activity statements

f. Provide access to safe deposit boxes

g. Reconcile cash drawer

The company benchmarks its operations against banks in other cities and has found that it has many more tellers in comparison to banks of similar size. Further, the company has a relatively unsophisticated Web site and call center.

***Required***

a. How does the company's Web site and call center affect the demand for teller activities and the cost of teller services?

b. Identify two or three ways that technology can be used to reduce the cost of teller services.

**PROBLEM 6-12. (Appendix) Activity-Based Management**    Each month, senior managers at Logan's Department Store review cost reports for the company's various departments. The report for the human resource (HR) group for April is as follows:

| **Human Resources**<br>**April, 2006** | |
| --- | --- |
| Salaries and benefits | $63,500 |
| Supplies | 1,900 |
| Depreciation of office equipment | 1,300 |
| Total | $66,700 |

Megan Capshaw, the new vice president of operations, expressed her dissatisfaction with the report at a meeting with the company president, CFO, and controller. "This report is garbage," she began. "It shows that $63,500 is being spent on salaries in HR but it doesn't provide any information on what we're paying for. We need to know the activities of HR and what they cost. How are we suppose to manage the activities without that information? At my previous company, we routinely did activity-based management studies and they really helped us get a handle on operations and our costs."

Ed Walters, the controller responded that he'd get to work on ABM studies right away. Two week later, his staff had developed the following information for the HR operation:

| Activities in HR | Monthly Cost |
|---|---|
| a. General administration of department | |
| Salary of HR head | $ 8,500 |
| Salary of assistant to HR head | 4,000 |
| Depreciation of equipment | 200 |
| Supplies | 150 |
| | 12,850 |
| | |
| b. Benefits administration | |
| Salary of administrator | 6,500 |
| Depreciation of equipment | 150 |
| Supplies | 300 |
| | 6,950 |
| | |
| c. HR Web site development/maintenance | |
| One half-time staff person | 2,000 |
| Depreciation of equipment | 400 |
| Supplies | 150 |
| | 2,550 |
| | |
| d. Operations | |
| Salary of 5 clerks who process paperwork related to hiring, retirements, and terminations | 12,500 |
| Depreciation of equipment | 600 |
| Supplies | 450 |
| | 13,550 |
| | |
| e. Training | |
| Salary of 6 staff members who train new employees on company policies, operation of cash-registers, etc. | 30,000 |
| Depreciation of equipment | 550 |
| Supplies | 250 |
| | 30,800 |
| Total | $66,700 |

**Additional Information:** The company has approximately 6,000 employees and annual employee turnover of approximately 15 percent.

*Required*

Comment on the insights provided by the ABM study to date. Where's the "low hanging fruit?" In other words, what activities appear to be good candidates for further study and significant cost savings?

# CASES

## 6-1 JANSEN ENGINEERING

In recent years, Jansen Engineering Corporation's computer system had been plagued by slow response times and frequent repairs. The cause was a substantial increase in computer-aided design work that pushed the system beyond its intended capacity. Bob Wilson, vice president of operations, decided that a new computer should be acquired to absorb some of the additional work. Surprisingly, six months after installing the new computer, he noticed that many of the engineers continued to use the old computer system, even though the new system had excess capacity and several features that simplified programming.

Bob discussed the situation with the supervisors of the company's six design teams. They explained that the controller's office allocates the cost of each computer to their work based on the number of hours they use the computer. One responded, "Look, the old computer didn't cost much and it's highly utilized—even the accounting department uses that machine. When the cost per hour of use is calculated, it's very low. The new machine, on the other hand, cost a bundle, and in the first couple of months we didn't use it much because it takes time to learn a new system. I was shocked when I saw how high my charges were for using the new machine. Because the cost is high and use is low, the cost per hour charged to my work was incredible. I'll tell you something, next month we'll probably use the new computer even less. Our job performance doesn't look very good when our jobs cost a fortune to complete because of huge allocations of computer cost."

"What a mess," Bob thought. "Even though the new computer is bought and paid for and has plenty of capacity, the engineers aren't using it. Don't they realize that most of the computer costs are fixed costs? It doesn't really cost the company much more to use the new computer 200 hours per month rather than 20 hours per month."

*Required*
Recommend a change in the allocation system at Jansen that will change the behavior of the design teams.

## 6-2 EASTSIDE MEDICAL TESTING

Eastside Medical Testing performs five different tests (T1–T5) to detect drug use. Most clients are referred to the company by potential employers who pay for the tests. Revenue and costs related to the tests, for the most recent fiscal year, are detailed in Table 1.

Setting up equipment to conduct a test is the responsibility of three highly skilled technicians, one of whom is Emmet Wilson, founder and owner of the company. Tests T2–T5 are high-volume tests that are conducted in batches of 100 tests per batch. Thus, for example, T5 is run approximately twice a day to annually process 70,000 tests in 700 batches. On the other hand, T1 is a test with relatively low demand. However, it is run almost every day (300 runs per year), so that results can be quickly communicated to employers. This fast turnaround represents a significant competitive advantage for the company.

Nuclear Systems, Inc., is one of the few companies that requires T1. Indeed, it accounted for almost half of the 3,000 T1 tests conducted in the past year. Recently, Ron Worth, vice president of operations at Nuclear Systems questioned the relatively high price being charged for T1. In a letter to Emmet Wilson he noted that

> We pay $31 for each T1 test, which is about 50% higher than your next most expensive test. Is this charge warranted? Frankly, this isn't just a matter of dollars and cents. We believe that we are being taken advantage of because we are one of the few companies that requires the test, and you are one of the few companies that provide it. If we believed that the high price was justified in terms of significantly higher costs, we would not be writing this letter.

Before responding to Worth's letter, Emmet reviewed the revenue and cost data presented in Table 1. As indicated, T1 produced a profit of $6.80 per test which was much higher than the profit per test of any of the other procedures. However, since taking a day-long continuing education course at City College (entitled "ABC and Managing by the Right Numbers!"), Emmet has wondered whether the profitability of tests is being distorted by the company's simple approach to allocating overhead—overhead allocation is based on direct labor cost. Direct labor consists of wages and benefits paid to relatively unskilled technicians who prepare samples for testing. This cost, $194,850, is only 10 percent of total overhead.

**Table 1  Profitability of Tests for the Fiscal Year Ending December 31, 2004**

|  | T1 | T2 | T3 | T4 | T5 | Total |
|---|---|---|---|---|---|---|
| Number of tests per year | 3,000 | 40,000 | 55,000 | 60,000 | 70,000 | 228,000 |
| Number of runs | 300 | 400 | 550 | 600 | 700 | 2,550 |
| Price per test | $ 31.00 | $ 22.00 | $ 20.00 | $ 18.00 | $ 17.00 | |
| Less: | | | | | | |
| Material cost | 11.00 | 9.00 | 7.00 | 6.85 | 5.35 | |
| Direct labor at $18 per hour | 1.20 | 0.85 | 0.85 | 0.85 | 0.85 | |
| Overhead at $10 per labor dollar | 12.00 | 8.50 | 8.50 | 8.50 | 8.50 | |
| Total cost | 24.20 | 18.35 | 16.35 | 16.20 | 14.70 | |
| Profit per test | $ 6.80 | $ 3.65 | $ 3.65 | $ 1.80 | $ 2.30 | |
| Total profit | $20,400 | $146,000 | $200,750 | $108,000 | $161,000 | $ 636,150 |
| Total overhead | $36,000 | $340,000 | $467,500 | $510,000 | $595,000 | $1,948,500 |
| Total labor | $ 3,600 | $ 34,000 | $ 46,750 | $ 51,000 | $ 59,500 | $ 194,850 |

With help from his bookkeeper, Emmet began to analyze overhead costs in an attempt to calculate the ABC cost of the five tests. In the past year, overhead amounted to $1,948,500 as follows.

| Overhead | Costs |
|---|---|
| Setup labor | $ 525,000 |
| Equipment | 1,050,000 |
| Rent | 140,000 |
| Billing | 84,000 |
| Clerical | 68,000 |
| Other | 81,500 |
| Total | $1,948,500 |

Emmet's analysis of these six overhead cost categories was as follows.

**Setup labor** ($525,000). This amount is essentially the salary and benefits paid to Emmet and the two other skilled technicians who set up equipment for testing batches of T1–T5. Emmet believes that the number of runs (batches of tests) is a valid driver for this cost pool. In the past year, there were 2,550 runs.

**Equipment** ($1,050,000). This amount is depreciation on equipment used to process the tests. All of the major pieces of equipment are used in each test. (In other words, no major piece of equipment is used exclusively for any individual test.) Emmet believes that the amount of direct labor cost is a valid driver for this cost pool. This follows because equipment hours vary with direct labor hours and direct labor cost. In the past year, total direct labor was $194,850.

**Rent** ($140,000). This amount is the annual rent on the facility occupied by Eastside Medical Testing. Emmet believes that the number of tests (228,000 in the prior year) is a valid driver for this cost pool since each test benefits equally from the incurrence of rent expense.

**Billing** ($84,000). This amount is the annual salary and benefits of two billing clerks as well as a variety of other charges (e.g., billing software costs). Emmet believes that the number of tests (228,000 in the prior year) is a valid driver for this cost pool since each test requires a separate billing charge.

**Clerical** ($68,000). This amount is the annual salary and benefits of two general clerical employees who process orders for supplies, file records, and so on. Emmet believes that the number of tests (228,000 in the prior year) is a valid driver for this cost pool since each test benefits equally from the incurrence of clerical expense.

**Other** ($81,500). This amount includes the salary and benefits of the bookkeeper, depreciation on office equipment, utilities, and so on. Emmet believes that the number of tests (228,000 in the prior year) is a valid driver for this cost pool since each test benefits equally from the incurrence of these expenses.

*Required*

a. Based on Emmet's assumptions, calculate the ABC cost per unit and profit per unit of each test.

b. Should Emmet lower the price of the T1 test, or keep the current price and risk losing the business of Nuclear Systems?

c. Assume that Emmet, based on his ABC analysis, decides not to lower the price of the T1 test. What will be the effect on annual company profit if the company loses the business of Nuclear Systems (i.e., T1 tests decrease by 1,500)?

# 6-3 WILTON INTERNATIONAL

Wilton International is a large conglomerate with divisions that produce chemicals, tires, specialty metals and pharmaceuticals. Two years ago, the chief financial officer noted that the company paid consultants more than $3,000,000 per year to help solve problems related to manufacturing efficiency, employee motivation, investment decisions and a variety of other matters. The $3,000,000 in charges reflect average fees of approximately $120 per hour. The CFO decided that substantial funds could be saved by setting up an internal consulting group. Accordingly, five senior consultants from a respected firm were hired to run an internal consulting group at an average salary of $150,000 per year. These new managers hired 15 additional employees at an average salary of $50,000 per year. Thus, the company had 20 full time internal consultants at a yearly cost of only $1,500,000. The 20 individuals can work approximately 38,000 hours per year in total.

In the first year of the consulting group, the CFO sent out a notice to all divisions that they would no longer be allowed to hire outside consultants for work that could be performed by the internal group. Further, each division was to be charged a flat annual fee for use of the consultants based on their relative size (measured in sales dollars) over the last four years. With this approach, the allocation was as follows:

|  | **Allocation** |
| --- | --- |
| Chemicals | $ 150,000 |
| Tires | 300,000 |
| Specialty Metals | 450,000 |
| Pharmaceuticals | 600,000 |
| Total | $1,500,000 |

With this allocation, the division managers made frequent demands for the services of the consultants. Indeed, because of the demand for the services of the internal consultants, there were frequent delays, often exceeding one month.

The following year, the CFO changed the method of allocation to a charge for hours worked. Since costs were $1,500,000 and 38,000 hours were available, the charge was $39.50 per hour. With this charge, demand for consulting services declined. In fact, the average consultant was only charging 70 percent of available hours. Further, all requests for service were easily answered within a day or two.

*Required*

a. Explain the difference in demand under the two allocation schemes.

b. Is the current charge of $39.50 per hour more or less than the opportunity cost of providing consulting services?

c. Because at a charge equal to the actual hourly wage paid to consultants, demand is less than internal consulting capacity, the CFO is considering closing the internal consulting department. Based on the limited information provided, what would you advise?

# 6-4 QuantumTM

QuantumTM manufactures electronic testing and measurement instruments. Many products are custom designed with recent orders for function generators, harmonic analyzers, logic analyzers, temperature measurement instruments, and data logging instruments. The company prices its instruments at 35 percent over estimated cost (excluding administrative and selling costs).

Recently, senior management has noted that it's product mix has changed. Specifically, the company is receiving fewer large orders for instruments that are relatively simple to produce and customers are saying that the company is not price competitive. On the other hand, the company is receiving more small orders for complex instruments and customers appear quite happy to pay QuantumTM's price. This situation was discussed at a weekly management meeting and Jason Norton, VP operations, blamed the company's antiquated cost accounting system. "Look," he said. "If you have bad cost information, you're going to have bad prices, and we're still doing product costing the way companies did it in the 1930s. I've been reading articles about activity-based costing and they indicate that out-of-date costing systems make simple products look too costly and complex products too cheap. If that's true, it would explain why we're not price competitive for simple products."

The meeting ended with a decision to hire a consultant to conduct a preliminary ABC study to determine how a switch to ABC would affect product cost. The consulting firm selected two recent orders for study: an 800 unit order for a temperature monitoring device and an order for 1 harmonic analyzer. The costs and prices charged were as follows:

**Exhibit 1   Cost Pools and Drivers**

| Cost Pools | Annual Cost | Annual Driver Value |
|---|---|---|
| Product design | $ 6,000,000 | 120,000 design hours |
| Material ordering and handling | 8,000,000 | 100,000 unique part numbers |
| Inspection | 2,500,000 | 400,000 inspections |
| Set-up | 1,500,000 | 50,000 set-ups |
| Labor related overhead | 6,000,000 | $8,000,000 direct labor cost |
| Depreciation of plant and equipment | 16,000,000 | 200,000 machine hours |
| | $40,000,000 | |

| | Temperature Monitor | Harmonic Analyzer |
|---|---|---|
| Component cost per unit | $200 | $2,000 |
| Direct labor per unit | 20 | 400 |
| Overhead per unit | 100 | 2,000 |
| Cost per unit | 320 | 4,400 |
| Mark-up at 30% | 96 | 1,320 |
| Price per unit | $416 | $5,720 |
| Number of units | 800 | 1 |
| Value of order | $332,800 | $5,720 |

In the current system, overhead is applied based on an estimate of $40,000,000 of annual overhead and $8,000,000 of direct labor cost. The consultants have broken the $40,000,000 of annual overhead down into six cost pools and identified related cost drivers as indicated in Exhibit 1. The consultants have also found that the monitor and analyzer make use of the cost drivers as indicated in Exhibit 2.

**Exhibit 2   Use of Cost Driver**

**The following values relate to the entire order of 800 Monitors (This is not per monitor.)**

| | |
|---|---|
| Number of design hours | 42 |
| Number of unique parts | 15 |
| Number of inspections | 200 |
| Number of setups | 1 |
| Machine hours | 100 |

**The following values relate to the order for 1 Analyzer**

| | |
|---|---|
| Number of design hours | 100 |
| Number of unique parts | 20 |
| Number of inspections | 15 |
| Number of setups | 1 |
| Machine hours | 5 |

*Required*

a. Based on the consultants work to date, calculate the ABC cost *per unit* of each product.

b. The consultants have completed their job and QuantumTM has adopted an ABC system as indicated in Exhibit 1. Recently, the company received an order for a unique data logging device. The device will require $8,000 of components and $2,000 of direct labor along with the following requirements.

**Use related to a data logging device**

| | |
|---|---|
| Number of design hours | 25 |
| Number of unique parts | 15 |
| Number of inspections | 10 |
| Number of set-ups | 1 |
| Machine hours | 8 |

The customer has indicated that they currently have a low bid from another company of $19,000. Calculate the ABC cost of the data logging device.

c. Suppose QuantumTM meets their competitors price and gets the job. What will be the impact on company profit? In answering this question, make the following assumptions:

   a. Forty percent of design costs are fixed and 60 percent vary with design hours.

   b. Thirty percent of material ordering and handling costs are fixed and 70 percent vary with the number of unique parts.

   c. Fifty percent of inspection costs are fixed and 50 percent are variable.

   d. Eighty percent of set-up costs are fixed and 20 percent are variable.

   e. Twenty percent of labor related costs are fixed and 80 percent are variable.

   f. Prices charged to this customer or other customers in the future will not be impacted by the current deal. This follows because each order is somewhat unique.

# chapter 7

## LEARNING OBJECTIVES

1. Explain the role of incremental analysis (analysis of incremental costs and revenues) in management decisions.

2. Define sunk cost, avoidable cost, and opportunity cost and understand how to use these concepts in analyzing decisions.

3. Analyze decisions involving joint costs.

4. Discuss the importance of qualitative considerations in management decisions.

# THE USE OF COST INFORMATION IN MANAGEMENT DECISION MAKING

At the start of the year, the president of General Refrigeration Company asked his three plant managers to examine their operations and search for ways to cut costs and improve profitability. Substantial bonuses were promised to managers who achieved cost savings in excess of $1,000,000.

Wendy Grant, manager of the Tennessee plant, thought she had a surefire way to save money. Her plant manufactures refrigeration units used by food processors and retail food stores. One of the main components of the refrigeration units is a compressor. Wendy anticipates producing 50,000 compressors in the coming year at a cost per unit of $345. Because she is concerned that production of compressors is not efficient, Wendy asked Dillard Compressor Corporation to bid on supplying the 50,000 units. After studying the specifications of the compressor, Dillard has indicated that it is willing to supply the compressors at $310 per unit.

"Look," Wendy explained to Ed Anderson, the plant accountant, "if we close the compressor operation and buy compressors from Dillard, we'll save about $1,750,000 a year! That kind of cost saving ought to really grab the president's attention." Ed seemed skeptical. "Wendy, let's look at the costs of producing the compressors. More than $1,000,000 of the cost is depreciation on plant and equipment purchased years ago. Another $500,000 represents the salaries of production supervisors. I don't think all of those costs will go away just because we shut down the compressor operation and turn to an outside supplier. Perhaps you'd better let me analyze the cost information in some detail before you make a recommendation."

Ed's point is well taken. Before making a decision, managers must gain a thorough understanding of the cost information that is relevant. In previous chapters, we have examined various issues involving costs: determining the costs of products and services using job-order and process costing systems (Chapters 2 and 3), examining cost-volume-profit relations (Chapter 4), and discussing the allocation of costs (Chapter 6). In the course of those discussions, we considered several examples of how cost information is used in decision making. Now, we discuss the topic in more detail.

**Decision Making/
Incremental Analysis**

Explain the role of
incremental analysis
(analysis of incremental
costs and revenues) in
management decisions.

# INCREMENTAL ANALYSIS

All decisions involve a choice among alternative courses of action. In Chapter 1, we learned that the solution to all business problems involves **incremental analysis**—the analysis of the *incremental* revenue and the *incremental* costs incurred when one decision alternative is chosen over another. **Incremental revenue** is the additional revenue received as a result of selecting one decision alternative over another. **Incremental cost** is the additional cost incurred as a result of selecting one decision alternative over another. If an alternative yields an incremental profit (the difference between incremental revenue and incremental cost), then it should be selected. Incremental costs are sometimes referred to as **relevant costs**, because they are the only costs that are *relevant* to consider when analyzing decision alternatives. They are also referred to as **differential costs**, because they are the costs that differ between decision alternatives.

Let's review a simple example of incremental analysis to ensure that the approach is understood. Then, in the next section we'll apply incremental analysis to somewhat more complicated decisions. Currently, Jensen Rapid Copy Center is open from 6 A.M. until 8 P.M. The owner of the company, Jon Jensen, is trying to decide whether or not hours should be extended until midnight. In this case, Jensen is facing a choice of two alternatives: closing at 8 P.M., which is the status quo, or closing at midnight. Jensen estimates that with the longer hours, revenue will increase by $800 per day. However, he will have to pay a part-time worker $20 per hour for 4 hours, there will be additional paper, toner, and other miscellaneous printing costs of $500, and additional utility costs of $10. In this case, incremental revenue associated with staying open until midnight is $800 per day, incremental costs are $590 per day and incremental profit is $210 per day. Since incremental profit is positive, staying open is the preferred alternative.

| Stay Open Until Midnight versus 8 P.M. | | |
|---|---:|---:|
| **Incremental revenue** per day | | $800 |
| **Incremental costs** per day: | | |
|   Salary | $ 80 | |
|   Paper, toner, etc. | 500 | |
|   Utilities | 10 | 590 |
| **Incremental profit** | | $210 |

Jensen pays rent for the space occupied by his company. Is the rent expense relevant to this decision? The answer is no. Jensen will pay the same amount of rent whether he sticks with the status quo or opts for staying open until midnight. Thus, rent is *not* an incremental expense.

Incremental analysis can be easily extended beyond two decision alternatives. Suppose Jensen is also considering the option of keeping the copy center open until 2 A.M. Now there are three alternatives: close at 8 P.M., close at midnight, or close at 2 A.M. There are two ways we can deal with the third alternative. We can compare it to the status quo and see if it yields an incremental profit greater than $210—if so, it is preferred to the midnight alternative. Or, we can compare the 2 A.M. alternative directly to the midnight option which, as we know, dominates the status quo. Let's do the latter. Suppose the incremental revenue per day associated with staying open from midnight to 2 A.M. is only $70. The incremental cost of salary is two hours at $20 per hour. Incremental paper, toner, and other printing costs are $27, and incremental utilities are $5. In this case, we should stick with the midnight option, since staying open until 2 A.M. yields an incremental *loss* of $2.

| Stay Open Until 2 A.M. versus Midnight | | |
|---|---:|---:|
| **Incremental revenue** per day | | $70 |
| **Incremental costs** per day: | | |
|   Salary | $40 | |
|   Paper, toner, etc. | 27 | |
|   Utilities | 5 | 72 |
| **Incremental loss** | | ($ 2) |

## WHEN YOUR BOSS ASKS "WHAT DOES THIS PRODUCT COST?" YOU SHOULD SAY "WHY DO YOU WANT TO KNOW?"

If you're ever in a situation where your boss asks you how much a product or service costs, you should reply "Why do you want to know?" While that reply may seem a bit rude, it makes an important point about incremental analysis. There is no single cost number that is relevant for all decisions. Thus, you need to know what decision your boss is planning to make so you can identify the incremental cost information that is applicable to the decision. Suppose your boss is trying to decide whether to accept a special order for a particular product. In this case, your boss wants to know whether the incremental cost of producing the order will exceed the incremental revenue from accepting it. Some costs such as the salary of a production supervisor will not change as a result of accepting the order and should not be considered as an incremental cost.

On the other hand, your boss may be considering dropping the product. If the product is dropped, the supervisor may be laid off and the cost savings related to the supervisor's salary is incremental. Thus, whether supervisory salary is an incremental cost and relevant to a decision depends on the decision being made. So, whenever, you're asked what a product or service costs, you want to respond "Why do you want to know?"

# ANALYSIS OF DECISIONS FACED BY MANAGERS

Now let's turn our attention to the use of incremental analysis for three decisions that managers frequently face:

1. The decision to engage in additional processing of a product.
2. The decision to make or buy a product.
3. The decision to drop a product line.

## ADDITIONAL PROCESSING DECISION

Occasionally, manufacturers must decide whether to sell a product in a partially completed stage or incur the additional processing costs required to complete the product. As an example, consider PowerComp, a manufacturer of personal computers. PowerComp has already decided to discontinue its Model 250 computer. Currently, it has 5,000 partially completed units on hand. To date, the company has spent $800 per unit, or $4,000,000, to bring these computers to their current stage of completion. The company estimates that costs of $400 per unit must be incurred to complete the computers. The costs are summarized below:

| **PowerComp** | | |
| --- | --- | --- |
| **Costs of Model 250 Computer** | | |
| | **Costs per Unit Incurred to Date** | **Costs per Unit to Complete** |
| Material | $300 | $200 |
| Labor | 200 | 100 |
| Variable overhead | 100 | 100 |
| Fixed overhead | 200 | |
| | $800 | $400 |

Because the company has announced that the Model 250 is going to be discontinued, the price of the computer has fallen. If the units are completed, they can only be sold for $1,000 per unit. That is less than the total cost of producing the computers—$1,200 per unit ($800 cost to date plus $400 of additional cost). An alternative to finishing the units is to sell them as they are. A small computer assembly company in another state is willing to buy the units in their current partial state of completion for $500 per unit.

Which action should be taken? Should the computers be sold in their current state of completion, or should the additional processing costs be incurred? Without a thorough understanding of accounting information and incremental analysis, a manager at PowerComp might conclude that further processing is not appropriate. After all, with further processing, total costs will amount to $1,200 per unit, which is more than the selling price of $1,000 per unit.

The error of this conclusion is revealed by incremental analysis. The facts for our analysis are presented in Illustration 7-1. Note that the illustration contains three columns. The first column lists the revenue and costs related to selling the computers in their current state of completion (Alternative 1). The second column lists the revenue and costs related to selling completed computers (Alternative 2). The third column lists the incremental revenue and costs that will be incurred by completing the computers.

We'll begin by examining incremental revenue. Recall that incremental revenue is simply the difference in revenue between two alternatives. PowerComp can sell completed units for $1,000 each, whereas it can sell the units in their current state of completion for $500 each. Thus, incremental revenue of $500 per unit is associated with choosing Alternative 2 and completing processing.

Now let's turn to incremental cost. Before going any further, we need to recall another cost term from Chapter 1—*sunk costs*, or costs incurred in the past. Sunk costs are not incremental costs. Since they've already been incurred, they won't increase or decrease with the choice of one alternative over another. In the case of PowerComp, the prior production costs are sunk costs, not incremental costs. Thus, they do not enter our analysis.

**Illustration 7-1**
Incremental analysis
of additional processing
decision

| | | | | |
|---|---|---|---|---|
| **PowerComp** | | | | |
| **Incremental Analysis of Additional Processing** | | | | |
| | **Sell in Current State of Completion (Alternative 1)** | **Complete Processing (Alternative 2)** | **Incremental Revenue and Costs (Alternative 2 minus Alternative 1)** | Incremental revenue associated with Alternative 2 |
| Revenue | $500 | $1,000 | $500 | |
| Less: | | | | |
| Prior production costs | | | | |
| Material | 300 | 300 | 0 | |
| Labor | 200 | 200 | 0 | |
| Variable overhead | 100 | 100 | 0 | |
| Fixed overhead | 200 | 200 | 0 | |
| | 800 | 800 | 0 | |
| Additional processing costs | | | | |
| Material | 0 | 200 | 200 | Incremental cost associated with Alternative 2 |
| Labor | 0 | 100 | 100 | |
| Variable overhead | 0 | 100 | 100 | |
| | 0 | 400 | 400 | |
| Gain (loss) per unit | ($300) | ($200) | $100 | |

Incremental profit associated with Alternative 2

What, then, are the incremental costs for PowerComp? An incremental cost, remember, is the difference in cost between two alternatives. The $400 cost of completing the units ($200 material, $100 labor, and $100 variable overhead) will be incurred if the units are completed and, thus, $400 is the incremental cost associated with completing processing.

You can see that by choosing Alternative 2 the company will be better off by $100 per unit ($500 incremental revenue − $400 incremental cost). In other words, choosing this alternative produces an incremental profit. As we noted earlier, if an alternative yields an incremental profit, it should be selected.

## MAKE-OR-BUY DECISIONS: THE GENERAL REFRIGERATION EXAMPLE

Most manufactured goods are made up of numerous components. In some cases, a company may purchase one or more of the components from another company. This may lead to considerable savings if the outside supplier is particularly efficient at manufacturing the component and can offer it at a reasonable price. Two decision alternatives arise in this situation: make or buy the component. No incremental revenues are involved. Therefore, the analysis of this decision concentrates solely on incremental costs.

Recall that Wendy Grant, manager of the Tennessee plant of General Refrigeration Company, is considering an offer by Dillard Compressor Corporation to supply 50,000 compressors at $310 per unit. Last year, when her plant produced 50,000 compressors, the following costs were incurred.

---

### ❄ GENERAL REFRIGERATION

**Cost of Manufacturing 50,000 Compressors**

| | |
|---|---:|
| Variable costs | |
| Direct material ($100 per unit) | $ 5,000,000 |
| Direct labor ($120 per unit) | 6,000,000 |
| Variable overhead ($80 per unit) | 4,000,000 |
| Total variable cost | 15,000,000 |
| Fixed costs | |
| Depreciation of building | 600,000 |
| Depreciation of equipment | 800,000 |
| Supervisory salaries | 500,000 |
| Other | 350,000 |
| Total fixed cost | 2,250,000 |
| Total cost | $17,250,000 |
| Cost per unit | $345 |

---

Additional analysis reveals the following: (1) The market value of the machinery used to produce the compressors is approximately zero. (2) Five of the six production supervisors will be fired if production of compressors is discontinued. However, one of the supervisors, who has more than 10 years of service, is protected by a clause in a labor contract, and will be reassigned to other duties, although his services are not really needed. His salary is $110,000.

**Illustration 7-2**
Incremental analysis
of make-or-buy decision

**GENERAL** REFRIGERATION

**Incremental Cost Analysis**

| | Cost of Manufacturing 50,000 Compressors | Cost of Buying 50,000 Compressors | Incremental Cost (Savings) |
|---|---|---|---|
| Variable costs | | | |
| Direct material | $ 5,000,000 | –0– | ($5,000,000) |
| Direct labor | 6,000,000 | –0– | (6,000,000) |
| Variable overhead | 4,000,000 | –0– | (4,000,000) |
| Total variable cost | 15,000,000 | –0– | (15,000,000) |
| Fixed costs | | | |
| Depreciation of building | 600,000 | 600,000 | –0– |
| Depreciation of equipment | 800,000 | 800,000 | –0– |
| Supervisory salaries | 500,000 | 110,000 | (390,000) |
| Other | 350,000 | 350,000 | –0– |
| Total fixed costs | 2,250,000 | 1,860,000 | (390,000) |
| Cost of buying compressors | –0– | 15,500,000 | 15,500,000 |
| Total | $17,250,000 | $17,360,000 | $ 110,000 |

At first, you might assume that General should buy the compressors rather than manufacture the units internally since the company can buy the units for $310 each, whereas the cost of manufacturing them is $345 each ($17,250,000 ÷ 50,000 units). However, careful consideration of the incremental costs reveals that it is cheaper to manufacture the compressors internally.

To demonstrate, we'll work through an incremental analysis, which is presented in Illustration 7-2. Like Illustration 7-1, Illustration 7-2 uses a three-column format. The first two columns present the costs of the two alternatives, while the third column presents the incremental costs. Another option is to use a single-column format that concentrates only on the incremental costs and benefits. A single-column analysis of the make or buy decision faced by the General Refrigeration Company is presented in Illustration 7-3.

**Illustration 7-3**
Single-column format
for incremental analysis

**GENERAL** REFRIGERATION

**Incremental Cost Analysis**

| | | |
|---|---|---|
| Cost of buying compressors outside (50,000 units @ $310) | | $15,500,000 |
| Cost savings (avoidable if purchase compressors outside): | | |
| Variable costs | $15,000,000 | |
| Supervisory salaries (salaries of 5 of 6 supervisors) | 390,000 | (15,390,000) |
| Excess cost of buying compressors outside | | $110,000 |

A key issue in our analysis involves determining which of the costs listed earlier are, in fact, incremental costs. Clearly, none of the $15,000,000 of variable manufacturing costs will be incurred if the compressors are purchased outside the company. Thus, this is an incremental cost *savings* between the two alternatives.

What about the fixed costs? Let's consider them item by item. The fixed costs associated with depreciation on the building and equipment do not represent a cost savings. The costs of purchasing the building and equipment were incurred in prior periods. Remember that the approach to analyzing decisions requires consideration of only the incremental revenues and costs of decision alternatives. The sunk costs related to purchasing the building and the pieces of equipment are not incremental costs because they have already been incurred and will not change no matter which decision alternative is selected.

The example assumes that fixed costs classified as "other" are also irrelevant sunk costs. But note that not all fixed costs are irrelevant sunk costs. Some fixed costs are **avoidable costs**—costs that can be avoided if a particular action is un-

## LINK TO PRACTICE

### *BP Outsources HR*

The make-or-buy decision that we just analyzed for General Refrigeration is much like the outsourcing decisions faced by many companies. In recent years, companies have been outsourcing more and more business processes including payroll, employee benefits, customer support, invoicing, and IT management. Companies claim that outsourcing leads to substantial cost savings, allows them

to focus on their core competencies, and ultimately increases shareholder value.

The trend is global. Consider BP (British Petroleum), the largest company in the UK. In 2000, the company signed a 600 million dollar, five-year deal to outsource the administration of human resources (HR). Interestingly, it signed the deal with Exult, a relatively small start-up in California. Using Internet-based technology and administrative centers, Exult deals with everything from pay and benefits to training, recruitment, and relocation.

The transition to Exult has not been trouble free. In Germany, for example, BP's third largest location with more than 10,000 employees, privacy laws make it difficult to process personnel information. In fact, BP workers outside Germany can't use technology to apply for jobs at BP's German locations. Also, BP held on to 1,500 HR employees as a "safety net" for the outsourcing experiment. This limited near-term cost savings. Still, BP expects the system to work well and even bought a 9 percent stake in Exult.

*Source:* Alison Maitland, "Giant Leap for Human Resources: Outsourcing," *Financial Times* (London), March 27, 2002, "Inside Track," pg. 12.

dertaken. In our example, if compressors are purchased outside the company, the salaries of five production supervisors will be saved. The saving totals $390,000 (total supervisory salaries of $500,000 less the $110,000 that must still be paid to the supervisor who will be retained). In other words, supervisory salaries of $390,000 represent an avoidable cost and thus an incremental cost.

We can see, then, that $15,000,000 of variable costs and $390,000 of fixed costs can be eliminated if the compressors are purchased from Dillard Compressor Corporation, for a total cost savings of $15,390,000. But the cost of purchasing the compressors from Dillard is $15,500,000 (50,000 units × $310). The difference is $110,000 ($15,500,000 purchase price − $15,390,000 cost saving), and the General Refrigeration Company would be $110,000 worse off if it decided to buy rather than make the compressors. Before a final decision is reached, however, qualitative factors should be considered. We'll discuss these factors later in the chapter.

A cost that must be considered in decision making is an opportunity cost. An **opportunity cost** is the value of benefits foregone by selecting one decision alternative over another. For example, if you chose to purchase a $1,000 stereo system rather than investing in a certificate of deposit (CD), the potential interest that could have been earned on the CD is an opportunity cost associated with buying the stereo. Since opportunity costs differ depending upon which decision alternative is selected, they are also incremental costs and are relevant in evaluating decision alternatives.

Suppose that the Tennessee plant is currently spending $500,000 per year to rent space for manufacturing metal shelving, which is used in the refrigeration units. If production of compressors is discontinued, the company will move the shelving operation to space currently occupied by the compressor operation. Thus, in continuing to produce the compressors the company gives up rent savings of $500,000. The foregone rent savings represents an opportunity cost. An analysis that includes this opportunity cost is presented in Illustration 7-4. According to this analysis, purchasing the compressors outside is the best alternative because it results in a net annual cost saving of $390,000.

**Illustration 7-4**
Make-or-buy analysis with opportunity costs considered

| ✳ GENERAL REFRIGERATION | | |
|---|---|---|
| **Incremental Cost Analysis** | | |
| Cost of buying compressors outside (50,000 units @ $310) | | $15,500,000 |
| Cost savings (avoidable if purchase compressors outside) | | |
| Variable costs | $15,000,000 | |
| Supervisory salaries (salaries of 5 of 6 supervisors) | 390,000 | |
| **Opportunity cost of using the plant to produce compressors (foregone rent savings)** | **500,000** | (15,890,000) |
| Net savings resulting from buying the compressors outside | | ($390,000) |

## DROPPING A PRODUCT LINE

Dropping a product line is a very significant decision and one that receives a great deal of attention. The proper approach to analyzing the problem is to calculate the change in income that will result from dropping the product line. If income will increase, the product line should be dropped. If income will decrease, the product line should be kept. This amounts to comparing the incremental revenues and costs that result from dropping the product line.

Let's consider an example involving a retailer. Magnolia Hardware sells three product lines: tools, hardware supplies, and garden supplies. Illustration 7-5 presents a product line income statement for the prior year. To arrive at net income for each product line, both direct fixed costs and allocated fixed costs are deducted from each product line's contribution margin.

Direct fixed costs are fixed costs that are directly traceable to a product line. For example, the salary of a worker who spends 100 percent of his or her time working in the tool section of the hardware store is a direct fixed cost to the tool product line.

Allocated fixed costs are those fixed costs that are not directly traceable to an individual product line. These costs are also referred to as **common costs**, because they are incurred for the common benefit of all product lines. An example of an allocated fixed cost is the salary of the owner/manager of the hardware store. Magnolia Hardware allocates common fixed costs to product lines based on their relative sales revenues. For example, sales of tools are 30 percent of sales ($120,000 tool sales ÷ $400,000 total sales). Thus, of the $80,000 of common costs, $24,000 (30% of $80,000) is allocated to tools.

In examining the product line income statement, the owner of Magnolia Hardware observes that the garden supplies line is currently showing a loss of $500. Would dropping this product line increase the profitability of the hardware store? To answer this question, we turn again to incremental analysis. As indicated in Illustration 7-6, sales revenue will decline by $80,000 if garden supplies are dropped. However, some costs will decrease or be eliminated altogether. Cost of goods sold will decrease by $60,000, and other variable costs will decrease by

**Illustration 7-5**
Product line income statement for Magnolia Hardware

| Magnolia Hardware | | | | |
|---|---|---|---|---|
| Product Line Income Statement<br>For the Year Ended December 31, 2006 | | | | |
| | **Tools** | **Hardware Supplies** | **Garden Supplies** | **Total** |
| Sales | $120,000 | $200,000 | $80,000 | $400,000 |
| Cost of goods sold | 81,000 | 90,000 | 60,000 | 231,000 |
| Gross margin | 39,000 | 110,000 | 20,000 | 169,000 |
| Other variable costs | 2,000 | 4,000 | 1,000 | 7,000 |
| Contribution margin | 37,000 | 106,000 | 19,000 | 162,000 |
| Direct fixed costs | 8,000 | 5,000 | 3,500 | 16,500 |
| Allocated fixed costs | 24,000 | 40,000 | 16,000 | 80,000 |
| Total fixed costs | 32,000 | 45,000 | 19,500 | 96,500 |
| Net income (loss) | $ 5,000 | 61,000 | $ (500) | $ 65,500 |

**Illustration 7-6**
Effect of dropping garden supplies at Magnolia Hardware

| | Income with Garden Supplies | | | | Income without Garden Supplies | | | Difference |
|---|---|---|---|---|---|---|---|---|
| | Tools | Hardware Supplies | Garden Supplies | Total | Tools | Hardware Supplies | Total | |
| Sales | $120,000 | $200,000 | $80,000 | $400,000 | $120,000 | $200,000 | $320,000 | $(80,000) |
| Cost of goods sold | 81,000 | 90,000 | 60,000 | 231,000 | 81,000 | 90,000 | 171,000 | (60,000) |
| Gross margin | 39,000 | 110,000 | 20,000 | 169,000 | 39,000 | 110,000 | 149,000 | (20,000) |
| Other variable costs | 2,000 | 4,000 | 1,000 | 7,000 | 2,000 | 4,000 | 6,000 | (1,000) |
| Contribution margin | 37,000 | 106,000 | 19,000 | 162,000 | 37,000 | 106,000 | 143,000 | (19,000) |
| Direct fixed costs | 8,000 | 5,000 | 3,500 | 16,500 | 8,000 | 5,000 | 13,000 | (3,500) |
| Allocated fixed costs | 24,000 | 40,000 | 16,000 | 80,000 | 30,000 | 50,000 | 80,000 | – |
| Total fixed costs | 32,000 | 45,000 | 19,500 | 96,500 | 38,000 | 55,000 | 93,000 | (3,500) |
| Net income | $ 5,000 | $ 61,000 | $ (500) | $ 65,500 | $ (1,000) | $ 51,000 | $ 50,000 | $(15,500) |

$1,000. Whether or not the direct fixed costs will decrease depends on the nature of these costs. For purposes of this example, assume that the direct fixed cost of $3,500 for garden supplies represents the wages paid to a part-time employee. If the garden supplies product line is dropped, this employee will not be retained by the store. In this case, the direct fixed cost of $3,500 is avoidable and represents a cost savings achieved by dropping garden supplies.

Allocated common fixed costs are generally not avoidable. Thus, no cost savings will be achieved with respect to the $16,000 of fixed costs allocated to garden supplies. For example, one component of the allocated fixed cost is rent of the hardware store. The rent will not decrease simply because one of the product lines is eliminated. Another allocated fixed cost is the cost of electricity. This cost is also unlikely to decrease if garden supplies are eliminated, because the store will still need approximately the same amount of heat and light. If garden supplies are eliminated, the share of fixed costs allocated to tools and hardware supplies will simply increase.

To summarize, the analysis of incremental costs and revenues indicates that income of $15,500 will be lost if garden supplies are dropped.

| Incremental Analysis Dropping Garden Supplies | |
|---|---|
| Lost sales | ($80,000) |
| Cost savings: | |
| Cost of goods sold | 60,000 |
| Other variable costs | 1,000 |
| Direct fixed costs | 3,500 |
| Total cost savings | 64,500 |
| Net loss from dropping | ($15,500) |

## BEWARE OF THE COST ALLOCATION DEATH SPIRAL!

Whenever you analyze a decision involving dropping a product or service, remember that common fixed costs are not incremental. This will allow you to avoid what is sometimes referred to as the *cost allocation death spiral*! In many cases, products or services may not appear to be profitable because they receive allocations of common fixed costs. But what will happen to the common costs if the product or service is dropped? They'll be allocated over the remaining products and services. That may result in another product or service appearing to be unprofitable.

Consider Magnolia Hardware as an example. If the company had decided to drop garden supplies, the $80,000 of common fixed costs would have been allocated over tools and hardware supplies. The new allocation would be $6,000 higher for tools, and it no longer would appear profitable—it would show a $1,000 loss. But what will happen to the common costs if it's dropped? That's right, they'll be allocated to hardware supplies. Before long, the store (which is reasonably profitable) would be out of business!

Define sunk cost, avoidable cost, and opportunity cost and understand how to use these concepts in analyzing decisions.

## SUMMARY OF INCREMENTAL, AVOIDABLE, SUNK, AND OPPORTUNITY COSTS

A number of costs terms have been used earlier, and in this section we briefly review them. Recall that the basic approach to decision making is to compare decision alternatives in terms of costs and revenues that are incremental. Costs that can be *avoided* by taking a particular course of action are always incremental costs and, therefore, relevant to the analysis of a decision. Costs that are *sunk* (i.e., already incurred and not reversible) are never incremental costs because they do not differ among the decision alternatives. Therefore, they are not relevant in making a decision.

Students of managerial accounting often assume that fixed costs are equivalent to sunk costs and are thus irrelevant (i.e., are not incremental costs), but this is not always the case. Fixed costs may be sunk and, therefore, irrelevant. Fixed costs may not be sunk but still irrelevant. Finally, fixed costs may not be sunk and may be relevant. Examples of these three possibilities are presented in Illustration 7-7.

Finally, *opportunity costs* represent the benefit foregone by selecting a particular decision alternative over another. By their nature, they are always incremental costs, and they must be considered when making a decision. To illustrate opportunity costs, consider the Magnolia Hardware example presented earlier. In this example, the company is considering dropping the garden supplies product line. Suppose that if garden supplies are dropped, more space can be devoted to selling tools, sales of tools will increase and the contribution margin associated with tools will increase by $20,000. In this case, there is a $20,000 opportunity

**Illustration 7-7**
Fixed costs and decision relevance

| Fixed costs | Classification |
| --- | --- |
| Depreciation on equipment already purchased | Sunk and irrelevant (not incremental) |
| President's salary which will not change for both action A and action B | Not sunk but still irrelevant (not incremental) |
| Salary of supervisor who will be retained if action A is taken and fired if action B is taken | Not sunk and relevant (incremental) |

cost associated with the decision to keep the garden supplies product line. This opportunity cost would make dropping the product line desirable rather than undesirable. Recall that our previous analysis indicated a $15,500 decrease in income from dropping the product line. However, considering the $20,000 opportunity cost due to foregone sales of tools, it appears that the store will be better off by $4,500 (i.e., $20,000 − $15,500) if garden supplies are dropped.

Analyze decisions involving joint costs.

# DECISIONS INVOLVING JOINT COSTS

When two or more products *always* result from common inputs, they are known as **joint products**. The costs of the common inputs are referred to as **joint costs**. Joint costs are common in the food processing, extractive, and chemical industries. For example, in the dairy processing business, the common input of raw milk is converted into cream, skim milk, and whole milk. For lumber companies, the common input of a log is converted into various grades of lumber. For fuel companies, the common input of crude oil is converted into a variety of fuels and lubricants.

A graphical treatment of a joint products and joint costs problem is presented in Illustration 7-8. In the illustration, joint costs are incurred, leading to two joint products. The stage of production at which individual products are identified is referred to as the **split-off point**. Beyond this point each product may undergo further separate processing and may incur additional costs.

## ALLOCATION OF JOINT COSTS

For financial reporting purposes, the cost of the common inputs must be allocated to the joint products. However, care must be taken to ensure that the resulting information does not mislead managers about the profitability of the

**Illustration 7-8**
Joint costs and joint products

### The Sunk Cost Effect

When managers make decisions, they need to be careful that they are not influenced by sunk costs. That's difficult because, psychologically, people are pre-disposed to take sunk costs into account. Psychologists refer to this "irrational" economic behavior as the *sunk cost effect*. Consider an immensely expensive waterway project that was scheduled for Congressional Review. Proponents of the project suggested that its elimination would be inappropriate because so much money had already been spent on its completion. That is, proponents rationalized continuation of the project in terms of sunk costs!

Two psychologists, Hal Arkes and Catherine Blumer, have investigated the sunk cost effect. In a research study, they presented 61 college students in Ohio and Oregon with the following question.

Assume that you have spent $100 on a ticket for a weekend ski trip to Michigan. Several weeks later you buy a $50 ticket for a weekend ski trip to Wisconsin. You think you will enjoy the Wisconsin ski trip more than the Michigan ski trip. As you are putting your just-purchased Wisconsin ski trip ticket in your wallet, you notice that the Michigan ski trip and the Wisconsin ski trip are for the same weekend! It's too late to sell either ticket, and you cannot return either one. You must use one ticket and not the other. Which trip will you go on?

More than half of the respondents chose the Michigan trip, even though the Wisconsin trip was identified as more enjoyable. Based on this result and other experiments, Arkes and Blumer suggest that the psychological justification for the irrational behavior is a desire not to appear wasteful.

Arkes and Blumer also presented the question above to a group of students enrolled in an economics course where they had studied the concept of sunk cost. Even in this group, about a third favored the Michigan trip. Apparently, training in economics does not greatly lessen the sunk cost effect. On the other hand, I gave the question to a group of students who had studied sunk cost in their managerial accounting course. Almost none of the students selected the Michigan trip. Maybe accounting instructors are more effective in getting across the message— Beware of sunk costs when making decisions!

*Source:* Arkes, H. R. and C. Blumer, "The Psychology of Sunk Cost," *Organizational Behavior and Human Decision Processes*, 35 (1985) pp. 124–140.

joint products. For example, suppose a lumber company spends $600 for an oak log and $20 to saw the log into two grades of lumber. The process results in 500 board feet of grade A lumber that sells for $1 per board foot and 500 board feet of grade B lumber that sells for $0.50 per board foot. How should the $620 joint cost be allocated to the joint products? One approach might be to allocate the cost based on the physical quantity of output. Since the production process results in equal quantities of physical output, it might seem reasonable to allocate an equal share of the joint cost to each of the grades of lumber. In this case both the grade A lumber and the grade B lumber would show a cost of $310. This allocation could lead managers to think that grade B lumber is not profitable and should be scrapped—after all, its cost is $310, while revenue from its sale is only $250. But this logic is faulty. If the grade B lumber were scrapped, the company would lose $250 that helped cover the joint cost of $620.

It is important to realize that the total joint cost will be incurred no matter what the company does with the joint products beyond the split-off point. Because the joint cost is not incremental to production of an individual joint product, it is irrelevant to any decision regarding an individual joint product. However, the joint cost is relevant to decisions involving the joint products as a group. If the total revenue from the sale of the joint products is less than the joint cost, production of all of the joint products should cease.

A better way of allocating the joint cost is to use the **relative sales value method**. With this method, the amount of joint cost allocated to products depends on the relative sales values of the products at the split-off point.

$$\frac{\text{Joint cost allocated}}{\text{to product A}} = \frac{\text{Sales value of A}}{\text{Sales value of A} + \text{Sales value of B}} \times \text{Joint Cost}$$

$$\frac{\text{Joint cost allocated}}{\text{to product B}} = \frac{\text{Sales value of B}}{\text{Sales value of A} + \text{Sales value of B}} \times \text{Joint Cost}$$

In the previous example, the grade A lumber would receive an allocation of $413.33 [i.e., $620 × ($500 ÷ $750)]. The grade B lumber would receive an allocation of $206.67 [i.e., $620 × ($250 ÷ $750)]. A good feature of this method is that the amount of joint cost allocated to a product cannot exceed its sales value at the split-off point. Thus, products that make a positive contribution to covering joint cost will not look unprofitable.

The costs allocated to the two grades of lumber using the physical quantity and the relative sales value approaches are compared in Illustration 7-9. In particular, note that for grade B lumber, the physical quantity approach yields a negative gross margin of $60, whereas the relative sales value approach yields a positive gross margin of $43.33.

## ADDITIONAL PROCESSING DECISIONS AND JOINT COSTS

Suppose the manager of a lumber company is considering whether or not to pressure-treat grade B lumber so that it will be resistant to rot. The additional processing costs per board foot will be $0.20. The pressure-treated lumber can be sold for $0.75 per board foot, compared with $0.50 for nontreated lumber. Should the additional processing be undertaken? Ask yourself, What will be the incremental revenue and the incremental costs? The incremental revenue will be $0.25 per board foot (i.e., $0.75 − $0.50). The incremental cost will be $0.20. Therefore, the incremental profit will be $0.05, indicating the further processing is warranted.

Where do the joint costs enter into this decision? They don't, because they are not incremental! Whether or not further processing will take place, the company must obtain a log and cut it into grade A and grade B lumber (unless the company wants to get out of the business of producing both grade A and grade B lumber).

**Illustration 7-9**
Comparison of physical quantity and relative sales value approaches to allocation of joint costs

Joint cost:

| | |
|---|---|
| Cost of log | $600.00 |
| Cost of sawing | 20.00 |
| Total | $620.00 |

Joint process yields:

500 board feet of grade A lumber selling for $1.00 per board foot

500 board feet of grade B lumber selling for $.50 per board foot

**Results using physical quantities to allocate joint costs**

| | Grade A | Grade B |
|---|---|---|
| Sales revenue | | |
| 500 b.f. × $1.00 | $500.00 | |
| 500 b.f. × $.50 | | $250.00 |
| Cost | | |
| $620 × (500 b.f. ÷ 1,000 b.f.) | 310.00 | |
| $620 × (500 b.f. ÷ 1,000 b.f.) | | 310.00 |
| Gross margin | $190.00 | ($60.00) |

**Results using relative sales values to allocate joint costs**

| | Grade A | Grade B |
|---|---|---|
| Sales revenue | | |
| 500 b.f. × $1.00 | $500.00 | |
| 500 b.f. × $.50 | | $250.00 |
| Cost | | |
| $620 × ($500 ÷ $750) | 413.33 | |
| $620 × ($250 ÷ $750) | | 206.67 |
| Gross margin | $ 86.67 | $ 43.33 |

Discuss the importance of qualitative considerations in management decisions.

# QUALITATIVE CONSIDERATIONS IN DECISION ANALYSIS

The solutions to the problems presented above have focused on the *quantitative* features of the decision situations. In particular, we have concentrated on quantitative differences in costs and revenues among decision alternatives. However, most important problems have one or more features that are very difficult, if not impossible, to quantify. These *qualitative* aspects of the problem must receive the same careful attention as the quantitative components.

The importance of qualitative considerations can be illustrated in the context of the make-or-buy decision discussed earlier. Recall that the Tennessee plant of the General Refrigeration Company was considering whether to continue producing compressors or purchase them from another firm. The goal of our analysis was to determine whether it would cost General more to produce the compressors or to buy them from an outside supplier. However, our analysis only considered the easily quantifiable differences in costs between the two decision alternatives. In addition, there are qualitative benefits and costs associated with using an outside supplier.

## LINK TO PRACTICE

### *United's Decision to Close Ticket Offices*

In June, 2002, United Airlines decided to shut down 23 of its 38 ticket offices west of Denver. No doubt United focused on the incremental cost savings associated with the closings (for example, savings related to salaries and rent that don't have to be paid when an office is shut down).

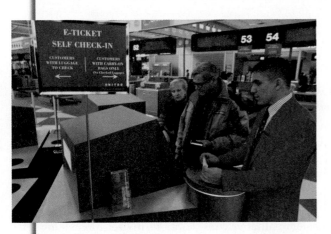

There is also no doubt that the company considered a number of qualitative factors, which are important to consider but are difficult, if not impossible, to quantity. Some examples:

- The offices proudly display the United name and are a form of advertising. Recognition of the United brand is reduced when offices are closed.

- The availability of electronic kiosks and Internet reservation systems will minimize negative customer reaction to the loss of the offices.

- United employees, in general, may react negatively to the news of the closing affecting morale and, ultimately, customer service.

Perhaps the primary benefit of using an outside supplier is that the adverse effect of a downturn in business is less severe. Suppose there is a temporary downturn in the demand for refrigeration units. In this case, General can simply order fewer compressors from its outside supplier, thus avoiding a major cost. In contrast, if General continues to manufacture the compressors and a temporary downturn in business is experienced, it is much more difficult to eliminate some of the fixed costs associated with manufacturing the compressors. For example, the company probably cannot eliminate the fixed costs of supervisors if the downturn is thought to be only temporary. Experienced supervisors are difficult to find, and they cannot be hired and fired based on temporary fluctuations in business.

A disadvantage of using an outside supplier is the associated loss of control over the production process. Purchased items may not be of sufficiently high quality and delivery schedules may not be honored. Furthermore, knowing that it would be costly for the company to restart internal production, the outside supplier may believe that it has the company "over a barrel" and that it can raise prices significantly in the future. Also, employee morale may suffer when a company decides to purchase a component outside and employees are fired or transferred as a result. The cost to the firm of reduced morale is difficult to quantify, but it may have a significant effect on the quantity and quality of the products produced by remaining employees.

# MAKING BUSINESS DECISIONS

Throughout the book, and in particular in this chapter, we've stressed the idea that decision making relies on incremental analysis. A problem with implementing this approach, however, is that some incremental costs and incremental benefits are very difficult to quantify. What if a decision has a negative impact on employee morale? How will we quantify this as an incremental cost? Or what if a decision has a positive impact on customer satisfaction? How do we go from knowledge of this qualitative benefit to an estimate of incremental revenue? Whenever you make a decision, carefully think about items that are difficult to quantify. These so-called qualitative factors may be the most important aspect of the decision.

## KNOWLEDGE AND SKILLS (K/S) CHECKLIST

*Knowledge and skills are needed to make good business decisions. Check off the knowledge and skills you've acquired from reading this chapter.*

❑ K/S 1. You have an expanded business vocabulary (see key terms).

❑ K/S 2. You have an enhanced ability to analyze decision alternatives using incremental analysis. In particular, you can appropriately deal with avoidable, sunk, and opportunity costs in decision making.

❑ K/S 3. You can appropriately analyze additional processing decisions involving joint costs.

❑ K/S 4. You understand the importance of qualitative considerations in decision making.

# SUMMARY OF LEARNING OBJECTIVES

**①** *Explain the role of incremental analysis (analysis of incremental costs and revenues) in management decisions.* Decisions involve a choice between two or more alternatives. The best decision can be determined by comparing alternatives in terms of the costs and revenue items that differ between them. These costs and revenues are referred to as incremental costs and revenues.

**②** *Define sunk cost, avoidable cost, and opportunity cost and understand how to use these concepts in analyzing decisions.* Sunk costs are costs that have been incurred in the past and are irrelevant to present and future decisions. Avoidable costs are costs that can be avoided by taking a particular action. The term *opportunity cost* refers to the benefit foregone by selecting a particular decision alternative over another. Avoidable costs and opportunity costs are always incremental and relevant in decision analysis.

**③** *Analyze decisions involving joint costs.* Joint costs are the costs of common inputs that result in two or more joint products. Joint costs are not relevant to analyzing decisions that involve only one of the joint products, because they are only incremental to producing all of the joint products. In analyzing decisions related to further processing beyond the split-off point, consider only the incremental revenue (the extra revenue related to further processing) and incremental costs (the costs incurred beyond the split-off point).

**④** *Discuss the importance of qualitative considerations in management decisions.* A variety of qualitative factors (e.g., quality of goods, employee morale, and customer service) need to be considered in making a decision. Qualitative factors are often even more important than costs and benefits that are easy to quantify.

# APPENDIX

# THE THEORY OF CONSTRAINTS (TOC)

In this chapter, we focused on the general approach to decision making—incremental analysis. Here we discuss decisions related to constraints and show how large increases in profit can be achieved by elimination of bottlenecks in production processes. Specifically, we will focus on the Theory of Constraints (TOC), which is an approach to production and constraint management, developed by Eli Goldratt.[1]

To facilitate our discussion, let's consider the production process of Dwyer Electronics, a producer of electronic measurement instruments. Production takes place in 4 departments as indicated in Illustration A7-1. Subassemblies are produced in Departments 1 and 2. The subassemblies are transferred to Department 3, which makes and tests connections and installs the subassemblies in housing units. Units are then transferred to Department 4, which completes final testing and packages units for shipping.

# THE FIVE-STEP PROCESS OF TOC

Goldratt specifies a five-step process for dealing with constraints. In this section, we discuss each step.

## STEP 1. IDENTIFY THE BINDING CONSTRAINT

The first step in the TOC process is to identify the bottleneck or binding constraint. This is the process that limits throughput (throughput is the amount of inventory produced in a period). Every manufacturing company has a binding constraint unless capacity in all departments exceeds demand for the company's product. And in this case, demand is the binding constraint. For Dwyer Electronics, lets assume that Department 3 is the bottleneck. Management has identified

**Illustration A7-1**
Production flow at dwyer electronics

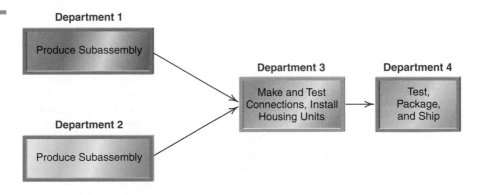

---

[1]For additional information on TOC, see E. Goldratt and J. Cox, *The Goal*, North River Press (1984). Also see D. Smith, *The Measurement Nightmare, How the Theory of Constraints Can Resolve Conflicting Strategies, Policies, and Measures*, The St. Lucie Press/APICS Series on Constraints Management (2000).

this department as the bottleneck since production from Departments 1 and 2 is stacking up in front of the Department 3 work area.

In the TOC, the department that is the bottleneck is equated to a drum since it "beats a rhythm" that coordinates the production in other departments. At Dwyer Electronics, the production in Departments 1 and 2 should be tied to the needs of Department 3. Even though they can produce more than Department 3, there is no need for them to do so. Production beyond the needs of Department 3 just ties up company funds in excess work in process inventory.

## STEP 2. OPTIMIZE USE OF THE CONSTRAINT

The second step is to optimize use of the constraint. This requires that the company use the constraint to produce products with the *highest contribution margin per unit of the constraint*.[2] Consider the following two testing instruments produced by Dwyer:

|  | Model A70 | Model B90 |
|---|---|---|
| Selling price per unit | $1,000 | $2,000 |
| Variable costs per unit: |  |  |
|    Direct materials | 400 | 900 |
|    Direct labor | 200 | 300 |
| **Contribution margin per unit** | **400** | **800** |
| Fixed costs per unit | 100 | 300 |
| Profit per unit | $ 300 | $ 500 |
| Time to complete 1 unit in Department 3 | .1 hour | .3 hour |
| Contribution margin per hour in Dept. 3 | $4,000 | $2,667 |

Which product optimizes use of the constraint—the Model A70 or the Model B90? The answer is the Model A70. Note that its contribution margin is $400 per unit but it only takes .1 hour to produce a unit in Department 3, which is the constrained department. Thus, each hour this product generates $4,000 of incremental profit. So if managers of Dwyer face a choice between using scarce time in Department 3 to produce the Model A70 or the Model B90, they should definitely choose the Model A70.

## STEP 3. SUBORDINATE EVERYTHING ELSE TO THE CONSTRAINT

The third step is to subordinate everything else to the constraint. This means that managers of Dwyer should focus their attention on trying to loosen the constraint and not concentrate on process improvements in other departments. Why, for example, should managers work to improve processes 1, 2, or 4 if they are not limiting production? Only the binding constraint limits production and attention should be focused completely on this department.

There are a number of things that managers can do to loosen the constraint in Department 3. For example, suppose the workers in Department 3 all take their

---

[2]Goldratt takes the somewhat extreme position that the only variable cost is material. While this is undoubtedly true in some situations, it is also undoubtedly true that in other situations additional cost elements are variable. For example, in the production of aluminum, which requires a great deal of electricity, power is clearly a variable cost.

breaks at the same time. Capacity could be gained by staggering breaks. And note that this would generate substantial sums of money. Product Model A70 generates $4,000 per hour. If breaks are staggered and the company gains an hour a day of additional capacity in Department 3, then it is generating an additional $20,000 of profit per week (5 hours × $4,000 per hour).

## STEP 4. BREAK THE CONSTRAINT

The fourth step in the TOC process is to break the constraint. This can be accomplished in many ways. Here are some examples:

- Cross-train workers in Departments 1 and 2 so they can help out in Department 3.
- Outsource some of Department 3's work.
- Purchase additional equipment for Department 3.
- Hire additional workers for Department 3.
- Train workers in Department 3 so that they can perform their jobs more efficiently.

## STEP 5. IDENTIFY A NEW BINDING CONSTRAINT

The final step is to identify a new binding constraint. Once, the constraint is broken in Department 3, either Department 1, 2, or 4 will become the bottleneck. Or, if the company has excess capacity in all departments, it should focus its attention on building demand.

# IMPLICATIONS OF TOC FOR INSPECTIONS, BATCH SIZES, AND ACROSS THE BOARD CUTS

TOC has implications for a number of decisions faced by managers. Here, we'll discuss three: implications for inspections, batch sizes, and across the board cuts.

**Inspections.** Time in a constrained department should never be wasted. Thus, whenever possible, inspections should take place *before* work is transferred to a constrained department. That way, the valuable time of the constrained department will not be wasted working on defective items.

**Batch Sizes.** In recent years, many companies have gone to small batch sizes to gain flexibility in responding to new orders and to avoid producing large quantities of defective items if a process goes out of control. However, when a production process is a binding constraint, it may be better to have large batch sizes. The reason is that then the valuable time of the constrained department is not wasted setting up equipment for numerous small batches of production.

**Across the Board Cuts.** The decision to have across the board cuts is completely at odds with TOC. Cuts in nonbottleneck departments may make sense, but across the board cuts, even to the department that is the binding constraint, can have a severe, negative impact on profit. Recall that at Dwyer Electronics, each hour gained in Department 3 results in $4,000 of incremental profit if the time is spent producing Model A70. Likewise, each hour lost reduces profit by $4,000. If an across the board cut reduced capacity by the equivalent of just an hour a day, more than a $1 million of profit would be lost in a year (1 hour × 5 days per week × 52 weeks × $4,000 per hour = $1,040,000).

**You Get What You Measure**

# YOU GET WHAT YOU MEASURE AND TOC

As you know, a major theme of this book is "You get what you measure!" In other words, performance measures drive the behavior of managers. TOC points out that performance measures related to production volume (e.g., units produced per hour) can have a negative impact on shareholder value *when they are applied to nonbottleneck departments*. Suppose at Dwyer Electronics, the company measures and rewards Departments 1 and 2 for units produced per hour. In this case, the departments have an incentive to produce more items than Department 3 can deal with since it is a bottleneck. The result will be large levels of work in process inventory accumulating in front of Department 3. That excess inventory is an investment of shareholder funds, but shareholders will not receive a reasonable return on the investment since it serves no useful purpose. Remember—be careful of performance measures that encourage overproduction in nonbottleneck departments!

# R E V I E W   P R O B L E M

Mayfield Software has a 2,000 square foot cafeteria located on the lower level of Building No. 3, the company's largest building. The vice president of operations for Mayfield insists that meal prices be reasonable so workers will stay on campus and avoid "wasting time" driving to restaurants with slow service. Employees at Mayfield are generally happy with the quality of food and the level of service in the cafeteria. Still, Mayfield is considering outsourcing to Regal Food Service. Mayfield is expanding and realizes that the future success of the company will require increased focus on its core competencies (and food service is not a core competency!).

A cafeteria profit report for 2006 follows. In the report, the cafeteria is charged $20 per year per square foot for space and three percent of sales for general overhead (to cover the centrally administered costs of Mayfield Software such as legal, brand advertising, salary of the CFO, etc.). All business units receive the same three percent charge.

### Cafeteria Profit Report for 2006

| | | |
|---|---:|---:|
| Sales | | $1,095,000 |
| Less expenses: | | |
| Cost of food and supplies | $657,000 | |
| Salaries | 342,000 | |
| Space charge | 40,000 | |
| Depreciation of equipment | 6,000 | |
| General overhead charge | 32,850 | 1,077,850 |
| Cafeteria profit | | $   17,150 |

The terms of the agreement with Regal (which has not yet been signed) call for Regal to provide similar quality meals and service at the same prices that were charged in

2006. Regal will use the current cafeteria space and existing equipment without cost to them. Regal will keep 96 percent of sales revenue and remit four percent of sales revenue back to Mayfield. Regal will pay for all food and supplies and hire and pay the salaries of all staff including the cafeteria manager, cooks and servers.

**Required**

Evaluate the annual financial impact of the outsourcing decision assuming sales in the coming year, under Regal, will be the same as in 2006.

**Answer**

### Incremental Revenue and Costs

| | |
|---|---:|
| Lost sales | ($1,095,000) |
| 4% payment from Regal | 43,800 |
| Food savings | 657,000 |
| Salary savings | 342,000 |
| Net effect | ($52,200) |

Food services should not be outsourced since the effect is to reduce profit by $52,200. Note that the general overhead charge is not included in the analysis because these costs will not actually change due to the outsourcing decision. Thus, they are not incremental costs.

# KEY TERMS

| | | |
|---|---|---|
| Avoidable costs (242) | Incremental cost (236) | Opportunity cost (243) |
| Common costs (244) | Incremental revenue (236) | Relative sales value method (249) |
| Differential costs (236) | Joint costs (247) | Relevant costs (236) |
| Incremental analysis (236) | Joint products (247) | Split-off point (247) |

# SELF ASSESSMENT *(Answers Below)*

1. Differential costs are sometimes referred to as _____ costs.

2. Which of the following costs should not be taken into consideration when making a decision?
   a. Opportunity costs.
   b. Sunk costs.
   c. Relevant costs.
   d. Differential costs.

3. Which of the following is often not a differential cost?
   a. Material.
   b. Labor.
   c. Variable overhead.
   d. Fixed overhead.

4. True or False? Fixed costs are never incremental costs.

5. Which of the following is not relevant when considering whether or not to drop a product?
   a. The contribution margin.
   b. Qualitative factors.
   c. The potential impact on demand for other products.
   d. Allocated common costs.

6. Opportunity costs are:
   a. Never incremental costs.
   b. Always incremental costs.
   c. Sometimes sunk costs.
   d. None of the above.

7. The joint costs incurred in a joint product situation:
   a. Are incurred before the split-off point.
   b. Are incurred after the split-off point.
   c. Should only be allocated based on physical attributes.
   d. None of the above.

8. A joint product's cost is $18, which includes $6 of allocated joint cost. Its sales price is $16. In this case:

   a. Profit will improve if the company discontinues production of the product.
   b. The company should sell as few of the items as possible to minimize the loss on sales.
   c. The data are misleading because the $6 allocated joint cost will be incurred even if the product is discontinued.
   d. Both a and b are correct.

9. (Appendix) According to the Theory of Constraints, optimizing use of a constraint requires:

   a. Production of the product with the highest profit per unit.
   b. Production of the product with the shortest production time.
   c. Production of the product with the highest contribution margin.
   d. Production of the product with the highest contribution margin per unit of the constrained resource.

10. (Appendix) True or False. Generally, parts should be inspected prior to being sent to a department that is a bottleneck.

**Answers to Self Assessment**

**1.** relevant;    **2.** b;    **3.** d;    **4.** False;    **5.** d;
**6.** b;    **7.** a;    **8.** c;    **9.** d;    **10.** True.

# INTERACTIVE LEARNING

**Enhance and test your knowledge of Chapter 7 using the interactive CD.**

1. Learning Objectives
2. Multiple Choice
3. Language of Business—Matching of Key Terms
4. Critical Thinking
5. Demonstration—The cost allocation death spiral!
6. Case—*West Coast Grocery Supply*; Incremental analysis

**Go to our dynamic Web site for more self-assessment, Web links, and additional information.**

# QUESTIONS

1. What are differential costs and revenues?
2. Why are sunk costs irrelevant in decision making?
3. What are avoidable costs?
4. Why are opportunity costs relevant when making decisions?
5. What is the proper approach to analyzing whether or not a product line should be dropped?
6. Give an example of a fixed cost that is not sunk but is still irrelevant.
7. What is a qualitative *advantage* of making rather than buying a component?
8. Why is the relative sales value a more logical basis for allocating joint costs compared to physical quantity?
9. (Appendix) Why are batch sizes generally larger in bottleneck departments?
10. (Appendix) Why is the bottleneck department referred to as a "drum" in the Theory of Constraints?

# EXERCISES

**EXERCISE 7-1. Group Assignment**    Describe a decision and provide an example of a fixed cost that is incremental in the context of the decision. Then, provide an example of a fixed cost that is *not* incremental in the context of the decision.

**EXERCISE 7-2. Writing Assignment**   Adrienne Ciello owns and operates an exclusive bridal boutique in Bellevue, Washington. Her accountant has prepared a product line income statement that is reproduced below (Adrienne's two lines are gowns and accessories). In preparing the income statement, the accountant allocated all common costs including rent, Adrienne's salary and the salary of her two assistants, utilities, and other common costs based on relative sales. His reason is that "Each product line needs to cover its share of common costs."

In light of this report, Adrienne is considering eliminating accessories and concentrating solely on the sale of gowns (although she does not expect an increase in gown sales).

|  | Gowns | Accessories | Total |
|---|---|---|---|
| Sales | $850,000 | $125,000 | $975,000 |
| Cost of merchandise | 595,000 | 93,750 | 688,750 |
| Gross margin | 255,000 | 31,250 | 286,250 |
| Rent | 41,760 | 6,240 | 48,000 |
| Salaries | 191,400 | 28,600 | 220,000 |
| Utilities | 5,220 | 780 | 6,000 |
| Other | 4,350 | 650 | 5,000 |
|  | 242,730 | 36,270 | 279,000 |
| Income before taxes | $ 12,270 | $ (5,020) | $ 7,250 |

*Required*

Analyze the effect on profit of dropping accessories. Then, write a paragraph explaining the role of common costs in your analysis and how allocation of common costs can lead to the cost allocation death spiral!

**EXERCISE 7-3. Internet Assignment**   Go to the financial glossary Investorwords.com at http://www.investorwords.com/ and look up the words "sunk cost" and "opportunity cost." Why is it that sunk costs are never relevant to a decision whereas opportunity costs are always relevant?

**EXERCISE 7-4. Incremental Analysis**   Nelson Design, a Kitchen and Bath design company, has experienced a drop in business due to an increase in interest rates and a corresponding slowdown in remodeling projects. To stimulate business, the company is considering exhibiting at the Atlanta Home Show. The exhibit will cost the company $10,000 for space. At the show, Nelson Design will present a slide show on a PC, pass out brochures that were printed previously (the company printed more than needed), and show its portfolio of previous jobs.

The company estimates that revenue will increase by $30,000 over the next year as a result of the exhibit. For the previous year, profit was as follows:

| | | |
|---|---|---|
| Revenue | | $170,000 |
| Less: | | |
| Design supplies | $10,000 | |
| Salary of Laura Nelson (owner) | 72,000 | |
| Salary of Emily Holder (full time employee) | 51,000 | |
| Rent | 18,000 | |
| Utilities | 4,000 | |
| Depreciation of office equipment | 2,500 | |
| Printing of advertising materials | 500 | |
| Advertising in Atlanta Home Magazine | 2,000 | |
| Travel expenses other than depreciation of autos | 1,000 | |
| Depreciation of company cars | 8,000 | 169,000 |
| Net income | | $ 1,000 |

*Required*

Calculate the impact of the exhibit on company profit. Should the company exhibit at the home show?

**EXERCISE 7-5. Incremental Analysis**    Each year, Knight Motors surveys 6,000 former and prospective customers regarding satisfaction and brand awareness. For the current year, the company is considering outsourcing the survey to RBG Associates who have offered to conduct the survey and summarize results for $25,000.

Craig Knight, the president of Knight Motors, believes that RBG will do a higher quality job than his company has been doing, but is unwilling to spend more than $10,000 above current costs.

The head of bookkeeping for Knight has prepared the following summary of costs related to the survey in the prior year.

| | |
|---|---:|
| Mailing | $12,000 |
| Printing (done by Lester Print Shop) | 3,000 |
| Salary of Pat Fisher, part-time employee who stuffed envelopes and summarized data when surveys were returned (90 hours × $15) | 1,350 |
| Share of depreciation of computer and software used to track survey responses and summarize results | 900 |
| Share of electricity/phone/etc. based on square feet of space occupied by Pat Fisher vs. entire company | 200 |
| Total | $17,450 |

*Required*

What is the incremental cost of going outside versus conducting the survey as in the past? Will Craig Knight accept the RBG offer?

 **EXERCISE 7-6. Incremental Analysis and Opportunity Costs**    Sawyer's Seafood Restaurant has been approached by Wellsworth Real Estate, which wants to hold an employee recognition dinner next month. Katie Miller, a manager of the restaurant agreed to a charge of $75 per person, for food, wine, and dessert, for 120 people. She estimates that the cost of unprepared food will be $20 per person and beverages will be $10 per person.

To be able to accommodate the group, Katie will have to close the restaurant for dinner that night. Typically, she would have served 130 people with an average bill of $45 per person. On a typical night, the cost of unprepared food is $15 per person and beverages are $12 per person. No additional staff will need to be hired to accommodate the group from Wellsworth.

*Required*

a. Calculate the incremental profit or loss associated with accepting the Wellsworth group.

b. What was the opportunity cost of accepting the Wellsworth group?

c. Should Katie have considered any qualitative factors in her decision? Explain.

**EXERCISE 7-7. Make or Buy Decision: Relevant Costs**    The Tufanzi Furniture Company manufactures leather furniture. The manufacturing process uses a variety of metal pieces such as brackets, braces, and casters. Carla Reid, the resource officer of Tufanzi, has been asked to determine if it is advisable to purchase these pieces rather than make them internally (the current practice). Identify which of the following items are relevant to her decision.

a. The original cost of equipment currently used to make metal pieces.

b. The market value of equipment currently used to make metal pieces.

c. The cost of buying metal pieces from suppliers.

d. The space freed up if metal pieces are not made internally.

e. The salary of the president of Tufanzi Furniture.

f. The quality of the metal pieces made internally.

g. The quality of the metal pieces purchased from suppliers.

h. Depreciation on equipment used to make metal pieces (ignore taxes).

i. The labor contract with production workers.

j. The selling prices of furniture pieces.

**EXERCISE 7-8. Make-or-Buy Decision**   Howell Corporation produces an executive jet. In this regard, the company is currently manufacturing a fuel valve and the cost of the valve is indicated below:

|  | Cost per Unit |
|---|---|
| Variable costs | |
| Direct material | $   800 |
| Direct labor | 500 |
| Variable overhead | 200 |
| Total variable costs | 1,500 |
| Fixed costs | |
| Depreciation of equipment | 400 |
| Depreciation of building | 100 |
| Supervisory salaries | 200 |
| Total fixed costs | 700 |
| Total cost | $2,200 |

The company has an offer from Duvall Valves to produce the part for $1,800 per unit and supply 1,000 valves (the number needed in the coming year). If the company accepts this offer and shuts down production of valves, production workers and supervisors will be reassigned to other areas needing their services. The equipment cannot be used elsewhere in the company, and it has no market value. However, the space occupied by the production of the valve can be used by another production group that is currently leasing space for $50,000 per year.

*Required*
Should the company make or buy the valve?

**EXERCISE 7-9. Sunk, Avoidable, and Opportunity Costs**   Consider the information in exercise 7-8 and identify the following statements as true or false.

a. Supervisory salary is an avoidable cost if the company decides to buy the valves.

b. Depreciation of building is an avoidable cost if the company decides to buy the valves.

c. The $50,000 cost of leasing space is an opportunity cost associated with continuing production of the valve.

d. The depreciation of equipment is an opportunity cost associated with continuing production of the valve.

e. Depreciation of building is a sunk cost even if the company continues with production of the valve.

f. Supervisory salary is a sunk cost even if the company continues with production of the valve.

**EXERCISE 7-10. Dropping a Product: Relevant Costs**   E-Teller Inc. manufactures ATM machines. Recently, the company has begun manufacturing and marketing a machine that can recognize customer fingerprints. Demand for this machine is very strong and the chief executive officer (CEO) of E-Teller is considering dropping production of the company's original model that relies on bankcards and passwords. This will allow the company to have increased capacity to devote to the new model.

Which of the following items are relevant to the CEO's decision to drop the old model machine?

a. The original cost of equipment used to manufacture the old model.

b. Depreciation of the equipment used to manufacture the old model (ignore taxes).

c. The CEO's salary.

d. The time it takes to manufacture each model.

e. The production manager's salary.

f. The selling price of the new model.

g. The variable cost of producing the new model.

h. The cost of retraining personnel to make the newer model.

i. Depreciation of the factory building allocated to the old model.

**EXERCISE 7-11. Additional Processing Decision**   CellCom Inc. has decided to discontinue manufacturing its Elite model cellular phone. Currently, the company has a number of partially completed phones on hand. The company has spent $95 per unit to manufacture these phones. To complete each unit, costs of $10 for material and $10 for direct labor will be incurred. In addition, $5 of variable overhead and $20 of allocated fixed overhead (relating primarily to depreciation of plant and equipment) will be added per unit.

If CellCom Inc. completes the phones, they can sell them for $110 per unit. On the other hand, another manufacturer is interested in purchasing the partially completed phones for $90 per unit and converting them into wireless inventory tracking devices. Determine if CellCom Inc. should complete the cellular phones or sell them in their current state.

**EXERCISE 7-12. Make or Buy Decision**   Eurospa Corp. produces whirlpool tubs. Currently, the company uses internally manufactured pumps to power water jets. Eurospa Corp. has found that 40 percent of the pumps have failed within their 12-month warranty period, causing huge warranty costs. Because of the company's inability to manufacture high quality pumps, management is considering buying pumps from a reputable manufacturer who will also bear any related warranty costs.

Eurospa's unit cost of manufacturing pumps is $83.75 per unit which includes $17.25 of allocated fixed overhead (primarily depreciation of plant and equipment). Also, the company has spent an average of $22.00 (labor and parts) repairing each pump returned. Eurospa Corp. can purchase pumps for $92.50 per pump.

*Required*

During 2003, Eurospa Corp. plans to sell 12,800 whirlpools (requiring 12,800 pumps). Determine whether the company should make or buy the pumps and the amount of cost savings related to the best alternative. What qualitative factors should be considered in the outsourcing decision?

**EXERCISE 7-13. Dropping a Product Line**   Computer Village sells computer equipment and home office furniture. Currently, the furniture product line takes up approximately 50 percent of the company's retail floor space.

The president of Computer Village is trying to decide whether the company should continue offering furniture or just concentrate on computer equipment.

Below is a product line income statement for the company. If furniture is dropped, salaries and other direct fixed costs can be avoided. In addition, sales of computer equipment can increase by 20 percent without affecting direct fixed costs. Allocated fixed costs are assigned based on relative sales.

|  | Computer Equipment | Home Office Furniture | Total |
|---|---|---|---|
| Sales | $1,000,000 | $700,000 | $1,700,000 |
| Less cost of goods sold | 600,000 | 420,000 | 1,020,000 |
| Contribution margin | 400,000 | 280,000 | 680,000 |
| Less direct fixed costs: |  |  |  |
|   Salaries | 150,000 | 150,000 | 300,000 |
|   Other | 50,000 | 50,000 | 100,000 |
| Less allocated fixed costs |  |  |  |
|   Rent | 11,765 | 8,235 | 20,000 |
|   Insurance | 2,941 | 2,059 | 5,000 |
|   Cleaning | 3,529 | 2,471 | 6,000 |
|   President's salary | 70,588 | 49,412 | 120,000 |
|   Other | 5,882 | 4,118 | 10,000 |
| Net income | $ 105,295 | $ 13,705 | $ 119,000 |

*Required*

Determine whether Computer Village should discontinue the furniture line and the financial benefit (cost) of dropping it.

**EXERCISE 7-14. Qualitative Factors in Decision Making**   For each of the following situations, indicate a qualitative factor that should be considered prior to making a decision:

a. A company that produces and sells bottled water is considering outsourcing its bottling operation. The company will still source the water and deliver it to bottling companies.

b. A wine producer is considering dropping its premium brand wine and concentrating exclusively on less costly wines.

c. A software company currently has a large facility for producing videos used in games and advertisements. The company is considering shutting down the facility and using resources provided by other companies.

**EXERCISE 7-15. Joint Cost Allocation with Physical Quantity of Output**   Baxter Products produces two joint products (A and B). Prior to the split-off point, the company incurs costs of $1,000. Product A weighs 20 pounds and product B weighs 40 pounds. Product A sells for $50 per pound and product B sells for $10 per pound.

*Required*

a. Based on a physical measure of output, allocate joint costs to products A and B.

b. Compare the costs to the selling prices. Should the company sell products whose selling price is less than the allocated joint cost?

**EXERCISE 7-16. Joint Cost Allocation with Relative Sales Values**   Baxter Products produces two joint products (A and B). Prior to the split-off point, the company incurs costs of $1,000. Product A weighs 20 pounds and product B weighs 40 pounds. Product A sells for $50 per pound and product B sells for $10 per pound.

*Required*

a. Based on relative sales values at the split-off point, allocate joint costs to products A and B.

b. Under what condition would the cost allocated using relative sales values be greater than the selling price of a joint product?

**EXERCISE 7-17. Allocating Joint Costs** The Fresh Produce Company purchased a truckload of watermelons (weighing 6,000 pounds) for $600. Fresh Produce separated the melons into two grades: superior and economy. The superior grade melons had a total weight of 4,000 pounds and the economy grade melons totaled 2,000 pounds. Fresh Produce sells the superior grade at $0.25 per pound and the economy grade at $0.10 per pound.

*Required*

Allocate the $600 cost of the truckload to the superior grade and economy grade melons using the physical quantity method and the relative sales value method.

**EXERCISE 7-18. (Appendix) Calculating the Value of Loosening a Constraint** At CF Rogers Corporation, the stamping department is a bottleneck, and the company is considering hiring an extra worker, whose salary will be $50,000 per year, to mitigate the problem.

With the extra worker, the company will be able to produce and sell 5,000 more units per year. The selling price per unit is $20. Cost per unit currently is $11 as follows:

| | |
|---|---|
| Direct material | $4.00 |
| Direct labor | 1.00 |
| Variable overhead | .50 |
| Fixed overhead (primarily depreciation of equipment) | 5.50 |
| Total | $11.00 |

*Required*

Calculate the annual financial impact of hiring the extra worker.

# PROBLEMS

**PROBLEM 7-1. Decision Making and Ethics** Sandra Winston, VP of marketing for Frontier Home and Car Stereo, has developed a marketing plan for presentation to the company's president. The plan calls for television ads, something the company has never used. As part of her presentation, she will indicate the impact of the TV ads on company profit as follows:

| | | |
|---|---|---|
| Incremental sales from increased exposure | | $7,000,000 |
| Less: | | |
| Incremental cost of goods sold | $3,000,000 | |
| Cost of TV ads | 2,000,000 | 5,000,000 |
| Incremental profit | | $2,000,000 |

While Sandra is quite confident in the cost of the ads and the incremental cost of goods sold if sales are $7,000,000, she is quite uncertain about the sales increase. In fact, she believes that her estimate is on the "high side." However, she also believes that if she puts in a more conservative estimate such as $6,000,000, the president will not go along with the TV ads even though they will still generate substantial profits at $6,000,000 of incremental sales.

*Required*

Is it unethical of Sandra to bias her estimate of incremental sales on the "high side" given she believes the ultimate outcome is in the best interest of the company?

**PROBLEM 7-2. Incremental Analysis of Outsourcing Decision** Oakland College is considering outsourcing their grounds maintenance. In this regard, Oakland has received a bid from Highline Grounds Maintenance for $250,000 per year. Highline states that their bid will cover all services and planting materials required to "keep

Oakland's grounds in a condition comparable to prior years." Oakland's cost for grounds maintenance in the preceding year were $267,000 as follows:

| | |
|---|---:|
| Salary of 3 full-time gardeners | $185,000 |
| Plant materials | 65,000 |
| Fertilizer | 5,000 |
| Fuel | 4,000 |
| Depreciation of tractor, mowers, and other miscellaneous equipment | 8,000 |
| Total | $267,000 |

If Oakland College outsources maintenance, it will be able to sell equipment for $20,000, and the three gardeners will be "laid off."

### Required

a. Analyze the one year financial impact of outsourcing grounds maintenance.

b. How will savings in the second year differ from year one?

c. Discuss qualitative factors that should be considered in the decision.

**PROBLEM 7-3. Make-or-Buy Decision** For most construction projects, Bradley Heating and Cooling buys sheet metal and forms the metal into heating/cooling ducts as needed. The company estimates the costs of making and installing ductwork for the Kerry Park shopping mall to be as follows:

| | |
|---|---:|
| Materials | $30,000 |
| Labor to form ductwork | 2,000 |
| Labor to install ductwork | 8,000 |
| Misc. variable costs | 1,000 |
| Fixed costs allocated based on labor hours | 2,500 |
| Total cost | $43,500 |

The fixed costs relate to the company's building, equipment, and office staff. The company plans on billing the Kerry Park developer $60,000 for services.

Bradley is currently behind schedule on other projects and is paying a late penalty of $1,000 per day. Walt Bradley, the owner of Bradley Heating and Cooling, is considering ordering prefabricated duct-work for the Kerry Park job. The prefabricated ductwork will cost $34,000 (including the cost of sheet metal). If Walt buys the prefabricated ductwork, he'll be able to reassign workers to another project and avoid 5 days of late fees.

### Required
Should Bradley make the ductwork or buy it prefabricated?

**PROBLEM 7-4. Make-or-Buy Decision** Curtis Corporation is beginning to manufacture Mighty Mint, a new mouthwash in a small spray container. The product will be sold to wholesalers and large drugstore chains in packages of 30 containers for $18 per package. Management allocates $200,000 of fixed manufacturing overhead costs to Mighty Mint. The manufacturing cost *per package* of Mighty Mint for expected production of 100,000 packages is as follows:

| | |
|---|---:|
| Direct material | $16.50 |
| Direct labor | 3.50 |
| Overhead (fixed and variable) | 3.00 |
| Total | $23.00 |

The company has contacted a number of packaging suppliers to determine whether it is better to buy or manufacture the spray *containers*. The lowest quote for the containers is $1.75 per 30 units. It is estimated that purchasing the containers from a supplier will save 10 percent of direct materials, 20 percent of direct labor, and 15 percent of variable overhead. Curtis's manufacturing space is highly constrained. By purchasing the spray containers, the company will not have to lease additional manufacturing space that is estimated to cost $15,000 per year. If the containers are purchased, one supervisory position can be eliminated. Salary plus benefits for this position are $70,000 per year.

### Required

Should Curtis make or buy the containers? What is the incremental cost (benefit) of buying the containers as opposed to making them?

**PROBLEM 7-5. Additional Processing Decision and Qualitative Factors**   Carpets Unlimited produced 1,000 yards of its economy grade carpet. In the coloring process, there was a pigment defect and the resulting color appeared to be faded. The carpet normally sells for $10 per yard: $5 of variable cost per yard and $3 of fixed cost per yard have been assigned to the carpet.

The company realizes that it cannot sell the carpet for $10 per yard, through its normal channels, unless the coloring process is repeated. The incremental cost of the process is $2 per yard. However, United Home Discount Store is willing to buy the carpet in its current faded condition for $7 per yard.

### Required

a. Should Carpets Unlimited repeat the coloring process or sell the carpet to United Home Discount Store?

b. Suppose United Home Discount Store is willing to buy the carpet for $9 per yard if Carpets Unlimited's brand is associated with the carpet by means of a tag indicating the carpet was produced by Carpets Unlimited (a highly regarded producer). Would you accept United's offer if you were the president of Carpets Unlimited?

**PROBLEM 7-6. Additional Processing Decision with a Production Constraint**   Mega Chemical Company produces ZylexA and a related product called ZylexB, along with other products. ZylexB, which sells for $13.50 per gallon, is made from a base of ZylexA plus additional ingredients. It takes 20 minutes to manufacture a gallon of ZylexA and an additional 10 minutes to manufacture a gallon of ZylexB. ZylexA sells for $9.75 per gallon. The cost per gallon of manufacturing ZylexA and the additional costs to convert it into ZylexB are:

|                   | ZylexA  | Additional Cost of ZylexB |
| ----------------- | ------- | ------------------------- |
| Material          | $2.25   | $1.90                     |
| Labor             | 1.80    | .70                       |
| Variable overhead | 2.60    | 1.20                      |

Both products have been successful and demand for both products is strong. However, Mega's other products are also in demand and the company is operating at capacity. Since it takes longer to manufacture ZylexB, the vice president of production is trying to determine whether ZylexB should be produced.

### Required

Which product makes the largest contribution to company profit given a capacity constraint measured in terms of production time?

**PROBLEM 7-7. Dropping a Product Line**   AVD Electronics, a consumer electronics retailer, has three product lines: audio, video, and communications (cell phones and pagers). Common costs are allocated based on relative sales. A product line income statement follows:

**AVD Electronics**
**Income Statement**
**for the Year Ended December 31, 2006**

|  | Audio | Video | Communi-cations | Total |
|---|---|---|---|---|
| Sales | $1,025,000 | $2,125,000 | $2,120,000 | $5,270,000 |
| Less cost of goods sold | 563,750 | 1,168,750 | 1,908,000 | 3,640,500 |
| Gross margin | 461,250 | 956,250 | 212,000 | 1,629,500 |
| Less other variable costs | 50,000 | 65,000 | 21,000 | 136,000 |
| Contribution margin | 411,250 | 891,250 | 191,000 | 1,493,500 |
| Less direct salaries | 125,000 | 140,000 | 56,000 | 321,000 |
| Less common fixed costs: |  |  |  |  |
|   Rent | 11,669 | 24,194 | 24,137 | 60,000 |
|   Utilities | 3,407 | 7,063 | 11,530 | 22,000 |
|   Depreciation | 8,492 | 17,605 | 3,903 | 30,000 |
|   Other administrative costs | 147,059 | 191,176 | 61,765 | 400,000 |
| Net income | $ 115,623 | $ 511,212 | $ 33,665 | $ 660,500 |

Since the profit for communication devices is relatively low, the company is considering dropping this product line.

*Required*

a. Determine the impact on profit of dropping communications products.

b. Discuss the potential qualitative effects of discontinuing the sale of communications products.

**PROBLEM 7-8. Drop a Product/Opportunity Cost**   Midwestern Sod Company produces two products: Fescue Grass and Bermuda Grass.

|  | Fescue Grass | Bermuda Grass |
|---|---|---|
| Selling price per square yard | $1.90 | $2.65 |
| Less variable cost per square yard | .40 | 1.00 |
|   (water, fertilizer, maintenance) |  |  |

The company has 100,000 square yards of growing space available. In the past year, the company dedicated 50,000 square yards to Fescue and 50,000 square yards to Bermuda grass. Annual fixed costs are $120,000, which the company allocates to products based on relative growing space.

Martha Lopez, the chief financial officer of Midwestern Sod, has suggested that in the coming year, all 100,000 square yards should be devoted to Bermuda grass. The president vetoed her suggestion saying "I know that right now home construction is booming in our area, and we can sell all the grass we can produce, irrespective of what type. But, you know a lot of developers really like that Fescue grass and I'd hate to disappoint them by not offering it."

*Required*
What is the opportunity cost of the president's decision to stick with both types of grass?

**PROBLEM 7-9. Drop a Product Decision**   Winslow Pumps manufactures three model pumps for industrial use. The standard selling price and cost of each pump follows:

|  | **Model 101** | **Model 201** | **Model 301** |
|---|---|---|---|
| Selling price | $5,000 | $10,000 | $13,000 |
| Unit cost: |  |  |  |
|   Material | 1,050 | 4,500 | 6,000 |
|   Direct labor | 500 | 2,000 | 4,000 |
|   Overhead | 769 | 3,077 | 6,154 |
| Unit profit (loss) | $2,681 | $   423 | ($3,154) |

Essentially, all overhead costs are fixed. Some of the fixed overhead costs are direct costs to particular models and others are common fixed costs.

**Estimated total overhead**

|  | **Model 101** | **Model 201** | **Model 301** | **Total** |
|---|---|---|---|---|
| Direct fixed | $4,000,000 | $1,500,000 | $500,000 | $ 6,000,000 |
| Common fixed |  |  |  | 4,000,000 |
|  |  |  | Total | $10,000,000 |

Winslow allocates overhead costs to products using a single overhead rate developed as follows. Estimated total overhead is divided by estimated direct labor cost. This results in an overhead rate per labor dollar. This rate is used to assign standard overhead to products.

Below are estimates of sales and direct labor. These values imply an overhead rate of $1.5385 per labor dollar ($10,000,000 ÷ $6,500,000).

|  | **Model 101** | **Model 201** | **Model 301** | **Total** |
|---|---|---|---|---|
| Estimated unit sales | 1,000 | 2,000 | 500 | 3,500 |
| Estimated labor | $500,000 | $4,000,000 | $2,000,000 | $6,500,000 |

*Required*

a. Because it is showing a loss, the controller of Winslow has asked you to analyze whether the Model 301 should be dropped. You should assume that direct fixed costs will be avoided if a model is dropped but common fixed costs will not be avoided if the model is dropped.

b. Explain why the method used to allocate costs at Winslow results in "unreasonably high" charges to the Model 301 pump.

**PROBLEM 7-10. Cost Allocation Death Spiral**  Carpets Unlimited produces and sells three lines of carpet (economy, standard, and deluxe). Jeff Choi, the chief financial officer of the company has prepared the following report on the profitability of the company in the past year. In the report, fixed costs are allocated based on yards of carpet.

|  | **Economy** | **Standard** | **Deluxe** | **Total** |
|---|---|---|---|---|
| **Yards of Carpet** | 20,000 | 30,000 | 50,000 | 100,000 |
| Sales | $200,000 | $450,000 | $1,000,000 | $1,650,000 |
| Less variable costs |  |  |  |  |
| (Dye, yarn, labor, etc.) | 100,000 | 270,000 | 600,000 | 970,000 |
| Less fixed costs (Depreciation, |  |  |  |  |
| supervisory salaries, etc.) | 110,000 | 165,000 | 275,000 | 550,000 |
| Profit (loss) | $(10,000) | $ 15,000 | $ 125,000 | $ 130,000 |

Upon seeing the report, Matt Williams, the president of Carpets Unlimited suggested that the company should consider dropping the Economy grade and concentrate on the two other lines. Jeff replied, however, that that would lead to the "cost allocation death spiral."

*Required*

a. Revise the report assuming the company drops the economy grade.

b. If either the standard or the deluxe grades is reporting a loss in part a, revise the report assuming that it is also dropped.

c. Explain what Jeff means by the "cost allocation death spiral."

**PROBLEM 7-11. Joint Costs and Decision Making** Olympic Wood Products purchases alder logs for $80 per log. After stripping the bark, the log is spun on a veneer cutter, which peels thin layers of wood (referred to as veneer) that are sold to furniture manufacturers for $140 per 3′ × 30′ sheet of veneer. The peeled log (referred to as a peeler) is sold for $40 to companies that use the logs to construct outdoor play equipment. On average, each alder log yields one, 3′ × 30′ sheet of veneer and (obviously) one peeled log. The cost of processing each log into a sheet of veneer and a peeled log is $20 in addition to the $80 cost of the alder log. On average, a peeled log weighs 60 pounds and an average 3′ × 30′ sheet of veneer weights 10 pounds.

*Required*

a. Suppose Olympic were to allocate all joint costs based on the weight of the joint products. Calculate expected profit per sheet of veneer and per peeler.

b. The profit per peeler in part a is negative. Does this imply that the company should not sell them?

c. Suppose Olympic were to allocate all joint costs based on the relative sales values of the joint products. Calculate expected profit per sheet of veneer and per peeler.

d. Briefly explain why the relative sales value approach is the preferred method for allocating joint costs.

**PROBLEM 7-12. Joint Costs and Additional Processing** Good Earth Products produces orange juice and candied orange peels. A 1,000 pound batch of oranges, costing $400, is transformed using labor of $40 into 100 pounds of orange peels and 300 pints of juice.

The company has determined that the sales value of 100 pounds of peels at the split-off point is $300 and the value of a pint of juice (not pasteurized or bottled) is $0.30. Beyond the split-off point, the cost of sugar-coating and packaging the 100 pounds of peels is $50. The cost of pasteurizing and packaging the 300 pints of juice is $150.

A 100 pound box of candied peels is sold to commercial baking companies for $500. Each pint of juice is sold for $1.

*Required*

a. Allocate joint costs using the relative sales values *at the split-off point* and calculate the profit per 100 pound box of sugarcoated peels and the profit per pint of juice.

b. What is the incremental benefit (cost) to the company of sugarcoating the peels rather than selling them in their condition at the split-off point?

c. What is the incremental benefit (cost) to the company of pasteurizing and packaging a pint of juice rather than selling the juice at the split-off point?

**PROBLEM 7-13. Joint Costs** Robert Gordon is a commercial fisherman and he has just returned from a trip off the coast of Alaska. Robert has calculated the cost of his catch as follows:

| | |
|---|---|
| Wages of deckhands | $20,000 |
| Robert's wage | 10,000 |
| Food, medical supplies, etc. | 2,000 |
| Depreciation of netting and other equipment | 4,000 |
| Depreciation of boat | 8,000 |
| Fuel | 10,000 |
| Total | $54,000 |

Robert's nets yielded a catch of 10,000 pounds of salmon, 10,000 pounds of halibut, and 20,000 pounds of flounder. Salmon sells for $4 per pound, halibut for $3 per pound, and Flounder for $1 per pound.

*Required*

a. Allocate joint costs based on weight. With these costs, what is the profit associated with each type of fish?

b. Allocate joint costs based on relative sales values. With these costs, what is the profit associated with each type of fish?

c. Robert is considering turning the flounder into fish paste. The incremental cost of this operation is $7,000. Each pound of flounder yields one half pound of paste, and the paste sells for $3 per pound. Will Robert be better off selling the flounder or turning it into paste? What role does the allocated joint cost play in this decision?

**PROBLEM 7-14. Joint Costs**   Northwest Minerals operates a mine. During July, the company obtained 400 tons of ore, which yielded 100 pounds of gold and 50,000 pounds of copper. The joint cost related to the operation was $400,000. Gold sells for $270 per ounce and copper sells for $0.68 per pound.

*Required*

a. Allocate the joint costs using relative weight. With these costs, what is the profit associated with each mineral? What is the drawback of this approach?

b. Allocate the joint costs using the relative sales values. With these costs, what is the profit associated with each mineral?

c. With the relative sales value approach to allocation, what is the smallest value of joint cost that would result in cooper showing a loss? What is the smallest value of joint cost that would result in gold showing a loss?

**PROBLEM 7-15. (Appendix) Batch Size Decision and Constraints**   At Jordan Outdoor Furniture, the powder coating process is a bottleneck. Typically, it takes approximately two hours to switch between jobs. The time is spent cleaning nozzles, and paint tanks, and recalibrating equipment. Currently, the company runs relatively small batch sizes through the process but is considering increasing them to reduce setup time.

   With small batch sizes, powder coating can process approximately 2,500 units per 8-hour shift and products have an average contribution margin of $40. With large batch sizes, powder coating can process approximately 3,000 units per 8-hour shift.

*Required*

a. Calculate the additional profit associated with running larger batch sizes through the powder coating process.

b. What potential problems are created by the larger batch sizes.

**PROBLEM 7-16. (Appendix) Managing Constraints**   Reece Herbal Supplements purchases, in bulk, a variety of dietary supplements that the company bottles, packages, and ships to health food stores and drugstores around the country. The company has a good reputation, and its products are in high demand. Last year, the company purchased mechanical packaging equipment for $260,000 and reduced it's shipping department by two people, eliminating an annual salary expense of $100,000. When it works, the equipment packages product 10 percent faster than the previous manual system. Unfortunately, the equipment has broken down on many occasions for up to four hours.

   Normally (when the packaging equipment is working), the company packages 2,000 bottles per hour and the average contribution margin per bottle is $0.50. The general manager of operations has suggested that the company rehire the two packaging workers as back up for the new packaging system. The company president doesn't think this is a good idea since the workers will be "sitting around doing nothing for 30 hours per week!"

*Required*

Comment on the general manager's suggestion and the president's reaction. Support your answer with an estimate of the financial impact of rehiring the two workers.

# CASES

## 7-1 PRIMUS CONSULTING GROUP

Primus is a firm of consultants that focuses on process reengineering and quality improvement initiatives. Northwood Industries has asked Primus to conduct a study aimed at improving on-time delivery. Normal practice for Primus is to bill for consultant time at standard rates plus actual travel costs and estimated overhead. However, Northwood has offered a flat $85,000 for the job. Currently, Primus has excess capacity in that it can take on the Northwood job without turning down other business and without hiring additional staff.

If normal practices were followed, the bill would be:

| Classification | Hours | Rate | Amount |
|---|---|---|---|
| Partner | 100 | $250 | $25,000 |
| Senior consultant | 200 | $150 | 30,000 |
| Staff consultant | 200 | $ 80 | 16,000 |
| Travel costs | | | 15,000 |
| Overhead at $20 per nonpartner hour | | | 8,000 |
| Total | | | $94,000 |

Overhead (computer costs, rent, utilities, paper, copying, etc.) is determined at the start of the year by dividing estimated annual overhead costs ($1,600,000) by total estimated nonpartner hours (80,000 hours). Approximately 10 percent of the total amount is variable costs.

All Primus employees receive a fixed wage (i.e., there is no compensation for overtime). Annual compensation in the previous year amounted to the following:

| | Per Hour |
|---|---|
| Partners | $260 |
| Senior consultant | $ 95 |
| Staff consultant | $ 45 |

### Required
What will be the effect on company profit related to accepting the Northwood Industries job? What qualitative factors should be considered in the decision as to whether or not to accept the job?

## 7-2 MAYFIELD SOFTWARE, VAM

Mark Pelton works for Mayfield Software and is the vendor account manager (VAM) responsible for Mayfield's relationship with Nelson Electronics. Nelson manufactures an ergonomic keyboard designed and marketed by Mayfield Software. In the past year, Mayfield purchased 83,400 keyboards at $55 per unit. Mayfield sells the keyboards for $64 wholesale and $79 retail.

Mark is in the process of negotiating a new contract with Nelson. Recognizing the relatively low profit margin on the keyboards, he would like Nelson to lower its price. Nelson, however, insists that it is only making 10 percent over its costs and has provided the following information to support its assertion.

| | |
|---|---|
| Component costs | $3,500,000 |
| Direct labor | 300,000 |
| Depreciation of equipment | 80,000 |
| Depreciation of building | 60,000 |
| Supervisory salaries | 80,000 |
| Advertising | 50,000 |
| General and admin. | 100,000 |
| Total costs | $4,170,000 |
| Number of units | ÷ 83,400 |
| Unit cost | $ 50 |
| Markup at 10% | $ 55 |

### Additional Facts:

1. Nelson has some excess capacity. Production of the keyboard for Mayfield does not necessitate turning down business from other customers.

2. Discussion with the vendor indicated that all costs other than component costs, direct labor, and supervisory salaries were allocated to the keyboard by Nelson on the basis of relative sales.

| | |
|---|---|
| Sales to Mayfield | $ 4,587,000 |
| Total company sales | $38,225,000 |
| Percent | 12 |

Thus, for example with total advertising costs in the prior year equal to $416,667, 12 percent of them ($50,000) were assigned to the ergonomic keyboard.

3. In the coming year, Mayfield estimates that demand for its keyboard will be 100,000 units (if the company maintains its current pricing structure).

*Required*

Mark would like Nelson to reduce its price to $52 per unit. To facilitate negotiations, he intends to prepare an analysis showing that Nelson will be better off if it accepts a price of $52 as compared to losing Mayfield's business.

Show the quantitative analysis that Mark can present to Nelson to, hopefully, get the company to reduce its price.

# 7-3 FIVE STAR TOOLS

(Note: This case relates to the appendix on the Theory of Constraints.)

Five Star Tools is a small family-owned firm that manufactures diamond-coated cutting tools (chisels and saws) used by jewelers. Production involves three major processes. First, steel "blanks" (tools without the diamond coating) are cut to size. Second, the blanks are sent to a chemical bath that prepares the tools for the coating process. In the third major process, the blanks are coated with diamond chips in a proprietary process that simultaneously coats and sharpens the blade of each tool. Following the coating process each tool is inspected and defects are repaired or scrapped.

In the past two years, the company has experienced significant growth and growing pains. The company is at capacity in the coating and sharpening process, which requires highly skilled workers and expensive equipment. Because of the bottleneck created by this operation, the company has missed deadlines on orders from several important customers.

Maxfield Turner the son of Frederick Turner, founder of Five Star Tools, is the president of the company. Over lunch he and Betty Spence, vice president of marketing, discussed the situation. "We've got to do something," Betty began. "If we don't think we can meet a customer's order deadline, we should turn down the business. We can't simply keep customers waiting for product or we'll develop a reputation as an unreliable supplier. You know as well as I do that this would be devastating to our business."

"I think there may be another approach, Betty," replied Max. "Some of our products are exceptionally profitable. Maybe we should concentrate on them and drop some of the less profitable ones. That would free up our production resources. Or, maybe we can figure out a way to run more product through the coating process. If we could just loosen that constraint, I know we could improve our response time and profitability. I'll tell you what I'll do. I'll get the accounting department to prepare an analysis of product profitability. That should help us figure out which products to concentrate on. And, I'll get the production people thinking about how to free up some time in coating. We'll meet early next month and try to get a handle on how to deal with our production constraints."

*Required*

a. What steps can be taken to loosen the constraint in Coating and Sharpening?

b. Consider the Model C210 and the Model D400 chisels. Which product should be "emphasized" given the constraint in Coating and Sharpening cannot be loosened?

|  | Model C210 Chisel | | Model D400 Chisel | |
|---|---|---|---|---|
| Selling price | | $400 | | $700 |
| Less variable costs: | | | | |
|    Direct labor | $ 70 | | $150 | |
|    Direct material | 120 | | 150 | |
|    Variable overhead | 10 | 200 | 50 | 350 |
| Contribution margin | | 200 | | 350 |
| Less allocated fixed costs | | 150 | | 190 |
| Profit per unit | | $ 50 | | $160 |
| Time in Coating and Sharpening to produce 1 unit | | .2 Hours | | .8 Hours |

c. Focusing only on the Model C210 Chisel and the Model D400 Chisel, what would be the benefit to the firm of gaining one more hour of production time in Coating and Sharpening?

d. In Coating and Sharpening, the operator begins by inspecting items that have arrived from the Chemical Bath. If rough edges or blemishes are detected, the operator smoothes and/or buffs the items before actual coating or sharpening takes place. (Note that this process is in addition to the inspection that takes place at a separate inspection station following coating and sharpening.)

In order to save valuable time in Coating and Sharpening, management is considering forming a separate inspection station before the coating and sharpening process. The inspection station can utilize existing smoothing and buffing equipment, and it can be staffed on an as needed basis by an employee who normally works in the Chemical Bath area, which has excess capacity (so the employee will not be missed for brief periods). Management estimates that this action will free up 240 hours in Coating and Sharpening (an average of 5 minutes per hour × 8 hours per day × 360 operating days per year). Management has calculated that the average contribution margin per unit for its products is $275. The average contribution margin per hour spent in Coating and Sharpening is $800.

Based on this information, estimate the incremental profit per year associated with adding the new inspection station.

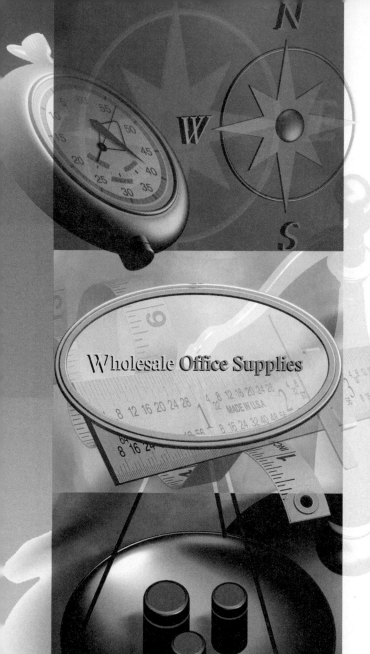

# chapter 8

## LEARNING OBJECTIVES

**1** Compute the profit maximizing price for a product or service.

**2** Perform incremental analysis related to pricing a special order.

**3** Explain the cost-plus approach to pricing and why it is inherently circular for manufacturing firms.

**4** Explain the target costing process for a new product.

**5** Analyze customer profitability.

**6** Explain the activity-based pricing approach.

# PRICING DECISIONS, ANALYZING CUSTOMER PROFITABILITY, AND ACTIVITY-BASED PRICING

Peter Spence, vice president of marketing for Wholesale Office Products, recently attended a management training seminar where the instructor made the following point:

*All customers are not the same—some are highly profitable and some are marginally profitable at best. To be successful, companies need to analyze the profitability of customers. Marginally profitable customers should be charged increased prices or their business should be dropped. The highly profitable customers—those are the ones you want to focus on. Direct your marketing campaigns towards them and you'll be on your way to achieving major increases in shareholder value!*

Driving home from the seminar, Peter thought about what he had learned and changes that needed to be made at Wholesale. In particular, he thought about his company's approach to pricing. Currently, the company charges all customers a 10 percent markup over the cost of products ordered. But some customers are much more difficult to deal with than others. In particular, some customers want frequent deliveries of relatively small orders. This means that relatively more time is spent picking and packing

their orders, and delivery costs are higher. "What we need to do," Peter decided, "is determine the profitability of our various customers and then come up with a more rational approach to pricing. First thing tomorrow, I'll set up a team with members from distribution, marketing, and accounting to work on customer profitability, measurement, and pricing."

Pricing decisions are often the most difficult decisions that managers face, and in this chapter we will examine them in some detail. We begin by discussing the profit maximizing price from the standpoint of economic theory. Then we discuss pricing special orders and prices set by marking up costs as well as determining the target cost for a new product. We will conclude the chapter with a discussion of measuring customer profitability and activity-based pricing—two topics that relate directly to the problem Peter Spence is facing at Wholesale Office Supplies.

Compute the profit
maximizing price for a
product or service.

# THE PROFIT MAXIMIZING PRICE

Economic theory suggests that the quantity demanded of a product or service is a function of the price that is charged and that generally, the higher the price, the lower the quantity demanded. If managers can estimate the quantity demanded at various prices (admittedly a difficult but not an impossible task), determining the optimal price is relatively straightforward. Simply subtract variable costs from price to obtain the contribution margin, multiply the contribution margin by the quantity demanded, subtract fixed costs, and estimate profit. The price with the highest profit should be selected. This is much simpler than it sounds. Consider the following example.

Next month, QuantumTM will begin to market a new electronic testing device called the Model TM20. The variable costs of producing and marketing the device are $1,500 per unit, and fixed costs are $7,000,000 per year. The market research team at QuantumTMs estimate demand at various prices as indicated in Illustration 8-1. Note that with a price of $6,000 per unit, the quantity demanded is only 1,000 units whereas demand increases to 19,000 units if the price is dropped to $2,500 per unit. By subtracting the variable cost of $1,500 per unit from each price we obtain the contribution margin per unit, which we multiply by the quantity demanded to estimate the total contribution margin. From the total contribution margin, we subtract fixed costs of $7,000,000 to obtain a measure of profit. In this case, the optimal price would be $3,500 per unit, because this price yields the highest total profit ($17,000,000 per year).[1]

The most difficult part of determining the profit maximizing price is determining the demand function, which is the relation between price and the quantity demanded. While this is as much art as science, a number of approaches can be used. For example, QuantumTM could ask sales managers in various regions to estimate the quantities they can sell at various prices and then sum their responses to estimate the total quantity demanded at various prices. Or the company could test-market the product with a number of potential customers and experiment with various prices. From this experience, the company would extrapolate to the entire market for the product. Still, it must be admitted that estimat-

**Illustration 8-1**
Estimating the profit
maximizing price

| A | B | C | D = A − C | E = B × D | F | G = E − F |
|---|---|---|---|---|---|---|
| Price per unit | Quantity demanded | Variable cost per unit | Contribution margin per unit | Total contribution margin | Fixed Costs | Profit |
| $6,000 | 1,000 | $1,500 | $4,500 | $ 4,500,000 | $7,000,000 | $(2,500,000) |
| 5,500 | 2,000 | 1,500 | 4,000 | 8,000,000 | 7,000,000 | 1,000,000 |
| 5,000 | 4,000 | 1,500 | 3,500 | 14,000,000 | 7,000,000 | 7,000,000 |
| 4,500 | 6,000 | 1,500 | 3,000 | 18,000,000 | 7,000,000 | 11,000,000 |
| 4,000 | 9,000 | 1,500 | 2,500 | 22,500,000 | 7,000,000 | 15,500,000 |
| 3,500 | 12,000 | 1,500 | 2,000 | 24,000,000 | 7,000,000 | 17,000,000 |
| 3,000 | 15,000 | 1,500 | 1,500 | 22,500,000 | 7,000,000 | 15,500,000 |
| 2,500 | 19,000 | 1,500 | 1,000 | 19,000,000 | 7,000,000 | 12,000,000 |

---

[1] The approach to pricing in Illustration 8-1 is equivalent to an approach you may have learned in economics; namely, select a price such that marginal revenue equals marginal cost.

ing the demand function is quite challenging and that's why some companies turn to a more simple approach—cost-plus pricing which we discuss later in the chapter. Now let's turn to the pricing of special orders and return to a concept we've stressed throughout the book—incremental analysis.

# PRICING SPECIAL ORDERS

In general, products are not sold for a price less than their full cost. In some circumstances, however, it may be beneficial to charge a lower price. This is often the case when companies are faced with special orders from customers. If granting a price below full cost for a special order will not affect demand for its other products, a company may actually be better off charging a price below full cost.

Consider a situation faced by Quality Lens Company, which manufactures camera lenses. Its lenses are sold through camera shops with a variety of mounting adapters to fit most popular 35-millimeter cameras. Recently, Nystrom Camera Company has asked Quality to produce 20,000 lenses for their compact 35-millimeter digital camera. The lens is identical to the Model A lens that Quality currently sells for $85. However, the model to be produced will substitute the Nystrom name for the Quality name stamped on the lens.

In the past year, Quality sold 280,000 units of the Model A. However, the company has been operating at only 75 percent of practical capacity and can easily accommodate production of the 20,000 additional units. The standard cost of producing the Model A is $75.

Nystrom Camera Company has offered to buy the 20,000 lenses for $73 each. Since the total standard cost is $75, it appears that the special order should be turned down. However, the incremental analysis presented in Illustration 8-2 indicates that the special order will make a substantial contribution to company income.

| Model A Standard Unit Cost | |
|---|---|
| Direct material | $30.00 |
| Direct labor | 15.00 |
| Variable overhead | 10.00 |
| Fixed overhead | 20.00 |
| Total | $75.00 |

The special-order decision presents two alternatives: accept or reject the special order. Since the income from the main business is the same under both alternatives, it is *not incremental* and need not be considered in the decision. The most obvious incremental item is the revenue associated with the special order. If Quality accepts the order, its revenue will increase by $1,460,000. In addition,

**Illustration 8-2**
Incremental analysis of special lens order

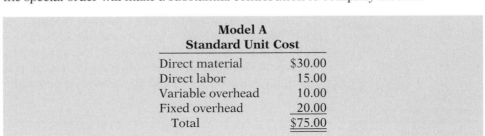

| | | |
|---|---|---|
| Incremental revenue (20,000 × $73) | | $1,460,000 |
| Less incremental costs: | | |
| Direct material (20,000 × $30) | $600,000 | |
| Direct labor (20,000 × $15) | 300,000 | |
| Variable overhead (20,000 × $10) | 200,000 | 1,100,000 |
| Net benefit of special order | | $ 360,000 |

direct material, direct labor, and variable overhead will increase by $1,100,000 if the special order is accepted. These costs are incremental, because they will be incurred if the special order is accepted and they will not be incurred if the special order is not accepted. Since incremental revenue exceeds incremental cost by $360,000, it appears to be quite beneficial to accept the special order.

Note that in the calculation of the net benefit of accepting the special order, none of the fixed costs of production are considered to be incremental costs. This is because these costs will be incurred whether or not the special order is accepted. This assumption seems reasonable given that the Quality Lens Company has excess capacity. However, suppose the management of Quality anticipates some increase in fixed costs if the special order is accepted. By how much could fixed costs increase before acceptance of the special order would be inadvisable? As long as fixed costs increase by less than $360,000, the excess of incremental revenue over incremental cost, acceptance of the special order will increase company income.

Explain the cost-plus approach to pricing and why it is inherently circular for manufacturing firms.

# COST-PLUS PRICING

Perhaps in part because of the difficulty of estimating demand functions, many companies use so-called **cost-plus pricing**. With a cost-plus approach, the company starts with an estimate of cost and adds a markup to arrive at a price that allows for a reasonable level of profit. To illustrate cost-plus pricing, suppose the Windsor Pump Company produces a variety of pumps used in the mining industry. The company has recently introduced the Model L50 pump. To produce the pump, the company must incur $1,000,000 of annual fixed costs and variable costs of $200 per unit. The company estimates that it can sell 10,000 pumps annually and marks up cost by 30 percent. In this case, as indicated in the top section of Illustration 8-3, the price will be $390 per unit, which includes total cost of $300 and markup of $90.

The obvious advantage of a cost-plus pricing approach is that it is simple to apply. Also, if a sufficient quantity can be sold at the specified price, the company will earn a reasonable profit. However, the approach also has limitations.

An obvious difficulty is choosing what markup percent to use. Is 30 percent an appropriate markup or should 10 percent, 20 percent, or 40 percent be used? Deter-

**Illustration 8-3**
Cost-plus pricing
for Model L50 Pump

| | |
|---|---:|
| Estimated quantity demanded in units | 10,000 |
| Total fixed costs | $1,000,000 |
| Fixed costs per unit ($1,000,000 ÷ 10,000) | $100 |
| Variable costs per unit | 200 |
| Total cost per unit | 300 |
| Markup at 30% | 90 |
| Price | $390 |
| Suppose the actual quantity demanded is less (say 9,000 units) | 9,000 |
| Total fixed costs | $1,000,000 |
| Fixed costs per unit ($1,000,000 ÷ 9,000) | $111 |
| Variable costs per unit | 200 |
| Total cost per unit | 311 |
| Markup at 30% | 93 |
| Price | $404 |

## With Technology, It's No Longer One Price for Everyone

You may think it's great or you may think it's terrible, but with technology, different people pay different prices for the same goods and services. Some examples:

- Hotels and airlines offer lower prices on their Internet sites when rooms and seats aren't filled.

- Grocery stores present shoppers with a posted price and a discount price for customers with frequent-shopper cards who allow their purchases to be tracked via computer programs.

- PNC Bank in Pittsburgh auctions certificates of deposit via a Web site. If your bid is among the top 25, you get the CD.

- Mortgage lenders charge different mortgage rates based on computer models of borrower risk.

*Source:* Wall Street Journal. Eastern Edition by David Wessel. Copyright 2001 by Dow Jones & Co., Inc. Reproduced with permission of Dow Jones & Co., Inc. in the format textbook via Copyright Clearance Center.

mination of an appropriate markup requires considerable judgment, and experimentation with different markups may be necessary before a final decision is reached.

Another problem is that cost-plus pricing is inherently circular for manufacturing firms.[2] You must estimate demand to determine fixed manufacturing costs per unit so that you can mark up cost to obtain a price. However, the price affects the quantity demanded; the higher the price, the lower the quantity demanded for most products. What would happen if demand for the Model L50 pump produced by Windsor Pump actually turned out to be 9,000 units? In this case, the cost per pump, as indicated in the bottom half of Illustration 8-3, would increase (because fixed costs would be spread over fewer units) and the price would be increased to $404. But what will happen to the quantity demanded when the price is increased? That's right, fewer units will be purchased, the cost per unit will go up, and the cost-plus price will be increased, resulting in lower demand! This circular process (increased price, decreased demand, increased cost per unit, increased price) is obviously not a strategy used by successful companies!

**Explain the target costing process for a new product.**

# TARGET COSTING

Manufacturing companies are always searching for ways to cut costs. Unfortunately, once a new product is designed (the product's features are specified, detailed engineering plans are made, and manufacturing of the product is ready to commence) it is very difficult to make changes that will reduce costs. In fact, it is commonly accepted that

---

[2]Cost-plus pricing is not inherently circular for retail firms. Such firms typically mark-up the cost of merchandise from supplies which is a variable cost. They do not mark-up fixed cost per unit which would require an estimate of the quantity demanded *before* setting price.

**Illustration 8-4**
The target costing process

80 percent of a product's costs can not be reduced once it is designed. The primary reason for this state of affairs is that product features drive costs. Consider the case of Kramer Home Appliances. The company is bringing a new coffeemaker to market designed with an automatic burr grinder, a water filter, and a stainless steel carafe that keeps coffee warm for six hours. These features will largely determine the cost of manufacturing the coffee pot and it will be very difficult to reduce them once the coffee pot is being produced. Indeed, costs related to purchases of equipment to produce the grinders, the filters, and the carafes are sunk costs and cannot be changed.

To confront this difficulty, a number of companies have turned to **target costing**, which is an integrated approach to determining product features, product price, product cost and product design that helps ensure a company will earn a reasonable profit on new products. The target costing process is presented in Illustration 8-4. The process begins with a careful analysis of competing products and customer needs and wants. This leads to a specification of product features and a price that the company believes will be attractive to customers given the product features. Suppose Kramer Home Appliances determines that, given the features of its new coffee maker, it can sell 50,000 units per year at $200 each. The second step in the target costing process is to specify a desired level of profit. Suppose that Kramer wants a profit margin of 30 percent or, alternatively, a profit of $60. The price and the desired profit determine the target cost, which is $140 (see Illustration 8-5). Finally, the product engineering department, working with substantial input from the cost accounting department, develops a detailed design for a product that can be produced for $140 or less. If the product cannot be produced for $140 per unit, then the company will reconsider features and price. For example, the company may decide to slightly lower its price and go with a plastic carafe as opposed to a more expensive stainless steel carafe.

Companies using target costing often set up cross-functional product development teams, including staff from engineering, marketing, and cost accounting. This helps ensure good communication among the parties involved in the product development/pricing process.

**Illustration 8-5**
Target cost of Kramer Appliance's new coffeemaker

| | |
|---|---|
| Quantity demanded given features | 50,000 units |
| Price given features | $200 |
| Required profit margin per unit (30% × $200) | 60 |
| Target cost | $140 |

**Companies Using Target Costing**

Target costing is widely used in Japan. In the United States, the approach has been slow to catch on although companies that have used it claim that it has lead to significant increases in profit. Well-known firms using target costing include Toyota, Boeing, Eastman Kodak, Honda of America, DaimlerChrysler and Caterpillar.

*Source:* Russ Banham "Off Target?" *CFO The Magazine for Senior Financial Executives.* May 2000, pp. 127–130.

Analyze customer profitability.

# ANALYZING CUSTOMER PROFITABILITY: Revisiting the Wholesale Office Supply Case

Recall that in the chapter opener, Peter Spence, vice president of Wholesale Office Supply, wanted to know the profitability of various customers as a basis for setting prices and targeting marketing campaigns. To accomplish his objective, he needs a **customer profitability measurement (CPM) system**. With a CPM system, the indirect costs of servicing customers including the cost of processing orders, the cost of handling returns, the cost of shipments, etc. are assigned to cost pools. Using cost drivers, these costs are then allocated to specific customers. Subtracting these costs and product costs from customer revenue yields a measure of customer profitability. A graphical presentation of CPM is presented in Illustration 8-6.

You probably notice a connection between activity-based costing (ABC) presented in Chapter 6 and CPM. In Chapter 6, we used ABC to allocate costs to products and services. In this section, we're going to use ABC to allocate costs to

**Illustration 8-6**
Graphical presentation of customer profitability measurement

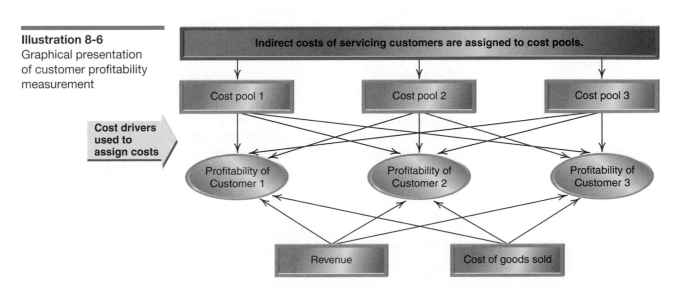

**Illustration 8-7**
Cost pools and drivers for indirect costs to service customers at Wholesale Office Supplies

| Cost pools | Annual Cost | Cost driver | Annual driver quantity | Allocation rate |
|---|---|---|---|---|
| Cost pool related to processing Internet orders | $ 434,400 | Number of Internet orders | 362,000 | $1.20 |
| Cost pool related to processing orders received via phone, fax, or mail | 576,000 | Number of fax/phone/ mail orders | 128,000 | $4.50 |
| Cost pool related to picking orders from stock in the warehouse | 7,200,000 | Number of line items in orders | 8,000,000 | $0.90 |
| Cost pool related to shipping | 720,000 | Miles to customer location | 2,000,000 | $0.36 |
| Cost pool related to packing orders | 6,000,000 | Weight of order | 15,000,000 | $0.40 |
| Cost pool related to processing returns | 52,000 | Number of items returned | 65,000 | $0.80 |
| | $14,982,400 | | | |

customers so that we can determine the full cost of serving them. To facilitate our discussion of customer profitability measurement, we will consider the situation facing Peter Spence at Wholesale Office Supply. Assuming his company has a reasonably sophisticated computerized information system, it can easily trace sales revenue and cost of goods sold to individual customers. The challenging task will be to trace the indirect costs of serving customers to individual customers.[3]

Suppose the team that investigated CPM at Wholesale Office Supplies determined the cost pools and cost drivers indicated in Illustration 8-7. In total, indirect costs amount to $14,982,400 per year. The first two cost pools relate to the costs of processing Internet orders versus orders placed by phone, fax, or mail. Note that the cost per Internet order is substantially less ($1.20 per order versus $4.50 per order). The next cost pool relates to the costs incurred in picking orders from stock in the warehouse. More time is spent as the number of different items in the order increases since different items are stored in different locations in the warehouse, and each line on an order form relates to a specific item. Thus, the cost driver is the number of line items in an order. The final three cost pools relate to shipping and packing orders and processing returned merchandise.

The next step in the customer profitability analysis is to apply the indirect costs to specific customers. Consider the two customers analyzed in Illustration 8-8. Although Customers 1 and 2 have about the same level of sales, Customer 2 imposes more than twice as much indirect costs on Wholesale Office Supplies ($8,658 for Customer 2 versus $3,498 for Customer 1). This results because Customer 2 places more orders and uses the more costly fax method rather than the Internet. Customer

---

[3]See L. Brem and V. G. Narayanan, "Owens and Minor (A) and (B)," *Harvard Business School Cases* (2000) for a description of customer profitability measurement at the company Owens and Minor. These cases also discuss an activity-based pricing system that we will cover at the end of this chapter.

**Illustration 8-8**
Customer profitability
analysis for two customers

**Customer 1**

| | | |
|---|---|---|
| Revenue | | $740,000.00 |
| Less cost of goods sold | | 666,000.00 |
| Gross margin | | 74,000.00 |
| Less indirect costs: | | |
| 165 Internet orders × $1.20 | $    198.00 | |
| 20 fax orders × $4.50 | 90.00 | |
| 2,500 line items × $0.90 | 2,250.00 | |
| 1,200 miles × $0.36 | 432.00 | |
| 900 pounds × $.40 | 360.00 | |
| 210 items returned × $0.80 | 168.00 | 3,498.00 |
| Customer profit | | $ 70,502.00 |
| Profit as a percent of sales | | 9.53% |

**Customer 2**

| | | |
|---|---|---|
| Revenue | | $735,000.00 |
| Less cost of goods sold | | 661,500.00 |
| Gross margin | | 73,500.00 |
| Less indirect costs: | | |
| 0 Internet orders × $1.20 | $      – | |
| 320 fax orders × $4.50 | 1,440.00 | |
| 5,100 line items × $0.90 | 4,590.00 | |
| 3,300 miles × $0.36 | 1,188.00 | |
| 870 pounds × $0.40 | 348.00 | |
| 910 items returned × $1.20 | 1,092.00 | 8,658.00 |
| Customer profit | | $ 64,842.00 |
| Profit as a percent of sales | | 8.82% |

2 also orders a greater variety of items (indicated by its 5,100 line items), which leads to higher order-picking costs. Finally, more miles are traveled to deliver orders for Customer 2, and Customer 2 returns more merchandise.

Wholesale Office Supplies could perform the same analysis for all of its customers and then sort them into groups based on their relative profitability. The most profitable customers may receive special treatment (e.g., occasional calls/visits from the president of Wholesale Office Supplies, special discounts or promotions, etc.) to ensure their continued business. The company may also study the characteristics of the most profitable companies in an effort to gain a better understanding of how to expand business to similar customers. With respect to the least profitable customers, the company may increase prices, try to move them to less costly service (e.g., require that they place orders over the Internet ordering system), or even drop them.

LEARNING
OBJECTIVE
6

Explain the activity-based
pricing approach.

# ACTIVITY-BASED PRICING

The same type of information used to analyze customer profitability can form the basis for an activity-based pricing system. Essentially, **activity-based pricing** is an approach to pricing in which customers are presented with separate prices for

**Illustration 8-9**
Activity-based pricing for indirect cost at Wholesale Office Supplies

| | |
|---|---|
| Charge for Internet orders | $1.25 |
| Charge for phone, fax, or mail orders | $4.75 |
| Charge per line item in an order | $1.00 |
| Delivery charge per mile | $0.40 |
| Packing charge per pound | $0.50 |
| Per item restocking charge for returned merchandise | $1.00 |

services they request in addition to the cost of goods they purchase. This causes customers to carefully consider the services they request and may lead them to impose less cost on their suppliers. Some companies refer to activity-based pricing as menu-based pricing since customers are presented with a menu of prices related to the various services they request in addition to the products they purchase.

Let's see how an activity-based pricing system might work at Wholesale Office Supplies. Suppose that, based on the study of indirect costs presented in Illustration 8-7, the company set the prices for services indicated in Illustration 8-9. As you can see, the company proposes to charge customers $1.25 for every order placed via the Internet whereas phone, fax, or mail orders are priced at $4.75 per order. Each line item in an order is associated with picking an item from the warehouse and the company charges $1 for this activity. Delivery charges are $0.40 per mile ($0.04 higher than cost), packing is $0.50 per pound ($0.10 higher than cost), and the company charges $1 to restock a returned item ($0.20 higher than cost).

Some customers might object to this pricing scheme by arguing that the price they pay for the goods they purchase should cover these costs. There are a number of ways to deal with this resistance. The company could lower its prices for goods (at least slightly) and then encourage customers to make fewer but larger purchases to reduce their overall costs. Customers could also be encouraged to limit the variety of goods they purchase, since variety leads to separate line items on order forms and higher cost (e.g., does the customer really need 10 different pens in four different colors?). Alternatively, the company might decide to just use the activity-based pricing approach for its less profitable customers. Then, the most profitable customers, who are still paying just for the goods they purchase, will perceive that they are getting a "break" because they are valued customers. And the least profitable customers will be paying for the extra costs they impose on the company.

# MAKING BUSINESS DECISIONS

When making a pricing decision, don't get overly focused on the current cost per unit. The quantity demanded is affected by the price and this quantity changes the cost per unit because fixed costs are spread out over more or less units.

Ideally, you want to determine the price that maximizes profit. The profit maximizing approach we learned in this chapter can be difficult to implement because of difficulty in estimating the relation between the quantity demanded and price. However, at a minimum, it provides a useful framework for thinking about pricing decisions since it takes into account price, demand, variable costs, and fixed costs.

## KNOWLEDGE AND SKILLS (K/S) CHECKLIST

*Knowledge and skills are needed to make good business decisions. Check off the knowledge and skills you've acquired from reading this chapter.*

☐ K/S 1. You have an expanded business vocabulary (see key terms).

☐ K/S 2. You can compute the profit maximizing price for a product or service.

☐ K/S 3. You can explain the target costing process.

☐ K/S 4. You can perform customer profitability measurement.

☐ K/S 5. You can explain how activity-based pricing will impact the costs customers impose on suppliers.

# SUMMARY OF LEARNING OBJECTIVES

**1** *Compute the profit maximizing price for a product or service.* The first step in computing the profit maximizing price is to estimate the quantity demanded at various prices. Then, variable costs are subtracted from price to determine the contribution margin per unit. From the total contribution margin, subtract fixed costs to determine profit. The price that yields the highest profit is the profit maximizing price.

**2** *Perform incremental analysis related to pricing a special order.* Special orders will yield an incremental profit as long as the selling price exceeds the incremental cost of filling the order. Fixed costs that are not affected by the special order are irrelevant to the decision as to whether the order should be taken.

**3** *Explain the cost-plus approach to pricing and why it is inherently circular for manufacturing firms.* In cost-plus pricing, the full cost per unit is determined and price is set by adding a prespecified markup to the cost. This process is circular for manufacturing firms in that the quantity demanded, which is needed to estimate full cost per unit, is determined prior to setting the price, which has a major impact on the quantity demanded.

**4** *Explain the target costing process for a new product.* Using target costing, companies analyze the marketplace and decide on a set of features and a price point for their product. They subtract a desired profit level from the price to solve for the target cost. The product is then designed to meet the target cost when it is produced. If the target cost cannot be achieved, the company may reconsider the set of features and the price or decide not to go ahead with the product.

**5** *Analyze customer profitability.* The profitability of a customer depends not just on what is purchased, but also on the set of services provided to the customer (e.g., order processing, shipping, handling returns, etc.). To analyze the profitability of a customer, the cost of such services must be subtracted from the customer's gross margin. This requires that service costs be grouped into cost pools and related cost drivers must be identified so that the cost per unit of service can be allocated to specific customers.

**6** *Explain the activity-based pricing approach.* In activity-based pricing, customers are presented with a menu of prices and are charged for *services* provided to them (in addition to being charged for the goods they purchase). The charge for such services is usually determined based on an analysis of their cost. Since they are charged for specific services, customers will carefully consider the services they request and may end up imposing less cost on suppliers.

# REVIEW PROBLEM

Heartland Tools is a large Midwest company that designs and manufactures dies, jigs, fixtures, roll-form tooling, and special machines. Equipment used by the company includes milling machines, HeliArc welders, drill presses, hydraulic presses, and heat treatment ovens. Due to intense competition from foreign companies, the firm currently has substantial excess capacity, and in the prior year, the company laid off 545 employees.

To price its product, the company estimates design and product costs and marks the total up by 40 percent to cover administrative and marketing costs and to earn a profit. Product costs include material, labor, depreciation of equipment, and other overhead. The costs in the "other overhead" cost pool are primarily fixed costs.

Costs are estimated as follows:

1. Design costs    Based on estimated engineering hours times a rate of $40 per hour.

2. Material    Estimate of the actual cost of materials.

3. Labor    Estimate of actual direct labor costs (estimate of actual hours multiplied by the wage rate of employees likely to be assigned to the job).

4. Depreciation of manufacturing equipment    Based on predetermined overhead rates for each type of equipment. For each type of equipment, the company divides estimated annual depreciation by estimated annual hours of use.

| Equipment type | Annual depreciation | Annual hours of use |
|---|---|---|
| Milling | $6,000,000 | 4,000 |
| Welding | $2,000,000 | 8,000 |
| Drill press | $1,000,000 | 5,000 |
| Hydraulic press | $4,000,000 | 4,000 |
| Heat treatment | $5,000,000 | 4,000 |

5. Other manufacturing overhead (i.e., other than depreciation)    Estimated as $50 per direct labor hour.

The company is currently pricing a job for Preston Manufacturing. A preliminary bid form indicates the following:

**Preliminary/incomplete cost estimate and bid for Preston Manufacturing**

| | | |
|---|---|---|
| Material | | $25,000 |
| Direct labor | 28 hours × $25 | $   700 |
| | 15 hours × $18 | $   270 |
| | 25 hours × $30 | $   750 |
| Design time | 18 hours | |
| Milling time | 9.0 hours | |
| Welding time | 5.0 hour | |
| Drill press time | 7.0 hours | |
| Hydraulic press time | 6.5 hours | |
| Heat treat time | 2.0 hours | |
| Other overhead | | _____ |
| Estimated total cost | | _____ |
| Mark up at 40% | | _____ |
| Bid | | _____ |

**Required**

a. Estimate total cost and the bid price with the 40 percent mark up.

b. Preston has told Heartland that it will use another supplier if Heartland's bid is over $50,000. Heartland's CFO strongly objects to a $50,000 price since it will not even cover full costs. Evaluate the CFO's position. Should the company price the job at $50,000?

**Answer**

a.

**Cost-Plus Price for Preston Manufacturing**

| | | | |
|---|---|---:|---:|
| Material | | | $25,000 |
| Direct labor | 28 hours × $25 | $   700 | |
| | 15 hours × $18 | 270 | |
| | 25 hours × $30 | 750 | 1,720 |
| Design time | 18 hours × $40 | | 720 |
| Milling time | 9.0 hours × $1,500 | 13,500 | |
| Welding time | 5.0 hour × $250 | 1,250 | |
| Drill press time | 7.0 hours × $200 | 1,400 | |
| Hydraulic press time | 6.5 hours × $1,000 | 6,500 | |
| Heat treatment time | 2.0 hours × $1,250 | 2,500 | 25,150 |
| Other overhead | 68 direct labor hours × $50 | | 3400 |
| Estimated total cost | | | $55,990 |
| Mark up at 40% | | | 22,396 |
| Bid | | | $78,386 |

| Equipment type | Annual depreciation | Annual hours of use | Overhead rate |
|---|---|---|---|
| Milling | $6,000,000 | 4,000 | $1,500 |
| Welding | $2,000,000 | 8,000 | $   250 |
| Drill press | $1,000,000 | 5,000 | $   200 |
| Hydraulic press | $4,000,000 | 4,000 | $1,000 |
| Heat treatment | $5,000,000 | 4,000 | $1,250 |

b. It appears that the only costs that are likely to be incremental are those related to design, material, and labor. Assuming this is the case, the company will generate an incremental profit of $22,560 at a price of $50,000. Given the company is operating below capacity (and assuming this "low" price does not negatively impact future prices to Preston or other customers), charging $50,000 for the job is a good decision.

| | | |
|---|---:|---:|
| Incremental revenue | | $50,000 |
| Incremental costs | | |
| Design costs | $   720 | |
| Material | 25,000 | |
| Labor | 1,720 | 27,440 |
| Incremental profit | | $22,560 |

# KEY TERMS

# S E L F   A S S E S S M E N T   *(Answers Below)*

1. To determine the profit-maximizing price a manager must:
   a. Estimate the quantity demanded for various prices.
   b. Estimate variable costs.
   c. Both a and b are correct.
   d. None of the above are correct.

2. Cost-plus pricing:
   a. Leads to profit maximization.
   b. Is inherently circular for manufacturing firms.
   c. Is difficult to perform.
   d. None of the above are correct.

3. Target costing:
   a. Requires specification of desired level of profit.
   b. Targets specific costs for reduction.
   c. Is used primarily with products that are already in production.
   d. Leads to profit maximization.

4. Customer profitability is measured as:
   a. Revenue − cost of goods sold.
   b. Revenue − indirect manufacturing costs.
   c. Revenue − cost of goods sold-indirect service costs.
   d. Revenue − cost of goods sold-indirect manufacturing costs.

5. With activity-based pricing:
   a. Customers face a menu of prices for various services.
   b. Customers are encouraged to consider the costs they impose on a supplier.
   c. Customers may be charged less if they request less product variety in their orders.
   d. All of the above are correct.

**Answers to Self Assessment**

**1.** c;     **2.** b;     **3.** a;     **4.** c;     **5.** d.

# I N T E R A C T I V E   L E A R N I N G

**Enhance and test your knowledge of Chapter 8 using the interactive CD.**

1. Learning Objectives
2. Multiple Choice
3. Language of Business—Matching of Key Terms
4. Critical Thinking
5. Demonstration—Target costing
6. Case—*Nelson Plumbing Products*; Determine the profit maximizing price

**Go to our dynamic Web site for more self-assessment, Web links, and additional information.**

# Q U E S T I O N S

1. According to economic theory, how would a manager determine the profit-maximizing price for a product or service?

2. Why is cost-plus pricing inherently circular for a manufacturing firm?

3. To implement target costing for a new product, companies often set up a cross-functional team with members from engineering, marketing, and cost accounting. Why is a cross-functional team desirable when implementing the target costing approach?

4. How is cost allocation used in customer profitability analysis?

5. Explain why less profitable customers may become more profitable if a supplier switches to activity-based pricing.

# EXERCISES

**EXERCISE 8-1. Group Assignment**   Consider a company that manufactures and sells personal computers (let's call the company Bell Computers). Recently the company lowered its prices dramatically. The company is very efficient and needs only five days of inventory, collects its receivables within 30 days, and has suppliers who are willing to wait 59 days for payment. A competitor commenting on the aggressive pricing stated that "We're in a commodity business and a price war in a commodity business is really dumb."

*Required*

Discuss the competitor's comment that lowering prices is a dumb move by Bell Computers.

**EXERCISE 8-2. Writing Assignment**   Brindle Corporation is considering an initiative to assess customer profitability. The company's CFO, John Bradley, stated his position as follows: "I strongly suspect that some of our customers are losers—in other words, they're not covering product costs and service costs. Think about our Weston account. Weston places a ton of small orders and they're always asking us to expedite them. Then our accounting department has to follow up because Weston misplaces billing records which really slows down their payments. We're going to make a $1,000,000 investment in CRM (customer relationship management) software to help us assess customer profitability, but I'm confident that the investment will really pay off when it helps us identify this type of loser customer."

The position of the company's marketing vice president, Jerry Brown, is quite different. "This $1,000,000 investment is a waste of money. We'll go through the exercise and find out that some customers are more profitable than others, but we're not going to change a thing. Even the less profitable customers make a contribution to covering overhead and we're not going to drop a single one."

*Required*

Write one or two paragraphs elaborating on the arguments of the CFO and the marketing vice president. In your discussion, consider the fact that the bonus compensation of the marketing VP is based on sales volume. Could this be influencing Jerry's position?

**EXERCISE 8-3. Internet Assignment**   Go to the Web and search for information on how customer relationship management (CRM) software is used to assess customer profitability. What is the relationship between the process used in profitability assessment and activity-based costing?

**EXERCISE 8-4. Profit maximizing price**   The editor of Spunk Magazine is considering three alternative prices for her new monthly periodical. Her estimate of price and quantity demanded are:

| Price | Quantity Demanded |
|-------|-------------------|
| $6.95 | 20,000 |
| $5.95 | 25,000 |
| $4.95 | 32,000 |

Monthly costs of producing and delivering the magazine include $80,000 of fixed costs and variable costs of $1.50 per issue.

*Required*

Which price will yield the largest monthly profit?

**EXERCISE 8-5. Analyzing a Special Order**   PowerDrive, Inc. produces a hard disk drive that sells for $140 per unit. The cost of producing 20,000 drives in the prior year was:

| | |
|---|---:|
| Direct material | $ 500,000 |
| Direct labor | 300,000 |
| Variable overhead | 100,000 |
| Fixed overhead | 1,200,000 |
| Total cost | $2,100,000 |

At the start of the current year, the company received an order for 2,000 drives from a computer company in China. Management of PowerDrive has mixed feelings about the order. On the one hand they welcome the order because they currently have excess capacity. Also, this is the company's first international order. On the other hand, the company in China is only willing to pay $100 per unit.

*Required*

What will be the affect on profit of accepting the order?

**EXERCISE 8-6. Cost-Plus Pricing**   World View is considering production of a lighted world globe that the company would price at a markup of 20 percent above full cost. Management estimates that the variable cost of the globe will be $50 per unit and fixed costs per year will be $100,000.

*Required*

a.  Assuming sales of 1,000 units, what is the full cost of a globe and what is the price with a 20 percent markup?

b.  Assume that the quantity demanded at the price calculated in Part a is only 500 units. What is the full cost of the globe and what is the price with a 20 percent markup?

c.  Is the company likely to sell 500 units at the price calculated in Part b?

**EXERCISE 8-7. Target costing**   A cross functional team at Mazzor Systems is developing a new product using the target costing methodology. Product features in comparison to competing products suggest a price of $2,000 per unit. The company requires a profit of 20 percent of selling price.

*Required*

a.  What is the target cost per unit?

b.  Suppose the engineering and cost accounting members of the team determine that the product cannot be produced for the cost calculated in Part a. What is the next step in the target costing process?

**EXERCISE 8-8. Customer Profitability Analysis**   Using CRM (customer relationship management) software, Delta Products has determined the following costs:

| | |
|---|---:|
| Order processing (per order) | $    5.00 |
| Additional handling costs if order marked rush (per order) | 8.50 |
| Customer service calls (per call) | 10.00 |
| Relationship management costs (per customer per year) | $2,000.00 |

In addition to these costs, product costs amount to 90 percent of sales.

In the prior year, Delta had the following experience with one of it's customers, Johnson Brands:

| | |
|---|---:|
| Sales | $53,800 |
| Number of orders | 200 |
| Percent of orders marked rush | 60 |
| Calls to customer service | 140 |

*Required*

Calculate the profitability of the Johnson Brands account.

**EXERCISE 8-9. Activity-Based Pricing**  Refer to the information in Exercise 8. For the coming year, Delta Products has told Johnson Brands that it will be switched to an activity-based pricing system or it will be dropped as a customer. In addition to regular prices, Johnson will be required to pay:

|  | **Price** |
|---|---|
| Order processing (per order) | $ 6.00 |
| Additional handling costs if order marked rush (per order) | 10.00 |
| Customer service calls (per call) | 15.00 |

*Required*

a. Calculate the profitability of the Johnson Brands account if activity is the same as in the prior year.

b. Assume that Johnson Brands decides to accept the activity-based pricing system offered by Delta Products. What changes will likely be made by Johnson?

# PROBLEMS

**PROBLEM 8-1. Determining the Profit Maximizing Price**  Spencer Electronics has just developed a low-end electronic calendar that it plans on selling via a cable channel marketing program. The cable program's fee for selling the item is 15 percent of revenue. For this fee, the program will sell the calendar over six 10-minute segments in September.

Spencer's fixed costs of producing the calendar are $120,000 per production run. The company plans on waiting for all orders to come in, and then it will produce exactly the number of units ordered. Production time will be less than three weeks. Variable production costs are $20 per unit. In addition, it will cost approximately $6 per unit to ship the calendars to customers.

Marsha Andersen, a product manager at Spencer, is charged with recommending a price for the item. Based on her experience with similar items, focus group responses, and survey information, she has estimated the number of units that can be sold at various prices:

| Price | Quantity |
|---|---|
| $69.99 | 10,000 |
| $59.99 | 15,000 |
| $49.99 | 25,000 |
| $39.99 | 40,000 |
| $29.99 | 60,000 |

*Required*

a. Calculate expected profit for each price.

b. Which price maximizes company profit?

 **PROBLEM 8-2. Ethics and Pricing Decisions**  LowCostDrugs.com is an on-line drugstore. Recently, the company used a computer program to analyze the purchase behavior of customers sorted by zip code and found that customers in some zip codes are, on average, less price sensitive than customers in other zip codes. Accordingly, the company has raised prices by three percent for the customers in the less price sensitive zip codes. Note that zip code is automatically identified when a customer comes to the company Web site.

*Required*

Is it ethical for LowCostDrugs.com to charge some customers a higher price based on their analysis of prior purchasing behavior?

**PROBLEM 8-3. Determining the Profit Maximizing Price**   RoverPlus, a pet product superstore, is considering pricing a new RoverPlus labeled dog food. The company will buy the premium dog food from a company in Indiana that packs the product with a RoverPlus label. Rover pays $6 for a 50-pound bag delivered to its store.

The company also sells Royal Dog Food (under the Royal Dog Food label), which it purchases for $9.00 per 50-pound bag and sells for $16.99. The company currently sells 25,000 bags of Royal Dog Food per month, but that is expected to change when the RoverPlus brand is introduced.

The company will continue to price the Royal Dog Food brand at $16.99. The quantity of RoverPlus and the quantity of Royal Dog Food that will be sold at various prices for Royal is estimated as:

| Price of RoverPlus | Quantity RoverPlus | Quantity Royal |
|---|---|---|
| $ 8.99 | 35,000 | 11,000 |
| $ 9.99 | 34,500 | 11,300 |
| $10.99 | 34,000 | 11,500 |
| $11.99 | 33,000 | 12,000 |
| $12.99 | 30,000 | 13,000 |
| $13.99 | 25,000 | 14,000 |
| $14.99 | 15,000 | 15,000 |
| $15.99 | 10,000 | 19,000 |
| $16.99 | 5,000 | 21,000 |

For example, if RoverPlus is priced at $8.99, the company will sell 35,000 bags of RoverPlus and 11,000 bags of Royal at $16.99. On the other hand, if the company prices RoverPlus at $16.99, it will sell 5,000 bags of RoverPlus and 21,000 bags of Royal at $16.99. This is 4,000 fewer bags of Royal than is currently being sold.

*Required*

a. Calculate the profit maximizing price for the RoverPlus brand taking into account the effect of the sales of RoverPlus on sales of the Royal Dog Food brand.

b. At the price calculated in Part a, what is the incremental profit over the profit earned before the introduction of the RoverPlus branded dog food?

**PROBLEM 8-4. Cost-Plus Pricing**   Wendel Stove Company is developing a "professional" model stove aimed at the home market. The company estimates that variable costs will be $2,000 per unit and fixed costs will be $10,000,000 per year.

*Required*

a. Suppose the company wants to set its price equal to full cost plus 30 percent. To determine cost, the company must estimate the number of units it will produce and sell in a year. Suppose the company estimates that it can sell 5,000 units. What price will the company set?

b. What is "odd" about setting the price based on an estimate of how many units will be sold?

c. Suppose the company sets a price as in Part a, but the number of units demanded at that price turns out to be 4,000. Revise the price in light of demand for 4,000 units.

d. What will happen to the number of units that will be sold if the price is raised to the one you calculated in Part c?

e. Explain why setting price by marking up cost is inherently circular for a manufacturing firm period.

**PROBLEM 8-5. Target Costing**   Baker Plumbing Fixtures is developing a pre-plumbed, acrylic shower unit. The team developing the product includes representatives from marketing, engineering, and cost accounting. To date, the team has developed a set of features that it plans on incorporating in the unit including a seat, two shower heads, 4 body sprays, and a steam unit. With this set of features, the team believes that a price of $3,500 will be attractive in the marketplace. Baker seeks to earn a per unit profit of 25 percent.

***Required***

a. Calculate the target cost per unit.

b. The team has estimated that the fixed production costs associated with the product will be $1,500,000 and variable costs to produce and sell the item will be $2,000 per unit. In light of this, how many units must be produced and sold to meet the target cost per unit?

c. Suppose the company decides that only 1,800 units can be sold at a price of $3,500 and, therefore, the target cost cannot be reached. The company is considering dropping the steam feature, which adds $600 of variable cost per unit. With this feature dropped, the company believes it can sell 2,500 units at $3,000 per unit. Will Baker be able to produce the item at the new target cost or less?

**PROBLEM 8-6. Analyzing Customer Profitability**   Lauden Conference Solutions specializes in the design and installation of meeting and conference centers for large corporations. When bidding on jobs, the company estimates product cost and direct labor for installers and marks the total cost up by 30 percent. On a recent job for Orvieto Industries, the company set its price as follows:

| | |
|---|---:|
| Product costs including podiums, seating, lighting, etc. | $140,000 |
| Installer salaries | 20,000 |
| Total | 160,000 |
| Markup at 30 percent | 48,000 |
| Bid price | $208,000 |

The job turned out to be a big hassle. Orvieto requested 20 change orders, although the dollar value of the products they requested changed very little. The company also returned 25 items that had extremely minor flaws (scratches that were barely visible and that would be expected in normal shipping). Orvieto also requested six meetings with designers taking 30 hours before its plan was finalized. Normally, only two or three meetings are necessary.

Nancy Jackson, controller for Lauden, decided to conduct a customer profitability analysis to determine the profitability of Orvieto. She grouped support costs into three categories with the following drivers:

| Driver | Annual value of driver | Annual cost |
|---|---|---|
| Change orders | 700 change orders | $175,000 |
| Number of returns | 850 product returns | 63,750 |
| Design meeting hours | 1,200 meeting hours | 60,000 |

***Required***

a. Calculate the indirect service costs related to the job performed for Orvieto Industries.

b. Assuming that Orvieto Industries causes a disproportionate amount of indirect service costs, how should Lauden deal with this situation?

**PROBLEM 8-7. Activity-Based Pricing**   Consider the information in Problem 8-6. Lauden Conference Solutions has decided to adopt an activity-based pricing scheme. On future jobs, the company will charge a 30 percent markup on the sum of product costs plus installer salaries. In addition, the company will charge $300 per change order, $100 per product return for products that are in excellent condition, and $75 per meeting hour with a Lauden conference room designer.

***Required***

a. What would the profit be on the order from Orvieto in Problem 8-6?

b. Identify pros and cons of adopting the activity-based pricing scheme.

# CASES

## 8-1 PRESTON CONCRETE

Preston Concrete is a major supplier of concrete to residential and commercial builders in the Pacific Northwest. The company's policy is to price deliveries at 20 percent over full cost per cubic yard (including an allowance for administrative costs). At the start of 2005, the company estimated costs as follows:

Material costs = $60 per cubic yard

Delivery costs = $200,000 per year
+ $8 (mile) + $40
(truck hour)

Yard operation costs = $200,000 per year
+ $10 per cubic yard

Administrative costs = $1,000,000 per year

Delivery costs include a *rate per mile* recognizing that more miles result in more gas and maintenance costs and a *rate per truck hour* since, even if a delivery truck is kept waiting at a job site, the truck must be kept running (so the concrete mix will not solidify) and the driver must be paid.

At the start of 2005, the company estimated that it would deliver 400,000 cubic yards.

### Required

a. On October 28, Fairview Construction Company asked Preston to deliver 5,000 cubic yards of concrete. The job will require driving 7,000 miles and 250 truck hours. What will the price be if Preston follows its normal pricing policy?

b. A sharp increase in interest rates has reduced housing starts and the demand for concrete. Fairview has indicated that it will only sign a firm order agreement if the price is $86 per cubic yard. Should Pearson accept the order? Briefly indicate factors that, while hard to quantify, should be taken into account in this decision.

## 8-2 EASTERN UNIVERSITY PHARMACY

Eastern University (EU) has a top rated medical facility that draws patients from a three state area. On the day of discharge from the EU hospital, most patients fill their prescriptions from the EU pharmacy. However, when it comes time to renew them, they turn to a local pharmacy because that is more convenient than driving back to the EU pharmacy. To encourage prescription renewals, Eastern is considering offering either free overnight delivery or reduced prices on renewal orders.

Currently, the EU pharmacy has revenue of $50,816,000 per year on 794,000 orders. The profit margin (price minus cost of drugs) is approximately 20 percent. Free overnight delivery is expected to cost $6 per order and result in 100,000 renewal orders per year. To deal with the increased volume, the pharmacy will need to hire two pharmacists at $80,000 each per year and an additional staff person at $40,000 per year.

Alternatively, the pharmacy can generate 100,000 renewal orders per year by offering 15 percent off on the prices of renewal orders. With this option, two pharmacists must be hired, but no additional staff person will be needed.

### Required

Estimate the impact on annual pharmacy profit of free delivery and "10 percent off on renewals." Which option should be selected?

# chapter 9

## LEARNING OBJECTIVES

**1** Define capital expenditure decisions and capital budgets.

**2** Evaluate investment opportunities using the net present value approach.

**3** Evaluate investment opportunities using the internal rate of return approach.

**4** Calculate the depreciation tax shield, and explain why depreciation is important in investment analysis only because of income taxes.

**5** Use the payback period and the accounting rate of return methods to evaluate investment opportunities.

**6** Explain why managers may concentrate erroneously on the short-run profitability of investments rather than their net present values.

# CAPITAL BUDGETING DECISIONS

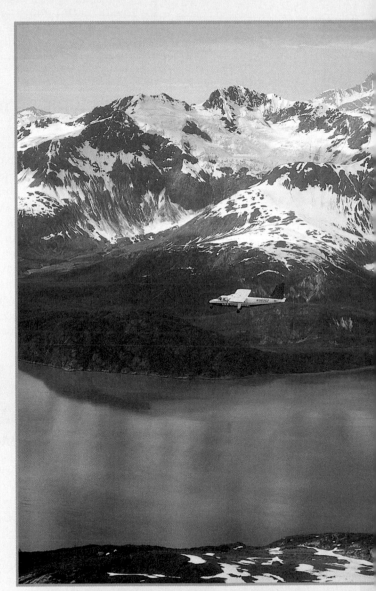

For several years, Steve Wilson, president of Wilson Air, has operated a successful business flying passengers between Seattle and resorts in Idaho and around Washington State. Now, Steve thinks it's time to consider adding to his "fleet" of three seven-passenger aircraft. "Look," he explains to his chief accountant, Ellen Ortega, "with another plane, we can service 3,500 additional round-trip passengers a year. At an average fare of $200, that's $700,000!" "But don't forget," Ellen points out, "a new plane will cost around $1,000,000, operating cost will be nearly $400,000 per year, and, after five years, that $1,000,000 plane will only be worth $500,000. It's not clear that buying another plane is a good business decision."

This chapter extends the discussion of decision making in Chapter 7 to include problems like the one facing Steve Wilson. Steve is considering investing cash *today* in order to receive cash in the *future*. Obviously, Steve will require a total cash inflow that is larger than his initial outflow, since he wants to earn a return on his investment in the plane. Here, we discuss how to determine whether future cash inflows are sufficient to earn a *satisfactory* return.

1. Starbucks invests in a new retail outlet
2. Ford Motor Company invests in robotic manufacturing equipment
3. Overlake Hospital invests in a filmless X-ray system
4. Cooper Mountain Ski Resort invests in a new chairlift
5. Holland America Cruise Line invests in a new ship
6. San Francisco Municipal Railway invests in articulated buses
7. Chateau St. Michelle winery invests in new bottling equipment
8. A Pizza Hut franchise invests in a new oven
9. *The Boston Globe* invests in a new printing press
10. Nordstrom invests in a new store on Long Island

**LEARNING OBJECTIVE 1**

Define capital expenditure decisions and capital budgets.

# CAPITAL BUDGETING DECISIONS

Individuals make investments in their homes, automobiles, major appliances, furniture, and other long-lived assets. Companies also make investments in long-lived assets. Examples of investment decisions are presented in Illustration 9-1. In each example, a firm is considering investing in one or more assets that will affect its operations for several years.

Investment decisions are extremely important because they have a major, long-term effect on a firm's operations. When BMW decided to expand its South Carolina plant, it made an investment in additional productive capacity that will affect its labor and transportation costs for many years to come. Labor to build the cars is supplied by American rather than German workers, so labor costs are largely determined by business conditions in the United States rather than in Germany. Transportation costs are greatly reduced for cars sold in the United States because cars can be shipped from South Carolina rather than continental Europe.

**LINK TO PRACTICE**

### BMW Invests in Its Spartanburg Plant

German auto maker BMW has decided to invest $400 million to expand its Spartanburg, SC plant. This is the facility devoted to the X5 SUV and the company's new Z4 roadster. The expansion will increase capacity by 30,000 vehicles per year to more than 150,000 annually.

In making the investment, BMW decided that the net future cash flows from producing and selling more vehicles will earn a *satisfactory* return on the $400 million investment. In this chapter, we'll see how to determine whether the return is, indeed, satisfactory.

*Sources:* "BMW to Expand Its South Carolina Plant," *Reuters*, September 27, 2002. "10 Years Later: BMW Manufacturing Corp. to Invest $400 Million and Add 400 Jobs," *BMW Group News: Corporate News*, September 26, 2002.

The investment decisions of small companies are also extremely important. Consider a small print shop that decides to make an investment in a computerized printing machine. The cost of the machine may represent 50 percent or more of the company's total assets. But the cost savings from the investment in new technology may make the difference between being a solid competitor in its market or being on the verge of financial failure.

Investment decisions involving the acquisition of long-lived assets are often referred to as **capital expenditure decisions** because they require that capital (company funds) be expended to acquire additional resources. Investment decisions are also called **capital budgeting decisions**. Most firms carefully analyze the potential projects in which they may invest. The process of evaluating the investment opportunities is referred to as capital budgeting, and the final list of approved projects is referred to as the **capital budget**.

# EVALUATING INVESTMENT OPPORTUNITIES: TIME VALUE OF MONEY APPROACHES

Crucial to an understanding of capital budgeting decisions is an understanding of the *time value of money*. In evaluating an investment opportunity, a company must know not only *how much* cash it receives from or pays for an investment but also *when* the cash is received or paid. The time value of money concept recognizes that it is better to receive a dollar today than it is to receive a dollar next year or any other time in the future. This is because the dollar received today can be invested so that at the end of the year it amounts to more than a dollar.

In an investment decision, a company invests money today in the hopes of receiving more money in the future. Obviously, the company would not invest money in a project unless it expected the total amount of funds received in the future to exceed the amount of the original investment. But by *how much* must the future cash flows exceed the original investment? Because money in the future is not equivalent to money today, we need to develop a way of converting future dollars into their equivalent current, or present, value. The techniques developed to equate future dollars to current dollars are referred to as present value techniques or time value of money methods.

Some readers of this book will have been introduced to present value techniques in their study of financial accounting and the valuation of long-term debt. We review the basics in the next section, "Basic Time Value of Money Calculations." After that, we discuss two approaches for evaluating investments that take into account the time value of money: the net present value method and the internal rate of return method.

## BASIC TIME VALUE OF MONEY CALCULATIONS

Suppose you invest $100 at an interest rate of 10 percent. At the end of one year, you will have $110.

$$\$100 \times (1 + .10) = \$110$$

Now, let's turn this problem around. Suppose you require a return of 10 percent on your investments. How much is a payment of $110, one year from now, worth today? A little algebra (dividing both sides by 1 + .10) indicates that it is worth $100. In other words, if your required return is 10 percent, the present value of $110 received one year from now is $100. Put another way, $100 is the amount you would have to invest today, at an interest rate of 10 percent, to have $110 at the end of one year.

$$\$100 = \frac{\$110}{(1 + .10)}$$

Now, suppose you invest $100 at 10 percent for two years. At the end of the first year you will have $100 times (1 + .10). At the end of the second year you will have this new amount times (1 + .10) which equals $121.

$$\$100 \times (1 + .10) \times (1 + .10) = \$100(1 + .10)^2 = \$121$$

Turning this problem around, if you require a return of 10 percent on your investments, then how much is a payment of $121, two years from now, worth today? The answer is $100.

$$\$100 = \frac{\$121}{(1 + .10)^2}$$

You may note that a pattern is emerging. In general, if your required rate of return is $i$, the present value (P) of any amount (F) received $n$ years in the future is

$$P = \frac{F}{(1 + i)^n}$$

That is, to calculate the present value (P) of an amount (F) received $n$ years in the future, we divide F by 1 plus the required rate of return ($i$) raised to the $n$th power.

Let's try out the formula. What is the present value of $1,000 received five years from now if your required rate of return is 12 percent? To answer the question, we divide $1,000 (the amount received in the future) by 1 plus the required return raised to the fifth power, since the cash is received at the end of year 5. The answer is $567.43.

$$P = \frac{F}{(1 = I)^n}$$

$$= \frac{\$1,000}{(1 + .12)^5}$$

$$= \frac{\$1,000}{1.7623417}$$

$$= \$567.43$$

To simplify calculations, managers can use present value tables to look up present value factors (also called discount factors).[1] Present value factors are simply calculations of $\frac{1}{(1 + i)^n}$. Thus, to calculate the present value of a future amount, you can multiply the future amount by the present value factor.

---

[1] Managers can also use financial calculators and spreadsheet programs rather than tables of present value factors. In fact, this is what most managers do. We discuss use of Excel® to perform present value calculations in Appendix A of this chapter.

For example, let's consider again the present value of $1,000 received five years from now if the required rate of return is 12 percent. The present value factor, or discount factor, is $\frac{1}{(1 + i)^n}$. Substituting values into this equation, and rounding the result to four places, we find that the factor is:

$$\text{Present value factor} = \frac{1}{(1 + i)^n}$$

$$= \frac{1}{1.7623417}$$

$$= .5674$$

Rather than working through this calculation, we can turn to the present value of $1 table, Table 1 in Appendix B. Going across the top of the table to a discount rate of 12 percent and down five rows (since the amount is to be received five years in the future), we come to a present value factor of .5674, the same as the value we calculated. Now we can find the present value itself by multiplying the factor times $1,000 (the amount to be received at the end of five years):

$$\text{Present value} = \$1,000 \times \text{Present value factor}$$

$$= \$1,000 \times .5674$$

$$= \$567.40$$

Except for a slight difference caused by rounding, this is the same answer calculated with the present value formula introduced earlier.

## THE NET PRESENT VALUE METHOD

The time value of money forms the basis of the net present value method for evaluating capital investments.

**Steps in the NPV Method.** The first step in using the net present value method is to identify the amount and time period of each cash flow associated with a potential investment. Investment projects have both cash inflows (which are positive) and cash outflows (which are negative). Consistent with our discussion in the previous chapter, the only relevant cash flows are those that are *incremental*—the cash flows that will be incurred if the project is undertaken. Cash flows that have already been incurred are sunk and have no bearing on a current investment decision.

The second step is to equate or discount the cash flows to their present values using a required rate of return. The required rate of return is discussed later. For now, simply assume that the **required rate of return** (also called the hurdle rate) is the minimum return that top management wants to earn on investments.

The third and final step is to evaluate the net present value. The sum of the present values of all cash flows (inflows and outflows) is the **net present value (NPV)** of the investment. If the NPV is zero, the investment is generating a rate of return exactly equal to the required rate of return. Thus, the investment should be undertaken. If the NPV is positive, it should also be undertaken because it is generating a rate of return that is even greater than the required rate of return. Investment opportunities that have a negative NPV are not accepted because their rate of return is less than the required rate of return. A graphical presentation of the NPV approach to evaluating investments is presented in Illustration 9-2.

**LEARNING OBJECTIVE 2**

Evaluate investment opportunities using the net present value approach.

**Decision Making/ Incremental Analysis**

**Illustration 9-2**
NPV approach to
evaluating investments

**See the interactive CD for an example of how Holland America-Westours uses the NPV approach to analyze investing in a cruise ship.**

**An Example of the NPV Approach.** An example will show how the NPV approach is used. Suppose an auto repair shop is considering purchasing automated paint-spraying equipment. The company estimates that the equipment will last five years. Each year, it will save the company $2,000 in paint wasted in the current manual spraying operation. It will also reduce labor costs by $20,000. It is estimated that the machine will require maintenance costs of $1,000 per year. The machine costs $70,000, and it is expected to have a residual value of $5,000 at the end of five years. Top management has determined that the required rate of return is 12 percent. Should the company invest in the new equipment?

The cash flows related to the investment opportunity are presented on the time line at the top of Illustration 9-3. In analyzing the cash flows, we make the assumption that all cash inflows and outflows (other than the cash outflow of $70,000 for purchasing the equipment) occur at the end of a year. To simplify analysis, managers commonly make this assumption, and it is unlikely to introduce significant error, even though cash flows actually take place throughout the year (not just at year end).

Illustration 9-3 also includes present value (PV) factors for each year's cash-flow total. Consider first the $70,000 cash outflow created by the purchase of the spraying equipment. Note that the present value factor associated with the $70,000 purchase price is 1.0000. Because this amount is going to be spent immediately, it is already expressed in terms of its present value. Now, consider the

**Illustration 9-3**
Evaluation of automated
paint-spraying equipment

| Time period | Present 0 | Year 1 | Year 2 | Year 3 | Year 4 | Year 5 |
|---|---|---|---|---|---|---|
| Cash Flow | | | | | | |
| Purchase Price | ($70,000) | | | | | |
| Labor Saving | | $20,000 | $20,000 | $20,000 | $20,000 | $20,000 |
| Paint Saving | | $2,000 | $2,000 | $2,000 | $2,000 | $2,000 |
| Maintenance | | ($1,000) | ($1,000) | ($1,000) | ($1,000) | ($1,000) |
| Salvage Value | | | | | | $5,000 |
| Total cash flow | ($70,000) | 21,000 | $21,000 | $21,000 | $21,000 | $26,000 |
| PV Factor | ×1.000 | ×.8929 | ×.7972 | ×.7118 | ×.6355 | ×.5674 |
| Total | ($70,000) | $18,751 | $16,741 | $14,948 | $13,346 | $14,752 = $8,538 (NPV) |

**Illustration 9-4**
Evaluation of automated
paint-spraying equipment
using present value
of an annuity approach

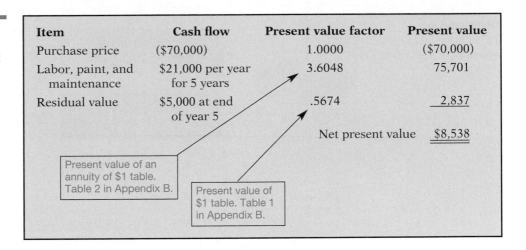

| Item | Cash flow | Present value factor | Present value |
|------|-----------|----------------------|---------------|
| Purchase price | ($70,000) | 1.0000 | ($70,000) |
| Labor, paint, and maintenance | $21,000 per year for 5 years | 3.6048 | 75,701 |
| Residual value | $5,000 at end of year 5 | .5674 | 2,837 |
| | | Net present value | $8,538 |

Present value of an annuity of $1 table. Table 2 in Appendix B.

Present value of $1 table. Table 1 in Appendix B.

cash flows in year 1. In this year, the net cash inflow is $21,000. The present value factor for an amount received at the end of year 1 using a 12 percent rate of return is .8929 (see Table 1 in Appendix B). Multiplying the present value factor by the cash inflow of $21,000 indicates that the present value of the net cash inflow in year 1 is $18,751. The net present value of the investment in spraying equipment is found by summing the present values of the cash flows in each year. This amounts to $8,538. Because the net present value is positive, the company should go ahead with plans to purchase the equipment.

In the preceding problem, the $20,000 labor savings, the $2,000 paint savings, and the $1,000 maintenance expense are identical in each of the five years. Thus, the net annual amount of $21,000 can be treated as a five-year annuity (series of equal payments) in calculating the present value. This treatment is presented in Illustration 9-4. Present value factors that apply to annuities are in Table 2 in Appendix B. The present value factor, using a 12 percent rate of return, for an annuity lasting five years is 3.6048 (see Table 2 in Appendix B). Multiplying this factor by the $21,000 annuity indicates a present value of $75,701. In other words, a five year annuity of $21,000 is worth $75,701 if you require a 12 percent rate of return. The present value of the $5,000 residual value in year 5 is calculated using a factor from the Present Value of $1 table (Appendix B). Note that the total net present value, $8,538, is equal to the amount calculated in Illustration 9-3.

## THE INTERNAL RATE OF RETURN METHOD

The internal rate of return method is an alternative to net present value for evaluating investment possibilities. Like net present value, it takes into account the time value of money. Specifically, the **internal rate of return (IRR)** is the rate of return that equates the present value of future cash flows to the investment outlay. If the IRR of a potential investment is equal to or greater than the required rate of return, the investment should be undertaken. In Illustration 9-5, the IRR approach to evaluating investments is outlined.

Consider a simple case where $100 is invested to yield $60 at the end of year 1 and $60 at the end of year 2. What rate of return equates the two-year, $60 annuity to $100? Recall that when we performed present value analysis for previous

**Illustration 9-5**
IRR approach to
evaluating investments

annuities, we multiplied a present value factor by the annuity to solve for a present value. That is:

$$\text{Present value} = \text{Present value factor} \times \text{Annuity}$$

In the current case, we set the present value equal to the initial outlay for the investment. Then, we can solve for the present value factor and use it to look up the rate of return implicit in the investment.

$$\text{Present value factor} = \frac{\text{Initial outlay}}{\text{Annuity amount}}$$

With a $100 cost of the investment and a $60 annuity, the present value factor is 1.667.

$$1.6667 = \frac{\$100}{\$60}$$

Because the $60 is to be received in each of two years, we use the annuity table (Table 2 in Appendix B) to look up the internal rate of return. In the row in Table 2 for two periods we find a present value factor of 1.6681 (very close to 1.6667) in the column for a 13 percent rate of return. Thus, the IRR on this investment is ap-

# LINK TO PRACTICE

## *Investment in Malaysian Pulp Mill Yields IRR of 30 Percent*

Although pulp mills are thought to be marginal investment opportunities in North America, Malaysia's Primary Industries Minister, Dr. Lim Keng Yaik, claims that investments in Malaysian pulp mills can yield internal rates of return of roughly 30 percent. The high returns are due, at least in part, to low cost input—so-called empty fruit bunches (EFB) that are what's left after oil is squeezed from palm fruits. Palm fruit is grown on 60 percent of the cultivated land in Malaysia and disposal of EFB has been a long-standing problem Dr. Lim visited China where mills are profitably producing pulp from "waster" fiber such as rice straws, corn stalks, and wheat straws. He hopes that Malaysia can follow China's lead.

*Sources:* Alice Chia, "Vast Potential in Pulp and Paper Production," *Business Times* (Malaysia), September 24, 2002, p. 4, Utusan Melayu (M) BHD., 46M, Jalan Lima of Jalan Chan Sow Lin, 55200 Kuala Lumpur. "First Pulping Demo Plant Using Oil Palm Waste to be Built," *Utusan Malaysia Online*, July 2, 2002. "Paving the Way for Commercial Exploitation of Oil Palm Biomass," *Malaysian Timber Council*, May 20, 2002.

proximately 13 percent. If the required rate of return is 13 percent or less, the investment should be undertaken.

Insight into the IRR can be gained by using it to calculate the net present value of the project. If we evaluated the previous project using a 13 percent required rate of return, what would be the net present value? The answer is zero, because the internal rate of return equates the present value of future cash flows to the investment outlay.

| Item | Cash flow | Present value factor | Present value |
|------|-----------|----------------------|---------------|
| Cash flow | $60 | 1.6681 | $100.09 |
| Initial investment | ($100) | 1.0000 | (100.00) |
| | | Difference (due to rounding) | $    .09 |

## THE INTERNAL RATE OF RETURN WITH UNEQUAL CASH FLOWS

For cases where cash flows are not equal each year, the approach previously presented cannot be used to calculate the IRR, because we cannot divide the initial investment by a single cash-flow annuity to yield a present value factor. Instead, we must estimate the internal rate of return and use the estimate to calculate the net present value of the project. If the net present value is greater than zero (implying an internal rate of return greater than the estimate), the estimate of the internal rate of return should be increased. If the net present value is less than zero (implying an internal rate of return less than the estimate), the estimate should be decreased. By estimating the internal rate of return in this trial and error fashion, it is possible to eventually arrive at the actual internal rate of return.

Let's consider an example to illustrate the method. Suppose a company is considering changes in its production process that will involve purchasing several pieces of equipment costing a total of $120,000. The changes are expected to yield cost savings of $49,500 in year 1; $45,000 in year 2; $35,000 in year 3; $22,000 in year 4; and $19,600 in year 5.

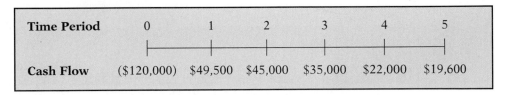

| Time Period | 0 | 1 | 2 | 3 | 4 | 5 |
|-------------|---|---|---|---|---|---|
| Cash Flow | ($120,000) | $49,500 | $45,000 | $35,000 | $22,000 | $19,600 |

The company wants to evaluate the potential project in terms of its internal rate of return. The first step is to estimate what the internal rate of return is likely to be. Since the cash flow are fairly large in relation to the initial investment, a reasonable "guess" as to the internal rate of return might be 14 percent. However, when we calculate the net present value of the investment as in Illustration 9-6 using 14 percent, we see that the present value is a positive $4,880. Thus, the true internal rate of return is greater than 14 percent. As a next approximation, we can try 18 percent. However, with this rate of return, the present value is a negative $4,514. This indicates that our second estimate of the internal rate of return was too high.

At this point, we know that the internal rate of return is somewhere between 14 percent and 18 percent. Thus, as a further attempt, we might try 16 percent. The present value using a rate of 16 percent is $26. This is sufficiently close to zero to allow us to conclude that the internal rate of return is approximately 16

**Illustration 9-6**
Calculating the IRR
when there are unequal
cash flows

| Time period | Cash flows | 14% | | 18% | | 16% | |
|---|---|---|---|---|---|---|---|
| | | Factor for 14% | Present value | Factor for 18% | Present value | Factor for 16% | Present value |
| 0 | ($120,000) | 1 | ($120,000) | 1 | ($120,000) | 1 | ($120,000) |
| 1 | $49,500 | 0.8772 | $43,421 | 0.8475 | $41,951 | 0.8621 | $42,674 |
| 2 | $45,000 | 0.7695 | $34,628 | 0.7182 | $32,319 | 0.7432 | $33,444 |
| 3 | $35,000 | 0.6750 | $23,625 | 0.6086 | $21,301 | 0.6407 | $22,425 |
| 4 | $22,000 | 0.5921 | $13,026 | 0.5158 | $11,348 | 0.5523 | $12,151 |
| 5 | $19,600 | 0.5194 | $10,180 | 0.4371 | $8,567 | 0.4761 | $9,332 |
| | | Total | $4,880 | | ($4,514) | | $26 |

percent. If management of the company believes that a return of 16 percent is sufficient, then the company should go ahead with the project.

It may appear that the need to estimate the internal rate of return using a trial and error approach presents a significant obstacle to its use. Actually, this is not the case. A spreadsheet program such as Excel and even some pocket calculators contain functions that easily estimate the internal rate of return of a project. The user simply inputs the cash flow information and the IRR is computed automatically.

## SUMMARY OF NET PRESENT VALUE AND INTERNAL RATE OF RETURN METHODS

Although both the net present value method and the internal rate of return method take into account the time value of money, they differ in their approach to evaluating investment alternatives. With net present value, any investment with

### Use of NPV and IRR by CFOs

John Graham and Campbell Harvey of Duke University recently conducted a survey of chief financial officers (CFOs) to assess their use of capital budgeting techniques. According to their results, 74.9 percent of CFOs always or almost always use NPV and 75.7 percent always or almost always use IRR. Moreover, large companies are significantly more likely to use NPV than small companies. After NPV and IRR, the payback method (discussed later in this chapter) is the most frequently used capital budgeting technique with 56.7 percent of the CFOs stating that they always or almost always use it.

*Source:* J. Graham and C. Harvey, "How Do CFOs Make Capital Budgeting and Capital Structure Decisions," *Journal of Applied Corporate Finance.* Spring 2002, p. 8–22.

a zero or positive net present value should be undertaken. With the internal rate of return method, any investment with an internal rate of return equal to or greater than the required rate of return should be undertaken.[2]

# CONSIDERING "SOFT" BENEFITS IN INVESTMENT DECISIONS

When managers make investment decisions, it is important that they consider so-called "soft" benefits in addition to a project's NPV or IRR. Soft benefits are ones that are hard to quantify.[3] Consider a situation faced by Dynamic Medical Equipment Company. The company is considering production of a high-tech wheelchair. The wheelchair would take advantage of advances in light-weight graphite construction techniques pioneered in the manufacturing of tennis rackets and design improvements suggested by athletes competing in wheelchair events. Suppose that in evaluating the project, the finance department fails to consider the fact that production of the high-tech wheelchair will improve the firm's reputation as an industry leader committed to innovation. Such a reputation is clearly valuable, since it has a positive effect on sales of the firm's entire product line. However, the value is also very difficult to quantify. Or consider the fact that producing the wheelchair will introduce new construction techniques that will help the firm produce future products made from graphite. This may be a major benefit to the firm, but it is very difficult to quantify.

Ignoring soft benefits may lead firms to pass up investments that are of strategic importance, especially investments in advanced manufacturing technology. For example, investment in robotics may be needed to reduce product defects. And defect-free production may be a source of competitive advantage. However, the NPV analysis of the investment may focus on the cash savings resulting from a reduction in labor, which is relatively easy to quantify, and ignore the cash savings resulting from increased product demand, which is relatively hard to quantify.

As a further example, consider an investment in a flexible manufacturing system. Such systems are generally highly automated and often involve computer controlled equipment. They are configured so that machines can be easily adjusted to produce a number of different products or variations of standard products. With a flexible manufacturing system, companies can easily respond to custom orders that meet the exact specifications of their individual customers. Flexible manufacturing systems also improve delivery times on orders and allow companies to introduce new products quickly. But while being able to improve delivery times and introduce new products quickly may greatly improve a company's competitive position, these benefits are quite difficult to quantify in dollar terms.

---

[2]Under some circumstances, the net present value and the internal rate of return methods may be inconsistent with one another in evaluating the desirability of an investment opportunity. This potential problem is discussed in introductory corporate finance texts.

[3]Firms may also have difficulty quantifying certain costs. For example, an investment in a new manufacturing process may result in additional pollution, the cost of which is hard to quantify. If "soft costs" are ignored in investment analysis, companies will tend to overinvest.

**Illustration 9-7**
Calculation of soft benefits needed to make the investment acceptable

$$\text{Needed present value} = \text{Discount factor} \times \text{Value of benefits}$$

$$\text{Value of benefits} = \frac{\text{Needed present value}}{\text{Discount factor}}$$

$$\text{Value of benefits} = \frac{\$80,000}{5.019}$$

$$\text{Value of benefits} = \$15,959$$

## CALCULATING THE VALUE OF SOFT BENEFITS REQUIRED TO MAKE AN INVESTMENT ACCEPTABLE

Managers should make a reasonable effort to calculate the cash value of soft benefits when analyzing investment opportunities. However, in some cases, they may decide that quantifying the benefits is too costly. In these cases, if the NPV of a potential investment is negative, managers should calculate the amount of additional cash inflows needed to have a positive NPV. Then, if managers believe that the value of soft benefits, while uncertain, will clearly exceed the additional cash inflows, they can decide to fund the investment.

For example, suppose the high-tech wheelchair project at Dynamic Medical Equipment has a NPV of negative $80,000. In calculating the NPV, the finance department used a required rate of return of 15 percent and assumed that the project would have a 10-year life. After 10 years, the chair will be out of date and replaced in the product line. As we know, the finance department did not consider soft benefits in calculating the NPV. But, what must be the value of the soft benefits each year before the wheelchair is an acceptable investment? The calculation needed to answer this question is presented in Illustration 9-7.

The present value of the soft benefits must be at least $80,000 before the project is acceptable. Using the present value of an annuity table, we find that the discount factor for 10 periods at 15 percent is 5.019. This implies that as long as the soft benefits are worth at least $15,959 per year, the project should be funded. Managers at Dynamic Medical Equipment will likely find this analysis to be very useful. For example, while they may unable to specify the exact value of the soft benefits, there may be generally agreement that the value will certainly exceed $16,000 each year. If this is the case, then the wheelchair appears to be a good investment. On the other hand, there may be general agreement that while there certainly will be some soft benefit, the value is unlikely to exceed even $10,000 per year. If this is the case, then the wheelchair is not a good investment.

# ESTIMATING THE REQUIRED RATE OF RETURN

In the problems presented earlier, we simply stated a required rate of return that could be used to calculate an investment's net present value or that could be compared with an investment's internal rate of return. In practice, the required rate of return must be estimated by management. Under certain conditions, the required rate of return should be equal to the cost of capital for the firm. The **cost of capital** is the weighted average of the costs of debt and equity financing used to generate capital for investments. The cost of debt arises because interest must be paid

### Cost of Capital for Various Business Sectors

The Stern School of New York University has a Web site listing the cost of capital by business sector. The values provide you with a good feel for differences in the cost of capital across companies.

http://pages.stern.nyu.edu/~adamodar/New_Home_Page/datafile/wacc.htm

Some examples as of July 15, 2002 are:

| | |
|---|---|
| Aerospace/defense | 8.18% |
| Apparel | 8.70% |
| Auto parts | 7.83% |
| Biotechnology | 10.74% |
| E-commerce | 18.36% |
| Entertainment | 10.79% |
| Food wholesalers | 7.84% |
| Grocery | 6.87% |
| Semiconductor | 15.59% |
| Wireless networking | 11.79% |

to individuals, banks, and other companies that lend money to the firm. Essentially, the cost of equity is the return demanded by shareholders for the risk they bear in supplying capital to the firm. Estimating the cost of capital, especially the cost due to equity capital, is a challenge even to sophisticated financial managers.[4] Because of this difficulty, many managers use their judgment to determine the required rate of return, following the general principle that the more risky the investment, the higher the required rate of return.

# ADDITIONAL CASH FLOW CONSIDERATIONS

To be useful in investment analysis, both the net present value and the internal rate of return methods require a proper specification of cash flows. It is particularly important to remember that *only cash inflows and outflows, not revenues and expenses*, are discounted back to present value. Thus, if a sale is expected to occur in period 1 but the collection of the sale is not anticipated until period 2, the cash flow that is discounted back to present value is a period 2 cash flow, even though the related revenue will be recorded in period 1. Similarly, if a cash payment is

---

[4]Complications arise, for example, because some debt issues allow for conversion to common stock. Also, some companies have multiple classes of stock with different voting rules and other features that make calculation of the cost of equity capital difficult.

anticipated at the start of period 1 to purchase an asset, and related depreciation is to be recorded in periods 1 through 5, only the start of period 1 cash outflow is used in the net present value analysis. Depreciation is a legitimate business cost, but it does not require a cash outflow in the period in which it is recorded. Present value analysis is concerned only with cash flows.

In this section, we consider two special topics related to cash flows. The first deals with depreciation. Although depreciation does not have a direct effect on cash flows, it does have an indirect effect because of taxes. The second topic deals with the effect of inflation on cash flows.

## CASH FLOWS, TAXES, AND THE DEPRECIATION TAX SHIELD

Calculate the depreciation tax shield, and explain why depreciation is important in investment analysis only because of income taxes.

In all of the previous examples, we ignored the effect of income taxes on cash flows. However, tax considerations play a major role in capital budgeting decisions, and we discuss them here. If an investment project generates taxable revenue, cash inflows from the project will be reduced by the taxes that must be paid on the revenue. Similarly, if an investment project generates tax-deductible expenses, cash inflows from the project will be increased by the tax savings resulting from the decrease in income taxes payable.

Earlier, we stated that depreciation is not relevant in a present value analysis of an investment opportunity because it is not a cash flow. But although depreciation does not *directly* affect cash flow, it *indirectly* affects cash flow because it reduces the amount of tax a company must pay. That is, it acts to shield income from taxes. The term **depreciation tax shield** is used to refer to the tax savings resulting from depreciation.

As an example, suppose the Party Supply Company is considering a new product, custom-imprinted T-shirts. Imprinting will require an investment in equipment costing $100,000. Each year, the company expects sales to amount to $70,000 and expenses (other than depreciation on the equipment) to amount to $40,000. Depreciation calculated on a straight-line basis for the expected 10-year life of the equipment is $10,000 per year. The company has a 40 percent tax rate.[5] Assume that revenue is collected in the period earned and expenses are paid in the period incurred. Thus, net income and cash flows related to the investment are as follows:

| | | |
|---|---:|---:|
| Revenue | | $70,000 |
| Less: Operating expenses | | |
| other than depreciation | $40,000 | |
| Depreciation | 10,000 | 50,000 |
| Income before taxes | | 20,000 |
| Income taxes (40% tax rate) | | 8,000 |
| Net income | | 12,000 |
| Add back: Depreciation | | 10,000 |
| Cash flow each period | | $22,000 |

---

[5]Our discussion and examples assume a 40 percent tax rate. This assumption ignores complexities in tax rates and rules in practice that may change from year to year. However, the assumption allows us to more clearly convey the essential role of taxes in investment decisions.

### *Depreciation Tax Shield at Amazon.com*

Although Amazon.com has tremendous potential, the company has yet to generate an annual profit. Indeed, in fiscal 2001 the company had a net loss of $567 million. How does this affect Amazon.com's calculation of the depreciation tax shield when the company does present value analysis?

When companies have net losses, they can carry the losses forward and offset future income in the determination of federal income taxes. Thus, if Amazon.com is considering an investment that will result in $500,000 of depreciation expense in the year 2004, but this expense will not reduce taxes until the year 2006 when the company expects to show a profit, the depreciation tax shield should be recognized in year 2006 when performing present value analysis. In other words, companies in loss positions need to recognize the depreciation tax shield in the year when taxes are reduced, not the year in which depreciation is calculated for financial reporting purposes.

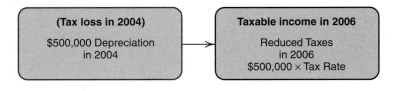

Note that depreciation is deducted to arrive at income before taxes and that it reduces the amount of income taxes that must be paid. However, depreciation is not itself a cash outflow. Therefore, it must be added back to net income to arrive at cash flow.

Because the project is fairly risky, top management of Party Supply has set a required rate of return of 16 percent. The net present value calculation for the investment under consideration is presented in Illustration 9-8. Note that because the amounts of revenue, expense, and tax are the same each year, we can work with the net amount and treat it as a 10-year annuity with a required rate of return of 16 percent. Because the net present value is a positive $6,326, the investment in the equipment should be undertaken.

**Illustration 9-8**
NPV analysis taking taxes into account

| Item | Cash flow | Present value factor | Present value |
|------|-----------|----------------------|---------------|
| Initial investment | ($100,000) | 1.000 | ($100,000) |
| Revenue | $70,000 | | |
| Expense (other than depreciation) | (40,000) | | |
| Taxes | (8,000) | 22,000 | 4.8332 | 106,330 |
| Net present value | | | $ 6,330 |

The fact that depreciation reduced taxes had a significant effect on the value of the investment project. With depreciation of $10,000 and a 40 percent tax rate, there is a $4,000 tax savings each year due to depreciation. The present value of this "tax shield" over 10 years at 16 percent is $19,333 ($4,000 × present value factor of 4.8332). Thus, it is apparent that without the tax shield afforded by depreciation, the investment would not have a positive net present value and would not be worth undertaking.

### ADJUSTING CASH FLOWS FOR INFLATION

An additional topic that must be addressed in estimating the cash flows of investments is how to handle inflation. During the 1970s and early 1980s, the United States experienced double-digit inflation. Because high rates of inflation are still common in many foreign countries, it may be quite important to consider inflation when estimating the cash flows associated with investment opportunities.

Inflation can be taken into account by multiplying the current level of cash flow by the expected rate of inflation. For example, if an investment is expected to yield a cash flow in period 1 of $100 and the rate of inflation is expected to be 5 percent per year in the foreseeable future, then a reasonable estimate of the cash flow would be $105 ($100 × 1.05) in period 2, $110.25 ($105 × 1.05) in period 3, $115.76 in period 4, and so forth. Estimates of inflation can be obtained from financial journals or can be purchased for a fee from firms that specialize in economic forecasts.

If inflation is ignored in net present value analysis, many worthwhile investment opportunities may be rejected. Why? Because current rates of return for debt and equity financing already include estimates of future inflation. For example, banks charge higher rates of interest on loans to companies when they estimate that inflation will be high. Suppose a company uses its current costs of debt and equity financing (which are high because a high rate of inflation is expected) to determine its required rate of return. Now, if the company does not take inflation into account in estimating future cash flows, the cash flows will be relatively low, whereas the required rate of return will be relatively high. The result may be that suitable projects will appear to have a negative net present value.

Use the payback period and the accounting rate of return methods to evaluate investment opportunities.

# SIMPLIFIED APPROACHES TO CAPITAL BUDGETING

The net present value and the internal rate of return methods are widely used in industry to evaluate capital projects. However, many companies continue to use other, simpler, approaches to evaluating capital projects. Two of these approaches, the payback period method and the accounting rate of return method, are discussed in this section. As you will see, both of these methods have significant limitations in comparison to net present value and internal rate of return.

### PAYBACK PERIOD METHOD

The **payback period** is the length of time it takes to recover the initial cost of an investment. Thus, if an investment opportunity costs $1,000 and yields cash flows of $500 per year, it has a payback period of two years. If an investment costs

$1,000 and yields cash flows of $300 per year, it has a payback period of 3-1/3 years. All else being equal, a company would like to have projects with short payback periods.

One approach to using the payback method is to accept investment projects that have a payback period less than some specified requirement. However, this can lead to extremely poor decisions. For example, suppose a company has two investment opportunities, both costing $1,000. The first investment yields cash flows of $500 per year for three years and has a payback period of two years. The second investment yields no cash flows in the first two years but has cash flows of $1,000 in the third year and $4,000 in the fourth year. Thus, it has a payback period of three years. Obviously, the second investment is preferable. However, if the company has a two-year payback requirement, it will select the first investment and reject the second. The problem is that the payback method *does not take into account the total stream of cash flows* related to an investment. It only considers the stream of cash flows up to the time the investment is paid back. Thus, in this example, the payback period method ignores the $4,000 cash inflow in the fourth year of the second investment.

A further limitation of the payback method is that it *does not consider the time value of money*. Consider two investments, each with a cost of $1,000. The first yields cash flows of $700 in the first year, $300 in the second year, and $300 in the third year. Thus, it has a payback of two years. The second investment yields cash flows of $300 in the first year, $700 in the second year, and $300 in the third year. Thus, it also has a payback period of two years. But although both investments have the same payback period (implying they are equally valuable) the first investment is actually more favorable, because the $700 cash inflow is received in the first year rather than the second year. In fact, the first investment has an internal rate of return of 17 percent, whereas the second investment has an internal rate of return of only 14 percent.

Although the payback method has significant limitations, some companies may find it useful, particularly if they have cash-flow problems. Companies with cash-flow problems may need to focus on investments that quickly return cash in order to avoid bankruptcy.

## ACCOUNTING RATE OF RETURN

The **accounting rate of return** is equal to the average after-tax income from a project divided by the average investment in the project.

$$\text{Accounting Rate of Return (ARR)} = \frac{\text{Average Net Income}}{\text{Average Investment}}$$

The accounting rate of return can be used to evaluate investment opportunities by comparing their accounting rates of return with a required accounting rate of return. The primary limitation of this approach is that, like the payback period method, it ignores the time value of money.

Consider two investment alternatives facing a firm with a cost of capital of 15 percent and a 40 percent tax rate. Both require investments in equipment costing $100,000, and both generate cash flows for two years. The investments are identical except that, while both have total revenue over two years of $180,000, project 1 has $90,000 of revenue in the first year, while project 2 has $70,000. In the second year, project 1 again has $90,000 of revenue, while project 2 has $110,000. Illustration 9-9 presents the net incomes and cash flows of the two alternatives for

**Illustration 9-9**
Net Income and cash flow data for alternative projects

| | | Project 1 | Project 2 |
|---|---|---|---|
| **Year 1** | | | |
| | Revenue | $90,000 | $70,000 |
| | Less: Operating expenses | | |
| |     other than depreciation | 20,000 | 20,000 |
| |     Depreciation | 50,000 | 50,000 |
| | Income before taxes | 20,000 | 0 |
| | Taxes | 8,000 | 0 |
| | Net income | 12,000 | 0 |
| | Plus: depreciation | 50,000 | 50,000 |
| | Cash flow | $62,000 | $ 50,000 |
| **Year 2** | | | |
| | Revenue | $90,000 | $110,000 |
| | Less: Operating expenses | | |
| |     other than depreciation | 20,000 | 20,000 |
| |     Depreciation | 50,000 | 50,000 |
| | Income before taxes | 20,000 | 40,000 |
| | Taxes | 8,000 | 16,000 |
| | Net income | 12,000 | 24,000 |
| | Plus: depreciation | 50,000 | 50,000 |
| | Cash flow | $62,000 | $ 74,000 |

the two years. We assume that all revenue items are collected in the period earned and all expense items (other than depreciation) are paid in the period incurred. Thus, the difference between net income and cash flow is simply the amount of depreciation.

Based on the information, it is easy to calculate the accounting rate of return for each project as indicated in Illustration 9-10. Both have identical accounting rates of return of 24 percent, indicating that the two projects are equally desirable. When we take into account the time value of money, however, it is clear that project 1 is more desirable than project 2. As indicated in Illustration 9-11, using a cost of capital of 15 percent, the net present value of project 1 is $793.40, whereas project 2 has a negative net present value of $568.60. Thus, taking into account the time value of money, project 1 is an acceptable investment while project 2 is not acceptable.

**Illustration 9-10**
Comparison of ARRs for alternative projects

$$\text{Accounting Rate of Return (ARR)} = \frac{\text{Average Net Income}}{\text{Average Investment}}$$

$$\text{ARR for Project 1} = \frac{(\$12,000 + \$12,000) \div 2}{(\$100,000 \div 2)} = .24$$

$$\text{ARR for Project 2} = \frac{(\$0 + \$24,000) \div 2}{(\$100,000 \div 2)} = .24$$

**Illustration 9-11**
NPV comparison of
alternative projects

**Project 1**

| Time period | Cash flow | Present value factor | Present value |
|---|---|---|---|
| –0– | ($100,000) | 1.0000 | ($100,000.00) |
| 1 | $62,000 | .8696 | 53,915.20 |
| 2 | $62,000 | .7561 | 46,878.20 |
| | | Net present value | $793.40 |

**Project 2**

| Time period | Cash flow | Present value factor | Present value |
|---|---|---|---|
| –0– | ($100,000) | 1.0000 | ($100,000.00) |
| 1 | $50,000 | .8696 | 43,480.00 |
| 2 | $74,000 | .7561 | 55,951.40 |
| | | Net present value | $ ($568.60) |

**6**

Explain why managers may
concentrate erroneously on
the short-run profitability of
investments rather than their
net present values.

**You Get
What You Measure**

# CONFLICT BETWEEN PERFORMANCE EVALUATION AND CAPITAL BUDGETING

An NPV greater than zero or an IRR greater than the required rate of return informs managers that an investment opportunity will increase their firm's value. Thus, managers who wish to maximize shareholder wealth should use these present value techniques to evaluate investments. However, in some companies, managers may be discouraged from using present value techniques for evaluating investments because of the way in which their own performance is evaluated.

For example, an investment may result in high amounts of depreciation in the early years of its life. At the same time, in these early start-up years, revenues may be quite low, resulting in low profits or even losses. However, revenues in later years may be large enough to ensure that the project has a positive net present value. If a manager knows that job performance is evaluated in terms of reported accounting income, he or she may fear being fired because of the low initial profits of this investment. If this is the case, the manager will likely ignore the fact that a project has a positive net present value and concentrate instead on reported income.

To illustrate this, suppose a manager is considering producing a new product that requires an investment of $1,000,000 in equipment. Depreciation on the equipment will be recorded using the straight-line method. Based on a 10-year life, depreciation will be $100,000 per year. The product is not expected to sell well in the early years. Expected first year revenue is only $40,000. However, by the end of the seventh year, expected revenue is up to $400,000 per year. In addition to depreciation, there are $40,000 of other expenses each year. The company has a 10 percent required rate of return.

Illustration 9-12 is a net present value analysis of the investment. The net present value is $26,998, indicating that the project should be undertaken. However, will the manager be motivated to undertake this project, which is in the best interest of the company? Note that the project shows a substantial loss in each of the first three years. The manager may fear that this will reflect badly on his or

**Illustration 9-12**
Net present value analysis
of new product*

| | Year 1 | Year 2 | Year 3 | Year 4 | Year 5 |
|---|---|---|---|---|---|
| Revenue | $40,000 | $60,000 | $100,000 | $150,000 | $200,000 |
| Less: Operating expenses other than depreciation | 40,000 | 40,000 | 40,000 | 40,000 | 40,000 |
| Depreciation | 100,000 | 100,000 | 100,000 | 100,000 | 100,000 |
| Net income | (100,000) | (80,000) | (40,000) | 10,000 | 60,000 |
| Plus: depreciation | 100,000 | 100,000 | 100,000 | 100,000 | 100,000 |
| Cash Flow | $0 | $20,000 | $60,000 | $110,000 | $160,000 |
| | **Year 6** | **Year 7** | **Year 8** | **Year 9** | **Year 10** |
| Revenue | $300,000 | $400,000 | $400,000 | $400,000 | $400,000 |
| Less: Operating expenses other than depreciation | 40,000 | 40,000 | 40,000 | 40,000 | 40,000 |
| Depreciation | 100,000 | 100,000 | 100,000 | 100,000 | 100,000 |
| Net income | 160,000 | 260,000 | 260,000 | 260,000 | 260,000 |
| Plus: depreciation | 100,000 | 100,000 | 100,000 | 100,000 | 100,000 |
| Cash Flow | $260,000 | $360,000 | $360,000 | $360,000 | $360,000 |

| Time period | Cash flows | Factor for 10% | Present value |
|---|---|---|---|
| 0 | ($1,000,000) | 1.0000 | ($1,000,000) |
| 1 | 0 | 0.9091 | 0 |
| 2 | 20,000 | 0.8264 | 16,528 |
| 3 | 60,000 | 0.7513 | 45,078 |
| 4 | 110,000 | 0.6830 | 75,130 |
| 5 | 160,000 | 0.6209 | 99,344 |
| 6 | 260,000 | 0.5645 | 146,770 |
| 7 | 360,000 | 0.5132 | 184,752 |
| 8 | 360,000 | 0.4665 | 167,940 |
| 9 | 360,000 | 0.4241 | 152,676 |
| 10 | 360,000 | 0.3855 | 138,780 |
| | Net present value | | $26,998 |

*Note that the example is simplified and ignores taxes. Therefore, there is no depreciation tax shield. Also, the example assumes that revenue is collected in the period earned and other expenses are paid in the period incurred.

her performance, perhaps leading to dismissal from the firm. If this is the case, the manager may opt to pass up this valuable investment opportunity.

At least a partial solution to this problem is to make sure managers realize that, if they approve projects with positive net present values that lower reported income in the short run, evaluations of their performance and their compensation will take the expected *future* benefits into account. Managers must be confident that their performance will be evaluated with respect to the long-run profitability of the firm, or they will not take a long-run perspective in evaluating capital projects.

At some firms, top managers are required to hold stock in the company they work for. The idea behind the requirement is that it aligns the interests of managers with the interests of shareholders. These managers will tend to take actions that maximize the value of the firm, because increasing firm value increases their own wealth. Hopefully, these mangers will tend to focus on present value techniques in evaluating investments because these techniques identify investments that increase the firm's value.

# WILSON AIR EXAMPLE REVISITED

At the beginning of the chapter, Steve Wilson, president of Wilson Air, was trying to decide whether or not he should purchase another plane. At this point, we have developed the tools needed to analyze problems like the one facing Steve.

Recall that a new plane costs $1,000,000. The residual value of the plane after five years will be $500,000, and annual depreciation using the straight-line method is $100,000. Revenue will increase by $700,000 per year, and operating costs (ignoring depreciation and taxes) will be $400,000. Revenue will be collected in the period earned, and operating costs other than depreciation will be paid in the period incurred. Assume the income tax rate is 40 percent. What is the net present value of the investment in the plane if the required rate of return is 10 percent? The answer is $144,426, as shown in Illustration 9-13. Because the NPV is positive, the investment should be undertaken.

**Illustration 9-13**
Present value of
investment in plane

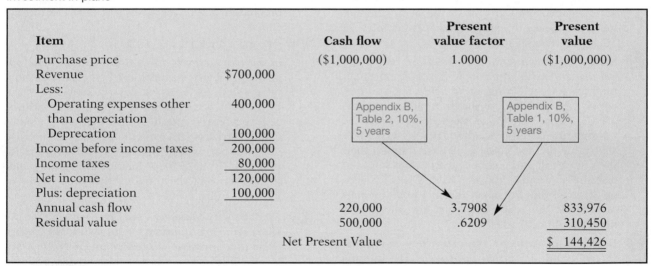

| Item | | Cash flow | Present value factor | Present value |
|---|---|---|---|---|
| Purchase price | | ($1,000,000) | 1.0000 | ($1,000,000) |
| Revenue | $700,000 | | | |
| Less: | | | | |
| Operating expenses other than depreciation | 400,000 | | | |
| Deprecation | 100,000 | | | |
| Income before income taxes | 200,000 | | | |
| Income taxes | 80,000 | | | |
| Net income | 120,000 | | | |
| Plus: depreciation | 100,000 | | | |
| Annual cash flow | | 220,000 | 3.7908 | 833,976 |
| Residual value | | 500,000 | .6209 | 310,450 |
| | Net Present Value | | | $ 144,426 |

Appendix B, Table 2, 10%, 5 years

Appendix B, Table 1, 10%, 5 years

# MAKING BUSINESS DECISIONS

Capital budgeting decisions involve estimation of incremental cash inflows and outflows. Since the cash flows don't occur in the same periods and because a dollar today is worth more than a dollar tomorrow, we need to take into account the time value of money by using the net present value (NPV) approach or the internal rate of return (IRR) approach.

However, managers may not make investments in projects with substantial NPVs (or projects with IRRs greater than the required rate of return) because they are evaluated in terms of short-run accounting profit, which may decrease when the projects are undertaken.

## KNOWLEDGE AND SKILLS (K/S) CHECKLIST

*Knowledge and skills are needed to make good business decisions. Check off the knowledge and skills you've acquired from reading this chapter.*

❏ K/S 1. You have an expanded business vocabulary (see key terms).

❏ K/S 2. You can calculate the net present value (NPV) of an investment.

❏ K/S 3. You can calculate the internal rate of return (IRR) of an investment.

❏ K/S 4. You understand the impact of the depreciation tax shield on an investment decision.

❏ K/S 5. You can calculate the payback period and the accounting rate of return for a potential investment, and you can explain the major limitation of these approaches.

❏ K/S 6. You understand that how a manager's performance is evaluated can impact the manager's approach to investment decision making.

# S U M M A R Y OF LEARNING OBJECTIVES

**1** *Define capital expenditure decisions and capital budgets.* Capital expenditure decisions are investment decisions involving the acquisition of long-lived assets. A capital budget is the final list of approved acquisitions.

**2** *Evaluate investment opportunities using the net present value approach.* Two of the primary methods for evaluating investment opportunities, which take into account the time value of money, are the net present value method (NPV) and the internal rate of return method (IRR). The net present value method equates all cash flows to their present values. If the sum of the present values of cash inflows and outflows (i.e., the NPV) is zero or positive, the return on the investment equals or exceeds the required return and the investment should be made.

**3** *Evaluate investment opportunities using the internal rate of return approach.* The internal rate of return method calculates the rate of return that equates the present value of the future cash flows to the initial investment. If this rate of return is equal to or greater than the required rate of return, the investment is warranted.

**4** *Calculate the depreciation tax shield, and explain why depreciation is important in investment analysis only because of income taxes.* In analyzing cash flows for a net present value analysis or an internal rate of return analysis, remember that depreciation is not a cash flow but

the tax savings generated by depreciation is relevant to the analysis. The tax savings owing to depreciation is referred to as the depreciation tax shield.

**5** *Use the payback period and the accounting rate of return methods to evaluate investment opportunities.* The payback method evaluates capital projects in terms of how quickly the initial investment is recovered by future cash inflows. The accounting rate of return method evaluates capital projects in terms of the ratio of average after-tax accounting income to the average investment. Both of these methods have the major limitation that they ignore the time value of money.

**6** *Explain why managers may concentrate on the short-run profitability of investments rather than their present values.* Managers who want to maximize shareholder wealth should evaluate investment opportunities using the net present value method or the internal rate of return method. In some cases, however, projects with a positive net present value or with an internal rate of return greater than required may have a negative effect on short-run income. Although these projects may be quite valuable to the long-run success of the firm, managers may not approve them because they fear that their own job performance will receive negative evaluations if short-run income is reduced.

# APPENDIX A

**LEARNING OBJECTIVE A1**

Use Excel to calculate the NPV and IRR of investment opportunities.

## USING Excel® TO CALCULATE NPV AND IRR

In this appendix, you will see how to use functions in Excel® to calculate the net present value (NPV) and internal rate of return (IRR) of investment opportunities. Let's focus on the data related to the paint-spraying equipment example presented in Illustration 9-3.

The first step in performing present value calculations in Excel is to input the relevant cash flows into a spreadsheet—cells B2–G2 in Illustration A9-1. As indicated, purchase of the paint-spraying equipment requires a $70,000 payment at time zero. The company buying the equipment will save $21,000 each year for five years and sell the equipment for $5,000 at the end of the fifth year. Thus, the cash inflow at the end of year 5 is $26,000 ($21,000 + $5,000). The required rate of return on the investment is 0.12, which we input in cell B5.

To calculate net present value, we need to input the NPV function into a cell, so first click on cell E8. Now, click on the function button ($f_x$), then click the financial category, and then click the NPV function name.

**Illustration A9-1**
Using Excel to calculate NPV and IRR

| | A | B | C | D | E | F | G | H | I | J |
|---|---|---|---|---|---|---|---|---|---|---|
| 1 | Year | 0 | 1 | 2 | 3 | 4 | 5 | | | |
| 2 | Cash flow | (70,000) | 21,000 | 21,000 | 21,000 | 21,000 | 26,000 | | | |
| 3 | | | | | | | | | | |
| 4 | Required rate | | | | | | | | | |
| 5 | of return | 0.12 | | | | | | | | |
| 6 | | | | | | | | | | |
| 7 | | Equation | | | Answer | | | | | |
| 8 | NPV | =NPV(B5,C2:G2)+B2 | | | | | | | | |
| 9 | | | | | | | | | | |
| 10 | IRR | =IRR(B2:G2,0.1) | | | | | | | | |
| 11 | | | | | | | | | | |

*Microsoft Excel - NPV_IRR Analyses*

After you complete these steps, you will see the following box:

The first item we input into the NPV function is the required rate of return, which is in cell B5. The NPV function calculates the present value of cash flows assuming the first cash flow occurs at the *end* of year 1. So, be careful—don't include the cash flow at time zero at this point Simply input the cash flows from C2 through G2. Now click OK, go back to cell E8 and add the cash flow occurring at time zero, which is in cell B2. As you can see, this gives us the project's NPV of $8,537.43.

Let's turn our attention now to the IRR function and put it in cell E10. Go to the function button, click the financial category, and click the IRR function name.

Now, input B2:G2, which highlights the project's cash flows. Then, input an estimated internal rate of return. This estimate simply helps the program have an efficient starting point for calculating the IRR. For our purposes, let's guess that the IRR is 0.10.

As you can see, the spreadsheet now calculates the IRR to be 16.68 percent. Since the NPV is positive and the IRR is greater than the required rate of 12 percent, the project should be undertaken. Your final spreadhsheet should look like the one presented in Illustration A9-2.

**Illustration A9-2**
Using Excel to calculate NPV and IRR

# APPENDIX B

**Table 1,** Present Value of $1 Due in *n* Periods

|    | 6% | 7% | 8% | 9% | 10% | 11% | 12% | 13% | 14% | 15% | 16% | 20% | 30% |
|----|--------|--------|--------|--------|--------|--------|--------|--------|--------|--------|--------|--------|--------|
| 1  | 0.9434 | 0.9346 | 0.9259 | 0.9174 | 0.9091 | 0.9009 | 0.8929 | 0.8850 | 0.8772 | 0.8696 | 0.8621 | 0.8333 | 0.7692 |
| 2  | 0.8900 | 0.8734 | 0.8573 | 0.8417 | 0.8264 | 0.8116 | 0.7972 | 0.7831 | 0.7695 | 0.7561 | 0.7432 | 0.6944 | 0.5917 |
| 3  | 0.8396 | 0.8163 | 0.7938 | 0.7722 | 0.7513 | 0.7312 | 0.7118 | 0.6931 | 0.6750 | 0.6575 | 0.6407 | 0.5787 | 0.4552 |
| 4  | 0.7921 | 0.7629 | 0.7350 | 0.7084 | 0.6830 | 0.6587 | 0.6355 | 0.6133 | 0.5921 | 0.5718 | 0.5523 | 0.4823 | 0.3501 |
| 5  | 0.7473 | 0.7130 | 0.6806 | 0.6499 | 0.6209 | 0.5935 | 0.5674 | 0.5428 | 0.5194 | 0.4972 | 0.4761 | 0.4019 | 0.2693 |
| 6  | 0.7050 | 0.6663 | 0.6302 | 0.5963 | 0.5645 | 0.5346 | 0.5066 | 0.4803 | 0.4556 | 0.4323 | 0.4104 | 0.3349 | 0.2072 |
| 7  | 0.6651 | 0.6227 | 0.5835 | 0.5470 | 0.5132 | 0.4817 | 0.4523 | 0.4251 | 0.3996 | 0.3759 | 0.3538 | 0.2791 | 0.1594 |
| 8  | 0.6274 | 0.5820 | 0.5403 | 0.5019 | 0.4665 | 0.4339 | 0.4039 | 0.3762 | 0.3506 | 0.3269 | 0.3050 | 0.2326 | 0.1226 |
| 9  | 0.5919 | 0.5439 | 0.5002 | 0.4604 | 0.4241 | 0.3909 | 0.3606 | 0.3329 | 0.3075 | 0.2843 | 0.2630 | 0.1938 | 0.0943 |
| 10 | 0.5584 | 0.5083 | 0.4632 | 0.4224 | 0.3855 | 0.3522 | 0.3220 | 0.2946 | 0.2697 | 0.2472 | 0.2267 | 0.1615 | 0.0725 |
| 11 | 0.5268 | 0.4751 | 0.4289 | 0.3875 | 0.3505 | 0.3173 | 0.2875 | 0.2607 | 0.2366 | 0.2149 | 0.1954 | 0.1346 | 0.0558 |
| 12 | 0.4970 | 0.4440 | 0.3971 | 0.3555 | 0.3186 | 0.2858 | 0.2567 | 0.2307 | 0.2076 | 0.1869 | 0.1685 | 0.1122 | 0.0429 |
| 13 | 0.4688 | 0.4150 | 0.3677 | 0.3262 | 0.2897 | 0.2575 | 0.2292 | 0.2042 | 0.1821 | 0.1625 | 0.1452 | 0.0935 | 0.0330 |
| 14 | 0.4423 | 0.3878 | 0.3405 | 0.2992 | 0.2633 | 0.2320 | 0.2046 | 0.1807 | 0.1597 | 0.1413 | 0.1252 | 0.0779 | 0.0254 |
| 15 | 0.4173 | 0.3624 | 0.3152 | 0.2745 | 0.2394 | 0.2090 | 0.1827 | 0.1599 | 0.1401 | 0.1229 | 0.1079 | 0.0649 | 0.0195 |
| 16 | 0.3936 | 0.3387 | 0.2919 | 0.2519 | 0.2176 | 0.1883 | 0.1631 | 0.1415 | 0.1229 | 0.1069 | 0.0930 | 0.0541 | 0.0150 |
| 17 | 0.3714 | 0.3166 | 0.2703 | 0.2311 | 0.1978 | 0.1696 | 0.1456 | 0.1252 | 0.1078 | 0.0929 | 0.0802 | 0.0451 | 0.0116 |
| 18 | 0.3503 | 0.2959 | 0.2502 | 0.2120 | 0.1799 | 0.1528 | 0.1300 | 0.1108 | 0.0946 | 0.0808 | 0.0691 | 0.0376 | 0.0089 |
| 19 | 0.3305 | 0.2765 | 0.2317 | 0.1945 | 0.1635 | 0.1377 | 0.1161 | 0.0981 | 0.0829 | 0.0703 | 0.0596 | 0.0313 | 0.0068 |
| 20 | 0.3118 | 0.2584 | 0.2145 | 0.1784 | 0.1486 | 0.1240 | 0.1037 | 0.0868 | 0.0728 | 0.0611 | 0.0514 | 0.0261 | 0.0053 |

**Table 2,** Present Value of an Annuity of $1 Per Period

|    | 6% | 7% | 8% | 9% | 10% | 11% | 12% | 13% | 14% | 15% | 16% | 20% | 30% |
|----|------|------|------|------|------|------|------|------|------|------|------|------|------|
| 1 | 0.9434 | 0.9346 | 0.9259 | 0.9174 | 0.9091 | 0.9009 | 0.8929 | 0.8850 | 0.8772 | 0.8696 | 0.8621 | 0.8333 | 0.7692 |
| 2 | 1.8334 | 1.8080 | 1.7833 | 1.7591 | 1.7355 | 1.7125 | 1.6901 | 1.6681 | 1.6467 | 1.6257 | 1.6052 | 1.5278 | 1.3609 |
| 3 | 2.6730 | 2.6243 | 2.5771 | 2.5313 | 2.4869 | 2.4437 | 2.4018 | 2.3612 | 2.3216 | 2.2832 | 2.2459 | 2.1065 | 1.8161 |
| 4 | 3.4651 | 3.3872 | 3.3121 | 3.2397 | 3.1699 | 3.1024 | 3.0373 | 2.9745 | 2.9137 | 2.8550 | 2.7982 | 2.5887 | 2.1662 |
| 5 | 4.2124 | 4.1002 | 3.9927 | 3.8897 | 3.7908 | 3.6959 | 3.6048 | 3.5172 | 3.4331 | 3.3522 | 3.2743 | 2.9906 | 2.4356 |
| 6 | 4.9173 | 4.7665 | 4.6229 | 4.4859 | 4.3553 | 4.2305 | 4.1114 | 3.9975 | 3.8887 | 3.7845 | 3.6847 | 3.3255 | 2.6427 |
| 7 | 5.5824 | 5.3893 | 5.2064 | 5.0330 | 4.8684 | 4.7122 | 4.5638 | 4.4226 | 4.2883 | 4.1604 | 4.0386 | 3.6046 | 2.8021 |
| 8 | 6.2098 | 5.9713 | 5.7466 | 5.5348 | 5.3349 | 5.1461 | 4.9676 | 4.7988 | 4.6389 | 4.4873 | 4.3436 | 3.8372 | 2.9247 |
| 9 | 6.8017 | 6.5152 | 6.2469 | 5.9952 | 5.7590 | 5.5370 | 5.3282 | 5.1317 | 4.9464 | 4.7716 | 4.6065 | 4.0310 | 3.0190 |
| 10 | 7.3601 | 7.0236 | 6.7101 | 6.4177 | 6.1446 | 5.8892 | 5.6502 | 5.4262 | 5.2161 | 5.0188 | 4.8332 | 4.1925 | 3.0915 |
| 11 | 7.8869 | 7.4987 | 7.1390 | 6.8052 | 6.4951 | 6.2065 | 5.9377 | 5.6869 | 5.4527 | 5.2337 | 5.0286 | 4.3271 | 3.1473 |
| 12 | 8.3838 | 7.9427 | 7.5361 | 7.1607 | 6.8137 | 6.4924 | 6.1944 | 5.9176 | 5.6603 | 5.4206 | 5.1971 | 4.4392 | 3.1903 |
| 13 | 8.8527 | 8.3577 | 7.9038 | 7.4869 | 7.1034 | 6.7499 | 6.4235 | 6.1218 | 5.8424 | 5.5831 | 5.3423 | 4.5327 | 3.2233 |
| 14 | 9.2950 | 8.7455 | 8.2442 | 7.7862 | 7.3667 | 6.9819 | 6.6282 | 6.3025 | 6.0021 | 5.7245 | 5.4675 | 4.6106 | 3.2487 |
| 15 | 9.7122 | 9.1079 | 8.5595 | 8.0607 | 7.6061 | 7.1909 | 6.8109 | 6.4624 | 6.1422 | 5.8474 | 5.5755 | 4.6755 | 3.2682 |
| 16 | 10.1059 | 9.4466 | 8.8514 | 8.3126 | 7.8237 | 7.3792 | 6.9740 | 6.6039 | 6.2651 | 5.9542 | 5.6685 | 4.7296 | 3.2832 |
| 17 | 10.4773 | 9.7632 | 9.1216 | 8.5436 | 8.0216 | 7.5488 | 7.1196 | 6.7291 | 6.3729 | 6.0472 | 5.7487 | 4.7746 | 3.2948 |
| 18 | 10.8276 | 10.0591 | 9.3719 | 8.7556 | 8.2014 | 7.7016 | 7.2497 | 6.8399 | 6.4674 | 6.1280 | 5.8178 | 4.8122 | 3.3037 |
| 19 | 11.1581 | 10.3356 | 9.6036 | 8.9501 | 8.3649 | 7.8393 | 7.3658 | 6.9380 | 6.5504 | 6.1982 | 5.8775 | 4.8435 | 3.3105 |
| 20 | 11.4699 | 10.5940 | 9.8181 | 9.1285 | 8.5136 | 7.9633 | 7.4694 | 7.0248 | 6.6231 | 6.2593 | 5.9288 | 4.8696 | 3.3158 |

# REVIEW PROBLEM

Summit Maintenance Technology sells a software package that companies can use to manage their facility and equipment maintenance functions. Features include work order tracking, maintenance history reporting, repair history reporting, and parts inventory management. The software is used mainly by large organizations such as airports, manufacturing plants, office complexes, hospitals, and commercial bakeries. A unique aspect of Summit's product is that it has a very intuitive interface and can be accessed via the Web with Summit providing application servers, database servers and security. Thus, firms that implement the system do not need to add IT staff or equipment.

Currently, Summit is negotiating with Ogden National Airport, which has considerable maintenance challenges. For example, the airport has six employees whose sole job is re-lamping (i.e., replacing light bulbs). In total, the maintenance department at Ogden has 45 employees who maintain escalators, elevators, trams, lighting, and perform painting and other miscellaneous maintenance duties.

Craig Bradley, a senior manager at Ogden National Airport, has held a series of meetings with Summit and has identified the following cost savings:

1. The company can avoid purchasing a server costing $10,000 next year.
2. Due to better tracking, parts inventory can be reduced. The effect on purchases is $30,000, $20,000, and $10,000 over the next three years.
3. The company will need one less maintenance employee with an annual salary and benefits of $60,000.
4. The company is currently paying $5,000 per year to upgrade its maintenance software.

Craig anticipates that the changes to Ogden for software and consulting services will be as follows:

Initial costs—$90,000 "program fee" plus $55,000 consultant charges for systems integration and customization of reports

Ongoing costs—$14,000 annual program fee after the initial year plus $6,000 per year consulting charges for ongoing customization beyond the initial year

**Required**

Calculate the net present value (NPV) assuming a required rate of return of 15 percent. Also calculate the internal rate of return (IRR). In performing your calculations, use a three-year time horizon and ignore taxes.

Should Ogden invest in the new software?

**Answer**

| Time | 0 | 1 | 2 | 3 |
|---|---|---|---|---|
| Initial program fee | (90,000.00) | | | |
| Initial consulting charges | (55,000.00) | | | |
| Ongoing charges | | (20,000.00) | (20,000.00) | (20,000.00) |
| | | | | |
| IT equipment | | 10,000.00 | | |
| Parts inventory | | 30,000.00 | 20,000.00 | 10,000.00 |
| Maintenance employee | | 60,000.00 | 60,000.00 | 60,000.00 |
| Old software upgrade | | 5,000.00 | 5,000.00 | 5,000.00 |
| | | | | |
| Total | (145,000.00) | 85,000.00 | 65,000.00 | 55,000.00 |
| Present value factors at 15% | 1.0000 | 0.8696 | 0.7561 | 0.6575 |
| | (145,000.00) | 73,916.00 | 49,146.50 | 36,162.50 |

| | |
|---|---|
| NPV | 14,225.00 |
| IRR, in % | 21.33 |

Note—IRR calculated using Excel® as explained in Appendix A

Since the NPV is greater than zero and the IRR is greater than the required rate of return, Ogden should invest in the software.

# KEY TERMS

| | | |
|---|---|---|
| Accounting rate of return (313) | Cost of capital (308) | Net present value (NPV) (301) |
| Capital budget (299) | Depreciation tax shield (310) | Payback period (312) |
| Capital budgeting decisions (299) | Internal rate of return (IRR) (303) | Required rate of return (301) |
| Capital expenditure decisions (299) | | |

# SELF ASSESSMENT   *(Answers Below)*

1. Which of the following is *not* a capital expenditure decision?

   a. Building a new factory
   b. Purchasing a new piece of equipment
   c. Purchasing a computer system
   d. All of the above are capital expenditure decisions

2. Which of the following methods equates future dollars to current dollars?

   a. Net present value method
   b. Internal rate of return method
   c. Payback period method
   d. Both a and b are correct

3. If you require a return of 8 percent, the present value of $100 received two years from now would be calculated as:

   a. $\dfrac{\$100}{(.08)^2}$

   b. $\dfrac{(1 + .08)^2}{\$100}$

   c. $\dfrac{\$100}{(1 + .08)^2}$

   d. None of the above

4. If the net present value of a project is zero, the project is earning a return equal to:

   a. Zero
   b. The rate of inflation
   c. The accounting rate of return
   d. The required rate of return

5. An investment should be made if:
   a. The IRR is equal to or greater than the required rate of return
   b. The IRR is equal to or greater than zero
   c. The IRR is greater than the accounting rate of return
   d. The IRR is greater than the present value factor

6. The cost of capital is:
   a. The cost of debt financing
   b. The cost of equity financing
   c. The weighted average of the costs of debt and equity financing
   d. The internal rate of return

7. A piece of equipment costs $100,000 and has a five year life. Assuming straight-line depreciation and a 40 percent tax rate, this investment:
   a. Will generate a positive cash inflow at time 0
   b. Will have a negative depreciation tax shield
   c. Will generate a $40,000 expense each year but will not affect cash flows beyond year 0
   d. Will generate a depreciation tax shield equivalent to an annual cash inflow of $8,000 for five years.

8. A project costs $200,000 and yields cash inflows of $50,000 per year for five years. In this case, the payback period is:
   a. Four years
   b. Five years
   c. $50,000
   d. None of the above

9. A project with a useful life of five years requires an investment of $100,000 and yields after-tax income of $20,000 per year for five years. Assuming the investment has no value at the end of five years, the accounting rate of return is:
   a. 40 percent
   b. 20 percent
   c. 10 percent
   d. None of the above

10. A project requires a $2,000,000 investment and has an internal rate of return of 20 percent. The cost of capital is only 15 percent. A manager with a short-run orientation may still reject this investment if:
    a. The net present value is positive
    b. The rate of inflation is high
    c. The accounting rate of return is high
    d. Accelerated depreciation leads to reported losses in the early years of the investment's useful life

11. A project has unequal cash flows, and a manager "guesses" that the internal rate of return will be 10 percent. If the net present value is positive at 10 percent, then:
    a. The internal rate of return is greater than 10 percent
    b. The internal rate of return is less than 10 percent
    c. The internal rate of return is exactly 10 percent
    d. None of the above are true

12. An example of a "soft" benefit is:
    a. Improved brand recognition
    b. Savings of material cost
    c. Savings of labor cost
    d. Increase in sales

### Answers to Self Assessment

**1.** d;   **2.** d;   **3.** c;   **4.** d;   **5.** a;   **6.** c;
**7.** d;   **8.** a;   **9.** a;   **10.** d;   **11.** a;   **12.** a.

# INTERACTIVE LEARNING

**Enhance and test your knowledge of Chapter 9 using the interactive CD.**

1. Learning Objectives
2. Multiple Choice
3. Language of Business—Matching of Key Terms
4. Critical Thinking
5. Demonstration—A trial and error approach to calculating the internal rate of return with uneven cash flows
6. Case—*Medford Valley Resort*; Test your knowledge of capital budgeting
7. Video—*Holland America-Westours*; Analyzing the acquisition of a cruise ship

**Go to our dynamic Web site for more self-assessment, Web links, and additional information.**

# QUESTIONS

1. What is a capital expenditure decision?

2. Why is it important to take into account the time value of money when making capital budgeting decisions?

3. What are the two approaches for evaluating investments that take into account the time value of money?

4. How do the net present value and the internal rate of return methods differ in their approach to evaluating investment alternatives?

5. What is the cost of equity financing?

6. How are cash flows affected as a result of the tax consequences of depreciation?

7. What are the advantages of evaluating projects using the net present value and internal rate of return methods instead of the payback and accounting rate of return methods?

8. Why may managers concentrate on the short run profitability of investments rather than their net present values?

9. How is the internal rate of return (IRR) determined if there are uneven cash flows?

10. Why does the failure to consider "soft" benefits discourage investment?

# EXERCISES

**EXERCISE 9-1. Group Assignment**  Explain why interest expense is not treated as a cash outflow in capital budgeting decisions made using net present value (NPV) analysis.

**EXERCISE 9-2. Writing Assignment**  Pauline Hsu is the manager of the office products division of Lomar Enterprises. In this position, her annual bonus is based on an appraisal of return on investment (ROI) measured as Division Income ÷ End-of-Year Division Assets (net of accumulated depreciation).

Currently, Pauline is considering investing $25,000,000 in modernization of the division plant in Tennessee. She estimates that the project will generate cash savings of $5,500,000 per year for 8 years. The plant improvements will be depreciated over 8 years ($25,000,000 ÷ 8 years = $3,125,000). Thus, the annual effect on income will be $2,375,000 ($5,500,000 − $3,125,000).

*Required*
Using a discount rate of 12 percent, calculate the NPV of the modernization project. Then, calculate the ROI of the project each year over it's eight-year life. (Calculate ROI as affect on income divided by end of year book value. Note that the value of ROI is not defined at the end of year eight when book value is zero.) Finally, write a paragraph explaining why Pauline may not make the investment even though it has a positive NPV.

**EXERCISE 9-3. Internet Assignment**  Go to Web site of Technology/Engineering Management, Inc. (http://www.temi.com/NewTechInvestments.htm) and read the note on justifying investments in new technology by Richard Mignogna, president of this consulting firm. What are the strategic benefits of investments in technology that, according to Mignogna, are seldom considered in investment decisions?

**EXERCISE 9-4. Investment Decisions**  Provide an example of an investment decision at Charles Schwab (a company that provides traditional and online brokerage services), McDonalds, and Wal-Mart. For each example, indicate the cash inflows and outflows that the company would estimate in analyzing the investment.

**EXERCISE 9-5. Using Present Value Tables**  What is the present value of $100 received at the end of five years if the required return is 10 percent (answer using Table 1 in Appendix B, *Present Value of $1 Due in n Periods*)?

**EXERCISE 9-6. Using Present Value Tables**   What is the present value of $100 per year for five years if the required return is 10 percent (answer using Table 2 in Appendix B, *Present Value of an Annuity of $1 Per Period*)?

**EXERCISE 9-7. Using Present Value Tables**   Examine Table 1 in Appendix B. Explain why the numbers decrease as you move from left to right in a given row. Explain why the numbers decrease as you move from top to bottom in a given column.

**EXERCISE 9-8. Calculate Present Value**   Suppose you face the prospect of receiving $200 per year for the next five years plus an extra $500 payment at the end of five years. Determine how much this prospect is worth today if the required rate of return is 10 percent.

**EXERCISE 9-9. Calculate Present Value**   Juanita Martinez is ready to retire and has a choice of three pension plans. Plan A provides for an immediate cash payment of $100,000. Plan B provides for the payment of $10,000 per year for 10 years and the payment of $100,000 at the end of year 10. Plan C will pay $20,000 per year for 10 years. Juanita Martinez desires a return of 8 percent. Determine the present value of each plan and select the best one.

**EXERCISE 9-10. Calculate Net Present Value**   An investment that costs $10,000 will return $4,000 per year for four years. Determine the net present value of the investment if the required rate of return is 12 percent. Ignore taxes. Should the investment be undertaken?

**EXERCISE 9-11. Calculate Net Present Value**   Magnolia Florist is considering replacing an old refrigeration unit with a larger unit to store flowers. Because the new refrigeration unit has a larger capacity, Magnolia estimates that they can sell an additional $6,000 of flowers a year (the cost of the flowers is $3,500). In addition, the new unit is energy efficient and should save $950 in electricity each year. It will cost an extra $1,800 per year for maintenance. The new refrigeration unit costs $20,000 and has an expected life of 10 years. The old unit is fully depreciated and can be sold for an amount equal to disposal cost. At the end of 10 years, the new unit has an expected residual value of $5,000. Determine the net present value of the investment if the required rate of return is 14 percent (ignore taxes). Should the investment be undertaken?

**EXERCISE 9-12. Choosing Among Alternative Investments**   Walker Shoe Corporation is considering investing in one of two machines that attach heels to shoes. Machine A costs $50,000 and is expected to save the company $15,000 per year for six years. Machine B costs $75,000 and is expected to save the company $20,000 per year for six years. Determine the net present value for each machine and decide which machine should be purchased if the required rate of return is 10 percent. Ignore taxes.

**EXERCISE 9-13. Calculate the Internal Rate of Return**   An investment that costs $79,100 will reduce operating costs by $14,000 per year for 10 years. Determine the internal rate of return of the investment (ignore taxes). Should the investment be undertaken if the required rate of return is 18 percent?

**EXERCISE 9-14. Calculate the Internal Rate of Return**   Nadine Roberts, owner of Roberts Fine Wine, is considering investing $79,137 in a temperature controlled wine storage room. She plans to rent space to customers and expects to generate $22,500 annually (rental charges less miscellaneous expenses other than depreciation).

*Required*

a. Assuming Nadine wishes to evaluate the project with a five-year time horizon, what is the internal rate of return of the investment (ignore taxes)?

b. Should Nadine make the investment if her required rate of return is 12 percent?

**EXERCISE 9-15. Depreciation Tax Shield**   Anton Corporation is making a $200,000 investment in equipment with a five-year life. The company uses the straight-line method of depreciation and has a tax rate of 40 percent. The company's required rate of return is 10 percent.

*Required*

What is the present value of the tax savings related to depreciation of the equipment?

**EXERCISE 9-16. Cash Flow Implications of Tax Losses**   WesternWear.com is expected to have operating losses of $100,000 in its first year of business and $50,000 in its second year. However, the company expects to have income before taxes of $120,000 in its third year and $ 200,000 in its fourth year. The company's required rate of return is 14 percent.

*Required*

Assume a tax rate of 40 percent and that current losses can be used to offset taxable income in future years. What is the present value of tax savings related to the operating losses in years one and two?

**EXERCISE 9-17. Net Present Value with Taxes**   Wilson Smoked Fish Corporation is contemplating the purchase of a new smoker. The smoker will cost $21,000 but will generate additional revenue of $15,500 per year for seven years. Additional costs, other than depreciation, will equal $8,000 per year. The smoker has an expected life of seven years, at which time it will have no residual value. Wilson uses the straight-line method of depreciation for tax purposes. Determine the net present value of the investment if the required rate of return is 12 percent and the tax rate is 40 percent. Should Wilson make the investment in the smoker?

**EXERCISE 9-18. Calculate the Payback Period**   The Lower Valley Wheat Cooperative is considering the construction of a new silo. It will cost $41,000 to construct the silo. Determine the payback period if the expected cash inflows are $5,000 per year.

**EXERCISE 9-19. Calculate the Accounting Rate of Return**   The Deaton Company is considering entering a new line of business. Starting the business will require an initial investment in equipment of $200,000. It is expected that the new business will increase net income by $30,000 per year for five years. The equipment will be depreciated over a five-year period using straight-line depreciation with no residual value. Determine the accounting rate of return of the new business.

**EXERCISE 9-20. IRR and Unequal Cash Flows**   Newport Department Store is considering development of an e-commerce business. The company estimates that development will require an initial outlay of $1,000,000. Other cash flows will be as follows:

| | |
|---|---|
| Year 1 | ($500,000) |
| Year 2 | $200,000 |
| Year 3 | $630,000 |
| Year 4 | $750,000 |
| Year 5 | $800,000 |

*Required*

Assuming the company limits its analysis to five years, estimate the internal rate of return on the e-commerce business. Should the company develop the e-commerce business if the required rate of return is 13 percent?

**EXERCISE 9-21. IRR and Unequal Cash Flows**   A company is making an investment of $2,200,100 that will yield the following cash flows:

| | |
|---|---|
| Year 1 | $200,000 |
| Year 2 | $400,000 |
| Year 3 | $600,000 |
| Year 4 | $800,000 |
| Year 5 | $1,000,000 |

*Required*

What is the internal rate of return of the investment?

**EXERCISE 9-22. "Soft" Benefits**   Sherman's Jewelry has 45 stores in major malls around the country. The company is considering starting an online business, Shermans.com, which will require a substantial investment in technology.

*Required*

Identify a potential benefit of the online business that would be difficult to quantify in a net present value analysis.

**EXERCISE 9-23. Quantifying "Soft" Benefits**   Pritchard Manufactured Products is considering investing in a flexible manufacturing system that will enable the company to respond rapidly to customer requests. Ben Jarvis, the controller of Pritchard, has estimated that the system will have a 10-year life and a net present value of a *negative* $500,000. However, he admits that he did not take into account the potential sales increases that will result from improvement in on-time delivery. According to Ben, "this is just too hard to estimate."

*Required*

Using a 10-year life and a required return of 12 percent, what must be the annual value of the soft benefits associated with the project to yield a zero net present value? Assume that there is general agreement that the annual "soft" benefits will be at least $90,000. In this case, should the investment be undertaken?

# P R O B L E M S

**PROBLEM 9-1. Present Value Analysis**   Carter "Flip" Allison recently rejected an $8,000,000, five-year contract with the Vancouver Seals. The contract offer called for an immediate signing bonus of $3,000,000 and annual payments of $1,000,000.

   To "sweeten" the deal, the president of player personnel for the Seals has now offered a $10,000,000, five-year contract. This contract calls for annual increases and a balloon payment at the end of five years.

| | |
|---|---:|
| Year 1 | $1,000,000 |
| Year 2 | 1,100,000 |
| Year 3 | 1,200,000 |
| Year 4 | 1,300,000 |
| Year 5 | 1,400,000 |
| Year 5 balloon payment | 4,000,000 |
| Total | $10,000,000 |

*Required*

Suppose you are Allison's agent and you wish to evaluate the two contracts using a required rate of return of 10 percent. In present value terms, how much better is the second contract?

**PROBLEM 9-2. Present Value and "What If" Analysis**   National Cruise Line, Inc. is considering the acquisition of a new ship that will cost $180,325,005. In this regard, the president of the company asked the CFO to analyze cash flows associated with operating the ship under two alternative itineraries: Itinerary 1, Caribbean Winter/Alaska Summer and Itinerary 2 Caribbean Winter/Eastern Canada Summer. The CFO estimated the following cash flows, which are expected to apply to each of the next 15 years:

|                           | **Caribbean/Alaska** | **Caribbean/East. Canada** |
|---------------------------|:--------------------:|:--------------------------:|
| Net revenue               | $119,789,010         | $103,904,336               |
| Less:                     |                      |                            |
|   Direct program expenses   | (24,091,051)         | (22,812,140)               |
|   Indirect program expenses | (19,437,162)         | (19,437,162)               |
|   Non-operating expenses    | (20,186,695)         | (20,186,401)               |
| Add back depreciation     | 12,021,667           | 12,021,667                 |
| Cash flow per year        | $ 68,095,769         | $ 53,490,300               |

### Required

a. For each of the itineraries, calculate the present values of the cash flows using required rates of return of both 10 and 15 percent. Assume a 15-year time horizon. Should the company purchase the ship with either or both required rates of return?

b. The president is uncertain as to whether a 10 percent or a 15 percent required return is appropriate. Explain why, in the present circumstance, spending a great deal of time to determine the correct required return may not be necessary.

c. Focusing on a 10-percent required rate of return, what would be the opportunity cost to the company of using the ship in a Caribbean/Eastern Canada itinerary rather than a Caribbean/Alaska itinerary?

(Note—this problem closely parallels the one facing Holland America Line-Westours Inc. in the video on the interactive CD. Be sure to watch this video before finishing the chapter.)

**PROBLEM 9-3. Net Present Value and Taxes**   Kreskie Productions is evaluating a film project. The president of Kreskie estimates that the film will cost $16,000,000 to produce. In its first year, the film is expected to generate $12,000,000 in net revenue, after which the film will be released to video. Video is expected to generate $6,000,000 in net revenue in its first year, $2,000,000 in its second year and $500,000 in its third year. For tax purposes, amortization of the cost of the film will be $12,000,000 in year 1 and $4,000,000 in year 2. The company's tax rate is 40 percent, and the company requires a 10 percent rate of return on its films.

### Required

What is the net present value of the film project? To simplify, assume that all outlays to produce the film occur at time 0. Should the company produce the film?

**PROBLEM 9-4. Internal Rate of Return and Taxes**   The Boston Culinary Institute is evaluating a classroom remodeling project. The cost of the remodel will be $200,000 and will be depreciated over five years using the straight-line method. The remodeled room will accommodate 5 extra students per year. Each student pays annual tuition of $15,000. The before-tax incremental cost of a student (e.g., the cost of food prepared and consumed by a student) is $1,360 per year. The company's tax rate is 40 percent, and the company requires a 12-percent rate of return on the remodeling project.

### Required

Assuming a five-year time horizon, what is the internal rate of return of the remodeling project? Should the company invest in the remodel?

**PROBLEM 9-5. Net Present Value, Internal Rate of Return, Payback, Accounting Rate of Return, and Taxes**   Walter Leland, the owner of Quality Motors, is considering the addition of a paint and body shop to his automobile dealership. Construction of a building and the purchase of necessary equipment is estimated to cost $700,000 and both the building and equipment will be depreciated over 10 years using the straight-line method. The building and equipment have zero estimated residual value at the end of 10 years. Leland's required rate of return for this project is 10 percent. Net income related to each year of the investment is as follows:

| | |
|---|---:|
| Revenue | $360,000 |
| Less: | |
| Material cost | 60,000 |
| Labor | 140,000 |
| Depreciation | 70,000 |
| Other | 5,000 |
| Income before taxes | 85,000 |
| Taxes at 40% | 34,000 |
| Net income | $ 51,000 |

*Required*

a. Determine the net present value of the investment in the paint and body shop. Should Leland invest in the paint and body shop?

b. Calculate the internal rate of return of the investment.

c. Calculate the payback period of the investment.

d. Calculate the accounting rate of return.

**PROBLEM 9-6. Choosing Among Alternative Investments**   Bright Spot Corporation, a chain of dry cleaning stores, has the opportunity to invest in one of two dry-cleaning machines. Machine A has a four-year expected life and a cost of $43,000. It will cost an additional $4,500 to have the machine delivered and installed and the expected residual value at the end of four years is $3,200. Machine B has a four-year expected life and a cost of $73,000. It will cost an additional $5,000 to have the machine delivered and installed and the expected residual value at the end of four years is $5,200. Bright Spot has a required rate of return of 14 percent. Additional cash flows related to the machines are as follows:

| | Machine A | | | |
|---|---|---|---|---|
| **Item** | **Year 1** | **Year 2** | **Year 3** | **Year 4** |
| Labor saving | $21,000 | $21,000 | $21,000 | $21,000 |
| Power saving | 1,300 | 1,300 | 1,300 | 1,300 |
| Chemical saving | 2,900 | 2,900 | 2,900 | 2,900 |
| Additional maintenance | (1,000) | (1,000) | (1,000) | (1,000) |
| Additional miscellaneous | (2,200) | (2,200) | (2,200) | (2,200) |

| | Machine B | | | |
|---|---|---|---|---|
| **Item** | **Year 1** | **Year 2** | **Year 3** | **Year 4** |
| Labor saving | $29,000 | $29,000 | $29,000 | $29,000 |
| Power saving | 1,900 | 1,900 | 1,900 | 1,900 |
| Chemical saving | 3,200 | 3,200 | 3,200 | 3,200 |
| Additional maintenance | (1,200) | (1,200) | (1,200) | (1,200) |
| Additional miscellaneous | (2,300) | (2,300) | (2,300) | (2,300) |

*Required*

a. Ignoring taxes, determine the net present value of investing in machine A.

b. Ignoring taxes, determine the net present value of investing in machine B.

c. Which, if any, machine should be purchased?

**PROBLEM 9-7. Net Present Value and Taxes**   Crown Limousine Service is considering acquisition of an additional vehicle. The model under consideration will cost $80,000, have a five-year life and a $20,000 residual value. The company anticipates that the effect on annual net income will be as follows:

| | |
|---|---:|
| Revenue | $109,500 |
| Less expenses: | |
| Driver | 60,000 |
| Fuel | 3,750 |
| Maintenance | 1,600 |
| Insurance | 1,500 |
| Depreciation | 12,000 |
| Miscellaneous | 1,000 |
| Total expense | 79,850 |
| Income before taxes | 29,650 |
| Taxes at 40% | 11,860 |
| Net income | $ 17,790 |

*Required*

Calculate the net present value of the investment assuming the company has a required rate of return of 14 percent. Should the company invest in the new limousine?

**PROBLEM 9-8. Net Present Value and Taxes** Island Ferry plans to expand operations by acquiring another boat. They have a bid of $828,000 from a boat manufacturer to provide a boat that can carry 40 passengers. The boat has an expected life of eight years with an expected residual value for financial reporting and tax purposes of $62,000. Island Ferry has a tax rate of 40 percent and uses straight-line depreciation for tax purposes. Their required rate of return is 12 percent. The following annual cash flows relate to the investment in the new boat.

| Item | Cash Flow |
|---|---|
| Passenger revenues | $293,000) |
| Labor cost | (84,000) |
| Fuel cost | (15,800) |
| Maintenance cost | (26,700) |
| Miscellaneous cost | ( 3,500) |
| Taxes | ? |

*Required*

Calculate the net present value of the investment in the boat. Should the company make the investment?

**PROBLEM 9-9. Comprehensive Capital Budgeting Problem** Clayton Corporation is considering producing a new product, Autodial. Marketing data indicate that the company will be able to sell 35,000 units per year at $35. The product will be produced in a section of an existing factory that is currently not in use.

To produce Autodial, Clayton must buy a machine that costs $310,000. The machine has an expected life of five years and will have an ending residual value of $10,000. Clayton will depreciate the machine over five years using the straight-line method for both tax and financial reporting purposes.

In addition to the cost of the machine, the company will incur incremental manufacturing costs of $300,000 for component parts, $400,000 for direct labor, and $180,000 of miscellaneous costs. Also, the company plans to spend $130,000 annually for advertising Autodial. Clayton has a tax rate of 40 percent, and the company's required rate of return is 14 percent.

*Required*

a. Compute the net present value.

b. Compute the payback period.

c. Compute the accounting rate of return.

d. Should Clayton make the investment required to produce Autodial?

**PROBLEM 9-10. Comprehensive Capital Budgeting Problem** Quality Grocery operates a chain of 40 grocery stores. Currently, the company is considering starting a new division, QualityGrocer.com, to provide home delivery services. Customers will be able to order groceries by phone or using the Internet, and QualityGrocer.com will deliver them within 24 hours at a price guaranteed to be identical to the prices charged in the company's stores.

The company has projected revenue and cost related to this business for the next seven years as follows:

| | Year 1 | Year 2 | Year 3 | Year 4 | Year 5 | Year 6 | Year 7 |
|---|---|---|---|---|---|---|---|
| Revenue | $1,500,000 | $1,575,000 | $1,653,751 | $1,736,438 | $1,823,259 | $1,914,422 | $2,010,143 |
| Less Expenses: | | | | | | | |
| Cost of merchandise | 1,050,000 | 1,102,500 | 1,157,625 | 1,215,506 | 1,276,281 | 1,340,096 | 1,407,100 |
| Salaries | 300,000 | 315,000 | 330,750 | 347,288 | 364,652 | 382,884 | 402,030 |
| Depreciation | 50,000 | 50,000 | 50,000 | 50,000 | 50,000 | 50,000 | 50,000 |
| Miscellaneous | 25,000 | 26,250 | 27,563 | 28,940 | 30,388 | 31,907 | 33,502 |
| Total Expense | 1,425,000 | 1,493,750 | 1,565,938 | 1,641,734 | 1,721,321 | 1,804,887 | 1,892,632 |
| Income before taxes | 75,000 | 81,250 | 87,813 | 94,704 | 101,938 | 109,535 | 117,511 |
| Taxes at 40% | 30,000 | 32,500 | 35,125 | 37,882 | 40,775 | 43,814 | 47,004 |
| Net income | $   45,000 | $   48,750 | $   52,688 | $   56,822 | $   61,163 | $   65,721 | $   70,507 |

The business will require an initial investment in delivery trucks and other equipment of $400,000. The trucks and equipment will be depreciated over a seven-year life using straight-line depreciation with a residual value of $50,000.

*Required*

Assume that Quality has decided to limit its analysis to seven years. Calculate the net present value of the new business using a 14-percent required rate of return. Should Quality make the investment in the new business?

**PROBLEM 9-11. Net Present Value and Inflation**   Lauren Edwards, an accountant with Sultan Industries, prepared the following analysis of an investment in manufacturing equipment.

| | |
|---|---|
| Cost savings: | |
| Labor savings | $   425,000.00 |
| Reduction in rework materials | 100,000.00 |
| Other | 50,000.00 |
| Total | 575,000.00 |
| Additional taxes related to cost savings | (201,250.00) |
| Tax savings related to depreciation of new equipment | 140,000.00 |
| Annual cash flow | $   513,750.00 |
| Present value at 10 percent for five years | $1,947,523.50 |
| Cost of equipment | 2,000,000.00 |
| Net present value | $   (52,476.50) |

Lauren's boss, Cynthia Sanchez, reviewed the calculation and made the following observation: "Lauren, you've assumed that there won't be inflation, but inflation is built into our 10-percent cost of capital. I think it's reasonable to assume that labor and costs other than depreciation will increase by four percent per year. Why don't you redo the analysis with that assumption."

*Required*

a. What does Cynthia Sanchez mean by "inflation is built into our 10-percent cost of capital"?

b. Redo Lauren Edwards' analysis assuming an inflation rate of 4 percent. Should the company make the investment in the equipment?

**PROBLEM 9-12. Internal Rate of Return with Uneven Cash Flows**   Based on the information in Problem 11, what is the internal rate of return of the investment, assuming an inflation rate of 4 percent applicable to labor and costs other than depreciation? Should the company make the investment if their cost of capital is 10 percent?

**PROBLEM 9-13. Risk and Cost of Capital**   Frankel Manufacturing company is considering investing in an automated welding system. The system employs a 300-watt laser with fiber optic beam delivery to weld dissimilar metals. The specifications of the system indicate that it can make hundreds of welds per minute—significantly faster than the company's current welding equipment—and improve the quality of welds.

In the recent past, Frankel has evaluated investments using a 12-percent cost of capital. However, the automated welding system is not in general use and, while the company expects that it will result in significant labor savings and improve quality leading to increased sales, the cash flows are not at all certain.

*Required*

Assume that the cash inflows associated with the automated welding system are more risky than those associated with the company's typical investment. Should the company evaluate the investment using the cost of capital of 12 percent, or should a higher or lower rate be used? Briefly explain the basis for your answer.

(See the Web site (*http://ce-toolkit.crd.ge.com/homepage.html*) of the *General Electric Research and Development Center—Manufacturing Technology Laboratory*, which performs research and development in a wide range of manufacturing and engineering design technologies leading to products like the one described in the problem.)

**PROBLEM 9-14. Conflict Between Performance Evaluation and Use of NPV**   Division managers at Creighton Aerospace are evaluated and rewarded based on ROI (return on investment) targets. In the current year, Delmar Richards, the president of the commercial products division, has an ROI target of 11 percent. If the division has an ROI of 11 percent or greater, Richards will receive 200,000 options on Creighton stock in addition to a base salary of $350,000.

The commercial products division is considering a major investment in product development, which has a net present value of $20,000,000. However, the investment will have a negative effect on reported profit over the next two years after which the investment will begin to have a significant positive effect on firm profitability for the next eight years.

*Required*

a. Discuss the potential conflict between the company's evaluation/compensation system and Richards focus on the NPV of the investment in product development.

b. Suppose Richards currently holds stock in Creighton Aerospace with a market value of $1,000,000 and has options on 400,000 shares (awarded in previous years). Is this likely to acerbate or mitigate the conflict you discussed in Part a?

**PROBLEM 9-15. Internal Rate of Return with Uneven Cash Flows**   Melrose Pizza is considering expanding operations by establishing a delivery business. This will require the purchase of an oven that will cost $42,000, including installation. The oven is expected to last five years, have a $2,000 residual value, and will be depreciated using the straight-line method. Cash flows associated with the delivery business are as follows:

| Item | Year 1 | Year 2 | Year 3 | Year 4 | Year 5 |
|---|---|---|---|---|---|
| Revenue | $63,000 | $69,300 | $76,230 | $83,853 | $92,238 |
| Ingredients | (25,200) | (27,720) | (30,492) | (33,541) | (36,895) |
| Salary | (25,000) | (27,000) | (29,000) | (31,000) | (33,000) |
| Additional miscellaneous | (2,200) | (2,400) | (2,600) | (2,800) | (3,000) |
| Residual value | | | | | 2,000 |

In addition to the above, there are tax consequences related to the new business, and the company's tax rate is 40 percent.

*Required*

Calculate the internal rate of return for the delivery business. (*Hint:* Try a range of rates between 9 percent and 14 percent.) Should Melrose invest in the delivery business if the required rate of return is 10 percent?

# CASES

## 9-1 ETHICS CASE: JUNIPER PACKAGING SOLUTIONS, INC.

Juniper Packaging Solutions, Inc. provides custom packaging products to companies all over the United States. With five production facilities, the company produces cardboard boxes, plastic and steel drums, aluminum bottles, and absorbent pouches and bags. Companies using their products ship everything from chemicals in 55-gallon containers to biological specimens in tamper evident pouches.

Spencer Williams is the vice president in charge of the Maryland production facility, and in the last year he's become concerned about plant performance. The plant needs a long lead time for orders and defect rates have increased—both hurting customer satisfaction. In Spencer's opinion, the problems are the result of outmoded production equipment. Recently, Spencer's team of production managers identified three pieces of "state of the art" equipment that they believe will turn the plant around and make it the most efficient of the company's five plants. Unfortunately, the price tag of the equipment is $1.5 million and the company has a freeze on capital expenditures greater than $300,000. The freeze was mandated by the company chief executive officer (CEO) after third-quarter earnings dropped by 10 percent due to a weakening of the Asian economy and reduced shipments to Japan and Korea by several of Juniper's major customers.

Spencer and the controller of the Maryland plant both believe that the new equipment is absolutely necessary for the company to maintain customer satisfaction and market share. Together they've devised a plan to circumvent the capital expenditure freeze. Each piece of equipment is actually a "system" with multiple components (e.g., conveyer belt, box molding unit, box taping unit, etc.). Spencer will ask the equipment manufacturers to break each system into components and submit multiple bills (e.g., a separate bill for the conveyer, a separate bill for the box molding unit, etc.) each less than $300,000. The plant controller will then approve the expenditures as being consistent with the guidelines that only prohibit expenditures on equipment costing more than $300,000.

### Required

Is the plan devised by Spencer and the CFO ethical? In answering this question, assume that Spencer and the controller are both firmly convinced that the new equipment will increase shareholder value.

## 9-2 SERGO GAMES

Sergo Games produces a variety of action games including a flight simulation game, *Rescue 2000*, which sold more than 700,000 copies in the past year. The games are played on computers, and the company operates an in-house production facility that manufactures and packages CDs for shipment to customers.

In 2006, the production plant prepared 2,000,000 CDs and incurred the following costs:

| | |
|---|---:|
| Units processed | 2,000,000 |
| Labor | $ 600,000 |
| Material | 4,000,000 |
| Supervisory salaries | 200,000 |
| Depreciation of equipment | 300,000 |
| Heat, light, phone, etc. | 100,000 |
| Total | $5,200,000 |

Cameron West, an accounting manager, has been given the responsibility to analyze outsourcing the production of CDs. His report is provided below.

### Required

Should production be outsourced? *Support your answer with appropriate calculations.*

**Sergo Games**

April 19, 2007

| | |
|---|---|
| *TO:* | Georgia Wilson, CFO |
| *FROM:* | Cameron West |
| *SUBJECT:* | Outsourcing CD production |

In 2006, total production and packaging costs were $5,200,000 or $2.60 per CD. The low cost outside bidder for this business was RTS. They are a highly respected firm, and their offer is $2.50 per CD. Although the savings related to outsourcing is only $0.10 per CD, with annual production of 2,000,000 units, this amounts to $200,000 per year. The present value with a five-year horizon and a 10-percent cost of capital is $758,157. Thus, I recommend that we outsource CD production.

You asked me to determine the selling price of the production equipment. I had a representative of RTS walk through the facility. In his opinion, the equipment is dated, and he believes that the market value is essentially zero. At any rate, his company is not interested in purchasing the equipment even if we select them as a supplier.

If we outsource, I do not believe that we can use the production facility for another purpose. As you know, the building is run down, and it's not a suitable space even for programmers!

Finally, I want to mention another aspect of the problem that enhances the appeal of outsourcing. We currently have equipment with a book value of $1,500,000 and an average remaining life of five years. This generates approximately $300,000 per year of depreciation. If we outsource, we'll have a $1,500,000 tax loss, which will save us approximately $525,000 (assuming a 35-percent tax rate). Thus, the total value of outsourcing is $1,283,157 (i.e., $758,157 + $525,000).

Please call me if you have any questions regarding my analysis.

# chapter 10

## LEARNING OBJECTIVES

**1** Discuss the use of budgets in planning and control.

**2** Prepare the budget schedules that make up the master budget.

**3** Explain why flexible budgets are needed for performance evaluation.

**4** Discuss the conflict between the planning and control uses of budgets.

# BUDGETARY PLANNING AND CONTROL

Preston Joystick produces a joystick that is the top choice for many serious game players. At a meeting of key managers, Alan Renton, president of Preston Joystick, reviewed the past successes and failures of his firm. "As you know," he concluded, "we've begun a new marketing campaign, and I am confident that next year sales will increase by at least 20 percent." Jack North, the production manager, seemed caught off guard by this good news. "Look, Alan," he said, "if you really think sales are going to take off, we've got to plan for the increase. I'll have to hire additional workers, and the people in purchasing will need to buy more parts so we don't run out." Pam Smith, Vice President of Finance, chimed in, "Also, more sales means more inventory, and more inventory means we'll have to borrow additional funds to finance the expansion. I'll need some lead time to arrange the loan."

The meeting ended with everyone agreeing that more attention should be devoted to planning company activities. Alan went back to his office

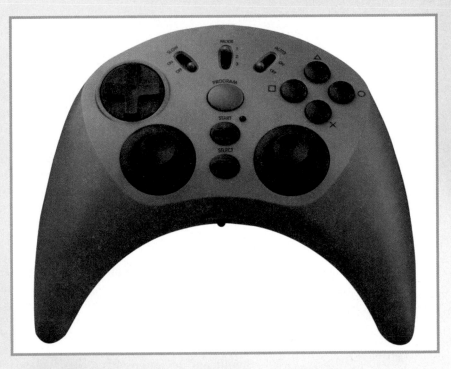

convinced that without a plan to guide and coordinate company activities, the coming year would be a series of near disasters. "The marketing, production, and finance people need to know what is anticipated so we can operate effectively and efficiently," he concluded.

In business, **budgets** are the formal documents that quantify a company's plans for achieving its goals. The entire planning and control process of many companies is built around budgets. This chapter illustrates the preparation of several budgets that are in common use. The chapter also describes the role of budgets in the performance evaluation process and discusses a number of issues associated with budgets.

Discuss the use of budgets in planning and control.

# USE OF BUDGETS IN PLANNING AND CONTROL

At companies from Microsoft to Marriott, from Wal-Mart to Wendy's, budgets are a high priority. As mentioned, the entire planning and control process of many companies is built around budgets. This section describes how budgets are used in planning and control

## PLANNING

Budgets are useful in the planning process because they enhance *communication* and *coordination*. The process of developing a formal plan—that is, a budget—forces managers to consider carefully their goals and objectives and to specify means of achieving them. Budgets become the vehicle for communicating information about where the company is heading, and they aid coordination of managers' activities. For example, the marketing department may prepare a budget that includes estimates of sales for each month of a future year. The production department may use the information contained in this budget to schedule workers and material deliveries. Thus, the necessary coordination of product sales and product production is achieved.

## CONTROL

Budgets are useful in the control process because they provide a basis for *evaluating performance*. To control a company—to make sure it is heading in the proper direction and operating efficiently—it is essential to assess the performance of managers and the operations for which they are responsible. Often, performance evaluation is carried out by comparing actual performance with planned or budgeted performance.

Significant deviations from planned performance are associated with three potential causes.

1. **It is possible that the plan or budget was poorly conceived.** If a budget is not carefully developed, it should not be surprising that actual results are different from planned results.

2. **It is possible that although the budget was carefully developed, conditions have changed.** For example, if the economy were to take a sudden downturn, actual sales might be less than budgeted sales.

3. **It is possible that managers have done a particularly good or poor job managing operations.** If this is the case, the managers will be rewarded for good performance (e.g., given a bonus or a promotion) or punished for poor performance (e.g., given reduced responsibility or even fired).

**You Get What You Measure**

A graphic presentation of the role of budgets in the planning and control process appears in Illustration 10-1. As you study this illustration, remember that **you get what you measure**! This idea is central to an understanding of the control process. If managers know that their performance will be evaluated with respect to the budget, they are likely to work especially hard to achieve budgeted goals. Thus, it is critical that the budgeted goals be well thought out and clearly communicated to managers.

**Illustration 10-1**
Role of budgets in planning and control process

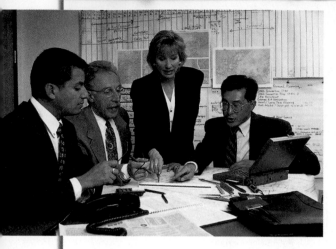

### CEOs Say Budgeting Is the CFO's Major Responsibility

Heidrick & Struggles, an executive search firm, surveyed the chief executive officers (CEOs) of the Fortune 1000 firms and asked them a number of questions regarding what they look for in a chief financial officer (CFO). The CEOs want the CFO to be an analytical thinker, a strategic partner, and a leader. Also, the CFO must be objective and creative and must communicate effectively. When asked to name the CFO's major finance duty, most respondents identified budgeting and planning as the key responsibility. Contributing to mergers and acquisitions, accounting and control, and investor relations were also noted as key qualities.

*Source:* "Measuring Up: CEO's Evaluation of Their Chief Financial Officers," *Financial Executive*, November 1, 1998.

# DEVELOPING THE BUDGET

Budgets are prepared for departments, for divisions of a company, and for the company as a whole. Often, the group within a company that is responsible for approval of the various budgets is the **budget committee**. This committee consists of senior managers, including the president, the chief financial officer, the vice president for operations, and the controller. Typically, the budget committee works with departments to develop realistic plans that are consistent with overall company goals. In some cases, however, the budget committee may impose a budget without soliciting input from department managers.

The extent to which departments are consulted relates to the distinction between top-down and bottom-up approaches to the development of a budget. In a top-down approach, budgets are developed at higher organizational levels without substantial input from lower level managers. In a bottom-up approach, lower-level managers are the primary source of information used in setting the budget. Most managers believe a successful budgeting process requires a bottom-up approach. After all, lower-level managers often have the best information regarding business conditions affecting their departments. If this is the case, their input is critical in developing realistic financial plans.

## BUDGET TIME PERIOD

Before a budget can be prepared, managers must decide on an appropriate budget period. A company may prepare budgets for a variety of time periods, depending on its needs. In some cases, long-run budgets are prepared for a 3-year or even a 5-year period. Short-run budgets may cover a month, a quarter, or a year. Generally, the longer the time period, the less detailed the budget.

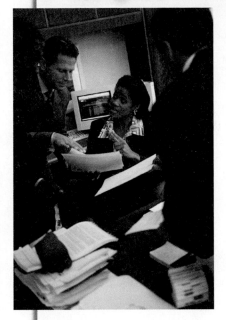

**LINK TO PRACTICE**

### Sometimes a Bottom-Up Approach Is Still Top Down!

Here's how a business unit manager describes the budgeting approach at a $30 billion U.S. bank.

"This past year the budgeting process wasn't so bad. We changed to top-down so there wasn't much work to do. They told us our number and we entered it. Of course, who knows if we can meet our target; it's not like we were involved in setting it. The year before was really painful. We did a bottom-up plan. So we worked really hard to figure out what we could deliver the following year. We started summarizing the plan up the organization and then the CEO and CFO started pushing back. Increase this and that; deliver more; iteration after iteration. Finally they told us the numbers they wanted us to use and we plugged them in. This year we eliminated the pain and wound up in the same place. Except it's still not our plan!"

*Source:* Nolan, G., "The End of Traditional Budgeting," *Bank Accounting and Finance*, Summer 1998.

## ZERO BASE BUDGETING

A common starting point in developing a budget is a consideration of the costs and revenues of the previous period. These amounts are adjusted up or down based on current information and assumptions or estimates of what will happen in the future. However, this approach may *not* lead to a fresh consideration of activities.

So called **zero base budgeting** is a method of budget preparation that requires budgeted amounts to be justified by each department at the start of each budget period, even if the amounts were supported in prior budget periods. That is, managers must start from zero in developing their budgets. This results in a fresh consideration of the validity of budget amounts, but the technique is time-consuming and expensive. Although zero base budgeting has gained some support in governmental budgeting, it is not widely practiced by business enterprises.

LEARNING OBJECTIVE **2**

Prepare the budget schedules that make up the master budget.

## THE MASTER BUDGET

The **master budget** is a comprehensive planning document that incorporates a number of individual budgets. Typically, it includes budgets for sales, production, direct materials, direct labor, manufacturing overhead, selling and administrative expenses, capital acquisitions, and cash receipts and disbursements, as well as a budgeted income statement and a budgeted balance sheet.

**Illustration 10-2**
Relationships among various budgets that comprise the master budget

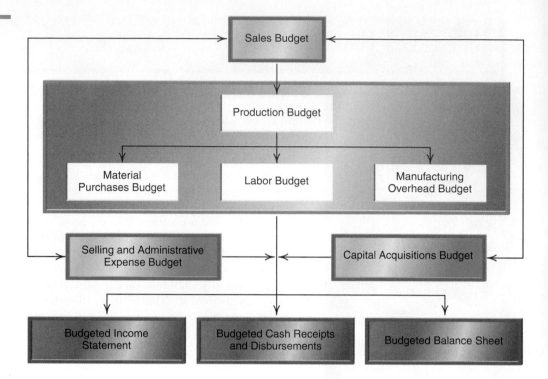

In this section, we present examples of each of these components of a master budget. For purposes of the example, budgetary information is prepared by quarter for Preston Joystick. As you will see, the various budgets are interrelated. In particular, the sales budget influences the production budget. The production budget, in turn, influences the material purchases budget, the direct labor budget, and the manufacturing overhead budget. The relationships among the various budgets are presented in Illustration 10-2.

## SALES BUDGET

The first step in the budget process involves preparation of sales forecasts and development of a sales budget. This budget comes first because other budgets cannot be prepared without an estimate of sales. For example, managers preparing the production budget must have an estimate of future sales before they can determine what level of production will be necessary to meet demand.

Companies use numerous methods to estimate sales. Very large companies may hire economists to prepare sales forecasts using sophisticated mathematical models that take into consideration the rate of inflation, national capital expenditures, and other economic data. Smaller companies may develop forecasts based on an analysis of the trend in their own sales data. Trade journals or magazines exist for almost every industry, and they may provide useful information for developing sales forecasts. Typically, these journals contain information on past industry sales. They may also make predictions about the growth of the industry. Sales personnel may be another good source of information for forecasting sales. Some companies periodically ask all of their salespersons to estimate sales in their territories for the coming year. These estimates may be highly accurate if

### Budget Process in Great Britain

In 2002, *Financial Director* (a business magazine) and Hyperion (a software company) conducted a survey of financial managers in Great Britain. Here are some of the major findings:

- Budget holders involved in preparing their budgets are more likely to take ownership of the results.
- Bottom-up budgeting is more common than "imposed" top-down budgets.
- The budget process is being completed much more quickly than four years ago.
- Large organizations believe that there is too little accountability when plans are not achieved.
- Half of the large companies surveyed believe there is some "game playing" in negotiating budgets.
- Large companies believe their budgets are too detailed.

*Source: Financial Director*, "Budgeting; More of the Same," November 1, 2002, p. 41.

the salespersons make their estimates based on a thorough knowledge of their customers' needs. In general, forecasts of sales are part science and part art. The forecasts of even the most sophisticated mathematical models are often adjusted based on the professional judgment of experienced managers.

Based on the trend of sales and taking into account a planned marketing campaign, Alan Renton, president of Preston Joystick, has predicted that unit sales will increase by 20 percent in the coming year. Sales personnel generally agree that this level of increase is realistic provided the company maintains a price per unit of $45. Accordingly, the company budgeted sales for each quarter simply by increasing prior year sales in units by 20 percent. The result is the sales budget presented in Illustration 10-3.

**Illustration 10-3**
Sales budget

**Preston Joystick**

|  | Sales Budget for the Year Ending December 31, 2006 | | | | |
| --- | --- | --- | --- | --- | --- |
|  | First Quarter | Second Quarter | Third Quarter | Fourth Quarter | Year |
| Prior year sales in units | 17,500 | 20,833 | 19,167 | 18,333 | 75,833 |
| Projected sales at 120% of prior year | 21,000 | 25,000 | 23,000 | 22,000 | 91,000 |
| Sales price per unit | $ 45 | $ 45 | $ 45 | $ 45 | $ 45 |
| Budgeted sales revenue | $945,000 | $1,125,000 | $1,035,000 | $990,000 | $4,095,000 |

## PRODUCTION BUDGET

Once the sales budget has been prepared, the production budget can be developed. In deciding how much to produce, managers must take into account how much they expect to sell, how much is in beginning inventory, and how much they want in ending inventory.[1]

The quantity that must be produced can be calculated from the following formula.

$$
\begin{array}{ccccc}
\text{Finished} & & \text{Expected} & \text{Desired} & \text{Beginning} \\
\text{units to be} & = & \text{sales in} & + \text{ending inventory} & - \text{inventory of} \\
\text{produced} & & \text{units} & \text{of finished units} & \text{finished units}
\end{array}
$$

Preston Joystick would like the ending inventory of finished goods to be equal to 10 percent of next quarter's sales. In the first quarter, Preston estimates that 21,000 units will be sold; 2,500 units are needed in ending inventory (i.e., 10 percent of 25,000 units expected to be sold in the second quarter). Thus, a total of 23,500 units are required. However, the company has 2,100 units in beginning inventory, so only 21,400 units must be produced. The production budget for Preston Joystick is presented in Illustration 10-4.

## DIRECT MATERIAL PURCHASE BUDGET

The amount of direct materials that must be purchased depends on the amount needed for production and the amount needed for ending inventory. Obviously, a company needs some direct materials on hand at the end of the period for use in production at the start of the subsequent period (although, as explained in Chapter 2, the amount would be small in a just-in-time environment). The amount that must be purchased can be calculated from the following formula.

$$
\begin{array}{ccccc}
\text{Required} & & \text{Amount} & \text{Desired ending} & \text{Beginning} \\
\text{purchases of} & = & \text{required for} & + \text{inventory of} & - \text{inventory of} \\
\text{direct materials} & & \text{production} & \text{direct materials} & \text{direct materials}
\end{array}
$$

**Illustration 10-4**
Production budget

**Preston Joystick**

**Production Budget**
**for the Year Ending December 31, 2006**

| | First Quarter | Second Quarter | Third Quarter | Fourth Quarter | Year |
|---|---|---|---|---|---|
| Unit sales[a] | 21,000 | 25,000 | 23,000 | 22,000 | 91,000 |
| Plus desired ending inventory of finished units[b] | 2,500 | 2,300 | 2,200 | 2,400[c] | 2,400 |
| Total needed | 23,500 | 27,300 | 25,200 | 24,400 | 93,400 |
| Less beginning inventory of finished units | 2,100 | 2,500 | 2,300 | 2,200 | 2,100 |
| Units to be produced | 21,400 | 24,800 | 22,900 | 22,200 | 91,300 |

[a]Information from sales budget in Illustration 10-3.
[b]Equals 10 percent of next quarter's sales.
[c]Based on estimate of sales in the first quarter of the following year.

---

[1]Preston Joystick does not have a significant amount of work-in-process inventory. Thus, we do not need to take work-in-process into account in our calculations of anticipated production.

**Illustration 10-5**
Direct material purchases
budget

**Preston Joystick**

### Direct Material Purchases Budget
### for the Year Ending December 31, 2006

| | First Quarter | Second Quarter | Third Quarter | Fourth Quarter | Year |
|---|---|---|---|---|---|
| Units to be produced[a] | 21,400 | 24,800 | 22,900 | 22,200 | 91,300 |
| Cost of parts per unit | $ 6 | $ 6 | $ 6 | $ 6 | $ 6 |
| Cost of parts needed for production | $128,400 | $148,800 | $137,400 | $133,200 | $547,800 |
| Plus desired ending inventory of parts[b] | 14,880 | 13,740 | 13,320 | 14,700[c] | 14,700 |
| Total needed | 143,280 | 162,540 | 150,720 | 147,900 | 562,500 |
| Less beginning inventory of parts | 12,840 | 14,880 | 13,740 | 13,320 | 12,840 |
| Cost of purchases | $130,440 | 147,660 | $136,980 | $134,580 | $549,660 |

[a]Information from production budget in Illustration 10-4.
[b]Equals 10 percent of parts required for next quarter's production.
[c]Based on estimate of parts required for production in the first quarter of next year.

Preston Joystick has established a policy of maintaining direct materials inventory equal to 10 percent of the amount required for production in the subsequent quarter. In the first quarter, the company plans on producing 21,400 units. Each unit requires parts costing $6. In addition, $14,880 of parts must be on hand at the end of the quarter (i.e., 10 percent of the amount required for next quarter's production) but $12,840 of parts are on hand at the start of the quarter. Thus, $130,440 of parts must be purchased in the first quarter. This information is presented in the purchases budget, Illustration 10-5.

## DIRECT LABOR BUDGET

The direct labor budget for Preston Joystick presents direct labor cost by quarter. Direct labor cost is calculated by multiplying the number of units produced each quarter by the labor hours per unit and the rate per hour. In the first quarter, the company expects to produce 21,400 units, and 1 labor hour per unit is required. At a rate of $15 per labor hour, this amounts to $321,000. Preston estimates that, on average, each employee works 480 hours per quarter. This information can be used to estimate the approximate number of employees needed each quarter. In the first quarter, 21,400 labor hours are required. Since an average employee works 480 hours per quarter, approximately 45 employees will be needed for production. The direct labor budget for Preston Joystick is presented in Illustration 10-6.

Note that the direct labor budget indicates that 52 employees are needed in the second quarter, whereas only 45 are needed in the first quarter. With this information, the company may decide to adjust its production plans to keep employment stable. If new employees are hired in the second quarter, operations may not be efficient. And if several of these employees are fired in the third quarter, when only 48 employees are needed, morale may suffer. A better idea may be to hire part-time workers or have full-time employees work overtime.

**Illustration 10-6**
Direct labor budget

**Preston Joystick**

**Direct Labor Budget**
**for the Year Ending December 31, 2006**

| | First Quarter | Second Quarter | Third Quarter | Fourth Quarter | Year |
|---|---|---|---|---|---|
| Direct labor hours per unit | 1.0 | 1.0 | 1.0 | 1.0 | 1.0 |
| Labor rate per hour | $ 15 | $ 15 | $ 15 | $ 15 | $ 15 |
| Direct labor cost per unit | 15 | 15 | 15 | 15 | 15 |
| Units to be produced$^a$ | 21,400 | 24,800 | 22,900 | 22,200 | 91,300 |
| Direct labor cost | $321,000 | $372,000 | $343,500 | $333,000 | $1,369,500 |
| Total hours | 21,400 | 24,800 | 22,900 | 22,200 | |
| Average hours per quarter per employee | 480 | 480 | 480 | 480 | |
| Approximate number of employees needed | 45 | 52 | 48 | 46 | |

$^a$Information from production budget in Illustration 10-4.

## MANUFACTURING OVERHEAD BUDGET

Preston Joystick separates variable and fixed costs in the budget for manufacturing overhead. The cost per unit of production of each variable cost item is multiplied by the quantity produced each quarter. The fixed costs are identical each quarter except for the amount of depreciation. This cost increases in the third and fourth quarters because of planned acquisitions of equipment that increase the level of depreciation.

The manufacturing overhead budget is presented in Illustration 10-7. Note that in the budget, we subtract depreciation from total overhead to determine the amount of cash paid out for overhead each quarter. This information will be used when we prepare the budget for cash receipts and disbursements.

## SELLING AND ADMINISTRATIVE EXPENSE BUDGET

To this point, we have presented only the sales budget and production-related budgets. However, budget information is also needed for selling and administrative expenses. Preston Joystick estimates that these expenses are all fixed. The 2006 selling and administrative expense budget is presented in Illustration 10-8.

## BUDGETED INCOME STATEMENT

Much of the information contained in the budgets already described is utilized in the preparation of a *budgeted income statement*. This budget is presented in Illustration 10-9. As you can see, the sales figures come directly from the sales budget (Illustration 10-3). Cost of goods sold requires a calculation of the unit cost of production. The direct material budget indicates that material cost is $6 per unit (Illustration 10-5). The direct labor budget indicates that direct labor is $15 per

**Illustration 10-7**
Manufacturing overhead
budget

| | First Quarter | Second Quarter | Third Quarter | Fourth Quarter | Year |
|---|---|---|---|---|---|
| **Manufacturing Overhead Budget for the Year Ending December 31, 2006** | | | | | |
| Units to be produced[a] | 21,400 | 24,800 | 22,900 | 22,200 | 91,300 |
| Variable costs: | | | | | |
|   Indirect material ($2/unit) | $ 42,800 | $ 49,600 | $ 45,800 | $ 44,400 | $182,600 |
|   Indirect labor ($1.50 per unit) | 32,100 | 37,200 | 34,350 | 33,300 | 136,950 |
|   Other variable costs ($1.00 per unit) | 21,400 | 24,800 | 22,900 | 22,200 | 91,300 |
| Total variable overhead | 96,300 | 111,600 | 103,050 | 99,900 | 410,850 |
| Fixed costs: | | | | | |
|   Supervisory salaries | 90,000 | 90,000 | 90,000 | 90,000 | 360,000 |
|   Depreciation of plant and equipment[b] | 20,000 | 20,000 | 26,000 | 28,000 | 94,000 |
|   Other | 5,000 | 5,000 | 5,000 | 5,000 | 20,000 |
| Total fixed overhead | 115,000 | 115,000 | 121,000 | 123,000 | 474,000 |
| Total overhead | $211,300 | $226,600 | $224,050 | $222,900 | $884,850 |
| Less depreciation | 20,000 | 20,000 | 26,000 | 28,000 | 94,000 |
| Cash payments for overhead | $191,300 | $206,600 | $198,050 | $194,900 | $790,850 |

Estimated overhead rate = annual overhead ÷ annual production = $884,850 ÷ 91,300 = $9.69 per unit

[a]Information from production budget, Illustration 10-4.
[b]Increase in third and fourth quarter due to acquisition of additional equipment. See capital acquisition budget in Illustration 10-10.

**Illustration 10-8**
Selling and administrative
expense budget

| | First Quarter | Second Quarter | Third Quarter | Fourth Quarter | Year |
|---|---|---|---|---|---|
| **Selling and Administrative Expense Budget for the Year Ending December 31, 2006** | | | | | |
| Salaries | $160,000 | $160,000 | $160,000 | $160,000 | $ 640,000 |
| Advertising | 70,000 | 70,000 | 70,000 | 70,000 | 280,000 |
| Depreciation of office equipment | 5,000 | 5,000 | 5,000 | 5,000 | 20,000 |
| Other | 15,000 | 15,000 | 15,000 | 15,000 | 60,000 |
| Total | $250,000 | $250,000 | $250,000 | $250,000 | $1,000,000 |
| Less depreciation | 5,000 | 5,000 | 5,000 | 5,000 | 20,000 |
| Cash disbursements for selling and administrative expense | $245,000 | $245,000 | $245,000 | $245,000 | $ 980,000 |

**Illustration 10-9**
Budgeted income
statement

**Preston Joystick**

**Budgeted Income Statement**
**for the Year Ending December 31, 2006**

|  | First Quarter | Second Quarter | Third Quarter | Fourth Quarter | Year |
|---|---|---|---|---|---|
| Sales[a] | $945,000 | $1,125,000 | $1,035,000 | $990,000 | $4,095,000 |
| Less cost of goods sold[b] | 644,490 | 767,250 | 705,870 | 675,180 | 2,792,790 |
| Gross margin | 300,510 | 357,750 | 329,130 | 314,820 | 1,302,210 |
| Less selling and administrative expenses[c] | 250,000 | 250,000 | 250,000 | 250,000 | 1,000,000 |
| Net income | $ 50,510 | $ 107,750 | $ 79,130 | $ 64,820 | $ 302,210 |

[a]Information per sales budget, Illustration 10-3.
[b]First quarter calculation is: 21,000 units × $30.69 = $644,490.
[c]Information per selling and administrative expense budget in Illustration 10-8.

unit. And the manufacturing overhead budget indicates that manufacturing overhead is $9.69 per unit. Thus, the unit cost of production is $30.69.

| Direct materials | $ 6.00 (Illustration 10-5) |
|---|---|
| Direct labor | 15.00 (Illustration 10-6) |
| Manufacturing overhead | 9.69 (Illustration 10-7) |
| Total | $30.69 per unit |

Management should carefully consider the budgeted income statement to make sure that anticipated profit is consistent with company goals. If budgeted profit is less than the amount management considers satisfactory, steps may be taken to increase sales and reduce costs. Perhaps the advertising campaign can be expanded to further increase sales. Or perhaps material costs can be reduced through negotiations with suppliers. If management decides to take steps to increase profit, then the previous budgets will need to be adjusted to reflect the anticipated changes.

## CAPITAL ACQUISITIONS BUDGET

Acquisitions of capital assets (property, plant, and equipment) must be carefully planned, in part because they may substantially reduce cash reserves. The budget for capital assets is referred to as the *capital acquisitions budget*. Preston Joystick anticipates purchases of office equipment and machinery during the coming year, and this is reflected in the capital acquisitions budget presented in Illustration 10-10.

## CASH RECEIPTS AND DISBURSEMENTS BUDGET

In the cash receipts and disbursements budget, managers plan the amount and timing of cash flows. The information in this budget is a necessary supplement to the information presented in the budgeted income statement. It is quite possible for a company to project a substantial amount of net income and still face finan-

**Illustration 10-10**
Capital acquisitions
budget

**Preston Joystick**

**Capital Acquisitions Budget**
**for the Year Ending December 31, 2006**

| | First Quarter | Second Quarter | Third Quarter | Fourth Quarter | Year |
|---|---|---|---|---|---|
| Office equipment (5-year life) | $10,000 | — | — | — | $ 10,000 |
| Machinery (5-year life) | — | — | $120,000[a] | $40,000[b] | $160,000 |
| Total | $10,000 | — | $120,000 | $40,000 | $170,000 |

[a]Increases depreciation by $6,000 in third quarter [i.e., ($120,000 ÷ 5 year life) × 1/4 for third quarter]. See manufacturing overhead budget in Illustration 10-7.
[b]Increases depreciation by $2,000 in fourth quarter [i.e., ($40,000 ÷ 5 year life) × 1/4 for fourth quarter]. See manufacturing overhead budget in Illustration 10-7.

cial distress because its entire set of plans imply more cash outflows than cash inflows. For example, a considerable amount of income may be recognized when a major sale is made. However, the cash received in payment for the sale may not arrive for many months. Or consider a company that makes a major equipment purchase. Although cash reserves may be reduced immediately by the *total* cost of the equipment, current period income will only be reduced by a *fraction* of the cost of the equipment (i.e., by the amount of depreciation). By carefully planning cash receipts and disbursements, companies can anticipate cash shortages and arrange to borrow funds to enhance their cash positions. Or if cash surpluses are anticipated, companies can seek additional investment opportunities or consider paying higher dividends to shareholders.

To prepare an estimate of cash collections, management must determine the percent of credit sales revenue that is collected in the period of sale and the percent collected in the subsequent period. The percentages can usually be estimated based on past collection experience. Preston Joystick has only credit sales. Fifty percent of the sales revenue is collected in the quarter of sale and 50 percent is collected in the next quarter.

To prepare an estimate of cash disbursements, management must determine the percent of material purchases that is paid in the period of purchase and the percent that is paid in the subsequent period. Preston Joystick determines that 70 percent is paid in the quarter of purchase and 30 percent is paid in the subsequent quarter. The company has determined that, for practical purposes, all other disbursements are made in the quarter in which the related cost is incurred.

In preparing a cash receipts and disbursements budget, it is important to remember that some expenses do not require cash outlays. For example, depreciation is part of manufacturing overhead, but it does not require a current outlay of cash. Cash is disbursed when an asset is purchased, not when depreciation is recorded. Another example of a non-cash expense is the amortization of prepaid insurance. Cash is disbursed when the insurance is purchased, not when the expense is recognized through the amortization of prepaid insurance.

In the cash receipts and disbursements budget for Preston Joystick, Illustration 10-11, note that cash disbursed for manufacturing overhead in the first quarter is only $191,300. This is $20,000 less than the $211,300 of overhead cost planned for the first quarter in the manufacturing overhead budget, Illustration 10-7. The $20,000 is the amount of depreciation in the first quarter.

As indicated in the illustration, the anticipated cash flows fluctuate significantly from quarter to quarter. The result is that at the end of the first quarter, the cash balance is expected to be only $28,147, whereas the cash balance at the end

**Illustration 10-11**
Cash receipts and
disbursements budget

**Preston Joystick**

**Cash Receipts and Disbursements Budget**
**for the Year Ending December 31, 2006**

| | First Quarter | Second Quarter | Third Quarter | Fourth Quarter | Year |
|---|---|---|---|---|---|
| Cash receipts | | | | | |
| Collection of credit sales[a] | | | | | |
| 4th quarter prior year | $430,435 | | | | $ 430,435 |
| 1st quarter ($945,000) | 472,500 | $ 472,500 | | | 945,000 |
| 2nd quarter ($1,125,000) | | 562,500 | $ 562,500 | | 1,125,000 |
| 3rd quarter ($1,035,000) | | | 517,500 | $ 517,500 | 1,035,000 |
| 4th quarter ($990,000) | | | | 495,000 | 495,000 |
| | 902,935 | 1,035,000 | 1,080,000 | 1,012,500 | 4,030,435 |
| Cash disbursements | | | | | |
| Purchases of materials[b] | | | | | |
| 4th quarter prior year | 36,180 | | | | 36,180 |
| 1st quarter ($130,440) | 91,308 | 39,132 | | | 130,440 |
| 2nd quarter ($147,660) | | 103,362 | 44,298 | | 147,660 |
| 3rd quarter ($136,980) | | | 95,886 | 41,094 | 136,980 |
| 4th quarter | | | | 94,206 | 94,206 |
| Total disbursement for purchases | 127,488 | 142,494 | 140,184 | 135,300 | 545,466 |
| Payment for direct labor[c] | 321,000 | 372,000 | 343,500 | 333,000 | 1,369,500 |
| Payment for manufacturing overhead[d] | 191,300 | 206,600 | 198,050 | 194,900 | 790,850 |
| Payment for sell. & adm. expense[e] | 245,000 | 245,000 | 245,000 | 245,000 | 980,000 |
| Capital acquisitions[f] | 10,000 | | 120,000 | 40,000 | 170,000 |
| Total cash disbursements | 894,788 | 966,094 | 1,046,734 | 948,200 | 3,855,816 |
| Excess of receipts over disbursements | 8,147 | 68,906 | 33,266 | 64,300 | 174,619 |
| Plus beginning cash balance | 20,000 | 28,147 | 97,053 | 130,319 | 20,000 |
| Ending cash balance | $ 28,147 | $ 97,053 | $ 130,319 | $ 194,619 | $ 194,619 |

[a]See Illustration 10-3 for sales information; 50% collected in quarter of sale and 50% collected in subsequent quarter.
[b]See Illustration 10-5 for purchase information; 70% paid in quarter of purchase and 30% paid in subsequent quarter.
[c]See Illustration 10-6 for labor cost information.
[d]Does not include depreciation indicated in manufacturing overhead budget (Illustration 10-7), since depreciation does not require a cash outlay.
[e]Does not include depreciation indicated in selling and administrative expense budget (Illustration 10-8), since depreciation does not require a cash outlay.
[f]See capital acquisitions budget (Illustration 10-10).

of the fourth quarter is expected to be $194,619. Obviously, a low cash balance is dangerous because the company may not have enough funds to pay employees and suppliers. Thus, Preston Joystick may wish to consider borrowing money to improve the cash position in the first quarter. The cash budget alerts management to such potential problems well in advance. This gives management sufficient time to arrange a loan on favorable terms. As the budget indicates, the loan can easily be repaid in the fourth quarter when cash reserves are high.

Excessively large cash balances should generally be avoided, because they earn little if any interest. If a company is building up financial reserves for expansion (purchasing a major piece of equipment or even another company), excess cash will generally be invested in low-risk, highly marketable securities. If the company is not building up reserves to expand, the excess cash may be distributed to shareholders as dividends.

## BUDGETED BALANCE SHEET

The last component of the master budget that we consider is the *budgeted balance sheet*. This budget is simply a planned balance sheet (sometimes called a pro forma balance sheet). Managers can use this budget to assess the effect of their planned decisions on the future financial position of the firm. The budgeted balance sheet for Preston Joystick is presented in Illustration 10-12.

**Illustration 10-12**
Budgeted balance sheet

**Preston Joystick**

### Budgeted Balance Sheet
### December 31, 2006

| | |
|---|---:|
| Current Assets | |
| Cash[a] | $ 194,619 |
| Accounts receivable[b] | 495,000 |
| Raw material inventory[c] | 14,700 |
| Finished goods inventory[d] | 73,656 |
| Property, plant and equipment (net) | 620,000 |
| Total assets | $1,397,975 |
| | |
| Current Liabilities | |
| Accounts payable[e] | $40,374 |
| Stockholders' Equity | |
| Common stock | 906,456 |
| Retained earnings | 451,145 |
| Total liabilities and stockholders' equity | $1,397,975 |

[a]Ending balance per cash receipts and disbursements budget (Illustration 10-10).
[b]50% of 4th quarter sales not yet collected per cash receipts and disbursements budget (Illustration 10-10).
[c]See direct material purchases budget in Illustration 10-5.
[d]Per the production budget (Illustration 10-3), 2,400 units of finished goods are required. The cost per unit is $30.69 ($6 of direct material per Illustration 10-5; $15 of direct labor per Illustration 10-6; and $9.69 of manufacturing overhead per Illustration 10-7).
[e]30% of 4th-quarter purchases of materials not yet paid per cash receipts and disbursements budget (Illustration 10-10).

# USE OF COMPUTERS IN THE BUDGET PLANNING PROCESS

The budget committee may review a budget and decide that it is inconsistent with company goals. This conclusion may lead managers to explore a variety of actions that affect future costs and revenues. If the managers decide to make changes, then they must also revise the budget. Since budgets are highly interdependent, a change in one can affect several others.

Computers are very useful in this situation. Most companies that use budgets define the budget relationships in a computer model using a spreadsheet program such as Excel® or a custom program specifically designed for them. With computerized budget information, an item in a budget can be changed, and the computer

## LINK TO PRACTICE

### *Software for Budgeting*

SRC Software is a market leader in enterprise-wide budgeting applications. Its product, Budget Advisor™ provides the following useful features:

- User-definable layouts and formats for different department types.
- Scenario management capability to conduct "what if" analyses.
- Allows for consolidation of multiple companies and multiple sites in the budget
- Intuitive spreadsheet interface
- Robust security over access to the budget
- Easily integrated with existing general ledger software

Check out the company's Web site if you would like to know more about this product and the use of software in budgeting: ⟨http://www.srcsoftware.com/⟩

| | Account Description | Red Flag | Last Year Actual | Cur Year Budget | YTD Actual Aug-03 | Cur Year Remainder | Cur Year Projected | Next Year Budget | Var $ | Va |
|---|---|---|---|---|---|---|---|---|---|---|
| | | | | | Annualized E | 50% | | | | |
| | **Units** | | | | | | | | | |
| 1400000 | Total Units Sold | | 10,311 | 9,838 | 7,649 | 4,254 | 11,903 | 12,164 | 260 | |
| | **Wages & Benefits** | | | | | | | | | |
| 602000 | Wages: Hourly Staff | ! | 171,170 | 175,928 | 100,876 | 50,438 | 151,314 | 192,771 | 41,457 | |
| 603000 | Wages: Salaried Staff | | 134,907 | 143,002 | 100,502 | 50,251 | 150,753 | 175,485 | 24,733 | |
| 610000 | Wages: Executive Staff | | 90,925 | 93,825 | 60,240 | 30,120 | 90,360 | 95,783 | 5,423 | |
| 620100 | Bonuses | ! | 19,670 | 20,363 | 6,039 | 3,019 | 9,058 | - | (9,058) | - |
| | Total Wages | | 416,671 | 433,118 | 267,656 | 133,828 | 401,484 | 464,039 | 62,555 | |
| 620200 | Paid Time Off | | 59,238 | 61,002 | 34,922 | 17,461 | 52,383 | 60,544 | 8,162 | |
| 620300 | Overtime Premium | | 22,522 | 22,895 | 12,693 | 6,347 | 19,040 | 18,000 | (1,040) | |
| 630100 | FICA | | 42,941 | 44,909 | 24,381 | 12,190 | 36,571 | 42,269 | 5,698 | |
| 630200 | FUTA | | 14,313 | 14,751 | 8,247 | 4,124 | 12,371 | 14,298 | 1,927 | |
| 630300 | SUTA | | 8,589 | 8,961 | 4,889 | 2,444 | 7,333 | 8,476 | 1,143 | |
| 631100 | Medical / Dental | | 8,809 | 9,201 | 5,996 | 2,998 | 8,994 | 11,229 | 2,235 | |
| | Payroll Taxes and Benefits | | 156,412 | 161,719 | 91,128 | 45,564 | 136,692 | 154,817 | 18,125 | |
| | **Payroll Recap** | | | | | | | | | |
| | Total Hours | | 24,387 | 25,858 | 16,840 | 8,420 | 25,260 | 29,494 | 4,234 | |

1110 - Miami - Sales Administration

Instructions / Summary / **Budget** / Payroll / Capital /

can recalculate that budget and any other budget affected by the change. Obviously, this results in a substantial savings in time and managerial effort.

"What if" analysis, discussed in Chapter 4, is also facilitated when budgets are prepared using a spreadsheet program. Suppose the management of Preston Joystick wants to know *what* the cash balance will be in the fourth quarter *if* sales in the first quarter are 22,000 instead of the 21,000 units budgeted. If all of the budgetary relationships have been properly specified in a spreadsheet, the answer can be found by simply changing the sales figure in the first-quarter sales budget from 21,000 to 22,000 and letting the computer recalculate the cash balance in the fourth-quarter cash receipts and disbursements budget.

# BUDGETARY CONTROL

Our discussion of the master budget and its components gave you some indication of how budgets are used in the planning process to communicate company goals and coordinate diverse activities. Budgets, as noted earlier, also facilitate *control* of operations. Next, we discuss that function in more detail.

## BUDGETS AS A STANDARD FOR EVALUATION

Budgets facilitate control by providing a standard for evaluation. The standard is the budgeted amount, against which actual results are compared. Differences between budgeted and actual amounts are referred to as **budget variances**, and reports that indicate budget variances are referred to as *performance reports*. If budgeted and actual costs are approximately equal, no action needs to be taken because results are consistent with management's expectations. However, if actual costs differ from budgeted costs by a material amount, management should launch an investigation to determine the cause of the difference.

How would performance be evaluated if budgets were not prepared? Most likely, actual performance in the current period would be compared with actual performance in the prior period. This is obviously an inferior approach, because conditions may change significantly from one period to the next, making a comparison of the two periods meaningless. For example, suppose Preston Joystick evaluates the performance of the marketing department by comparing sales in the current year with sales in the past year. Further, suppose sales in the prior year are 75,833 units and actual sales in the current year are 85,000 units. An evaluation of performance based on a comparison with the prior year would lead to a favorable evaluation of the marketing department, because sales are up by approximately 12 percent. However, senior managers at Preston anticipated that, given an expanded advertising campaign, the company should have sales of 91,000 units, a 20 percent increase that is reflected in the budget. A comparison of actual sales to budgeted sales indicates that rather than receiving a favorable evaluation, the marketing department should be asked to explain why actual sales are only 85,000 units instead of the 91,000 units forecasted.

## STATIC AND FLEXIBLE BUDGETS

In evaluating performance by using budgets, care must be taken to make sure that the level of activity used in the budget is equal to the *actual* level of activity. Let's consider an example to see why this is the case. Suppose the manager responsible for manufacturing overhead at Preston Joystick is evaluated at the end

Explain why flexible budgets are needed for performance evaluation.

**Illustration 10-13**
Performance evaluation
with a static budget

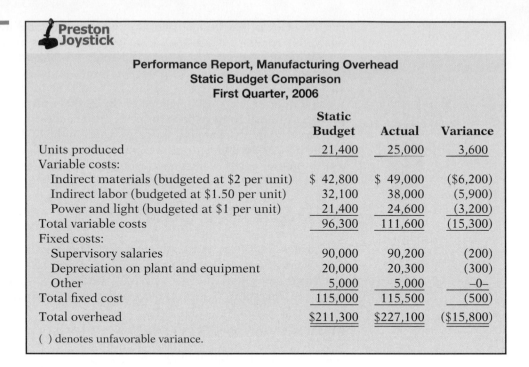

**Preston Joystick**

**Performance Report, Manufacturing Overhead**
**Static Budget Comparison**
**First Quarter, 2006**

|  | Static Budget | Actual | Variance |
|---|---|---|---|
| Units produced | 21,400 | 25,000 | 3,600 |
| Variable costs: |  |  |  |
|   Indirect materials (budgeted at $2 per unit) | $ 42,800 | $ 49,000 | ($6,200) |
|   Indirect labor (budgeted at $1.50 per unit) | 32,100 | 38,000 | (5,900) |
|   Power and light (budgeted at $1 per unit) | 21,400 | 24,600 | (3,200) |
| Total variable costs | 96,300 | 111,600 | (15,300) |
| Fixed costs: |  |  |  |
|   Supervisory salaries | 90,000 | 90,200 | (200) |
|   Depreciation on plant and equipment | 20,000 | 20,300 | (300) |
|   Other | 5,000 | 5,000 | –0– |
| Total fixed cost | 115,000 | 115,500 | (500) |
| Total overhead | $211,300 | $227,100 | ($15,800) |

( ) denotes unfavorable variance.

of the first quarter by comparing the actual level of overhead cost to the overhead costs budgeted at the start of the year. This comparison is presented in Illustration 10-13.

The analysis implies that the manager responsible for overhead costs has not done a good job of cost control. After all, total variable overhead costs are $15,300 higher than planned, and total fixed overhead costs are $500 higher than planned. However, note that actual production was 25,000 units, whereas planned production was only 21,400 units. The extra production may be due to an unexpected increase in sales necessitating increased production. With the increase in production, an increase in variable costs is expected. Fixed costs, however, would be expected to remain the same. Since changes in cost are expected when actual production is different from planned production, the analysis presented is not very useful for evaluating performance.

The budget presented in Illustration 10-13 is referred to as a **static budget** because it is not adjusted for the actual level of production. A more appropriate analysis of performance would make use of a **flexible budget**, which is a set of budget relationships that can be adjusted to various activity levels. Thus, flexible budgets take into account the fact that when production increases or decreases, variable costs change. Fixed costs, however, stay the same. Consider a company that anticipates variable production costs of $10 per unit and fixed production costs of $500,000. With this cost structure, flexible budgets for production levels of 20,000 units, 30,000 units, and 40,000 units can be prepared as in Illustration 10-14.

In Illustration 10-15, a flexible budget is used to evaluate the performance of the manager responsible for manufacturing overhead at Preston Joystick. Note that the variable costs are adjusted to the actual level of units produced. The fixed costs are at the same level as in the static budget, because they are not expected to change when production increases or decreases. Comparison of actual overhead

**Illustration 10-14**
Flexible budgets for
various production levels

| Flexible Budgets for Production Levels of 20,000, 30,000, and 40,000 Units | | | |
|---|---|---|---|
| Units produced | 20,000 | 30,000 | 40,000 |
| Variable costs ($10 per unit) | $200,000 | $300,000 | $400,000 |
| Fixed costs | 500,000 | 500,000 | 500,000 |
| Total | $700,000 | $800,000 | $900,000 |

**Illustration 10-15**
Performance evaluation
with a flexible budget

**Preston Joystick**

**Performance Report, Manufacturing Overhead**
**Flexible Budget Comparison**
**First Quarter, 2006**

| | Flexible Budget | Actual | Variance |
|---|---|---|---|
| Units produced | 25,000 | 25,000 | –0– |
| Variable costs: | | | |
| Indirect materials (budgeted at $2 per unit) | $ 50,000 | $ 49,000 | $1,000 |
| Indirect labor (budgeted at $1.50 per unit) | 37,500 | 38,000 | (500) |
| Power and light (budgeted at $1 per unit) | 25,000 | 24,600 | 400 |
| Total variable costs | 112,500 | 111,600 | $ 900 |
| Fixed costs: | | | |
| Supervisory salaries | 90,000 | 90,200 | (200) |
| Depreciation on plant and equipment | 20,000 | 20,300 | (300) |
| Other | 5,000 | 5,000 | –0– |
| Total fixed cost | 115,000 | 115,500 | (500) |
| Total overhead | $227,500 | $227,100 | $ 400 |

( ) denotes unfavorable variances.

costs with the overhead costs in a flexible budget is, potentially, more revealing about the manager's ability to control costs. Actual variable costs are $900 less than the *flexible* budget amount. This contrasts sharply with the $15,300 amount by which actual costs were greater than the *static* budget amount for variable costs. The variance with respect to fixed costs is still $500 more than budgeted—the same as in the static budget comparison.

# INVESTIGATING BUDGET VARIANCES

As noted at the beginning of the chapter, significant deviations from the budget (i.e., significant variances) may have three causes:

1. The budget may not have been well conceived.

2. Conditions may have changed.

3. Managers may have performed their jobs particularly well or poorly.

If the budget is not carefully developed with reasonable estimates of cost, it should not be surprising if actual costs are not equal to the budgeted amounts. In

## Any Questions?

**Q** The chapter provides an example of a "favorable" variance from the budget that is actually unfavorable from the standpoint of increasing shareholder value. Can there also be "unfavorable" variances that are associated with increasing shareholder value?

**A** It is quite possible that an "unfavorable" budget variance could be due to an action that increased shareholder value. Here's an example. Suppose a manager decides to spend much more on customer service than budgeted. But the outcome of the additional expenditures is that the company makes great strides in customer satisfaction and sales increase dramatically. In this case, there's an unfavorable variance but the action that generated the variance increased shareholder value.

this case budget variances should not be blamed on the manager responsible for meeting the budget.

Even if the budget is carefully developed, the company may nonetheless experience unforeseen and unavoidable price increases. As a result, the actual costs will be different from budgeted costs.

Finally, budget variances are sometimes due to inefficiencies resulting from poor management techniques or decisions. In this case, top management may adjust the compensation of the manager responsible for meeting the budget (e.g., reduce or eliminate his or her bonus compensation) and suggest ways the manager can improve the performance of his or her operation. In some cases it may even be necessary to fire a manager who is incapable of improving.

The cause of a variance cannot be determined without an investigation. However, because of the cost of investigation, it is not practical to investigate all budget variances. A **management by exception** approach is more economical. Under this approach, only exceptional variances are investigated. Generally, variances that are large in absolute dollars or relative to budgeted amounts are considered to be exceptional. It is important to point out that both exceptional "unfavorable" *and* exceptional "favorable" variances should be investigated. For example, in the preceding performance report (Illustration 10-13), there is a $1,000 "favorable" variance for indirect materials, indicating that actual costs are less than budgeted costs. This seems to indicate a favorable state of affairs. However, it is possible that cheap, low-quality materials are being used. This could result in substandard products that damage the reputation of the company.

Discuss the conflict between the planning and control uses of budgets.

# CONFLICT IN PLANNING AND CONTROL USES OF BUDGETS

As previously discussed, budgets are used for both planning and control. With respect to planning, they communicate company goals and help coordinate various activities. With respect to control, they focus the attention of managers on meeting or beating budget targets. This is because a manager's total compensation, including his or her bonus, may depend on meeting or beating budget targets.

Unfortunately, there is an inherent conflict when budgets are used for both planning and control. The result of the conflict is that managers may (1) pad their budgets and (2) shift income between periods to increase their compensation.[2] Both problems are discussed in the next section.

## WHY BUDGET-BASED COMPENSATION CAN LEAD TO BUDGET PADDING AND INCOME SHIFTING

Illustration 10-16 helps understanding of the two related problems. The illustration shows a common budget-based compensation scheme in which a manager receives a "hurdle" bonus once he or she hits a target that is commonly 80 percent of budgeted performance. (Here, the budget could be in sales dollars, units of output, profit, or some other performance measure. For our purposes, we will assume the performance measure is profit.) Performance better than 80 percent of budgeted profit results in additional "variable" bonus compensation until a cap is reached. This is commonly 120 percent of the budget. At this point no additional compensation is earned for the budget period under consideration.

Now, let's examine the two potential problems. Recall that managers who are evaluated with respect to a budget are likely to provide information used in setting it. This follows because they are likely to have better information about costs and revenues compared to their superiors. This leads to the first problem, which is that managers have an incentive to pad a budget and create budget **slack**—that is, a budget with targets that are easy to achieve. That's because the lower the budget target, the more likely it is that the managers will receive the hurdle bonus and the maximum variable bonus. Managers can create slack by lowering their forecasts of sales and increasing their forecasts of costs.

**Illustration 10-16**
Common budget-based compensation scheme

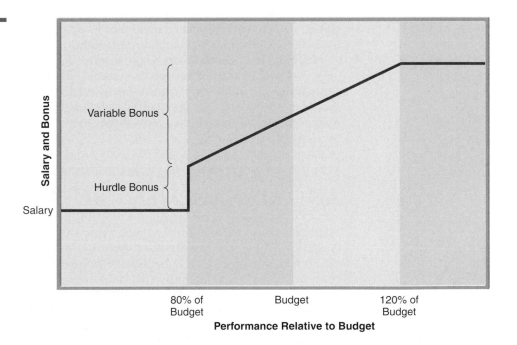

[2]The well known economist, Michael Jensen, has an excellent discussion of the two problems (and their solution) in his article "Corporate Budgeting Is Broken—Let's Fix It," *Harvard Business Review*, November 2001. Illustration 10-16 is taken from this article.

The second problem relates to the fact that managers who are evaluated with respect to the budget may have an incentive to shift income from one period to another. Consider a manager who estimates that it is unlikely he or she will meet the hurdle target. This manager has an incentive to shift income from a future period into the current period so that the hurdle target (80 percent of the budget) is reached and the hurdle bonus is received. This might be done by cutting back research and development expenditures in the current year and delaying them until a future year. Or, a manager could recognize revenue in the current year on goods that are not going to be shipped until the start of the next year. This latter option violates generally accepted accounting principles (GAAP) and is, most likely, illegal. But, the action has certainly been used over the years by a number of ethically challenged managers.

Now consider a manager who estimates that the performance of his or her business unit is likely to exceed 120 percent of the budget target. This manager has an incentive to shift income from the current period to a future period. The excess performance (performance in excess of 120 percent of the budget) won't help the manager's compensation since the bonus is capped once 120 percent of the budget is reached. The manager might delay shipments scheduled at year end so that revenue won't be recognized in the current period but will be recognized at the start of the next year when goods are finally shipped. The extra revenue in the next year will make achievement of the budget target in that year relatively easy.

A factor that deters both budget padding and income shifting is the chance of getting caught. There is always a chance that senior managers will detect that a lower level manager has padded a budget and punish this behavior by, for example, firing the manager. That certainly reduces the incentive to build in excessive budget slack. And with respect to income shifting, there is also a chance that it will be detected and punished by higher level managers. And, if the income shifting is illegal, penalties may be quite stiff indeed.

Perhaps the best that can be done to mitigate the conflict between the planning and control uses of budgets is to assure managers that their performance in comparison to the budget will be fairly evaluated and compensated. Managers should be confident that they will be allowed to comment on the real causes of budget variances and tell their side of the story.

# EVALUATION, MEASUREMENT, AND MANAGEMENT BEHAVIOR

**You Get What You Measure**

Managers pay close attention to those aspects of their jobs that are measured and evaluated. Thus, it is important to quantify in budgets key "success factors" for the company. Historically, budgets have primarily included dollar amounts. However, including some nonmonetary measures of performance in the budget is likely to be advantageous. For example, if a key aspect of a company's success is high-quality, defect-free products, it may be useful to budget the number of defects and the number of customer complaints at levels consistent with high quality. The actual number of defects and complaints can be compared with the budgeted quantities to evaluate performance. Or if a company is experiencing problems with employee absenteeism, it may be useful to budget an acceptable number of days missed and compare actual days missed with the target. Remember, **you get what you measure**!

# THE PRESTON JOYSTICK CASE REVISITED

At the start of the chapter, Alan Renton, president of Preston Joystick, noted that "The marketing, production, and financing people need to know what is anticipated so we can operate effectively and efficiently." How can Alan plan and coordinate the activities of his company?

As you know from reading the preceding material, the answer lies in developing budgets. Once a sales budget is produced, the production group can develop budgets for labor, material, and overhead that are consistent with the production level needed to meet expected sales. Once these budgets are produced, the finance group can prepare budgets that take into account the cash inflows and outflows anticipated in the sales and production budgets as well as the cash flows related to selling and administrative activities and capital acquisitions.

# MAKING BUSINESS DECISIONS

Budget-based compensation schemes can encourage budget padding (e.g., overestimation of expense and underestimation of revenue). But can this hurt decision making? Absolutely. Suppose a manager underestimates next year's sales so that his or her budgeted income target will be relatively easy to beat. Since the sales figures in the budget are used to prepare the production budget, it may be that production managers will fail to make optimal hiring and material acquisition decisions. The result could be needless overtime and more costly rush orders for materials when sales turn out to be higher than anticipated by the people in production.

## KNOWLEDGE AND SKILLS (K/S) CHECKLIST

*Knowledge and skills are needed to make good business decisions. Check off the knowledge and skills you've acquired from reading this chapter.*

❏ K/S 1. You have an expanded business vocabulary (see key terms).

❏ K/S 2. You can prepare the budget schedules that make up the master budget.

❏ K/S 3. You understand the difference between a static and a flexible budget.

❏ K/S 4. You know that budget-based compensation can lead to budget padding and income shifting.

❏ K/S 5. You know the causes of budget variances.

# SUMMARY OF LEARNING OBJECTIVES

**1** *Discuss the use of budgets in planning and control.* Budgets are useful in the planning process because they enhance communication and coordination. Budgets are also useful in the control process because they provide a standard for evaluating performance.

**2** *Prepare the budget schedules that make up the master budget.* The master budget is a comprehensive planning document and usually includes budgets for sales, production, direct materials, direct labor, manufacturing overhead, selling and administrative expenses, capital acquisitions, cash receipts and disbursements, a budgeted income statement, and a budgeted balance sheet. These budgets are highly interrelated in that the amounts presented in one budget may be dependent on the amounts in one or more other budgets.

**3** *Explain why flexible budgets are needed for performance evaluation.* In evaluating performance, flexible budgets should be used because they present amounts adjusted to the actual level of production. Comparing actual performance with a static budget is not very useful because variable costs are expected to differ from the budget if actual production is different from the production level indicated in the static budget.

**4** *Discuss the conflict between the planning and control uses of budgets.* The fact that budgets are used for both planning and performance evaluation presents a difficulty in that managers who participate in the development of their own budgets may tend to understate budgeted revenues and overstate budgeted expenses. The result is a budget that is easy to achieve and contains budget slack. Managers may also shift income from one budget period to the next to improve their chances of receiving the "hurdle bonus" and the maximum "variable bonus."

# REVIEW PROBLEM

The results of operations for the Jackson Manufacturing Company for the fourth quarter of 2005 were as follows (in thousands):

| | | |
|---|---:|---:|
| Sales | | $600,000 |
| Less variable cost of sales | | 240,000 |
| Contribution margin | | 360,000 |
| Less fixed production costs | $ 65,000 | |
| Less fixed selling and administrative expenses | 105,000 | 170,000 |
| Income before taxes | | 190,000 |
| Less taxes on income | | 76,000 |
| Net income | | $114,000 |

*Note:* Jackson Manufacturing uses the variable costing method. Thus, only variable production costs are included in inventory and cost of goods sold. Fixed production costs are charged to expense in the period incurred.

The company's balance sheet as of the end of the fourth quarter of 2005 was as follows (in thousands):

| | |
|---|---:|
| Cash | $200,000 |
| Accounts receivable | 120,000 |
| Inventory | 400,000 |
| Total current assets | 720,000 |
| Property, plant, and equipment | 200,000 |
| Less accumulated depreciation | (100,000) |
| Total assets | $820,000 |
| Accounts payable | $ 12,000 |
| Retained earnings | 208,000 |
| Common stock | 600,000 |
| Total liabilities and owners' equity | $820,000 |

Additional information:

1. Sales and variable costs of sales are expected to increase by 10 percent in the next quarter.
2. All sales are on credit with 80 percent collected in the quarter of sale and 20 percent collected in the following quarter.
3. Variable cost of sales consists of 50 percent materials, 30 percent direct labor, and 20 percent variable overhead. Materials are purchased on credit: 90 percent are paid for in the quarter of purchase and the remaining amount is paid for in the quarter after purchase. The inventory balance is not expected to change. Also, direct labor and variable overhead are paid in the quarter the expenses are incurred.

4. Fixed production costs (other than $10,000 of depreciation) are expected to increase by 5 percent. Fixed production costs requiring payment are paid in the quarter they are incurred.

5. Fixed selling and administrative costs (other than $5,000 of depreciation expense) are expected to increase by 5 percent. Fixed selling and administrative costs requiring payment are paid in the quarter they are incurred.

6. The tax rate is expected to be 40 percent. All taxes are paid in the quarter they are incurred.

7. No purchases of property, plant, or equipment are expected in the first quarter of 2006.

**Required**

a. Prepare a budgeted income statement for the first quarter of 2006.

b. Prepare a budgeted statement of cash receipts and disbursements for the first quarter of 2006.

c. Prepare a budgeted balance sheet as of the end of the first quarter of 2006.

**Answer**

a.

**Jackson Manufacturing Company**
**Budgeted Income Statement**
**for the Quarter Ended 3/31/2006**

| | | | |
|---|---:|---:|---|
| Sales | | $660,000 | 10% increase over prior quarter |
| Less variable cost of sales | | 264,000 | 10% increase over prior quarter |
| Contribution margin | | 396,000 | |
| Less fixed production costs | $ 67,750 | | $10,000 + 1.05 ($65,000 − $10,000) |
| Less fixed selling and adm. | 110,000 | 177,750 | $5,000 + 1.05 ($105,000 − $5,000) |
| Income before taxes | | 218,250 | |
| Less taxes on income | | 87,300 | 40% of income before taxes |
| Net income | | $130,950 | |

b.

**Jackson Manufacturing Company**
**Budgeted Statement of Cash Receipts and Disbursements**
**for the Quarter Ended 3/31/2006**

| | |
|---|---:|
| Cash collected from sales: | |
| $120,000 + .8 ($660,000)[1] | $648,000 |
| Cash payments: | |
| Payment of material ($12,000 + 0.9 × $132,000)[2] | 130,800 |
| Payment for labor[3] | 79,200 |
| Payment for variable overhead[4] | 52,800 |
| Payment for fixed production costs | 57,750 |
| ($67,750 − $10,000 depreciation) | |
| Payment for fixed selling and administrative | 105,000 |
| expenses ($110,000 − $5,000 depreciation) | |
| Payment of income taxes | 87,300 |
| Total cash payments | 512,850 |
| Plus beginning cash balance | 200,000 |
| Ending cash balance | $335,150 |

[1]20% of prior quarter sales collected in next quarter (0.2 × $600,000 = $120,000)

| | |
|---|---:|
| [2]Material used in prior quarter (0.5 × $240,000) | $120,000 |
| 10% paid in next quarter | $12,000 |
| Material used in current quarter (0.5 × $264,000) | $132,000 |
| [3]Direct labor used (0.3 × $264,000) | $79,200 |
| [4]Variable overhead incurred (0.2 × $264,000) | $52,800 |

c.

**Jackson Manufacturing Company**
**Budgeted Balance Sheet**
**as of 3/31/2006**

Assets:
| | | |
|---|---|---|
| Cash | $335,150 | |
| Accounts receivable | 132,000 | (0.2 × $660,000) |
| Inventory | 400,000 | |
| Total current assets | 867,150 | |
| Property plant, and equipment | 200,000 | |
| Less accumulated depreciation | (115,000) | ($100,000 + $10,000 + $5,000) |
| Total assets | $952,150 | |

Liabilities and owners' equity:
| | | |
|---|---|---|
| Accounts payable | $ 13,200 | (0.1 × $132,000) |
| Retained earnings | 338,950 | ($208,000 + $130,950) |
| Common stock | 600,000 | |
| Total liabilities and owners' equity | $952,150 | |

# KEY TERMS

Budgets (339)
Budget committee (342)
Budget variance (355)

Flexible budget (356)
Management by exception (358)
Master budget (343)

Slack (359)
Static budget (356)
Zero base budgeting (343)

# SELF ASSESSMENT *(Answers Below)*

1. Which of the following statements regarding budgets is false?

   a. They are formal documents that quantify a company's plans.
   b. They enhance communication and coordination.
   c. They are useful in planning but not in control.
   d. They provide a basis for evaluating performance.

2. Budgets are useful in the planning process because they enhance _____ and _____.

3. Which of the following statements regarding a sales budget is false?

   a. Input from the sales force may be useful in predicting sales
   b. Very large companies may hire economists to help forecast sales
   c. The sales budget is prepared before the cash receipts and disbursements budget
   d. The sales budget is developed after the production budget

4. Which of the following is the correct formula to determine required purchases of direct materials?

   a. Quantity required for production + Desired ending quantity − Beginning quantity
   b. Quantity required for production − Desired ending quantity + Beginning quantity
   c. Quantity required for production + Desired ending quantity + Beginning quantity
   d. Beginning quantity + Purchases − Desired ending quantity

5. Which of the following items do *not* require a cash outflow?

   a. Salaries
   b. Purchase of raw materials
   c. Advertising
   d. Depreciation

6. Differences between budgeted and actual amounts are referred to _____.

7. A _____ budget is not adjusted for the actual level of production whereas a _____ budget is adjusted for the actual level of production.

8. Which of the following is true about management by exception?

   a. Only large favorable variances are investigated
   b. Management by exception is an economical approach to cost control
   c. Management by exception can only be used with computers
   d. Large favorable variances should not be investigated

9. True or False? There is never a conflict between the planning and control use of budgets.

10. Which of the following is false?

    a. Including some nonmonetary measures of performance in a budget is not likely to be advantageous

    b. If a key aspect of a company's success is high quality, defect free products, it may be useful to budget the number of defects and the number of customer complaints at levels consistent with high quality
    c. The actual number of defects and complaints can be compared with the budgeted quantities to evaluate performance
    d. If a company is experiencing problems with employee absenteeism, it may be useful to budget an acceptable number of days missed and compare actual days missed with the target

**Answers to Self Assessment**

**1.** c;   **2.** communication and coordination;   **3.** d;
**4.** a;   **5.** d;   **6.** budget variances;   **7.** static,
flexible;   **8.** b;   **9.** False;   **10.** a.

# I N T E R A C T I V E   L E A R N I N G

**Enhance and test your knowledge of Chapter 10 using the interactive CD.**

1. Learning Objectives
2. Multiple Choice
3. Language of Business—Matching of Key Terms
4. Critical Thinking
5. Demonstration—The interdependence of budgets and using computers to update budgets for changes
6. Case—*Toscona Coffee*; Preparation of a production budget

**Go to our dynamic Web site for more self-assessment, Web links, and additional information.**

# Q U E S T I O N S

1. Why are budgets useful in the planning process?
2. Why are budgets useful in the control process?
3. What is the difference between the top-down and bottom-up approach to developing a budget?
4. What is meant by a zero base budget?
5. How does use of a spreadsheet program facilitate "what if" analysis in budgeting?
6. What are the main purposes of preparing a cash receipts and disbursements budget?

7. Explain the difference between a static and a flexible budget.
8. The number of defects in a manufacturing process is an example of a nonmonetary measure of employee performance. Describe a financial measure that captures the effect of defects.
9. How would performance be evaluated if there were no budgets?
10. Why is there an inherent conflict between the planning and control uses of budgets?

# EXERCISES

**EXERCISE 10-1. Group Assignment** Explain why a budget-based compensation scheme may encourage a manager to shift income from the current period to a future period if expected performance is quite high (e.g., greater than 120 percent of budgeted performance). How could the income shifting be accomplished?

**EXERCISE 10-2. Writing Assignment** Write a paragraph explaining why a budget-based compensation scheme may lead managers to create budget slack.

**EXERCISE 10-3. Internet Assignment** Go to the Web site of Hyperion, a leading provider of budgeting software (⟨http://hyperion.com/⟩). Locate information on the key features of the product, Hyperion Planning. List five features that make this product (or a similar software application from another company) useful to a large company with offices in many locations.

**EXERCISE 10-4. Order of Budgets** Determine the order in which the following budgets are generally prepared.

a. Material purchases budget

b. Sales budget

c. Budgeted income statement

d. Production budget

**EXERCISE 10-5. Sales Budget** Locksafe Company manufactures burglar-resistant commercial door locks. Recently, the company began selling locks on the Web, and the company expects sales to increase dramatically compared with the prior year. For the past year, 2006, unit sales were as follows:

| | |
|---|---|
| First quarter | 21,000 |
| Second quarter | 26,000 |
| Third quarter | 25,000 |
| Fourth quarter | 30,000 |

*Required*

Assume that sales for each quarter in 2007 will be 30 percent higher than they were in 2006 and the selling price per lock is $20. Prepare a sales budget.

**EXERCISE 10-6. Production Budget** SunnyM produces a sports drink that is sold in southern California. The company expects sales to be 15,600 bottles in January, 16,500 bottles in February, 16,000 bottles in March, and 18,500 bottles in April. There are 1,600 bottles on hand at the start of January. SunnyM desires to maintain monthly ending inventory equal to 10 percent of next month's expected sales.

*Required*

Prepare the production budget for SunnyM for the months of January, February, and March.

**EXERCISE 10-7. Direct Materials Purchases Budget** Ajax Chemical company has estimated that production for the next five quarters will be:

### Production Information

| | |
|---|---|
| Quarter 1, 2006 | 46,000 units |
| Quarter 2, 2006 | 42,000 units |
| Quarter 3, 2006 | 50,000 units |
| Quarter 4, 2006 | 39,000 units |
| Quarter 1, 2007 | 48,000 units |

Finished units of production require 4 pounds of raw material per unit. The raw material cost is $4 per pound. There are 45,000 pounds of raw material on hand at the beginning of quarter 1, 2006. Ajax desires to have 30 percent of next quarter's material requirements on hand at the end of each quarter.

*Required*
Prepare quarterly direct materials purchases budgets for Ajax Chemical Company for 2006.

**EXERCISE 10-8. Direct Labor Budget**   Prepare quarterly direct labor budgets for Ajax Chemical Company for 2006 using the production information in Exercise 8. It takes 2.5 hours of direct labor to produce each finished unit of product. Direct labor costs are $20 per hour. Each employee can work 450 hours per quarter.

**EXERCISE 10-9. Manufacturing Overhead Budget**   Prepare quarterly manufacturing overhead budgets for Ajax Chemical Company for 2006 using the production information from Exercise 8. Ajax has overhead costs as follows:

| Variable Costs | | Fixed Costs per Quarter | |
| --- | --- | --- | --- |
| Indirect material | $2.25 per unit | Supervisory salaries | $80,000 |
| Indirect labor | 1.50 per unit | Factory depreciation | 30,000 |
| Utilities | 1.00 per unit | Other | 4,100 |

**EXERCISE 10-10. Budgeted Sales and Cash Receipts**   R. Johnson Old Time Guitar Emporium budgeted Credit sales in the first quarter of 2007 to be as follows:

| | |
| --- | --- |
| January | $60,000 |
| February | 80,000 |
| March | 90,000 |

Credit sales in December of 2006 are expected to be $100,000. The company expects to collect 80 percent of a month's sales in the month of sale and 20 percent in the following month.

*Required*
Estimate cash receipts for each month of the first quarter of 2007.

**EXERCISE 10-11. Cash Disbursements for Purchases**   R. Johnson Old Time Guitar Emporium expects to make instrument purchases in the first quarter of 2007 as follows:

| | |
| --- | --- |
| January | $42,000 |
| February | 56,000 |
| March | 63,000 |

Purchases in December of 2006 are expected to be $70,000. The company expects that 10 percent of a month's purchases will be paid in the month of purchase and 90 percent will be paid in the following month

*Required*
Estimate cash disbursements related to purchases for each month of the first quarter of 2007.

**EXERCISE 10-12. Budgeted Sales and Cash Receipts**   Mississippi Retailers expects Credit sales in the next quarter as follows:

| | |
| --- | --- |
| April | $ 75,000 |
| May | 85,000 |
| June | 108,000 |

Prior experience has shown that 50 percent of a month's sales are collected in the month of sale, 30 percent in the month following sale, and the remaining 20 percent in the second month following sale. February and March sales were $85,000 and $95,000 respectively.

*Required*

Estimate budgeted cash receipts for April, May, and June.

**EXERCISE 10-13. Cash Disbursements for Purchases**  Mississippi Retailers expects to make inventory purchases in the next quarter as follows:

| | |
|---|---|
| April | $55,000 |
| May | 65,000 |
| June | 88,000 |

Prior experience has shown that 20 percent of a month's purchases are paid in the month of purchase and 80 percent in the month following purchase. March purchases were $50,000.

*Required*

Estimate cash disbursements related to purchases for April, May, and June.

**EXERCISE 10-14. Flexible Budget**  Bookbinder Company's expected manufacturing costs are as follows:

| Variable Costs | | Fixed Costs per Month | |
|---|---|---|---|
| Direct material | $5.30/unit | Supervisory salaries | $14,000 |
| Direct labor | 2.50/unit | Factory depreciation | 8,500 |
| Variable overhead | 1.20/unit | Other factory costs | 1,100 |

*Required*

Estimate manufacturing costs for production levels of 8,000 units, 10,000 units, and 12,000 units per month.

**EXERCISE 10-15. Performance Report**  Prepare a performance report for Bookbinder Company using the budget information from Exercise 14 and the following performance information. During the period, Bookbinder produced 12,000 units and incurred the following costs:

| Variable Costs | | Fixed Costs per Month | |
|---|---|---|---|
| Direct material | $71,900 | Supervisory salaries | $13,750 |
| Direct labor | 28,500 | Factory depreciation | 8,500 |
| Variable overhead | 15,300 | Other factory costs | 1,360 |

**EXERCISE 10-16. Performance Report**  At the start of 2007, La Patisserie Bakery budgeted before tax income as follows:

| | | |
|---|---|---|
| Sales | | $500,000 |
| Less: | | |
| Material cost | $100,000 | |
| Labor cost | 200,000 | |
| Owner's salary | 60,000 | |
| Rent | 50,000 | |
| Depreciation | 40,000 | |
| Utilities | 20,000 | 470,000 |
| Income before taxes | | $ 30,000 |

Actual before tax income for 2004 was:

| | | |
|---|---|---|
| Sales | | $600,000 |
| Less: | | |
| Material cost | $119,000 | |
| Labor cost | 260,000 | |
| Owner's salary | 60,000 | |
| Rent | 50,000 | |
| Depreciation | 40,000 | |
| Utilities | 19,000 | 548,000 |
| Income before taxes | | $ 52,000 |

*Required*

Michelle Girard, the owner of the bakery is pleased that sales were much higher than planned, but she is also concerned that expenses were $78,000 higher than the amounts she budgeted. Should she be concerned with the level of actual expenses? Prepare a performance report that will help her focus on areas needing attention.

**EXERCISE 10-17. Conflict in Planning and Control**   Riemers Jewelry operates 45 stores in major shopping malls around the country, and Walter Chan is the manager of a store in Dallas. The company is in the third quarter of 2006 and is beginning preparation of its fiscal 2007 budget. Typically, the company begins its profit-planning process by asking store managers to forecast sales and expenses. Individual profit plans are developed for each store and aggregated to develop a profit plan for the company as a whole.

In the control process, company executives compare actual profit performance to the plan on a store by store basis. Managers of stores that beat their budgeted profit levels are rewarded with significant bonuses.

*Required*

Will Walter Chan be motivated to provide unbiased forecasts of revenue and expense for the Dallas store? If not, what will be the direction of the bias for revenue and for expense?

# PROBLEMS

**PROBLEM 10-1. Master Budget**   (*Note:* This problem is similar to the chapter review problem—only the numbers have been changed. Students who get "stuck" should consult the solution to the review problem.)

The results of operations for the Preston Manufacturing Company for the fourth quarter of 2005 were as follows (in thousands):

| | | |
|---|---:|---:|
| Sales | | $500,000 |
| Less variable cost of sales | | 300,000 |
| Contribution margin | | 200,000 |
| Less fixed production costs | $100,000 | |
| Less fixed selling and administrative expenses | 50,000 | 150,000 |
| Income before taxes | | 50,000 |
| Less taxes on income | | 20,000 |
| Net income | | $ 30,000 |

*Note:* Preston Manufacturing uses the variable costing method. Thus, only variable production costs are included in inventory and cost of goods sold. Fixed production costs are charged to expense in the period incurred.

The company's balance sheet as of the end of the fourth quarter of 2005 was as follows (in thousands):

| | |
|---|---:|
| Assets: | |
| Cash | $ 150,000 |
| Accounts receivable | 250,000 |
| Inventory | 350,000 |
| Total current assets | 750,000 |
| Property, plant, and equipment | 400,000 |
| Less accumulated depreciation | (100,000) |
| Total assets | $1,050,000 |

Liabilities and owners' equity:

| | |
|---|---:|
| Accounts payable | $ 48,000 |
| Retained earnings | 502,000 |
| Common stock | 500,000 |
| Total liabilities and owners' equity | $1,050,000 |

Additional information:

1. Sales and variable costs of sales are expected to increase by five percent in the next quarter.

2. All sales are on credit with 50 percent collected in the quarter of sale and 50 percent collected in the following quarter.

3. Variable cost of sales consists of 40 percent materials, 40 percent direct labor, and 20 percent variable overhead. Materials are purchased on credit and 60 percent are paid for in the quarter of purchase and the remaining amount is paid for in the quarter after purchase. The inventory balance is not expected to change. Also, direct labor and variable overhead are paid in the quarter the expenses are incurred.

4. Fixed production costs (other than $8,000 of depreciation) are expected to increase by two percent. Fixed production costs requiring payment are paid in the quarter they are incurred.

5. Fixed selling and administrative costs (other than $7,000 of depreciation expense) are expected to increase by two percent. Fixed selling and administrative costs requiring payment are paid in the quarter they are incurred.

6. The tax rate is expected to be 40 percent. All taxes are paid in the quarter they are incurred.

7. No purchases of property, plant, or equipment are expected in the first quarter of 2006.

*Required*

a. Prepare a budgeted income statement for the first quarter of 2006.

b. Prepare a budgeted statement of cash receipts and disbursements for the first quarter of 2006.

c. Prepare a budgeted balance sheet as of the end of the first quarter of 2006.

**PROBLEM 10-2. Master Budget** Techlabs operates a computer training center. The following data relate to the preparation of a master budget for January of 2007.

1. At the end of 2006, the company's general ledger indicated the following balances

| **Debits** | | **Credits** | |
|---|---:|---|---:|
| Cash | $ 40,000 | Accounts payable | $ 30,000 |
| Accounts receivable | 30,000 | Note payable | 50,000 |
| Equipment (net) | 100,000 | Retained earnings | 70,000 |
| | | Common stock | 20,000 |
| Total | $170,000 | | $170,000 |

2. Tuition revenue in December of 2006 was $60,000 and tuition revenue budgeted for January, 2007 is $70,000.

3. Fifty percent of tuition revenue is collected in the month earned and 50 percent is collected in the subsequent month. The receivable balance at the end of 2006 reflects tuition earned in December 2006.

4. Monthly expenses (excluding interest expense) are budgeted as follows: salaries, $30,000; rent, $2,000; depreciation on equipment, $5,000; utilities, $500; other, $1,000.

5. Expenses are paid in the month incurred. Purchases of equipment are paid in the month after purchase. The $30,000 payable at the end of 2006 represents money owed for the purchase of computer equipment in December 2006.

6. The company intends to purchase $20,000 of computer equipment in January of 2007. The anticipated $5,000 per month of depreciation (see number 4) reflects the addition of $800 of monthly depreciation related to this purchase.

7. The note is at 10 percent per annum and requires monthly interest payments of $417. The payments are made on the 20th of each month. The principal must be paid in February of 2008.

8. The tax rate is 35 percent.

*Required*
Complete the following budgets:

**Part A.**
**Budgeted Cash Receipts and Disbursements**
**For January 2007**

**Cash receipts**

| | |
|---|---|
| Collection of December 2006 tuition | $_____ |
| Collection of January 2005 tuition | _____ |
| Total cash receipts | _____ |

**Cash disbursements**

| | |
|---|---|
| Payment of salaries | _____ |
| Payment of rent | |
| Payment of utilities | |
| Payment of other expenses | |
| Payment for purchases of computer equipment | |
| Payment of interest on note | |
| Payment of taxes | _____ |
| Total disbursements | |
| Plus beginning cash balance | _____ |
| Ending cash balance | $_____ |

**Part B.**
**Budget Income Statement**
**For January 2007**

| | |
|---|---|
| Tuition revenue | $_____ |
| Less: | |
|   Salaries | |
|   Rent | |
|   Utilities | |
|   Depreciation | |
|   Other | |
|   Interest expense | _____ |
| Total expense | _____ |
| Income before taxes | |
| Taxes on income | _____ |
| Net income | $_____ |

**Part C.**
**Budgeted Balance Sheet**
**As of January 30, 2007**

| | |
|---|---|
| Assets | |
| Cash | $ |
| Accounts receivable | |
| Equipment (net) | _____ |
| Total assets | $_____ |
| Liabilities | |
| Accounts payable | $ |
| Note payable | _____ |
| Total liabilities | _____ |
| Owner equity | |
| Retained earnings | |
| Common stock | _____ |
| Total owner's equity | _____ |
| Total liabilities and owner's equity | $_____ |

**PROBLEM 10-3. Master Budget**   The Botanical Soap Company operates a retail store in a local shopping mall. The results of operations for the fourth quarter of 2006 are as follows:

| | |
|---|---:|
| Sales | $200,000 |
| Less cost of sales | 100,000 |
| Gross margin | 100,000 |
| Less selling, general, and administrative expenses | 40,000 |
| Income before taxes | 60,000 |
| Less income taxes | 21,000 |
| Net income | $ 39,000 |

Additional information:

1. Sales and cost of sales are expected to increase by 10 percent in each of the next two quarters.
2. Ninety percent of sales are collected in the quarter of sale and 10 percent are collected in the quarter following sale.
3. The balance in accounts receivable at the end of 2006 relates to sales in the fourth quarter of 2006.
4. Inventory purchases in the fourth quarter of 2006 are $80,000.
5. The balance in accounts payable at the end of 2006 relates to purchases in the fourth quarter of 2006.
6. Inventory at the end of 2006 is $82,500. The company plans on holding ending inventory equal to 75 percent of subsequent quarter cost of sales.
7. Selling, general, and administrative expenses are expected to increase by $7,000 owing to increases in advertising and salaries. All other expenses in this category are expected to remain constant.
8. Eighty percent of inventory purchases are paid in the quarter of purchase and 20 percent are paid in the following quarter. All other expenses, including taxes, are paid in the quarter incurred.
9. Selling, general, and administrative expense includes $1,000 of depreciation related to furniture and fixtures with a book value (net of accumulated depreciation) of $40,000 at the end of 2006.
10. The tax rate is expected to remain at 35 percent.
11. The cash balance at the end of 2006 is $24,000.

12. Common stock at the end of 2006 is $60,000 and retained earnings is $90,500.

13. Asset accounts are cash, accounts receivable, and furniture and fixtures. The only liability account is accounts payable. Owner's equity accounts are common stock and retained earnings.

**Required**

a. Prepare a budgeted income statement for the first quarter of 2007.

b. Prepare a cash receipts and disbursements budget for the first quarter of 2007.

c. Prepare a budgeted balance sheet as of the end of the first quarter of 2007.

d. The company is discussing the possibility of opening a new store late in the first quarter of 2007. A store opening would require cash payments of $40,000. Assuming the company wants a minimum cash balance of $25,000 at the end of quarter 1, can a new store be opened without obtaining additional funds?

**PROBLEM 10-4. Budgeted Income Statement** Modern Healthcare, a group practice clinic with 10 physicians, had the following income in 2006:

| | |
|---|---:|
| Revenue | $2,400,000 |
| Less operating expenses: | |
| Salaries | |
|    Physicians | 1,000,000 |
|    Nurses | 140,000 |
|    Nursing aid | 62,375 |
|    Receptionist | 45,200 |
| Accounting services | 34,450 |
| Training | 155,000 |
| Supplies | 191,250 |
| Phone and fax | 2,500 |
| Insurance | 250,000 |
| Depreciation | 200,000 |
| Utilities | 18,000 |
| Miscellaneous | 60,000 |
|    Total operating expenses | 2,158,775 |
| Income before taxes | 241,225 |
| Less taxes on income | 84,429 |
| Net income | $ 156,796 |

The following changes are expected in 2007:

1. The clinic is expecting a five percent decline in revenues because of increasing pressure from insurance companies.

2. Physicians are planning to hire a physician assistant at a salary of $70,000 per year.

3. Training costs are expected to increase by $15,000.

4. Supplies are expected to increase to 8.5 percent of revenue.

5. Phone, fax, and insurance amounts will stay the same.

6. Depreciation expense will increase by $20,000 per year, since the clinic is planning to purchase equipment for $100,000.

7. Utilities and miscellaneous expenses are expected to increase next year by five percent.

8. Taxes on income will be 35 percent.

**Required**

Prepare a budgeted income statement for Modern Healthcare for the year 2007.

**PROBLEM 10-5. Combined Production and Purchases Budgets**   BugAway, Inc. produces and sells bug repellent. Information about the budget for the year 2007 is as follows:

1. The company expects to sell 40,000 bottles of BugAway in the first quarter, 50,000 in the second quarter, 93,000 in the third quarter, and 36,000 in the fourth quarter.

2. A bottle of BugAway requires 6 ounces of Chemical A and 10 ounces of Chemical B.

3. The desired ending inventory of finished goods is equal to 20 percent of next quarter's sales whereas the desired ending inventory for material is 15 percent of next quarter's production requirements.

4. There are 11,000 bottles of BugAway, 57,000 ounces of Chemical A, and 97,000 ounces of Chemical B on hand at the beginning of the first quarter.

5. At the end of the fourth quarter, the company must have 12,000 bottles of Bug-Away, 60,000 ounces of Chemical A, and 102,000 ounces of Chemical B to meet its needs in the first quarter of 2008.

6. The cost of Chemical A is $0.12 per ounce, the cost of Chemical B is $0.09 per ounce, and the selling price of BugAway is $9.95 per bottle.

7. The cost of direct labor is $0.60 per bottle and the cost of variable overhead is $0.90 per bottle. Fixed manufacturing overhead is $40,000 per quarter.

8. Variable selling and administrative expense is 4 percent of sales and fixed selling and administrative expenses is $50,000 per quarter.

*Required*

a. Prepare a production budget for each quarter of 2007.

b. Prepare a material purchases budget for each quarter of 2007.

c. Prepare a budgeted income statement for each quarter of 2007 (ignore taxes).

**PROBLEM 10-6. Cash Budget**   In the fourth quarter of 2006, Casey Wholesalers had the following net income:

| | |
|---|---:|
| Sales | $500,000 |
| Less cost of sales | 250,000 |
| Gross margin | 250,000 |
| Selling and administration | 200,000 |
| Income before taxes | 50,000 |
| Income taxes | 17,500 |
| Net income | $ 32,500 |

Purchases in the fourth quarter amounted to $300,000.
Estimated data for Casey Wholesalers, Inc. for 2007 are as follows:

| | **Quarter 1** | **Quarter 2** | **Quarter 3** | **Quarter 4** |
|---|---|---|---|---|
| Sales | $600,000 | $700,000 | $800,000 | $900,000 |
| Cost of sales | 300,000 | 350,000 | 400,000 | 450,000 |
| Purchases | 350,000 | 400,000 | 450,000 | 485,000 |
| Selling and adm. | 200,000 | 200,000 | 200,000 | 200,000 |

Taxes are 35 percent of pretax income. Sixty percent of sales are collected in the quarter of sale and 40 percent in the next quarter. Eighty percent of purchases are paid in the quarter of purchase and 20 percent in the next quarter. Selling and administrative expenses are paid in the quarter incurred except for $10,000 of depreciation included in selling and administrative expense. A capital expenditure for $50,000 is planned for the fourth quarter of 2007.

*Required*

Prepare a cash receipts and disbursements budget for each quarter of 2007.

**PROBLEM 10-7. Budget Relationships**  The accountant at Supreme Audio resigned while he was in the midst of preparing the budget for 2007. His work papers indicated the following:

**Budgeted Sales and Inventory Purchases for 2007**

|  | Quarter 1 | Quarter 2 | Quarter 3 | Quarter 4 | Total |
|---|---|---|---|---|---|
| Sales in 2006 | $200,000 | $250,000 | $300,000 | $400,000 | $1,150,000 |
| **Expected sales in 2007** | $250,000 | $ | $ | $ | |
| Cost of Sales | $150,000 | $ | $ | $ | |
| Beginning inventory | $ 75,000 | $ | $ | $ | |
| Ending inventory | $ | $ | $ | $ | |
| **Purchases** | $ | $ | $ | $ | |

*Assumptions:*
Sales will increase by 25 percent over 2006.
Cost of sales equals 60 percent of sales.
Ending inventory should equal 50 percent of the amount needed for next quarter sales.
Sales in the first quarter of 2008 will be $280,000.

*Required*
Fill in the missing information to determine the **sales** and **purchases** budgets for 2007.

**PROBLEM 10-8. "What If" Analysis Using a Spreadsheet**  Cynthia Morton is in the process of developing a spreadsheet to budget annual sales and purchases of inventory for her company, Morton Fine Carpets, a retail store that sells handmade carpets from the Middle East. In 2006, sales were as follows.

| Quarter 1 | Quarter 2 | Quarter 3 | Quarter 4 |
|---|---|---|---|
| $200,000 | $210,000 | $220,000 | $185,000 |

Inventory at the end of 2006 is $66,000.

*Required*
Help Cynthia build a spreadsheet that will allow her to examine the impact on purchases of inventory of the following three items:

1. Sales growth from 2006 to 2007. Cynthia believes that quarterly sales will grow by 10 percent in 2007 compared to the corresponding quarter in 2006. And sales in the first quarter of 2008 will be 10 percent higher than in 2007. However, she would also like to explore the effect on purchases of alternative growth rates. Thus, your spreadsheet must allow you to change this value and observe the effect on all other values.

2. Inventory on hand at the end of each quarter. Cynthia is tentatively planning on having ending inventory equal to 20 percent of the amount needed to meet next quarter's sales. She would also like to explore the effect on purchases of alternative rates. Thus, your spreadsheet must allow you to change this value and observe the effect on purchases.

3. Cynthia estimates that cost of goods sold as a percent of sales will be 30 percent. She would also like to explore the effect on purchases of different rates. Thus, your spreadsheet must allow you to change this value.

   After you have developed your spreadsheet, calculate purchases in the first through the fourth quarter of 2007 for the following combinations:

   Combination 1—Sales growth of 10 percent, Ending inventory of 22 percent, Cost of goods sold of 33 percent.
   Combination 2—Sales growth of 15 percent, Ending inventory of 24 percent, Cost of goods sold of 28 percent.
   Combination 3—Sales growth of 9 percent, Ending inventory of 34 percent, Cost of goods sold of 40 percent.

**PROBLEM 10-9. Budgeting Process**    Debra Green is the divisional manager of the Consumer Banking Division of Pennywise Bank. Each year Debra submits an annual budget to Barney Stringer, the chief financial officer of the bank. Debra's bonus, salary increases, and promotion opportunities are based on how her performance compares with budgeted divisional income. Debra has to negotiate the budget with the CFO each year.

In the past, Barney has insisted that Debra underestimates revenue and overestimates expenses, whereas Debra tells Barney that he is expecting too much from her division.

During 2006, the Consumer Banking Division had a record year and Debra received a huge bonus. For 2007, Barney insisted that Debra's budget be at least equal to the prior year's performance level. Debra stated that the prior year was exceptional and performance could not be repeated. After getting into a rather heated argument, they scheduled a meeting with the President and CEO of the bank to resolve their conflict.

*Required*

a. Explain why Barney and Debra have conflicting opinions.

b. If you were the president of Pennywise Bank, how would you resolve the argument between Barney and Debra?

**PROBLEM 10-10. Performance report**    The Customer Support Department at Silvan.com budgeted for the following costs in June assuming 40 customer consultants responding to 10,000 customer calls.

|  |  |
|---|---|
| Salaries of customer consultants | $120,000 |
| Salaries of supervisors | 18,000 |
| Office space charge | 5,000 |
| Depreciation on equipment | 4,000 |
| Total | $147,000 |

The department is located in a wing of the company's new office building and has space to accommodate extra customer consultants. Each customer consultant works at a computer/telecommunications center. Depreciation on equipment relates to the equipment used by each customer consultant.

During the month of June, the department handled 12,000 customer calls and incurred the following costs:

|  |  |
|---|---|
| Salaries of customer consultants | $160,000 |
| Salaries of supervisors | 17,500 |
| Office space charge | 5,000 |
| Depreciation on equipment | 5,000 |
| Total | $187,500 |

*Required*

a. Making assumptions about fixed and variable costs, prepare a performance report comparing actual costs with flexible budget costs applicable to handling 12,000 customer calls.

b. List possible causes for significant variances in the performance report.

c. In addition to the variances calculated above, what nonfinancial measures could be used to evaluate the Customer Support Department?

**PROBLEM 10-11. Performance Report** The Athletic Equipment Division of Physique Inc. had significant problems in 2007. Sales and production were down by almost 30 percent as compared with the budget. Manufacturing was plagued by quality problems and had frequent customer complaints.

John Martin, the division's manager, recently received a report comparing his division's actual costs with the costs in the master budget prepared at the start of 2007. Surprisingly, actual costs were less than budgeted, indicating favorable variances.

John was upbeat when told that the president had scheduled a meeting with him to discuss the Athletic Equipment Division's performance. Although sales were down, at least he could point to a large number of favorable cost variances.

*Required*

Briefly explain why the variances are positive, and discuss what John should know about flexible budgets. Assuming that the president understands flexible budgets, will the president be impressed by the favorable cost variances?

**PROBLEM 10-12. Conflict in Planning and Control** Jack Norton is the president of Wynn Electronics, a wholly owned subsidiary of Mammoth Industries. His annual salary is $400,000. In addition, he receives a $100,000 bonus if Wynn's profit exceeds 80 percent of budget. He also receives 1 percent of any profit over 80 percent of budget. His total bonus is capped when Wynn's profit exceeds 120 percent of budget.

*Required*

a. Each year, Jack spends hours negotiating the profit budget for Wynn with the senior management team of Mammoth Industries. Invariably he claims that their sales estimates are too high and their cost estimates too low. They in turn claim that Jack is padding his budget. In this context, what is meant by budget padding? Explain why Jack may, indeed, have an incentive to pad his budget. Provide an example of how budget padding may hurt company performance.

b. For the current year, the profit budget was set at $40,000,000. Late in the fourth quarter of the current year, Jack received a report from Wynn's CFO indicating that actual profit would be close to $50,000,000. Jack then ordered that planned shipments for the last two weeks of the quarter be delayed until the start of the next year. Why did Jack take this step? What is the effect of this action on shareholder value?

**PROBLEM 10-13. Budgeting and Nonmonetary Measures** Xtreme Board Company manufactures skateboards. The president of the company, Greg Conklin, believes that "you get what you measure!" Accordingly, he would like to include a number of nonmonetary measures, related to factors that affect the success of the company, in the annual budget. In Greg's opinion, this will get his management team focused on important success factors, and the budgeted amounts can be compared to actual values at year end to determine if goals have been achieved.

*Required*

Suggest four nonmonetary measures that Greg Conklin can include in the annual budget for Xtreme Board Company.

# CASES

## 10-1 ETHICS CASE: COLUMBUS PARK— WASTE TREATMENT FACILITY

As manager of the waste treatment facility for the city of Columbus Park, Illinois, Ann Paxton is in the process of preparing an annual expense budget. While eating lunch at her desk she thought about the coming year. "Next year, my department will probably be asked to process some 8,000,000 gallons of waste. Our variable costs are about $.10 per gallon and our fixed costs are about $1,100,000. So, the total cost should be somewhere around $1,900,000. I better submit a budget of around $2,300,000. The city's tax revenues are down and the city controller will probably reduce whatever budget I submit by 10 percent. And what if I end up incurring higher expenses than anticipated? A new labor contract, for instance, could increase costs by more than $100,000. Or waste could be 500,000 gallons higher than estimated. The last thing I want is to incur more costs than budgeted. I've got to stay within budget to have any chance for a promotion out of this stinking department!"

### Required

Discuss whether or not it is ethical for Ann to submit a budget for an amount higher than the cost expected to be incurred?

## 10-2 ABRUZZI OLIVE OIL COMPANY

Abruzzi Olive Oil Company is a small producer of premium olive oil. Cheryl Sounders, the owner of Abruzzi is currently developing a budget spreedsheet to explore the impact of various sales goals on production. In 2005, the company had monthly sales as follows:

| Month | Sales (gallons) |
| --- | --- |
| January | 9,100 |
| February | 9,000 |
| March | 8,600 |
| April | 8,400 |
| May | 8,100 |
| June | 8,200 |
| July | 8,000 |
| August | 8,100 |
| September | 8,500 |
| October | 8,800 |
| November | 8,900 |
| December | 9,000 |

At a planning meeting in November 2005, Jay Peters, the marketing manager for Abruzzi told Cheryl that he expected monthly sales to increase by 5 to 15 percent in the coming year. But in late December 2005, Jay rushed into Cheryl's office with some good news. "Cheryl, I just had a meeting with Consolidated Restaurants, and they're considering an order for 1,000 gallons each month for all of 2006."

"Gosh," Cheryl replied, "that's an exciting bit of news, but I'm concerned about whether we have the capacity to accept such a large order. I'll prepare budgets assuming we don't get the Consolidated business but we increase monthly sales by 5, 10 or 15 percent. Then, I'll assume the Consolidated order comes through and on top of that we have monthly sales increases of 5, 10 and 15 percent. This should give us a good idea of whether or not we'll bump up against capacity."

Jay thought that this sounded fine, but he wondered if Cheryl had the time to do this much work. Cheryl indicated that the analysis was relatively easy since she was preparing the budget on a spreadsheet and each analysis would require only a simple change.

### Required

1. Using a spreadsheet, prepare the six monthly budget schedules that Cheryl suggested (i.e., monthly budgets with and without the Consolidated business assuming other sales increases of 5, 10, and 15 percent). As a general rule, Cheryl likes to have ending inventory equal to 15 percent of next month's sales. Assume the company ended 2005 with an inventory of 1,500 gallons of olive oil. In order to calculate ending inventory at the end of December 2006, assume that sales in January of 2007 will be the same as December 2006 sales.

2. Suppose that capacity is 11,000 gallons. Is the company likely to encounter a capacity problem?

3. Abruzzi sells its oil for $20 per gallon. The variable cost per gallon is $8. What will be the annual impact on profit of obtaining the Consolidated business (assuming there is not a capacity problem)?

# 10-3 TEXAS STYLE, INC.

Texas Style is a small manufacturer of western clothes sold at specialty shops throughout the Southwest. All production takes place at a factory located outside Austin, Texas. To improve communication of company goals and coordination of activities, Paul Rodriguez, the president of Texas Style, has asked Marilyn Ritter, the controller, to set up a formal budgeting system.

At a recent meeting to discuss the new system, Paul mentioned an article related to budgeting that he had read in a management journal. "The article made two interesting points," he began. "First, the article suggested that the budget be set with the full participation of the workers responsible for achieving the budget. According to the author, participation makes the workers feel more involved and committed to achieving the budget. So, in our case, you really need to get the plant manager, Harold, involved when developing the budget for production costs."

"A second point is that budgets should include nonmonetary as well as dollar measures of performance. Marilyn, you know as well as I do that key success factors for our business are delivering orders on time and without defects in the garments. Why don't we include in the budget a specified percent of on-time orders, say 95 percent? And, we can also budget the number of defect-related returns each quarter."

Marilyn agreed that the two suggestions had merit and promised to consider them in the budgeting process.

### Required
1. Do you believe that Harold will be more "committed to the budget" if he participates in budgeting production costs? Identify a potential problem in having Harold participate in the budget process.

2. Do you believe that including nonmonetary measures of performance in the budget is appropriate? Justify your response. Suggest two additional nonmonetary measures of performance that would be reasonable to include in the budget for Texas Style.

# chapter 11

## LEARNING OBJECTIVES

**1** Explain how standard costs are developed.

**2** Calculate and interpret variances for direct material.

**3** Calculate and interpret variances for direct labor.

**4** Calculate and interpret variances for manufacturing overhead.

**5** Calculate the financial impact of operating at more or less than planned capacity.

**6** Discuss how the management by exception approach is applied to investigation of standard cost variances.

**7** Explain why a "favorable" variance may be unfavorable, how process improvements may lead to "unfavorable" variances, and why evaluation in terms of variances may lead to overproduction.

# STANDARD COSTS AND VARIANCE ANALYSIS

At the start of the year, Darrington Ice Cream budgeted material costs at $2 per gallon. During the year, the company produced 1,000,000 gallons, and the material cost was approximately $2,200,000. Linda Evert, director of operations, immediately called a meeting of the plant manager and the production supervisor. Linda's opening statement grabbed their attention. "What's going on? Our actual costs are 10 percent higher than budgeted." Both managers assured her that the increased costs were not due to waste in the use of materials. The plant manager was confident that the increased costs resulted from a sudden jump in sugar and milk prices. And, he observed, "price changes are beyond our control. Talk to the guys in purchasing—they'll back me up on the price increase."

Linda went back to her office and continued to think about the situation. "What would really be useful," she concluded, "would be a report that broke the material cost increase out into two parts: the part due to using more material than planned and the part due to paying a higher price than planned. I wonder if Jane in the accounting department can help out with the calculations?"

Fortunately, Linda is on the right track. An accountant can help her with the needed calculations and, ultimately, help the company develop a standard costing system. In such systems, manufactured goods are not recorded at their actual product cost but rather at the cost that *should have been incurred* to produce the items. This cost is referred to as the standard cost.

A primary benefit of a standard costing system is that it allows managers to compare differences between standard and actual costs. Such differences are referred to as standard cost variances. For material costs, the standard cost variances distinguish between the variance due to a difference between the actual price and the standard price and the variance due to a difference between the actual quantity of raw material and the standard quantity. Standard costing systems also generate variances for direct labor and manufacturing overhead. Large or unusual variances are investigated by management to determine if production is inefficient. If problems exist, corrective action can be taken. Thus, standard costs play an important role in *controlling operations* as well as in determining *product costs*. This chapter illustrates both of these uses of standard costs.

# STANDARD COSTS

The term **standard cost** refers to the cost that management believes *should be incurred* to produce a good or service under anticipated conditions. A tool manufacturing company may set a standard cost for the production of a hammer, whereas a bank may set a standard cost for processing a check. In the following examples we concentrate on standard costing in a manufacturing setting. But much of the discussion also applies to service companies, like banks, that also use standard costs.

## STANDARD COSTS AND BUDGETS

Some accountants use the terms **budgeted cost** and standard cost interchangeably. However, the term *standard cost* often refers to the cost of a single unit, whereas the term *budgeted cost* often refers to the cost, at standard, of the total number of budgeted units. The cost information contained in budgets must be consistent with standard costs. For example, suppose the standard cost of a unit of production is:

| Standard Cost per Unit | |
| --- | --- |
| Direct material (2 lbs. at $5 per lb.) | $10.00 |
| Direct labor (3 hours at $10 per hour) | 30.00 |
| Manufacturing overhead ($5 per labor hour) | 15.00 |
| Standard cost per unit | $55.00 |

If the budget for direct material purchases calls for purchasing 5,000 pounds of raw material, the budget would show an expected cost of $25,000 (i.e., 5,000 pounds at the standard price of $5 per pound). Similarly, if the direct labor bud-

### Starbucks Uses Standard Costs

When we think of companies that use standard costing, manufacturing companies like Boeing and General Motors and chemical producers, like Dow Chemical, come to mind. But even companies in the food services industry use standard costing. See the video on the interactive CD for details on how Starbucks uses standard costing to control the cost of beans in its roasting operation.

get is prepared for an expected production level of 1,000 units, it would indicate 3,000 hours of labor costing $30,000.

## DEVELOPMENT OF STANDARD COSTS

Explain how standard costs are developed.

Standard costs for material, labor, and overhead are developed in a variety of ways. The standard quantity of material may be specified in engineering plans that provide detailed lists of raw materials needed in production. For some companies, the standard quantity of raw material is actually specified in recipes or formulas. This is the case in large commercial bakeries and other companies that manufacture food products. The standard price of the materials is often determined from price lists provided by suppliers.

The standard quantity of direct labor can be determined by time and motion studies conducted by industrial engineers. In time and motion studies, standard labor hours are determined based on observation of workers under simulated or actual working conditions. Standard labor hours can also be estimated from an analysis of past data. For example, suppose a company developed the following information on production and labor hours.

|  | Production in Units | Labor Hours |
|---|---|---|
| First quarter, 2006 | 2,025 | 6,500 |
| Second quarter, 2006 | 2,500 | 7,400 |
| Third quarter, 2006 | 2,100 | 6,800 |
| Fourth quarter, 2006 | 2,600 | 7,900 |
| Total | 9,225 | 28,600 |

Based on these data, the average time to produce one unit is approximately 3.10 hours (28,600 hours ÷ 9,225 units). If the company does not anticipate any major changes in the production process, this average could be used as the standard quantity of labor. However, if the company has operated inefficiently in the past, basing current standards on past performance will result in standards that do not reflect efficient production practices. The standard labor wage rates are usually set at the rates management expects to pay the various categories of workers. In many cases, the wage rates are set equal to the rates specified in labor contracts.

Developing standard costs for overhead involves procedures similar to the ones used to develop the predetermined overhead rates discussed earlier in the book. Dividing the amount of anticipated overhead by the standard quantity of the allocation base results in a standard cost of overhead. For example, suppose a company anticipates that $60,000 of overhead will be incurred if the company works 5,000 standard labor hours. In this case, the standard overhead rate would be $12 per standard labor hour. At companies that use activity-based costing, standard costs are developed for a number of overhead cost drivers, such as the number of setups, the number of purchase orders, and the number of shipments received.

### IDEAL VERSUS ATTAINABLE STANDARDS

In developing standard costs, some managers emphasize **ideal standards,** whereas other managers emphasize **attainable standards**. Ideal standards are developed under the assumption that no obstacles to the production process will be encountered. Thus, they do not allow for a breakdown of equipment that would increase the quantity of labor hours, or defects in raw material that would increase the quantity of material required for production. Ideal standards are sometimes referred to as perfection standards because they emphasize production in a "perfect" environment. However, if a company expects occasional equipment failure, occasional substitution of inexperienced for experienced workers, and some raw material defects, then standards should be set at a level that allows for the cost of these events. Currently attainable standards are standard costs that take into account the possibility that a variety of circumstances may lead to costs that are greater than "ideal."

Managers who support ideal standards believe they motivate employees to strive for the best possible control over production costs. Such managers argue that if the cost of defects and breakdowns is built into the standards, the result will be an acceptance of defects and breakdowns rather than an effort to eliminate them. However, because they do not allow for *expected* deviations from ideal conditions, ideal standards may not be useful for planning. If equipment breakdowns and defects are a "fact of life," then it makes sense to plan for their associated costs. Most managers support the use of attainable standards.

# A GENERAL APPROACH TO VARIANCE ANALYSIS

Companies that have standard costing systems can analyze the difference between a standard and an actual cost, referred to as a **standard cost variance**, to determine if operations are being performed efficiently. The analysis—referred to as **variance analysis**—generally involves decomposing (breaking down) the difference between standard and actual cost into two components. For direct material, the two components are the material price and the material quantity variances. For direct labor, the two components are the labor rate variance and the labor efficiency variance. And for manufacturing overhead, the two components are the overhead volume variance and the controllable overhead variance.

Variance analysis helps companies control operations by highlighting potential problems in operations. In the following sections, we examine the variance calculations for National Compound Company, a producer of a synthetic rubber compound used in molding operations. The standard cost for a 50-gallon drum of the compound (the standard production unit) is as follows:

| | | |
|---|---|---|
| Material | | |
| 400 pounds @ $10 per pound | | $4,000 |
| Labor | | |
| 4 hours @ $15 per hour | | 60 |
| Overhead | | |
| $50 per unit | | 50 |
| Total per 50-gallon drum | | $4,110 |

**LEARNING OBJECTIVE 2**

Calculate and interpret variances for direct material.

# MATERIAL VARIANCES

The difference between standard and actual material cost can be divided into two material variances—a material price variance and a material quantity variance. The formulas used to calculate the variances are presented in Illustration 11-1 and are discussed next.

**Illustration 11-1**
Direct material variance formulas

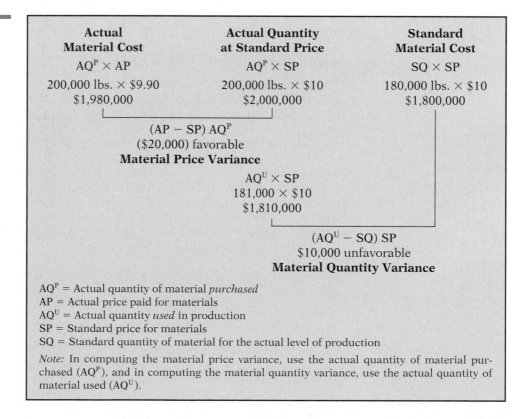

| Actual Material Cost | Actual Quantity at Standard Price | Standard Material Cost |
|---|---|---|
| $AQ^P \times AP$ | $AQ^P \times SP$ | $SQ \times SP$ |
| 200,000 lbs. × $9.90 | 200,000 lbs. × $10 | 180,000 lbs. × $10 |
| $1,980,000 | $2,000,000 | $1,800,000 |

$(AP - SP) AQ^P$
($20,000) favorable
**Material Price Variance**

$AQ^U \times SP$
181,000 × $10
$1,810,000

$(AQ^U - SQ) SP$
$10,000 unfavorable
**Material Quantity Variance**

$AQ^P$ = Actual quantity of material *purchased*
AP = Actual price paid for materials
$AQ^U$ = Actual quantity *used* in production
SP = Standard price for materials
SQ = Standard quantity of material for the actual level of production

*Note:* In computing the material price variance, use the actual quantity of material purchased ($AQ^P$), and in computing the material quantity variance, use the actual quantity of material used ($AQ^U$).

## MATERIAL PRICE VARIANCE

The **material price variance** is equal to the difference between the actual price per unit of material (AP) and the standard price per unit of material (SP), times the actual quantity of material purchased ($AQ^P$).

$$\text{Material price variance} = (AP - SP)\, AQ^P$$

Let's see how to calculate this variance for the National Compound Company. Suppose the company purchased 200,000 pounds of material and actually paid $9.90 per pound rather than the standard price of $10. In this case, there would be a favorable $20,000 material price variance.

$$\text{Material price variance} = (AP - SP)\, AQ^P$$
$$= (\$9.90 - \$10.00)\, 200{,}000$$
$$= (\$20{,}000) \text{ favorable}$$

In thinking about this variance, note that material costs $0.10 less per pound than planned, and this saving is realized on 200,000 pounds purchased. That is why the material price variance is labeled "favorable," because the actual price per pound is less than the standard price.

In the variance formulas presented in this chapter, negative variances will be favorable and positive variances will be unfavorable. Rather than concentrating on the sign of the variance, however, you can simply remember that:

- Actual prices or quantities greater than standard are labeled *unfavorable*.
- Actual prices or quantities less than standard are labeled *favorable*.

## MATERIAL QUANTITY VARIANCE

The **material quantity variance** is equal to the difference between the actual quantity of material used($AQ^U$) and the standard quantity of material allowed for the number of units produced (SQ) times the standard price of material (SP)

$$\text{Material Quantity Variance} = (AQ^U - SQ)\, SP$$

Suppose National Compound produces 450 of the 50-gallon drums of molding compound. The standard quantity of material is 400 pounds per drum. Thus, the standard quantity of material allowed for the 450 units produced is 180,000 pounds (i.e., 450 drums × 400 lbs. per drum). Recall that the standard price of material is $10 per pound. Thus, if 181,000 pounds of material are actually used, the material quantity variance is $10,000 and unfavorable.

$$\text{Material quantity variance} = (AQ^U - SQ)\, SP$$
$$= (181{,}000 - 180{,}000)\, \$10$$
$$= \$10{,}000 \text{ unfavorable}$$

In other words, 1,000 extra pounds are used at a standard cost of $10 per pound. Note that the material quantity variance is labeled "unfavorable." This is because more material is actually used than called for by the standards. This is considered an unfavorable outcome because it has a negative effect on company profit.

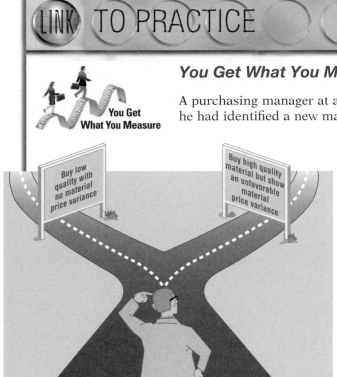

## LINK TO PRACTICE

### *You Get What You Measure!*

A purchasing manager at a large Midwestern manufacturing firm recounted how he had identified a new material that would result in higher quality and cost savings for the company. However, the material would cost a bit more than the standard price of the current inferior material. Buying the new material would make the purchasing department look bad because it would be charged with a material price variance. Any savings in manufacturing would be credited to the manufacturing department.

Guess what happened. The company stuck with the inferior material. This example illustrates that placing too much emphasis on price variances when evaluating performance can ultimately hurt company profitability.

Rather than concentrating only on purchase price variances, purchasing managers should also be evaluated on developing strong relationships with suppliers that lead to on-time deliveries and minimal quality problems.

# DIRECT LABOR VARIANCES

**LEARNING OBJECTIVE 3**

Calculate and interpret variances for direct labor.

As we just saw, there are two material variances: a material price variance and a material quantity variance. Similarly, there are two direct labor variances: a labor rate variance and a labor efficiency variance. The formulas used to calculate these variances are presented in Illustration 11-2 and are discussed next.

**Illustration 11-2**
Direct labor variance formulas

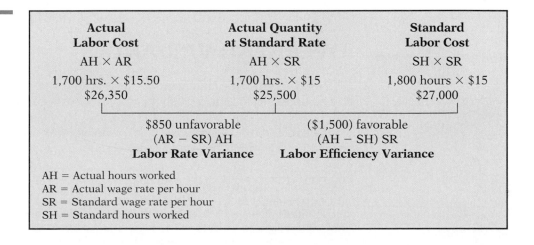

| Actual Labor Cost | Actual Quantity at Standard Rate | Standard Labor Cost |
|---|---|---|
| AH × AR | AH × SR | SH × SR |
| 1,700 hrs. × $15.50 | 1,700 hrs. × $15 | 1,800 hours × $15 |
| $26,350 | $25,500 | $27,000 |

| $850 unfavorable | ($1,500) favorable |
|---|---|
| (AR − SR) AH | (AH − SH) SR |
| **Labor Rate Variance** | **Labor Efficiency Variance** |

AH = Actual hours worked
AR = Actual wage rate per hour
SR = Standard wage rate per hour
SH = Standard hours worked

### LABOR RATE VARIANCE

The **labor rate variance** is equal to the difference between the actual wage rate (AR) and the standard wage rate (SR) times the actual number of labor hours worked (AH). This variance is very similar to the material price variance.

$$\text{Labor rate variance} = (AR - SR)\,AH$$

The standards for National Compound call for a standard wage rate of $15 per hour. Suppose that the actual wage rate is $15.50 and 1,700 hours are worked. In this case, the labor rate variance is an unfavorable $850.

$$\text{Labor rate variance} = (AR - SR)\,AH$$
$$= (\$15.50 - \$15.00)\,1{,}700$$
$$= \$850 \text{ unfavorable}$$

In other words, the company paid $0.50 more per hour than planned for each of the 1,700 hours worked.

### LABOR EFFICIENCY VARIANCE

The **labor efficiency variance** is equal to the difference between the actual number of hours worked (AH) and the standard labor hours allowed for the number of units produced (SH) times the standard labor wage rate (SR). This variance is similar to the material quantity variance.

$$\text{Labor efficiency variance} = (AH - SH)\,SR$$

National Compound Company used 1,700 hours to produce 450 units. Standards call for 4 hours per unit at a standard wage rate of $15 per hour. Thus, the standard number of hours for 450 units is 1,800 (450 units × 4 hours per unit). In this case, the labor efficiency variance is $1,500 favorable.

$$\text{Labor efficiency variance} = (AH - SH)\,SR$$
$$= (1{,}700 - 1{,}800)\,\$15$$
$$= (\$1{,}500) \text{ favorable}$$

In other words, the company worked 100 hours less than planned, saving $15 per hour at the planned rate.

Calculate and interpret variances for manufacturing overhead.

# OVERHEAD VARIANCES

The total variance for manufacturing overhead is the difference between the overhead applied to inventory at standard and actual overhead costs. The total overhead variance can be separated into an overhead volume variance and a controllable overhead variance.[1] The formulas for the overhead variances are presented in Illustration 11-3 and are discussed next.

---

[1]It is possible to decompose the difference between variable overhead applied at standard and actual variable overhead into a *variable* overhead spending and a *variable* overhead efficiency variance. And the difference between applied and actual *fixed* overhead can be decomposed into a *fixed* overhead budget variance and a *fixed* overhead volume variance. This "four-way analysis" of overhead variances is covered in cost accounting textbooks.

**Illustration 11-3**
Manufacturing overhead
variance formulas

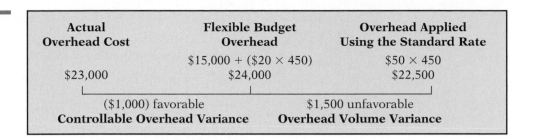

| Actual Overhead Cost | Flexible Budget Overhead | Overhead Applied Using the Standard Rate |
|---|---|---|
| | $15,000 + ($20 × 450) | $50 × 450 |
| $23,000 | $24,000 | $22,500 |

($1,000) favorable — **Controllable Overhead Variance**

$1,500 unfavorable — **Overhead Volume Variance**

## CONTROLLABLE OVERHEAD VARIANCE

The **controllable overhead variance** is the difference between the actual amount of overhead and the amount of overhead that would be included in a flexible budget for the actual level of production. The variance is referred to as "controllable" because managers are expected to be able to control costs so that they are not substantially different from the amount that would be included in the flexible budget.

$$\text{Controllable overhead variance} = \text{Actual overhead} - \text{Flexible budget level of overhead for actual level of production}$$

Suppose the National Compound Company expects $15,000 of fixed overhead and $20 of variable overhead per unit. In this case, the flexible budget for the actual level of production (450 units) is $24,000 [$15,000 + ($20 × 450)]. During the period, National incurs $23,000 of overhead. Thus, there is a $1,000 favorable controllable overhead variance.

$$\text{Controllable overhead variance} = \text{Actual overhead} - \text{Flexible budget level of overhead for actual level of production}$$

$$= \$23,000 - (\$15,000 + (\$20 \times 450))$$

$$= (\$1,000) \text{ favorable}$$

Again, the variance is labeled "favorable" because the actual amount of cost is less than the amount indicated in the flexible budget.

## OVERHEAD VOLUME VARIANCE

The **overhead volume variance** is equal to the difference between the amount of overhead included in the flexible budget and the amount of overhead applied to production using the standard overhead rate.

$$\text{Overhead volume variance} = \text{Flexible budget level of overhead for actual level of production} - \text{Overhead applied to production using standard overhead rate}$$

Before calculating the volume variance, let's review the calculation of the standard overhead rate. Suppose that at the start of its accounting period, National Compound anticipates producing 500 of the 50-gallon drums of compound. Further, the company anticipates having $15,000 of fixed manufacturing overhead and variable overhead equal to $20 per unit. In this case, total expected overhead is $25,000 [$15,000 + ($20 × 500 units)], and the overhead rate is $50 per unit (i.e., $25,000 ÷ 500 units).

| $15,000 + ($20 × 500 units) | $25,000 |
|---|---|
| ÷ Expected production | 500 units |
| = Standard overhead rate | 50 per unit |

*168500*
*75000*
*2.246*

Note that the standard overhead rate in this example is expressed on a per-unit basis. This is because National only produces a single product. When multiple products are produced, the overhead rate should be based on labor hours, machine hours, or some other measure of activity that is common to the various products. Or, an activity-based costing system can be used with standard rates for each driver of overhead cost.

*2.10*

**Computing the Overhead Volume Variance.** Now, if National actually produces 450 units, $22,500 of standard overhead would be applied to production (450 × $50). However, the flexible budget amount for 450 units of production is $24,000. Thus, the overhead volume variance is $1,500 unfavorable.

$$\text{Overhead volume variance} = \text{Flexible budget level of overhead for actual level of production} - \text{Overhead applied to production using standard overhead rate}$$

$$\text{Overhead volume variance} = 15,000 + (\$20 \times 450) - (\$50 \times 450 \text{ units})$$

$$\$1,500 \text{ unfavorable} = \$24,000 - \$22,500$$

Why is this variance labeled "unfavorable"? We turn to that question next.

**Interpreting the Overhead Volume Variance.** Volume variances do not signal that overhead costs are in or out of control. That signal is provided by the controllable overhead variance, discussed earlier. An overhead volume variance simply signals that the quantity of production was greater or less than anticipated when the standard overhead rate was developed. When more units are produced than anticipated, the amount of overhead applied to inventory exceeds the flexible budget because the amount of fixed cost per unit is being applied to more units than anticipated.

Consider the standard overhead rate of the National Compound Company. The rate of $50 per unit is composed of $20 per unit of variable cost and $30 of fixed cost. The $30 of fixed cost per unit results from dividing the expected amount of fixed cost ($15,000) by the anticipated production of 500 units.

| Standard Overhead Rate | |
|---|---|
| Variable cost per unit | $20 |
| Fixed cost per unit ($15,000 ÷ 500 expected units) | 30 |
| Total | $50 |

When this rate is applied to 450 units, a fixed cost of $13,500 is applied to inventory rather than the expected amount of fixed cost, which is $15,000. Thus, the amount of fixed cost applied to inventory is $1,500 less than the amount of fixed cost in the flexible budget (which is not affected by the level of activity).

|  | Standard Cost Applied to 450 Units | Flexible Budget for 450 Units | Difference |
|---|---|---|---|
| Variable cost | $ 9,000 ($20 × 450) | $ 9,000 ($20 × 450) | –0– |
| Fixed cost | 13,500 ($30 × 450) | 15,000 | $1,500 |
| Total | $22,500 | $24,000 | $1,500 |

If the company had anticipated that 450 units would be produced, the fixed cost per unit would have been $33.3333, and the standard overhead rate would have been set at $53.3333.

| Standard Overhead Rate | |
|---|---|
| Variable cost per unit | $20.0000 |
| Fixed cost per unit ($15,000 ÷ 450 expected units) | 33.3333 |
| Total | $53.3333 |

With a rate of $53.3333 per unit, $24,000 of overhead would have been applied to the 450 units produced, and the volume variance would be zero.

The usefulness of the volume variance is limited. It only signals that more or fewer units have been produced than planned when the standard overhead rate was set. If more units are produced than were originally planned, the variance is labeled "favorable" because additional production often (but not always) reflects unexpectedly high customer demand (a favorable outcome). If fewer units are produced, the variance is referred to as "unfavorable."

**LEARNING OBJECTIVE 5**

Calculate the financial impact of operating at more or less than planned capacity.

**Decision Making/ Incremental Analysis**

## CALCULATING THE FINANCIAL IMPACT OF OPERATING AT MORE OR LESS THAN PLANNED CAPACITY

As just explained, the volume variance really doesn't measure the financial impact of operating at more or less than planned capacity. So you are probably wondering how one would go about calculating the financial impact of producing more or fewer units than planned. To perform the calculation, we return to a familiar concept—incremental analysis.

Recall that at the start of the accounting period, National Compound anticipated producing 500 units. As it turned out, the company operated at less than planned capacity and produced only 450 units. Let's assume that a unit (a 50-gallon drum of compound) sells for $5,000. How much profit does the company lose when a unit is not produced and sold? The company obviously loses the selling price per unit but it saves the variable cost per unit of production. Fixed costs are not saved since they are not affected by production volume. In other words, the company loses the contribution margin per unit. The contribution margin of a 50-gallon drum is $920.

| | | |
|---|---|---|
| Selling price per unit | | $5,000 |
| Less variable costs: | | |
|   Material | $4,000 | |
|   Labor | 60 | |
|   Variable overhead | 20 | 4,080 |
| Contribution margin | | $ 920 |

Since 50 units were not produced and sold, National lost $46,000 of profit.

| | |
|---|---:|
| Number of units not produced and sold | 50 |
| Contribution margin per unit | × $   920 |
| Financial effect of not producing and selling 50 units | $46,000 |

Similarly, if 50 units more than planned were produced and sold, the company would have gained $46,000 of incremental profit.

# COMPREHENSIVE EXAMPLE: DARRINGTON ICE CREAM

Let's apply the information just discussed to the Darrington Ice Cream Company. Recall from the scenario at the start of the chapter that Linda Evert, director of operations for Darrington, was concerned about a 10 percent increase in material cost. The plant manager assured her that the increase was not due to waste in the use of raw materials. The material variances we calculate next will provide insight into the validity of the plant manager's statement.

At the start of the year, Darrington Ice Cream planned on producing 900,000 gallons of ice cream. Production of ice cream requires various raw materials (e.g., milk, cream, sugar, and flavorings). Most likely, Darrington develops separate standards for each. To simplify the setting, however, we assume that Darrington uses only one raw material. Each gallon of ice cream requires .8 gallons of raw material costing $2.50 per gallon—a gallon of ice cream does not require a gallon of raw material, because air is incorporated in the production process. Each gallon of ice cream also requires .125 hours of direct labor costing $12 per hour.

The company estimates that fixed overhead costs will equal $450,000 per year and variable overhead costs will equal $0.25 per gallon. Thus, the standard overhead rate is set at $0.75 per gallon [$0.50 of fixed overhead per gallon ($450,000 ÷ 900,000 gallons) + $0.25 of variable overhead per gallon].

In summary, the standard cost per unit are:

| | Standard Cost per Unit |
|---|:---:|
| Direct material (.8 gallons × $2.50) | $2.00 |
| Direct labor (.125 hours × $12) | 1.50 |
| Manufacturing overhead | .75 |
| Total | $4.25 |

Actual demand during the year is somewhat greater than anticipated, necessitating production of 1,000,000 gallons. Darrington purchases 810,000 gallons and uses 809,000 gallons of material, at a cost of $2.72 per gallon, to produce the 1,000,000 gallons of ice cream. Actual direct labor costs of $1,573,000 are incurred for 130,000 actual hours. Thus, the actual wage rate is $12.10 per hour ($1,573,000 ÷ 130,000). Finally, actual overhead costs of $680,000 are incurred.

At this point, you should attempt to calculate the standard cost variances for the Darrington Ice Cream data. For your convenience in working through the example and in solving problems at the end of the chapter, a summary of the variance formulas is presented in Illustration 11-4. Some key figures needed in the calculation of the variances for Darrington Ice Cream are summarized in Illustration 11-5.

**Illustration 11-4**
Standard cost variance
formulas

**Material Price Variance** $= (AP - SP) AQ^P$
$AP$ = actual price per unit of material
$SP$ = standard price per unit of material
$AQ^P$ = actual quantity of material purchased

**Material Quantity Variance** $= (AQ^U - SQ) SP$
$AQ^U$ = actual quantity of material used
$SQ$ = standard quantity of material for the actual level of production
$SP$ = standard price per unit of material

**Labor Rate Variance** $= (AR - SR) AH$
$AR$ = actual labor rate per hour
$SR$ = standard labor rate per hour
$AH$ = actual hours worked

**Labor Efficiency Variance** $= (AH - SH) SR$
$AH$ = actual hours worked
$SH$ = standard hours of labor for the actual level of production
$SR$ = standard labor rate per hour

$$\text{Controllable Overhead Variance} = \text{Actual overhead} - \begin{array}{c}\text{Flexible budget level}\\\text{of overhead for actual}\\\text{level of production}\end{array}$$

$$\text{Overhead Volume Variance} = \begin{array}{c}\text{Flexible budget level}\\\text{of overhead for}\\\text{actual level of production}\end{array} - \begin{array}{c}\text{Overhead applied to}\\\text{production using}\\\text{standard overhead rate}\end{array}$$

**Illustration 11-5**
Summary of data for
production of 1,000,000
gallons of ice cream

| | Standard Cost Information | Actual Cost Information |
|---|---|---|
| Direct material | 800,000 gallons at $2.50 per gallon | 810,000 gallons purchased at $2.72 per gallon<br>809,000 gallons used in production |
| Direct labor | 125,000 hours at $12 per hour | 130,000 hours at $12.10 per hour |
| Overhead applied at standard | $0.75 × 1,000,000 gallons = $750,000 | |
| Flexible budget overhead | $450,000 + ($0.25 × 1,000,000 gallons) = $700,000 | Actual overhead    $680,000 |

## MATERIAL VARIANCES

The actual price of material is $2.72 per gallon, whereas the standard price is $2.50 per gallon. The actual quantity of material purchased is 810,000 gallons. Thus, the material price variance is:

$$\text{Material price variance} = (\$2.72 - \$2.50)\, 810,000$$

$$= \$178,200 \text{ unfavorable}$$

Note that the material price variance is based on the quantity of material *purchased*, not the quantity used.

The actual quantity of material used is 809,000 gallons. Since 1,000,000 gallons of ice cream were produced, and the standard quantity of material per gallon is .8 gallons, the standard quantity of material for the total units produced is 800,000 gallons. The standard price is $2.50 per gallon. Thus, the material quantity variance is:

$$\text{Material quantity variance} = (809,000 - 800,000)\, \$2.50$$

$$= \$22,500 \text{ unfavorable}$$

Note that these results support the plant manager's contention that the large material variance was not due to wasting materials. Of the total $200,700 unfavorable variance, only $22,500 is due to using more material than planned. Most of the variance is due to paying more per gallon for raw material than planned.

## LABOR VARIANCES

The actual wage rate is $12.10 per hour, whereas the standard wage rate is $12 per hour. Because 130,000 actual hours are worked, the labor rate variance is:

$$\text{Labor rate variance} = (\$12.10 - \$12)\, 130,000$$

$$= \$13,000 \text{ unfavorable}$$

The actual quantity of labor is 130,000 hours, whereas the standard quantity of labor for the 1,000,000 gallons produced is 125,000 hours (1,000,000 gallons × .125 hours per gallon). The standard wage rate is $12 per hour. Thus, the labor efficiency variance is:

$$\text{Labor efficiency variance} = (130,000 - 125,000)\, \$12$$

$$= \$60,000 \text{ unfavorable}$$

## OVERHEAD VARIANCES

The actual amount of overhead is $680,000, whereas the flexible budget amount of overhead for 1,000,000 gallons produced is $700,000 [$450,000 + ($0.25 × 1,000,000 gallons)]. Thus, the controllable overhead variance is:

$$\text{Controllable overhead variance} = \$680,000 - \$700,000$$

$$= (\$20,000) \text{ favorable}$$

The amount of overhead applied to production is equal to the standard overhead rate of $0.75 per gallon times the 1,000,000 gallons produced. This amounts to $750,000. The flexible budget amount of overhead is $700,000. The difference between the flexible budget amount of overhead and the amount of overhead applied is the overhead volume variance, which is $50,000.

$$\text{Overhead volume variance} = \$700,000 - \$750,000$$

$$= (\$50,000) \text{ favorable}$$

# INVESTIGATION OF STANDARD COST VARIANCES

Once standard cost variances have been computed, how should they be used? It is important to note that standard cost variances do not provide definitive evidence that costs are "out of control" and that managers are not performing effectively. Rather, they should be viewed as indicators of *potential* problem areas. The only way to determine whether or not costs are being effectively controlled is to investigate the facts behind the variances.

To illustrate, consider again the standard cost variances just computed for Darrington Ice Cream. The variances are summarized in Illustration 11-6. As indicated in the illustration, there is a $178,200 unfavorable material price variance. Does this imply that the purchasing department is not doing a good job of searching for the lowest-cost material consistent with desired quality levels? Not necessarily. Investigation may reveal that price increases were unavoidable. Obviously, the purchasing department can do very little if all of the company's suppliers increase their prices.

As another example, consider the $60,000 unfavorable labor efficiency variance indicated in Illustration 11-6. What factors might account for this unfavorable variance? The first explanation that comes to mind may be that the manager responsible for supervising the production workforce has not done a competent job. However, this is just one possibility. Perhaps workers went on strike, and inexperienced substitutes were hired. These substitutes would have a difficult time meeting standard allowable production times even if they were properly supervised. Another possibility is that a new piece of equipment was placed into production during the period. Workers may simply require additional time to become familiar with the new equipment. Which of these, among other possible explanations, is correct can only be determined by an investigation to determine the real cause of the variance.

**Illustration 11-6**
Variance summary

DARRINGTON
ICE CREAM

**Variance Summary**
**for the Period Ended 12/31/x1**

| | | |
|---|---:|---|
| Material price variance | $178,200 | unfavorable |
| Material quantity variance | 22,500 | unfavorable |
| Labor rate variance | 13,000 | unfavorable |
| Labor efficiency variance | 60,000 | unfavorable |
| Controllable overhead variance | (20,000) | favorable |
| Overhead volume variance | (50,000) | favorable |
| Total | $203,700 | unfavorable |

## Any Questions?

**Q** In the previous chapter, we learned that there are three reasons why actual results may be different from the budget. Does the same logic apply to standard cost variances?

**A** That's exactly right. Actual costs may differ from standard because:
1. The standards were not properly developed;
2. The standards were properly developed but conditions changed; or
3. Management performance was particularly good (or bad).

An investigation is usually needed to determine which of these factors caused a particular variance.

Discuss how the management by exception approach is applied to investigation of standard cost variances.

## MANAGEMENT BY EXCEPTION

Because investigation of standard cost variances is itself a costly activity, management must decide which variances to investigate. Most managers take a "management by exception" approach and investigate only those variances that they deem to be exceptional. Of course, this implies that some criterion for determining what is meant by "exceptional" must be established. The absolute dollar value of the variance or the variance as a percent of actual or standard cost is often used as the criterion.

Suppose, for example, that Darrington Ice Cream decides to investigate any variance in excess of $40,000. This implies that the material price variance, the labor efficiency variance, and the overhead volume variance should be investigated. However, the cause of the overhead volume variance is quite obvious—more units were produced than anticipated when the standard overhead rate was developed. Thus, management need only investigate the material price variance and the labor efficiency variance.

Explain why a "favorable" variance may be unfavorable, how process improvements may lead to "unfavorable" variances, and why evaluation in terms of variances may lead to overproduction.

## "FAVORABLE" VARIANCES MAY BE UNFAVORABLE

The fact that a variance is "favorable" does not mean that it should not be investigated. Indeed, a favorable variance may be indicative of poor management decisions. For example, suppose the price of raw materials increases. In order to avoid an unfavorable material price variance, a manager could order the purchase of cheap, inferior materials. This could generate a favorable material price variance if the price of the inferior goods is less than the standard price of materials. However, the inferior materials may result in undetected product defects and cause the company to lose its reputation as a high-quality producer. If the defects are detected, items would be scrapped or "reworked." This would lead to an unfavorable material quantity variance, because additional materials would be used to replace or rework defective items.

## CAN PROCESS IMPROVEMENTS LEAD TO "UNFAVORABLE" VARIANCES?

A surprising reason why a firm may have an unfavorable variance is because it engaged in process improvements! Recall that at National Compound the standard labor hours for a unit of production is four hours and the company anticipated producing 500 units. Thus, the company anticipates needing 2,000 labor hours and staffs its production department to this level. Now suppose production workers at National Compound suggest a change in a manufacturing process such that they can produce a unit with only three hours of labor instead of four and standards are changed accordingly. If the company produces 500 units, standard labor will be 1,500 hours. But what will actual labor be? Unless the company fires workers, actual labor will still be 2,000 hours and there will be an unfavorable variance. And, it will be very difficult to fire workers who just improved the production process!

| Company anticipates production of 500 units at 4 labor hours per unit | 2,000 labor hours |
| Process improvement results in standard labor for 500 units of only 3 hours per unit | 1,500 labor hours |
| Unfavorable labor hour variance | 500 labor hours |

What the company really needs to do is stimulate demand for its product so it can produce and sell more than 500 units and take advantage of the extra "free capacity" generated by the process improvement.

## BEWARE—EVALUATION IN TERMS OF VARIANCES CAN LEAD TO EXCESS PRODUCTION

**You Get What You Measure**

If you read the appendix on the Theory of Constraints in Chapter 7, you know that a production department in front of a bottleneck department should not produce more units than the bottleneck can handle. If it does, the company will be making an investment in excess work-in-process inventory with a negative impact on shareholder value. However, evaluation in terms of standard cost variances might just encourage such counter-productive behavior.

Let's see why this is the case. Suppose a company has two production departments: Assembly and Finishing. The company anticipates that both departments will process 1,000 units per month and standard labor is 1.92 hours per unit in the Assembly department. Since Assembly anticipates the need for 1,920 labor hours per month, it hires 12 full-time workers (1,920 hours per month ÷ 160 hours per employee per month). Now suppose the Finishing department becomes a bottleneck due to sporadic failure of a paint curing device. In this case, the Assembly department should cut back its production until the Finishing department has solved the problem of the paint curing device. Let's assume that the Assembly department cuts back production to 900 units. With 900 units, standard labor hours are only 1,728. But, unless the Assembly department fires workers, it will have an unfavorable labor hour variance of 192 hours if only 900 units are produced.

| Staffing for 1,000 units (1,000 × 1.92 hours per unit) | 1,920 hours |
| Standard for 900 units needed (900 × 1.92 hours per unit) | 1,728 hours |
| Unfavorable variance unless the Assembly department fires workers | 192 hours |

Since the Assembly department does not want to fire workers for a short-term problem, it may go ahead and produce 1,000 units (100 more than needed) to avoid an unfavorable labor efficiency variance. Remember that "You get what you measure!" And if you measure efficiency in terms of the labor efficiency variance, you just might get "over production" in a nonbottleneck department.

# RESPONSIBILITY ACCOUNTING AND VARIANCES

As noted previously, the central idea of responsibility accounting is that managers should be held responsible only for costs they can control. The implication for variances is that managers and workers should only be held responsible for *variances* they can control. Thus, a supervisor who can control material usage but has no control over the price paid for materials should be held responsible for the material quantity variance but not for the material price variance. The purchasing agent responsible for buying material at the lowest price consistent with quality considerations should be held responsible for the price variance.

# MAKING BUSINESS DECISIONS

Managers need to assure their subordinates that they recognize that an unfavorable variance does not necessarily imply poor performance. Otherwise, subordinates may make decisions that hurt shareholder value. Let's see why this is the case. Suppose a manager unfairly criticizes a subordinate for having an unfavorable material price variance when, beyond the control of the subordinate, suppliers increase prices. What will happen the next time prices increase? It may be that the subordinate will turn to a lower quality (and lower price) supplier in an effort to avoid an unfavorable material price variance. That decision, however, could have a major negative impact on shareholder value.

## KNOWLEDGE AND SKILLS (K/S) CHECKLIST

*Knowledge and skills are needed to make good business decisions. Check off the knowledge and skills you've acquired from reading this chapter.*

❏ K/S 1. You have an expanded business vocabulary (see key terms).

❏ K/S 2. You can compute material, labor, and overhead variances.

❏ K/S 3. You understand that variances must be investigated to determine if a manager has performed particularly well or poorly. In particular, you know that a "favorable" variance may be unfavorable.

❏ K/S 4. You know that the overhead volume variance does not signal that overhead costs are in or out of control. It simply indicates that more or less was produced than anticipated when the overhead rate was developed.

❏ K/S 5. You know that performance evaluation using standard cost variances can lead to overproduction.

# SUMMARY OF LEARNING OBJECTIVES

① *Explain how standard costs are developed.* Standard costs are developed in a variety of ways. Standard material quantities may be determined by engineering studies. Supplier price lists may be used to determine standard prices of materials. Time and motion studies are sometimes used to determine standard labor hours.

② *Calculate and interpret variances for direct material.* The total material variance can be di-

vided into a material price variance and a material quantity variance.

③ *Calculate and interpret variances for direct labor.* The total labor variance can be divided into labor rate and labor efficiency variances.

④ *Calculate and interpret variances for manufacturing overhead.* The total overhead variance can be divided into an overhead volume variance and a controllable overhead variance.

**5** *Calculate the financial impact of operating at more or less than planned capacity.* When a company produces and sells more (less) units than planned, the company gains (loses) an amount equal to the contribution margin per unit times the number of units.

**6** *Discuss how the management by exception approach is applied to the investigation of standard cost variances.* Because the investigation of variances is costly, managers only investigate exceptional variances. Variances that are large in absolute dollar value or as a percent of actual or standard cost are generally considered exceptional.

**7** *Explain why a "favorable" variance may be unfavorable, how process improvements may lead to "unfavorable" variances, and why evalua-* tion in terms of variances may lead to overproduction. A favorable material price variance may result from buying inferior materials at a price lower than standard.

A process improvement might result in the need for less labor and lower standard labor hours per unit. Then, unless a firm fires workers or increases output, an unfavorable labor efficiency variance will result.

A production department generally should not produce more units than required by downstream production departments. However, if a downstream department is a bottleneck and requires fewer units than planned, the nonbottleneck department will have an unfavorable labor efficiency variance if it decreases production to the level required by the bottleneck (unless it fires or lays off workers).

# A P P E N D I X

Record standard costs in the accounts of a manufacturing firm.

# RECORDING STANDARD COSTS IN ACCOUNTS

Standard costing systems are used to control the operations of manufacturing companies and to determine product costs. In this chapter, we have illustrated the calculation of standard cost variances and discussed how they can be used to evaluate operations. Now, we'll see how product costs are recorded at the standard rate in the accounts of a manufacturing company. In a standard costing system, the costs added to the Raw Material Inventory, Work in Process Inventory, Finished Goods Inventory, and Cost of Goods Sold accounts are all recorded at standard rather than actual cost. In the process of recording inventory at standard cost, variances are also calculated and recorded for management's use in performance evaluation. As a concrete example, we will present the entries for recording material, labor, and manufacturing overhead using the information presented for Darrington Ice Cream (see Illustration 11-5).

## RECORDING MATERIAL COSTS

Darrington Ice Cream purchased 810,000 gallons of raw materials. The company actually paid $2.72 per gallon, or $2,203,200. This amount is recorded as a credit to accounts payable. The Raw Material Inventory account, however, is debited for the standard cost of the material purchased. Because the standard price is $2.50 per gallon, this amounts to $2,025,000 in total. The difference between actual and the standard cost is the material price variance of $178,200.

| (date) | Raw Material Inventory | 2,025,000 | |
|--------|------------------------|-----------|-----------|
| | Material Price Variance | 178,200 | |
| | Accounts payable | | 2,203,200 |
| | To record material purchases | | |

Darrington Ice Cream used 809,000 gallons of material in production. The standard cost of this material (809,000 × $2.50 = $2,022,500) is removed from Raw Material Inventory by crediting that account. The standard quantity of material to produce 1,000,000 gallons of ice cream is 800,000 gallons. At the standard price of $2.50 per gallon, the standard material cost is $2,000,000. The standard amount is recorded as a debit in Work in Process Inventory. The difference between the debit and the credit is due to the material quantity variance ($22,500).

Variance accounts are temporary accounts and are always closed before financial statements are prepared. We demonstrate the closing process later. Note that in this example, both the material price variance and the material quantity variance are unfavorable and recorded as debits. Unfavorable variances are associated with increases in the expenses of a company and have a debit balance like expense accounts. Favorable variances are associated with reductions in the expenses of a company and have a credit balance.

| (date) | Work in Process Inventory | 2,000,000 | |
| | Material Quantity Variance | 22,500 | |
| |     Raw Material Inventory | | 2,022,500 |
| | | | |
| | To record material used in production. | | |

## RECORDING LABOR COST

During the year, 130,000 actual labor hours are worked at a rate of $12.10 per hour for a total cost of $1,573,000. The standard number of hours is 125,000, and the standard wage rate is $12 per hour. Thus, the total standard cost of labor to be added to Work in Process Inventory is $1,500,000. The difference between the total actual labor cost payable and the total standard labor cost assigned to Work in Process Inventory is the sum of the labor rate and labor efficiency variances.

| (date) | Work in Process Inventory | 1,500,000 | |
| | Labor Rate Variance | 13,000 | |
| | Labor Efficiency Variance | 60,000 | |
| |     Wages and Salaries Payable | | 1,573,000 |
| | | | |
| | To record labor cost. | | |

## RECORDING MANUFACTURING OVERHEAD

Recording manufacturing overhead in a standard costing system is a three-step process.

1. Actual overhead is recorded in the manufacturing overhead account.
2. Overhead is applied to Work in Process Inventory at the standard cost.
3. The difference between actual overhead and overhead applied at standard is closed and overhead variances are identified.

These three steps are illustrated next.

Actual overhead incurred during the year is $680,000. Various accounts (e.g., indirect wages payable, utilities payable, and accumulated depreciation) are credited to record this amount, and the actual cost of overhead is debited in the Manufacturing Overhead account.

| (date) | Manufacturing Overhead | 680,000 | |
| | Various Accounts | | 680,000 |
| | | | |
| | To record actual overhead cost. | | |

Work in Process Inventory is assigned the standard cost of overhead, which is equal to the standard overhead rate times the number of units produced. In the example, this amounts to $750,000 (i.e., 1,000,000 gallons × $0.75 per gallon). When this amount is applied to Work in Process Inventory, Manufacturing Overhead is reduced by the same amount.

| (date) | Work in Process Inventory | 750,000 | |
| | Manufacturing Overhead | | 750,000 |
| | | | |
| | To apply overhead cost to inventory at standard. | | |

At this point, Manufacturing Overhead has been debited for the actual amount of overhead and credited for the amount of overhead applied to Work in Process Inventory at the standard overhead rate. The difference between the actual overhead cost and the standard overhead applied to inventory ($70,000) is equal to the sum of the overhead volume variance and the controllable overhead variance. These two variances are identified when the journal entry to close out manufacturing overhead is recorded.

| (date) | Manufacturing Overhead | 70,000 | |
| | Overhead Volume Variance | | 50,000 |
| | Controllable Overhead Variance | | 20,000 |
| | | | |
| | To close out Manufacturing Overhead and Record Overhead Variances. | | |

## RECORDING FINISHED GOODS

At this point, Work in Process Inventory contains the following costs:

| Raw material | $2,000,000 |
| Direct labor | 1,500,000 |
| Overhead | 750,000 |
| Total | $4,250,000 |

The total of $4,250,000 is equal to the 1,000,000 gallons produced at a standard cost per gallon of $4.25. When the units are completed, the cost is transferred from Work in Process Inventory to Finished Goods Inventory.

| (date) | Finished Goods Inventory | 4,250,000 | |
| | Work in Process Inventory | | 4,250,000 |
| | | | |
| | To record completed units in Finished Goods Inventory. | | |

## RECORDING COST OF GOODS SOLD

When units are sold, the cost of Finished Goods Inventory is reduced and Cost of Goods Sold is increased by the standard cost of the units sold. Assume that all

1,000,000 gallons of ice cream produced are sold. The standard cost is $4.25 per gallon. Therefore, the entry to record the Cost of Goods Sold is:

| (date) | Cost of Goods Sold | 4,250,000 | |
|--------|--------------------|-----------|--|
| | Finished Goods Inventory | | 4,250,000 |
| | | | |
| | To record Cost of Goods Sold. | | |

## CLOSING VARIANCE ACCOUNTS

At the end of the accounting period, the temporary variance accounts must be closed. As a practical matter, this is usually accomplished by debiting or crediting the variances to Cost of Goods Sold. Before closing the variance accounts, Cost of Goods Sold is recorded at standard cost. Thus, closing the variances results in the account being adjusted to approximate actual cost. It would be more accurate to adjust Work in Process Inventory and Finished Goods Inventory (as well as Cost of Goods Sold) to actual cost by allocating part of the total variance to these accounts. However, unless the variances are significant and the balances in Work in Process Inventory and Finished Goods Inventory are large relative to Cost of Goods Sold, closing the total variance to Cost of Goods Sold is convenient and not misleading. In the case of Darrington Ice Cream, there is no work in process or finished goods inventory at the end of the year (all of the ice cream produced was sold). Therefore, the variances are closed to Cost of Goods Sold.

The journal entry to close the variance accounts is as follows. Note that a favorable variance reduces the amount of Cost of Goods Sold, whereas an unfavorable variance increases the account.

| (date) | Cost of Goods Sold | 203,700 | |
|--------|--------------------|---------|--|
| | Overhead Volume Variance | 50,000 | |
| | Controllable Overhead Variance | 20,000 | |
| | Material Price Variance | | 178,200 |
| | Material Quantity Variance | | 22,500 |
| | Labor Rate Variance | | 13,000 |
| | Labor Efficiency Variance | | 60,000 |
| | | | |
| | To close variance accounts to Cost of Goods Sold | | |

# REVIEW PROBLEM

RampUp Storage Containers produces a 1,000 cubic foot metal storage unit that is used by storage companies and other businesses needing low-cost, mobile storage units. The units sell for $3,000 per unit.

The company uses a standard costing system. At the start of 2004, standard costs were set as follows:

**Standard cost per unit:**

| | |
|---|---|
| Material cost (6 prefabricated metal sheets × $200) | $1,200 |
| Direct labor (10 hours × $20) | 200 |
| Overhead ($500 per unit) | 500 |
| Total | $1,900 |

**The overhead rate was calculated as follows:** At the start of 2004 the company estimated that it would produce and sell 5,000 units, incur $500,000 of variable overhead costs and $2,000,000 of fixed overhead costs.

| | |
|---|---:|
| Variable overhead | $ 500,000 |
| Fixed overhead | 2,000,000 |
| Total | 2,500,000 |
| Divided by estimated production | 5,000 |
| Overhead cost per unit | $      500 |

Based on estimated sales, standard costs, and other information, the following budget was prepared:

**2004 budget (expected production and sales of 5,000 units)**

| | |
|---|---:|
| Sales | $15,000,000 |
| Cost of sales | 9,500,000 |
| Gross profit | 5,500,000 |
| Selling, general, and administrative expense | 3,900,000 |
| Income from operations | $ 1,600,000 |

During 2004, the company received an unexpected large order (1,000 units) from a national storage company. The result was a substantial increase in the number of units produced and sold (6,000 units in total). Of the 6,000 units, 5,000 were sold at the standard price of $3,000 per unit and the 1,000 units sold to the national storage company were sold at $2,800 per unit.

To produce the 6,000 units, the company incurred the following production costs:

| | |
|---|---:|
| Material purchased and used | |
| (36,200 metal sheets × $200) | $ 7,240,000 |
| Direct labor | |
| (62,000 hours × $21) | 1,302,000 |
| Variable overhead | 594,000 |
| Fixed overhead | 2,480,000 |
| Total actual production costs | $11,616,000 |

**Required**
a. Calculate the production cost variances and indicate whether they are favorable or unfavorable.
b. Provide a brief interpretation of the overhead volume variance. In other words, answer the question: "What is the meaning of an overhead volume variance?"
c. Calculate the financial impact of the 1,000 unit special order from the national storage company.

**Answer**
a. **Material price variance**
   (AP − SP) AQ
   ($200 − $200) 36,200 =                                         –0–

   **Material quantity variance**
   (AQ − SQ) SP
   (36,200 − 36,000) $200 =                       $40,000 unfavorable

   **Labor rate variance**
   (SR − AR) AH
   ($20 − $21) 62,000 =                           $62,000 unfavorable

**Labor efficiency variance**

(AH − SH) SR
(62,000 − 60,000) $20 =                                          $40,000 unfavorable

**Controllable overhead variance**

Actual overhead − Flexible budget for actual production
$3,074,000 − [$2,000,000 + $100 (6,000)] =       $474,000 unfavorable

**Overhead volume variance**

Flexible budget for actual production − Overhead applied
[$2,000,000 + $100 (6,000)] − ($500 × 6,000) = $400,000 favorable

b. The overhead volume variance results from applying a predetermined fixed overhead rate to more or less units than originally planned when the rate was determined. If more units are produced than planned, more fixed overhead than
anticipated will be applied at the standard rate. If fewer units are produced than
planned, less fixed overhead than anticipated will be applied at the standard
rate.

c. The selling price per unit for the 1,000 unit order is                    $2,800
Variable costs at standard are:

| | | |
|---|---:|---:|
| Material | $1,200 | |
| Labor | 200 | |
| Variable overhead | 100 | 1,500 |
| Contribution margin | | $1,300 |

1,000 extra units results in $1,300,000 of incremental profit.

| | |
|---|---:|
| Contribution margin per unit | $1,300 |
| Number of units | 1,000 |
| Incremental profit | $1,300,000 |

# KEY TERMS

Attainable standards (384)
Budgeted cost (382)
Controllable overhead
 variance (389)
Ideal standards (384)

Labor efficiency variance (388)
Labor rate variance (388)
Material price variance (386)
Material quantity variance (386)

Overhead volume variance (389)
Standard cost (382)
Standard cost variance (384)
Variance analysis (384)

# SELF ASSESSMENT   *(Answers Below)*

1. What is the primary benefit of a standard costing
system?

   a. It records costs at what should have been incurred.
   b. It allows for a comparison of differences between actual and standard costs.
   c. It is easy to implement.
   d. It is inexpensive and easy to use.

2. Which of the following is not a way to develop a
standard cost?

   a. By using a fixed rate that is higher every
period.
   b. By performing time and motion studies.
   c. By analyzing past data.
   d. By using what is specified in engineering
plans.

**3.** The total material variance can be divided into a material _____ variance and a material _____ variance.

**4.** Which of the following statements correctly describes an unfavorable material price variance?

   a. Too much material was purchased.
   b. A higher price was paid for material purchased compared with the standard price.
   c. More material was used than called for by the standard.
   d. Less material was used than called for by the standard.

**5.** True or False? The labor rate variance is equal to the difference between the actual wage rate and the standard wage rate times the standard number of labor hours worked.

**6.** What does a favorable labor efficiency variance mean?

   a. Labor rates were higher than called for by standards.
   b. Inexperienced labor was used, causing the rate to be lower than standard.
   c. More labor was used than called for by standards.

   d. Less labor was used than called for by standards.

**7.** What does an unfavorable overhead volume variance mean?

   a. Overhead costs are out of control.
   b. Overhead costs are in control.
   c. Production was greater than anticipated.
   d. Production was less than anticipated.

**8.** True or False? Standard cost variances provide definitive evidence that costs are "out of control" and managers are not performing effectively.

**9.** True or False? A *favorable* variance may be due to a *poor* management decision.

**10.** (Appendix) At the end of the accounting period, a journal entry is made to close variance accounts to _____ or _____, _____, and _____.

## Answers to Self Assessment

**1.** b;    **2.** a;    **3.** price, quantity;    **4.** b;
**5.** False;    **6.** d;    **7.** d;    **8.** False;    **9.** True;
**10.** Cost of Goods Sold or Work in Process, Finished Goods and Cost of Goods Sold.

# INTERACTIVE LEARNING

**Enhance and test your knowledge of Chapter 11 using the interactive CD.**

1. Learning Objectives
2. Multiple Choice
3. Language of Business—Matching of Key Terms
4. Critical Thinking
5. Demonstration—The calculation of variances.
6. Case—*Crowley Industries*; Standard cost variances.
7. Video—Starbucks; Variance analysis

**Go to our dynamic Web site for more self-assessment, Web links, and additional information.**

# QUESTIONS

**1.** What role do standard costs play in controlling the operations of a business?

**2.** How are standard costs developed for direct materials, direct labor, and manufacturing overhead?

**3.** What is the difference between an ideal standard and an attainable standard?

**4.** "You get what you measure!" If so, what problem might be created by managers attempting to achieve favorable material price variances?

**5.** How might a favorable material price variance or a favorable labor rate variance be related to an unfavorable material quantity variance?

**6.** Should managers investigate only unfavorable variances?

**7.** "Overhead volume variances do not signal that overhead costs are in or out of control." Do you agree? Explain.

**8.** What factors should be considered when investigating variances?

**9.** What is management by exception?

**10.** What does responsibility accounting imply with respect to holding managers responsible for standard cost variances?

**11.** (Appendix) What are the alternative methods for closing variance accounts?

# EXERCISES

**EXERCISE 11-1. Group Assignment**[1]   Five Star Tools is a small family-owned firm that manufactures diamond-coated cutting tools (chisels and saws) used by jewelers. Production involves three major processes. First, steel "blanks" (tools without the diamond coating) are cut to size. Second, the blanks are sent to a chemical bath that prepares the tools for the coating process. In coating, the third major process, the blanks are coated with diamond chips in a proprietary process that simultaneously coats and sharpens the blade of each tool. Following the coating process each tool is inspected and defects are repaired or scrapped.

Production process at five star tools

Currently, the Chemical Bath Department is a bottleneck due to intermittent failures related to an antiquated dipping tank. The result is that the department can only process 500 items per hour from the Cutting Department rather than the 600 items per hour that are normally processed.

*Required*
Explain why the Cutting Department should cut back production from 600 items per hour to 500. Further, explain why if the Cutting Department does cut back, as it should, it is likely to have an unfavorable labor efficiency variance.

**EXERCISE 11-2. Writing Assignment**   Write a paragraph explaining how, if workers improve a production process, they may actually generate an unfavorable labor efficiency variance.

**EXERCISE 11-3. Internet Assignment**   SAP provides enterprise resource planning software (discussed in Chapter 1 of this book). Go to the Web site ⟨*http://searchsap.techtarget.com*⟩, which has a search feature that you can use to locate information on SAP features. Type in "What is a standard cost variance?" You'll find a discussion entitled "Product variances explained."

*Required*
a. According to this article, what is the definition of a production variance in SAP?

b. In the example where a manager buys blue widgets for $1 less per unit than standard, should the standard be adjusted in the SAP program?

---

[1]Note that this exercise is related to a case in Chapter 7 that dealt with decision making and constraints.

**EXERCISE 11-4. Calculating Material Variances**   At Midwest Refrigeration, the standard price for the Z240 electrical relay (a component used in the production of a commercial refrigeration unit) is $25. Standards call for 2 relays per unit of finished product. In July, the company purchased 100 relays for $2,600. The company used 83 relays in the production of 40 refrigeration units (three relays were damaged in the installation process).

*Required*
Calculate the material price variance and the material quantity variance related to the Z240 electrical relay. Indicate whether the variances are favorable or unfavorable.

**EXERCISE 11-5. Calculating Labor Variances**   At Midwest Refrigeration, the standard quantity of labor is 20 hours per refrigeration unit. The standard wage rate is $25. In July, the company produced 40 refrigeration units, and incurred 820 labor hours at a cost of $21,320.

*Required*
Calculate the labor rate variance and the labor efficiency variance. Indicate whether the variances are favorable or unfavorable.

**EXERCISE 11-6. Calculating Overhead Variances**   At the start of the year, Midwest Refrigeration estimated that the company would produce 504 refrigeration units during the year (42 per month). Annual fixed overhead costs were estimated to be $599,760 ($49,980 per month), and estimated variable overhead costs were estimated to be $600 per unit.

During July, the company produced 40 refrigeration units and incurred $76,000 of actual overhead cost.

*Required*

a. What is the standard overhead rate used to apply overhead to units produced?

b. Calculate the controllable overhead variance for July and indicate whether it is favorable or unfavorable.

c. Calculate the overhead volume variance for July and indicate whether it is favorable or unfavorable.

**EXERCISE 11-7. Calculating Material Variances**   Crown Jewelry produced 1,300 rings during March. The standard cost of each ounce of gold used in a ring is $295 per ounce. The standard quantity of material for each ring is a half ounce of gold per ring. The cost of gold purchased and used in March was $198,900 at $300 per ounce. Determine the material price variance and the material quantity variance for March. Indicate whether each variance is favorable or unfavorable.

**EXERCISE 11-8. Calculating Material Variances**   Kent Space Products uses a standard costing system. For production of a fuel cell, standards call for four model K4Q valves per cell costing $2,000 each. During 2006, the company purchased 110 valves for $209,000. The company used 105 valves in the production of 25 fuel cells (5 valves were ruined through installation error).

*Required*
Calculate material price and quantity variances for the model K4Q valves.

**EXERCISE 11-9. Calculating Labor Variances**   The standard labor cost in the production of a pair of Tukor Brand athletic shoes is .5 hours at $18 per hour. During the month of June, 20,000 pairs were produced. Actual labor costs were $172,900 for 9,500 hours. Compute the labor rate and labor efficiency variances for the month of June.

**EXERCISE 11-10. Calculating Material and Labor Variances** Texas Boots uses a standard costing system. The standard material and labor costs for producing each pair of boots are as follows:

| | |
|---|---|
| Materials (1.5 yards × $9.00) | $13.50 |
| Direct labor (.5 hours × $15) | 7.50 |

During May, the company produced 7,000 pairs of boots; 10,000 yards of material were purchased for $80,000, and 11,000 yards of material were used in production. Also during May, 3,800 direct labor hours were worked at a cost of $58,900. Calculate material price and quantity variances and labor rate and efficiency variances. Indicate whether the variances are favorable or unfavorable.

**EXERCISE 11-11. Calculating Overhead Variances—Service Example** Barret Hospital is interested in analyzing overhead related to laundry services. The hospital administrator estimated that monthly fixed costs would be $80,000 and variable costs would be $1.20 per patient day.

During the month of September, the hospital had 5,000 patient days. Total laundry costs were $91,000.

*Required*
Analyze laundry costs for the month of September using the procedures for calculating a controllable overhead variance. Is the variance favorable or unfavorable?

**EXERCISE 11-12. Calculating Labor and Overhead Variances** At the start of 2006, Western Thread company determined its standard labor cost to be 1.5 hours per unit at $12.30 per hour. The budget for variable overhead was $6 per unit and budgeted fixed overhead was $135,000 for the year. Expected annual production was 30,000 units. During 2006, the actual cost of labor was $12.75 per hour. Western Thread produced 32,500 units requiring 52,000 direct labor hours. Actual overhead for the year was $326,800.

*Required*
Calculate labor rate and efficiency variances and the controllable overhead variance and the overhead volume variance.

**EXERCISE 11-13. Investigating Variances** At the start of the year, Midwest Refrigeration estimated that the company would produce 504 refrigeration units during the year (42 per month). Annual fixed overhead costs were estimated to be $599,760 ($49,980 per month), and estimated variable overhead costs were estimated to be $600 per unit. Standard cost per unit was set at $3,290:

| | |
|---|---|
| Standard material cost | $1,000 |
| Standard labor cost | 500 |
| Standard overhead volume rate per unit | 1,790 |
| Total | $3,290 |

During the year, the company experienced stiff competition and ended up producing and selling only 420 units. Actual annual production costs were $1,498,807 and standard cost variances were as follows:

**Summary of Production Variances**

| | |
|---|---|
| Material price variance | $ 2,349 unfavorable |
| Material quantity variance | 10,468 unfavorable |
| Labor rate variance | 1,452 favorable |
| Labor efficiency variance | 4,682 unfavorable |
| Controllable overhead variance | 1,000 unfavorable |
| Overhead volume variance | 99,960 unfavorable |
| Total | $117,007 unfavorable |

*Required*

Suppose you are the CFO of Midwest Refrigeration and you want to determine the cause of significant variances. Given the demands on your time, you don't want to investigate variances that have an obvious explanation or that are less than 1/2 percent of actual production cost. Which variance(s) would you investigate? Explain the basis for your answer.

**EXERCISE 11-14. (Appendix) Calculating Material Variances and Recording Material Costs** Quality Cabinet Company uses a standard costing system and produced 2,200 cabinets during May. The standard cost of wood is $25 per linear foot, and the standard quantity for each cabinet is 30 linear feet.

During May, the company purchased 70,000 linear feet of wood for $1,680,000, and 65,000 feet were used in production.

Determine the material price variance, the material quantity variance, and record the related journal entries for May.

**EXERCISE 11-15. (Appendix) Recording Labor Variances** Reliance Company uses a standard costing system. In August, 9,328 actual labor hours were worked at a rate of $11.75 per hour. The standard number of hours is 9,400 and the standard wage rate is $11.90 per hour. Prepare a journal entry to record labor cost and related variances during the month.

**EXERCISE 11-16. (Appendix) Recording Manufacturing Overhead Variances** Menton Company uses a standard costing system. During 2006, the company incurred actual overhead of $381,000. The standard rate for applying overhead is $2.25 per unit and 180,000 units were produced in 2006. One-third of the total overhead variance is attributed to the volume variance and the remainder is attributed to the controllable overhead variance. Prepare the journal entries to record overhead incurred (you should credit "various accounts") and the overhead variances.

**EXERCISE 11-17. (Appendix) Closing variance accounts** The variance summary for Bell Computers is as follows

**Bell Computer Company**
**Variance Summary**
**for the Year Ended December 31, 2006**

| | | |
|---|---:|---|
| Material price variance | $(4,150) | Favorable |
| Material quantity variance | 3,250 | Unfavorable |
| Labor rate variance | (115) | Favorable |
| Labor efficiency variance | 2,600 | Unfavorable |
| Controllable overhead variance | 2,500 | Unfavorable |
| Overhead volume variance | 4,500 | Unfavorable |
| Total | $8,585 | Unfavorable |

*Required*

Prepare a journal entry to close the variance accounts at Bell Computers. Assume that the total variance is not material and is closed to cost of goods sold.

**EXERCISE 11-18. (Appendix) Closing Variance Accounts** Refer to the summary of variances in Exercise 17. At Bell Computers, the ending balance in Finished Goods Inventory is $100,000; the ending balance in Work in Process Inventory is $50,000 and the balance in Cost of Goods Sold is $350,000.

*Required*

Prepare a journal entry to close the variance accounts at Bell Computers. Assume that the total variance is material and is apportioned among Finished Goods Inventory, Work in Process Inventory, and Cost of Goods Sold.

# PROBLEMS

**PROBLEM 11-1. Material Variances**   Hank's is a chain of 54 coffee shops. The standard amount of ground coffee per cup is .8 ounces. During the month of September, the company sold 324,000 cups of coffee (reported via electronic cash registers) and the 54 shops reported using 16,800 pounds of coffee. Also during September, the company purchased 15,900 pounds of coffee at a cost of $135,150. The standard price per pound is $8.

*Required*

a. Compute material price and quantity variances.

b. Do either or both of the variances warrant investigation?

**PROBLEM 11-2. Comprehensive Variance Problem**   Hayes Chemical Company produces a chemical used in dry cleaning. Its accounting system uses standard costs.

The standards per half gallon can of chemical call for .5 gallons of material and 1.5 hours of labor. The standard cost per gallon of material is $6.50. The standard cost per hour for labor is $9.00. Overhead is applied at the rate of $10.50 per can. Expected production is 15,000 cans with fixed overhead per year of $30,000, and variable overhead of $8.50 per unit (a half gallon can).

During 2006, 17,500 cans were produced; 10,000 gallons of material were purchased at a cost of $66,000; 9,100 gallons of material were used in production. The cost of direct labor incurred in 2006 was $229,643.75 based on an average actual wage rate of $9.05 per hour. Actual overhead for 2006 was $169,750.

*Required*

a. Determine the standard cost per unit.

b. Calculate material, labor, and overhead variances.

c. List a possible cause for each variance.

**PROBLEM 11-3. Comprehensive Variance Problem**   Dante's Statue Company produces lawn statues. The standard cost of producing one statue is:

| | |
|---|---|
| Material (2 pounds × $2.25) | $ 4.50 |
| Labor (.5 hours × $10) | $ 5.00 |
| Overhead | $ 9.90 |
| Total | $19.40 |

Standard variable overhead is $5.40 per unit and fixed annual overhead is $90,000. At the start of 2005, expected production was 20,000 units.

During 2005, 22,000 statues were produced. The following information, related to actual costs incurred in 2005, is available:

1. Purchased 44,000 pounds of material for $96,800.

2. Used 46,200 pounds of material.

3. Worked 10,300 labor hours costing $113,300.

4. Actual overhead incurred was $208,000.

*Required*

a. Show the calculation of the standard overhead rate per unit of $9.90.

b. Calculate all material, labor, and overhead variances.

c. Prepare a variance summary, and briefly comment on variances that should be investigated.

**PROBLEM 11-4. Comprehensive Variance Problem**  Bowser Products operates a small plant in New Mexico that produces dog food in batches of 1,000 pounds. The product sells for $3 per pound.

Standard costs for 2006 are:
Standard direct labor cost = $15 per hour.
Standard direct labor hours per batch = 8 hours.
Standard cost of material A = $0.20 per pound
Standard pounds of material A per batch = 800 pounds
Standard cost of material B = $0.40 per pound
Standard pounds of material B per batch = 200 pounds
Fixed overhead cost per batch = $400

At the start of 2006, the company estimated monthly production and sales of 40 batches. The company estimated that all overhead costs were fixed and amounted to $16,000 per month.

During the month of June, 2006 (typically a somewhat slow month) 30 batches were produced (not an unusual level of production for this month). The following costs were incurred:

Direct labor costs were $4,800 for 300 hours.
24,500 pounds of material A costing $4,655 were purchased and used.
5,900 pounds of material B costing $2,419 were purchased and used.
Fixed overhead of $15,500 was incurred

*Required*

a. Calculate variances for material, labor, and overhead.

b. Prepare a summary of the variances. Does the unfavorable overhead volume variance suggest that overhead costs are out of control?

**PROBLEM 11-5. Comprehensive Variance Problem**  Vulkan Company produces rubber seals used in the aerospace industry. Standards call for 3.5 pounds of material at $3.40 per pound for each seal. The standard cost for labor is .5 hours at $20 per hour. Standard overhead is $7 per unit. For the year 2006, expected production is 100,000 seals with fixed overhead of $100,000 and variable overhead of $6 per seal.

During 2006, a total of 99,000 seals were produced. The company purchased 350,000 pounds of material for $1,260,000. Production required 341,550 pounds of material. The cost of direct labor incurred was $1,039,500 with an actual average wage rate of $21 per hour. Actual overhead for the year was $650,000.

*Required*

a. Determine the standard cost per seal.

b. Calculate the material, labor, and overhead variances.

c. Prepare a summary of the variances and indicate which variances should be investigated.

**PROBLEM 11-6. Labor Variances**  Northwest Medical Testing draws blood samples from approximately 2,000 clients each month. The standard time for a technician to draw and prepare a blood sample for testing is 9.5 minutes.

The standard wage rate for technicians is $25 per hour. During August, Northwest hired a temporary employee at $40 per hour to fill in for a technician who quit unexpectedly. During the month, technicians processed 1,910 samples and were paid $10,480 for 322 hours of work related to drawing and preparing blood samples.

*Required*

Calculate labor rate and efficiency variances for August, and comment on whether or not labor costs for technicians appear to be in or out of control.

**PROBLEM 11-7. Variance Analysis** Will Norton, the general manager of Cummings Manufactured Siding, is reviewing a monthly variance summary. The summary reveals a large favorable material price variance and large unfavorable material quantity and labor efficiency variances. All other variances are small. Will's initial instinct is to reward the purchasing manager with a substantial bonus, and withhold the plant manager's monthly bonus until material quantity and labor efficiency variances improve.

*Required*

a. Should Will act according to his initial instinct?

b. What scenario(s) other than "good performance in purchasing and poor performance in manufacturing" could lead to the same variances as those noted?

c. What should Will do to determine whether or not the purchasing manager's performance is especially good and the plant manager's performance is poor?

**PROBLEM 11-8. Variance Analysis—Nonmonetary Measures** XcomSoftware operates a 24-hour help line to answer customer questions. To control the cost of operations, the company compares the actual time required to answer customer questions with a standard time of five minutes per customer call. Monthly bonuses are awarded if the standard is achieved.

In the past five months, the number of calls has decreased from approximately 8,000 to approximately 7,000. And the average time per call has decreased from 7 minutes to 4.98 minutes. However, a software magazine recently gave the company a poor evaluation in an article that reviewed the support that software companies provide customers.

*Required*

a. Does the favorable variance for response time indicate good performance?

b. What might account for the "improvement" in performance related to time per call and the poor rating of customer support?

**PROBLEM 11-9. Relationships Among Variances** In her review of annual production variances, Taylor Abboud, CFO of Edwards Manufacturing, noted that there was an $80,000 favorable material price variance, a $65,000 unfavorable material quantity variance, a $90,000 favorable labor rate variance, and a $200,000 unfavorable labor efficiency variance. From her previous discussions with factory supervisors and other managers, she knows that the purchasing department was able to buy materials at a "bargain" price. However, the material often failed stress tests and a large number of items needed to be reworked. Also, the company had a brief strike. During the strike, the company hired a number of inexperienced, temporary replacement workers at wage rates significantly below those paid to the workers on strike.

*Required*

a. Explain how the favorable material price variance and the favorable labor rate variance may be related to the unfavorable material quantity variance and the unfavorable labor efficiency variance.

b. Would you characterize the favorable material price variance as indicative of a good decision by the purchasing department?

**PROBLEM 11-10. Interpreting the Overhead Volume Variance; Calculating the Financial Impact of Operating Below Capacity** National Battery Company produces a wide variety of batteries for home, automobile, and marine use. One example of its many products is the Road Guardian automobile battery. The standard cost for this battery is as follows:

**Standard Cost, Road Guardian**

| | |
|---|---|
| Material | $ 3.00 |
| Labor | 2.00 |
| Overhead | 10.00 |
| Total | $15.00 |

At the start of the current year, 2006, the company estimated that it would incur $40,000,000 of overhead costs and $8,000,000 of direct labor costs. Thus, $5 of overhead is applied at standard for each dollar of direct labor. Overhead is, essentially, completely fixed, which reflects the high level of investment in automated manufacturing.

During 2006, the company experienced a labor strike that severely limited production and standard labor cost was only $7,000,000. At a recent meeting in early January of 2007, C.W. Rogers, the president of National, asked the company controller, Walter Cox, to estimate the effect of the strike on company profit. The following morning, Walter sent the president a memo:

Date:      January 7, 2007

To:        C.W.
From:      Walter
Subject:   Effect of strike on company profit.

As you know, profit in 2006 was greatly affected by a strike, which reduced productive capacity. The way to measure the impact of the reduced capacity is to examine the overhead volume variance.

At the start of the year, we budgeted overhead to be $40,000,000. Actual overhead was $39,400,000 so we had a favorable overhead budget variance of $600,000. However, we only applied $35,000,000 of overhead to inventory ($5 overhead rate × $7,000,000 standard labor). Thus, we had an unfavorable overhead volume variance of $5,000,000.

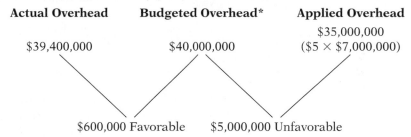

| **Actual Overhead** | **Budgeted Overhead*** | **Applied Overhead** |
|---|---|---|
| | | $35,000,000 |
| $39,400,000 | $40,000,000 | ($5 × $7,000,000) |

$600,000 Favorable     $5,000,000 Unfavorable

*Note that budgeted overhead does not need to be adjusted for actual production since overhead costs are, for practical purposes, fixed. Thus, overhead in a static and in a flexible budget are equal.

In my opinion, the $5,000,000 unfavorable volume variance tells the story of our poor profit performance. If we did not have the strike, production would have been at a higher level (a level requiring $8,000,000 of standard labor cost) and this variance would have been avoided.

C.W., I realize that you are not an accountant, so please call me if you have any questions about my analysis.

*Required*

Suppose the result of the strike was to restrict production of the Road Guardian battery—a battery for which there is excess demand. Without the strike, 500,000 more of these batteries could have been produced and sold ($1,000,000 of direct labor not available ÷ $2 of labor per battery). The selling price of the battery is $30. Taking this into account, calculate the effect of the strike on company profit, and comment on the controller's analysis.

**PROBLEM 11-11.   (Appendix) Recording Standard Costs**   Bechtel Technical Clothing produces parkas used by arctic explorers, mountain climbers, and people living in Minnesota. The company uses a standard costing system and standards call for three yards of material at $40 per yard for each parka. The standard cost for labor is five hours at $20 per hour. Standard overhead is $10 per unit. For the year 2006, expected production is 5,000 parkas with fixed overhead of $30,000 and variable overhead of $4 per parka.

During 2006, 5,100 parkas were manufactured. The company purchased 16,000 yards of material at a cost of $656,000. Production required 15,800 yards of material. The cost of direct labor was $527,100 for 25,100 hours. Actual overhead for the year was $50,200.

### Required

a.  Prepare a journal entry to record the purchase of material.

b.  Prepare a journal entry to record material used in production.

c.  Prepare a journal entry to record direct labor.

d.  Prepare a journal entry to record actual overhead and overhead applied.

e.  Prepare a journal entry to close the variances in requirements a through d to Cost of Goods Sold.

# CASES

## 11-1 BRANDON AMPLIFICATION

Brandon Amplification produces amplifiers and mixing boards in a modern production facility. The company is well known for its quality products—each item is thoroughly tested before it leaves the plant. Workers are highly skilled and the company considers direct labor to be a fixed cost because it does not reduce the workforce when there is a small downturn in business, and it can accommodate production increases of up to 10 percent due to excess capacity.

In the production process, workers in the *circuit department* prepare circuit boards that are sent to the *case department* for installation in custom cases. In the past six months, the workers in the circuit department have pursued a number of process improvement initiatives that have resulted in much shorter production times. For example, the model K25 amplifier used to require 10.5 standard labor hours in the circuit department, but the standard was revised last month to only 8.4 standard hours.

Although the circuit department has made production improvements, the chief financial officer of

the company, Carlie Cristopherson, is concerned about a major buildup of in-process inventory that is occurring between the circuit department and the case department. "What's going on?" she asked her assistant Amy Blake. "I was walking through the plant yesterday and I saw a tremendous amount of in-process inventory. I thought we had implemented a JIT system and we were working to balance our production processes. That investment in Work in Process is just going to drag down company performance."

Amy replied that the source of the problem might be related to the process improvements and the fact that bonuses for production workers are tied to standard cost performance. Carlie, however, didn't see how a process improvement could actually make things worse!

### Required

Assume that the company is reluctant to fire workers in the circuit department even if they are not really needed (after all they have just worked hard to improve productivity). Given the production improvements and the institution of new standards, explain why the circuit department has an incentive to overproduce (i.e., produce more output than can be handled by the case department). (*Hint:* If the circuit department does not overproduce, what will be the effect of the process improvements on the labor efficiency variance?)

# 11-2 CHAMPION INDUSTRIES

Stan Holbert, the purchasing manager for Champion Industries, recently attended a meeting with a potential supplier, Wallace Materials. At the meeting a Wallace manager demonstrated a material that was easier to handle and shape than the material currently used by Champion Industries.

Current standards call for 10 pounds of material per unit costing $20 per pound. Direct labor per unit is two hours at $20 per hour.

The new material will cost $22 per pound. However, only 9 pounds of material will be needed per unit due to reduced waste. Also, direct labor per unit will be reduced to 1.5 hours because the new material is less toxic and easier to handle.

*Required*

a. Assume that annual production is 100,000 units. Calculate the cost savings associated with using the new material.

b. Stan knows that because of an overworked accounting department, standard costs will not be updated in a timely manner. Suppose that the company switches to the new material. What are the expected material and labor variances if standards are not updated?

c. Suppose purchase price variances play a prominent role in the evaluation of Stan's job performance. Will he be inclined to suggest use of the new material?

# chapter 12

## LEARNING OBJECTIVES

**1** List and explain the advantages and disadvantages of decentralization.

**2** Explain why companies evaluate the performance of subunits and subunit managers.

**3** Identify cost centers, profit centers, and investment centers.

**4** Calculate and interpret return on investment (ROI).

**5** Explain why using a measure of profit to evaluate performance can lead to overinvestment and why using a measure of return on investment (ROI) can lead to underinvestment.

**6** Calculate and interpret residual income (RI) and economic value added (EVA).

**7** Explain the potential benefits of using a Balanced Scorecard to assess performance.

# DECENTRALIZATION AND PERFORMANCE EVALUATION

Action Industries is a diversified corporation whose divisions manufacture office products, home products, janitorial supplies, storage containers, and a variety of plastic products. At a recent meeting of the board of directors of Action Industries, Bill Stern, president and CEO, rose to address board members. "As I'm sure you know," he began, "Marie Greco is doing a really superb job as manager of our Home Products division. Five years ago, we gave her a mandate to turn this sleepy division around, and we granted her the authority to make the key decisions that would improve the division's performance. The result is that her division has increased profit by 10 to 15 percent each year, and her division has gone from being our fifth to our second largest! Marie's operation is really making a contribution to our bottom line. Maybe it's time to think of moving her into corporate. The position of VP of Operations is opening up, and I want a results-oriented person in the job."

At this point, Alister Hurd, the founder and chairman of the board of Action Industries, spoke up. "Bill, I'm not so sure that Home Products is a top performer. After all, we expect profit to increase with the size of a division. Is the profit of Home

Products that great if we take our investment into account? I think it's time we moved away from our focus on division profit and growth in profit. When I talk to my friends at other companies, I find they focus on ROI, and some of them are starting to use EVA and the Balanced Scorecard approach to evaluating performance. I wonder if our approach is out of step with current thinking. We need to be sure that our performance measures are giving us a clear picture of performance and driving the right manager behaviors." The meeting ended with Bill committed to a thorough review of alternative performance measures, which he would present at the next board meeting.

As firms increase in size and complexity, business segments or subunits (such as the Home Products division at Action Industries) are organized, and the managers of the segments are granted decision making authority so that the firm will function efficiently and effectively. Firms that grant substantial decision making authority to the managers of subunits are referred to as **decentralized organizations**.

Most firms are neither totally centralized nor totally decentralized. Decentralization is a matter of degree. To the extent that more decision making authority is delegated to subunit managers, a firm is more decentralized. Action Industries is a decentralized organization in that substantial decision making authority has been given to Marie Greco, the manager of the Home Products division.

In this chapter, we examine various types of subunits, and we illustrate how performance evaluation can be used to control the behavior of subunit managers. The goal is to ensure that subunit managers make decisions that are in the best interest of the entire firm.

List and explain the advantages and disadvantages of decentralization.

# WHY FIRMS DECENTRALIZE

Firms decentralize for a number of reasons. Here, we look first at what firms hope to gain by decentralizing. Then we examine some disadvantages of decentralization.

## ADVANTAGES OF DECENTRALIZATION

A primary reason for decentralization is that subunit managers have *better information* than top management and they can *respond quicker* to changing circumstances. Consider an electronics firm that has two primary divisions: a copier division and a camera division. Division managers report to top management responsible for both divisions. As shown in Illustration 12–1, each division operates in a unique environment. Competition, customer needs, and the supply of workers and raw materials are different for each of these product lines.

Suppose a new personal copier is to be introduced in the coming year and a pricing decision must be made. Who has superior information as to an appropri-

**Illustration 12–1**
Firm and subunit environments

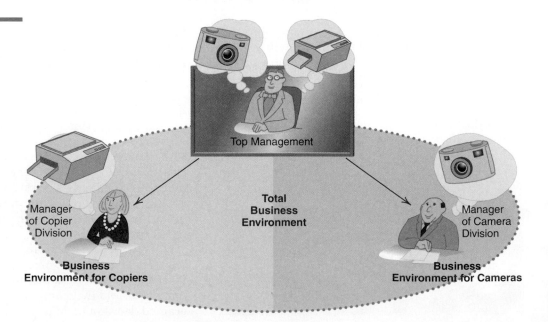

ate price to charge—the manager of the copier division or top management? Because of his or her daily involvement with the market for copiers, the manager of the division probably has a better understanding of how the market will react to a particular price. If this is the case, then the pricing decision should be delegated to the divisional manager, further enhancing the decentralization of the firm.

Suppose the manager of the camera division learns that a supplier of camera lenses is facing excess capacity and is willing to supply the division with lenses at a bargain price. In a decentralized organization, the manager can react quickly to this opportunity and increase the profitability of the division and the firm. However, if the firm is more centralized, the manager of the division may have to present the facts to top management, which will make the decision as to whether the lenses should be purchased. This can be a time-consuming process, and by the time a decision is made, the supplier may no longer have excess capacity. Worse, other camera companies may take advantage of the situation and gain a competitive edge.

Some firms decentralize because they believe that managers who are given significant decision making authority are *more motivated* and work harder than managers in centralized organizations. If managers are given broad decision making responsibility, they may identify so strongly with their subunits that they work as hard as they would if they actually owned the business.

Finally, decentralized organizations provide excellent *training* for future top-level executives. Managers in decentralized organizations are used to making important decisions and taking responsibility for their actions. Thus, when high-level positions in the firm need to be filled, the firm has a ready supply of managers with the required decision making experience.

## DISADVANTAGES OF DECENTRALIZATION

Although decentralization has several beneficial features, it may create problems. One potential problem is that decentralization may result in a costly *duplication of activities*. For example, two subunit managers may decide to develop their own purchasing departments when one purchasing department would be more economical. Or each major subunit may have its own sales force, when a single coordinated sales force would be more effective.

A second problem with a decentralized organization is that managers of subunits may pursue personal goals that are incompatible with the goals of the company as a whole. This problem is referred to as a **lack of goal congruence**. An example of a goal congruence problem is "empire building." Some managers derive substantial satisfaction from running large subunits (their *empires*). Perhaps this satisfaction comes from impressing friends and business associates with the size of their staff and the size of the facilities under their control. However, maximizing the size of the subunit, which satisfies the manager's personal goal, may be incompatible with the overall company goal of profit maximization. Bigger operations are not necessarily more profitable operations.

To control goal congruence problems in decentralized organizations, companies evaluate the performance of subunit managers. As we will see later in this chapter, the evaluation process should encourage managers of subunits to take actions that are in the interest of the company as a whole. That is, performance evaluation should encourage managers to behave as if their own personal goals were congruent with the goals of the company as a whole.

A summary of these advantages and disadvantages of decentralization is presented in Illustration 12–2.

**Illustration 12–2**
Some advantages
and disadvantages
of decentralization

> **Advantages of Decentralization**
> 1. Better information, leading to superior decisions
> 2. Faster response to changing circumstances
> 3. Increased motivation of managers
> 4. Excellent training for future top level executives
>
> **Disadvantages of Decentralization**
> 1. Costly duplication of activities.
> 2. Lack of goal congruence

**LEARNING OBJECTIVE 2**

Explain why companies
evaluate the performance
of subunits and subunit
managers.

**You Get
What You Measure**

# WHY COMPANIES EVALUATE THE PERFORMANCE OF SUBUNITS AND SUBUNIT MANAGERS

Decentralization leads naturally to the need to evaluate subunits and their managers. In general, companies evaluate the performance of subunits and subunit managers for two reasons. First, evaluation identifies successful operations and areas needing improvement. Managers can then continue to develop successful operations and work to improve or eliminate those that have not met expectations. A second reason for evaluating performance is that the evaluation influences the behavior of managers. As first discussed in Chapter 1, "You get what you measure!" In other words, performance measures can be used to drive the behavior of managers.

For example, suppose Marie Greco, the manager of the Home Products division of Action Industries, has historically been evaluated in terms of *total sales*. In the current year, she is also being evaluated in terms of *sales to new customers*. Do you think her behavior will change? Quite likely, she will spend more time focusing the attention of her sales team on developing *new* customers, because she will want to perform at a high level with respect to the new performance measure. If developing new customers is critical to the company's success, then it is a good idea to encourage this behavior by focusing on the new performance measure—sales to new customers.

Note that the heading for this section distinguishes between evaluating the performance of a subunit and evaluating the performance of a subunit manager. This distinction is important: We evaluate subunits in order to decide if we should expand or contract them or change their operations in some way. We evaluate subunit managers in order to motivate them to take actions that maximize the value of the firm. You should keep in mind that it is possible to have a good manager and a bad subunit. A manager may do all that is reasonably possible to improve a subunit, but the subunit may not be a line of business that the company believes has good long-run profit potential. In this case, the company may reward the performance of the manager but still exit the subunit's line of business.

## RESPONSIBILITY ACCOUNTING AND PERFORMANCE EVALUATION

The discussion of cost allocation in Chapter 6 introduced the topic of *responsibility accounting*, a technique that holds managers responsible only for costs and revenues that they can control. This idea should play a prominent role in the design of accounting systems used to evaluate the performance of managers in a decentralized organization. To implement responsibility accounting in a decentralized organization, costs and revenues are traced to the organizational level where they can be controlled.

For example, consider the information presented for the Jones Tool Co. in Illustration 12–3. Jones Tool Co. produces a variety of small tools in two plants: the Eastern Plant and the Western Plant. Each plant has a plant manager who is responsible for operations. Currently, two production shifts are run each day, with work supervised by individuals with the title *production supervisor*. A vice president of manufacturing is responsible for production in both the Eastern Plant and the Western Plant.

The illustration indicates, in a simplified setting, how implementation of responsibility accounting would suggest that costs be accumulated for assessing performance. Only labor costs and material costs are traced to the individual shift supervisors. This follows because at Jones Tool Co., the production supervisors make numerous decisions that affect the amount of labor and material costs incurred. However, plant overhead costs are not traced to the supervisors, because these supervisors are not involved in decisions that affect the amount of overhead incurred. Instead, overhead costs are traced to the individual plant managers, who can control overhead costs. The manager of the Eastern Plant, for example, is responsible for $500,000 of labor costs ($300,000 from the first shift and $200,000 from the second shift), $400,000 of material costs ($250,000 from the first shift and $150,000 from the second shift), and $600,000 of overhead costs incurred in the Eastern Plant.

**Illustration 12–3**
Tracing costs to the organizational level where they can be controlled

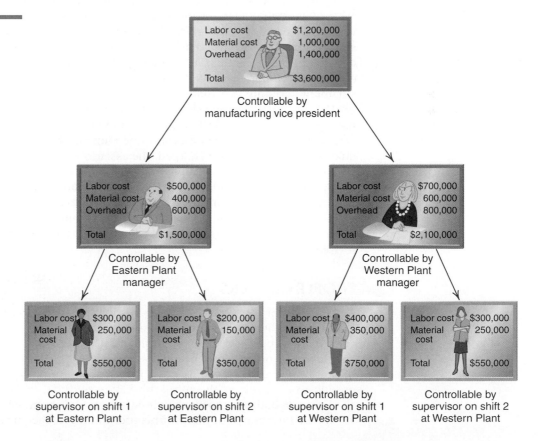

Labor cost $1,200,000
Material cost 1,000,000
Overhead 1,400,000

Total $3,600,000

Controllable by
manufacturing vice president

Labor cost $500,000
Material cost 400,000
Overhead 600,000

Total $1,500,000

Controllable by
Eastern Plant
manager

Labor cost $700,000
Material cost 600,000
Overhead 800,000

Total $2,100,000

Controllable by
Western Plant
manager

Labor cost $300,000
Material cost 250,000

Total $550,000

Controllable by
supervisor on shift 1
at Eastern Plant

Labor cost $200,000
Material cost 150,000

Total $350,000

Controllable by
supervisor on shift 2
at Eastern Plant

Labor cost $400,000
Material cost 350,000

Total $750,000

Controllable by
supervisor on shift 1
at Western Plant

Labor cost $300,000
Material cost 250,000

Total $550,000

Controllable by
supervisor on shift 2
at Western Plant

The vice president of manufacturing is responsible for all of the costs incurred at both the Eastern Plant and the Western Plant. Therefore, all production costs are traced to the vice president. For example, the overhead costs traced to the vice president are $1,400,000, which includes $600,000 from the Eastern Plant and $800,000 from the Western Plant.

Identify cost centers, profit centers, and investment centers.

# COST CENTERS, PROFIT CENTERS, AND INVESTMENT CENTERS

Subunits are organizational units with identifiable collections of related resources and activities. A subunit may be a department, a subsidiary, or a division. Subunits are sometimes referred to as **responsibility centers**, defined as organizational units responsible for the generation of revenue and/or the incurrence of costs. Responsibility centers are typically classified as being either cost centers, profit centers, or investment centers. Let's look at the types of performance measures that are appropriate for each of these subunits.

## COST CENTERS

A **cost center** is a subunit that has responsibility for controlling costs but does not have responsibility for generating revenue. Most service departments (e.g., the machine maintenance department, the janitorial services department, and the computer services department) are classified as cost centers. The managers of these departments are responsible for making sure that their services are provided at a reasonable cost to the company, but they typically do not have responsibility for generating revenue for the firm. Production departments are also classified as cost centers. As an example, consider a department that assembles electronic components into desktop computers. The manager of the assembly department certainly is responsible for making sure that the computers are assembled at the lowest cost consistent with acceptable quality standards. However, the manager probably has little input into how the computers will be marketed and what price will be charged. Because the manager has little direct control over the quantity sold or the price charged, the assembly department would be considered a cost center.

A common approach to controlling cost centers is to compare their actual costs with standard or budgeted costs. If variances from standard are significant, an investigation into the activities of the cost center should be undertaken to determine if costs are out of control or, alternatively, if cost standards need to be revised.

## PROFIT CENTERS

A **profit center** is a subunit that has responsibility for generating revenue as well as for controlling costs. Consider our earlier example of an electronics firm that consists of a copier division and a camera division. Each of these divisions can be classified as a profit center because each has responsibility for generating revenue through sales and controlling costs associated with producing and marketing its products.

Because both revenues and costs (the two elements that determine income) are under the control of the profit-center manager, the performance of the profit center can be evaluated in terms of profitability. Evaluation in terms of profitability is useful because it motivates managers to focus their attention on ways of maximizing profit-center profitability.

Companies use a variety of methods to evaluate the profitability of profit centers. Income earned in the current year may be compared with an income target or budget. Or income earned may be compared with income earned in the prior year. Some firms evaluate profit centers using **relative performance evaluation**. Relative performance evaluation of profit centers involves evaluating the profitability of each profit center relative to the profitability of other, similar profit centers.

For example, the Chicken King Company operates 10 fast-food restaurants in a major Midwestern city. Each outlet (restaurant) is treated as a profit center because it is responsible for generating revenue (sales of chicken sandwiches, sodas, ice cream, etc.) and controlling costs (food costs, labor, heat and light, etc.). If each outlet is *reasonably* similar in terms of size, appearance, and menu, comparing the income earned by each outlet with the income earned by other outlets may be a useful means of assessing the effectiveness of outlet managers.

## INVESTMENT CENTERS

An **investment center** is a subunit that is responsible for generating revenue, controlling costs, and investing in assets. Because it is responsible for revenue, costs, and investment, an investment center is charged with earning income consistent with the amount of assets invested in the segment. Most divisions of a company can be treated as either profit centers or investment centers. If the division manager can significantly influence decisions affecting investment in divisional assets, the division should be considered an investment center. If the division manager cannot influence investment decisions, the division should be considered a profit center. Since Marie Greco, the manager of the Home Products division of Action Industries, is granted authority to make investment decisions, her operation is an investment center.

### Subunits at Nordstrom

NORDSTROM

Think about the subunits at Nordstrom, Inc. The company has 80 full line stores selling apparel, shoes, and accessories for women, men, and children. In addition, the company operates 45 discount stores under the name Nordstrom Rack. The company also operates four specialty boutiques under the name Façonnable. Each of these operations is a profit center or an investment center, depending on how much autonomy the managers have over investments. The individual stores (e.g., the Nordstrom store in San Francisco) are also profit centers or investment centers. The advertising, maintenance, and accounting departments at Nordstrom are cost centers. Managers in these subunits are responsible for controlling their costs, but they do not have responsibility for generating revenue.

Investment center managers generally play a major role in determining the level of inventory, the level of accounts receivable, and the investment in equipment and other assets held by the investment center. Thus, it seems reasonable to hold them responsible for earning a return on these assets. However, although investment center managers play a major role, they are generally not given complete autonomy in investing in assets. Typically, central management has final approval of all major investments. Guidelines may specify that investment center managers must have central management approval for all investments greater than some specified dollar amount (e.g., investments greater than $200,000).

Calculate and interpret return on investment (ROI).

# EVALUATING INVESTMENT CENTERS WITH ROI

One of the primary tools for evaluating the performance of investment centers is **return on investment**, or ROI. ROI is calculated as the ratio of investment center income to invested capital. The idea of evaluating performance using ROI was developed in the early part of the twentieth century by Du Pont (known then as the Du Pont Powder Company) and has now gained widespread acceptance.[1]

ROI has a distinct advantage over income as a measure of performance. It focuses the attention of managers not only on income (the numerator of ROI) but also on investment (the denominator of ROI). Suppose two business units earn the same income—$100,000. A performance measure based solely on income would rate the two units as equally successful. However, suppose the first business unit required an investment in assets of $1,000,000, while the second business unit required only $500,000. The second unit has performed much better than the first because it required only half the investment to earn the same level of income. This allows the company to invest the funds not required by the second unit in another project and earn additional income.

|  | | Business Unit 1 | | Business Unit 2 | |
|---|---|---|---|---|---|
| ROI = | $\dfrac{\text{Income}}{\text{Invested capital}}$ | $\dfrac{\$100,000}{\$1,000,000}$ = | .10 or 10% | $\dfrac{\$100,000}{\$500,000}$ = | .20 or 20% |

Note that, unlike income, ROI does not rate these two units as equally successful. The first unit has an ROI of only 10 percent while the second unit has a much higher ROI of 20 percent.

Some companies break ROI down into two components: profit margin and investment turnover.

$$\text{ROI} = \frac{\text{Income}}{\text{Invested capital}} = \underbrace{\frac{\text{Income}}{\text{Sales}}}_{\substack{\textbf{Profit} \\ \textbf{Margin}}} \times \underbrace{\frac{\text{Sales}}{\text{Invested capital}}}_{\substack{\textbf{Investment} \\ \textbf{Turnover}}}$$

**Profit margin** is the ratio of income to sales, while **investment turnover** is the ratio of sales to invested capital. Breaking down ROI into these components clearly indicates to managers that there are two ways in which ROI can be im-

---

[1]See Chapter 4, H. Thomas Johnson and Robert S. Kaplan, *Relevance Lost: The Rise and Fall of Management Accounting*, Harvard Business School Press, 1987.

### *Focus on Shareholder Value and Financial Performance Not the Same in Germany as in the United States*

In 1998, German auto maker Daimler-Benz and U.S. auto maker Chrysler merged creating the firm of DaimlerChrysler. Following the merger, James Donlon, a financial executive with Chrysler became controller of the combined company and found that the focus on shareholder value, so common in the U.S., was not universally accepted in Germany. In a test of their focus on shareholder value, 10 managers were asked to give the company's stock price—seven didn't know and three were wrong! Donlon also found that some managers resisted his efforts to measure financial performance in terms of return on investment with a requirement that the return be at least as high as the cost of capital.

*Source*: Scott Miller, "American Drives Lonely Road at Daimler," *Wall Street Journal*, June 9, 2000, pg. A16.

proved. Managers can take actions to improve the income earned on each dollar of sales (i.e., increase the margin), or managers can take actions to generate more sales for each dollar invested (i.e., increase turnover).

## MEASURING INCOME AND INVESTED CAPITAL WHEN CALCULATING ROI

In calculating ROI, companies measure "income" in a variety of ways (net income, income before interest and taxes, controllable profit, etc.). For purposes of this book, and consistent with the practice of many companies, we'll measure investment center income as net operating profit after taxes, known by the abbreviation **NOPAT**.

Because NOPAT is focused on *operating* profit after taxes, it excludes interest expense which is a nonoperating expense and it excludes nonoperating gains and losses such as gains and losses on the sale of marketable securities. Therefore, to calculate NOPAT, we must add nonoperating items back to net income and adjust tax expense accordingly. Consider the data in Illustration 12–4, which relates to the Home Products division of Action Industries. As indicated, net income is $3,900,000. We add back interest expense of $1,000,000, and we subtract the tax savings on interest equal to the 35 percent tax rate times $1,000,000. The result is a NOPAT value of $4,550,000. A benefit of using NOPAT is that it does not hold the investment center manager responsible for interest expense. This is appropriate because investment center managers frequently do not have responsibility for decisions related to financing their operations.

As with "income," companies measure "invested capital" in a variety of ways (total assets, total assets after adding back accumulated depreciation, total assets less current liabilities, etc.). We'll measure invested capital as total assets less noninterest-bearing current liabilities (accounts payable, income taxes payable, accrued liabilities, etc.). Noninterest-bearing current liabilities are deducted from the total assets because they are a "free" source of funds and reduce the cost of the investment in assets. As indicated in Illustration 12–4, invested capital

**Illustration 12–4**
Calculation of investment center income and invested capital for the home products division of action industries

| **Net Income** | |
|---|---:|
| Sales | $40,000,000 |
| Less cost of goods sold | 25,000,000 |
| Gross margin | 15,000,000 |
| Less selling and administrative expenses | 8,000,000 |
| Income from operations | 7,000,000 |
| Less interest expense | 1,000,000 |
| Income before taxes | 6,000,000 |
| Less taxes | 2,100,000 |
| Net income | $ 3,900,000 |
| **NOPAT** | |
| Net income | $ 3,900,000 |
| Plus interest expense | 1,000,000 |
| Less tax savings related to interest (equals .35 × $1,000,000) | (350,000) |
| NOPAT | $ 4,550,000 |
| **Invested Capital** | |
| Book value of total assets | $70,000,000 |
| Less noninterest-bearing current liabilities | 5,000,000 |
| Invested capital | $65,000,000 |
| ROI = NOPAT ÷ invested capital | 0.07 or 7% |

calculated as total assets less noninterest-bearing current liabilities is $65,000,000. Thus, ROI (the ratio of NOPAT to invested capital) is 7 percent.

Given the relatively low ROI earned by the Home Products division, it is appropriate for Alister Hurd, the chairman of the board, to question the performance of the operation. While Home Products is generating a substantial profit, the profit is low relative to the level of investment in the operation. That is the essential insight provided by ROI.

## Any Questions?

**Q.** In illustration 12–4, NOPAT is calculated by adding interest back to net income and then subtracting the tax savings on interest. Why not just take income from operations and then subtract related taxes? You get the same answer.

| Income from operations (see Illustration 12–4) | $7,000,000 |
|---|---:|
| Less taxes at 35% | 2,450,000 |
| NOPAT | $4,550,000 |

**A.** It is perfectly fine to start with income from operations and then subtract related taxes. As you can see, you get the same answer. However, some income statements do not break out an "income from operations" number. In such cases, *you* have to first calculate income from operations and then subtract related taxes. Either approach works—just remember that NOPAT does not include nonoperating items such as interest expense, interest income, or gains and losses on investments.

## PROBLEMS WITH USING ROI

In spite of its advantages, using ROI can present problems. One problem with ROI is that investment in assets is typically measured using historical costs. Recall that the historical cost of total assets is affected by depreciation of plant and equipment. As assets become fully depreciated, the measure of investment becomes very low, and ROI becomes quite large. This makes comparison of investment centers using ROI difficult.

Consider two investment centers that are alike in all respects except one: Investment Center 1 was started five years ago, and its investment in fixed assets is substantially depreciated, whereas Investment Center 2 was started in the current year. Both earn exactly the same level of net operating profit after taxes, $100,000. As indicated in Illustration 12–5, the ROI of Investment Center 1 is 29.41 percent, while the ROI of Investment Center 2 is 23.81 percent. The difference of 5.6 percent is due to the fact that the fixed assets of Investment Center 1 are substantially depreciated. Thus, its investment base is much lower than the investment base of Investment Center 2.

Now, suppose additional funds become available to invest in either of the two business segments. Will Investment Center 1 earn a higher return than Investment Center 2 on the incremental investment? Although Investment Center 1 has the higher ROI, the two business segments are identical in all respects except for the age of their equipment. Thus, we would expect both segments to generate the same income with the funds. The point is that using ROI to rank the attractiveness of investment centers can be difficult if the remaining useful lives of their depreciable assets are very different.

Some critics of ROI have suggested that undue emphasis on ROI may lead managers to delay the purchase of modern equipment needed to stay competitive. Old equipment has a low carrying value because it is substantially depreciated. Thus, the denominator of ROI (total assets less noninterest-bearing current liabilities) is low, and ROI is high. If new equipment is purchased, it may significantly raise the level of investment and reduce ROI. If managers are evaluated in terms of ROI, they may fear that the decline in ROI will lead to low ratings of their job

**Illustration 12–5**
Comparison of investment centers with differences in accumulated depreciation

| | Investment Center 1 | | Investment Center 2 | |
|---|---|---|---|---|
| NOPAT | | $100,000 | | $100,000 |
| Investment: | | | | |
| Cash | | $ 20,000 | | $ 20,000 |
| Accounts receivable | | 80,000 | | 80,000 |
| Inventory | | 150,000 | | 150,000 |
| Plant and equipment | | | | |
| Cost | 200,000 | | 200,000 | |
| Less: Accumulated depreciation | 100,000 | | 20,000 | |
| Carrying amount of equipment | | 100,000 | | 180,000 |
| Total assets | | 350,000 | | 430,000 |
| Less noninterest-bearing current liabilities | | 10,000 | | 10,000 |
| Invested capital | | $340,000 | | $420,000 |
| ROI | | 29.41% | | 23.81% |

performance. In situations like this, managers may fail to purchase equipment necessary for the long-run success of the company.

Recall that in an earlier chapter, we recommended that investment alternatives should be evaluated in terms of their net present values. Investment opportunities with positive net present values should be undertaken, while investment opportunities with negative net present values should be rejected. However, if the performance of managers is evaluated using ROI, they may *not* be motivated to invest in projects with positive net present values. The reason is that, in the short run, projects with positive net present values may have low levels of income and correspondingly low ROI's. If managers are evaluated in terms of ROI, they will be quite concerned about how ROI will be affected by additional investments. The result is that managers may consider the effect on ROI, instead of net present value, in evaluating investment alternatives.

# PROBLEMS OF OVERINVESTMENT AND UNDERINVESTMENT: YOU GET WHAT YOU MEASURE!

**LEARNING OBJECTIVE 5**

Explain why using a measure of profit to evaluate performance can lead to overinvestment and why using a measure of return on investment (ROI) can lead to underinvestment.

A related problem with ROI is that managers of investment centers with high ROI's may be unwilling to invest in assets that will earn a return that is satisfactory to central management if that return is less than their current, high, ROI. That is, managers may underinvest. As illustrated later, this problem can be minimized by evaluating managers using residual income or economic value added (EVA). For now, let's compare the tendency for underinvestment, which is related to the use of ROI as a performance measure, to the tendency for overinvestment, which is related to the use of profit as a performance measure.

**You Get What You Measure**

**Evaluation in Terms of Profit Can Lead to Overinvestment.** As discussed in Chapter 9, we would like managers to invest in assets that earn a return in excess of the cost of capital. But remember, "You get what you measure." If we evaluate managers in terms of growth in profit, they may be motivated to make investments that earn a return that is less than the cost of capital—that is, they may overinvest in assets.

I may not be a very good manager, but I can increase the profit of any company as long as shareholders will provide me with the assets to make investments. And while I'm increasing profit, I'll be decreasing shareholder value! How will I achieve these apparently conflicting outcomes? I'll do it by growing the company and investing in projects that earn returns that are less than the cost of capital (i.e., I'll do it by overinvesting). For example, suppose the cost of capital relevant to my subunit is 9 percent, and the subunit currently earns a profit of $100,000 on an investment of $1,000,000. This means the subunit is earning a 10 percent return. Now, I'll grow the subunit using funds provided by shareholders (so there is no interest charge to reduce my profit!). Suppose I double the size of the investment in my subunit to $2,000,000 and earn a profit of $150,000. Note that I've had a 50 percent increase in profit, so my performance will look good if I'm evaluated in terms of growth in profit. But what return have I earned on the incremental investment of $1,000,000? The increase in profit is only $50,000, so I only earned a return of 5 percent, which is less than the cost of capital.

**Evaluation in Terms of ROI Can Lead to Underinvestment.** Perhaps an obvious solution to the overinvestment problem is to evaluate managers in terms of ROI.

Managers won't want to take on projects that have a low return just to increase profit if they are evaluated in terms of the return they earn. As we have just seen, however, ROI has its own set of problems, and one of them is that it may lead managers to underinvest—that is, they may pass up projects that earn a return that is greater than the cost of capital.

Suppose you were the manager of a subunit with an ROI of 15 percent and a cost of capital of 10 percent. If you were evaluated in terms of ROI, would you take on a new project that had a return of 12 percent? Probably not. Although the project has a return greater than the cost of capital and will increase shareholder wealth, it will lower your reported ROI and possibly reflect negatively on your performance. In fact, you may try to get rid of some of your current projects that are earning a return greater than 10 percent but less than 15 percent in an effort to increase your reported ROI.

Calculate and interpret residual income (RI) and economic value added (EVA).

# EVALUATION USING ECONOMIC VALUE ADDED (EVA)

An approach to solving overinvestment and underinvestment problems involves the use of a performance measure known as economic value added (EVA). Firms that use EVA typically tie bonus compensation to the measure. Thus, managers become very focused on achieving high levels of EVA. EVA was developed based on an earlier concept known as residual income. In the next section, we will review residual income and then consider the extension to EVA.

## RESIDUAL INCOME (RI)

**Residual income**, or RI, is the net operating profit after taxes of an investment center in excess of its required profit. And required profit is equal to the investment center's required rate of return times the level of investment in the center (i.e., RI = NOPAT − Required Profit). Generally, the required rate of return is the cost of capital for the investment center. Although a number of alternative measures of investment exist, we'll use total assets minus noninterest-bearing current liabilities as a measure of investment. Under these conditions, the formula for calculating residual income is:

$$\text{Residual Income} = \text{NOPAT} - \text{Required Profit}$$

$$= \text{NOPAT} - \text{Cost of Capital} \times \text{Investment}$$

$$= \text{NOPAT} - \text{Cost of Capital} \times (\text{Total Assets} - \text{NIBCL})$$

Here NIBCL stands for Noninterest-Bearing Current Liabilities. Why is NIBCL deducted from total assets to determine the level of investment? The answer is that these liabilities are a free source of funds. Suppose you open an audio/video store and purchase a million dollars of inventory. Further, suppose your suppliers agree that you do not have to pay for the inventory until it is sold. Thus, you have total assets of $1,000,000 related to inventory and $1,000,000 of accounts payable (a noninterest-bearing current liability). But, what is your investment in the company? The answer, of course, is zero and this is precisely what you will calculate if you measure investment as total assets less NIBCL.

**Revisiting the Situation at Action Industries.** Consider the situation of the Home Products division of Action Industries presented at the start of the Chapter. As we saw in Illustration 12–4, it has NOPAT of $4,550,000 and invested capital (total assets minus NIBCL) of $65,000,000. Assume that cost of capital for Home Products is 10 percent. In this case, residual income is a loss of $1,950,000.

$$\text{Residual Income} = \text{NOPAT} - \text{Required Profit}$$
$$= \text{NOPAT} - \text{Cost of Capital} \times \text{Investment}$$
$$= \text{NOPAT} - \text{Cost of Capital} \times (\text{Total Assets} - \text{NIBCL})$$
$$= \$4,550,000 - (10\% \times \$6,500,000)$$
$$= \$4,550,000 - \$6,500,000$$
$$= (\$1,950,000)$$

The Home Products division had a net operating profit after taxes of $4,500,000, but given the company had an investment of $65,000,000 it should have had net operating profit after taxes of $6,500,000. Thus, the company has a negative residual income of $1,950,000. So instead of helping improve the company's economic well being, the division has destroyed almost $2,000,000 of shareholder value! This is only clear after we calculate an appropriate level of income given the investment in the Home Products division.

## SOLVING THE OVERINVESTMENT AND UNDERINVESTMENT PROBLEMS

RI has the potential to solve the overinvestment problem and the underinvestment problem. Let's see how. Suppose a project comes along that will earn a return on its incremental investment of nine percent. Would the manager make the investment? Not if the manager is evaluated using RI and the cost of capital is 10 percent. Since the manager receives a capital charge on investments of 10 percent, the manager knows that residual income will be reduced if the investment is made. Thus, there is no incentive for overinvestment. Now suppose a project comes along that will earn a return of 11 percent. Will the manager make the investment? The answer is yes, since residual income will increase (because the capital charge is less than the amount earned by the project). Thus, there is no incentive to underinvest.

## ECONOMIC VALUE ADDED (EVA)

**Economic value added**, better known as simply EVA, is a performance measure developed by the consulting firm Stern Stewart.[2] In essence, EVA is simply residual income adjusted for what Stern Stewart refers to as "accounting distortions" that arise from following generally accepted accounting principles (GAAP). A primary distortion is related to research and development (R&D). GAAP requires that R&D be expensed in the period incurred. However, in many if not most cases, R&D creates benefits for future periods. Thus, with EVA, R&D is capitalized as an asset and amortized over the future periods that benefit from the incurrence of the R&D. An advantage of this approach is that managers are less

---

[2]EVA is described in an article by Shawn Tully, "The Real Key to Creating Wealth," *Fortune*, September 20, 1993, p. 38.

### Companies that Use EVA

Here are a number of well-known companies that use EVA:

| | | |
|---|---|---|
| Bausch & Lomb | Georgia-Pacific | Toys "R" Us |
| Briggs & Stratton | HermanMiller | Tupperware |
| Coca-Cola | JC Penney | Whirlpool |
| Eli Lilly | Sprint | |

An excellent Web site for information on EVA is by EVANOMICS at (*http://evanomics.com*).

tempted to cut R&D; an act that increases short-term income but destroys shareholder value. Marketing programs that benefit future periods are also capitalized under EVA although the cost of such programs is expensed under GAAP. In total, there are more than 100 adjustments that Stern Stewart might make on a particular EVA consulting engagement. However, in practice the number of adjustments is likely to be five or less.

The adjustments made using EVA affect both the computation of NOPAT and the computation of investment. Thus, the formula for EVA is:

$$\text{EVA} = \text{NOPAT}^{\text{adjusted}} - (\text{Cost of Capital} \times \text{Investment}^{\text{adjusted}})$$

**EVA Example.** Let's review the calculation of EVA using the example of InterfaceSolutions, a company that manufactures and sells a variety of connectivity products used in the audio/video, telecom, and computer industries (e.g., fiber optic cables, FireWire products, USB devices, high-definition video and audio cables, modular plugs, etc.). The company's financial information is presented in Illustration 12-6.

Note that between 2005 and 2006, net income increased from $3,266,000 to $3,334,000. Is that increase consistent with good performance? Let's calculate EVA for both years to help us answer that question. In doing so, we'll assume that R&D has a three-year life with one third amortized in the year it's incurred.

The calculation of EVA is presented in Illustration 12-7. Basically, the calculation of EVA is a three-step process. First we calculate adjusted NOPAT, then we calculate adjusted Investment, and third we calculate EVA as (adjusted NOPAT − Cost of Capital × adjusted Investment). Note that in calculating adjusted NOPAT for 2006 we start with income before taxes and add back interest and the current

**Illustration 12–6**
Financial information
for interface solutions

| (In Thousands) **Comparative Income Statements** | 2006 | 2005 |
|---|---|---|
| Sales | $29,059 | $27,287 |
| Less: | | |
| Cost of sales | 19,361 | 17,981 |
| Research and development | 1,400 | 1,600 |
| Selling, general and administrative expense | 3,031 | 2,537 |
| Interest expense | 138 | 144 |
| Income before income taxes | 5,129 | 5,025 |
| Income taxes | 1,795 | 1,759 |
| Net income | $ 3,334 | $ 3,266 |

| **Comparative Balance Sheets** | 2006 | 2005 |
|---|---|---|
| Assets | | |
| Cash and cash equivalents | $   147 | $ 1,286 |
| Accounts receivable | 4,588 | 2,568 |
| Inventory | 3,420 | 1,902 |
| Prepaid expenses | 47 | 45 |
| Total current assets | 8,202 | 5,801 |
| Land | 1,342 | 1,342 |
| Building, furniture, fixtures (net) | 8,438 | 8,523 |
| Total noncurrent assets | 9,780 | 9,865 |
| Total assets | $17,982 | $15,666 |
| **Liabilities** | | |
| Accounts payable | $   209 | $   199 |
| Accrued liabilities | 57 | 45 |
| Taxes payable | 60 | 49 |
| Current portion of long-term debt | 175 | 188 |
| Total current liabilities | 501 | 481 |
| Long-term debt | 795 | 863 |
| Total liabilities | 1,296 | 1,344 |
| **Stockholders' Equity** | | |
| Common stock | 5,080 | 5,080 |
| Retained earnings | 11,606 | 9,242 |
| Total stockholders' equity | 16,686 | 14,322 |
| Total liabilities and stockholders' equity | $17,982 | $15,666 |

*Note*: Research and development was $1,500,000 in 2004 and $1,400,000 in 2003.

period R&D. Unless we add back interest, we will be double-counting a financing charge (interest would be deducted from income and it would be deducted again when we multiply the cost of capital times the level of investment to calculate the return.) R&D is added back because we treat R&D as an intangible asset in EVA. We then deduct R&D expense related to amortizing the current and prior years' R&D amounts over three years (i.e., we deduct one-third of R&D from 2006, 2005, and 2004). Note that this results in adjusted NOPAT of $3,359,000 for 2006.

Now let's go on to the second step—calculation of adjusted investment. We start with total assets and then add unamortized R&D. Only one-third of R&D in

**Illustration 12–7**
EVA calculations
for interface solutions

| Step 1 | | Step 2 | | Step 3 | |
|---|---|---|---|---|---|
| **2006** | | | | | |
| Income before taxes | $5,129 | Total assets | $17,982 | Adjusted NOPAT | $3,359 |
| Add interest expense | 138 | Plus unamortized R&D | | Less cost of capital × | |
| Add current period R&D | 1,400 | 2006: 2/3 × $1,400 | 933 | adjusted investment | |
| Less amortization of prior R&D | | 2006: 1/3 × $1,600 | 533 | (.18 × $19,122) | (3,442) |
| 2006: 1/3 × $1,400 | (467) | | 19,448 | EVA | $  (83) |
| 2005: 1/3 × $1,600 | (533) | Less NIBCL | | | |
| 2004: 1/3 × $1,500 | (500) | Accounts payable | (209) | | |
| | 5,167 | Accrued liabilities | (57) | | |
| Less taxes at 35% | (1,808) | Taxes payable | (60) | | |
| Adjusted NOPAT | $3,359 | | (326) | | |
| | | Adjusted Investment | $19,122 | | |
| **2005** | | | | | |
| Income before taxes | $5,025 | Total assets | $15,666 | Adjusted NOPAT | $3,425 |
| Add interest expense | 144 | Plus unamortized R&D | | Less cost of capital × | |
| Add current period R&D | 1,600 | 2005: 2/3 × $1,600 | 1,067 | adjusted investment | |
| Less amortization of prior R&D | | 2004: 1/3 × $1,500 | 500 | (.18 × $16,940) | (3,049) |
| 2005: 1/3 × $1,600 | (533) | | 17,233 | EVA | $  376 |
| 2004: 1/3 × $1,500 | (500) | Less NIBCL | | | |
| 2003: 1/3 × $1,400 | (467) | Accounts payable | (199) | | |
| | 5,269 | Accrued liabilities | (45) | | |
| Less taxes at 35% | (1,844) | Taxes payable | (49) | | |
| Adjusted NOPAT | $3,425 | | (293) | | |
| | | Adjusted Investment | $16,940 | | |

2006 became an expense so two-thirds are still an intangible asset. Of the R&D in 2005, one-third was expensed in 2005, and one-third was expensed in 2006, which means that one-third remains an intangible asset at the end of 2006. In total, adjusted investment is $19,122,000 for 2006.

The last step is to calculate EVA. Assuming a cost of capital of 18 percent (the cost of capital for technology companies is often quite high), EVA is equal to a loss of $83,000. A similar process is followed to calculate EVA for 2005. Here we find that EVA is a positive $376,000.

Now, why is it that accounting profit is up in 2006 but EVA is down? Look at what happened to the level of investment. It went from $16,940,000 to $19,122,000. Although income is up in 2006, *it's not up enough* given the increased investment, especially in accounts receivable and inventory. This is an important insight provided by EVA—firms need to have earnings consistent with their cost of capital and their investment in assets. Most likely, if the senior managers of InterfaceSolutions were evaluated and compensated based on EVA, they would have paid more attention to the investment the company was making in additional assets, and analyzing whether or not the investment was likely to result in a payoff greater than the cost of capital.

### Kodak Drops EVA When Performance and Bonuses Drop

In 2000, the board of directors of Kodak was widely criticized. In fact a majority of shareholders voted to eliminate Kodak's staggered board terms so that more new directors could be appointed. Their wishes were ignored—company bylaws state that a supermajority of 80 percent is needed to change the way the board is elected.

Why were shareholders critical of the board? Consider the following. In 1999 the board adopted EVA as the sole performance measure that would determine the size of management's bonus pool. But with the company's weak financial performance, EVA was low and so was the senior management bonus pool. In fact CEO Dan Carp's bonus was cut in half. The compensation committee of the board then announced that it was dropping EVA in favor of 19 performance measures. The committee can pick and choose among the measures, and since performance is likely to be good for at least one of them, management is virtually guaranteed a cushy bonus. This occurred when Kodak's stock was 40 percent lower than its 52-week high.

(*Source*: Matthew Boyle, "The Dirty Half-Dozen: America's Worst Boards," *Fortune*, May 14, 2001, p. 250.

Explain the potential benefits of using a Balanced Scorecard to assess performance.

# USING A BALANCED SCORECARD TO EVALUATE PERFORMANCE

A problem with just assessing performance with financial measures like profit, ROI, and EVA is that the financial measures are "backward looking." In other words, today's financial measures tell you about the accomplishments and failures of the past. And the lag may be quite long. Suppose you work for a biotech company and have a tremendous "day at the office": You develop a drug that cures the common cold! When will this tremendous accomplishment play out in accounting earnings? Given the regulatory process, it's likely that the drug will not be marketed and profit recognized for more than 10 years! Now suppose a new CEO is hired 10 years from now. Even if the executive performs poorly, it's likely that profit, ROI, and EVA will be high. It won't be because of the CEO's performance. It will be because of accomplishments that took place in the distant past! Illustration 12–8 graphically presents the backward looking nature of financial performance measures.

An approach to performance measurement that also focuses on what managers are doing today to create future shareholder value is the Balanced Scorecard, a technique developed by Robert Kaplan, a Harvard professor, and David Norton, a consultant.[3] Essentially, a **Balanced Scorecard** is a set of performance

---

[3]Seminal articles on the Balanced Scorecard include Robert S. Kaplan and David Norton, "The Balanced Scorecard—Measures that Drive Performance," *Harvard Business Review*, January–February 1992, and Robert S. Kaplan and David Norton, "Putting the Balanced Scorecard to Work," *Harvard Business Review*, September–October 1993.

**Illustration 12–8**
Financial performance measures are "backward looking"

measures constructed for four dimensions of performance. As indicated in Illustration 12–9, the dimensions are financial, customer, internal processes, and learning and growth. Having financial measures is critical even if they are backward looking. After all, they have a great affect on the evaluation of the company by shareholders and creditors. Customer measures examine the company's success in meeting customer expectations. Internal process measures examine the company's success in improving critical business processes. And learning and growth measures examine the company's success in improving its ability to adapt, innovate, and grow. The customer, internal processes, and learning and growth measures are generally thought to be predictive of *future* success (i.e., they are not backward looking).

**Tying the Balanced Scorecard Measures to the Strategy for Success.** Typically, a company using a balanced scorecard will develop three to five performance measures for each dimension. To the extent possible, the measures on a balanced scorecard should be tied to a company's strategy for success. For example, consider the customer dimension. If it is critical to success that the company's product be easy to use, the company may survey customers to measure this aspect of performance. If on-time delivery is critical to customers, then it will be used as a performance measure. With respect to internal processes, a company may decide that it needs to reduce the number of defective units produced. In this case, number of defects might be an appropriate measure for the internal-process dimension. With respect to the learning and growth dimension, a company may decide that to remain innovative it is crucial to retain its highly skilled workforce. In this

**Illustration 12–9**
The balanced scorecard

Financial Perspective

Customer Perspective ← Strategy → Internal Process Perspective

Learning and Growth

case a measure of employee job satisfaction might be an appropriate measure for the learning and growth dimension. Another potential learning and growth measure is the number of new products developed.

As you well know, "You get what you measure!" and companies need measures that drive behaviors consistent with their strategy for success. Let's consider four scenarios for a software company, to further illustrate how performance measures are tied to strategy for each dimension of a balanced scorecard.

**Scenario 1. Learning and Growth Dimension.** At Mayfield Software, many of the product managers are former programmers who have little or no training in business management. The company believes that to continue to grow sales and adapt to changes in the industry these managers need to become more knowledgeable about business concepts and practices. In this case, the company might develop a learning and growth measure that assesses the average number of hours of business training received by a product manager. Also, the company might survey product managers and have them rate the quality of business training provided by the company.

**Scenario 2. Internal Process Dimension.** Mayfield Software has been severely hampered by viruses that shut down all computer systems for 15 days in the prior year. This led to delays and provided an advantage to a competitor who was first to market with a product that was also under development by Mayfield. In this case, the company might develop an internal process measure that assesses the company's ability to detect and block viruses. Such a measure might be *number of hours computers are locked down to prevent the spread of a virus*.

**Scenario 3. Customer Dimension.** Critical to the success of Mayfield Software is brand awareness. In this case, the company might commission a survey to measure brand awareness from a random sample of potential customers. The results of the measure would be posted to the company's balanced scorecard under the customer dimension.

**Scenario 4. Financial Dimension.** At Mayfield Software, fixed costs such as R&D are high but variable costs are quite low. For example, its project management software program sells for $200 but the variable cost per unit is only $5 (including the cost of a CD, its packaging, and shipping). Thus, the contribution margin ratio of the product (the amount of profit per dollar of sales) is 97.5 percent. In light of this cost structure, the company's strategy for success focuses on sales volume. In this case, an important financial measure that will drive a focus on sales volume, is *growth in sales*.

## HOW BALANCE IS ACHIEVED IN A BALANCED SCORECARD

A variety of potential measures for each dimension of a Balanced Scorecard are indicated in Illustration 12–10. After reviewing these measures, note how "balance" is achieved:

1. Performance is assessed across a *balanced set of dimensions* (financial, customer, internal processes, and innovation).
2. *Quantitative* measures (e.g., number of defects) are balanced with *qualitative* measures (e.g., ratings of customer satisfaction).
3. There is a balance of *backward-looking* measures (e.g., financial measures like growth in sales) and *forward-looking* measures (e.g., number of new patents as an innovation measure).

**Illustration 12–10**
Examples of measures
for the four perspectives
of a balanced scorecard

| | | Measures |
|---|---|---|
| **Financial** | Is the company achieving its financial goals? | Operating income<br>Return on assets<br>Sales growth<br>Cash flow from operations<br>Reduction of administrative expense |
| **Customer** | Is the company meeting customer expectations? | Customer satisfaction<br>Customer retention<br>New customer acquisition<br>Market share<br>On-time delivery<br>Time to fill orders |
| **Internal Processes** | Is the company improving critical internal processes? | Defect rate<br>Lead time<br>Number of suppliers<br>Material turnover<br>Percent of practical capacity |
| **Learning and Growth** | Is the company improving its ability to innovate? | Amount spent on employee training<br>Employee satisfaction<br>Employee retention<br>Number of new products<br>New product sales as a percent of total sales<br>Number of patents |

**You Get What You Measure**

Underlying the Balanced Scorecard is an idea that we have emphasized throughout this book—"You get what you measure!" If you believe that customer satisfaction is critical for success, then you had better measure it so that managers will focus their attention on it. If you believe that reducing cycle time (the time it takes to make a product) is critical for success, then drive your managers to reduce cycle time by evaluating their performance in relation to this aspect of performance.

**LINK TO PRACTICE**

### *Trouble Related to Linking Executive Pay to Sales*

Merck & Co. is alleged to have included in revenue billions of dollars in co-payments that the company did not actually receive. Why would the previously respected company engage in such financial shenanigans? A plausible answer is that the bonus compensation of Merck executives is tied to growth in revenue. So, when executives record unearned revenue, they receive higher bonuses.

*Source*: Gretchen Morgenson, "Linking Pay of Execs to Sales is Haywire Idea," *Eastside Journal*, July 14, 2002, p. 1, Section C. Penelope Patsuris, "The Corporate Scandal Sheet," *Forbes.com*, August 26,2002. Stephen Taub, "Cash-and-Apothecary," *CFO.com*, June 24, 2002.

# MAKING BUSINESS DECISIONS

In the chapter, we saw that various financial performance measures can cause managers to make poor investment decisions. Evaluation in terms of growth in profit can lead to overinvestment (making investments that should not be made because the return is too low). Evaluation in terms of return on investment (ROI) can lead to underinvestment (not making investments that earn an adequate return) for business units with high current ROIs. Arguably, evaluation in terms of economic value added (EVA) influences managers to make good investment decisions since EVA increases when managers take on projects that earn a return in excess of the cost of capital.

## KNOWLEDGE AND SKILLS (K/S) CHECKLIST

*Knowledge and skills are needed to make good business decisions. Check off the knowledge and skills you've acquired from reading this chapter.*

☐ K/S 1. You have an expanded business vocabulary (see key terms).

☐ K/S 2. You can compute return on investment.

☐ K/S 3. You can compute economic value added (EVA).

☐ K/S 4. You can explain why NOPAT and investment are adjusted for so-called accounting distortions in the calculation of EVA.

☐ K/S 5. You can explain why growth in profit as a performance measure can encourage overinvestment.

☐ K/S 6. You can explain why use of ROI as a performance measure can encourage a very successful business unit to underinvest.

☐ K/S 7. You can identify performance measures that should be included on a Balanced Scorecard to drive a company's strategy for success.

# SUMMARY OF LEARNING OBJECTIVES

**① List and explain the advantages and disadvantages of decentralization.** Decentralization may lead to better information, faster responses to changing circumstances, and increased motivation of managers. Decentralized organizations also may provide excellent training for future top-level executives. On the other hand, decentralization may lead to costly duplication of activities and problems of goal congruence.

**② Explain why companies evaluate the performance of subunits and subunit managers.** Companies evaluate the performance of subunits to identify successful operations and areas needing improvement. Companies evaluate subunit managers to influence the behavior of the managers (because you get what you measure).

**③ Identify cost centers, profit centers, and investment centers.** Managers of cost centers are responsible only for controlling costs. Managers of profit centers are responsible for generating revenue as well as for controlling costs. Investment center managers are responsible for income and the level of assets used to generate income.

**④ Calculate and interpret return on investment (ROI).** Return on investment is calculated as the ratio of investment center income to invested capital. We measure income as net operating profit after taxes (NOPAT), and we measure invested capital as total assets less noninterest-bearing current liabilities.

**⑤ Explain why using a measure of profit to evaluate performance can lead to overinvestment and using ROI can lead to underinvestment.** Managers who are evaluated in terms of profit know that it is easy to increase profit by growing their company and taking on projects that earn a low return (i.e., overinvesting). In this case, profit increases, but the return is not adequate. If managers are evaluated in terms of ROI and their operation is already earning a high ROI, they may be reluctant to take on projects that earn a return greater than the cost of capital but lower than the current ROI. In this case, the managers are underinvesting.

**6** ***Calculate and interpret residual income (RI) and economic value added (EVA).*** Residual income is equal to the net operating profit after taxes of an investment center in excess of the profit required for the level of investment. EVA is conceptually similar, although adjustments are made for accounting distortions such as expensing R&D costs.

**7** ***Explain the potential benefits of using a Balanced Scorecard to assess performance.*** A Balanced Scorecard assesses performance with respect to four dimensions: financial, customer, internal processes, and learning and growth. The specific measures should be linked to a company's strategy for success. Whereas financial measures focus on past performance, the other dimensions assess what the company is doing to create future shareholder value.

# A P P E N D I X

Discuss the use of market price, variable cost, full cost plus profit, and negotiation in setting transfer prices.

# TRANSFER PRICING

In many cases, subunits of a company "sell" goods or services to other subunits within the same company. For example, a university print plant may sell printing services to other university departments. Similarly, a car manufacturing company may have one division that produces cars and another division that produces a variety of auto batteries. Most likely the car-producing division will use auto batteries produced by the battery division.

The price that is used to value internal transfers of goods or services is referred to as a **transfer price**. If the battery division transfers 10,000 batteries to the car division at a transfer price of $15 per unit, the battery division will have revenue of $150,000. However, this revenue is only recognized for internal reporting purposes. For external financial reporting purposes, a company cannot recognize revenue on the sale of goods between responsibility centers within the firm, because the revenue has not been realized.

Revenue, for financial reporting purposes, is realized when goods or services are sold to customers outside the firm. Sales within a company are not "arm's length" transactions (transactions entered into by unrelated parties). Without this restriction, companies could inflate sales and income by engaging in numerous unnecessary internal sales transactions.

In practice, a number of different approaches are taken to setting transfer prices. The primary alternatives in practice are transfer prices based on (1) market prices, (2) variable costs, (3) full cost plus profit, and (4) negotiated prices. These alternatives are discussed next. Which of the transfer prices is most appropriate depends on the circumstances. What is desired is a transfer price that will lead the subunit managers to make decisions that maximize firm value. The transfer price that motivates the best decisions is the *opportunity cost of producing an item and transferring it inside the company*. Recall that an opportunity cost is the foregone benefit (increased cost) of selecting one alternative over another.

# MARKET PRICE AS THE TRANSFER PRICE

For purposes of discussion, let's assume that the subunits buying and selling internally are divisions of a company. In some cases, the producing division transfers a product internally to a buying division and also sells the same product outside the firm. For example, the battery division of the auto company may sell batteries to various auto supply companies and also "sell" batteries internally to the car-producing division.

When the product is sold outside the firm, a market price exists, and it can be used as the transfer price. The external market price is an excellent internal transfer price because it allows both the buying division and the selling division to be treated as "stand-alone," independent companies. Generally, market prices are perceived as fair and reasonable by both the buying and the selling divisions. The buying division cannot complain that the transfer price is too high, because it represents the same price the buying division would have to pay in the open market. For the same reason, the selling division cannot complain that the transfer price is too low.

In some cases the selling division experiences cost savings from selling internally rather than in an external market. For example, shipping costs may be reduced if the buying division is close to the selling division. Advertising costs may also be lower, and reduced production costs may be achieved if the selling division finds it easier to schedule production for internal sales than for external sales. If cost savings exist, the market price should be reduced by the cost savings to arrive at the transfer price.

Consider an example. Suppose the Processor division of Tectron Manufacturing Co. produces a microprocessor that it sells to a large number of companies at a market price of $300 each. The Computer division of Tectron produces personal computers that utilize the microprocessor produced by the Processor division. By selling the microprocessor internally, the Processor division saves approximately $2 per unit in shipping costs and $1 per unit in manufacturing costs. In this case, a reasonable transfer price would be $297 (i.e., $300 market price less the $3 cost savings).

| | |
|---|---|
| Market price | $300.00 |
| Savings due to reduced shipping costs | 2.00 |
| Savings due to reduced manufacturing costs | 1.00 |
| Adjusted transfer price | $297.00 |

# MARKET PRICE AND OPPORTUNITY COST

Earlier, we suggested that the best transfer price should be the *opportunity cost of producing an item and transferring it to the buying division*. When a market price exits, it is a good transfer price because it is equal to the opportunity cost.

Suppose the Sweet Company is composed of two divisions. The Syrup division produces corn syrup, and the Candy division produces a variety of candies using corn syrup as a sweetener. The Syrup division can sell corn syrup to outside buyers for $8 per gallon. If the market price is used as a transfer price for sales of corn syrup from the Syrup division to the Candy division, the transfer price, too, will be $8. But is $8 the opportunity cost of transferring the corn syrup from the Syrup division to the Candy division?

An opportunity cost is the foregone benefit or increased cost of selecting one alternative over another. What benefit is foregone by transferring corn syrup internally? The answer is that the $8 that could be earned selling the corn syrup externally is foregone when the corn syrup is transferred to the Candy division. Thus, the opportunity cost is equal to the market price of the transferred product.

To illustrate, suppose that one gallon of syrup is used to produce every 10 pounds of rock candy manufactured by the Candy division. The rock candy sells for $50 for a 10-pound container. Variable costs are as follows.

| 10-Pound Container | |
|---|---|
| Variable production cost excluding corn syrup | $43 |
| Transfer price of corn syrup | 8 |
| Total variable cost per container | $51 |

In this situation, because the candy sells for $50 for a 10-pound container, the Candy division has a negative contribution margin of $1 per container and will not be willing to produce rock candy.

Now suppose the Candy division argues that if the transfer price of corn syrup is reduced to $5 (the variable cost of producing corn syrup), its variable costs will only be $48, and rock candy will have a positive contribution margin. Should the transfer price be lowered? The answer is no. The income of the Syrup division and the total income of the Sweet Company will be reduced if the Candy division is subsidized by a transfer price lower than the market price. If the Candy division cannot earn a profit paying a transfer price equal to what it would pay for syrup in the open market, then consideration should be given to eliminating the product.

The effect on the company's contribution margin of lowering the transfer price and transferring the syrup inside to the Candy division is presented in Illustration 12A–1. If the transfer price is the market price of $8, the Candy division will not find production of rock candy profitable. No syrup will be demanded by the Candy division, and all syrup will be sold in the marketplace. In this case, the

**Illustration 12A–1**
Analysis of lowering the transfer price below the market price

**Sell Syrup at Market Price**

| Contribution Margin of Syrup Division per Gallon of Syrup | | Contribution Margin of Candy Division per 10-Pound Container | Contribution Margin of Company |
|---|---|---|---|
| Selling price | $ 8 | | |
| Variable cost | 5 | | |
| Cont. margin | $ 3 | -0-[b] | $ 3[a] |

**Transfer Syrup to Candy Division at $5**

| Contribution Margin of Syrup Division per Gallon of Syrup | | Contribution Margin of Candy Division per 10-Pound Container | | Contribution Margin of Company |
|---|---|---|---|---|
| Transfer price | $ 5 | Selling price | $50 | |
| Variable cost | 5 | Own variable costs | 43 | |
| Cont. margin | $-0- | Transfer price | 5 | |
| | | Cont. margin | $ 2 | $ 2[a] |

[a] Note that a gallon of syrup is required to produce a 10-pound container of candy. Thus, a gallon of syrup is equivalent to a 10-pound container of candy.

[b] Contribution margin is zero because Candy division will not demand any corn syrup at a transfer price of $8.

Syrup division will earn $3 of contribution margin on every gallon of syrup, the Candy division will earn no contribution margin, and the contribution margin of the company as a whole will be $3. Alternatively, if the syrup is transferred to the Candy division at a transfer price of $5, the Syrup division will earn no contribution margin because the transfer price will be equal to the variable cost of producing the syrup. For each gallon of syrup, however, the Candy division can produce a 10-pound container of rock candy that sells for $50. The Candy division will have $43 of variable costs in addition to the $5 transfer price it must pay for each gallon of syrup. Thus, the Candy division will earn a contribution margin of $2. The contribution margin to the company will also be $2 because the Syrup division will have a contribution margin of zero. Note that although the Candy division is certainly better off with a transfer price of $5, the Syrup division is worse off, and the company as a whole is worse off by $1 for each gallon of syrup transferred at the $5 transfer price.

# VARIABLE COST AS THE TRANSFER PRICE

In some cases, the transferred product is unique and is not sold by the producing division in the open market. Obviously, no market price exists, and some other transfer price must be chosen. The variable cost of producing the transferred good may be the best transfer price in this situation. The reason for selecting the variable cost of production as the transfer price is that it conveys accurate opportunity cost information. When no external market exists, the opportunity cost of producing and selling an item internally is simply the variable costs of producing the item.[4] Each time an additional unit is produced, the company must incur additional costs equal to the variable cost of production.

Again, knowing the opportunity cost of the transferred product can lead the buying division to make well-informed decisions. For example, suppose the buying division is considering a request for a special order from a customer. To produce the product, the buying division must use a component that will be supplied by another division of the firm (the selling division). In addition to the transfer price, the buying division will incur variable production costs of $50 per unit. Further, the selling division will incur variable costs of $25 in producing the component. What is the minimum price that could be accepted for the special order? The answer is $75, which is equal to the $50 of variable cost incurred by the buying division plus the $25 of variable cost incurred by the selling division. Any price above $75 will increase the overall contribution margin of the company and its income.

But suppose the transfer price is set at an amount greater than the variable cost of the selling division? For example, suppose the transfer price is set at $40. In this case, the manager of the buying division will perceive that the minimum acceptable selling price for the special order is $90, not $75. The $90 amount is equal to the $40 transfer price paid for each unit by the buying division plus the other variable costs incurred by the buying division, which are equal to $50. The

---

[4]This assumes that the selling division has excess capacity. If not, the opportunity cost must include the income lost on items that cannot be produced when capacity is used to produce goods for internal transfer.

special order would be turned down by the manager of the buying division at prices between $75 and $90, at a definite loss of income for the company as a whole. A failure to know the real opportunity cost of production may thus lead to poor decisions by the buying division manager.

# FULL COST PLUS PROFIT AS THE TRANSFER PRICE

A very significant problem with using variable cost as the transfer price is that the selling division cannot earn a profit on production of the transferred product. Thus, use of variable costs as a transfer price may not be acceptable to division managers. For this reason, many companies add a profit margin to the full cost of an item and use the resulting amount as the transfer price.

For example, suppose the variable cost of producing an item for internal sale to a buying division is $100 per unit. Further, 1,000 units are expected to be transferred in the coming year, and fixed costs per year will amount to $200,000. The fixed costs relate to depreciation on equipment that is not currently being used to capacity. In this case, the full cost per unit is $300 ($100 variable cost and $200 fixed cost). At a transfer price of $300 the selling division will just break even on the internal transfer. However, suppose the company utilizes a transfer pricing policy whereby the transfer price is equal to full cost plus 10 percent of full cost. In this case, the transfer price will be $330, and the selling division will earn income of $30 on each item produced.

Although full cost plus profit may be more acceptable as a transfer price to division managers, the transfer price may not measure the opportunity cost of producing the transferred product. As we saw earlier, this can result in decisions that do not maximize the profitability of the whole company. Suppose the buying division of the company described above must incur $400 of variable costs in addition to the transfer price. The market price for the item produced by the buying division is $690. The buying division will not continue producing the product unless it makes a positive contribution toward covering its fixed costs. With a transfer price of $330, the contribution margin faced by the buying division is a negative $40 ($690 selling price less variable cost of $400 and transfer price of $330). Thus, the buying division will be inclined to drop the product. However, the product does, in fact, make a positive contribution to firm income. The selling price of $690 is greater than the variable cost of the buying division ($400) plus the variable cost of the selling division ($100) by $190. Thus, the company as a whole is actually better off by $190 for each unit sold.

|  | Transfer Price Equals Full Cost Plus Profit | Transfer Price Equals Variable Cost |
|---|---|---|
| Selling price of final product | $690 | $690 |
| Less: variable cost of the buying division except for the transfer price | 400 | 400 |
| Less: transfer price | 330 | 100 |
| Contribution margin of buying division | ($40) | $190 |

# NEGOTIATED TRANSFER PRICES

As discussed at the start of this chapter, one of the benefits of decentralization is that managers who are delegated significant decision making responsibility tend to be highly motivated. To encourage the sense of autonomy, some companies allow division managers to negotiate a transfer price. This presents the subunit managers with the same situation faced by an independent business that must negotiate a price for specialized items. However, the resulting transfer price may reflect the relative negotiating skills of the subunit managers and fail to reflect the underlying opportunity cost associated with producing goods and transferring them internally.

# TRANSFER PRICING AND INCOME TAXES IN AN INTERNATIONAL CONTEXT

When goods are transferred between profit centers in different countries, the income tax situations in the countries may create incentives for relatively high or relatively low transfer prices. For example, suppose the tax rate in Country A is 10 percent, whereas the tax rate in Country B is 40 percent. Holding everything else constant, this creates an incentive to have high transfer prices when goods are transferred from a profit center in Country A to a profit center in Country B. With this approach, the profit center in Country A will have relatively high income (which is taxed at a low rate), and the profit center in Country B will have relatively low income (which is taxed at a high rate). Thus, overall taxes of company income for the two profit centers will be reduced. If goods were to be transferred from a profit center in Country B to a profit center in Country A, there would be an incentive for a relatively low transfer price. The Internal Revenue Service in the United States and the taxing authorities in other countries are aware of these incentives and try to make sure that transfer prices are not unreasonably high or low in response to the incentives created by differences in income tax rates between countries.

# REVIEW PROBLEM

Merlin Appliances founded by Morgan D. Edwards in 1976, is a closely held company that operates five stores in Michigan selling refrigerators, stoves, washers and dryers, and other household appliances. The company's stock is owned by various members of the Morgan D. Edwards family, and five family members serve on the board of directors. The president and CEO of Merlin is David Bell. David, who is not a family member, was hired in 2003 and he is responsible for all day-to-day company decisions. He reports to Brandon Edwards, who is chairman of the board.

At the end of fiscal 2005, David was asked to prepare a brief memo to the board reviewing the company's performance. A copy of the memo is presented below along with comparative financial statements. A board meeting is scheduled for early February at which time the board will review company performance and David's compensation including his performance bonus for 2005.

**Merlin Appliances**

*Selection, Service, and Magically Low Prices*
*Serving Michigan Residents Since 1976*

January 26, 2006

TO: Board of Directors of Merlin Appliances

FROM: David Bell, President and CEO

SUBJECT: Financial performance in fiscal 2005

At the start of 2005 we discussed the fact that the market for appliances was likely to be soft due to economic conditions in the state of Michigan. Specifically, at the start of 2005, unemployment had risen to 7.1 percent and several major companies (especially Ford) had made plans for substantial job cuts. In light of this, I am very happy to report that we have had an outstanding year. Sales have increased by 7.68 percent and profit is up by 14.11 percent.

How was this accomplished? Here's a brief outline of the three strategies we employed—I'll review them in detail at the February 7th board meeting.

1. Market research indicated that sales could be increased if we held the line on prices, displayed a wider selection of items at each store, and had more items available in our warehouse so that we could offer 1- or 2-day delivery. This strategy was implemented, with obvious good results, in early 2005.

2. We adjusted our quarterly sales events. In addition to offering our normal discounts at these events, we also offered terms with no payments (and no interest charges) for 6 months. This strategy was successful in attracting customers who might have delayed purchases in the current year.

3. We retired all short-term and all long-term debt. As you know, we had cash reserves of approximately $1.6 million at the end of 2004 (the money had been accumulated in anticipation of expansion but expansion plans have been put on hold). Paying down debt reduces company risk and appears to be a good use of the funds.

I also want to note that our exceptional performance in fiscal 2005 could not have been achieved without the support of the 138 Merlin team members whose hard work and dedication to the company's success is evident in every sale and every delivery!

Finally, as you know, we paid out approximately $1,000,000 in dividends in fiscal 2005—no dividends were paid in 2004, and dividends in 2003 were only $500,000.

See you on February 7th.

| Comparative Income Statements | 2005 | 2004 | % Change |
|---|---|---|---|
| Sales | $27,659,548 | $25,687,240 | 7.68% |
| Less: | | | |
| Cost of sales | 19,361,684 | 17,981,068 | |
| Selling, general and administrative expense | 5,531,910 | 5,137,448 | |
| Interest expense | – | 144,711 | |
| Income before income taxes | 2,765,954 | 2,424,013 | |
| Income taxes | 968,084 | 848,405 | |
| Net income | $ 1,797,870 | $ 1,575,608 | 14.11% |

| Comparative Balance Sheets | 2005 | 2004 |
|---|---|---|
| Assets | | |
| Cash and cash equivalents | $    147,636 | $  1,586,250 |
| Accounts receivable | 2,990,221 | 2,568,724 |
| Inventory | 2,420,211 | 1,997,896 |
| Prepaid expenses | 47,399 | 45,265 |
| Total current assets | 5,605,467 | 6,198,135 |
| Land | 1,342,350 | 1,342,350 |
| Building, furniture, fixtures (net) | 8,438,088 | 8,523,321 |
| Total noncurrent assets | 9,780,438 | 9,865,671 |
| Total assets | $15,385,905 | $16,063,806 |
| **Liabilities** | | |
| Accounts payable | $    210,240 | $    199,790 |
| Accrued liabilities | 57,010 | 45,685 |
| Taxes payable | 60,690 | 49,321 |
| Current portion of long-term debt | – | 188,754 |
| Total current liabilities | 327,940 | 483,550 |
| Long-term debt | – | 1,258,360 |
| Total liabilities | 327,940 | 1,741,910 |
| **Stockholders' Equity** | | |
| Common stock | 5,079,315 | 5,079,315 |
| Retained earnings | 9,978,650 | 9,242,581 |
| Total stockholders' equity | 15,057,965 | 14,321,896 |
| Total liabilities and stockholders' equity | $15,385,905 | $16,063,806 |

**Required**

a. Evaluate performance in fiscal 2005 and 2004 in terms of economic value added (EVA). Assume a weighted average cost of capital of 15 percent in 2005 and 14 percent in 2004. Briefly comment on whether or not this evaluation supports a significant bonus for David Bell.

b. Suppose that the entire increase in net operating profit after taxes in 2005 is due to having more inventory and "no payments or interest" for 6 months which led to an increase in accounts receivable. Evaluate the impact of these strategies in terms of their impact on EVA using a 15 percent cost of capital.

**Answer**

a.

| | 2005 | 2004 |
|---|---|---|
| Net income | $ 1,797,870.00 | $ 1,575,608.00 |
| Add interest | | 144,711.00 |
| Less taxes related to interest | – | (50,648.85) |
| NOPAT | $ 1,797,870.00 | $ 1,669,670.15 |
| Investment | | |
| Total assets | $15,385,905.00 | $16,063,806.00 |
| Less NIBCL: | | |
|    Acct. pay. | (210,240.00) | (199,790.00) |
|    Accrued liab. | (57,010.00) | (45,685.00) |
|    Taxes pay. | (60,690.00) | (49,321.00) |
| Investment | 15,057,965.00 | $15,769,010.00 |
| Cost of capital | 0.15 | 0.14 |
| Required NOPAT | 2,258,694.75 | 2,207,661.40 |
| EVA (NOPAT − Required NOPAT) | $   (460,824.75) | $   (537,991.25) |

It does not appear that a substantial bonus is warranted since EVA is negative in 2005 indicating that shareholder value has actually declined. This follows because net operating profit is less than the level required given the investment in the company. Note that EVA was also negative in 2004. Also note that EVA and residual income are identical in this problem since there are no adjustments for "accounting distortions."

b. The company increased inventory. And the policy of no payments or interest for six months increased accounts receivable. Together, these two items increased investment by $843,812. With a 15 percent cost of capital, NOPAT would need to increase by $126,572 to "break even." In actuality, NOPAT increased by $128,200 for a net benefit of $1,628. While positive, this rather small amount is hardly in line with the financial gains claimed in David Bell's memo.

| | |
|---|---:|
| Increase in inventory ($2,420,211–$1,997,896) | $422,315 |
| Increase in receivables ($2,990,221–$2,568,724) | 421,497 |
| Increase in investment | 843,812 |
| Cost of capital | × .15 |
| Required additional NOPAT | 126,572 |
| Actual additional NOPAT ($1,797,870.00–$1,669,670.15) | 128,200 |
| Net benefit | $   1,628 |

# KEY TERMS

| | | |
|---|---|---|
| Balanced Scorecard (434) | Investment turnover (424) | Relative performance evaluation (423) |
| Cost center (422) | Lack of goal congruence (419) | Residual income (RI) (429) |
| Decentralized organizations (418) | NOPAT (425) | Responsibility centers (422) |
| Economic value added (EVA) (430) | Profit center (422) | Return on investment (ROI) (424) |
| Investment center (423) | Profit margin (424) | Transfer price (Appendix) (439) |

# SELF ASSESSMENT *(Answers Below)*

1. Which of the following is not a reason for having decentralized organizations?

   a. Better information at the local level leads to superior decisions.
   b. Goal congruence is enhanced.
   c. Quicker response to changing circumstances.
   d. Increased motivation of managers.

2. Which of the following is most indicative of a decentralized organization?

   a. The physical facilities of the company are widely dispersed geographically.
   b. The organization is divided into several operating divisions.
   c. Accounting is performed, in part, in the several operating divisions.
   d. The company grants substantial decision making authority to the heads of each of its several operating divisions.

3. Which of the following should *not* be used to evaluate the performance of a plant manager in a decentralized organization?

   a. Direct labor expense in the plant.
   b. Depreciation expense on equipment the manager authorized.
   c. Variable overhead expenses in the plant.
   d. Interest expense on bonds used to finance expansion of the plant.

4. Responsibility accounting suggests that:

   a. A department manager should be held responsible for the cost of computers used in his or her department even if the manager did not make the decision to purchase the computers.
   b. A department manager should be held responsible for a share of the rent paid to lease a large administrative office building.
   c. A department manager should be held responsible for general and administrative costs allocated to his or her department based on head count (the number of workers in the manager's department).
   d. None of the above.

5. Which of the following is not a cost center?

   a. An accounting department.
   b. A production department.
   c. A retail sales outlet.
   d. A maintenance department.

6. An investment center is responsible for:

   a. Investing in long term assets.
   b. Controlling costs.
   c. Generating revenues.
   d. All of the above.

7. A profit center is responsible for all of the following except:

   a. Investing in long term assets.
   b. Controlling costs.
   c. Generating revenues.
   d. All of the above are the responsibility of a profit center.

8. A cost center is responsible for which of the following?

   a. Investing in long-term assets.
   b. Controlling costs.
   c. Generating revenues.
   d. All of the above.

9. Use of profit as a performance measure:

   a. May lead to overinvestment in assets.
   b. Is appropriate for an investment center
   c. Is appropriate as long as profit is calculated using GAAP.
   d. Encourages managers to finance operations with debt rather than equity.

10. Return on investment (ROI) is calculated as:

    a. Sales ÷ Total assets.
    b. Gross margin ÷ Invested capital.
    c. Investment center income ÷ Invested capital.
    d. Income ÷ Sales.

11. Cost centers are often evaluated using:

    a. Variance analysis.
    b. Operating margin.
    c. Return on investment.
    d. Residual income.

12. Profit centers are often evaluated using:

    a. Investment turnover.
    b. Income targets or profit budgets.
    c. Return on investment.
    d. Residual income.

13. Investment centers are often evaluated using:

    a. Standard cost variances.
    b. Return on investment.

    c. Residual income/EVA.
    d. Both b and c.

14. Which of the following is a problem in using return on investment to evaluate managers?

    a. Managers of investment centers with high ROIs may not invest in some projects with returns greater than the required rate of return.
    b. Managers may overinvest in high ROI projects.
    c. Managers' morale may suffer from being evaluated.
    d. None of the above.

15. Which of the following is not a part of the calculation of residual income?

    a. NOPAT.
    b. Invested capital.
    c. Required rate of return.
    d. Interest expense.

16. Which of the following is a true statement regarding the evaluation of an investment center?

    a. Return on investment may be high because of old equipment that is fully depreciated.
    b. Residual income does not take into account the level of investment in fixed assets.
    c. Return on investment does not take into account the level of investment in fixed assets.
    d. None of the above.

17. Which of the following are included in the calculation of net income but excluded in the calculation of NOPAT?

    a. Interest expense.
    b. Gains on investments.
    c. Losses on investments.
    d. All of the above.

18. What is the difference between residual income and EVA?

    a. Residual income is a new concept.
    b. EVA makes adjustments for "accounting distortions."
    c. Residual income excludes research and development as an expense.
    d. EVA includes a capital charge.

19. Which of the following is not a dimension of the Balanced Scorecard?

    a. Customer.
    b. Internal processes.
    c. Innovation.
    d. Stakeholder.

20. (Appendix) When a ready market exists, the best transfer price will probably be the:

a. Market price.
b. Variable cost.
c. Full cost plus profit.
d. Negotiated transfer price.

21. (Appendix) In an international context, there is an incentive to set a high transfer price when:

a. Goods are transferred from a high-tax country to a low-tax country.
b. Goods are transferred from a low-tax country to a high-tax country.
c. Goods are transferred to an international subsidiary.
d. None of the above.

22. (Appendix) The transfer price that motivates the best decisions is one that measures:

a. The full cost of goods produced.
b. The opportunity cost of producing and transferring an item.
c. The selling division's variable cost.
d. None of the above.

**Answers to Self Assessment**

**1.** b;   **2.** d;   **3.** d;   **4.** d;   **5.** c;   **6.** d;
**7.** a;   **8.** b;   **9.** a;   **10.** c;   **11.** a;   **12.** b;
**13.** d;   **14.** a;   **15.** d;   **16.** a;   **17.** d;
**18.** b;   **19.** d;   **20.** a;   **21.** b;   **22.** b.

# INTERACTIVE LEARNING

**Enhance and test your knowledge of Chapter 10 using the interactive CD.**

1. Learning Objectives
2. Multiple Choice
3. Language of Business—Matching of key terms
4. Critical Thinking
5. Demonstration—The calculation of residual income/EVA
6. Case—*Nelson Tool Company*; A Balanced Scorecard
7. Video—SAFECO; A Balanced Scorecard

**Go to our dynamic Web site for more self-assessment, Web links, and additional information.**

# QUESTIONS

1. List four advantages related to decentralization of a firm's operations.

2. List two disadvantages associated with decentralization of a firm's operations.

3. What is empire building in a managerial context?

4. How could costly duplication of activities occur in a decentralized operating environment?

5. Discuss goal congruence and how it impacts the decision to decentralize.

6. Distinguish between cost centers, profit centers, and investment centers.

7. Discuss why evaluation in terms of profit may lead to overinvestment, whereas evaluation in terms of ROI may lead to underinvestment.

8. Why is it not advisable to hold production supervisors responsible for depreciation on equipment used by workers they supervise?

9. What is the formula for return on investment?

10. What is the formula for residual income?

11. What is the difference between residual income and EVA?

12. What is NOPAT?

13. What is the problem with using only financial measures of performance?

14. Provide two measures for each perspective of a Balanced Scorecard.

15. What problem may be created by evaluating managers using market share?

16. (Appendix) Explain the advantages of using market price as a transfer price.

17. (Appendix) When would a variable-cost transfer price measure opportunity cost?

18. (Appendix) How do the taxes affect transfer prices when goods are transferred between countries?

# EXERCISES

**EXERCISE 12-1. Group Assignment** Explain why, in the calculation of EVA, the profit measure used (NOPAT) excludes interest expense.

**EXERCISE 12-2. Writing Assignment** Write a paragraph explaining why, in the calculation of a company's EVA, noninterest-bearing current liabilities are subtracted from total assets to determine investment.

**EXERCISE 12-3. Internet Assignment** Go to the Web site of Art Schneiderman, a consultant, at (*http://www.schneiderman.com/AMS.htm*). Art worked for Analog Devices when it became the first company to develop and use a Balanced Scorecard. Click on the link to his electronic article that documents the development of a Balanced Scorecard at Analog Devices.

*Required*

Read the section on "How the Balanced Scorecard Became Balanced." What was the conflict between Jerry (the chief operating officer) and Art? And how was it resolved?

**EXERCISE 12-4. Why Firms Decentralize** Malcort Glass Company is a manufacturer of automotive glass and glass products used in the home. Discuss the advantages of forming two divisions (an Automotive division and a Home Products division) and allowing the division managers substantial decision making autonomy.

**EXERCISE 12-5. Responsibility Centers and Performance Measures** Department managers at Engstrom Department Stores are allowed considerable discretion in sourcing and pricing products based on local tastes and competition. They are also responsible for staffing their departments.

*Required*

Suggest two financial performance measures that would be useful in evaluating the performance of department managers at Engstrom Department Stores.

**EXERCISE 12-6. Responsibility Centers** A major software company has established customer service centers in India, Ireland, and Israel to provide support to its U.S. customers with foreign operations. The prices that the company charges for software reflect estimated costs in operating the centers (i.e., there is no separate charge for service). How should these centers be organized—as cost centers, profit centers, or investment centers? Support your answer.

**EXERCISE 12-7. Responsibility Centers** Mayfield Software operates a training facility that offers classes in the use of its software products. Historically, the classes have been offered at a modest charge that covers the cost of the instructor's salary but not overhead related to the training facility (e.g., janitorial cost, utilities, rent, and administration).

Lauren Walters had recently been named director of customer training, and she will be given considerable freedom in operating the training facility and in marketing classes. Top management at Mayfield, however, has told Lauren that they want her operation to earn a before-tax profit of at least $250,000.

*Required*

Discuss the wisdom of requiring the training operation to earn a profit.

**EXERCISE 12-8. Calculating ROI** Lowery Mills is a division of Spencer Woolen Products, Inc. For the most recent year, Lowery had net income of $10,000,000. Included in income was interest expense of $1,000,000. The operation's tax rate is 35 percent.

Total assets of Lowery Mills are $200,000,000, current liabilities are $40,000,000, and $25,000,000 of the current liabilities are noninterest-bearing.

*Required*
Calculate NOPAT, invested capital, and ROI for Lowery Mills.

**EXERCISE 12-9. Calculating ROI**    For fiscal year 2005, Kitchencraft Products had income as follows:

| | |
|---|---:|
| Sales | $40,000,000 |
| Less: | |
|     Cost of goods sold | 25,000,000 |
|     Selling and administrative expense | 5,000,000 |
|     Interest expense | 1,000,000 |
| Income before taxes | 9,000,000 |
| Less income taxes | 3,150,000 |
| Net income | $ 5,850,000 |

Total assets were $104,000,000 and noninterest-bearing current liabilities were $2,000,000. The company has a required rate of return on invested capital equal to 12 percent.

*Required*
Calculate NOPAT, invested capital and ROI for Kitchencraft Products and comment on the company's profitability.

**EXERCISE 12-10. Calculating Residual Income**    For fiscal year 2006, Zander's Department Store had net income of $1,950,000. Interest expense was $2,000,000 and the company's tax rate on income was 35 percent. Total assets were $65,000,000 and noninterest-bearing current liabilities were $4,000,000. The company's cost of capital (required rate of return) is 10 percent.

*Required*
Calculate NOPAT, invested capital and residual income for Zander's Department Store and comment on the company's profitability.

**EXERCISE 12-11. Evaluating Investment Centers with Residual Income**    Midwest Hospital is a division of Nationwide Healthcare organized as an investment center. In the past year, the hospital reported an after-tax income of $3,000,000. Total interest expense was $1,000,000, and the hospital's tax rate was 35 percent.

Hospital assets totaled $35,000,000 and noninterest-bearing current liabilities were $10,000,000. Nationwide has established a required rate of return equal to 20 percent of invested capital.

*Required*
Calculate the residual income/EVA of Midwest Hospital.

**EXERCISE 12-12. Evaluating Investment Centers; ROI Versus RI**    Consider the following data, which relate to the two divisions of MBR Products.

| | Division 1 | Division 2 |
|---|---|---|
| Total assets | $40,000,000 | $20,000,000 |
| Noninterest bearing current liabilities | 2,000,000 | 1,000,000 |
| NOPAT | 5,500,000 | 3,000,000 |
| Required return | 10% | 10% |

*Required*
Compare the two divisions in terms of return on investment and residual income. In the past year, which division has created the most wealth for MBR shareholders?

**EXERCISE 12-13. Overinvestment and Underinvestment**    Consider two companies. Criterion Products and Vulcan Products. Senior managers at Criterion Products are evaluated in terms of increases in profit. In fiscal 2006, Criterion Products had a net operating profit after taxes of $2,000,000 and invested capital of $20,000,000. In fiscal 2007, the company had net operating profit after taxes of $2,500,000 and invested capital of

$30,000,000. Senior managers at Vulcan Products are evaluated in terms of ROI. In fiscal 2006, ROI was 18 percent while the cost of capital was only 14 percent. Near the end of fiscal 2006, managers had an opportunity to make an investment that would have yielded a return of 16 percent. However, the senior managers did not support making the investment.

*Required*

a. Explain why the senior managers at Criterion Products have an incentive to overinvest.

b. Explain why the senior managers at Vulcan Products have an incentive to underinvest.

**EXERCISE 12-14. Adjusting *NOPAT* and Adjusting *Investment* in the Calculation of EVA**   The following income statements and other information are available for Norris Company:

|  | 2005 | 2004 | 2003 |
|---|---|---|---|
| Sales | $200,000,000 | $180,000,000 | $150,000,000 |
| Less cost of goods sold | 80,000,000 | 72,000,000 | 65,000,000 |
| Gross margin | 120,000,000 | 108,000,000 | 85,000,000 |
| Less: |  |  |  |
|   Selling and administrative costs | 24,000,000 | 21,600,000 | 17,000,000 |
|   Research and development | 15,000,000 | 12,000,000 | 9,000,000 |
| Income from operations | 81,000,000 | 74,400,000 | 59,000,000 |
| Less taxes on income | 28,350,000 | 26,040,000 | 20,650,000 |
| Net income | $ 52,650,000 | $ 48,360,000 | $ 38,350,000 |
|  |  |  |  |
| Total assets | $579,150,000 | $483,600,000 | $345,150,000 |
| Noninterest-bearing current liabilities | 10,500,000 | 9,600,000 | 8,500,000 |
| Cost of capital | 10% | 10% | 10% |

*Required*

Calculate EVA for 2005. Assume that for purposes of calculating EVA, the company capitalizes research and development expenditures and amortizes them over three years including the year they are incurred. For external reporting purposes, research and development is expensed in the year incurred as indicated in the income statements above.

**EXERCISE 12-15. Balanced Scorecard**   Some advocates of the Balanced Scorecard have argued that managing a company with just financial performance measures is like driving a car and just looking in the rearview mirror. That's why they recommend customer, internal process, and learning and growth measures which, they believe, focus attention on what a company is doing today to create future value.

*Required*

Explain the analogy between financial measures and driving using just the rearview mirror.

**EXERCISE 12-16. Customer-Focused Measures for a Balanced Scorecard**
Olympic Health Club operates a 20,000 square foot facility in Dallas. For the coming year, the company is considering development of a Balanced Scorecard.

*Required*

Help the company by identifying three customer-focused measures that can be used on the Balanced Scorecard.

**EXERCISE 12-17. (Appendix) Transfer Pricing in Healthcare, Market Price**
Northeast Medical Services has two outpatient clinics and a pathology laboratory, which are organized as separate profit centers. When the pathology laboratory conducts tests ordered by the clinics, the clinics are charged the basic market price of the tests. The managers of the clinics object to this practice and argue that because they

are all part of the same company, they should be charged for the *cost* of the procedures rather than market price.

*Required*

Support the use of market prices or cost-based prices for charging clinics for tests performed by the pathology laboratory.

**EXERCISE 12-18. (Appendix) Transfer Pricing, Full Cost Plus Profit**    National Chemical Company has a number of divisions that produce and market paints, varnishes, and other chemical products. The company also has a small plant that manufactures metal containers for the divisions' various products. The plant, which has substantial excess capacity, is organized as a cost center and transfers containers to the divisions at various cost.

John Elders, the container plant manager, has approached the corporate executive committee with the suggestion that the plant he administers be organized as a profit center. This would be accomplished by changing the transfer price to be equal to full cost plus a markup of 10 percent.

*Required*

Comment on John's suggestion. Could his proposal lead to suboptimal decisions from the standpoint of the company as a whole?

# P R O B L E M S

**PROBLEM 12-1. Cost Centers and Performance Measures**    Magnus Materials manufactures metal and plastic gutters for use in commercial and residential construction. Production occurs in two separate plants. Distribution is from a central warehouse and there is a centrally managed sales office. Both production plants are currently treated as cost centers, and their budgets are prepared in close consultation with the central office. Analysis of standard cost variances is used as a control mechanism in the two plants.

*Required*

a. Explain how budgets and variance analysis provide a means of controlling cost in the production plants.

b. List four nonfinancial performance measures that plant managers can use to assess the operations they control.

**PROBLEM 12-2. Investment Centers and Performance Measures**    SEI Corporation has five divisions, each of which is managed by a divisional president who reports to the chief executive officer (CEO) of SEI. SEI is decentralized, and divisional presidents are granted authority to make investments under $2,000,000 without prior approval by the CEO.

*Required*

Suggest three financial performance measures that could be used to evaluate the divisions and the divisional presidents.

**PROBLEM 12-3. Return on Investment**    Consider the following information for Binder and Conners, Inc.

|  | 12/31/05 | 12/31/06 |
|---|---|---|
| Total assets | $80,000,000 | $85,000,000 |
| Noninterest-bearing current liabilities | 3,000,000 | 3,200,000 |
| Net income | 5,510,000 | 5,600,000 |
| Interest expense | 1,000,000 | 1,200,000 |
| Tax rate | 35% | 35% |

*Required*

a. Evaluate the company in terms of return on investment (ROI).

b. While income has increased in fiscal 2006, is it clear that the company's performance has improved?

**PROBLEM 12-4. Residual Income/Economic Value Added**   Consider the following information for Everett Electronics.

|  | 12/31/05 | 12/31/06 |
|---|---|---|
| Total assets | $20,000,000 | $19,540,000 |
| Noninterest-bearing current liabilities | 800,000 | 900,000 |
| Net income | 1,240,000 | 1,586,800 |
| Interest expense | 4,000,000 | 1,000,000 |
| Tax rate | 35% | 35% |
| Required rate of return | 12% | 14% |

*Required*

a. Evaluate the company in terms of residual income (RI) which is equivalent to EVA since there are no adjustments for "accounting distortions."

b. While income has increased in fiscal 2006, is it clear that the company's performance has improved?

c. (**Optional**) Explain why the required rate of return increased in fiscal 2006. (Hint—note that while total assets are approximately the same in both years, interest expense has declined sharply in 2006.)

**PROBLEM 12-5. Return on Investment, Effect of Depreciation**   The Chief Operating Officer of the Baldwin Corporation is considering the effect of depreciation on company ROI. In the most recent year, net operating profit after taxes was $10,000,000 and investment (total assets of $120,000,000 less noninterest-bearing current liabilities of $20,000,000) was $100,000,000.

*Required*

a. Assuming that total assets will decline each year by 5 percent due to depreciation of plant and equipment but NOPAT will remain constant, calculate ROI for each of the next five years.

b. Explain why evaluation in terms of ROI may lead managers to delay purchases of equipment that, in the long run, will be needed to remain competitive.

**PROBLEM 12-6. Return on Investment, Profit Margin, and Investment Turnover**   Consider the following information for Vulcan Stores for 2005 and 2006.

|  | 2005 | 2006 |
|---|---|---|
| Total assets | $80,000,000 | $90,000,000 |
| Noninterest-bearing current liabilities | 7,000,000 | 8,000,000 |
| Net income | 6,000,000 | 8,000,000 |
| Interest expense | 4,000,000 | 5,000,000 |
| Sales | 120,000,000 | 180,000,000 |
| Tax rate | 35% | 35% |

*Required*

a. Compute ROI for both years.

b. Break ROI down into profit margin and investment turnover.

c. Comment on the change in financial performance between 2005 and 2006.

**PROBLEM 12-7. ROI and EVA**   Eastern Waste Management has a subsidiary that disposes of hazardous waste and a subsidiary that collects and disposes of residential garbage. Information related to the two subsidiaries follows:

|                                           | Hazardous Waste | Residential Waste |
|-------------------------------------------|-----------------|-------------------|
| Total assets                              | $10,000,000     | $60,000,000       |
| Noninterest-bearing current liabilities   | 2,000,000       | 8,000,000         |
| Net income                                | 1,500,000       | 4,000,000         |
| Interest expense                          | 1,000,000       | 5,000,000         |
| Required rate of return                   | 14%             | 10%               |
| Tax rate                                  | 35%             | 35%               |

*Required:*

a. Calculate ROI for both subsidiaries.

b. Calculate EVA for both subsidiaries. Note that since no adjustments for "accounting distortions" are being made, EVA is equivalent to residual income.

c. Which subsidiary has added the most to shareholder value in the last year?

d. Based on the limited information, which subsidiary is the best candidate for expansion? Explain.

**PROBLEM 12-8. EVA**   Phillips Electronics is considering instituting a plan whereby managers will be evaluated and rewarded based on a measure of economic value added (EVA). Before adopting the plan, management wants you to calculate what EVA will be in 2006 based on financial forecasts for 2006 and prior financial data.

|                                           | Forecast Fiscal 2006 |
|-------------------------------------------|----------------------|
| Total assets                              | $54,000,000          |
| Noninterest-bearing current liabilities   | 20,000,000           |
| Sales                                     | 98,000,000           |
| Net income                                | 5,000,000            |
| Interest expense                          | 1,000,000            |
| Research and development                  | 2,100,000            |
| Tax rate                                  | 35%                  |
| Cost of capital                           | 14%                  |

Research and development expenditures in 2004 and 2005 were $600,000 and $1,500,000, respectively. In calculating EVA, prior research and development will be capitalized and amortized assuming a three-year life (i.e., one-third will be expensed in the year incurred, and two-thirds will be capitalized and expensed in the following two years).

*Required*

a. Explain why it is important to capitalize research and development if managers are to be rewarded based on EVA.

b. Calculate forecasted EVA for 2006.

c. Will management be likely to support use of EVA as a financial performance measure?

**PROBLEM 12-9. EVA and Control of the Investment in Company Assets**   Optimum Electronics is a new public company that operates ten stores in Washington, Oregon, and California selling consumer electronics including stereo equipment and home theater systems. The following financial information is available for 2006 and 2005.

|                                           | 2006         | 2005         |
|-------------------------------------------|--------------|--------------|
| Income from operations                    | $ 6,200,000  | $ 5,800,000  |
| Net income                                | 4,004,000    | 3,737,500    |
| Interest expense                          | 40,000       | 50,000       |
| Total assets                              | 30,000,000   | 27,000,000   |
| Noninterest-bearing current liabilities   | 2,000,000    | 2,000,000    |
| Tax rate                                  | 35%          | 35%          |
| Cost of capital                           | 15%          | 15%          |

### Required

a. Although net income has increased by 7 percent, a shareholder evaluating the company's financial performance asserts that, in spite of the increase, financial performance has deteriorated in 2006. Support this assertion with appropriate calculations of EVA. Note that no adjustments are needed for "accounting distortions."

b. Management asserts that the increased investment in company's assets was clearly warranted since income increased. Briefly evaluate this assertion.

c. Briefly explain why evaluation in terms of EVA will drive managers to focus on carefully evaluating the investment in assets while this will not be the case if managers are evaluated in terms of growth in profit.

**PROBLEM 12-10. Economic Value Added and the Balanced Scorecard**   Mountain Book Company has two divisions—the Brick and Mortar division sells books through more than 100 bookstores throughout the United States; the Internet division was formed 16 months ago and sells books via the Internet. Data for the past year are:

|  | Brick and Mortar Division | Internet Division |
|---|---|---|
| Total assets | $80,000,000 | $6,000,000 |
| Noninterest-bearing current liabilities | 3,000,000 | 1,000,000 |
| Interest expense | 500,000 | 200,000 |
| Net income (loss) | $15,000,000 | (1,000,000) |
| Tax rate | 35% | –0– |
| Cost of capital | 12% | 15% |

### Required

a. Evaluate the two divisions in terms of Economic Value Added (EVA).

b. Explain why it might be better to evaluate the Internet division in terms of a balanced scorecard rather than just using EVA.

c. Consider the customer and internal process dimensions of the Balanced Scorecard. Suggest two measures for each dimension that would be appropriate for the Brick and Mortar division and two measures for each dimension that would be appropriate for the Internet division.

**PROBLEM 12-11. Growth in Profit, Overinvestment, and ROI**   Consider the following data related to the financial performance of Sanders Company.

|  | 2003 | 2004 | 2005 | 2006 |
|---|---|---|---|---|
| (in 000s) |  |  |  |  |
| Net income | $1,000 | $1,150 | $1,360 | $1,630 |
| % change in income | – | 15% | 18% | 20% |
| Total assets | $10,000 | $12,780 | $17,000 | $23,290 |

Between 2003 and 2006, income increased by 63 percent, showing a significant increase in income each year. In light of this performance, the board of directors has awarded large bonuses to senior executives. However, the stock price has fallen from $60 per share in 2003 to $42 per share at the end of 2006.

### Required

a. Calculate ROI for each year. To simplify the calculation, assume that there is no interest expense and there are no noninterest-bearing current liabilities (thus, net income equals NOPAT and total assets are a reasonable measure of investment).

b. Explain why the stock price has dropped and why rewarding managers based on increases in profit can lead to overinvestment.

c. Calculate Economic Value Added (EVA) for 2003–2006 using a cost of capital (required return) of 9.5 percent. Does performance measured in terms of EVA help explain the decline in stock price?

**PROBLEM 12-12. The Balanced Scorecard**  The strategy for success at Vamp Jeans calls for rapid growth, a limited number of units for each design to enhance exclusivity, perfect fit, on-time delivery to commercial customers, retaining employees who contribute to innovation, and control of inventory.

*Required*
Keeping in mind Vamp Jeans' strategy for success, suggest one performance measure for each dimension of a balanced scorecard.

**PROBLEM 12-13. You Get What You Measure and a Balanced Scorecard**  Jarrett Company produces custom molds that are used by producers of molded products (e.g., ski boots and snowboards). Many of its customers use just-in-time (JIT) manufacturing and on-time delivery of the molds is critical because customer production is halted if the molds are not available when needed.

In the past, managers (including Bill Thompson, the vice president of operations) at Jarrett have been rewarded based on financial performance and this has led to actions that are not consistent with maximizing shareholder value. Near the end of each quarter, Thompson evaluates expected profit in relation to the company's profit goal. If expected profit is below the goal, he rushes into production customer orders that have a high profit margin—even if the orders are not due for two or three weeks. Thus, deliveries of high profit margin jobs are often early and deliveries of low profit margin jobs (displaced in Jarrett's production schedule) are often late. And the company has not performed well on a dimension of performance that is critical for long-run success.

*Required*
a. A consultant to Jarrett Company has suggested that the company use a balanced scorecard. Suggest a customer measure and an internal process measure that will help the company track its performance with respect to on-time delivery and other improvements that meet the needs of customers.

b. Suppose that Bill Thompson continues to manage production to meet short-run profit goals. Explain how his actions will be detected by the customer and internal process measures you suggested in Part a.

**PROBLEM 12-14. (Appendix) Transfer Pricing**  The Century Steel Company has a coal mining subsidiary in West Virginia. A substantial amount of the coal produced by the subsidiary is used by Century's steel foundries located in Pennsylvania.

*Required*
a. Recommend and defend a transfer price (market price, variable cost, or full cost plus profit) for the coal shipped by the mining subsidiary to the foundries.

b. Indicate how the price you recommended in Part a compares with the opportunity cost related to using the coal internally.

**PROBLEM 12-15. (Appendix) Decentralization and Transfer Pricing**  The city of Medina Park operates a plumbing and electrical maintenance department, responsible for maintaining all water and electric service functions in buildings owned by the city. The city administration is concerned about the rising costs of the maintenance department, which is currently organized as a cost center.

Marie Esposito, the manager of the maintenance department, says that many of the department's service calls are strictly nuisance calls. She cites examples of numerous calls for defective electrical outlets, which turn out to be unplugged equipment, burned-out lightbulbs (which can easily be changed by the users), and drains clogged by coffee grounds. In Marie's opinion, these nuisance calls would be avoided if the departments using her department's services were "billed." Essentially, Marie suggests that there be a transfer price related to using her department's services and that the price should approximate the cost of these services in the "market" ($35–$50 per hour of service time). This would turn her operation into a profit center and, she believes, her department would operate more efficiently because demand for services would decline and she would need fewer employees.

### Required

Evaluate Marie's proposal. Do you support use of a transfer price for maintenance services? If so, should the price approximate the market price of service or should it be based on cost?

**PROBLEM 12-16. (Appendix) Transfer Pricing** Celtic Woolen Products has two divisions: a Fabric division that manufactures woolen fabrics, and a Clothing division that manufactures woolen dresses, coats, shirts, and accessories. All fabric used by the Clothing division is supplied by the Fabric division, which also supplies fabric to outside companies.

### Required

a. Suggest a transfer price for the fabric assuming that the Fabric division is operating at only 60 percent of capacity due to a surge in popularity of "easy-care" fabrics made of polyester and rayon.

b. Suggest a transfer price for fabric assuming that the Fabric division is operating at capacity due to a revival of consumer interest in natural products and development of lightweight, wrinkle-resistant woolen fabrics.

c. Explain how your choices in Parts a and b are related to the opportunity cost concept.

# CASES

## 12–1 MAYFIELD SOFTWARE, PACKAGED SOFTWARE DIVISION

Packaged Software is a division of Mayfield Software. The division was formed 10 years ago and is focused on games, learning, personal finance, and reference categories ("titles" include *Dogfight*, *Mathmagic*, *Money-Manager*, and *World Today*). It currently has two titles that are in the top 10 in the games and reference categories. A long-run goal of the division is to have the leading title in each product category.

At a recent retreat for senior managers, the president and CFO of Mayfield Software, together with the division's management team, outlined a strategy for success.

### Strategy for Success
1. Concentrate on a relatively small number of "killer" products.

2. Offer low-cost annual updates for selected titles.

3. Set rather than follow trends.

4. Hire and retain the top product developers in each category.

5. Be "best in class" in terms of user satisfaction.

Mayfield Software has begun using a Balanced Scorecard and the chief financial officer, Bob Wilson, has asked Erica Moore, the head of the Packaged Software division, to investigate using a Balanced Scorecard for her division. In Bob's opinion, the scorecard can be used to drive the strategy for success throughout Erica's organization.

Erica, in turn, asked each member of her management team to suggest two measures for each dimension of the Balanced Scorecard. Their suggestions will be summarized and debated at an upcoming meeting.

### Required

Assume that you are a member of Erica's management team. Suggest two measures of performance for each dimension of the Balanced Scorecard (indicated below).

Try to make the measures consistent with the division's strategy for success.

### Balanced Scorecard for the Packaged Software Division

**Financial** Measures to assess financial performance keeping in mind the assessment of Mayfield Software by its shareholders.

**Customer** Measures that track what the division needs to do in terms of customer desires and expectations.

**Internal Business Process** Measures that track what the division needs to do to improve key business processes.

**Learning and Growth** Measures that track the division's ability to innovate.

## 12–2 SUPER CLUB STORES

Super Club Stores operates 253 membership warehouse stores in the United States, Europe, and Asia. The company offers low prices on a limited selection of household and grocery products. In the past year, sales increased by approximately 7.5 percent and net earnings increased by 11 percent. The company opened only two stores in 2005 and 2006 and closed one of its stores due to poor performance.

Thomas Moreland and Benson Hunt are on the board of directors of Super Club and serve on the company's compensation committee. At a recent lunch meeting, they discussed the company's performance (see Table 1 for a balance sheet and an income

**Table 1  Comparative Income Statements and Balance Sheets for 2006 and 2005**

| In Thousands | 2006 | 2005 |
|---|---|---|
| Sales | $17,123,531 | $15,922,891 |
| Merchandise costs | 13,120,054 | 12,175,606 |
| Operating, general and administrative | 3,196,889 | 2,998,366 |
| Rent | 221,057 | 218,857 |
| Depreciation and amortization | 209,614 | 192,722 |
| Interest expense | 65,784 | 58,806 |
| Total | 16,813,398 | 15,644,357 |
| Earnings before taxes based on income | 310,133 | 278,534 |
| Taxes based on income | 108,547 | 97,487 |
| Net Earnings | $ 201,586 | $ 181,047 |
| **Assets** | | |
| Cash and temporary investments | $ 51,510 | $ 57,209 |
| Receivables | 215,414 | 204,062 |
| Inventories | 1,742,854 | 1,403,626 |
| Prepaid and other current assets | 119,431 | 114,049 |
| Total current assets | 2,129,209 | 1,778,946 |
| Land | 181,487 | 134,731 |
| Buildings and equipment (net) | 501,895 | 428,478 |
| | 683,382 | 563,209 |
| Total assets | $ 2,812,591 | $ 2,342,155 |
| **Liabilities** | | |
| Accounts payable | $ 586,248 | $ 524,287 |
| Current portion of long-term debt | 35,730 | 57,233 |
| Accrued income taxes | 89,124 | 69,783 |
| Total current liabilities | 711,102 | 651,303 |
| Long-term debt | 786,570 | 677,842 |
| Total liabilities | 1,497,672 | 1,329,145 |
| **Shareowners' equity** | | |
| Common stock | 771,286 | 670,963 |
| Retained earnings | 543,633 | 342,047 |
| Total shareholder's equity | 1,314,919 | 1,013,010 |
| Total liabilities and shareowners' equity | $ 2,812,591 | $ 2,342,155 |

statement). Both were pleased with the increase in profit, and decided to recommend a contract extension and a substantial six-figure bonus for the company's CEO. They anticipated, however, that the third member of the compensation committee, Sara Nelson, would object to the bonus. Sara believes that accounting profit is a poor measure of *future* firm performance and, in her opinion, the company should be focused on what it is doing today to create *future* value for shareholders. She has also pointed out that, although the company showed quarterly profit increases, its stock price remained flat.

### Required

a. To prepare for an upcoming board meeting, Sara has asked you to evaluate financial performance for *2005 and 2006* taking into account both the level of investment and the cost of capital. Specifically, she would like you to calculate the level of profit (loss) that was earned in excess of the amount required given the investment in the company. Assume that the cost of capital is 12 percent. Is it clear that the company has had superior financial performance?

b. In fiscal 2007, the CEO of Super Club Stores retired. His successor is concerned that warehouse managers do not understand how their actions are linked to the company's strategy and how they can affect future firm value. In his opinion, while monthly earnings are important, managers are focused almost exclusively on how their actions affect these numbers.

Suggest a performance measurement technique that can be used to address the new CEO's concerns.

## 12–3 WinTechMotors

In 2003, five retired software developers opened an auto dealership in Redmond, Washington, which they named WinTechMotors. The company specializes in "high end" sports and luxury autos, and has one of the largest inventories of used Porsches on the West coast (more than 50 Porsches are always in stock). The inventory is listed on the company's Web site (WinTechMotors.Com) and the company has shipped cars to Web-customers as far away as Florida, although most customers are located in Washington, Oregon, and California. In 2005, an industry publication (*Motor Watch*) listed WinTech as the fastest growing luxury auto dealership on the West coast.

Comparative income statements and balance sheets are presented in Table 2. As indicated, the company had sales of $15,600,000 in 2005 (a 28 percent increase over 2004) and net income of $344,240 (a 101 percent increase over 2004). The owners were delighted with the company's financial performance and quite proud that they had developed a successful business. However, at a recent meeting, their company's external accountants introduced them to the concept of EVA and noted that, with an assumed weighted average cost of capital of 16 percent, their EVA had been negative in both years. Accordingly, the owners have contracted with an EVA consultant to help them with financial planning.

### Required

a. Calculate EVA for 2005 and 2004 using a cost of capital of 16 percent. No adjustments for "accounting distortions" are needed. Explain why sales and income have increased substantially in 2005, and yet EVA is negative. What is not captured in income that is captured in EVA?

b. The owners realize they must cut back on inventory to earn a zero or positive EVA in the coming year. To get a handle on this, they would like you to calculate the maximum amount of inventory that could have been on hand at the end of 2005 for the company to achieve a zero level of EVA.

c. Assume the average car has a cost of $40,000. Also assume that sales, expenses, assets (except inventory) and liabilities are roughly the same in 2006 as in 2005. How many cars must be cut from inventory to achieve a zero EVA in 2006?

**Table 2 Comparative Financial Statements**

|  | 2005 | 2004 |
|---|---|---|
| Sales | $15,600,000 | $12,187,500 |
| Less cost of autos sold | 14,040,000 | 10,968,750 |
| Gross margin | 1,560,00 | 1,218,750 |
| Less selling and administrative expense | 965,400 | 895,650 |
| Interest | 65,000 | 60,000 |
| Income before taxes | 529,600 | 263,100 |
| Income taxes | 185,360 | 92,085 |
| Net income | $    344,240 | $    171,015 |
| Increase in sales | 28.00% |  |
| Increase in net income | 101.29% |  |

| Assets | 2005 | 2004 |
|---|---|---|
| Cash and short-term investments | $      55,000 | $      60,000 |
| Receivables | 365,000 | 300,000 |
| Inventory | 6,150,000 | 5,500,000 |
| Current assets | 6,570,000 | 5,860,000 |
| Building and equipment (net) | 895,000 | 900,000 |
| Other assets | 46,000 | 50,000 |
| Total assets | $ 7,511,000 | $ 6,810,000 |

| Liabilities and Owners' Equity | | |
|---|---|---|
| Accounts payable | $    296,760 | $    120,000 |
| Short term debt payable | 85,000 | 70,000 |
| Taxes payable | 110,000 | 35,000 |
| Current liabilities | 491,760 | 225,000 |
| Long term debt payable | 690,000 | 600,000 |
| Total liabilities | 1,181,760 | 825,000 |
| Retained earnings | 829,240 | 485,000 |
| Common stock | 5,500,000 | 5,500,000 |
| Total liabilities and owners' equity | $ 7,511,000 | $ 6,810,000 |

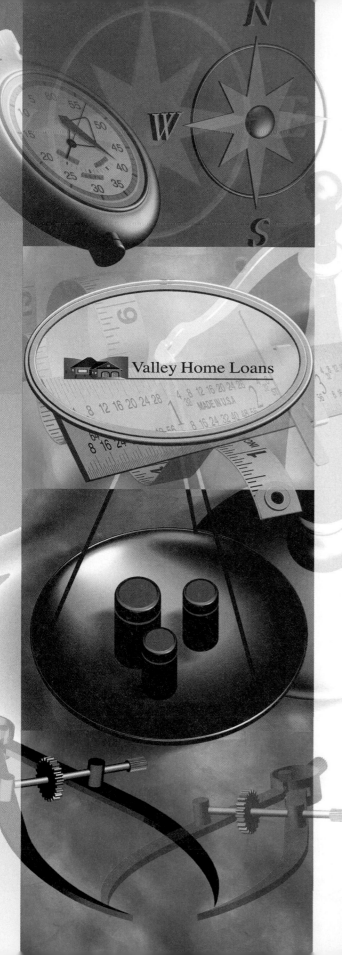

# chapter 13

## LEARNING OBJECTIVES

1. Explain why managers analyze financial statements.

2. Perform horizontal and vertical analysis of the balance sheet and the income statement.

3. Discuss earnings management and the importance of comparing net income to cash flow from operations.

4. Understand how MD&A, credit reports, and news articles can be used to gain insight into a company's current and future financial performance.

5. Calculate and interpret profitability ratios.

6. Calculate and interpret turnover ratios.

7. Calculate and interpret debt-related ratios.

# ANALYZING FINANCIAL STATEMENTS: A MANAGERIAL PERSPECTIVE

**B**ill Reston is the chief operating officer of Valley Home Loans, a residential mortgage lender located in Philadelphia, Pennsylvania. His company has expanded rapidly in the last three years and has just begun offering insurance and investment products as well as financial planning services to consumers. Bill believes that to be successful his company must focus on its core business activities, especially its new product lines. With this in mind, he is considering outsourcing the company's Web site development and hosting to CosmosSolutions, Inc. The jobs to be performed by Cosmos will include development of IT systems and e-business solutions, management of Valley's consumer Web site, and integration with existing systems. Bill knows that the tasks to be performed by Cosmos are "mission critical" in that system failures have tremendous costs to Valley Home Loans. Thus, it is important that Cosmos be a stable company. If Cosmos were to go out of business, and Valley had

## Valley Home Loans

### Building opportunity and security

www.ValleyHomeLoans.com

**Mortgages**
Fixed
Adjustable

**Investments**
IRAs
Stocks and bonds

**Insurance**
Home
Life

**Financial Advice**
Build wealth
Retirement planning

| BUSINESS | NEWS | INVESTOR RELATIONS |

to transition to another Web hosting company, it's likely that the company's Web site would experience technical difficulties that would translate into a loss of business and reduced profitability for Valley.

Bill, or a member of his staff, will conduct an analysis of CosmosSolutions' financial statements to gain assurance that the company is financially viable and likely to continue in existence in the next few years. This chapter discusses ways to analyze financial statements that provide insight into the viability of vendors—the type of insight that Bill

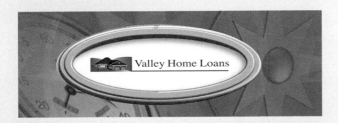
Valley Home Loans

Reston needs before signing an agreement with CosmosSolutions. Financial statements are also analyzed to evaluate and control operations and to assess how one's company appears to investors and creditors. Each of these perspectives is discussed in the chapter.

Explain why managers analyze financial statements.

# WHY MANAGERS ANALYZE FINANCIAL STATEMENTS

Managers analyze financial statements for a variety of reasons including: (1) to control operations; (2) to assess the financial stability of vendors, customers, and other business partners; and (3) to assess how their companies appear to investors and creditors. In this section, we discuss each of these motivations for analyzing financial statements.

## CONTROL OF OPERATIONS

Managers frequently set goals and develop financial plans related to various aspects of their businesses. To gain insight into whether their goals have been achieved or the plans have been successfully implemented, managers analyze financial statements. In part, this is how they control operations. Managers expect that successful implementation of their plan will be reflected in subsequent financial information. If the financial information is inconsistent with successful implementation, managers launch an investigation to determine why this is the case. On the other hand, if the information is consistent with successful implementation, then managers assume that their plan is working and direct their attention to other pressing issues.

For example, consider the case of Redmond Appliances. During 2005, the company had cost of goods sold of $80,000,000 and inventory at the end of 2005 of $20,000,000. Thus, inventory turnover (the ratio of cost of goods sold to ending inventory) was four. Senior management of Redmond Appliances knows that the industry average is closer to six and concludes that the company has too much invested in inventory given its sales levels. In light of this, the company develops plans to better monitor inventory and sales data and gets commitments from suppliers to provide merchandise on a timely basis. This should allow Redmond to reduce the amount of inventory it keeps on hand. Has the plan been successful? At the end of 2006 (or quarterly) the company can monitor inventory turnover. Suppose that during 2006 cost of goods sold was $90,000,000 and that inventory at the end of 2006 is $15,700,000. In this case, inventory turnover is 5.73 ($90,000,000 ÷ $15,700,000), which is much closer to the industry average of 6. Given this result, senior management can reasonably conclude that its plans for controlling the amount invested in inventory are achieving considerable success.

## ASSESSMENT OF VENDORS, CUSTOMERS, AND OTHER BUSINESS PARTNERS

Another important reason for analyzing financial statements is to assess the financial stability of vendors (i.e., suppliers), customers, and other business partners. Increasingly, companies are establishing strong relationships with a relatively small number of vendors who are willing to commit to high-quality levels and short lead times. In part, the short lead times are facilitated by sharing sales and other key data with vendors. Before committing substantial funds to integrate the vendor's information system with the company's system (which facilitates data sharing and reduces lead times), managers want to be confident that the vendor will be stable and continue in existence over the foreseeable future. In short, managers want to avoid developing systems to coordinate with a vendor only to have the vendor go out of business.

Companies analyze the financial statements of customers to assess whether they will be able to pay the amounts they owe on a timely basis. Companies are also concerned about the long-term viability of customers, especially if they need to make substantial investments in equipment to produce goods for them.

Many companies are also developing partnerships with other firms to produce and sell products and services. Obviously, they do not want to enter such a partnership with a firm that is in financial difficulty. How can a manager assess the financial stability of potential vendors, customers, and other business partners? Analysis of financial statements can be very helpful. We will go into more detail in following sections, but for now we'll consider one financial ratio, *times interest earned*, which is the ratio of operating income to interest expense. If this ratio is less than one, it suggests that the company will not be able to make required debt payments, which may lead to bankruptcy. Thus, this ratio and others that we will be discussing should be calculated for companies that are potential vendors, customers, or business partners.

## ASSESSMENT OF APPEARANCE TO INVESTORS AND CREDITORS

Investors and creditors carefully analyze a company's financial statements and managers should anticipate how their financial information will appear to these important stakeholders. If, for example, managers know that the financial statements will show a marked difference between cash flow from operations and net income and that such a difference is likely to cause investor concern, then they can communicate with investors via notes in their financial statements, press releases, or other news articles to explain the difference and, hopefully, alleviate concern. Alternatively, they can avoid transactions leading to such differences. In general, managers should analyze financial statements from the perspective of their investors and creditors so they can anticipate, and fully answer, questions from these stakeholders.

# REVIEW OF THE THREE BASIC FINANCIAL STATEMENTS

There are three basic financial statements: the balance sheet, the income statement, and the statement of cash flows. Most readers of this book have already studied financial accounting and are familiar with these statements. Therefore, we will only briefly review them here and introduce you to the financial statements of Home and Garden Warehouse (HGW) the company we will be analyzing throughout the chapter. HGW is a large home improvement retailer much like Home Depot or Lowe's.

## THE BALANCE SHEET

Think of the balance sheet as a snapshot of a company. At a given *point in time*, it shows a company's assets, its liabilities, and the ownership position of investors. In essence, the balance sheet presents the details of the so-called accounting equation:

$$\text{Assets} = \text{Liabilities} + \text{Shareholders' Equity}$$

This equation recognizes that a company has assets and there are claims on the assets by creditors (measured in terms of the company's liabilities) and company owners (measured in terms of stockholders' equity). The balance sheet for HGW is presented in Illustration 13-1. Note that as of the end of 2005, total assets are $2,084,308 while total liabilities are $602,106 (composed of $347,581 of current liabilities and $254,525 of long-term debt). Total stockholders' equity is $1,482,202. Thus, for HGW, the accounting equation as of December 31, 2005 is:

$$\text{Assets} = \text{Liabilities} + \text{Shareholders' Equity}$$

$$\$2,084,308 = \$602,106 + \$1,482,202$$

**Current and Noncurrent Assets and Liabilities.** The assets and liabilities on the balance sheet are classified into two categories: current and noncurrent. Current assets are those that will be used up or converted into cash within one year, and noncurrent assets are all other assets. Current liabilities are those liabilities that will be satisfied or paid within one year, whereas noncurrent liabilities are all other liabilities.

## THE INCOME STATEMENT

While a balance sheet is like a snapshot at a *point in time*, an income statement (also called a statement of earnings) covers a *period of time* showing how the company generated a profit (or incurred a loss) for the period. The relationships in an income statement are:

$$\text{Sales} - \frac{\text{Cost of}}{\text{Goods Sold}} - \frac{\text{Operating}}{\text{Expenses}} + \frac{\text{Nonoperating}}{\text{Income (Expense)}} - \frac{\text{Income}}{\text{Taxes}} = \text{Net Earnings}$$

In the calculation of net earnings, the distinction between operating expenses and nonoperating items is a bit confusing. Operating expenses relate to activities having to do with production, selling, and administration. Nonoperating items relate to interest expense and investment income and investment losses. The income statement for HGW is presented in Illustration 13-2. For this company the key components of earnings for fiscal 2005 are:

| Sales | − | Cost of Goods Sold | − | Operating Expenses | + | Nonoperating Income (Expense) | − | Income Taxes | = | Net Earnings |
|-------|---|-------|---|-------|---|-------|---|-------|---|-------|
| $2,766,425 | − | $1,942,654 | − | $569,343 | + | ($14,747) | − | 83,888 | = | $155,793 |

## THE STATEMENT OF CASH FLOWS

The statement of cash flows shows how the firm generated and used cash for a *period of time*. Essentially, cash flows are related to three types of activities: operating activities, investing activities, and financing activities.

**Illustration 13-1**
The balance sheet
for HGW

| Home and Garden Warehouse Balance Sheets (In Thousands) | December 31, 2005 | December 31, 2004 | Change | Percent Change* |
|---|---|---|---|---|
| **Assets** | | | | |
| Current assets: | | | | |
| Cash and cash equivalents | $    17,201 | $    16,968 | $      233 | 1.4% |
| Receivables, net | 70,150 | 59,287 | 10,863 | 18.3% |
| Merchandise inventories | 641,280 | 554,389 | 86,891 | 15.7% |
| Other current assets | 15,003 | 14,544 | 459 | 3.2% |
| Total current assets | 743,634 | 645,188 | 98,446 | 15.3% |
| Property and equipment: | | | | |
| Land | 427,230 | 328,048 | 99,182 | 30.2% |
| Buildings, net | 622,867 | 488,234 | 134,633 | 27.6% |
| Furniture, fixtures, and equipment, net | 290,577 | 230,179 | 60,398 | 26.2% |
| Net Property and Equipment | 1,340,674 | 1,046,461 | 294,213 | 28.1% |
| Total assets | $2,084,308 | $1,691,649 | $392,659 | 23.2% |
| **Liabilities and stockholders' equity** | | | | |
| Current liabilities: | | | | |
| Accounts payable | $  244,905 | $  199,420 | $ 45,485 | 22.8% |
| Accrued salaries and related expenses | 62,725 | 54,123 | 8,602 | 15.9% |
| Other accrued expenses | 29,886 | 26,943 | 2,943 | 10.9% |
| Income taxes payable | 6,807 | 6,158 | 649 | 10.5% |
| Current portion of long-term debt | 3,258 | 2,968 | 290 | 9.8% |
| Total current liabilities | 347,581 | 289,612 | 57,969 | 20.0% |
| Long-term debt | 254,525 | 75,628 | 178,897 | 236.5% |
| Total liabilities | 602,106 | 365,240 | 236,866 | 64.9% |
| Stockholders' equity: | | | | |
| Common stock | 440,538 | 440,538 | – | 0.0% |
| Additional paid-in capital | 16,413 | 16,413 | – | 0.0% |
| Retailed earnings | 1,025,251 | 869,458 | 155,793 | 17.9% |
| Total stockholders' equity | 1,482,202 | 1,326,409 | 155,793 | 11.7% |
| Total liabilities and stockholders' equity | $2,084,308 | $1,691,649 | $392,659 | 23.2% |

*Percent change equals change divided by 2004 balance.

**Operating Activities.** Operating activities are core business activities such as buying and selling goods and services. Thus, the cash collected from sales of merchandise is an operating cash inflow and cash paid to purchase merchandise is an operating cash outflow. Cash payments for general and administrative expenses are also operating cash outflows.

**Investing Activities.** Investing activities are activities related to the buying and selling of long-term assets such as property and equipment. They are called investing activities because a company is altering its investment in assets. When a company buys a machine, the cash outflow related to the purchase is classified as a cash outflow under investing activities. And when a company sells land, the related cash inflow is classified under investing activities.

**Illustration 13-2**
The income statement
for HGW

| Home and Garden Warehouse Statements of Earnings (In Thousands) | For the Year Ended December 31, 2005 | For the Year Ended December 31, 2004 | Change | Percent Change* |
|---|---|---|---|---|
| Net sales | $2,766,425 | $1,940,917 | $825,508 | 42.5% |
| Cost of merchandise sold | 1,942,654 | 1,364,662 | 577,992 | 42.4% |
| Gross profit | 823,771 | 576,255 | 247,516 | 43.0% |
| Operating expenses: | | | | |
|   Selling and store operating expenses | 518,742 | 344,360 | 174,382 | 50.6% |
|   General and administrative expenses | 50,601 | 33,886 | 16,715 | 49.3% |
|   Total operating expenses | 569,343 | 378,246 | 191,097 | 50.5% |
| Operating income | 254,428 | 198,009 | 56,419 | 28.5% |
| Interest expense | 14,747 | 3,737 | 11,010 | 294.6% |
| Earnings before income taxes | 239,681 | 194,272 | 45,409 | 23.4% |
| Income taxes | 83,888 | 67,995 | 15,893 | 23.4% |
| Net earnings | $ 155,793 | $ 126,277 | $ 29,516 | 23.4% |

*Percent change equals change divided by 2004 balance.

**Financing Activities.** Financing activities are activities related to acquiring capital, paying off loans to debt holders, and making payments to investors. Thus, the proceeds related to the sale of bonds would be a cash inflow classified under financing activities. Cash payments for dividends would be a cash outflow classified under financing activities.

Illustration 13-3 presents specific examples of activities and how they would be classified with respect to operating, investing, and financing activities in the statement of cash flows.

**Illustration 13-3**
Examples of operating, investing, and financing activities

**Operating Activities**

Cash collected on sale of merchandise
Cash paid to purchase merchandise
Cash paid for general and administrative expenses
Cash paid for income taxes

**Investing Activities**

Cash paid to buy a machine
Cash paid to buy a building
Cash paid to buy a business
Cash received on the sale of a machine no longer in use

**Financing Activities**

Cash received from selling bonds
Cash received from using a line of credit
Cash received from issuing common stock
Cash paid to retire long-term debt
Cash dividends paid

**Illustration 13-4**
The statement of cash flows for HGW

| Home and Garden Warehouse<br>Consolidated Statement of Cash Flows<br>(In Thousands) | For the Year<br>Ended<br>December 31,<br>2005 |
|---|---|
| **Cash provided from operations** | |
| Net earnings | $155,793 |
| Reconciliation of net earnings to cash provided by operations: | |
| Depreciation and amortization | 29,013 |
| Increase in receivables | (10,863) |
| Increase in merchandise inventories | (86,891) |
| Increase in other current assets | (459) |
| Increase in accounts payable | 45,485 |
| Increase in accrued salaries and related expenses | 8,602 |
| Increase in other accrued expenses | 2,943 |
| Increase in income taxes payable | 649 |
| Increase in current portion of long-term debt | 290 |
| Net cash provided by operations | 144,562 |
| **Cash flow from investing activities** | |
| Additions to property and equipment | (323,226) |
| **Cash flow from financing activities** | |
| Issuance of long-term debt | 178,897 |
| Increase in cash and cash equivalents | 233 |
| Cash and cash equivalents at beginning of year | 16,968 |
| Cash and cash equivalents at end of year | $ 17,201 |

The statements of cash flow for HGW for fiscal 2005 is presented in Illustration 13-4.

Perform horizontal and vertical analysis of the balance sheet and the income statement.

# HORIZONTAL AND VERTICAL ANALYSIS

Let's begin our analysis of HGW by performing two types of analyses: horizontal analysis and vertical analysis. **Horizontal analysis** consists of analyzing the dollar value and percentage changes in financial statement amounts across time. **Vertical analysis** (also called common size analysis) consists of analyzing financial statement amounts in comparison to a base amount (total assets when analyzing the balance sheet and net sales when analyzing the income statement). The calculations for either horizontal or vertical analyses are easy to do using a spreadsheet program.

## ANALYSIS OF THE BALANCE SHEET

The results of performing an horizontal analysis of the balance sheet for HGW is presented in Illustration 13-1. What are the major changes in HGW between 2004 and 2005? Somewhat arbitrarily, we'll define a major change to be a change exceeding $10 million (obviously a very large amount, but keep in mind that total assets are over $2 billion). For assets, these changes relate to receivables, merchandise inventory, land, buildings, and furniture and fixtures (all of which have increased). For liabilities and stockholders' equity, major changes relate to accounts payable, long-term debt, and retained earnings.

What can we conclude? It appears that HGW is expanding (hence the increases in land, buildings, and furniture, fixtures, and equipment) and building up receivables and inventories. The expansion is partly funded by increased long-term debt, and partly by internally generated funds (hence the increase in retained earnings).

A vertical analysis of the balance sheets of HGW is presented in Illustration 13-5. Note that the base in this analysis is total assets. The analysis indicates that the primary asset accounts are merchandise inventory, land, and buildings (all greater than 20 percent of total assets). In terms of liabilities and shareholders' equity balances, only common stock and retained earnings exceed 20 percent of total assets (or alternatively 20 percent of liabilities and owners' equity, which

**Illustration 13-5**
Vertical analysis of the balance sheet for HGW

| Home and Garden Warehouse Balance Sheets (In Thousands) | December 31, 2005 | | December 31, 2004 | |
|---|---|---|---|---|
| **Assets** | | | | |
| Current assets: | | | | |
| Cash and cash equivalents | $ 17,201 | 0.8% | $ 16,968 | 1.0% |
| Receivables, net | 70,150 | 3.4% | 59,287 | 3.5% |
| Merchandise inventories | 641,280 | 30.8% | 554,389 | 32.8% |
| Other current assets | 15,003 | 0.7% | 14,544 | 0.9% |
| Total current assets | 743,634 | 35.7% | 645,188 | 38.1% |
| Property and equipment: | | 0.0% | | 0.0% |
| Land | 427,230 | 20.5% | 328,048 | 19.4% |
| Buildings, net | 622,867 | 29.9% | 488,234 | 28.9% |
| Furniture, fixtures, and equipment, net | 290,577 | 13.9% | 230,179 | 13.6% |
| Net Property and Equipment | 1,340,674 | 64.3% | 1,046,461 | 61.9% |
| Total assets | $2,084,308 | 100.0% | 1,691,649 | 100.0% |
| **Liabilities and stockholders' equity** | | | | |
| Current liabilities: | | | | |
| Accounts payable: | $ 244,905 | 11.7% | $ 199,420 | 11.8% |
| Accrued salaries and related expenses | 62,725 | 3.0% | 54,123 | 3.2% |
| Other accrued expenses | 29,886 | 1.4% | 26,943 | 1.6% |
| Income taxes payable | 6,807 | 0.3% | 6,158 | 0.4% |
| Current portion of long-term debt | 3,258 | 0.2% | 2,968 | 0.2% |
| Total current liabilities | 347,581 | 16.7% | 289,612 | 17.1% |
| | | | | 4.5% |
| Long-term debt | 254,525 | 12.2% | 75,628 | 4.5% |
| Total liabilities | 602,106 | 28.9% | 365,240 | 21.6% |
| Stockholders' equity: | | | | |
| Common stock | 440,538 | 21.1% | 440,538 | 26.0% |
| Additional paid-in capital | 16,413 | 0.8% | 16,413 | 1.0% |
| Retained earnings | 1,025,251 | 49.2% | 869,458 | 51.4% |
| Total stockholders' equity | 1,482,202 | 71.1% | 1,326,409 | 78.4% |
| Total liabilities and stockholders' equity | $2,084,308 | 100.0% | $1,691,649 | 100.0% |

equals total assets). Note that except for long-term debt which has increased from 4.5 percent to 12.2 percent of total assets, balances as a percent of total assets are quite consistent between 2004 and 2005.

## ANALYZING THE INCOME STATEMENT

Similar to our analyses related to the balance sheet, let's perform horizontal and vertical analyses of the income statement. The horizontal analysis is presented in Illustration 13-2. The most obvious change between 2004 and fiscal 2005 is the $825,508 increase in net sales. This represents a 42.5 percent increase over fiscal 2004. Cost of merchandise sold increased by $577,992 and this was a 42.4 percent increase. The result of these two changes is an increase in gross profit of 43 percent. Recall from our analysis of the balance sheet that HGW appeared to be expanding operations (e.g., the cost of buildings increased by 28 percent). Thus, it appears that HGW is opening new stores, which, at least in part, accounts for the very substantial increase in sales. It may also be that the economy improved in 2005, which would increase sales of the types of products sold by HGW.

The other major change in 2005 is the $191,097 increase in operating expenses. This increase was 50.5 percent exceeding the percentage increase in sales. Overall, we can see that HGW had a substantial increase in sales that was partially offset by increases in expenses. Net earnings for fiscal 2005 increased by $29,516, a 23.4 percent increase over fiscal 2004.

A vertical (common size) analysis of the income statements is presented in Illustration 13-6. Note that in this analysis, the base is sales (in the analysis of the balance sheet, the base was total assets). As indicated, net income has declined from 6.5 percent of sales to 5.6 percent. What's the culprit for this decline? The most obvious cause of the decline is the relative increase in selling and store operating expenses. This was only 17.7 percent in fiscal 2004 but it increased to 18.8 percent in fiscal 2005. While this may appear to be only a minor increase, remember that these values are percentages of sales and sales are quite large (over $2.7 billion in fiscal 2005).

**Illustration 13-6**
Vertical analysis of the statement of earnings (also called income statement) for HGW

| Home and Garden Warehouse Statements of Earnings (In Thousands) | For the Year Ended December 31, 2005 | | For the Year Ended December 31, 2004 | |
|---|---|---|---|---|
| Net sales | $2,766,425 | 100.0% | $1,940,917 | 100.0% |
| Cost of merchandise sold | 1,942,654 | 70.2% | 1,364,662 | 70.3% |
| Gross profit | 823,771 | 29.8% | 576,255 | 29.7% |
| Operating expenses: | | | | |
| Selling and store operating expenses | 518,742 | 18.8% | 344,360 | 17.7% |
| General and administrative expenses | 50,601 | 1.8% | 33,886 | 1.7% |
| Total operating expenses | 569,343 | 20.6% | 378,246 | 19.5% |
| Operating income | 254,428 | 9.2% | 198,009 | 10.2% |
| Interest expense | 14,747 | 0.5% | 3,737 | 0.2% |
| Earnings before income taxes | 239,681 | 8.7% | 194,272 | 10.0% |
| Income taxes | 83,888 | 3.0% | 67,995 | 3.5% |
| Net earnings | $ 155,793 | 5.6% | $ 126,277 | 6.5% |

Discuss earnings management and the importance of comparing net income to cash flow from operations.

# EARNINGS MANAGEMENT AND THE NEED TO COMPARE EARNINGS AND CASH-FLOW INFORMATION

It is well-known that accounting earnings can be manipulated to make financial performance appear stronger than it actually is, and allegations of financial improprieties have been leveled against such firms as Cendant, Computer Associates, Enron, Kroger, Lucent, Sunbeam, and Waste Management. An analyst with Deutsche Bank in San Francisco, noted: "We are getting so much of this accounting irregularities stuff. As an analyst, it spooks you because you don't know how much of this is really going on behind the scenes."[1] Why do some managers manipulate earnings? As you well know, "you get what you measure," and managers are often evaluated and rewarded based on the level of firm earnings. Thus, for example, if earnings are below the level specified for achieving a bonus, managers have strong incentives to manipulate earnings upwards. Another reason to manage earnings upwards might be to inflate stock prices so managers can profit from exercising their stock options.

A "red flag" suggesting that accounting irregularities may be a problem is a substantial difference between reported net income and operating cash flows. Why is this comparison informative? Suppose a firm records fictitious sales. Income will increase, but operating cash flows will not be affected (since companies don't collect cash from fictitious sales!) and, thus, there will be a difference between income and operating cash flows. Likewise, if a company understates expenses (which increases income) but still makes payments related to the actual expenses, there also will be a difference between income and operating cash flows. In the case of HGW, net earnings for fiscal 2005 was $155,793 (see Illustration 13-2) while net cash provided by operations was only $144,562 (see Illustration 13-3). The more than $10 million difference (recall values are in thousands) does indeed suggest that earnings may have been managed upward at HGW. This, of course, is not definitive proof that earnings have been manipulated, but, as already stated, it's a "red flag" sending the signal—beware!

Understand how MD&A, credit reports, and news articles can be used to gain insight into a company's current and future financial performance.

# OTHER SOURCES OF INFORMATION ON FINANCIAL PERFORMANCE

In addition to analyzing the basic financial statements, there are a number of other information sources that can be used to gain insight into a company's current and future financial performance. Here we will discuss three such sources: management discussion and analysis; credit reports; and news articles.

## MANAGEMENT DISCUSSION AND ANALYSIS

The annual report of public companies contains a section called **Management Discussion and Analysis** (abbreviated as MD&A). In this section, management provides stockholders and other financial statement users with explanations for

---

[1]"Kroger Restates Profits, Cites Accounting Issues," *Los Angeles Times*, Tuesday, March 6, 2001, Business, p. 1.

**Fiscal Year ended December 31, 2005 compared to December 31, 2004**    Net sales for fiscal 2005 increased 42.5% to $2.8 billion from $1.9 billion in fiscal 2004. This increase is attributable to, among other things, full year sales from the 35 new stores opened during fiscal 2004, and 15 new store openings in 2005 as well as an eight percent comparable store-for-store sales increase.

Gross profit as a percent of sales was 29.8 percent for fiscal 2005 compared to 29.7 percent for fiscal 2004. The increase was primarily attributable to a lower cost of merchandise resulting from product line reviews and benefits from our global sourcing programs.

financial results that are not obvious from simply reading the basic financial statements. Illustration 13-7 provides an excerpt from the MD&A of HGW in the annual report for fiscal 2005. Note that the information is consistent with our brief analysis of the financial statements that indicated that HGW is engaged in substantial expansion.

## CREDIT REPORTS

A number of firms (e.g., Dun & Bradstreet) sell credit reports that provide information on a company's credit history. A picture of the Web page of Dun & Bradstreet's small-business solutions service, which offers credit ratings, is provided in Illustration 13-8. The ratings help managers evaluate the likelihood that a company they do business with will pay its bills on time.

## NEWS ARTICLES

News articles are another very valuable source of information with financial implications. For example, a recent article indicated that William Nelson, chief operating officer of HGW resigned. Such a departure could be a signal of serious internal problems. However, the article also noted that HGW is deep in talent related to merchandising and the company's stock price actually increased the day of the announcement. This suggests that the stock market did not view the departure as a major negative event.

Nexis-Lexis is a company that, for a fee, provides access to articles from major newspapers, magazines, and news wire services. A free service, and one that is targeted at financial performance, is provided by Yahoo! Finance (http://finance.yahoo.com/). On this Web site, you can search for news articles for publicly traded companies by inserting their stock ticker symbol.

# RATIO ANALYSIS

To control operations, to assess the stability of vendors, customers, and other business partners, and to assess how their companies appear to investors and creditors, managers frequently perform financial analyses using various ratios. We will examine a number of ratios in common use, and group them into three categories: those dealing with the profitability of a company; those dealing with asset turnover; and those dealing with a company's debt-paying ability.

## PROFITABILITY RATIOS

Calculate and interpret profitability ratios.

Let's begin by examining the profitability ratios presented in Illustration 13-9 using the data for HGW (see Illustrations 13-1 and 13-2). The first ratio we will examine is earnings per share (EPS) calculated as net income less preferred dividends divided by the number of shares of common stock that are outstanding. For fiscal 2005, HGW had net earnings of $155,793 thousand and it had 465,000 thousand shares of common stock outstanding at the end of 2005. Thus, its earnings per share is $0.335.

The second profitability ratio is the price–earnings ratio calculated as the market price per share divided by earnings per share. For HGW, the market price per share at the end of 2005 was $5.02 and thus its price–earnings ratio is 14.99. This ratio has increased slightly from the prior year. While a variety of factors affect the price–earnings ratio, including interest rates and other factors that relate to general economic conditions, a major factor is investors' expectations of future profitability.

The gross margin percentage is simply the gross margin divided by net sales, which provides a rough estimate of the incremental profit generated by each dollar of sales. This ratio (0.298) has stayed relatively constant between fiscal 2004 and fiscal 2005.

Return on total assets is equal to net income (adjusted for interest expense net of taxes) divided by total assets. The adjustment for interest is made so that the assessment of profitability is independent of how the firm is financed. (Debt financing reduces income (due to interest expense) but equity financing does not reduce reported income.) The tax rate is determined by dividing income taxes ($83,888 thousand in fiscal 2005) by earnings before income taxes ($239,681 thousand in fiscal 2005) yielding a tax rate of 35 percent. Return on total assets

**Illustration 13-9**
Profitability ratios for HGW

| | |
|---|---|
| **Earnings per share** = | (Net income − Preferred dividends) ÷ Number of common shares outstanding |
| 2005 | ($155,793 − 0) ÷ 465,000 = **$0.335** |
| 2004 | ($126,277 − 0) ÷ 465,000 = **$0.272** |
| **Price–earnings ratio** = | Market price per share ÷ Earnings per share |
| 2005 | $5.02 ÷ $0.335 = **$14.99** |
| 2004 | $4.05 ÷ $0.272 = **$14.89** |
| **Gross margin percentage** = | Gross margin ÷ Net sales |
| 2005 | $823,771 ÷ $2,766,425 = **0.298** |
| 2004 | $576,255 ÷ $1,940,917 = **0.297** |
| **Return on total assets** = | [Net income + (Interest expense × (1 − Tax rate))] ÷ Total assets |
| 2005 | [$155,793 + ($14,747 (1 − 0.35))] ÷ $2,084,308 = **0.079** |
| 2004 | [$126,277 + ($3,737 (1 − 0.35))] ÷ $1,691,649 = **0.076** |
| **Return on common stockholders' equity** = | (Net income − Preferred dividends) ÷ Common stockholders' equity |
| 2005 | ($155,793 − 0) ÷ $1,482,202 = **0.105** |
| 2004 | ($126,277 − 0) ÷ $1,326,409 = **0.095** |

was 0.079 in fiscal 2005 and 0.076 in fiscal 2004. This indicates only a slight increase in profitability.

The final profitability ratio that we will examine is return on common stockholders' equity, which is equal to net income less preferred dividends divided by common stockholders' equity. Consistent with the increase in the return on total assets, the return on common stockholders' equity has increased from 0.095 in fiscal 2004 to 0.105 in fiscal 2005.

**Financial Leverage.** Note that the return on common equity is higher than the return on assets (0.105 versus 0.079 for fiscal 2005). This indicates that the company is making good use of **financial leverage**, which relates to the use of debt financing to acquire assets. Whenever the cost of debt is less than the return that the company can earn on its assets, financing with debt will increase the percentage return to shareholders.

**Summary of the Profitability Ratios.** Let's summarize what we've learned from the profitability ratios. It appears that the profitability of HGW has increased but not dramatically. Earnings per share is up and so is the price–earnings ratio. The gross margin percentage, return on total assets and return on stockholders' equity are also up, but only slightly.

LEARNING OBJECTIVE 6

Calculate and interpret turnover ratios.

# TURNOVER RATIOS

Turnover ratios reveal the efficiency with which a company uses its assets. The turnover ratios we will use in examining HGW are presented in Illustration 13-10. The first turnover ratio that we will discuss is asset turnover defined as net sales

**Illustration 13-10**
Turnover ratios for HGW

| | |
|---|---|
| **Asset turnover** = | Net sales ÷ Total assets |
| 2005 | $2,766,425 ÷ $2,084,308 = **1.327** |
| 2004 | $1,940,917 ÷ $1,691,649 = **1.147** |
| **Accounts receivable turnover** = | Net credit sales ÷ Accounts receivable |
| 2005 | $2,766,425 ÷ $70,150 = **39.436** |
| 2004 | $1,940,917 ÷ $59,287 = **32.738** |
| **Days' sales in receivables** = | 365 ÷ Accounts receivable turnover |
| 2005 | 365 ÷ 39.436 = **9.256** |
| 2004 | 365 ÷ 32.738 = **11.149** |
| **Inventory turnover** = | Cost of goods sold ÷ Inventory |
| 2005 | $1,942,654 ÷ $641,280 = **3.029** |
| 2004 | $1,364,662 ÷ $554,389 = **2.462** |
| **Days' sales in inventory** = | 365 ÷ Inventory turnover |
| 2005 | 365 ÷ 3.029 = **120.502** |
| 2004 | 365 ÷ 2.462 = **148.253** |

divided by total assets.[2] Note that this ratio has increased from 1.147 to 1.327 suggesting an improvement in the efficient use of assets. Now let's take a look at two particular assets: accounts receivable and inventory.

The accounts receivable turnover ratio is defined as net credit sales divided by accounts receivable. Generally, financial statements do not indicate the breakdown of credit and cash sales so most analysts assume that all sales are credit sales. This assumption would not be reasonable for HGW since, for this company, cash sales predominate. Recall from Illustration 13-1 that receivables are relatively unimportant for HGW since they make up only 3.5 percent of total assets. Thus, the fact that we cannot obtain credit sales information that facilitates calculation of the accounts receivable turnover ratio is not unduly troubling.

Whereas the assumption that total sales is roughly equivalent to credit sales is inappropriate for HGW, let's make it simply to illustrate the calculation of the accounts receivable turnover ratio. Making the assumption, we can see that the turnover in receivables has increased from 32.738 in fiscal 2004 to 39.436 in fiscal 2005. Additional insight into receivables can be achieved by converting the accounts receivable turnover ratio into a measure of how many days' sales are in receivables. This is done by dividing the turnover ratio into 365 days. As indicated in Illustration 13-10, the days' sales in receivables was 11.149 days for fiscal 2004 and 9.256 days for fiscal 2005. These values are quite low and reflect the fact that most sales are actually cash sales. For a company that had credit sales with payment due in 30 days, we would expect to see values in the 30–50 day range.

---

[2]Using ending total assets in the denominator of this ratio is consistent with the approach used in a number of finance textbooks (e.g., Robert Higgins, *Analysis for Financial Management*, Irwin, McGraw-Hill, 2001). However, it is also common to calculate the ratio using the average of beginning and ending total assets in the denominator. Similarly, some books using ending inventory in the inventory turnover ratio and ending accounts receivable in the accounts receivable turnover ratio, while others use average values in the denominator. There are pros and cons to both approaches. Most importantly, however, you should use the same approach in each year when comparing performance from one year to another.

## Any Questions?

**Q** After we calculate a ratio, how do we know if it's too high or too low? Is this one of those "it's more art than science" things?

**A** In short, yes! No ratio has an unequivocally "correct" value. Consider the inventory turnover ratio. We can, for example, compare a company's inventory turnover ratio to those of its major competitors. But the average value of the ratio for competitors isn't necessarily the optimal value for a particular company. What if a company's ratio is lower than the industry average? That could mean that the company has excess inventory, or it could mean that the company has a great selection of items that is leading to high sales. Or, suppose a company's inventory turnover ratio is higher than the average ratio value of competitors. This could mean that the company is doing a great job of controlling inventory or it could mean that there's a problem and the company is frequently missing sales because inventory is backordered.

It's best to think of ratios as clues to a company's financial condition. You need to organize the clues and compare them to other pieces of information (such as credit reports, news articles, knowledge of economic conditions, etc.). With some experience, you'll find that the clues are providing you with important insights and helping you solve the "mystery" of a company's financial condition.

A measure of the efficient use of inventory is provided by the inventory turnover ratio defined as cost of goods sold divided by inventory. This ratio increased from 2.462 to 3.029. We can also convert this ratio into a days' sales in inventory measure by dividing 365 days by the inventory turnover ratio. This reveals that HGW has 120.502 days of sales in inventory for fiscal 2005 compared to 148.253 days for fiscal 2004. While there has been some improvement in days' sales in inventory, the number of days is quite high given the nature of HGW's business. In comparison, the number of days' sales in inventory for Home Depot is less than 70 days.

**Summary of Turnover Ratios.** From the turnover ratios, we can see that HGW appears to have been more efficient in its use of assets in fiscal 2005 compared to fiscal 2004. Asset turnover has increased, which is due in part to an increase in the turnover of inventory. Given the high-dollar value of inventory, it is appropriate to note especially that while days' sales in inventory has improved, it is quite high in comparison to the ratio of HGW's major competitors.

LEARNING OBJECTIVE 7

Calculate and interpret debt-related ratios.

## DEBT-RELATED RATIOS

The last set of ratios we will examine relate to the amount of debt a company has and its ability to repay its obligations. The debt-related ratios we will use to examine HGW are presented in Illustration 13-11.

The current ratio is computed as current assets divided by current liabilities, and it provides an indication of a company's ability to meet its short-term obligations. For HGW, the current ratio declined slightly from 2.228 to 2.139. However, given that the ratio is substantially greater than one, it appears that there is little doubt that HGW will be able to pay its current liabilities.

A more stringent test of short-term debt paying ability is provided by the acid-test ratio (also known as the quick ratio). This ratio compares cash, marketable

**Illustration 13-11**
Debt-related ratios
for HGW

| | |
|---|---|
| **Current ratio** = | Current assets ÷ Current liabilities |
| 2005 | $743,634 ÷ $347,581 = **2.139** |
| 2004 | $645,188 ÷ $289,612 − **2.228** |
| **Acid-test (Quick ratio)** = | [(Cash + Marketable securities) + Short-term receivables] ÷ Current liabilities |
| 2005 | ($17,201 + $70,150) ÷ $347,581 = **0.251** |
| 2004 | ($16,698 + $59,287) ÷ $289,612 = **0.262** |
| **Debt-to-equity ratio** = | Total liabilities ÷ Stockholders' equity |
| 2005 | $602,106 ÷ $1,482,202 = **0.406** |
| 2004 | $365,240 ÷ $1,326,409 = **0.275** |
| **Times interest earned** = | Operating income ÷ Interest expense |
| 2005 | $254,428 ÷ $14,747 = **17.253** |
| 2004 | $198,009 ÷ 3,737 = **52.986** |

securities, and short-term receivables to current liabilities. Note that the numerator of this ratio only includes a company's most liquid assets. For HGW, this ratio also decreased slightly from 0.263 to 0.251. For many companies, an acid-test ratio less than one is troubling, and this is the case for HGW. Recall that the company is not able to quickly convert its inventory into sales and then to cash to satisfy current liabilities—it has 120.502 days' sales in inventory implying that the company requires about four months to convert its inventory into sales which in turn generate cash which can be used to satisfy current liabilities.

The debt-to-equity ratio is calculated as the ratio of total liabilities to stockholders' equity, and it provides an assessment of a company's debt position. The higher the ratio, the more debt the company has and the more risky the company becomes because it must continue to make principal and interest payments on its debt even if sales decline. Further, potential creditors hesitate to grant additional financing to a company with a high debt-to-equity ratio since repayment is at least somewhat doubtful. For HGW, the ratio increased from 0.275 to 0.406 consistent with the increase in debt that we noted in the horizontal analysis of HGW's balance sheet.

In conjunction with the debt-to-equity ratio, it is useful to examine the ratio referred to as "times interest earned." This ratio is computed as operating income divided by interest expense. For HGW, the ratio is quite high, 17.253, although it has decreased from 52.986. Since the level of operating income is so high compared to the amount of interest expense, it seems highly likely that the company will be able to make its debt payments in spite of the fact that debt financing has increased.

**Summary of Debt-Related Ratios.** From the debt-related ratios, we can see that HGW has current assets in excess of current liabilities, indicating that the company should be able to cover its short-term obligations. And, while debt financing has increased, the company has operating income many times higher than the amount of interest it must pay on its debt. Thus, it appears that the company will be quite able to satisfy its long-term obligations as well as its short-term obligations. A concern, however, relates to the acid-test ratio, which is only 0.251. This is particularly troubling given our earlier finding that the company has 120.502 days' sales in inventory.

# A MANAGERIAL PERSPECTIVE ON THE ANALYSIS OF HGW'S FINANCIAL STATEMENTS

At the start of the chapter, we noted that managers analyze financial statements for three reasons: (1) to control operations; (2) to assess the stability of vendors, customers, and other business partners; and (3) to assess how their companies appear to investors and creditors. Now let's see how these objectives would be addressed in terms of the analyses we've performed for HGW.

## CONTROL OF OPERATIONS

Suppose that at the start of fiscal 2005, HGW decided to press for discounts from suppliers and to work to reduce selling and store operating expenses. Has the company been successful in achieving these goals? Our analysis suggests that its plans have not been effective. The gross margin percentage has remained at approximately 0.30, which implies that cost of merchandise sold is approximately the same percent of sales in fiscal 2005 as in fiscal 2004. Further, selling and store operating expenses have actually increased as a percentage of sales. Thus, financial analysis would suggest that the management of HGW should reexamine its plans and their implementation.

## STABILITY OF VENDORS, CUSTOMERS, AND OTHER BUSINESS PARTNERS

Suppose a company was considering a strategic partnership with HGW. For example, John Deere might be interested in developing a line of power mowers, edgers, and blowers that would be marketed exclusively at HGW with special pricing. In this arrangement, Deere might consider linking its information system to the information systems at the more than 200 HGW locations so it could track sales and efficiently schedule its production.

Should Deere be concerned about the financial stability of HGW? Our analysis suggested that HGW needs to do a better job controlling its inventory levels. However, the financial viability of HGW is not in question since the company is still reasonably profitable and in no danger of failing to meet its financial obligations. Thus, Deere should not be concerned that an alliance with HGW will be jeopardized by financial problems.

**Returning to the Situation Facing Valley Home Loan.** Note that in the opening vignette to the chapter, Bill Reston, chief operating officer of Valley Home Loans, was concerned about outsourcing IT services to CosmosSolutions, Inc. What type of analysis should Bill perform before entering an agreement with this company? All of the techniques we've discussed would be useful, including a horizontal and vertical analysis of the company's balance sheets and income statements, and an analysis of profitability, turnover, and debt related ratios. Valley should also obtain a credit report on Cosmos and consider a search of news articles to obtain additional information to help decide if Cosmos is a desirable business partner.

## APPEARANCE TO INVESTORS AND CREDITORS

Suppose you were the CEO at HGW, and you were going to meet with shareholders and financial analysts. Given the analyses we've performed, what questions would you anticipate? Quite possibly, questions would focus on the day's sales in

### Comparative Ratio Data

In this chapter, we've gained insight into HGW by comparing its ratios in fiscal 2005 to its ratios in fiscal 2004. It's also useful to compare a company's ratios to those of its primary competitor or to industry averages. Here's how to find competitors (the process may seem involved, but it will take less than five minutes!).

1. Go to Yahoo! Finance ⟨http://finance.yahoo.com/⟩
2. Insert the ticker symbol of the company you are analyzing.
3. Under **More Info**, click <u>Profile</u>.
4. Under **Market Guide**, click <u>Highlights</u>
5. Under **Analysis**, click <u>Comparisons</u>

This will lead you to a list of competitors sorted by market value

Once you have determined the competitor of interest, go to that company's Web site to obtain its annual report, or go to the SEC (Securities and Exchange Commission) Web site where you can download the company's form 10K (the annual filing with the SEC that contains the company's financial statements and a great deal of additional information that would be useful in analysis. The SEC Web site (known as EDGAR) is found at ⟨http://www.sec.gov/cgi-bin/srch-edgar⟩.

Industry ratios can be found in the *Annual Statement Studies* published by RMA (The Risk Management Association, formerly known as Robert Morris Associates). This publication is available in many libraries or by subscribing on-line.

inventory, which is more than 120 days. By performing financial analysis, the CEO can anticipate questions from investors and be prepared with solid answers. The same point would hold in regard to a meeting with creditors.

## SUMMARY OF ANALYSES

Let's briefly summarize the types of analyses we've performed in this chapter. We began by performing horizontal and vertical analyses of the balance sheets and income statements. We also performed ratio analysis. The ratios we examined were grouped into three categories: profitability ratios (which provide insight into the overall profitability of a company), turnover ratios (which provide insight into the efficient use of assets), and debt-related ratios (which provide insight into a company's ability to satisfy its short-term and long-term obligations). The specific formulas for the ratios we've covered are summarized in Illustration 13-12.

When conducting financial analysis, it is important to get "beyond the numbers." As we discussed, it is often useful to read the MD&A section of the annual report to learn management's explanation for financial results. Also, news articles and credit reports can provide insight into a firm's current and future performance.

**Illustration 13-12**
Summary of ratio formulas

| PROFITABILITY RATIOS | |
| --- | --- |
| Earnings per share | (Net income − Preferred dividends) ÷ Number of common shares outstanding |
| Price–earnings ratio | Market price per share ÷ Earnings per share |
| Gross margin percentage | Gross margin ÷ Net sales |
| Return on total assets | [Net income + (Interest expense × (1 − Tax rate))] ÷ Total assets |
| Return on common stockholders' equity | (Net income − Preferred dividends) ÷ Common stockholders' equity |
| **TURNOVER RATIOS** | |
| Asset turnover | Net sales ÷ Total assets |
| Accounts receivable turnover | Net credit sales ÷ Accounts receivable |
| Days' sales in receivables | 365 ÷ Accounts receivable turnover |
| Inventory turnover | Cost of goods sold ÷ Inventory |
| Days' sales in inventory | 365 ÷ Inventory turnover |
| **DEBT RELATED RATIOS** | |
| Current ratio | Current assets ÷ Current liabilities |
| Acid test (Quick ratio) | [(Cash + Marketable securities) + Short-term receivables] ÷ Current liabilities |
| Debt-to-equity ratio | Total liabilities ÷ Stockholders' equity |
| Times interest earned | Operating income ÷ Interest expense |

# MAKING BUSINESS DECISIONS

Many companies are trying to drive down the costs of their supply chain by integrating their information system with the information systems of their major suppliers who are referred to as "strategic partners." Critical to the success of such efforts is the choice of strategic partners. Financial analysis can help ensure that a company will not partner with a firm that isn't profitable and may go out of business in the near future. Systems integration is very costly and not appropriate if a partner's ability to continue doing business is doubtful.

## KNOWLEDGE AND SKILLS (K/S) CHECKLIST

*Knowledge and skills are needed to make good business decisions. Check off the knowledge and skills you've acquired from reading this chapter.*

☐ K/S 1. You have an expanded business vocabulary (see key terms).

☐ K/S 2. You can explain why managers analyze financial statements.

☐ K/S 3. You can perform horizontal and vertical analyses of income statements and balance sheets.

☐ K/S 4. You know why the difference between operating income and cash flow from operations may be informative about earnings management.

☐ K/S 5. You can calculate and interpret profitability ratios.

☐ K/S 6. You can calculate and interpret turnover ratios.

☐ K/S 7. You can calculate and interpret debt-related ratios.

# SUMMARY OF LEARNING OBJECTIVES

**1** *Explain why managers analyze financial statements.* Managers analyze financial statements for three reasons: (1) to control operations; (2) to assess the stability of vendors, customers, and other business partners; and (3) to assess how their companies appear to investors and creditors.

**2** *Perform horizontal and vertical analyses of balance sheets and income statements.* Horizontal analysis involves comparing the dollar value of balances and percentage changes between years; vertical analysis involves comparing individual balances to total assets (when analyzing balance sheet accounts) or sales (when analyzing income statement balances).

**3** *Discuss earnings management and the importance of comparing net income to cash flow from operations.* In analyzing financial information, it is important to recognize that earnings can be managed in an effort to make a company appear more profitable. Thus, it is useful to compare net income to cash flow from operations since cash flow is more difficult to manage. Income much higher than cash flow suggests (but, certainly, does not definitively indicate) that the earnings information is not reliable.

**4** *Understand how MD&A, credit reports, and news articles can be used to gain insight into a*

company's current and future financial performance. In addition to the insights from analyzing the basic financial statements, useful information can be obtained from the section of the annual report titled management discussion and analysis (MD&A), from credit reports, and from news articles. A good source of news articles is the Web site Yahoo! Finance.

**5** *Calculate and interpret profitability ratios.* The profitability ratios are earnings per share, the price–earnings ratio, the gross margin percentage, return on total assets, and return on common stockholders' equity. These ratios can be used to assess the overall profitability of a firm.

**6** *Calculate and interpret turnover ratios.* The turnover ratios are asset turnover, accounts receivable turnover (and the related ratio, days' sales in receivables), and inventory turnover (and the related ratio, days' sales in inventory). These ratios can be used to assess whether a company uses its assets to generate sales in an efficient manner.

**7** *Calculate and interpret debt-related ratios.* The debt-related ratios are the current ratio, the acid-test ratio (also known as the quick ratio), the debt-to-equity ratio, and times interest earned. These ratios can be used to assess a company's ability to meet its obligations to short-term and long-term creditors.

# REVIEW PROBLEM

Blast Tennis Rackets has asked Norton Industries to produce its new line of carbon fiber rackets. The initial order is for 20,000 rackets at $75 each (a $1,500,000 order). Blast will make a $200,000 deposit and the remaining $1,300,000 will be paid within 90 days of shipment.

This is an especially large order for Norton and the company wants to make sure that Blast will be able to pay its bill when it comes due. To gain confidence, Norton will analyze Blast's financial statements.

| **Blast Tennis Rackets** **Balance Sheets** **(In Thousands)** | **December 31, 2005** | **December 31, 2004** |
|---|---|---|
| **Assets** | | |
| Current assets: | | |
| Cash and cash equivalents | $ 302 | $ 405 |
| Accounts receivable | 2,433 | 2,658 |
| Inventory | 16,104 | 15,685 |
| Prepaid expenses | 42 | 23 |
| Total current assets | 18,881 | 18,771 |
| Plant and equipment, net | 1,302 | 1,256 |
| Total assets | $20,183 | $20,027 |

| | December 31, 2005 | December 31, 2004 |
|---|---|---|
| **Liabilities and stockholders' equity** | | |
| Current liabilities: | | |
| Accounts payable | $ 2,808 | $ 2,738 |
| Bank loan payable | 5,987 | 6,259 |
| Other accrued payables | 881 | 760 |
| Total current liabilities | 9,676 | 9,757 |
| Long-term debt | 1,585 | 1,677 |
| Total liabilities | 11,261 | 11,434 |
| Stockholders' equity: | | |
| Common stock | 3,500 | 3,500 |
| Retained earnings | 5,422 | 5,093 |
| Total stockholders' equity | 8,922 | 8,593 |
| **Total liabilities and stockholders' equity** | $20,183 | $20,027 |

| **Blast Tennis Rackets** **Consolidated Statement of Earnings** **(In Thousands)** | **Year Ended December 31, 2005** | **Year Ended December 31, 2004** |
|---|---|---|
| Net sales | $19,288 | $25,057 |
| Cost of goods sold | 12,151 | 15,034 |
| Gross margin | 7,137 | 10,023 |
| Operating expenses: | | |
| Selling expenses | 3,086 | 3,007 |
| General and administrative expenses | 2,377 | 2,255 |
| Total operating expenses | 5,463 | 5,262 |
| Operating income | 1,674 | 4,761 |
| Interest expense | 1,168 | 1,254 |
| Income before taxes | 506 | 3,507 |
| Income taxes | 177 | 1,227 |
| Net income | $    329 | $ 2,280 |

**Required**

a. Calculate the following ratios for Blast for 2005 and 2004: Return on total assets, inventory turnover, days' sales in inventory, current ratio, acid-test (quick ratio), the debt-to-equity ratio, and times interest earned.

b. Based on your analysis in Part a, do you recommend that Norton take on the order for Blast?

**Answer**

a.

**Return on total assets** = [Net income + (Interest expense × (1 − Tax rate))] ÷ Total assets

| 2005 | [$329 + ($1,168 × (1 − .35)] ÷ $20,183 = **0.054** |
|---|---|
| 2004 | [$2,280 + ($1,254 × (1 − .35)] ÷ $20,027 = **0.155** |

**Inventory turnover** = Cost of goods sold ÷ Inventory

| 2005 | $12,151 ÷ $16,104 = **0.755** |
|---|---|
| 2004 | $15,034 ÷ $15,685 = **0.958** |

**Day's sales in inventory** = 365 ÷ Inventory turnover

| 2005 | 365 ÷ 0.755 = **483.443** |
|---|---|
| 2004 | 365 ÷ 0.958 = **381.002** |

**Current ratio =**    Current assets ÷ Current liabilities

2005                   $18,881 ÷ $9,676 = **1.951**
2004                   $18,771 ÷ $9,757 = **1.924**

**Acid-test (Quick ratio)  =**    [(Cash + Marketable securities) + Short-term
                        receivables] ÷ Current liabilities

2005                   ($302 + $2,433) ÷ $9,676 = **0.282**
2004                   ($405 + $2,658) ÷ $9,757 = **0.314**

**Debt-to-equity ratio =**    Total liabilities ÷ Stockholders' equity

2005                   $11,261 ÷ $8,922 = **1.262**
2004                   $11,434 ÷ $8,593 = **1.331**

**Times interest earned =**    Operating income ÷ Interest expense

2005                   $1,674 ÷ $1,168 = **1.433**
2004                   $4,761 ÷ $1,254 = **3.797**

b. Norton should be very cautious about entering into a large transaction with Blast Tennis Rackets. Blast's profitability is down substantially, as indicated by the decline in return on assets. Most importantly, the company is holding 483 days of inventory—more than the amount needed for an entire year. This suggests that the inventory may be more obsolete and the cost on the balance sheet may be higher than the market value of the inventory. Also, note that the acid-test ratio (which excludes inventory) is only 0.28 suggesting that if the inventory cannot be sold, the company will have a great deal of difficulty satisfying its current liabilities. In addition, times interest earned has declined indicating that the company may have difficulty meeting required interest payments in the future.

In light of this information, Norton should not enter into the transaction unless Blast is able to pay for all or most of the order in advance of production.

# KEY TERMS

Financial leverage (475)          Management Discussion and          Vertical analysis (469)
Horizontal analysis (469)             Analysis (MD&A) (472)

# SELF ASSESSMENT    *(Answers Below)*

**1.** Why do managers analyze financial statements?

a. To evaluate and control operations
b. To evaluate vendors and customers.
c. To anticipate questions from shareholders and creditors.
d. All of the above.

**2.** Horizontal analysis analyzes:

a. Comparable companies.
b. Changes in expenses as a percent of sales.
c. Changes in expenses as a percent of total assets.
d. Changes in balances from one year to another.

**3.** Net income substantially higher than cash flow from operations may indicate:

a. Exceptional profitability.
b. Manipulation of income.
c. Exceptional control of expenses.
d. That a company has a lot of depreciation expense.

**4.** In connection with a company's annual report, MD&A stands for:

a. Management discussion and analysis.
b. More depreciation and amortization.
c. Monthly depreciation and amortization.
d. Monthly discounts and advertising.

**5.** The fact that the *return on common stockholders' equity* is higher than the *return on total assets* suggests that a company:

    a. Has made good use of financial leverage.
    b. Has funded asset acquisition primarily with debt.
    c. Has excessive debt financing.
    d. Has good control of operations.

**6.** A primary difference between the current ratio and the acid-test (quick) ratio is:

    a. The current ratio takes into account depreciation expense.
    b. The acid-test ratio is computed using monthly data.
    c. The acid-test ratio excludes inventory from the numerator.
    d. All of the above.

**7.** Day's sales in inventory is equal to:

    a. 365 ÷ inventory turnover.
    b. Sales ÷ inventory turnover.
    c. 365 × inventory ÷ sales.
    d. 365 × sales ÷ inventory.

**8.** The ratio *times interest earned* can be used to evaluate:

    a. The amount of debt versus equity financing.
    b. The extent to which interest income exceeds interest expense.
    c. The extent to which interest expense exceeds interest income.
    d. The likelihood that a company will be able to make required interest payments.

**9.** The efficient use of assets is indicated by:

    a. Turnover ratios.
    b. Debt-related ratios.
    c. The ratio of debt to equity.
    d. The ratio of current assets to current liabilities.

**10.** Which of the following items is not included in the calculation of income from operations?

    a. Gains on the sale of short-term investments.
    b. Interest income.
    c. Interest expense.
    d. None of the above are included in the calculation of income from operations.

**Answers to Self Assessment**

**1.** d;   **2.** d;   **3.** b;   **4.** a;   **5.** a;   **6.** c;
**7.** a;   **8.** d;   **9.** a;   **10.** d.

# INTERACTIVE LEARNING

**Enhance and test your knowledge of Chapter 13 using the interactive CD.**

**1.** Learning Objectives

**2.** Multiple Choice

**3.** Language of Business—Matching of Key Terms

**4.** Critical Thinking

**5.** Demonstration—Days' sales in accounts receivable

**6.** Case—*Ranger Company*; Vertical analysis

**Go to our dynamic Web site for more self-assessment, Web links, and additional information.**

# QUESTIONS

**1.** List three reasons why managers analyze financial statements.

**2.** Explain what is meant by horizontal and vertical analysis of the balance sheet and the income statement.

**3.** Suppose net income is much higher than cash flow from operations. Why is this potentially indicative of earnings management?

**4.** In addition to the three basic financial statements, what other information sources can be used to gain insight into a company's current and future financial performance?

**5.** List three profitability ratios.

**6.** List three turnover ratios.

**7.** List three debt-related ratios.

# EXERCISES

**EXERCISE 13-1. Group Assignment**   Explain why companies are concerned about the financial viability of suppliers and customers.

**EXERCISE 13-2. Writing Assignment**   Write a paragraph explaining why net income substantially higher than cash flow from operations may indicate manipulation of earnings.

**EXERCISE 13-3. Internet Assignment**   Go to the Web site of Yahoo! Finance (http://finance.yahoo.com). Enter the ticker symbol for Home Depot (HD) and Lowe's (LOW). For each firm, click on *Profile* and note the ratio for Profit Margin (the ratio we called Gross Margin Percentage) and the Debt/Equity ratio. How do the two companies stack up in terms of these ratios?

**EXERCISE 13-4. Financial News and Analysis**   For a company recommended by your instructor, read current financial news articles (available on Yahoo! Finance) and summarize how the stories relate to the financial condition of the company.

**EXERCISE 13-5. Reading the MD&A Section of the Annual Report**   For a company recommended by your instructor, go to the company's corporate Web site and obtain its annual report (most likely, you will have to click through to investor relations). Briefly summarize how information in the management discussion and analysis (MD&A) section of the annual report helps explain the results in the most recent fiscal year.

**EXERCISES 6–11.**   The following information for Westfield Furniture, a retail furniture and design firm, relates to exercises 6 through 11.

| Westfield Furniture Balance Sheets | December 31, 2005 | December 31, 2004 |
|---|---|---|
| **Assets** | | |
| Current assets: | | |
| Cash | $   35,684 | $   45,850 |
| Accounts receivable | 523,489 | 410,378 |
| Inventory | 4,675,540 | 4,457,540 |
| Prepaid expenses | 80,147 | 79,585 |
| Total current assets | 5,314,860 | 4,993,353 |
| Building and equipment, net | 1,013,021 | 1,012,256 |
| Total assets | $6,327,881 | $6,005,609 |
| **Liabilities and stockholders' equity** | | |
| Current liabilities: | | |
| Accounts payable | $  556,940 | $  577,668 |
| Bank loan payable | 625,871 | 578,526 |
| Other accrued payables | 195,965 | 287,125 |
| Total current liabilities | 1,378,776 | 1,443,319 |
| Long-term debt | 1,592,460 | 1,658,000 |
| Total liabilities | 2,971,236 | 3,101,319 |
| Stockholders' equity: | | |
| Common stock | 1,258,400 | 1,258,400 |
| Retained earnings | 2,098,245 | 1,645,890 |
| Total stockholders' equity | 3,356,645 | 2,904,290 |
| Total liabilities and stockholders' equity | $6,327,881 | $6,005,609 |

| Westfield Furniture Statements of Earnings | Year Ended December 31, 2005 | Year Ended December 31, 2004 |
|---|---|---|
| Net Sales | $5,136,628 | $4,845,875 |
| Cost of goods sold | 2,619,680 | 2,422,938 |
| Gross margin | 2,516,948 | 2,422,937 |
| Operating expenses: | | |
| Selling expenses | 462,297 | 581,505 |
| General and administrative expenses | 770,494 | 726,881 |
| Total operating expenses | 1,232,791 | 1,308,386 |
| Operating income | 1,284,157 | 1,114,551 |
| Interest expense | 126,687 | 145,687 |
| Income before taxes | 1,157,470 | 968,864 |
| Income taxes | 405,115 | 339,102 |
| Net income | $ 752,355 | $ 629,762 |

**EXERCISE 13-6. Horizontal Analysis**   Perform a horizontal analysis of the balance sheets and income statements for Westfield Furniture. Highlight changes that are greater than 10 percent.

**EXERCISE 13-7. Vertical Analysis**   Perform a vertical analysis of the balance sheets and income statements for Westfield Furniture. Are there any major changes between 2004 and 2005?

**EXERCISE 13-8. Profitability Ratios**   Calculate earnings per share, the price–earnings ratio, the gross margin percentage, return on total assets and return on common stockholders' equity for 2004 and 2005. There were 100,000 shares of common stock outstanding at the end of both 2004 and 2005. The price per share was $102 at the end of 2004 and $124 at the end of 2005.

**EXERCISE 13-9. Turnover Ratios**   Calculate asset turnover, accounts receivable turnover, days' sales in receivables, inventory turnover, and days' sales in inventory for 2004 and 2005.

**EXERCISE 13-10. Debt Related Ratios**   Calculate the current ratio, the acid-test ratio, the debt-to-equity ratio and times interest earned for 2004 and 2005.

**EXERCISE 13-11. Net Income Versus Cash Flow from Operations**   Cash flow from operations was $645,590 for 2004 and $795,823 for 2005. Does this suggest that management of Westfield Furniture has manipulated earnings upward in these years?

**EXERCISE 13-12. Inventory Turnover for Safeway**   Safeway, Inc. is a large food and drug retailer with more than 1,700 stores in the U.S. and Canada. The following financial information relates to fiscal 2001 and 2000.

| (In Millions) | 2001 | 2000 |
|---|---|---|
| Sales | $34,301.0 | $31,976.9 |
| Cost of goods sold | 23,696.7 | 22,482.4 |
| Receivables | 391.4 | 374.5 |
| Merchandise inventory | 2,576.8 | 2,508.2 |

*Required*

Calculate inventory turnover and days' sales in inventory.

# PROBLEMS

 **PROBLEMS 1–4**    HG Lang Designs operates an exclusive bridal boutique in Manhattan. All gowns are designed by Lang but are manufactured by various small firms in France and Italy. The following financial information for the company relates to Problems 1 through 4.

| HG Lang Designs Balance Sheets | December 31, 2005 | December 31, 2004 |
|---|---|---|
| **Assets** | | |
| Current assets: | | |
| Cash | $ 62,541 | $ 84,584 |
| Accounts receivable | 338,652 | 320,378 |
| Inventory | 1,725,425 | 1,695,785 |
| Other current assets | 59,859 | 62,587 |
| Total current assets | 2,186,477 | 2,163,334 |
| Buildings, furniture, and fixtures, net | 1,548,942 | 1,548,942 |
| **Total assets** | $ 3,735,419 | $ 3,712,276 |
| | | |
| **Liabilities and stockholders' equity** | | |
| Current liabilities: | | |
| Accounts payable | $ 69,852 | $ 62,854 |
| Bank loan payable | 85,625 | 105,421 |
| Other accrued payables | 12,695 | 10,569 |
| Total current liabilities | 168,172 | 178,844 |
| Long-term debt | 298,584 | 352,054 |
| Total liabilities | 466,756 | 530,898 |
| Stockholders' equity: | | |
| Common stock | 1,200,000 | 1,200,000 |
| Retained earnings | 2,068,663 | 1,981,378 |
| Total stockholders' equity | 3,268,663 | 3,181,378 |
| **Total liabilities and stockholders' equity** | $ 3,735,419 | $ 3,712,276 |

| HG Lang Designs Income Statements | December 31, 2005 | December 31, 2004 |
|---|---|---|
| Net sales | $19,838,074 | $18,540,256 |
| Cost of goods sold | 13,886,652 | 12,051,166 |
| Gross margin | 5,951,422 | 6,489,090 |
| Operating expenses: | | |
| Selling expenses | 614,980 | 556,208 |
| General and administrative expenses | 2,578,950 | 2,224,831 |
| Total operating expenses | 3,193,930 | 2,781,039 |
| Operating income | 2,757,492 | 3,708,051 |
| Interest expense | 27,844 | 36,598 |
| Income before taxes | 2,729,648 | 3,671,453 |
| Income taxes | 955,377 | 1,285,009 |
| Net income | $ 1,774,271 | $ 2,386,444 |

**PROBLEM 13-1. Vertical Analysis of the Income Statement**    Assume you are the vice president of operations for HG Lang and you are preparing for a meeting to discuss the 2005 financial results with Adrienne Aiello, the company president.

*Required*

a. Prepare a vertical analysis of the income statements for 2004 and 2005. Based on this analysis, what is Adrienne Aiello likely to focus on in your upcoming meeting?

b. During 2005, the company had price increases from its European gown manufacturers. Ms. Aiello has asked you to estimate what the gross margin would have been for 2005 if the price increase had not occurred.

**PROBLEM 13-2. Inventory Turnover**  Assume you are the vice president of operations of HG Lang. To prepare for a meeting with Adrienne Aiello, the company president, you are in the process of analyzing inventory.

*Required*

a. Compute inventory turnover and days' sales in inventory.

b. Based on your contacts in the industry, you know that inventory turnover at similar companies is generally around seven and days' sales in inventory is around 52. How does HG Lang's performance compare to these averages?

**PROBLEM 13-3. Assessing the Ability of a Company to Pay Its Liabilities**  Mode Milano is a bridal gown manufacturing company in Milan. Recently, the company received an order for $400,000 of merchandise from HG Lang with payment to be made within 60 days of delivery. Mode asked Lang to provide a copy of its audited financial statements from 2005 and 2004 so that it could analyze them before accepting the order.

*Required*

a. Compute the following ratios to help Mode Milano decide whether to accept the order from HG Lang: Current ratio, acid-test, debt-to-equity ratio, times interest earned, and return on total assets.

b. Based on the analysis in Part a, does it appear that HG Lang will have any difficulty paying its bill to Mode Milano?

**PROBLEM 13-4. Debt-to-Equity Ratio**  HG Lang is planning on opening a new store in Miami that will be financed in part by a new bank loan of $1,000,000.

*Required*

a. Assuming debt was $1,000,000 higher in 2005, what would the debt-to-equity ratio have been?

b. Assume that the additional debt will add $80,000 of interest expense. What would times interest earned have been in 2005 if interest expense had been $80,000 higher?

c. Assume you are a bank manager evaluating the potential $1,000,000 loan to HG Lang. Explain why you would or would not be favorably inclined to make the loan.

**PROBLEM 13-5. Comparing Income to Cash Flow from Operations; Ethics**  Alex Rembol is the CEO of Antura Corporation, a company that manufactures and sells contact lenses, lens cleaning and wetting solutions, and other miscellaneous eye care products. Alex's annual bonus depends on meeting a profit target of $6,000,000, but late in the fourth quarter the CFO brought Alex the bad news that, based on current orders, it appeared that earnings would be closer to $5,000,000.

To deal with the situation, Alex and the CFO decided on the following strategies:

1. The company has firm orders for $1.5 million of merchandise to be delivered in January and February of next year (the company's fiscal year ends on December 31). Alex proposes that the goods be shipped in December to a warehouse where they will be held until required by customers. Customers will be billed in December and receive a special 15 percent discount for accepting ownership upon shipment to the warehouse. Antura will pay for storage and insurance until the goods are actually delivered to customer locations.

2. The company had taken a $5 million restructuring charge in the prior year with cash payments of $2 million and a $3 million reserve. Alex and the CFO have decided that the cost of the restructuring was overestimated and, accordingly, $1 million should be taken back into income (with a corresponding reduction of the reserve) in the current year.

3. The company has a claim against a shipping company that had an accident on Highway 5, destroying $800,000 of Antura's merchandise. The shipping company claims it is not at fault and that liability relates to the driver of another vehicle who, unfortunately, did not have insurance. At this point, ultimate collection of the claim is not clear. However, Alex has directed that a receivable for $800,000 be recorded along with a reduction of current period expenses.

### Required

a. Do you believe that the three strategies constitute manipulation of earnings?

b. Comment on why a comparison of net income versus cash flow from operations may reveal that these actions were undertaken.

c. Do you consider the three strategies to be consistent with ethical business behavior?

**PROBLEM 13-6. Analyzing Financial Ratios and Cash Flows**   Venture Auto Parts is a chain of 35 stores offering a full line of auto parts and supplies to consumers and independent auto repair shops. Danny's Brake and Muffler has over 80 stores in the cities serviced by Venture. Recently, Danny Morton, the founder of Danny's Brake and Muffler was approached by Venture with an interesting offer. Venture wants to be the sole supplier of mufflers and brake parts to Danny's. In exchange, Venture will invest in technology to monitor Danny's inventory levels and make timely deliveries to all locations. Venture asserts that the deal will lead to lower part prices and greater inventory turnover for Danny's.

Prior to the final phase of negotiation, Danny's chief accountant, Sarah Wilson, was assigned the task of analyzing the confidential audited financial statements of Venture. As part of her work, Sarah calculated the following ratios and obtained Venture's Statement of Cash Flow for fiscal 2005.

|  | **Fiscal 2005** | **Fiscal 2004** |
| --- | --- | --- |
| Current ratio | 1.60 | 1.50 |
| Quick ratio | 0.65 | 0.85 |
| Inventory turnover | 3.82 | 5.25 |
| Debt to equity | 2.76 | 2.03 |
| Times interest earned | 1.02 | 2.34 |

| **Venture Auto Parts**<br>**Statement of Cash Flows** | **Year Ended**<br>**December 31,**<br>**2005** |
| --- | --- |
| **Cash provided from operations** |  |
| Net earnings | $ 8,567,483 |
| Reconciliation of net earnings to net cash provided by operations |  |
| Depreciation and amortization | 883,567 |
| Increase in receivables | (3,278,247) |
| Increase in merchandise inventories | (1,058,430) |
| Increase in accounts payable | 685,740 |
| Increase in income taxes payable | 98,351 |
| Net cash provided by operations | 5,898,464 |
| Cash flows from investing activities |  |
| Purchase of Dundee Stores | (4,558,630) |
| Purchase of property | (6,875,432) |
| Net cash used in investing activities | (11,434,062) |

| Cash flows from financing activities | |
|---|---|
| Proceeds from long-term borrowings | 5,785,648 |
| Net cash provided by financing activities | 5,785,648 |
| Increase in cash and cash equivalents | 250,050 |
| Cash and cash equivalents at beginning of year | 258,640 |
| Cash and cash equivalents at end of year | $   508,690 |

### Required

Based on this limited information, would you recommend that Danny pursue the deal with Venture?

**PROBLEM 13-7. Gross Margin Percentage and Inventory Turnover for Longs Drug Stores Corp; MD&A**   Longs is a West coast company with more than 400 drug stores. Financial information for fiscal 2002 and 2001 follows.

| (In Thousands) | Fiscal 2002 | Fiscal 2001 |
|---|---|---|
| Sales | $4,304,704 | $4,027,132 |
| Cost of merchandise sold | 3,201,945 | 2,977,422 |
| Merchandise inventory | 406,383 | 424,339 |

An excerpt from management discussion and analysis (MD&A) in the fiscal 2002 annual reported stated:

> Gross margin as a percent of sales was 25.6 percent in fiscal 2002, down from 26.1 percent and 26.5 percent in fiscal 2001 and 2000. The declining gross margin percentages reflect the increase in pharmacy sales as a percentage of total sales. Pharmacy sales have lower margins than front-end sales. In addition, pharmacy margin percentages continue to decline throughout the retail drug store industry due to the increasing percentage of pharmacy sales reimbursed by third-party health plans. Third-party health plans continue to reduce reimbursement levels, resulting in lower gross margins for these sales than for nonthird-party sales. However, despite decreases in pharmacy gross margin percentages, pharmacy gross profit in dollars has continued to rise with the growth in sales.

### Required

a. Compute the gross margin percentage for both years.

b. Based on your evaluation of the change in the gross margin percentage and the discussion in the MD&A, comment on how well the company has managed its gross margin.

c. Compute inventory turnover and days' sales in inventory for both years.

d. Based on your analysis in Part c, briefly comment on how well the company has controlled its investment in inventory.

**PROBLEM 13-8. Comparing Dell and Gateway**   Financial information for Dell and Gateway follows:

| (In Millions) | Dell 2/1/02 | Dell 2/1/01 | Gateway 12/31/01 | Gateway 12/31/00 |
|---|---|---|---|---|
| Sales | $31,168 | $31,888 | $6,079 | $9,601 |
| Cost of sales | 25,661 | 25,445 | 5,241 | 7,542 |
| Gross margin | $ 5,507 | $ 6,443 | $ 838 | $2,059 |
| Inventory | $   278 | $   400 | $ 120 | $ 315 |

Note that Dell's fiscal year ends on February 1. Thus, its fiscal year ending 2/1/02 is comparable to Gateway's fiscal year ending 12/31/01.

*Required*

a. Compare Dell and Gateway in terms of their percentage changes in sales and gross margin.

b. Compare Dell and Gateway in terms of their gross margin percentages.

c. Compare Dell and Gateway in terms of inventory turnover and days' sales in inventory.

d. In your opinion, which firm has had the best financial performance? Support your answer using your calculations in Parts a, b, and c.

**PROBLEM 13-9. Dell's MD&A—Follow Up to Problem 8**  Below is an excerpt from Dell's Management Discussion and Analysis:

> Gross margin decreased during fiscal 2002 across all geographies and product categories. This erosion began in the fourth quarter of fiscal 2001, when the Company saw industry demand starting to decline and began an aggressive pricing strategy to gain share and maximize profitability that resulted in gross margin declining to 17.7 percent from 20.2 percent the previous year. Throughout fiscal 2002, the Company focused on stabilizing and improving net operating margins. Gross margins in fiscal 2002 were roughly comparable to the fiscal 2001 exit rate. The year-to-year decrease occurred primarily as a result of this intense price competition and the continued execution of the Company's strategy to drive profitable market share growth. Based on the industry, economic, and other factors discussed above, the Company currently expects that this gross margin environment will continue to be challenging, but the Company's intent is to focus on improving operating margins as the economy improves. Management believes that the strength of the Company's direct-to-customer business model, as well as its strong liquidity position, makes the Company better positioned than its competitors to profitably grow market share in the current business climate.

*Required*

Compare your gross margin percentage calculations in Problem 8 to the statistics cited in the MD&A. Does the MD&A help you understand why the gross margin percentage changed between fiscal 2001 and fiscal 2002? In your own words (which may be much more clear than the verbiage in the MD&A) summarize what happened.

**PROBLEMS 10 AND 11**  Mandrake Motorcycles was started three years ago. The company manufactures and sells "classic" cycles similar in style to Harley Davidson and Indian motorcycles made in the late 1940s. The following financial information for the company relates to Problems 10 and 11.

| Mandrake Motor Cycles Balance Sheets | December 31, 2005 | December 31, 2004 |
|---|---|---|
| **Assets** | | |
| Current assets: | | |
| Cash and cash equivalents | $ 208,579 | $ 399,339 |
| Accounts receivable | 157,450 | 162,618 |
| Inventory | 785,657 | 568,880 |
| Other current assets | 175,864 | 187,982 |
| Total current assets | 1,327,550 | 1,318,819 |
| Property, plant and equipment, net | 998,547 | 1,099,544 |
| Total assets | $2,326,097 | $2,418,363 |

**Liabilities and stockholders' equity**

Current liabilities:

| | | |
|---|---|---|
| Accounts payable | $ 243,785 | $ 189,911 |
| Short-term debt payable | 341,680 | 293,553 |
| Other current liabilities | 255,642 | 252,971 |
| Total current liabilities | 841,107 | 736,435 |
| Long-term debt | 137,579 | 355,000 |
| Total liabilities | 978,686 | 1,091,435 |
| Stockholders' equity: | | |
| Common stock | 1,250,000 | 1,250,000 |
| Retained earnings | 97,411 | 76,928 |
| Total stockholders' equity | 1,347,411 | 1,326,928 |
| Total liabilities and stockholders' equity | $2,326,097 | $2,418,363 |

| Mandrake Motor Cycles Income Statements | Year Ended December 31, 2005 | Year Ended December 31, 2004 |
|---|---|---|
| Net sales | $1,476,941 | $1,576,941 |
| Cost of goods sold | 912,386 | 1,103,859 |
| Gross margin | 564,555 | 473,082 |
| Operating expenses: | | |
| Selling expenses | 295,388 | 201,564 |
| General and administrative expenses | 192,002 | 185,460 |
| Total operating expenses | 487,390 | 387,024 |
| Operating income | 77,165 | 86,058 |
| Interest expense | 45,652 | 70,248 |
| Income before taxes | 31,513 | 15,810 |
| Income taxes | 11,030 | 5,534 |
| Net income | $ 20,483 | $ 10,276 |

**PROBLEM 13-10. Comprehensive Financial Statement Analysis Problem**  Marty "Monk" Fisher owns the largest motorcycle dealership in southern Ohio. Recently, he was approached by Bob Sherman, founder of Mandrake Motorcycles and offered the opportunity to be the sole distributor of Mandrake cycles in the state. Acceptance of the offer will require Monk to open a dedicated Mandrake showroom and repair facility and, obviously, stock Mandrake cycles and parts. Monk is quite impressed by the Mandrake product but before making a major investment, he wants to be confident that the company will be around for "the long haul." Accordingly, he has asked you to analyze the audited financial statements of Mandrake for the previous two years.

*Required*

a. Prepare a horizontal and a vertical analysis of the 2005 and 2004 financial statements.

b. Calculate the following ratios for 2005 and 2004: return on assets; gross margin percentage, receivables turnover, days' sales in receivables; inventory turnover; days' sales in inventory; debt to equity; and times interest earned.

c. Based on your analysis in Parts a and b, comment on any matters that Monk should probe in an upcoming meeting with Bob Sherman from Mandrake.

d. Based on the limited information available, do you think Monk should open a Mandrake showroom?

**PROBLEM 13-11. Additional Information Related to Problem 10**   In 2006, Mandrake Motorcycles declared bankruptcy. Subsequently, it was determined that in fiscal 2005, the company produced more units than needed to fill pending orders. The result was a substantial decrease in production cost per unit. The company uses the LIFO inventory method.

*Required*

Discuss how (or if) this information is consistent with the results of the analysis conducted in Problem 10 Parts (a) and (b).

# CASES

## 13-1 JORDAN-WILLIAMS, INCORPORATED

Jordan-Williams, Incorporated (JWI) is a major publisher of college textbooks focused on business education. At the company's quarterly strategy meeting, senior management decided to expand into business education materials aimed at corporations that require entry-level and mid-level managers to complete training courses to improve their business skills. For such training, content (in the opinion of JWI's senior management) is best delivered via the Internet since it has cost advantages and allows for flexibility in scheduling employee training.

JWI has existing content in almost all business areas including accounting, finance, marketing, management, and information systems as well as connections to authors who can develop new materials. However, the firm does not have experience delivering content over the Internet and does not have a sales force with experience selling to the corporate training market. Given JWI wants a rapid entry into this market, it plans on developing a strategic alliance with a company that has experience in selling to the corporate market and in delivery of content via the Internet.

One of the companies JWI is considering as a partner is NetKnowledge, Inc. NetKnowledge is an infrastructure and services company that supports corporate communication and training. The company has approximately 65 satellite-linked communication centers that corporations can use for live video conferencing or training. NetKnowledge has also developed a platform to deliver pre-recorded training to personal computers via the Internet. For clients that need help developing training materials, NetKnowledge has three production studios for designing and recording client content.

A due diligence team from JWI has met with executives from NetKnowledge, viewed demonstrations of content delivered over the Internet using the NetKnowledge platform, and visited a NetKnowledge production facility. The team is quite impressed with NetKnowledge and believes an alliance with the company would be a great fit since NetKnowledge does not specialize in developing content (it only assists companies with designing and recording content) whereas JWI is a content expert.

JWI is going to be investing heavily to modify its existing content to make it more focused on the corporate training market and to make it compatible with NetKnowledge's delivery platform. Thus, it wants to gain some assurance that NetKnowledge will be around in the foreseeable future to continue selling and delivering the materials to the corporate market. To assess the financial stability of NetKnowledge, the JWI due diligence team performed financial analysis and held discussions with various executives and NetKnowledge. When finished with its investigation, the due diligence team prepared the following memo supporting a partnership with NetKnowledge.

March 25, 2005

**TO:**     Peter Gandrell (CEO), Christine Sayers (CFO), and Drew Marshall (Director of New Initiatives)
**FROM:**   Ted Chapman, lead manager, due diligence team investigating NetKnowledge
**SUBJECT:** Report on Financial Condition of NetKnowledge

In fiscal 2004/fiscal 2003, NetKnowledge (NK) suffered losses of $26,693,086/$19,909,857. In spite of these losses, the team recommends forming an alliance with NK. NK, like most companies in this space, is an early stage company and losses are not unexpected. The important questions to ask are "does NK have a reasonable plan to become profitable?" and "does NK have the cash to survive until profitability is achieved?" We believe the answer to both questions is yes.

In 2004, operating expenses increased substantially resulting in an increased loss. However, per our discussions with executives at NK, the increased operating expenses are due in large part to a major advertising campaign and expansion of the sales force. The result is that NK achieved substantial brand recognition, and in 2004 revenue increased by 20 percent. The company believes that, now that it has achieved its brand recognition goals, it can cut operating expenditures (including advertising and sales force salaries) back to a level of 80 percent of the amounts in fiscal 2003, or $27,609,269 (80% × 34,511,586). With current revenue at $17,547,648, and assuming an ongoing revenue growth rate of 20 percent, the company will be profitable in three years (i.e., at the end of fiscal 2007, revenue of $30,322,337 will exceed expenses of $27,609,269).

### Calculation of revenue estimate for year 3

| | |
|---|---|
| Revenue in Fiscal 2004 | $17,547,648 |
| Revenue in fiscal 2005 (fiscal 2004 with 20% increase) | 21,057,178 |
| Revenue in fiscal 2006 (fiscal 2005 with 20% increase) | 25,268,614 |
| Revenue in fiscal 2007 (fiscal 2006 with 20% increase) | 30,322,337 |

It appears to us that achieving profitability in three years is a very feasible goal. The company has expanded its Web hosting options to a 24/7 basis and is now able to service clients with training demands around the world. In the fourth quarter of fiscal 2004, the company signed contracts with three additional Fortune 500 clients to deliver services in 2005. The revenue from this prestigious group of clients is, of course, not reflected in the financial statements for 2004. Also, keep in mind that our partnership with NK will provide incremental revenue to the company.

Of course, achieving profitability will only be possible if the company does not run out of cash. At the end of fiscal 2004, NK had approximately $20,000,000 in cash and cash equivalents. The net decrease in cash and cash equivalents in fiscal 2004 was approximately $10,000,000. Thus, it appears that the company will be able to survive for at least two years (through fiscal 2006). At that point, assuming our net initiative is a success, we may want to make an equity investment in NK to provide the company with the cash it will need to survive a third year beyond 2006 (i.e., through fiscal 2007). Assuming an annual decrease in cash of $10,000,000, we would need to make an equity investment of $10,000,000. At the end of year 3, as discussed above, NK will be profitable and likely able to fund itself internally. An investment of $10,000,000 would give us a substantial equity position in a firm that we predict will be successful. Furthermore, it would allow us to have a substantial say in the direction of NK, thus insuring that the company remains focused on our long-run needs in addition to the needs of its other clients. Alternatively, in light of the fact that the company will be only a year away from profitability at the end of fiscal 2006, if we decide not to make an equity investment, NK should be able to obtain additional debt or equity financing from creditors or investors.

If you have any questions, please give me a call. I'll be in the rest of this week, and next week on Monday. After that, I'll be in Chicago working with the group from Balmer Consulting that is developing our new Authors' Web site.

*Required:*

The financial statements for NetKnowledge for fiscal 2004 and fiscal 2003 are provided below. You should analyze them as you deem appropriate. Based on your work, comment on the memo from Ted Chapman. Do you agree or disagree with his analysis and conclusions? Would you recommend pursuing an alliance with NK?

| NetKnowledge, Inc. Income Statements | Year Ended December 31, 2004 | Year Ended December 31, 2003 |
|---|---|---|
| Revenue | $17,547,648 | $14,568,200 |
| Expenses: | | |
| Wages and salaries expense | 20,683,471 | 14,462,540 |
| Depreciation of property and equipment | 4,061,739 | 4,287,653 |
| Other general, selling, and administrative | 22,274,924 | 15,761,393 |
| | 47,020,134 | 34,511,586 |
| Other income (expense): | | |
| Interest income | 1,120,000 | 1,462,000 |
| (Interest expense) | (1,340,600) | (1,428,471) |
| | (220,600) | 33,529 |
| Net loss | $(29,693,086) | $(19,909,857) |

| NetKnowledge, Inc. Balance Sheets | As of December 31, 2004 | As of December 31, 2003 |
|---|---|---|
| Assets | | |
| Current assets: | | |
| Cash and cash equivalents | $19,951,468 | $30,022,146 |
| Accounts receivable | 2,894,587 | 3,671,664 |
| Prepaid expenses and other assets | 256,874 | 483,651 |
| **Total current assets** | **23,102,929** | **34,177,461** |
| **Property and equipment** | **33,016,763** | **32,334,303** |
| **Less accumulated depreciation** | **(12,520,394)** | **(8,458,655)** |
| **Total assets** | **$43,599,298** | **$58,053,109** |
| Liabilities and stockholders' equity | | |
| Current liabilities: | | |
| Accounts payable and accrued expenses | $ 5,568,442 | $ 4,687,852 |
| Current portion of capital lease obligations | 5,657,142 | 3,485,214 |
| **Total current liabilities** | **11,225,584** | **8,173,066** |
| **Capital lease obligations less current portion** | **10,751,610** | **12,965,437** |
| **Bonds payable** | **14,400,584** | **—** |
| **Total liabilities** | **36,377,778** | **21,138,503** |
| Stockholders' equity | | |
| Common stock: | | |
| Shares issued and outstanding: 2,543,872 in 2001 and 2000 | | |
| Common stock par value | 125,480 | 125,480 |
| Additional paid-in capital | 79,485,662 | 79,485,662 |
| Accumulated deficit | (72,389,622) | (42,696,536) |
| **Total stockholders' equity** | **7,221,520** | **36,914,606** |
| **Total liabilities and stockholders' equity** | **$43,599,298** | **$58,053,109** |

| NetKnowledge, Inc.<br>Statements of Cash Flows | Year Ended<br>December 31,<br>2004 | Year Ended<br>December 31,<br>2003 |
|---|---|---|
| **Operating Activities** | | |
| **Net Loss** | $(29,693,086) | $(19,909,857) |
| Adjustment to reconcile net loss to net cash used<br>in operating activities: | | |
| Depreciation and amortization | 4,061,739 | 4,287,653 |
| **Changes in operating assets and liabilities:** | | |
| Decrease in accounts receivable | 777,077 | (124,587) |
| Decrease in prepaid expenses and other assets | 226,777 | (106,440) |
| Increase in accounts payable and accrued expenses | 880,590 | (65,804) |
| **Net cash used in operating activities** | (23,746,903) | (15,919,035) |
| | | |
| **Investing activities:** | | |
| Purchase of property and equipment | (682,460) | 2,696,874 |
| | | |
| **Financing activities:** | | |
| Issuance of bonds | 14,400,584 | — |
| Payment of capital lease obligations | (41,899) | (18,564) |
| **Net cash provided by financing activities** | 14,358,685 | (18,564) |
| **Net increase (decrease) in cash and cash equivalents** | (10,070,678) | (13,240,725) |
| **Cash and cash equivalents, beginning of period** | 30,022,146 | 43,262,871 |
| **Cash and cash equivalents, end of period** | $19,951,468 | $30,022,146 |

# GLOSSARY

## A

**Ability to bear costs (6)** The notion in cost allocation that the allocation base should result in more costs being allocated to products, service, or departments that are more profitable.

**Absorption costing (5)** An approach to product costing that includes direct material, direct labor, and both fixed and variable manufacturing overhead in product cost. Also referred to as *full costing*. The alternative to absorption costing is variable costing, which includes direct material, direct labor, and variable (but not fixed) manufacturing overhead.

**Account analysis (4)** A method of estimating cost behavior that requires professional judgment to classify costs as either fixed or variable. The total of the costs classified as variable are divided by a measure of activity to calculate the variable cost per unit of activity. The total of the costs classified as fixed provides the estimate of fixed cost.

**Accounting rate of return (9)** The average after-tax income from a project divided by the average investment.

**Activity-based costing (ABC) (2, 6)** A method of assigning overhead costs that identifies key activities and accumulates the costs associated with them. Cost drivers (volume- or nonvolume-related measure of activity) are used to assign the various cost categories to products or services.

**Activity-based management (ABM) (6)** A management approach that involves analyzing and costing activities with the goal of improving efficiency and effectiveness. See also activity-based costing.

**Activity-based pricing (8)** An approach to pricing in which customers are presented with separate prices for services they request in addition to the cost of goods they purchase. Activity-based pricing is also referred to as menu-based pricing since customers are presented with a menu of prices related to the various services they request in addition to the products they purchase.

**Allocation base (2)** The measure of activity used to calculate an overhead rate. Also referred to as a cost driver.

**Attainable standards (11)** A standard that takes into account the possibility that a variety of circumstances may lead to costs that are greater than ideal.

**Avoidable costs (7)** Costs that can be avoided if a company takes a particular action.

## B

**Balanced scorecard (12)** A set of performance measures (linked to a company's strategy) for four categories: financial, customer, internal processes, and learning and growth.

**Break-even point (4)** The number of units a company must sell to earn a zero profit.

**Budget (1, 10)** A formal document that quantifies a company's plan for achieving its goals.

**Budget committee (10)** The group responsible for preparing budgets.

**Budget variance (10)** The difference between budgeted and actual cost.

**Budgeted cost (11)** The cost, at standard, for a number of budgeted units.

## C

**Capital budget (9)** The final list of approved investments.

**Capital budgeting decision (9)** Investment decision involving the acquisition of long-lived assets. See also capital expenditure decision.

**Capital expenditure decision (9)** Investment decision involving the acquisition of long-lived assets. See also capital budgeting decision.

**Cause-and-effect relationship (6)** An allocation of cost to the cost objective that caused it to be incurred.

**Chief financial officer (CFO) (1)** The senior executive responsible for both accounting and financial operations.

**Chief information officer (CIO) (1)** The manager responsible for a company's information technology and computer systems.

**Committed fixed costs (4)** Fixed costs that cannot be easily changed in the short run.

**Common costs (7)** Cost incurred for the benefit of multiple departments or products.

**Computer-controlled manufacturing system (2)** Highly automated manufacturing system that uses computers to control equipment and generally increases the flexibility and accuracy of the production process.

**Contribution margin (4)** The difference between sales and variable costs.

**Contribution margin ratio (4)** The contribution margin divided by sales or the contribution margin per unit divided by the selling price.

**Controllable cost (1, 6)** A cost that a manager can influence by the decisions he or she makes.

**Controllable overhead variance (11)** The difference between the amount of overhead that would be included in a flexible budget for the actual level of production and the actual amount of overhead.

**Controller (1)** The top accounting executive responsible for financial and managerial accounting information and tax filings.

**Conversion costs (3)** The total costs of labor and overhead.

**Cost allocation (6)** The process of assigning indirect costs.

**Cost center (12)** A business segment responsible for controlling costs, not for generating revenues.

**Cost driver (2, 6)** A measure of the activity, related to a cost pool, that is used to allocate cost.

**Cost objective (6)** The object of cost allocation.

**Cost of capital (9)** The weighted average of the costs of debt and equity financing used to generate capital for investments.

**Cost of goods available for sale (2)** The sum of the beginning balance in Finished Goods plus the cost of goods manufactured.

**Cost of goods manufactured (2)** The cost of items that have been completed in the current accounting period.

**Cost per equivalent unit (3)** The sum of the cost in beginning Work in Process and the cost incurred in the current period divided by the sum of the units completed and the equivalent units in ending Work in Process.

**Cost pool (2, 6)** A grouping of overhead costs based on the major activity that created them. Also, a grouping of individual costs whose total is allocated using one allocation base.

**Cost-plus pricing (8)** An approach to pricing in which a prespecified markup is added to cost in order to determine price.

**Cost-volume-profit (C-V-P) analysis (4)** The analysis of how costs and profit change when volume changes.

**Customer profitability measurement (CPM) system (8)** A system in which the indirect costs of serving customers including the cost of processing orders, the cost of handling returns, the cost of shipments, etc. are assigned to cost pools. Using cost drivers, these costs are then allocated to specific customers. Subtracting these costs as well as product costs from customer revenue yields a measure of customer profitability.

**Customer relationship management (CRM) systems (1)** Systems that automate call centers and customer services. The systems also provide customer data analysis and support of e-commerce storefronts.

## D

**Decentralized organization (12)** A firm that grants substantial decision-making authority to the managers of subunits.

**Depreciation tax shield (9)** The tax savings resulting from depreciation.

**Differential costs (7)** Costs that differ between decision alternatives.

**Direct cost (1)** A cost that is directly traceable to a product, activity, or department.

**Direct labor cost (2)** The cost of labor that is directly traced to items produced.

**Direct material cost (2)** The cost of all materials and parts that are directly traced to items produced.

**Direct method of allocating cost (6)**   A method of allocating service department costs to production departments that does not allow for allocation of costs among service departments.

**Discretionary fixed costs (4)**   Fixed costs that management can easily change in the short run.

## E

**Economic value added (EVA) (12)**   A performance measure equal to net operating profit after taxes (adjusted for accounting distortions) less a charge based on the level of investment.

**Enterprise resource planning (ERP) systems (1)**   Systems that computerize inventory and production planning, support accounting, human resources, and various e-commerce applications.

**Equity approach to allocation (6)**   An attempt to allocate costs in a way that is fair to interested parties.

**Equivalent units (3)**   Partially completed units expressed as a comparable number of whole units.

## F

**Financial leverage (13)**   Portion of a firm's assets financed with debt as opposed to equity—the more debt, the higher the financial leverage.

**Finished Goods Inventory (2)**   The cost of goods that are completed and ready to sell.

**Fixed cost (1, 4)**   Costs that do not change when there is a change in business activity.

**Flexible budget (10)**   A budget that is adjusted for the actual level of activity.

**Full cost (2, 5)**   An approach to product costing that includes direct material, direct labor, and both fixed and variable manufacturing overhead in product cost. Also referred to as *absorption costing*. The alternative to full costing is variable costing which includes direct material, direct labor, and variable (but not fixed) manufacturing overhead.

## G

**General and administrative expenses (2)**   Expenses associated with the firm's general management. These include the salaries of the company president and accounting personnel, depreciation of the general office building, depreciation of office equipment, and the cost of supplies.

## H

**High-low method (4)**   A method of estimating fixed and variable cost components in which a straight line is fitted to the data points representing the highest and lowest levels of activity.

**Horizontal analysis (13)**   An analysis that focuses on the dollar value and percentage changes in financial statement amounts across time.

## I

**Ideal standards (11)**   Standards developed under the assumption that no obstacles to the production process will be encountered.

**Incremental analysis (1, 7)**   An analysis of the revenues and costs that will change if a decision alternative is selected.

**Incremental cost (1, 7)**   Costs that increase or decrease if a decision alternative is selected.

**Incremental revenue (1, 7)**   Revenue that increases or decreases if a decision alternative is selected.

**Indirect costs (1)**   A cost that either is not directly traceable to a product, activity, or department or is not worth tracing.

**Indirect labor cost (2)**   All labor costs that are not directly traced to items produced.

**Indirect materials (2)**   Materials and parts that are not directly traced to items produced.

**Internal rate of return (IRR) (9)**   The rate of return that equates the present value of future cash flows to the investment outlay.

**Investment center (12)**   A business segment responsible for generating revenue, controlling costs, and investing in assets.

**Investment turnover (12)**   A performance measure equal to sales divided by invested capital.

## J

**Job cost sheet (2)**   A form used to accumulate the cost of producing an item for order or for inventory.

**Job-order costing system (2)**   A system of accounting for product cost used by companies that produce individual products or batches of products that are unique.

**Joint costs (7)**   The costs of the common inputs that result in two or more products.

**Joint products (7)** Two or more products that arise from common inputs.

**Just-in-time (JIT) manufacturing (2)** A manufacturing system designed to minimize inventories of raw materials and works in process. In a JIT system, goods are manufactured just before they are sold and purchases are made just before goods are needed in production.

## L

**Labor efficiency variance (11)** The difference between the standard labor hours allowed for the number of units produced and the actual number of labor hours worked times the standard labor wage rate.

**Labor rate variance (11)** The difference between the standard and actual wage rates times the actual number of labor hours worked.

**Lack of goal congruence (12)** A situation where managers pursue personal goals that are incompatible with the goals of the company as a whole.

**Lump-sum allocations (6)** Allocations of fixed costs in which predetermined amounts are allocated regardless of changes in the level of activity.

## M

**Management by exception (1, 10)** Policy by which managers investigate departures (or variances) from planned results that appear to be exceptional; they do not investigate minor departures (or variances) from the plan.

**Management Discussion and Analysis (MD&A) (13)** The section of the annual report where firm management discusses the reason for changes in the results of operations, asset accounts and other matters.

**Managerial accounting (1)** Accounting that stresses concepts and procedures relevant to preparing reports for internal users of accounting information. It focuses on information that is useful in planning, control, and decision making.

**Manufacturing costs (2)** All costs associated with the production of goods (i.e., direct material, direct labor, and manufacturing overhead).

**Manufacturing overhead (2)** The costs of manufacturing activities other than direct material and direct labor.

**Margin of safety (4)** The difference between the expected level of sales and break-even sales.

**Master budget (10)** A comprehensive planning document that incorporates a number of individual budgets.

**Material price variance (11)** The difference between the standard and actual prices per unit of material times the actual quantity of material used.

**Material quantity variance (11)** The difference between the standard quantity of material allowed for the number of units produced and the actual quantity of material used times the standard price of the material.

**Mixed cost (4)** Cost that contain both variable and fixed cost elements.

## N

**Net present value (NPV) (9)** The sum of the present values of all cash flows (alternatively, the present value of future cash inflows less the cost of an investment).

**Noncontrollable costs (1)** Costs that a manager cannot influence.

**Nonmanufacturing costs (2)** Costs that are not associated with the production of goods (e.g., selling and administrative costs).

**NOPAT (12)** Net operating profit after taxes.

## O

**Operating leverage (4)** Level of fixed versus variable costs in a firm's cost structure. Firms that have relatively high levels of fixed cost are said to have high operating leverage.

**Opportunity cost (1, 7)** The values of benefits foregone by selecting one decision alternative over another.

**Overapplied overhead (2)** The excess of overhead applied to inventory using a predetermined rate over actual overhead incurred.

**Overhead allocation (2)** The process of assigning overhead to specific cost objectives (e.g., products or departments).

**Overhead allocation rate (2)** A measure of overhead cost divided by a measure of the overhead allocation base.

**Overhead applied (2)** The amount of overhead assigned to jobs.

**Overhead volume variance (11)** The difference between the amount of overhead applied to production at standard and the amount of overhead included in a flexible budget for the actual level of production.

## P

**Payback period (9)** The length of time it takes to recover the initial cost of an investment.

**Performance report (1)** A report used to evaluate managers and the operations they control. Frequently, performance reports involve a comparison of planned and actual results.

**Period cost (2)** Cost identified with accounting periods rather than with goods produced (i.e., nonmanufacturing costs).

**Predetermined overhead rate (2)** The estimated level of overhead cost divided by the estimated level of the allocation base.

**Present value analysis (9)** A method of investment analysis that expresses future cash flows in terms of their value today.

**Process costing system (2)** A product costing system used by companies that produce large numbers of identical items in a continuous production process.

**Product costing systems (2)** An integrated set of documents, ledgers, accounts, and accounting procedures used to measure and record the cost of manufactured products.

**Product costs (2)** Costs assigned to goods produced (i.e., manufacturing costs).

**Production cost report (3)** A report in a process costing system that provides a reconciliation of units and a reconciliation of costs as well as the details of the cost per equivalent unit calculations.

**Profit center (12)** A business segment responsible for generating revenue and controlling costs. It is not responsible for investing in assets.

**Profit equation (4)** Equation that states that profit is equal to revenue (selling price times quantity) minus variable cost (variable cost per unit times quantity) minus total fixed cost.

**Profit margin (12)** Net income divided by revenue.

## R

**Raw Materials Inventory (2)** An account that includes the cost of materials on hand that are used to produce a company's products.

**Regression analysis (4)** A statistical technique that can be used to estimate the intercept (an estimate of fixed cost) and the slope (an estimate of variable cost) of a cost equation.

**Relative benefits approach to allocation (6)** The notion in cost allocation that the allocation base should result in more cost being allocated to the cost objectives that benefit most from incurring the cost.

**Relative performance evaluation (12)** The evaluation of a subunit in comparison to similar subunits within a company.

**Relative sales value method (7)** A method of allocating joint costs in which the allocation is based on the relative sales value of the products at the split-off point.

**Relevant costs (7)** The only cost items that managers need to consider when analyzing decision alternatives because they differ between decision alternatives.

**Relevant range (4)** The range of activity for which estimates and predictions are likely to be accurate.

**Required rate of return (9)** The minimum acceptable return on an investment; also referred to as a hurdle rate.

**Residual income (RI) (12)** A performance measure equal to NOPAT less a charge for the level of investment.

**Responsibility accounting system (6)** A system of accounting that traces revenues and costs to organizational units and individuals with related responsibility for generating revenue and controlling costs.

**Responsibility centers (12)** Organizational units responsible for the generation of revenue or for the incurrence of costs.

**Return on investment (ROI) (12)** A performance measure equal to investment center income divided by invested capital.

## S

**Scattergraph (4)** A graph of costs at various activity levels.

**Selling costs (2)** Costs associated with securing and filling customer orders.

**Slack (10)** Amounts (padding) managers include in budgets to assure that budgeted goals can be easily achieved.

**Split-off point (7)** Stage of production when joint products are individually identifiable.

**Standard cost (11)**   The cost that management believes should be incurred to produce a good or service under anticipated conditions.

**Standard cost variance (11)**   The difference between standard cost and actual cost.

**Static budget (10)**   A budget that is not adjusted for the actual level of activity.

**Step costs (4)**   Costs that are fixed for a range of volume but increase to a higher level when the upper bound of the range is exceeded.

**Sunk costs (1)**   Costs incurred in the past—they are irrelevant to current decisions.

**Supply chain management (SCM) systems (1)**   Software systems that support the planning of the best way to fill orders and help tracking of products and components among companies in the supply chain.

## T

**Target costing (8)**   An integrated approach to determining product features, product price, product cost and product design that helps ensure a company will earn a reasonable profit on new products. Target cost is equal to price less desired profit and the product is designed to achieve the target cost.

**Time tickets (2)**   Forms completed by workers to keep track of the amount of time spent on each job.

**Total quality management (TQM) (2)**   Programs designed to ensure high-quality products that involve listening to customers' needs, making products right the first time, reducing defective products, and encouraging workers to improve their production processes continuously.

**Transfer price (Appendix) (12)**   The price used to value internal transfers of goods or services.

**Transferred-in costs (3)**   The cost a preceding processing department incurs and transfers to the next processing department.

**Treasurer (1)**   Company official who has custody of cash and funds invested in various marketable securities. In addition to money management duties, the treasurer is generally responsible for maintaining relationships with investors, banks, and other creditors.

## U

**Underapplied overhead (2)**   The amount by which actual overhead exceeds the amount applied to inventory using a predetermined overhead rate.

**Unitized fixed costs (6)**   Fixed costs stated on a per unit basis.

## V

**Value chain (1)**   The internal operations of a company and its relationships and interactions with suppliers and customers aimed at creating maximum value for the least possible cost.

**Variable cost (1)**   A cost that increases or decreases in response to increases or decreases in business activity.

**Variable costing (5)**   An alternative to full costing in which only variable production costs are included in inventory: Fixed production costs are treated as period costs.

**Variable costs (4)**   Those costs that increase or decrease in response to increases or decreases in business activity.

**Variance analysis (11)**   An analysis of the difference between actual and standard cost.

**Vertical analysis (13)**   An analysis that focuses on various financial statement account balances as a percent of some base. The base is sales when analyzing income statement accounts and total assets when analyzing balance sheet accounts. Vertical analysis is also referred to as common size analysis.

## W

**"What-if" analysis (4)**   An examination of the results of various courses of action.

**Work in Process Inventory (2)**   An account that includes the cost of goods that are only partially complete.

## Z

**Zero base budgeting (10)**   A method of budget preparation that requires each department to justify budgeted amounts at the start of each budget period, even if the amounts were supported in prior periods.

# PHOTO CREDITS

**Chapter 1**
**Page 1 (top):** Digital Vision/Getty Images. **Page 1 (center):** Walter Hodges/Stone/Getty Images. **Page 1 (bottom):** Strauss/Curtis/Corbis Images. **Page 3:** FoodPix/Brian Hagiwara/Getty Images. **Page 18:** (c)1989, Institute of Certified Management Accountants.

**Chapter 2**
**Page 31:** Okoniewski/The Image Works. **Page 36:** Dell Computer Corporation. **Page 57:** Lester Lefkowitz/Corbis Images. **Page 59:** Courtesy Baldridge National Quality Program/National Institute of Standards and Technology.

**Chapter 3**
**Page 79:** The Stock Market. **Page 80:** Kimberly-Clark Corp. **Page 83 (top):** Canadian Springs Water Industry. **Page 83 (center):** Endot Industries, Inc. **Page 83 (bottom):** Courtesy Monitor Sugar Company.

**Chapter 4**
**Page 111:** Lester Lefkowitz/Corbis Images. **Page 130:** Julie Toy/The Image Bank/Getty Images.

**Chapter 5**
**Page 165:** Tony Freeman/PhotoEdit.

**Chapter 6**
**Page 188:** Linc Cornell/Index Stock.

**Chapter 7**
**Page 237:** Stone/Getty Images. **Page 244:** Ian Waldie/Getty Images News and Sport Services. **Page 253:** Ralf-Finn Hestoft/SABA.

**Chapter 8**
**Page 277:** Tom Carter/PhotoEdit.

**Chapter 9**
**Page 299:** B. Daemmrich/The Image Works. **Page 300:** BMW of North America, Inc.

**Chapter 10**
**Page 341:** Corbis Images. **Page 344:** Index Stock. **Page 345:** EyeWire, Inc./Getty Images. **Page 356:** SRC Software.

**Chapter 11**
**Page 383:** The Image Bank. **Page 385:** Courtesy Starbucks Coffee Company. Photo by Nick Gunderson.

**Chapter 12**
**Page 419:** SUPERSTOCK. **Page 433:** EVA® is a registered trademark of Stern Stewart & Company.

**Chapter 13**
**Page 475:** Courtesy of D&B—Dunn & Bradstreet.

# INDEX